Lecture Notes in Computer Science 13148

More information about this subseries at https://link.springer.com/bookseries/7407

Hong Shen · Yingpeng Sang · Yong Zhang ·
Nong Xiao · Hamid R. Arabnia · Geoffrey Fox ·
Ajay Gupta · Manu Malek (Eds.)

Parallel and Distributed Computing, Applications and Technologies

22nd International Conference, PDCAT 2021
Guangzhou, China, December 17–19, 2021
Proceedings

 Springer

Editors
Hong Shen
Sun Yat-sen University
Guangzhou, Guangdong, China

Yingpeng Sang
Sun Yat-sen University
Guangzhou, China

Yong Zhang
Shenzhen Institute of Advanced Technology
Shenzhen, China

Nong Xiao
Sun Yat-sen University
Guangzhou, China

Hamid R. Arabnia
University of Georgia
Athens, GA, USA

Geoffrey Fox
University of Utah
Salt Lake City, USA

Ajay Gupta
Western Michigan University
Kalamazoo, MI, USA

Manu Malek
Stevens Institute of Technology
Hoboken, NJ, USA

ISSN 0302-9743   ISSN 1611-3349 (electronic)
Lecture Notes in Computer Science
ISBN 978-3-030-96771-0   ISBN 978-3-030-96772-7 (eBook)
https://doi.org/10.1007/978-3-030-96772-7

LNCS Sublibrary: SL1 – Theoretical Computer Science and General Issues

This Springer imprint is published by the registered company Springer Nature Switzerland AG
The registered company address is: Gewerbestrasse 11, 6330 Cham, Switzerland

Preface

It is our great pleasure to introduce this collection of research papers which were presented at the 22nd International Conference on Parallel and Distributed Computing, Applications and Technologies (PDCAT 2021). PDCAT is a major forum for scientists, engineers, and practitioners throughout the world to present the latest research, results, ideas, developments, and applications in all areas of parallel and distributed computing.

The conference started in Hong Kong in 2000, and PDCAT 2021 took place in Guangzhou, China, after 21 years of success in different countries/regions including Taiwan, Japan, China, South Korea, Singapore, Australia, and New Zealand. Due to the impact of the COVID-19 pandemic, this year's conference was conducted both online for external participants and offline for local participants.

This year we received 97 submissions from authors in 15 different countries and regions across the world. Out of these submissions, we have accepted 24 regular papers and 34 short papers. This represents an acceptance rate of 25% for regular papers and 35% for short papers. The submissions were in general of high quality, making paper selection a tough task. The paper review process involved all Program Committee members. To ensure a high-quality program and provide sufficient feedback to authors, we made great effort to have each paper reviewed by three independent reviewers on average. All accepted papers are included in the proceedings.

It would not have been possible for PDCAT 2021 to take place without the help and support of various people. The efforts of the authors, Program Committee members, and reviewers were essential to the conference's quality and deserve our utmost appreciation. We also wish to thank the local organization committee members for all their hard work in making PDCAT 2021 a great success, and we thank our sponsors, Sun Yat-sen University and Springer, for their support. Last but not least, we wish to thank Guoliang Chen from the Nanjing University of Posts and Telecommunications and Shenzhen University, China; Depei Qian from Beihang University, China; Manu Malek as the Editor-in-Chief of the Computers and Electrical Engineering journal; Jiannong Cao from the Hong Kong Polytechnic University, China; Haibing Guan from Shanghai Jiao Tong University, China; Zhiwen Yu from the Northwestern Polytechnical University, China; Chengzhong Xu from the University of Macau, Macao SAR, China; Ajay Gupta from Western Michigan University, USA; and Hiroyuki Takizawa from Tohoku University, Japan, who delivered keynote speeches and helped attain the objectives of the conference.

We are grateful to all authors for submitting their up-to-date research results to the conference and all participants for attending the conference. We hope that you found the conference rewarding.

December 2021

Hong Shen
Yingpeng Sang
Yong Zhang
Nong Xiao
Hamid Arabnia
Geoffrey Fox
Ajay Gupta
Manu Malek

Organization

Organizing Committee

General Chair

Hong Shen   Sun Yat-sen University, China

Program Chairs

Nong Xiao   Sun Yat-sen University, China
Hamid Arabnia   University of Georgia, USA
Geoffrey Fox   University of Utah, USA
Ajay Gupta   Western Michigan University, USA
Manu Malek   Stevens Institute of Technology, USA

Workshop and Tutorial Chair

Di Wu   Sun Yat-sen University, China

Publicity Chairs

Shi-Jinn Horng   National Taiwan University of Science and Technology, China
Hiroyuki Takizawa   Tohoku University, Japan

Publications Chairs

Yingpeng Sang   Sun Yat-sen University, China
Yong Zhang   Shenzhen Institute of Advanced Technology, China

Local Arrangement Chairs

Yuedong Yang   Sun Yat-sen University, China
Chao Yu   Sun Yat-sen University, China

Registration and Finance Chair

Xiangyin Liu   Sun Yat-sen University, China

Program Committee

Yuebin Bai	Beihang University, China
Raj Bayyar	University of Melbourne, Australia
Ümit V. Çatalyürek	Georgia Institute of Technology, USA
Zhansheng Chen	Beijing Union University, China
Yawen Chen	University of Otago, New Zealand
Shi-Jin Horng	National Taiwan University of Science and Technology, China
Zhengxiong Hou	Northwestern Polytechnical University, China
Mirjana Ivanovic	University of Novi Sad, Serbia
Teofilo Gonzalez	University of California, Santa Barbara, USA
Huaxi Gu	Xidian University, China
Haibing Guan	Shanghai Jiao Tong University, China
Longkun Guo	Fuzhou University, China
Hai Jin	Huazhong University of Science and Technology, China
Haibin Kan	Fudan University, China
Francis Lau	University of Hong Kong, China
Kenli Li	Hunan University, China
Keqiu Li	Tianjin University, China
Yidong Li	Beijing Jiaotong University, China
Yamin Li	Hosei University, Japan
Weifa Liang	Australian National University, Australia
Shangsong Liang	Sun Yat-sen University, China
Li Ma	North China University of Technology, China
Rui Mao	Shenzhen University, China
Koji Nakano	University of Hiroshima, Japan
James J. Park	Seoul National University of Science and Technology, South Korea
Depei Qian	Beihang University, China
Jiangbo Qian	Ningbo University, China
Yingpeng Sang	Sun Yat-sen University, China
Michael Sheng	Maquarie University, Australia
Jiwu Shu	Xiamen University, China
Hiroyuki Takizawa	Tohoku University, Japan
Hui Tian	Griffith University, Australia
Rangding Wang	Ningbo University, China
Xun Wang	Zhejiang Gongshang University, China
Jian Weng	Jinan University, China
Di Wu	Sun Yat-sen University, China
Jigang Wu	Guangdong University of Technology, China
Weigang Wu	Sun Yat-sen University, China

Chengzhong Xu	University of Macau, China
Jingling Xue	University of New South Wales, Australia
Yuedong Yang	Sun Yat-sen University, China
Chao Yu	Sun Yat-sen University, China
Jiguo Yu	Qilu University of Technology, China
Zhiwen Yu	Northwestern Polytechnical University, China
Haibo Zhang	University of Otago, New Zealand
Jianbiao Zhang	Beijing Polytechnic University, China
Yong Zhang	Shenzhen Institute of Advanced Technology, China
Zonghua Zhang	Huawei Paris, France
Xiaofan Zhao	Police University of China, China
Yuanjie Zheng	Shandong Normal University, China
Cheng Zhong	Guangxi University, China
Albert Zomaya	University of Sydney, Australia

Organizers

Hosted by

Sun Yat-sen University

In Cooperation with

Springer

Contents

Software Systems and Technologies

Security and Privacy

Networking and Architectures

Accelerating GPU-Based Out-of-Core Stencil Computation with On-the-Fly Compression

Jingcheng Shen$^{(\boxtimes)}$ (iD), Yifan Wu, Masao Okita, and Fumihiko Ino

Osaka University, 565-0871 Osaka, Japan
jc-shen@ist.osaka-u.ac.jp

Abstract. Stencil computation is an important class of scientific applications that can be efficiently executed by graphics processing units (GPUs). Out-of-core approaches help run large scale stencil codes that process data with sizes larger than the limited capacity of GPU memory. Nevertheless, performance of out-of-core approaches is always limited by the data transfer between the CPU and GPU. Many optimizations have been explored to reduce such data transfer, however, published results on the use of on-the-fly compression are insufficient. In this study, we propose a method that accelerates GPU-based out-of-core stencil computation with on-the-fly compression, introducing a novel data compression scheme that solves the data dependency between contiguous decomposed data blocks. We also modify a widely used GPU-based compression library to support pipelining that overlaps data transfer with computation. Experimental results show that the proposed method achieved a speedup of 1.2× compared with a method that involves no compression. Moreover, although precision loss caused by compression increased with the number of time steps, it was trivial up to 4,320 time steps, demonstrating the usefulness of the proposed method.

Keywords: High performance computing · On-the-fly compression · Stencil computation · Simulation · GPGPU

1 Introduction

Stencil computation is the backbone of many scientific applications, such as geophysics simulations [4,15,16], computational electromagnetics [1], and image processing [22]. The key principle of stencil computation is to iteratively apply a fixed calculation pattern (stencil) to every element of the input datasets. Such a single-instruction multiple-data (SIMD) characteristic of stencil computation makes itself a perfect scenario to use the graphics processing units (GPUs) for acceleration. A GPU has thousands of cores and its memory bandwidth is 5–10 times higher than that of a CPU, thus excelling at accelerating both compute- and memory-intensive scientific applications [5,13,18,19]. However, as a GPU

© Springer Nature Switzerland AG 2022
H. Shen et al. (Eds.): PDCAT 2021, LNCS 13148, pp. 3–14, 2022.
https://doi.org/10.1007/978-3-030-96772-7_1

has a limited capacity of device memory (tens of GBs), it fails to directly run a large stencil code whose data size exceeds the memory capacity.

A large entity of research on GPU-based out-of-core stencil computation has been performed to address this issue [6,9,16,20,21]. For a large dataset whose data size exceeds the capacity of the device memory, out-of-core computation first decomposes the dataset into smaller blocks and then streams the blocks to and from the GPU to process. Nevertheless, the performance of this approach is often limited by data transfer between the CPU and GPU because the interconnects fail to catch up with the development of the computation capability of GPUs as described in [19]. Data-centric strategies are thus necessary to reduce the data transfer. Studies have introduced strategies such as temporal blocking and region sharing to reuse the on-GPU data and to avoid extra data transfer [6,9,16]. Nevertheless, according to [16], the performance of out-of-core code was still limited by data transfer despite these strategies. We therefore need to further optimize the methods to reduce data transfer time. A potential solution is to use on-the-fly compression to compress the data on the GPU before transferring it back to the CPU, and decompress the data on the GPU before processing. However, hitherto studies on the acceleration of GPU-based out-of-core stencil computation with on-the-fly compression are really rare. According to a comprehensive review [3], studies on leveraging compression techniques in scientific applications mainly focused on scenarios such as post-analysis and failure recovery. We think that the scarcity of relevant research raises two research questions:

- Would the overhead of compression/decompression outweighs the reduced data transfer time?
- Would the precision loss involved by data compression be so huge that the output becomes useless?

In this study, we (1) propose a method to accelerate out-of-core stencil computation with on-the-fly compression on the GPU and (2) try to give answers to the two above-mentioned questions. The contribution of this work is three-fold:

- We introduced a novel approach to integrate an on-the-fly lossy compression into the workflow of a 25-point stencil computation. For large datasets that are decomposed into blocks, this approach solves the data dependency between contiguous blocks and thus secures the accessibility to the common regions between contiguous blocks after compression.
- We modified a widely-used GPU-based compression library [8] to support pipelining, which is mandatory for the purpose of overlapping CPU-GPU data transfer with GPU computation.
- We analyzed experimental results to answer the aforementioned questions, i.e., on-the-fly compression is useful in reducing the overall execution time of out-of-core stencil computation, and the precision loss is tolerable.

The remainder of this study is organized as follows: Related studies on accelerating stencil and similar scientific applications with compression techniques are introduced in Sect. 2. Background of stencil computation and challenges in applying on-the-fly compression to stencil computation are briefly described in Sect. 3. Section 4 discusses the selection of an appropriate GPU-based compression library. The proposed method to integrate the compression processes into the workflow of out-of-core stencil computation is described in Sect. 5. In Sect. 6, experimental results are presented and analyzed. Finally, Sect. 7 concludes the present study and proposes future research directions.

2 Previous Work

Nagayasu *et al.* [10] proposed a decompression pipeline to accelerate out-of-core volume rendering of time-varying data. Their method was specified to handle RGB data and the decompression procedure was partially performed on the CPU.

Tao *et al.* [23] proposed a lossy checkpointing scheme, which significantly improved the checkpointing performance of iterative methods with lossy compressors. Their scheme reduced the fault tolerance overhead for iterative methods by 23%–70% and 20%–58% compared to traditional checkpointing and lossless-compressed checkpointing, respectively.

Calhoun *et al.* [2] proposed metrics to evaluate loss of accuracy caused by using lossy compression to reduce the snapshot data used for checkpoint restart. They improved efficiency in checkpoint restart for partial differential equation (PDE) simulations by compressing the snapshot data, and found that this compression did not affect overall accuracy in the simulation.

Wu *et al.* [25] proposed a method to simulate large quantum circuits using lossy or/and lossless compression techniques adaptively. They managed to increase the simulation size by 2–16 qubits. However, their method was designed for CPU-based supercomputers and thus the compression libraries cannot be used for GPU-based scenarios. Moreover, the adaptive selection between lossy and lossless compression, i.e., using lossy compression if lossless one failed, is impractical in GPU-based high performance applications because such failures heavily impair the computational performance.

Jin *et al.* [7] proposed a method to use GPU-based lossy compression for extreme-scale cosmological simulations. Their findings show that GPU-based lossy compression can enable sufficient accuracy on post-analysis for cosmological simulations and high compression and decompression throughputs.

Tian *et al.* [24] proposed Cusz, an efficient GPU-based error-bounded lossy compression framework for scientific computing. This framework reported high compression and decompression throughputs and a good compression ratio. However, according to their study, Cusz has sequential subprocedures, which prevents us to use this framework as on-the-fly compression in our work due to the concern of the overhead to shift from GPU to CPU computation.

Zhou *et al.* [26] designed high-performance MPI libraries with on-the-fly compression for modern GPU clusters. In their work, they reduced the inter-node communication time by compressing the messages transferred between nodes, and the size of messages was up to 32 MB. On the other hand, our method

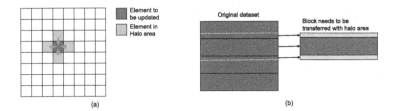

Fig. 1. Five-point stencil computation. (a): Update of an element relies on its four neighboring elements. (b): The decomposed blocks must be transferred with the halo data.

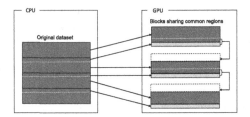

Fig. 2. The contiguous blocks can share common regions on the GPU, thus avoid transferring the amount of data equivalent to that of the halo areas.

compressed large datasets for stencil computation that were more than 10 GB to reduce the data transfer time between the CPU and GPU (i.e., intra-node communication time). Moreover, our method is specified to handle out-of-core stencil code, solving the data dependency between decomposed data blocks.

3   Out-of-Core Stencil Computation

Stencil computation is an iterative computation that updates each element of input datasets according to a fixed pattern that updates an element based on the elements surrounding it. A hello-world application of stencil computation is the solver of Laplace's equation, which can describe the phenomenon of heat conduction: A five-point stencil code, where the temperature of each data point at the $(t+1)$-th time step is obtained by taking the average temperature of the four surrounding points at the t-th time step (Fig. 1(a)).

To use out-of-core approaches that handle excess data, we decompose the original datasets into smaller blocks and stream the blocks to and from the GPU for processing. Due to data dependency of stencil computation, when we transfer a block to the GPU, we must also piggyback the neighbor data ("halo area") with the block (Fig. 1(b)). The size of halo data we must transfer along with the block increases in conformity with the number of time steps we want to process the block on the GPU. As two contiguous blocks share common regions, a block can get common regions from its former block as well as provide its later block with common regions. By doing so, we can effectively reduce the amount of data transfer equivalent to the size of halo data (Fig. 2).

One challenge in integrating on-the-fly compression into the workflow of out-of-core stencil computation is that we must solve the aforementioned data dependency. Naively compressing each block not only consumes more memory space but also prevents sharing of common regions across contiguous blocks. Therefore, sophisticated compression strategy is necessary, and will be introduced in Sect. 5.1.

4   On-the-Fly Compression

Another concern in leveraging on-the-fly compression in out-of-core stencil code is the overheads of compression and decompression that are often considerable. GPU-based compression libraries such as cuZFP [8], Cusz [24], and nvComp [12] report high speeds in compression and decompression. The cuZFP and Cusz libraries are based on lossy compression, whereas the nvComp is lossless.

In this study, we used cuZFP given that it is a library of high performance with source code relatively easy to modify to implement functionalities we need. The library allows users to specify the number of bits used to preserve a value. For example, specifying 32 bits to preserve a double-precision floating-point (i.e., double-type) value achieves a compression ratio of $1/2$.

We avoided using the lossless nvComp due to the concern of compression ratio. In our preliminary experiments, we found the size of data compressed with nvComp was larger than that of the original data. Therefore, we chose not use nvComp in the present study because we could not estimate the upper bound of the size of the compressed data, and we must allocate device memory every time the compression happens instead of reusing pre-allocated device buffers with fixed sizes. The reason why we avoided using Cusz was explained in Sect. 2.

5   Proposed Method

In this section, we introduce our proposed method, including separate compression that solves the data dependency between contiguous blocks and thus allows us to compress the decomposed datasets freely, and a pipelining version of cuZFP that supports overlapping compression/decompression with CPU-GPU data transfer.

5.1   Separate Compression

As shown in Fig. 2, two contiguous blocks have common regions that are shareable. The bottom halo areas needed by the i-th block lie in the $(i + 1)$-th block, and the top halo areas needed by the $(i + 1)$-th block lie in the i-th block. Therefore, the common region between the two blocks consist of the top areas and a part of the $(i + 1)$-th block whose size is equivalent to that of the top halo areas. If we transfer the i-th block together with its bottom halo areas, we can avoid transferring the common regions for the $(i + 1)$-th block.

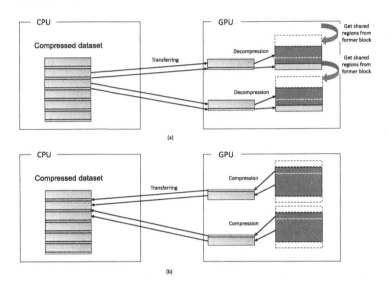

Fig. 3. Separate compression approach to solve data dependency between contiguous blocks. In this approach, the remainder and the common region are compressed separately for each block. As shown in (a), the i-th compressed remainder and common region are decompressed on the GPU for computation; and in (b), after computation, the remainder and common region are compressed and transferred back to CPU to update the i-th remainder and $(i-1)$-th common region, respectively.

Similarly, each block only needs to be transferred with its remainder and bottom halo areas, so the two parts, i.e., the remainder and half of the common region, must be exclusively readable and writable to the according contiguous blocks. Based on this observation, we propose a separate compression approach that compresses the two parts separately. As shown in Fig. 3(a), prior to computation, the i-th compressed remainder and the common region are decompressed, therefore the i-th block can be computed on and provides the data needed by the $(i + 1)$-th block. As shown in Fig. 2(b), after computation, the $(i + 1)$-th block is compressed as the $(i + 1)$-th remainder and i-th common region.

5.2 Pipelining cuZFP

The cuZFP library [8] is mainly designed as a standalone tool that can be seamlessly used for post-analysis and CPU-centric scientific computations. However, as an on-the-fly process in the out-of-core stencil computation, we have to modify the source code to support pipelining that overlaps CPU-GPU data transfer with GPU computations. Thanks to the good maintenance of the cuZFP project, we managed to modify the source code to add such functionality with a reasonable amount of programming effort. In pipelining cuZFP, we use three CUDA [11] streams (Fig. 4).

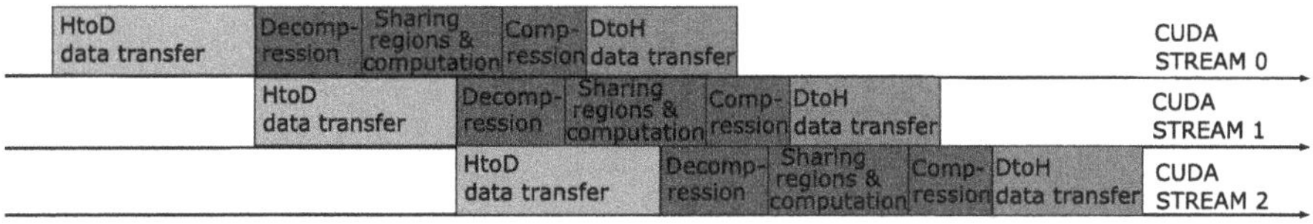

Fig. 4. Modified cuZFP that supports pipelining. Three CUDA streams are used to perform operations, overlapping CPU-GPU data transfer with GPU kernels including compression, decompression, and computation.

Table 1. Target stencil code.

No. of datasets	Data type	Dim. info.		Entire data size
4	Double	$(1152+2\times\text{HALO})^3$, HALO $= 4$		46 GB

Table 2. Testbed for experiments.

GPU	NVIDIA Tesla V100-PCIe
Device memory	32 GB
CPU	Xeon Silver 4110
Host memory	500 GB
OS	Ubuntu 16.04.6
CUDA	10.1
cuZFP	0.5.5

6 Experimental Results

In this section, we analyze the experimental results to evaluate the benefits of using on-the-fly compression in out-of-core stencil computation on a GPU. The stencil code we used is an acoustic wave propagator from a previous work [16]. The code is a 25-point stencil code that has two read-write datasets, a write-only dataset, and a read-only dataset. The two read-write datasets store the updated elements that need to be transferred to and from the GPU. The write-only dataset stores intermediate results at run-time and does not need to be transferred at all. The read-only dataset are constant values that must be referenced at run-time and thus needs to be transferred to the GPU. The values are of double-type because it is more preferable compared to single-precision floating-point format (i.e. `float`-type) in iterative scientific applications. According to a previous work [17], the CPU version of a code using float-type data leads to outputs different from that of the GPU version. Such divergence becomes a more severe problem with the increase of the total number of iterations. On the other hand, when using double-type, results of the CPU and GPU versions of the same code were consistent. Table 1 shows the detail of the datasets used by the stencil code.

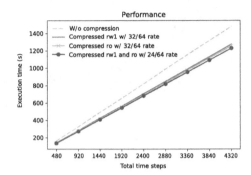

Fig. 5. Performance of the four stencil codes.

Moreover, we used four codes in our experiments to evaluate the performance and precision loss. The four codes include:

1. The original stencil code.
2. The stencil code with one read-write dataset compressed using a 32/64 rate (i.e., using 32 bits to preserve each double value).
3. The stencil code with the read-only dataset compressed using a 32/64 rate.
4. The stencil code with one read-write dataset and the read-only dataset compressed using a 24/64 rate. Note that we used 24 bits to preserve each double value to reduce memory usage in conformity with the limited device memory capacity.

The configuration to run the stencil codes is as the one described in [16] where the number of division is 8 and the number of temporal blocking time steps is 12. Accordingly, we divide the data into 8 blocks, and when a block is transferred to the GPU, it will be computed on for 12 times before transferred back to the CPU. For the total time steps, we used numbers from 480 to 4,320 with an increment of 480. For specifications of the testbed for all experiments performed, see Table 2.

6.1   Evaluation of Performance Benefits

As shown in Fig. 5, the three codes using on-the-fly compression ran faster than the original code. The code compressing one of the read-write datasets and the read-only dataset outperformed the others, running 1.20× as fast as the original code. The code compressing the read-only dataset and the code compressing one of the read-write datasets achieved speedups of 1.18× and 1.16×, respectively. Based on these results, our proposed method is beneficial for GPU-based out-of-core stencil computation in terms of performance. A detailed analysis of the achieved performance improvement will be given in next section.

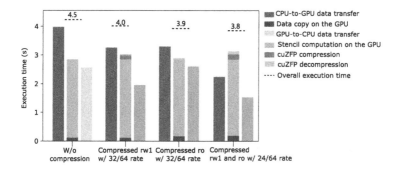

Fig. 6. Breakdown of the execution time of the four GPU-based codes that ran for 12 time steps. The execution time of a CPU-based code was measured to show the performance benefits of using GPU acceleration. Note that the bounding operation time for the fourth GPU-based code was GPU computation time (bars in the middle), whereas the bounding operation time for the other three GPU-based codes was CPU-to-GPU data transfer time (dark green bars). (Color figure online)

6.2 Detailed Analysis of Achieved Performance Improvement

In this experiment, we ran the four GPU-based codes individually for 12 time steps and profiled the breakdown of execution time. Moreover, we also ran a CPU-based code for 12 time steps to show the advanced performance of GPU-based code, compared to that of the CPU-based code. The CPU-based code was parallelized with OpenMP [14] and executed with 40 CPU threads. As shown in Fig. 6, we can see the three codes using compression reduced the CPU-to-GPU time (dark green bars) that limited the overall performance. The most interesting finding is that the fourth GPU-based code shifted from data-transfer-bounding to computation-bounding compared to the former three GPU-based codes, which is favorable because it theoretically means that the data transfer time can be fully hidden by the computation time.

Moreover, although the code compressing the read-only dataset did not reduce the GPU-to-CPU data transfer time, nor did it involve relatively significant compression time (dark purple). Therefore, the code compressing the read-only dataset slightly outperformed the code compressing one of the read-write datasets. Nevertheless, the gaps between the overall execution time and the bounding operation time (i.e., longest bar) of the three codes with compression are larger than that of the original GPU-based code. This suggests that the compression or/and decompression involved some unidentified overheads that compromised the efficiency of overlapping data transfer with GPU computation, otherwise the overall execution time should have been closer to the bounding operation time. Therefore, more sophisticated measures to orchestrate the pipelining could achieve further improvement, providing a direction for future work.

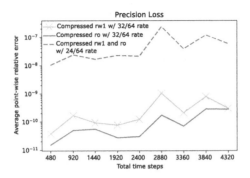

Fig. 7. Change in precision loss as total time steps increase.

6.3 Evaluation of Precision Loss

Besides showing performance benefits, demonstrating that the compression involves no significant precision loss is crucial. After completing the total time steps, we sampled 115,200 points (i.e., 100 points per plane) and compared the point values of the three codes using compression with that of the original code to calculate the average point-wise relative errors (Fig. 7). Although the relative errors increased with an increase in the total time steps, they were still far from significant at 4,320 time steps. The code compressing the read-only dataset had the lowest precision loss because the read-only dataset does not need to be compressed repeatedly. The code compressing one of the read-write datasets and the read-only dataset using 24/64 rate resulted in the largest precision loss due to the fewer bits we used to preserve the double values. Nevertheless, the code is useful because the relative error was trivial (between 10^{-6} and 10^{-7}). Given this, the proposed method will not lead to intolerable precision loss at least for a moderate number of time steps.

7   Conclusions and Future Work

In this study, we introduced a method to accelerate GPU-based out-of-core stencil computation with on-the-fly compression. To realize the method, we proposed a novel approach to compress the decomposed data, solving the data dependency between contiguous blocks. We also modified the cuZFP library [8] to support pipelining for overlapping data transfer with GPU computation. Experimental results show that the proposed method achieved a speedup of 1.2× at the expense of a trivial precision loss, i.e., an average point-wise relative error between 10^{-6} and 10^{-7}. The results answer the two research questions mentioned in Sect. 1. First, the reduction of CPU-GPU data transfer time achieved by using on-the-fly compression outweighs the overhead of compression/decompression, improving the overall performance of GPU-based out-of-core stencil computation. Secondly, the on-the-fly compression does not cause severe precision loss for thousands of time steps. Future work includes (1) comparing other on-the-fly compression algorithms to cuZFP and (2) orchestrating the pipelining for better efficiency in overlapping data transfer with GPU computation.

Acknowledgment. This study was supported in part by the Japan Society for the Promotion of Science KAKENHI under grant 20K21794 and "Program for Leading Graduate Schools" of the Ministry of Education, Culture, Sports, Science, and Technology, Japan.

References

1. Adams, S., Payne, J., Boppana, R.: Finite difference time domain (FDTD) simulations using graphics processors. In: 2007 DoD High Performance Computing Modernization Program Users Group Conference, pp. 334–338. IEEE (2007)
2. Calhoun, J., Cappello, F., Olson, L.N., Snir, M., Gropp, W.D.: Exploring the feasibility of lossy compression for PDE simulations. Int. J. High Perf. Comput. Appl. **33**(2), 397–410 (2019)
3. Cappello, F., Di, S., Gok, A.M.: Fulfilling the promises of lossy compression for scientific applications. In: Nichols, J., Verastegui, B., Maccabe, A.B., Hernandez, O., Parete-Koon, S., Ahearn, T. (eds.) SMC 2020. CCIS, vol. 1315, pp. 99–116. Springer, Cham (2020). https://doi.org/10.1007/978-3-030-63393-6_7
4. Farres, A., Rosas, C., Hanzich, M., Jordà, M., Peña, A.: Performance evaluation of fully anisotropic elastic wave propagation on NVIDIA volta GPUs. In: 81st EAGE Conference and Exhibition 2019, vol. 2019, pp. 1–5. European Association of Geoscientists & Engineers (2019)
5. Ikeda, K., Ino, F., Hagihara, K.: Efficient acceleration of mutual information computation for nonrigid registration using CUDA. IEEE J. Biomed. Health Inf. **18**(3), 956–968 (2014)
6. Jin, G., Lin, J., Endo, T.: Efficient utilization of memory hierarchy to enable the computation on bigger domains for stencil computation in CPU-GPU based systems. In: 2014 International Conference on High Performance Computing and Applications (ICHPCA), pp. 1–6. IEEE (2014)
7. Jin, S., et al.: Understanding GPU-based lossy compression for extreme-scale cosmological simulations. In: 2020 IEEE International Parallel and Distributed Processing Symposium (IPDPS), pp. 105–115. IEEE (2020)
8. Lindstrom, P.: Fixed-rate compressed floating-point arrays. IEEE Trans. Vis. Comput. Graph. **20**(12), 2674–2683 (2014)
9. Miki, N., Ino, F., Hagihara, K.: PACC: a directive-based programming framework for out-of-core stencil computation on accelerators. Int. J. High Perf. Comput. Netw. **13**(1), 19–34 (2019)
10. Nagayasu, D., Ino, F., Hagihara, K.: A decompression pipeline for accelerating out-of-core volume rendering of time-varying data. Comput. Graph. **32**(3), 350–362 (2008)
11. NVIDIA Corporation: CUDA C++ Programming Guide v11.4 (2021)
12. NVIDIA Developer: nvComp: High Speed Data Compression Using NVIDIA GPUs (2021)
13. Okuyama, T., et al.: Accelerating ode-based simulation of general and heterogeneous biophysical models using a GPU. IEEE Trans. Parallel Distrib. Syst. **25**(8), 1966–1975 (2013)

14. Van der Pas, R., Stotzer, E., Terboven, C.: Using OpenMP# The Next Step: Affinity, Accelerators, Tasking, and SIMD. MIT press, Cambridge (2017)
15. Serpa, M.S., et al.: Strategies to improve the performance of a geophysics model for different manycore systems. In: 2017 International Symposium on Computer Architecture and High Performance Computing Workshops (SBAC-PADW), pp. 49–54. IEEE (2017)
16. Shen, J., Ino, F., Farrés, A., Hanzich, M.: A data-centric directive-based framework to accelerate out-of-core stencil computation on a GPU. IEICE Trans. Inf. Syst. **103**(12), 2421–2434 (2020)
17. Shen, J., Mei, J., Walldén, M., Ino, F.: Integrating GPU support for freesurfer with openacc. In: 2020 IEEE 6th International Conference on Computer and Communications (ICCC), pp. 1622–1628. IEEE (2020)
18. Shen, J., Shigeoka, K., Ino, F., Hagihara, K.: An out-of-core branch and bound method for solving the 0-1 knapsack problem on a GPU. In: Ibrahim, S., Choo, K.-K.R., Yan, Z., Pedrycz, W. (eds.) ICA3PP 2017. LNCS, vol. 10393, pp. 254–267. Springer, Cham (2017). https://doi.org/10.1007/978-3-319-65482-9_17
19. Shen, J., Shigeoka, K., Ino, F., Hagihara, K.: GPU-based branch-and-bound method to solve large 0–1 knapsack problems with data-centric strategies. Concurr. Comput. Pract. Exp. **31**(4), e4954 (2019)
20. Shimokawabe, T., Endo, T., Onodera, N., Aoki, T.: A stencil framework to realize large-scale computations beyond device memory capacity on GPU supercomputers. In: 2017 IEEE International Conference on Cluster Computing (CLUSTER), pp. 525–529. IEEE (2017)
21. Sourouri, M., Baden, S.B., Cai, X.: Panda: a compiler framework for concurrent CPU+ GPU execution of 3D stencil computations on GPU-accelerated supercomputers. Int. J. Parallel Program. **45**(3), 711–729 (2017)
22. Tabik, S., Peemen, M., Romero, L.F.: A tuning approach for iterative multiple 3d stencil pipeline on GPUs: anisotropic nonlinear diffusion algorithm as case study. J. Supercomput. **74**(4), 1580–1608 (2018)
23. Tao, D., Di, S., Liang, X., Chen, Z., Cappello, F.: Improving performance of iterative methods by lossy checkpointing. In: Proceedings of the 27th International Symposium on High-Performance Parallel and Distributed Computing, pp. 52–65 (2018)
24. Tian, J., et al.: Cusz: an efficient GPU-based error-bounded lossy compression framework for scientific data. arXiv preprint arXiv:2007.09625 (2020)
25. Wu, X.C., et al.: Full-state quantum circuit simulation by using data compression. In: Proceedings of the International Conference for High Performance Computing, Networking, Storage and Analysis, pp. 1–24 (2019)
26. Zhou, Q., et al.: Designing high-performance MPI libraries with on-the-fly compression for modern gpu clusters. In: 2021 IEEE International Parallel and Distributed Processing Symposium (IPDPS), pp. 444–453. IEEE (2021)

Routing with Ant Colony Optimization in Wireless Mesh Networks

Jiadong Peng[1] ⓘ, Zhanmao Cao[1](✉), and Qisong Huang[2]

[1] South China Normal University, Tianhe District, Guangzhou 510631, China
20162180043@m.scnu.edu.cn, caozhanmao@scnu.edu.cn
[2] Agricultural Bank of China, Guangdong Branch, Tianhe District, Guangzhou 510623, China
2018022617@m.scnu.edu.cn

Abstract. Multiple-radio multiple-channel wireless mesh networks (MRMC WMNs) are fitting as the wireless backbone networks for ubiquitous Internet access. It is quite a challenge to satisfy the multiple traffic requests from multiple source-destination pairs with different data transmission requirements. The multiple pair traffic flows may cause heavy conflict via the nature of wireless media. To take almost full use of the limited resources, we design a routing algorithm based on ant colony optimization. The pheromone leads the finding of primary paths. The various simulations show the efficiency of the algorithm performance.

Keywords: Routing · Ant colony optimization · Wireless mesh networks · Link interference

1 Introduction

Multi-radio multi-channel wireless mesh networks (MRMC WMNs) have become a promising solution to provide convenient and ubiquitous broadband access to the Internet, while aiming to provide ubiquitous information services [1]. WMNs can offer high levels of service and wide coverage, while the deployment takes relatively inexpensive costs [2].

Different from the traditional wireless network, WMNs is a dynamic self-organizing and self-configuring network [3]. In other words, each node of a mesh network automatically creates and maintain the network connection. The special features of WMNs also present as high reliability and easy access to Internet for mobile devices. Compared with traditional wireless network, MRMC WMNs provide higher capacity, but ant colony method is rarely used in discussing multiple flow problem in MRMC WMNs.

It is common traffic mode for multiple users to transmit data at the same time. It is a challenge to satisfy multiple traffic flows from different source-destination pairs. We will try use ant colony to find nearly optimal routing and scheduling scheme for those simultaneous traffic flows.

The interference is a nature character for wireless links, while interference will decrease the performance significantly. Near neighbor nodes and links share the same

H. Shen et al. (Eds.): PDCAT 2021, LNCS 13148, pp. 15–26, 2022.
https://doi.org/10.1007/978-3-030-96772-7_2

channel will cause heavy interference. As interference will decrease the network performance and waste the wireless network resources. Thus, interference free channel assignment is also critical [4]. To get rid of the interference, we need design efficient routing and channel assignment scheme for every real applications. If we can use ant colony to find an effective scheme automatically, it will make sense to deploy various MRMC WMNs.

For full usage of the limited network resources, to reduce link interference is a key issue to improve network performance. The optimal multiple concurrent traffic flows is a challenge problem from multi-pair requests, which is the common phenomenon of the data stream and transmission requests [5]. Each data flow should have a path to forward data packets hop by hop. An uncooperative scheduling of multiple flows may result in unbalanced load, even serious interference. A simple fact is the transmission task not completed in time [6].

The shortest path routing, which simply based on hop count, cannot achieve better network performance [7]. Hence, we need consider some critical factors, such as the topology, the radio interfaces, and the channels, etc. Although ant colony algorithms were explored for sensor network, even for Ad Hoc, there are still few related conclusions that meet the multiple flow problem of MRMC WMNs.

The main contribution of this paper is to propose an optimization routing algorithm based on ant colony, which aims at effective use of network resources and improve transmission performance. In order to find more multiple pair active paths by more interference free links over independent orthogonal channels, pheromone based algorithm is used to create optimal routing in WMNs. Through the regulation of pheromone, we connect the characteristics of MRMC WMNs to produce a better scheme, toward concurrent transmission and channel interference free.

The rest of the paper is as following. Section 2 gives a survey of related work. Section 3 designs a routing algorithm. Section 4 evaluates the performance of our algorithm. Section 5 is a short conclusion.

2   Related Work

In WMNs, routing the multiple flows is quite complex because more constraints have to be considered for optimization, scheduling, routing, channel allocation, and interference avoidance. For the combinatorial problem, even only one aspect involving, it is hard to get an exact optimal solution. For example, if we schedule the multiple paths, we first need give the channel assignment for real-time data flows. However, the CA problem is NP-complete, because it can be reduced to the 3-partition problem [8]. The problem to perform routing to achieve maximum utilization of network resources is also NP-complete.

Various solutions from different angles have been proposed. For example, a distributed multi-flow opportunistic routing algorithm combining candidate node selection and rate allocation is proposed by He *et al.* [9]. Chu *et al.* reported a distributed algorithm to minimize the maximum channel congestion and solve the routing problem of multiple concurrent flows based on MIMO [10]. They focused on the traffic load, but other factors were not involved.

Qiao *et al.* propose a loose joint cooperative routing and channel allocation algorithm to promote network throughput effectively [11]. Bezzina *et al.* propose an interference aware routing metric, which considers intra flow and inter flow as well as link rate [12]. Yan *et al.* propose a cross layer joint channel allocation and routing algorithm, which greedily selects the channel with the least link interference in the channel allocation phase [13]. However, there are rare discussion on multiple concurrent flows.

For ant colony algorithm, there are a lot research on sensor networks and other simple cases of the radio and the channel. For example, an energy consumption optimization algorithm based on ant colony algorithm is proposed for wireless sensor network by Li [14]. These conclusions of wireless sensor network is not suitable to our MRMC WMNs. Most of researches do not consider multi-channel, multi-radio and link interference. Even though Amudhavel *et al.* introduce a recursive scheme of ant colony optimization in the WMNs [15], while they subdivide the large routing problem into smaller ones and achieved some results, their algorithm does not make good use of the advantages of MRMC.

Few reported algorithms are meeting the multiple concurrent flow problem. Those ant colony algorithms for sensor networks have no attention on link interference avoidance. In addition, most of the similar research pay attention on the deployed network, while our algorithm can play a role in the precomputing for the network deployment.

As above, multiple pair concurrent paths problem in MRMC WMNs is a challenging and not thoroughly studied one. In the aspect of routing, most of the existing solutions to the concurrency problem need to use all the information of the network, like topology, the radio interfaces and the available channels, which should be collected in advance.

In this paper, we tackle the optimal problem to maximize the utilization of wireless network resources. Inspired by the beneficial studies, we propose a routing algorithm based on ant colony optimization by using resources efficiently, in order to improve the network performance.

3 Routing Algorithm

The Cartesian Product of Graph (CPG) model is useful to reduce the CA complexity for the path selection criteria under the condition of multiple concurrent flows [16]. It divides the network topology into different virtual layers according to the number of channels like Fig. 1. When one link of a neighbor pair is working over a certain channel layer, its other links over other layers can also work concurrently. It can intuitively help us deal with channel conflicts. To facilitate a rigorous formulation of the problem, we provide some symbols for both the model and the algorithm in Table 1.

For routing the multiple pair traffic, we need to combine channel allocation and scheduling. For each request, routing algorithm should search a path from the source node to the destination node. To facilitate expression, it can be represented by a sequential node sequence. Our routing algorithm will take the channel allocation information and resource information into account in the process of routing, so that the subsequent channel allocation and scheduling can take full usage of the limited resources. If we split the routing, channel allocation and scheduling with each alone, it is hard to reach the optimal scheme.

Table 1. List of the notations

Notations	The symbolic meaning
(s_i, d_i)	The ith source-destination node pair
$l_{(i,j)}$	The potential link of neighbor i and j
P_{ij}^k	The probability of the kth ant passing $l_{(i,j)}$
A_k	The node set that the kth ant can reach
$\tau_{ij}(t)$	The pheromones in $l_{(i,j)}$ at iteration t
$\eta_{ij}(t)$	The influence factor in $l_{(i,j)}$ at iteration t
ρ	The residue coefficient of pheromone
C	The available channel set
R	The available radio interfaces
$|C|$	The number of available channels
$|R|$	The number of available interfaces
m	The number of ants for each (s_i, d_i)

According to the number of orthogonal channels, the CPG model maps the MRMC mesh into the virtual channel layers [17]. Each channel layer has the same topology, as shown in Fig. 1. A link can only transmit over one available channel. Multiple links can coexist to forward packets if and only if those links meet the following link interference free conditions. For the senders, any two different sender's distance is not less than two hops. For the receivers, any two different receiver's distance is not less than one hop. For a sender and a receiver, the distance is more than one hop. The colored links can coexist in each channel as in Fig. 1.

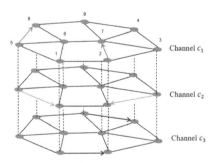

Fig. 1. A mesh. (Color figure online)

For the problem of multiple concurrent traffic flows, it is not suitable to consider only the shortest path [18]. Because of interference and resource allocation, only considering the shortest path can easily lead to overload, which makes the network performance worse. Our algorithm does not simply find the shortest path. We will illustrate this problem with a simple example based on Fig. 1, shown in Fig. 2.

We layer the topology by the number of channels, and each layer represents the usage of the channel. For example, this simple topology has three orthogonal channels c_1 c_2 and c_3, so we divide it into three layers. When a link is working in a certain layer, other links near it become unusable. We can calculate which links will conflict according to the previously mentioned interference conditions.

Suppose a traffic request of node pair (1,9) gets the turn to transmit. Let denote the potential link along a path from node i to node j as $l_{(i,j)}$. Figure 2(a) shows one of the shortest paths, which contains three potential links, $l_{(1,6)}$, $l_{(6,7)}$ and $l_{(7,9)}$. The links can be scheduled simultaneously over the channel of c_1, c_2 and c_3 respectively. If only one path, this choice is fine. However, for multiple pair requests, as we need to deal with many concurrent requests, it may cause serious interference.

For example, if $l_{(7,3)}$ is working over channel c_1, it interferes with $l_{(1,6)}$ in Fig. 2(a). We may need to consider choosing another path to avoid congestion. In that case, the path in Fig. 2(b) may reduce conflicts and get better performance. This path consists of three links of $l_{(1,6)}$, $l_{(6,7)}$ and $l_{(7,9)}$, over the channels c_1,c_2 and c_3. Sometimes the ant chooses longer new path, while the path may lead to better performance.

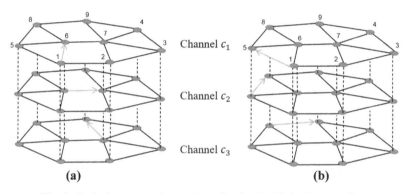

Fig. 2. Paths for source-destination pair of (1,9). (Color figure online)

The better performance path should be the choice via pheromone in ant colony algorithm, in order to improve the network performance. Ant colony optimization is an algorithm that mimics the real ant colony behavior. When searching for food, ants will leave pheromones on the path and other ants will choose the path according to the pheromone concentrations. As the pheromones evaporate over time, the pheromones get rapidly accumulated in the shorter paths. After repeated times, a shortest path will be found. When there are multiple paths, ants spread into these directions at an equal chance in the beginning. After some iterations, due to the accumulation of pheromones, ants tend to choose the shorter path.

As the simple shortest path cannot avoid the conflicts, our algorithm focuses on designing the pheromones. The pheromone in our algorithm will also evaporate over time, but it will accumulate in the links with surplus resources. When there are multiple paths, ants also spread in these directions with the same opportunity at the beginning. Later, due to the accumulation of pheromones, ants tend to choose a more optimized path rather than the shortest path. The formula of pheromone is defined as (3) in detail.

Our algorithm is executed in a host to find the routing scheme for a given multiple pairs of (s_i, d_i), $i = 1, 2, \ldots, k$. The paths are found on demand for the first time. It will be a proactive solution for the future if the perspective multiple pairs emerge again. Our ant colony optimization algorithm steps are as follow:

1. Each link in the network topology is given the same initial pheromone value, in order to reduce the impact caused by ants at the beginning of the algorithm.
2. One source node generates m ants, which explore the path from the source node.
3. Each ant selects the next hop node according to the transfer formula until it reaches the destination node or exceeds the maximum hop count.
4. When all m ants complete a path search from the source point to the destination node, the pheromone values will be updated.
5. Check whether the iteration is finished. If the paths converge, the iteration is finished. Then, we get an available path. Otherwise, repeat steps 2 to 5.
6. Repeating the above steps to select paths for each request.

Algorithm 1. ACO routing algorithm

Algorithm 1 Ant Colony Optimization routing algorithm
Input: network topology, nodes position, traffics set
Output: path scheme S
1.   Initialize S is empty set
2.   **for** each traffic requests of pairs (s_i, d_i) in traffics mode **do**
3.   Initialize ants set m
4.   **for** iteration I **do**
5.   **for** each ant in m **do**
6.   Initialize candidate paths set P
7.   Initialize node set N of a candidate path
8.   **while** current node $\neq d_i$ **do**
9.   search the node set A that the ant can reach in current node
10.   **for** each node in A **do**
11.   calculate the probability
12.   **end for**
13.   random select the next hop node h based on probability
14. $N \leftarrow N \cup h$
15. $P \leftarrow P \cup N$
16.   **end while**
17.   update pheromone
18.   **end for**
19.   **end for**
20.   if paths in P have converged **then**
21.   get the path pa
22. $S \leftarrow S \cup pa$
23.   update network information
24.   **end if**
25. **end for**

The above contents are the steps of the algorithm and the pseudo code of our algorithm. Some contents need to be described in more detail. In step 1, we set an initial pheromone value. This value needs to be set according to the size of the topology. A suitable initial value can make the algorithm converge faster. The initial value of the 64-node topology shown in Fig. 3 used in this paper is set to 20.

The number of ants m used in each iteration, which is mentioned in step 2, is set according to the shortest-hop path between the pair. In this paper, we use 5 times of the shortest hops.

When an ant selects a link, the algorithm will modify the resource data of the related nodes, which will affect the selection of another ant serving other pairs. When an ant is in the intermediate node, its next hop is determined by transfer formula, so it is an important part of our algorithm.

The state transfer formula determines the rules that ant colony should follow, while moving from the current state to the next. The rationality of the parameters will affect the quality of paths selection. The formula of the transition probability P_{ij}^k is as follow:

$$P_{ij}^k = \begin{cases} \frac{\tau_{ij}(t) * \eta_{ij}(t)}{\sum_{s \in A_k} \tau_{ij}(t) * \eta_{ij}(t)}, j \in A_k \\ 0, otherwise \end{cases} \tag{1}$$

Where $\tau_{ij}(t)$ is defined as the value of pheromones on link $l_{(i,j)}$ at iteration t. A_k is the node set which k^{th} ant can reach with one hop on node i. The formula of the transition in the routing algorithm is used as the basis for ants to select the next hop node. For a possible node that the ant may reach in the next hop, the probability will be computed through the formula. We normalize the formula so that the sum of the probability of ants selecting the next hop node is 1. Then, we describe each parameter in (1).

$$\eta_{ij}(t) = \frac{1}{|C| * |R| + 1} \tag{2}$$

$\eta_{ij}(t)$ is the value of resource surplus for $l_{(i,j)}$. It is calculated from the number of available channels and the number of available interfaces. After an ant completes its path, the pheromone of the path is updated. According to the ant colony algorithm, the pheromone on the link is defined as (3):

$$\tau_{ij}(t+1) = \tau_{ij}(t) * (1 - \rho) + \Delta\tau_{ij}, 0 < \rho < 1 \tag{3}$$

Where ρ denotes the residue coefficient of pheromone and t represents the number of iterations. In the simulation, ρ is set to 0.2, that is, 20% of the pheromone will be dispersed each time the pheromone is updated. $\Delta\tau_{ij}$ is the sum of pheromones released by all ants walking through the $l_{(i,j)}$. We define the increment of pheromone by (4):

$$\Delta\tau_{ij} = \sum_{k=1}^{m} \Delta\tau_{ij}^k \tag{4}$$

Where $\Delta\tau_{ij}^k$ denotes pheromone released by k^{th} ant on $l_{(i,j)}$. Our algorithm is optimized based on ant colony algorithm and applied to wireless mesh network, aiming at maximizing the utilization of network resources and reducing the link interference between paths under multiple concurrent requests. For the problem of multiple concurrent paths, the algorithm can give a path scheme without the global information collected.

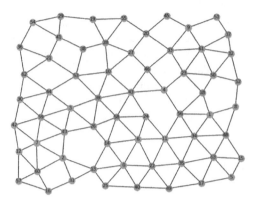

Fig. 3. Mesh topology

4 Performance Evaluation

The simulations are carried out under various network resource combinations and traffic requests. We evaluate the performance of our ACO algorithm based on maximum throughput. Therefore, we choose Dijkstra algorithm (DA) and joint optimal scheduling scheme (COSS) for comparison.

The parameters and values are listed in following. The resource combinations are virtually deployed with the numbers of available interfaces as one in {4,8,12,16,20}, and the number of interference free channels as one in {8,16,32}. Time duration is set to be 5ms, packet size is set to be 1MB, and each link capacity is set to be 200 MB/s. In general, the computing time depends on both the topology and the number of pairs. The topology has two aspects: the size, and the special local distribution. On the topology in the paper, a convergence solution takes after about 200 iterations.

To evaluate the performance of our algorithm, we conduct the simulation with a random mesh topology of 64-node, as showed in Fig. 3.

The tendency of maximum throughput with different combinations of radios and channels. By changing the number of radios and channels, we analyze the performance of ACO as Fig. 4.

In Fig. 4, when $|C| = 8$, the maximum throughput of the network does not increase significantly with the increase number of radios, which indicate that the dominant factor limiting the maximum throughput of the network in this example is the number of channels. When |C|=16, the maximum throughput of the network increases rapidly with the increase number of radios. This shows that the dominant factor limiting the maximum throughput of the network is the number of radios. When the number of radios is enough, the dominant factor limiting the maximum throughput of the network becomes the number of channels. When $|C| = 32$, the maximum throughput of the network increase with the increase number of radios. The number of available channels is sufficient and the maximum throughput of the network is no longer significantly improved by it. Through Fig. 4, we can find that our algorithm can make full use of network resources. As long as there are still available resources, the performance of our algorithm can be improved steadily.

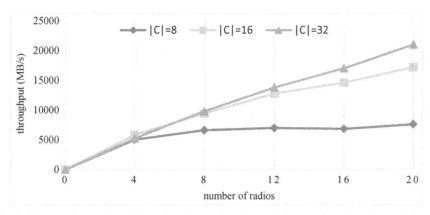

Fig. 4. The maximum throughputs for the combinations of the number of radios and that of channels

Network resource combinations are set as $|C| = 8 \land |R| = 8$, $|C| = 16 \land |R| = 12$, $|C| = 32 \land |R| = 16$, to evaluate the ACO algorithm for various traffic requests. When the number of source-destination pairs varies from 20 to 200, the maximum throughput improves slowly for one resource combination. However, it has significant jumps compared to the lower resource deployment, as in Fig. 5.

The more the source-destination pairs, the bigger of maximum throughput. Meanwhile, the increasing tendency is greater with the more plenty resources. It is easy to reason this fact, because the more network resource available means the more network capacity can be accessed. Hence, more compatible paths can be scheduled over the WMNs in a time slot.

At the same time, the maximum throughput of the network tends to a stable value, this is because the number of source-destination pairs has exceeded the network capacity and the number of compatible paths in the same time slot has reached the peak, so the maximum throughput of the network is no longer significantly improved.

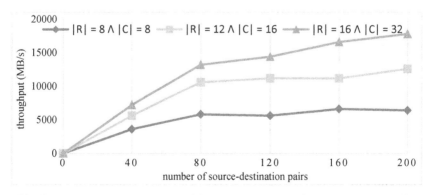

Fig. 5. The maximum throughputs with different numbers of source-destination pairs

Given different network resource combinations, Fig. 6 shows that the maximum throughput of ACO algorithm is better than that of DA. With the increase of traffic requests, our algorithm gradually exceeds COSS. Our algorithm can surpass the existing algorithms without the need for global network information. This scheme can save a lot of resources, because our algorithm is blind search one.

To evaluate the efficiency of ACO, we conduct comparison with DA and COSS on maximum throughput. As a single source shortest path algorithm, DA does not consider the available resource and mesh property, and it will lead to the overload of some nodes. COSS is a combinatorial optimization algorithm. It uses heuristic methods to find many compatible paths to realize the combinatorial optimization of compatible paths. When there are a large number of traffic requests, DA will bring local overload and reduce performance. The performance of COSS is also worse than ours in this case.

Moreover, with the increasing of network resource, the throughput performance of ACO algorithm is getting better. In the routing stage, path selection criteria of ACO algorithm can intelligently select the path of the maximum available resources under the current network status, meanwhile, it may effectively reduce the overlaps between multiple paths. With the resource intelligence, ACO realizes the node load balancing and improve the network performance.

In order to achieve the multi-path simultaneous optimization, we proposed an ACO algorithm for wireless mesh networks in which each path is avoiding interference. It can improve the performance of this network and balance the load of nodes and channels. Simulation results show that the ACO algorithm can achieve better performance under different network resource combinations and various traffic requests. Through the throughput performance comparison, we can see that it is slightly better than DA and COSS algorithm in the case of fewer conditions and resources.

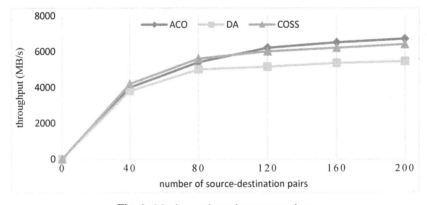

Fig. 6. Maximum throughput comparison

5 Conclusion

This work mainly focuses on the routing in WMNs and evaluates the performance by simulations. Paths are built upon the pheromone. The routing algorithm is based on ant colony optimization. The performance of the algorithm is verified via various simulations, which show the algorithm efficiency.

In the research of routing algorithm optimization, we found that there are still some points to tackle in future, such as how to use the solutions for those already known traffic mode. We want to achieve the continuous optimization of the path scheme. After obtaining the corresponding path scheme through the algorithm, we carry out the experimental calculation. If we find that the effect is not good, we need to adjust the path selection again. It would be better to get assistant of the last ant colony optimization, and to support the new optimization. We may introduce localized scheme to improve in a distributed way.

References

1. Akyildiz, I.F., Wang, X., Wang, W.: Wireless mesh networks: a survey. Comput. Netw. **47**(4), 445–487 (2005)
2. Cheng, H., Xiong, N., Yang, L.T., et al.: Links organization for channel assignment in multi-radio wireless mesh networks. Multimedia Tools Appl. **65**(2), 239–258 (2013)
3. Al Islam, A.B.M.A., Islam, M.J., Nurain, N., Raghunathan, V.: Channel assignment techniques for multi-radio wireless mesh networks: a survey. IEEE Commun. Surv. Tutor. **18**(2), 988–1017 (2016)
4. Tian, Y., Yoshihiro, T.: Traffic-demand-aware collision-free channel assignment for multi-channel multi-radio wireless mesh networks. IEEE Access **8**, 120712–120723 (2020)
5. Cao, Z., Wu, C.Q., Berry, M.L.: An optimization scheme for routing and scheduling of concurrent user requests in wireless mesh networks. Comput. Sci. Inf. Syst. **14**(3), 661–684 (2017)
6. Singh, A.R., Devaraj, D., Banu, R.N.: Genetic algorithm-based optimization of load-balanced routing for AMI with wireless mesh networks. Appl. Soft Comput. **74**, 122–132 (2019)
7. Bhojannawar, S., Mangalwede, S.: Interference, traffic load and delay aware routing metric for wireless mesh network. Adv. Electric. Comput. Eng. **21**(1), 57–64 (2021)
8. Cao, L., Zheng, H.: On the efficiency and complexity of distributed spectrum allocation. In: Cognitive Radio Oriented Wireless Networks and Communications, pp. 357–366 (2007)
9. He, S., Zhang, D., Xie, K.: Opportunistic routing for multi- flow in wireless mesh networks. Chin. J. Electron. **42**(5), 1004–1008 (2014). (in Chinese)
10. Chu, S., Wang, X.: MIMO-aware routing in wireless mesh networks. In: 2010 Proceedings IEEE INFOCOM, pp. 1–9 (2010)
11. Qiao, H., Zhang, D., Xie, K., et al.: Joint cooperative routing and channel assignment in multi-radio wireless mesh network. Chin. J. Electron. **44**(6), 1400–1405 (2016)
12. Bezzina, A., Ayari, M., Langar, R., Kamoun, F.: An interference-aware routing metric for multi-radio multi-channel wireless mesh networks. In: 2012 IEEE 8th International Conference on Wireless and Mobile Computing, Networking and Communications (WiMob), pp. 284–291 (2012)
13. Yan, W., Pan, X.: Egwra: QoS routing algorithm in wireless mesh networks based on evolutionary game theory. In: 2017 International Conference on Computer Network, Electronic and Automation (ICCNEA), pp. 272–275 (2017)
14. Peng, L., Nie, H., Qiu, L., Wang, R.: Energy optimization of ant colony algorithm in wireless sensor network. Int. J. Distrib. Sensor Netw. **13** (2017)

15. Amudhavel, J., Padmapriya, S., Nandhini, R., Kavipriya, G., Dhavachelvan, P., Venkatachala-pathy, V.S.K.: Recursive ant colony optimization routing in wireless mesh network. In: Sata-pathy, S.C., Srujan Raju, K., Mandal, J.K., Bhateja, Vikrant (eds.) Proceedings of the Second International Conference on Computer and Communication Technologies. AISC, vol. 381, pp. 341–351. Springer, New Delhi (2016). https://doi.org/10.1007/978-81-322-2526-3_36
16. Cao, Z., Wu, C.Q., Berry, M.L.: On routing of multiple concurrent user requests in multi-radio multi-channel wireless mesh networks. In: 2016 17th International Conference on Parallel and Distributed Computing, Applications and Technologies (PDCAT), pp. 24–29 (2016)
17. Cao, Z., Wu, C.Q., Zhang, Y., et al.: On modeling and analysis of MIMO wireless mesh networks with triangular overlay topology. Math. Prob. Eng. Article ID 185262, pp. 1–11 (2015)
18. Zhang, C., Liu, S., Sun, Z., Sun, S.: A breadth-first and disjoint multi-path routing algorithm in wireless mesh networks. In: 2013 15th IEEE International Conference on Communication Technology, pp. 560–564 (2013)

A Light-Weight Scheme for Detecting Component Structure of Network Traffic

Zihui Wu, Yi Xie$^{(\boxtimes)}$, and Ziyang Wu

School of Computer Science and Engineering, Guangdong Key Laboratory
of Information Security, Sun Yet-sen University, 510275 GuangZhou, China
`xieyi5@mail.sysu.edu.cn`

Abstract. The rapid development of network services not only expands
the scale of Internet traffic, but also diversifies the types of traffic. In
this work, we design a light-weight compromise scheme to meet the
management requirements of large-scale and business sensitive scenarios.
The proposed scheme regards the mixed traffic as a whole and directly
analyzes the component structure for it. It converts the structural and
attribute features into a traffic profile by encoding, embedding and mapping. Then the traffic profile is used to infer the component structure
based on CNN. The proposed scheme has no need to perform flow-by-
flow classification, it is not limited to the "quantity" balance of traffic,
but also considers the types of traffic in each link. Based on the experiments with actual dataset, the results show that the proposed scheme
can infer component structure for mixed traffic quickly and accurately.

Keywords: Component structure · Proportion analysis · Traffic profile

1 Background

The rapid development of network services has brought huge network traffic
with different requirements to the Internet, which results in new challenges to
the network. First, new devices and services bring massive traffic, which needs
to be transmitted through the Internet. Second, the increase of service types and
the access of heterogeneous devices lead to the complexity of network traffic. The
"best effort" service provided by traditional TCP/IP can not meet the diversified
and customized requirements of different business flows [1].

Existing work on this area mainly includes two major categories: improving
resource utilization [6] and guaranteeing end-to-end QoS [2]. These two kinds
of schemes have their own advantages and disadvantages. The schemes focusing on the resource management can achieve balanced load distribution at the
resource level and improve the utilization of resources. However, they treat each
kind of traffic equally and can only achieve load balance from the perspective of
"quantity", without considering the needs of different traffic at the business level,
which results the difficulty of guaranteeing the service quality. The schemes that
are designed for end-to-end QoS guarantee distinguishes service types through

© Springer Nature Switzerland AG 2022
H. Shen et al. (Eds.): PDCAT 2021, LNCS 13148, pp. 27–35, 2022.
https://doi.org/10.1007/978-3-030-96772-7_3

traffic classification method, and meets resource requirements of different service. However, these schemes need to perform flow-by-flow identification. In large-scale traffic scenarios, the performance is affected by the scale of the flow, leading to huge computational overhead. In general, both the traditional resource management and end-to-end QoS guarantee are not suitable for large-scale, business sensitive network scenarios.

To meet these challenges, we propose a light-weight component structure analysis scheme for large-scale, business sensitive scenarios. The scheme regards the mixed traffic as a whole, and uses the attribute and structure features of the mixed traffic to analyze the component structure, that is, the proportion of various service. The main contributions of this work include two aspects:

(1) Compared with QoS guarantee scheme, there is no need to identify the flows one by one so that it can avoid huge and meaningless overhead.
(2) Compared with resource management scheme based on "quantity", our scheme can realize load balancing in "quantity" and meet the link traffic composition ratio at the business level of different scenarios, which is more flexible.

2   Methodology

2.1   Overview

In order to formally define the problem, we use $u \subseteq \{1, 2, ..., U\}$ to represent the type of network traffic, and its proportion is calculated as follows:

$$P_u = \frac{N_u}{N} \tag{1}$$

where P_u defines the ratio of N_u to N, N_u the number of five-tuple flow with type u and N represents the number of all the five-tuple flows in the mixed network traffic. In addition, the proportion of the rest of the network traffic is represented as P_{U+1}. Network traffic component structure analysis is to identify the proportion of each type of traffic $[P_1, P_2, ..., P_U, P_{U+1}]$ in the mixed traffic.

As shown in Fig. 1, the proposed scheme to solve component structure analysis problem consists of three modules: Preprocessing, Traffic analysis and Proportion analysis, which are described in detail below.

2.2   Preprocessing

The Preprocessing module is responsible for extracting information from mixed traffic and representing it in the traffic topology.

Traffic capture tool is deployed on the network link and collect IPs and communication relationship which are stored in the IP set $\mathbb{S}_{IP}$ and relationship set $\mathbb{S}_{\langle IP,IP' \rangle}$ respectively. Then, for each IP in $\mathbb{S}_{IP}$, we extract its eigenvector $\vec{f}_{IP}$ and store them in the communication IP eigenvector set $\mathbb{S}_{\vec{f}_{IP}} = \left\{ \vec{f}_{IP} \mid IP \in \mathbb{S}_{IP} \right\}$.

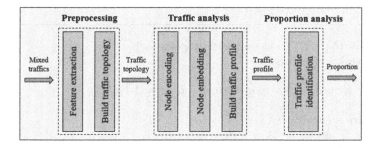

Fig. 1. Architecture

The information extracted from the original traffic sample is represented in the traffic topology $G = (V, E, F)$, where V represents the node set of G and each node v in V represents each IP in $\mathbb{S}_{IP}$; F represents the node's eigenvector set and each item $\vec{f}_v \in F$ corresponds to the $\vec{f}_{IP} \in \mathbb{S}_{\vec{f}_{IP}}$ which IP maps to the node v; E represents the edge set of G, for every IP pair $\langle IP_i, IP_j \rangle \in \mathbb{S}_{\langle IP, IP' \rangle}$, there exists a edge e_{v_i, v_j} between node v_i and v_j.

2.3   Traffic Analysis

Obviously, the specifications of traffic topology generated by different traffic samples are different, so it is difficult to use a unified model for analysis. Therefore, the design idea of the Traffic analysis module is to map the information in the irregular traffic topology to a regular traffic profile, and then a unified model can be used to analyze the component structure of the traffic profile.

Node encoding sub-module encodes all nodes according to its attribution which maps nodes in different traffic topology to the same coding space and divides the nodes into limited types, so that the traffic topology can be regarded as constructed by finite types of nodes. In our scheme, we use the degree of the node itself and its first-order neighbor to encode the node. Each node v_i is encoded as a two-tuple $C_{v_i} = \left(Deg(v_i), \frac{\sum_{v_j}^{v_j \in N_{v_i}} Deg(v_j)}{|N_{v_i}|} \right)$, where N_{v_i} represents the first-order neighbor nodes. It should be emphasized that the encoding attribution is not unique. Only the following two requirements need to be met:

(1) The value of this attribute is rich enough to divide the nodes into enough categories to facilitate the subsequent construction of traffic profiles.
(2) This attribute is distinguishable enough to effectively realize node classification.

Various connection modes of nodes lead to different structural characteristics of traffic topology. Node embedding technology is used to learn the node context relationship in the traffic topology and the procedure is shown as **Algorithm** 1. For all samples $\mathbb{G}'$, R round random walkings are performed in each traffic topology to generate sequence. The sequence set *sequences* is used to train the

---

Algorithm 1.CODE2VEC($\mathbb{G}'$, δ)

Input:
    $\mathbb{G}' = \{G'_1, G'_2, ..., G'_n\}$: encoded traffic topology set
    δ : dimension of embedding
Output:
    Φ : map for node's code to node's embedding, and $\Phi(C_{v_i}) \in \mathbb{R}^\delta$

 1: **initialize** $sequences = \{\}$
 2: **for** $G'_i \in \mathbb{G}'$ **do**
 3:    **for** $r = 1 \rightarrow R$ **do**
 4:      **for** $v_j \in V_i$ **do**
 5:         $sequence = \text{randomWalk}(G'_i, v_j, L)$
 6:         $sequences.\text{add}(sequence)$
 7:      **end for**
 8:    **end for**
 9: **end for**
10: $\Phi \leftarrow \text{word2vec}(sentences)$
11: **return** Φ

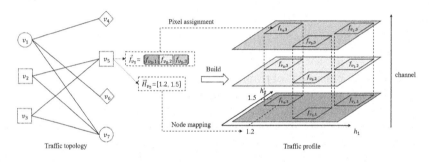

Fig. 2. Building traffic profile, where N^f is 3 and δ is 2

word2vec model, which is used to get node's embedding here. Then the map Φ for node's code to node's embedding is outputted, where $\vec{H}_{C_{v_i}} = \Phi(C_{v_i}) \in \mathbb{R}^\delta$.

For each encoded traffic topology G', each node v_i in V can get its node's embedding through Φ. And the encoded traffic topology can be updated to embedded traffic topology $G'' = (V, E, F, C, H)$, where $H = \{\vec{H}_{v_i} \mid 1 \le i \le |V|\}$ and each node's embedding $\vec{H}_{v_i} \in \mathbb{R}^{1 \times \delta}$.

After completing the node embedding, we use the proposed method of building traffic profile to transform the irregular traffic topology into regular traffic profile. It includes two steps: Node mapping and pixel assignment.

Node mapping is to map each node v_i in the node set V to the δ-dimensional space formed by the δ-dimensional embedding. For each node v_i in the traffic topology, the node's embedding $\vec{H}_{v_i}$ is regarded as the coordinate in the δ-dimensional traffic profile, and the node is mapped to the corresponding pixel of the traffic profile according to the coordinate. If the embedding of two nodes $\vec{H}_{v_i}, \vec{H}_{v_j}$ are the same, the two nodes v_i, v_j will be mapped to the same pixel.

The pixel assignment operation is to assign each channel of the pixel after mapping the node v_i to the corresponding pixel. Firstly, the N^f channel values of each pixel in the traffic profile are initialized to 0. where N^f is the same as the dimension of the node's eigenvector $|\vec{f}_{v_i}|$. Then, for the target pixel to be mapped, the values of its N^f channels are set to the eigenvector $\vec{f}_{v_i}$ of the node v_i mapped to the pixel. If multiple nodes are mapped to the same pixel, the value of the pixel is assigned to the mean value of the eigenvectors of all the nodes, and for the pixels that are not mapped to, the default value is kept.

Figure 2 shows how to build a traffic profile when $\delta = 2$ and $N^f = 3$. In the same way, when the value of δ is greater than 2, the δ-dimensional traffic profile can also be built according to the method described above. The structure information of the original traffic topology will be expressed in the pixel coordinates, and the attribute information will be expressed in the value of the pixels.

2.4 Proportion Analysis

The Proportion analysis module analyzes the inputted multi-dimensional traffic profile, and obtains the proportion results. The information of traffic profile is contained in the arrangement and value of pixels, which is similar to images. Therefore, we use the multi-dimensional CNN that is often used in image analysis tasks to extract features in the traffic profile. Finally, these features are used to predict the proportion of the original traffic sample.

For the convolutional layer in δ-dimensional CNN, the convolution kernel's size is defined as $S_1^k \times S_2^k \times ... \times S_\delta^k$, and the convolution operation is defined as:

$$y_{j_1 \sim j_\delta}^p = b^p + \sum_{c=1}^{c=N^f} \sum_{s_1=1}^{S_1^k} \sum_{s_2=1}^{S_2^k} ... \sum_{s_\delta=1}^{S_\delta^k} W_{s_1 \sim s_\delta}^{pc} x_{(j_1+s_1-1)(j_2+s_2-1)...(j_\delta+s_\delta-1)}^c \quad (2)$$

where $y_{j_1 \sim j_\delta}^p$ is the output value of the pixel with the coordinate $(j_1, j_2, ..., j_\delta)$ of the p-th output feature map; b_p is the bias corresponding to the p-th output feature map; c represents a channel of the input feature map. For the input traffic profile, there are N^f channels; $S_1^k \times S_2^k \times ... \times S_\delta^k$ is convolutional kernel size; $W_{s_1 \sim s_\delta}^{pc}$ is the weight corresponding to the position $(s1, s2, .., s_\delta)$ of the convolution kernel corresponding to the p-th output feature map and the c-th input channel. $x_{(j_1+s_1-1)(j_2+s_2-1)...(j_\delta+s_\delta-1)}^c$ is the value of the pixel's c-th channel which locate in the position $(j_1 + s_1 - 1, j_2 + s_2 - 1, ..., j_\delta + s_\delta - 1)$.

For the pooling layer of δ-dimensional CNN, the pooling window's size is defined as $S_1^p \times S_2^p \times ... \times S_\delta^p$. Maximum pooling is to find the maximum value in the window, and average pooling is to calculate the average of all pixel values in the pooling window.

$$\sum_{u=1}^{U+1} \hat{P}_u = 1 \quad (3)$$

Since our prediction goal is a multi-dimensional proportion vector and the vector satisfies the constraint of sum 1, we add a fully connected network with

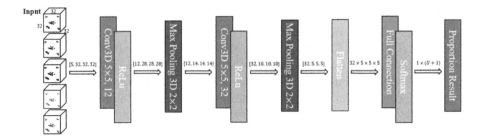

Fig. 3. proportion analysis model architecture

softmax as the activation function to analyze the features extracted by CNN and make the output proportion result $\hat{P}_1, \hat{P}_2, ..., \hat{P}_U, \hat{P}_{U+1}$ meet the constraint.

3 Evaluation

3.1 Data Set

To demonstrate the performance of our scheme, We construct a mixed traffic data set containing three types of traffic(web, P2P, and live), including a total of 2000 samples with proportion label. Each sample contains traffic data for 30 seconds through the collection point. Among them, 1600 traffic samples are divided into training sets, and the rest are divided into test sets.

3.2 Experiment Setting

For feature extracting, we first collect the communication IP and communication relationship in the sample, and extract the following features for each IP: Average/Variance of traffics that the IP communicates with other IPs; Number of different destination ports for the IP's communication; Number of source ports used for the IP's communication; Ratio of the number of destination IP and the number of destination ports for the IP's communication.

For scheme setting, the embedding dimension is set as 3 and the profile size is set as $32 \times 32 \times 32 \times 5$. The proportion analysis model is shown as Fig. 3. Since the proportion analysis model is a regression model, we choose RMSE as the loss function and Adam as optimizer with learning rate 0.0001.

For model evaluation, it mainly includes accuracy evaluation and real-time evaluation. We firstly define an accuracy metric SOMP to measure the error between the predicted proportions and the ground truth:

$$\text{SOMP} = \sum_{u=1}^{U+1} min(\hat{P}_u, P_u) \tag{4}$$

where SOMP means sum of maximal proportion and U is the number of types of traffic. Moreover, the mean number of SOMP $\overline{\text{SOMP}}$ and standard deviation

Table 1. Experiment result

	S_{SOMP}	$\overline{\mathrm{SOMP}}$	$\overline{T^{\mathrm{P}}}(\mathrm{s})$	$S_{T^{\mathrm{P}}}$	$\overline{T^{\mathrm{A}}}(\mathrm{s})$	$S_{T^{\mathrm{A}}}$	$\overline{T}(\mathrm{s})$	S_T
FS-Net[4]	**99.7%**	**0.003**	1.225	1.065	0.870	0.521	2.095	1.195
TRF+C4.5[3]	89.1%	0.102	2.429	1.429	1.879	0.867	2.472	1.441
CNN+LSTM[5]	87.3%	0.114	1.741	1.155	3.600	1.504	5.341	2.367
Traffics2Profile	94.9%	0.043	**1.056**	**0.652**	**0.007**	**0.001**	**1.063**	**0.652**

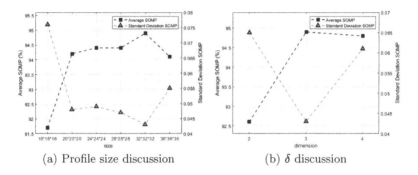

(a) Profile size discussion   (b) δ discussion

Fig. 4. Parameter discussion experiment result

S_{SOMP} are used to measure global error among the training set. For measuring time performance, we separately calculate the traffic processing time T^{P} and the proportion analysis time T^{A}. Among them, the traffic processing time is the time to obtain the traffic profile from the original traffic sample, and the proportion analysis time is the time to predict the traffic proportion based on the traffic profile. Same as accuracy evaluation, we use mean number and standard deviation of process time and analysis time to measure global time performance.

3.3 Experiment

We compare with three traffic classification methods and show results in Table 1. According to Table 1, we can obtain two conclusions about accuracy and time performance evaluation. Firstly, for accuracy evaluation, FS-Net achieve highest average SOMP value of 99.7% and its performance is very stable. FS-Net is a SOTA method in traffic classification field, and it realizes proportion prediction through one-by-one classification. Therefore, it is very reasonable for such fine-grained method to achieve higher accuracy. The average accuracy of our coarse-grained method Traffics2Profile has also reached 94.9%. Although the accuracy and stability are not as good as those traffic classification methods, the accuracy can meet most of the coarse-grained network management scenes. Secondly, for time performance evaluation, Traffics2Profile outperforms all the other methods. Among them, the traffic processing time slightly exceeds other methods, because no matter which method needs to extract features from the original traffic, how to extract features efficiently is not the focus of this article. As for the proportion analysis time, our method greatly exceeds other traffic classification methods due to its overall analysis which meets our expectations.

Profile's size may have an impact on the prediction effectiveness, we set profile's size to $16, 20, 24, 28, 32$ and 36 to explore its impact. According to experiment result shown in Fig 4a, With the increase of traffic profile's size, the accuracy of the method first improves and then slightly decreases. When the size of the traffic profile is small, the resolution of the traffic profile is also low. The nodes with similar embedding will be mapped to the same pixel, thus losing part of the structural information in the original traffic. However, excessively increasing the profile's size will result in an increase of invalid pixels in the traffic profile. These noisy pixels have a negative impact on the accuracy performance.

Embedding dimension δ is also an important parameter to affect method's accuracy. We set δ to $2, 3, 4$ and use CNN with corresponding dimension to analysis traffic profile. According to experiment result shown in Fig. 4b, when the embedding dimension is 3 or 4, the accuracy is significantly better than the accuracy when the embedding dimension is 2. This is because higher-dimensional embedded vector representations can represent richer structure information, which can better realize the proportion analysis. However, when the embedding dimension is 3 and 4, the difference in accuracy is very small, which shows that there is a boundary for the embedding dimension to improve accuracy.

4   Conclusion

In this paper, we proposed a component structure analysis scheme, which can effectively analyze the proportion of various traffic components in the mixed flow. A mixed traffic data set was collected to verify the effectiveness of our proposed scheme. The result shows that our scheme had a significant advantage in both time consumption and performance for traffic proportion analysis task.

Funding Information. This work was supported by the Natural Science Foundation of China (No. 61972431,U2001204,61873290), and the Natural Science Foundation of Guangdong Province, China (No.2018A030313303).

References

1. Barakabitze, A.A.: QoE management of multimedia streaming services in future networks: a tutorial and survey. IEEE Commun. Surv. Tutor. **22**(1), 526–565 (2020)
2. Blake, S., Black, D., Carlson, M., Davies, E., Wang, Z., Weiss, W.: Rfc2475: an architecture for differentiated service (1998)
3. Draper-Gil, G., Lashkari, A.H., Mamun, M.S.I., Ghorbani, A.A.: Characterization of encrypted and vpn traffic using time-related. In: Proceedings of the 2nd International Conference on Information Systems Security and Privacy (ICISSP), pp. 407–414 (2016)

4. Liu, C., He, L., Xiong, G., Cao, Z., Li, Z.: FS-NET: a flow sequence network for encrypted traffic classification. In: IEEE INFOCOM 2019-IEEE Conference on Computer Communications, pp. 1171–1179. IEEE (2019)
5. Lopez-Martin, M., Carro, B., Sanchez-Esguevillas, A., Lloret, J.: Network traffic classifier with convolutional and recurrent neural networks for internet of things. IEEE Access **5**, 18042–18050 (2017)
6. Zhang, J., Yu, F.R., Wang, S., Huang, T., Liu, Z., Liu, Y.: Load balancing in data center networks: a survey. IEEE Commun. Surv. Tutor. **20**(3), 2324–2352 (2018)

Evaluating the Performance and Conformance of a SYCL Implementation for SX-Aurora TSUBASA

Jiahao Li[1]([⊠]), Mulya Agung[2], and Hiroyuki Takizawa[1]

[1] Cyberscience Center, Tohoku University, Sendai, Japan
lijiahao@hpc.is.tohoku.ac.jp, takizawa@tohoku.ac.jp
[2] MRC Human Genetics Unit, Institute of Genetics and Cancer,
University of Edinburgh, Edinburgh, UK
mulya.agung@ed.ac.uk

Abstract. SX-Aurora TSUBASA (SX-AT) is a vector supercomputer equipped with Vector Engines (VEs). SX-AT has not only such a new system architecture, but also some execution modes to achieve high performance on executing a real-world application that often consists of vector friendly and unfriendly parts. Vector Engine Offloading (VEO) is a programming framework to offload only a vector-friendly part to VEs, and neoSYCL has been developed on top of VEO to allow programmers to use the standard SYCL interface at offload programming on SX-AT. However, it is unclear how much neoSYCL based on VEO can conform to the SYCL standard, which is primarily based on OpenCL. Therefore, this paper discusses the conformance of neoSYCL to the SYCL standard, and also the performance. Our thorough evaluation with SYCL-Bench kernels demonstrates that neoSYCL is conformant to the SYCL standard except for OpenCL-related features. In addition, the runtime overhead for using the SYCL interface on top of VEO is negligible in most cases, allowing the neoSYCL codes to achieve comparable performance with the VEO codes.

Keywords: SX-Aurora TSUBASA · SYCL · Benchmarking

1 Introduction

SYCL is an open industry standard for programming a wide range of heterogeneous architectures [5]. The design of SYCL allows standard C++ source code to be written such that it can run on either an accelerator device or on the host. It features high-level abstractions, easing many of the burdens commonly encountered in parallel programming, while still allowing for fine-grained control over performance and hardware features.

NEC SX-Aurora TSUBASA (SX-AT) is the latest vector supercomputer [9]. An SX-AT system is equipped with two kinds of processors, Vector Hosts (VHs)

© Springer Nature Switzerland AG 2022
H. Shen et al. (Eds.): PDCAT 2021, LNCS 13148, pp. 36–47, 2022.
https://doi.org/10.1007/978-3-030-96772-7_4

and Vector Engines (VEs). A VH is a standard x86 processor for running the Linux operating system and hosting VEs, while a VE is NEC's vector processor of eight cores implemented as a PCI-e device card. Having six High-Bandwidth Memory 2E (HBM2E) modules, a VE can provide high memory bandwidth of 1.53 TB/s [6]. Despite of the heterogeneous hardware configuration, users can run a program on the VE as if the whole program is running on the standard Linux environment. However, since a practical application is often a mix of vector friendly and unfriendly parts, there is a demand for offloading only the vector friendly parts to VEs and executing the rest on VHs. Thus, an offload programming model called Vector Engine Offloading (VEO) [10] is also provided by NEC. However, the programming interface of VEO is not only low-level but also non-portable to other platforms.

A SYCL implementation named *neoSYCL* is the first and only SYCL implementation for SX-AT based on VEO [4]. At the source code level, neoSYCL provides a simple tool to identify and separate the kernel part of a SYCL application, and thereby converting it to a distinct function. Relying on this simple approach, neoSYCL has been implemented as a collection of only header files, internally using VEO functions. Due to architectural differences between the vector processor and GPU, some of OpenCL's concepts employed in the SYCL standard do not fit in the vector architecture as discussed in [12]. Hence, neoSYCL implements only a subset of the standard SYCL specification. In addition, for VEs to achieve high sustained performance, the kernel code should be vector-friendly, containing vectorizable long loops. Therefore, this paper discusses the conformance and performance of neoSYCL through some evaluation results.

The purpose of this paper is to demonstrate that neoSYCL is conformant to the SYCL standard at offload programming for SX-AT. There are a large number of features defined in the SYCL standard, and some of them are used mostly for GPU platforms, not for others such as Field Programmable Gate Arrays (FPGAs) [13]. Consequently, this paper focuses on basic and popular SYCL features to be likely used for SX-AT, and discusses the conformance of neoSYCL. In addition, this paper also experimentally discusses the runtime overheads induced by neoSYCL's abstraction layer.

The main contributions of this paper are as follows.

1. This is the first work to demonstrate the conformance and performance of the neoSYCL implementation with a variety of benchmark programs.
2. Based on SYCL-Bench [7], we have developed a portable benchmark suite, named VEO-SYCL-Bench, to compare neoSYCL and VEO versions of a program.
3. We investigate the performance gain of using another framework, Alternative VE Offloading (AVEO) [2], instead of VEO.

2   NEC SX-Aurora TSUBASA

SX-AT is a new generation of NEC's SX-series supercomputers with dedicated vector processors. SX-AT employs a heterogeneous hardware configuration consisting of VHs and VEs. A VH is a standard x86 processor for running the Linux

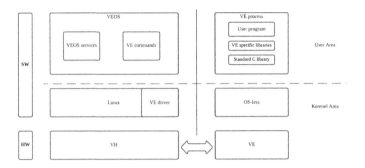

Fig. 1. Software stack of SX-AT.

operating system (OS) as well as hosting VEs. To control VEs, VEOS is a Linux process running on the VH and providing OS functionality to VE programs running on VEs. Each VE is packaged in the form factor of a PCI-e card. The vector processor consists of eight cores, six HBM2E modules, and one Last-Level Cache (LLC) of 16 MB shared by all the cores. Figure 1 shows an overview of an SX-AT system. Since there is no OS kernel on the VE side, VEOS running on the VH provides the OS functionality to a user process running on the VE.

VEOS consists of the `ve_exec` command and the VEOS service. The `ve_exec` command loads a VE program, requests permission to create a VE process, and handles the system calls and exceptions of the VE process. The VE driver installed in the VH Linux kernel space is a PCI device driver that provides VE resource accessibility and handles interrupts from the VEs. NEC provides C, C++, and Fortran compilers to build a program executable on a VE. Since the vector processors can achieve high performance on executing the vectorized code, these compilers support automatic vectorization of loops. In other words, to achieve high performance, the application code should be vector-friendly, meaning that the execution time of the code is mostly spent for executing vectorizable long loops.

There are two execution models to run a program with the VE. The first execution model is the native execution that simply runs the whole program on a VE to avoid the data transfer between VHs and VEs. However, in some applications and application areas, it might not be straightforward to vectorize the whole of an application, and thus non-vectorized parts of the application could critically degrade the overall performance. Since most execution time of a scientific program is likely spent only on a particular loop (expressed as a kernel in SYCL), the second execution model is VEO, which is one of the accelerator-style programming models such as OpenCL [8] and CUDA [11]. In VEO, a compute-intensive kernel part of an application is offloaded to VEs while the rest is executed on the VH. It provides a set of APIs that allow loading a shared library into the VE, locate functions and symbols in the library, allocate and free memory chunks on the VE, transfer data to and from the VE as well as asynchronously execute functions on the VE side. By properly offloading only a kernel part of an application to the VE, the total performance is improved in many cases. However, programmers need to invest more effort in modifying the original source code. In addition, an application developed with VEO is not portable to other platforms because the VEO programming interface is dedicated to SX-AT. Therefore, we need a standard offload programming interface available for the SX-AT platform.

3   Overview of neoSYCL

neoSYCL is a new SYCL implementation that aims to address the productivity issue of offload programming on SX-AT. The SYCL standard is designed to encourage and support a data-parallel programming style. A SYCL single source code contains both host code that runs natively on the host CPU, and device code that is executed on SYCL devices. Although the host code and device code can be written within a single source file, we need to use different compilers for VHs and VEs. Thus, neoSYCL first extracts a kernel part from the source code and writes it to another file as a distinct function. This is so-called *kernel outlining*, and the neoSYCL project provides a kernel generator tool for it. The tool can extract and transform a kernel part at the source-code level. Since the kernel part has been converted to a C/C++ function, the function can be compiled by a device compiler for VEs and linked to the host program to be run on the VH.

The proof-of-concept implementation of neoSYCL in [4] provides important SYCL concepts, including buffers, accessors, and queues. All of them are implemented by internally using VEO APIs.

In the SYCL specification, data storage and data access are handled by `sycl::buffer` and `sycl::accessor` classes, respectively. A `sycl::accessor` instance is created by calling `sycl::buffer::get_access()` to represent basic operations to the data storage associated with the instance. A `sycl::buffer` instance can be associated with a 1D, 2D, or 3D array that is accessible from kernels by using the corresponding `sycl::accessor` instance. The `sycl::buffer` class is a C++ template with two parameters, the type and dimension of the data stored in the buffer. In the neoSYCL implementation, a `sycl::buffer` instance is implemented as a standard C++ array, and copying data to the VE can be done by just copying the whole array to the VE's memory space. Accordingly, the original neoSYCL implementation provides buffers and accessors conformant to the SYCL specification.

Unlike buffers and accessors, queues in the original neoSYCL implementation are not conformant to the SYCL specification. A `sycl::queue` instance represents a mechanism, through which a host code submits work to a device for execution in the future. A `sycl::queue` instance passes kernels to devices in an asynchronous manner. In neoSYCL, there are two kinds of devices available. One is a VE device as a device or an accelerator, and the other is a VH device working also as a host. A `sycl::queue` instance is by default bound to the VH running the application. Any task submitted to the queue is executed on the

VH without any data transfers between VH memory and VE memory. In the original neoSYCL implementation [4], only a `sycl::ve_queue` instance could be bound to a VE to execute the kernel part on the VE. Although a SYCL application should be able to bind a queue to the host device or other accelerator devices by using the `sycl::device_selector` class, the original version of the neoSYCL implementation does not support the `sycl::device_selector` class. With the original neoSYCL implementation, it has been needed to replace every queue with a special one, `sycl::ve_queue`, to run a standard SYCL program on a VE. Therefore, to improve the conformance to the SYCL standard, we have modified the neoSYCL implementation to support the `sycl::device_selector` class compatible with the SYCL specification.

In this way, we have reviewed neoSYCL classes one by one to check if they are conformant to the SYCL specifications. Some classes are rewritten if they are needed for offload programming on SX-AT but not conformant to the SYCL specification.

In the SYCL specification, there are two ways of invoking a kernel. One is to use `sycl::queue::single_task()` (or its variant) to create a single thread on the device side to execute a kernel. If necessary, the single thread could later become the master thread and swan other worker threads for multi-thread execution. For example, we can use OpenMP directives [1] for multi-thread execution of the kernel loop. The other way is to use `sycl::queue::parallel_for()` (or its variant) to create multiple threads on the device side to execute a kernel. The **nd_item** and **nd_range** classes are used to express the information about kernel invocation, such as the number of threads (work items) to be created. The latter way is a basic SYCL feature inherited from OpenCL, which has originally been designed with keeping GPU computing in mind. However, although GPUs need to create a large number of concurrent threads for efficient data parallel processing, its execution model does not necessarily fit in non-GPU platforms. Accordingly, we have decided that the current neoSYCL implementation should not support SYCL features relevant to the **nd_item** and **nd_range** classes, and thus this paper discusses the conformance and performance of neoSYCL except for the unsupported features.

4 Evaluation and Discussions

This section discusses the conformance of the original and new neoSYCL implementations through testing the basic test cases provided by DPC++ [3]. Meanwhile, we use SYCL-Bench kernels to further measure the conformance and performance of the neoSYCL implementations. The neoSYCL implementations support only SX-AT, while other SYCL implementations are not available on SX-AT. Therefore, existing SYCL implementations cannot be directly compared to neoSYCL. However, this paper can still discuss the runtime overhead introduced by neoSYCL by comparing its performance to that of two offloading frameworks for SX-AT, VEO and AVEO. The specifications of the system used in the following experiments are listed in Table 1. We use the default optimization level for VH and VE compilers to compile the programs used in our evaluations.

Table 1. System specifications.

	NEC SX-Aurora TSUBASA A100-1
VH processor	Intel xeon gold 6126 CPU
VH memory	96 Gbytes
VH compiler	Clang version 12.0.0
VE processor	NEC vector engine type-10C
VE memory	24 Gbytes
VE compiler	NEC ncc compiler 2.5.1
Operating system	CentOS Linux 7.9.2009
	VEOS 2.7.4
	VEO 2.5.0
Software	DPC++ source code[1]
	SYCL-Bench[2]

[1]https://github.com/intel/llvm/tree/sycl/sycl/test
[2]https://github.com/bcosenza/sycl-bench

4.1   Conformance Test Cases

DPC++ provides test cases that cover various aspects of the SYCL specification [3]. In this work, our neoSYCL implementations are compared in terms of conformance by using DPC++ test cases, while the conformance is quantified by the number of test cases passed. Note that some of their test cases are designed for Intel hardware and additional extensions. Therefore, we use only the most basic and important test cases in the following evaluation. Specifically, 37 test cases including runtime classes (device selection, device, platform, context, queue and event), data access and storage (buffer and accessor) are used because they are the most common APIs in SYCL applications.

We evaluate the conformance of the original and new neoSYCL implementations by running these test cases on SX-AT. In the original neoSYCL implementation, an instance of special class, `ve_queue`, must first be created, and a task is submitted to the VE via the `ve_queue` instance. However, in the SYCL specification, at any point where the SYCL runtime needs to select a SYCL device through an explicit `device_selector` specialization or through the implicit `default_selector`, the system will call `select_device()`, which will query all available SYCL devices in the system, pass each to this function call operator and select one device. In order to make neoSYCL more conformant to the SYCL standard, the `ve_queue` is deprecated in this work and the `device_selector` classes are implemented. Since a VE can be seen as a kind of accelerator, `accelerator_selector` is defined as a derived SYCL `device_selector` class that selects a VE as a SYCL device. As a result, standard SYCL applications can be executed on SX-AT without code modification. Therefore, the original neoSYCL implementation can only pass 20 test cases (54%), while the new neoSYCL implementation can pass 35 test cases (95%).

Table 2. The detailed list of benchmarks included in the VEO-SYCL-Bench suite.

Benchmark name	Short	Domain
lin_reg_coeff	LRC	Data analytics
lin_reg_error	LRE	Data analytics
median	MEDIAN	Image processing
mol_dyn	MD	Physics simulation
scalar_prod	SP	Linear algebra
sobel3/5/7	SOBEL3/5/7	Image processing
vec_add	VA	Linear algebra
2DConvolution	2DCON	Image processing
2mm	2MM	Linear algebra
3DConvolution	3DCON	Image processing
3mm	3MM	Linear algebra
atax	ATAX	Linear algebra
bicg	BICG	Linear algebra
correlation	CORR	Data mining
covariance	COV	Data mining
fdtd2d	FTD2D	Stencils
gemm	GEMM	Linear algebra
gesummv	GESUM	Linear algebra
gramschmidt	GRAMS	Linear algebra
mvt	MVT	Linear algebra
syr2k	SYR2K	Linear algebra
syrk	SYRK	Linear algebra

The SYCL specification inherits some concepts from OpenCL, and some of those features are not supported by neoSYCL at present. However, there are still two test cases not passed even by the new neoSYCL implementation. This is because two functions `parallel_for_work_group` and `parallel_for_work_item` used in test cases are not supported by the neoSYCL implementations. Due to a great disparity between VEs and GPUs, it is difficult for VEs to efficiently support those OpenCL-related functions [12]. Although the new neoSYCL implementation does not currently support those APIs, the results demonstrate that the new neoSYCL implementation conforms to most important and commonly-used SYCL APIs.

4.2 VEO-SYCL-Bench

The SYCL-Bench suite [7] contains a number of benchmarks which are real-world applications and kernels from different domains such as linear algebra, image processing, and molecular dynamics. It is a benchmarking framework that provides a

```
1  void setup() {
2    input1.resize(args.problem_size);
3    input2.resize(args.problem_size);
4    output.resize(args.problem_size);
5    for (size_t i =0; i < args.problem_size; i++) {
6      input1[i] = static_cast<T>(i);
7      input2[i] = static_cast<T>(i);
8      output[i] = static_cast<T>(0);
9    }
10   input1_buf.initialize(args.device_queue, input1.data(), s::range<1>(args.problem_
11   input2_buf.initialize(args.device_queue, input2.data(), s::range<1>(args.problem_
12   output_buf.initialize(args.device_queue, output.data(), s::range<1>(args.problem_
13 }
14 void run(std::vector<cl::sycl::event>& events) {
15   events.push_back(args.device_queue.submit(
16     [&](cl::sycl::handler& cgh) {
17       auto in1 = input1_buf.template get_access<s::access::mode::read>(cgh);
18       auto in2 = input2_buf.template get_access<s::access::mode::read>(cgh);
19       auto out = output_buf.template get_access<s::access::mode::read_write>(cgh);
20       cl::sycl::range<1> ndrange {args.problem_size};
21       cgh.parallel_for<class VecAddKernel<T>>(ndrange,
22         [=](cl::sycl::id<1> gid) {
23           out[gid] = in1[gid] + in2[gid];
24         });
25   }));
26 }
```

(a) vec_add benchmark of SYCL-Bench.

```
1  int main(int argc, char** argv) {
2    accelerator_selector as;
3    queue q(as);
4    vector<float> input1(LENGTH, 0);
5    vector<float> input2(LENGTH, 0);
6    vector<float> output(LENGTH, 0);
7    for (size_t i = 0; i < LENGTH; i++) {
8      input1[i] = static_cast<float>(i);
9      input2[i] = static_cast<float>(i);
10     output[i] = static_cast<float>(0);
11   }
12   buffer<float> input1_buf(input1.data(), range<1>(LENGTH));
13   buffer<float> input2_buf(input2.data(), range<1>(LENGTH));
14   buffer<float> output_buf(output.data(), range<1>(LENGTH));
15   q.submit([&](handler& cgh) {
16     auto in1 = input1_buf.template get_access<access::mode::read>(cgh);
17     auto in2 = input2_buf.template get_access<access::mode::read>(cgh);
18     auto out = output_buf.template get_access<access::mode::read_write>(cgh);
19     cgh.parallel_for<class VecAddKernel>(range<1>(LENGTH), [=](id<1> gid) {
20       out[gid] = in1[gid] + in2[gid];
21     });
22   });
23   q.wait();
24   return 0;
25 }
```

(b) vec_add benchmark of VEO-SYCL-Bench.

Fig. 2. SYCL-Bench and VEO-SYCL-Bench versions of the vec add benchmark.

lot of features, such as the command line arguments, a verification layer for all benchmarks and the automated execution of the entire benchmark suite. However, SYCL-Bench is not portable because some of APIs used in the framework are not conformant to the standard SYCL specification, and thus neither DPC++ nor neoSYCL can compile the original SYCL-Bench. Hence, based on SYCL-Bench, we have developed a simple but portable version of those benchmarks. To discuss the runtime overhead induced by the neoSYCL's abstraction layer, we also developed a VEO version of those benchmarks. The collection of our SYCL benchmarks and VEO benchmarks is named VEO-SYCL-Bench[1]. Table 2 is the list of the benchmarks.

In SYCL-Bench, many of benchmarks provide variants for different kernel invocation mechanisms mentioned in Sect. 3. Since neoSYCL supports only `single_task()` and `parallel_for()`, we have copied only the kernels invoked

---

[1] https://github.com/Tohoku-University-Takizawa-Lab/veo-sycl-bench.

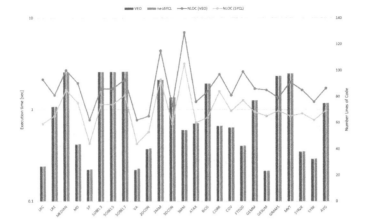

Fig. 3. Performance and code complexity comparison between VEO and neoSYCL versions of benchmark programs.

with `parallel_for()` from SYCL-Bench to VEO-SYCL-Bench, and rewrote the other parts such as buffer allocation and initialization that are performance insensitive. Figure 2 serves as an illustrating example. Figure 2a shows the original vec_add benchmark consists of the most important parts including buffer initialization and kernel function, while the arguments, queue and device selection are initialized through the framework. Hence, we simplify the SYCL-Bench code for VEO-SYCL-Bench as shown in Fig. 2b. The queue is bound to VE as a device by explicitly passing a `sycl::accelerator_selector` instance to the constructor. Data required by the kernel are initialized by using `sycl::buffer` instances. The kernel part is almost the same as that of the SYCL-Bench version. Since our VEO-SYCL-Bench only uses standard SYCL APIs, it can be easily used by other SYCL implementations.

Figure 3 shows the execution time of benchmarks using two different implementations. At the time measurement, we run each benchmark 10 times with a small input size, and then calculate the average execution time. The results show that the neoSYCL version is only 0.42% slower than the native VEO version on average. Although it is common that high-level abstraction introduces some runtime overhead, the results show that the overhead caused by the neoSYCL runtime is small enough and negligible. Furthermore, to evaluate the impacts of SYCL on productivity, a code complexity analyzer, called Lizard [14], is used to measure the code complexities of different implementations. Figure 3 also shows the NLOC (the number of lines of code without comments) of two implementations for each benchmark. Other metrics including CCN (cyclomatic complexity number) and the token (the number of distinct operators and distinct operands) are also calculated in our experiments. The average CCN and token values of SYCL versions are 10 and 653, respectively. On the other hand, the average CCN and token values of VEO versions are 12 and 764.5, respectively. All results show

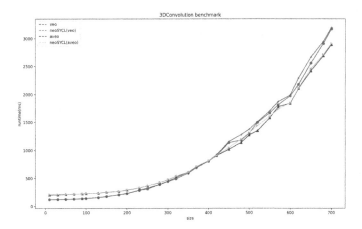

Fig. 4. Performance comparison between the VEO and AVEO implementations.

that SYCL versions are less complex and thus easier to maintain. In conclusion, because of employing the SYCL programming interface, neoSYCL can decrease the code complexity with achieving almost the same performance.

AVEO is an alternative implementation of the VEO framework, which is fully compatible with the original VEO [2]. It has been redesigned to solve a set of problems in VEO and improve the kernel invocation latency as well as the data transfer bandwidth. Therefore, in this paper, we also evaluate the performance of the neoSYCL implementation with AVEO while changing the input data size. The neoSYCL implementations on top of VEO and AVEO are called neoSYCL-VEO and neoSYCL-AVEO, respectively.

The kernel invocation latency of the original VEO is about 100 μs, while Focht [2] has shown that the kernel invocation latency of AVEO is in the range of 5.5–6 μs. In this work, however, most benchmarks invoke kernels only a few times. As a result, the time spent on kernel invocation is almost negligible in comparison with the time spent on executing the kernel. Therefore, a reduction in the kernel invocation latency may not significantly decrease the total execution time.

On the other hand, the data transfer bandwidth between a VH and a VE is essential even for those benchmarks, because the benchmarks usually need to transfer a certain amount of data between the VH and the VE. For example, 3D Convolution is an image processing benchmark from SYCL-Bench, and stores a large amount of data on both of the VH memory and the VE memory. Therefore, the improvement in data transfer bandwidth could potentially decrease the total execution time.

Figure 4 shows the performance comparison between neoSYCL-VEO and neoSYCL-AVEO for the 3D Convolution benchmark. In the case of a small buffer size, VEO and neoSYCL-VEO can achieve a better performance than AVEO and neoSYCL-AVEO. However, by increasing the input size, AVEO and neoSYCL-AVEO outperform VEO and neoSYCL-VEO. This is because the architecture of

AVEO is more complex than that of VEO, resulting in some overhead in small input cases. Since the performance for large input data is more important in practice, these results suggest that it is more promising to use AVEO for implementing neoSYCL, though the performance difference is not very significant in this particular benchmark. The results also show that both neoSYCL-VEO and neoSYCL-AVEO can always achieve comparable performance respectively with VEO and AVEO no matter of the input size. Thus, it is again demonstrated that the abstraction penalty induced by the neoSYCL implementation is negligible.

5   Conclusions

SX-AT is a heterogeneous computing system equipped with VEs, which can provide the world's highest memory bandwidth, and neoSYCL is a SYCL implementation for enabling offload programming on SX-AT with the standard programming interface. Although the original neoSYCL implementation has already supported most of the major SYCL features, there are some unsupported ones. In this work, therefore, we demonstrate the conformance and performance of the neoSYCL implementation with a variety of benchmark programs. We have reviewed the SYCL classes one by one, and modified some classes to improve the conformance. Although the improved neoSYCL implementation still has some unsupported features due to the hardware limitations, our evaluation has shown that most SYCL benchmarks can be executed on SX-AT.

For the performance evaluation, we also have developed a benchmark suite, named VEO-SYCL-Bench. The evaluation results indicate that the performance difference between neoSYCL and VEO versions of a program is small and thus the runtime overhead induced by neoSYCL is negligible in practice. Meanwhile, the results of code complexity metrics show that neoSYCL can always outperform the native implementation. Moreover, we investigate the performance gain of using AVEO. Our results show that VEO can perform better than AVEO for small input data, while for large input data, AVEO can outperform VEO.

In our future work, we will improve the neoSYCL implementation to support more SYCL features and various devices. Meanwhile, due to a great distinction among computing architectures, an efficient device selection mechanism is required to fully utilize computing resources. Thus, we will discuss the automation of a task-to-device mapping mechanism.

Acknowledgement. This work is partially supported by MEXT Next Generation High-Performance Computing Infrastructures and Applications R&D Program "R&D of A Quantum-Annealing-Assisted Next Generation HPC Infrastructure and its Applications," Grant-in-Aid for Scientific Research(A) #20H00593 and Grant-in-Aid for Scientific Research(B) #21H03449.

References

1. Chandra, R., Dagum, L., Kohr, D., Menon, R., Maydan, D., McDonald, J.: Parallel Programming in OpenMP. Morgan kaufmann, Burlington (2001)
2. Focht, E.: Speeding up vector engine offloading with AVEO, pp. 35–47 (2021)
3. Intel: Data Parallel C++ language. https://software.intel.com/content/www/cn/zh/develop/tools/oneapi/data-parallel-c-plus-plus.html
4. Ke, Y., Agung, M., Takizawa, H.: neosycl: a sycl implementation for sx-aurora tsubasa. In: The International Conference on High Performance Computing in Asia-Pacific Region, pp. 50–57. HPC Asia 2021, Association for Computing Machinery, New York (2021). https://doi.org/10.1145/3432261.3432268
5. Khronos: SYCL 1.2.1. Technical report, Khronos Group, Inc. (2020). https://www.khronos.org/registry/SYCL/specs/sycl-1.2.1.pdf
6. Komatsu, K., et al.: Performance evaluation of a vector supercomputer sx-aurora tsubasa. In: SC18: International Conference for High Performance Computing, Networking, Storage and Analysis, pp. 685–696 (2018). https://doi.org/10.1109/SC.2018.00057
7. Lal, S.: SYCL-bench: a versatile cross-platform benchmark suite for heterogeneous computing. In: Malawski, M., Rzadca, K. (eds.) Euro-Par 2020. LNCS, vol. 12247, pp. 629–644. Springer, Cham (2020). https://doi.org/10.1007/978-3-030-57675-2_39
8. Munshi, A.: The opencl specification. In: 2009 IEEE Hot Chips 21 Symposium (HCS), pp. 1–314 (2009). https://doi.org/10.1109/HOTCHIPS.2009.7478342
9. NEC: SX-Aurora TSUBASA - Vector Engine. https://www.nec.com/en/global/solutions/hpc/sx/vector_engine.html
10. Noack, M., Focht, E., Steinke, T.: Heterogeneous active messages for offloading on the nec sx-aurora tsubasa. In: 2019 IEEE International Parallel and Distributed Processing Symposium Workshops (IPDPSW), pp. 26–35 (2019). https://doi.org/10.1109/IPDPSW.2019.00014
11. Sanders, J., Kandrot, E.: CUDA by Example: An Introduction to General-Purpose GPU Programming. Addison-Wesley Professional, Boston (2010)
12. Takizawa, H., Shiotsuki, S., Ebata, N., Egawa, R.: An opencl-like offload programming framework for sx-aurora tsubasa. In: 2019 20th International Conference on Parallel and Distributed Computing, Applications and Technologies (PDCAT), pp. 282–288 (2019). https://doi.org/10.1109/PDCAT46702.2019.00059
13. Waidyasooriya, H.M., Takei, Y., Tatsumi, S., Hariyama, M.: Opencl-based FPGA-platform for stencil computation and its optimization methodology. IEEE Trans. Parallel Distrib. Syst. **28**(5), 1390–1402 (2017). https://doi.org/10.1109/TPDS.2016.2614981
14. Yin, T.: Lizard: An extensible Cyclomatic Complexity Analyzer (2019)

Bayesian Optimization-Based Task Scheduling Algorithm on Heterogeneous System

Tan Cai and Hong Shen[✉]

School of Computer Science and Engineering, Sun Yat-sen University,
Guangzhou, China
{cait7,shenh3}@mail2.sysu.edu.cn

Abstract. In heterogeneous computing systems, efficient task scheduling is essential for utilizing resources and reducing computing time. This problem has been shown NP-complete in the general case. Existing solutions are mainly heuristic-based that would easily track into optimal local solutions and reinforcement learning-based that need an expensive computation cost for data training on neural networks. To overcome the shortcomings, we propose a Bayesian optimization based task scheduling algorithm that automatically searches for the best heuristic strategy in the problem space. Our algorithm builds a Bayesian optimization model on heuristic strategy and scheduling performance, and updates the model by interacting with the environment to find the optimal solutions globally. To enhance the confidence of our experiments, we measure the average (weighted) makespans and running time of our algorithm. The experimental results show that our approach can improve the scheduling performance compared to the baselines.

Keywords: Task scheduling · Bayesian optimization · Heuristic

1 Introduction

A cloud data center containing heterogeneous servers interconnected in a high-speed network supports parallel execution of multiple tasks. In this paper, we study the problem of job (workflow) scheduling in a data center. For a given set of jobs, each job is represented as a task graph (directed acyclic graph or DAG), where nodes represent tasks in the job and edges represent the dependencies between the tasks. Under the task dependency constraints, we need to jointly determine the execution order of each task and the task-to-server allocation plan to minimize the overall makespan of all jobs.

Improving the performance of task scheduling is remarkably challenging and has critical importance in boosting the profit of cloud computing platforms. Existing static task scheduling methods can be roughly classified into three categories (heuristic-based scheduling, meta-heuristic scheduling, and machine learning-based scheduling algorithms). The heuristic-based scheduling algorithms [1, 11, 12]

ⓒ Springer Nature Switzerland AG 2022
H. Shen et al. (Eds.): PDCAT 2021, LNCS 13148, pp. 48–56, 2022.
https://doi.org/10.1007/978-3-030-96772-7_5

have advantages over execution time. In contrast, the performance of those algorithms relies on the specific heuristic strategy, so is poor in robustness. Meta-heuristic [8] is another type of popular algorithms, which provide good quality of schedules but the scheduling latency is much higher than other categories. In recent years, with the rapid development of machine learning technique, many researchers have attempted to address the problem of task scheduling with reinforcement learning [3,4,7] that can interact with the environment and automatically generate the scheduling strategy but requires expensive costs in computing with the neural network.

We propose a Bayesian optimization based task scheduling algorithm for the static task schedules on a heterogeneous system to handle the above problems. We summarize the main contributions of the paper as follows:

– We propose a Bayesian optimization based scheduling algorithm to handle the problem of task scheduling. Our algorithm searches for the best heuristic strategy in the problem space, effectively improving the performance and reducing the latency in the scheduling.
– We analyze the mathematical property of our algorithm and provide a guarantee for convergence in theory. The worst time complexity of our algorithm is less than other search methods (random search, grid search, etc.).
– We conduct simulation experiments to validate our algorithm. The experimental result illustrates that our algorithm can improve the scheduling performance compared against the baselines.

2 Related Work

Existing research efforts have been proposed for the task scheduling problem, and various algorithms are provided in the literature, which can be traditionally classified into three categories (heuristic-based scheduling, meta-heuristic scheduling, and machine learning-based scheduling algorithms).

The heuristic is a kind of traditional algorithms to solve the scheduling problem, utilizing the heuristic strategy to guide the scheduling process. Heterogeneous Earliest-Finish Time (HEFT) [11] is the most well-known list-based scheduling algorithm. Predict Earliest-Finish Time (PEFT) [1], Lookahead [2], Critical-Path-on-a-server (CPOP) [11] have been proposed as extensions of HEFT. The heuristic-based algorithms have low computational complexity but easily get the optimal local solution, so that poor in robustness and often need a slight change in the problem space.

Meta-heuristic is another popular algorithm, such as genetic algorithm, simulated annealing algorithm, ant colony optimization. Manasrah [8] proposes a hybrid GA-PSO algorithm that aims to reduce the makespan and the cost and balance the load of the dependent tasks over the heterogeneous resources in cloud computing environments. Meta-heuristic algorithms have the main disadvantage of the high computational cost.

In recent years, with the rapid development of machine learning, machine learning-based scheduling algorithms have been proposed which reduce the computation time. In [9], the authors use reinforcement learning (Q-learning and

SARSA) to solve the workflow scheduling problem for computation resources that reduces the task execution time. In [5,7], and [4], reinforcement learning and deep learning are combined to solve more difficult problems in real life. The machine learning-based scheduling algorithms have the main disadvantage on the high cost of training and computing in the neural network.

3   Problem Description

3.1   Scheduling Model

In this section, we formulate the task scheduling model. In a heterogeneous computing system, the user submits jobs (workflows) $\{j_i\}_{i=1}^{N}$ to be executed, and each job can be represented as a directed acyclic graph, where vertices indicate tasks and edges indicates dependencies between tasks. We call a task node without any parent as an entry node and a task node without any child as an exit node. The task scheduling process always begins with the entry nodes. We assume the heterogeneous environment consists of servers $\{p_i\}_{i=1}^{M}$.

For each job j_n, it contains tasks $\{t_{n,i}\}_{i=1}^{K_n}$, where the required resource $\{r_{n,i}\}_{i=1}^{K_n}$ and the workload $\{w_{n,i}\}_{i=1}^{K_n}$ are known in advance. For a task $t_{n,i}$ to be execute on a server p_j, the execution time is obtained as:

$$c_{n,i}^{j} = \frac{w_{n,i}}{W_j}. \tag{1}$$

In this paper, we aim to minimize the total weighted Job Completion Time (JCT):

$$T = min \sum_{n=1}^{N} W_n \cdot J_n \tag{2}$$

where W_n indicates the weight of job j_n and J_n shows the completion time, respectively. We suppose that important jobs are assigned higher weights.

3.2   Constraints

Resources Capacity Constraint. We use $\mathcal{V}_u$ to present a set of tasks running in server p_u, and introduce Eq. 3 to ensure that resources are sufficient enough to support performing tasks:

$$\sum_{t \in \mathcal{V}_u} r_t \leq \mathcal{R}_{\mathbf{u}} \tag{3}$$

Task Dependency Constraint. For each job j_n, the completion time J_n has the following constraint:

$$J_n = \max_{i \in \{1,...,K_n\}} C_{n,i} \tag{4}$$

where $C_{n,i}$ indicates the completion time of task $t_{n,i}$. It's noticeable that $C_{n,i}$ starts timing after the job j_n arrives. The completion time of a job depends on the completion time of the latest task that composes it. Similarly, a task $t_{n,i}$ can be scheduled after the job j_n is released, which has the following constraint:

$$R_n = \min_{i \in \{1,\dots,K_n\}} S_{n,i} \tag{5}$$

where $S_{n,i}$ indicates the start time of task $t_{n,i}$, and R_n indicates the releasing time of j_n. Consider the dependencies in each job, one task can start after the tasks it depends on has completed the transmission. The dependency constraint can be expressed as:

$$S_{n,i} = \max_{t' \in succ(t_{n,i})} (C_{t'} + m(t', t_{n,i})) \tag{6}$$

Algorithm 1: Bayesian optimization based scheduling algorithm.

Input: A set of jobs to be scheduled: $\{j_i\}_{i=1}^N$; A set of servers $\{p_i\}_{i=1}^M$.
Output: The weighted job completion time T.

1 Init a multivariate Gaussian process model $M : \{w_i\}_{i=1}^4 \to T$; /* Ref to 1.1 */
2 **repeat**
3 | Get the most promising candidate $\{w_i^*\}_{i=1}^4$ by minimizing M; /* Ref to 1.2 */
4 | $T' \leftarrow 0$;
5 | $S \leftarrow \emptyset$;
6 | $J \leftarrow \{j_i\}_{i=1}^N$;
7 | **foreach** *job j_i in J* **do**
8 | | **foreach** *task $t_{i,n}$ in j_i* **do**
9 | | | **if** *indegree$(t_{i,n})$ is equal to 0* **then**
10 | | | | $S \leftarrow S \cup \{t_{i,n}\}$; /* Ref to 2.2 */
11 | | | | $j_i \leftarrow j_i/t_{i,n}$;
12 | | | **end**
13 | | **end**
14 | **end**
15 | **while** *S is not empty* **do**
16 | | Select (t,p) from $t \in S$ and $p \in \{P_i\}_{i=1}^M$ with the highest priority according to f^*; /* Ref to 2.3 */
17 | | $S \leftarrow S/t$;
18 | | Release the dependencies from t to its predecessors and append new tasks without dependencies to S;
19 | | **if** *all the task in j' is completed* **then**
20 | | | $T' \leftarrow T' + W_{j'} * J'$;
21 | | **end**
22 | **end**
23 | $M \leftarrow$ FITMODEL$(M, (w^*, T'))$; /* Ref to 1.2 */
24 | $T = \min(T, T')$; /* Ref to 2.4 */
25 **until** *The result T is acceptable*;

---

where $succ(\cdot)$ indicates the set of immediate successors, and $m(\cdot, \cdot)$ indicates the transmission time.

4 Algorithm

In this section, we first introduce the scheduling strategy and then present our algorithm for finding the best scheduling strategy in the problem space automatically.

4.1 Scheduling Strategy

In heuristic-based scheduling, the scheduling strategy assigns priorities to tasks and decides the execution order. The format of the scheduling strategy is also different with various algorithms. In this paper, we present the strategy f as a linear combination of some scheduling indicators (such as resource utilization rate, upward rank, and so on) and express it as:

$$f(t, p) = w_1 \cdot x_{ru}(t, p) + w_2 \cdot x_{up}(t) + w_3 \cdot x_{down}(c) + w_4 \cdot x_{exec}(t, p), \qquad (7)$$

where $f(t, p)$ measures the priority of an executable pair (t, p), and the definition of resource utilization rate x_{ru}, upward rank x_{up}, downward rank x_{down}, and execution time x_{exec} are introduced next.

Resource utilization rate for one task t executing on the server p can be represented as:

$$x_{ru}(t, p) = \frac{r_t + \sum\limits_{t' \in \mathcal{V}_p} \mathbf{r}_{t'}}{\mathcal{R}_p}, \qquad (8)$$

Execution time is defined in the Eq. 1.
Upward rank can be represented below:

$$x_{up}(t) = w_t + \max_{t' \in succ(t)} (x_{up}(t') + m(t, t')) \qquad (9)$$

where w_t is the workload of t, $succ(t)$ is the set of immediate successors of t, and $m(t, t'))$ is the transmission cost between task t' and task t.
Downward rank can be represented below:

$$x_{down}(t) = \max_{t' \in pred(t)} (x_{down}(t') + w_{t'} + m(t, t')), \qquad (10)$$

where $pred(t)$ is the set of immediate predecessors of task t.

According the the Eq. 7, the quality of f is determined with the parameters $\{w_i\}_{i=1}^4$. We divide the scheduling process of our algorithm into two phases, which are introduced in the next subsection.

4.2   First phase: Bayesian optimization training

We regard the relationship between the parameters and the total completion time as a black-box function, and describe it with the help of Bayesian optimization:

1.1 Propose a Gaussian process model $M : \{w_i\}_{i=1}^4 \to T$, where $\{w_i\}_{i=1}^4$ indicates the parameters in Eq. 7 and T is defined in Eq. 2;

1.2 Fetch parameter $\{w'\}_{i=1}^n$ by minimizing M, gain the observe data $(\{w_i''\}_{i=1}^4, T')$ by simulating the scheduling process, and update M with the observe data;

1.3 Repeat 1.2 until we obtain an acceptable result.

4.3   Second Phase: Task Scheduling Simulation

In this phase, we predict the total completion time T' with $\{w_i'\}_{i=1}^4$.

2.1 Determine the heuristic strategy f' with the given parameters $\{w_i'\}_{i=1}^4$;

2.2 For the input $\{j_i\}_{i=1}^N$, define a set of all executable task list $l_{execute}$ and initialize the $l_{execute}$ with the entry nodes in $\{j_i\}_{i=1}^N$;

2.3 With the help of the heuristic strategy f', we fetch a pair (t, p) having the highest priority assigned with f compared with all the candidates, where t is from $l_{execute}$ and p is a server. If the task t is selected, it should be removed from $l_{execute}$ and release the dependencies with other tasks. Other tasks without dependencies should be appended to the $l_{execute}$;

2.4 Repeat 2.3 until the $l_{execute}$ is empty, then we obtain the reward T' defined in Eq. 2.

4.4   Theoretical Analysis

In this subsection, we explore the effectiveness of our algorithm. We first introduce the assumption about Gradients of GP Sample Paths [6]:

Lemma 1. *For the optimal solutions* $T = F(w^*)$ *in Bayesian optimization which can be represented as* $F(w^*) = max_{i=1,...,j} F(w_i)$, *we have*

$$F(w^*) - \max_{i=1,2,...,j} F(w_i) \le \mathbb{E}[F(w^*) - F(w_j)] \le \mathbb{E}[L\|w^* - w_j\|] \le \frac{d}{\tau_j}\mathbb{E}[L]$$

$$\le \frac{d}{\tau_j} \int_0^{inf} ae^{\frac{t^2}{b^2}} dt = \frac{dab\sqrt{\pi}}{2\tau_j} = \frac{1}{2j^2}$$

where j indicates the iteration times and w_i indicates the most promising candidate w from M in the i-th iteration. The first step bounds the difference in the function values by the largest partial derivative and the L distance between the points. The second step uses the properties of the discretization.

We follow Lemma 1 and have the ratio between the optimal solution $F(w^*)$ and the best observed solution $\max_{i=1,2,...,j} F(w_i)$ at the j-th iteration:

$$\frac{F(w^*)}{\max_{i=1,2,...,j} F(w_i)} \le 1 + \frac{1}{2j^2 \cdot \max_{i=1,2,...,j} F(w_i)} 1 + \frac{1}{\Psi_j \cdot 2j^2}. \tag{11}$$

And we apply the result here [10]

$$\mathbb{E}[\Psi_j] = \mu_j + \sigma_j \Phi^{-1}\left(\frac{j - \frac{\pi}{8}}{j - \frac{\pi}{4} + 1}\right). \tag{12}$$

The result below is workable:

$$\frac{F(w^*)}{\max_{i=1,2,\ldots,j} F(w_i)} \leq 1 + \frac{1}{2j^2\mu_j + 2j^2\sigma_j\Phi^{-1}(1 + \frac{\pi-8}{16-4\pi})}$$

$$\leq 1 + \frac{1}{2j^2\mu_j + 2.36j^2\sigma_j} \tag{13}$$

where $\phi(x) = \frac{1}{\sqrt{2\pi}exp(-\frac{1}{2}x^2)}$ and $\Phi(x) = \int_{-\infty}^{x} \phi(z)dz$. The Eq.13 indicates that our algorithm can guarantee the convergence.

5 Experimental Results

5.1 Research Questions

We discuss the research questions in the remainder of the section:

RQ1 Does the algorithm we propose workable and effective? Does our algorithm obtain high-quality scheduling results compared with other scheduling algorithms?

RQ2 Does the running time of our algorithm better than other algorithms? How does the running speed of our algorithm differ from others?

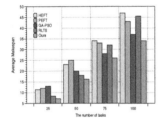
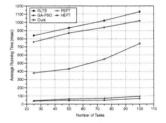

Fig. 1. The total weighted makespans of our algorithm and baselines with the number of tasks changing.

Fig. 2. Average running time (over 100 runs on randomly generated job) of our algorithm and baselines.

5.2 Baselines

In this subsection, we compare the performance with four typical algorithms: HEFT [11], PEFT [1], GA-PSO [8], and RLTS [5], where HEFT and PEFT belong to heuristic-based scheduling, GA-PSO belongs to meta-heuristic scheduling, and RLTS belongs to reinforcement learning-based scheduling (Figs. 1 and 2).

5.3 Experiments

We set up two main experiments to answer the research questions listed above. In the first experiment, we examine the performance of our algorithm compared with other task scheduling algorithms. We can see that all the values of makespan calculated by our algorithm are less than other algorithms. This is because our algorithm tries to search for the best heuristic strategy in the problem space and interact with the scheduling environment to avoid presenting local optimal solutions. In the second experiment, we evaluated the average running time of those algorithms. We can see that the running time of our algorithm is less than RLTS and GA-PSO, which indicates that our algorithm has less time complexity than the reinforcement learning-based algorithm and meta-heuristic algorithm. The running time of our algorithm is more than HEFT and PEFT because those algorithms have low computational complexity but can often be ended at local optimal solutions.

6 Conclusion

We propose a Bayesian optimization based scheduling algorithm to automatically search for the best heuristic strategy in the problem space. We also show theoretical guarantee of convergence of our algorithm. The experimental results show that our algorithm can improve the scheduling performance compared to the baselines.

Acknowledgement. This work is supported by Key-Area Research and Development Plan of Guangdong Province #2020B010164003.

References

1. Arabnejad, H., Barbosa, J.G.: List scheduling algorithm for heterogeneous systems by an optimistic cost table. IEEE Trans. Parallel Distrib. Syst. **25**(3), 682–694 (2014)
2. Bittencourt, L.F., Sakellariou, R., Madeira, E.R.M.: Dag scheduling using a lookahead variant of the heterogeneous earliest finish time algorithm. In: 2010 18th Euromicro Conference on Parallel, Distributed and Network-based Processing, pp. 27–34 (2010)
3. Chen, X., Zhang, H., Wu, C., Mao, S., Ji, Y., Bennis, M.: Optimized computation offloading performance in virtual edge computing systems via deep reinforcement learning. IEEE Internet Things J. **6**(3), 4005–4018 (2019)
4. Dai, H., Khalil, E.B., Zhang, Y., Dilkina, B., Song, L.: Learning combinatorial optimization algorithms over graphs (2018)
5. Dong, T., Xue, F., Xiao, C., Li, J.: Task scheduling based on deep reinforcement learning in a cloud manufacturing environment. Concurr. Comput. Pract. Exper. **32**(11), e5654 (2020)

6. Kandasamy, K., Krishnamurthy, A., Schneider, J., Poczos, B.: Parallelised bayesian optimisation via thompson sampling. In: Storkey, A., Perez-Cruz, F. (eds.) Proceedings of the Twenty-First International Conference on Artificial Intelligence and Statistics. Proceedings of Machine Learning Research, 09–11 April 2018, vol. 84, pp. 133–142. PMLR (2018). https://proceedings.mlr.press/v84/kandasamy18a.html

7. Lin, C.C., Deng, D.J., Chih, Y.L., Chiu, H.T.: Smart manufacturing scheduling with edge computing using multiclass deep q network. IEEE Trans. Ind. Inf. **15**(7), 4276–4284 (2019)

8. Manasrah, A.M., Ba Ali, H., Gupta, B.B.: Workflow scheduling using hybrid gapso algorithm in cloud computing. Wirel. Commun. Mob. Comput. 2018 (2018). https://doi.org/10.1155/2018/1934784

9. Orhean, A.I., Pop, F., Raicu, I.: New scheduling approach using reinforcement learning for heterogeneous distributed systems. J. Parallel Distrib. Comput. **117**, 292–302 (2018). https://www.sciencedirect.com/science/article/pii/S0743731517301521

10. Royston, J.P.: Algorithm as 177: expected normal order statistics (exact and approximate). J. Roy. Stat. Soc. Series C (Appl. Stat.) **31**(2), 161–165 (1982). http://www.jstor.org/stable/2347982

11. Topcuoglu, H., Hariri, S., Wu, M.Y.: Performance-effective and low-complexity task scheduling for heterogeneous computing. IEEE Trans. Parallel Distrib. Syst. **13**(3), 260–274 (2002)

12. Wang, H., Sinnen, O.: List-scheduling versus cluster-scheduling. IEEE Trans. Parallel Distrib. Syst. **29**(8), 1736–1749 (2018)

Optimizing Uplink Bandwidth Utilization for Crowdsourced Livecast

Xianzhi Zhang[1,2], Guoqiao Ye[1,2], Miao Hu[1,2], and Di Wu[1,2(✉)]

[1] School of Computer Science and Engineering, Sun Yat-Sen University,
Guangzhou 510006, China
{zhangxzh9,yegq3}@mail2.sysu.edu.cn, {humiao5,wudi27}@mail.sysu.edu.cn
[2] Guangdong Key Laboratory of Big Data Analysis and Processing,
Guangzhou 510006, China

Abstract. Driven by the prevalence of video generation devices and the development of network infrastructures, there has been an explosive growth of Crowdsourced Video Livecast (CVL) services in the past few years. Significant efforts have been made to provide high quality CVL services with limited bandwidth availability. However, most of the existing works focused on optimizing downlink bandwidth for video distribution rather than uplink bandwidth for video uploading. For example, uploaders (i.e., broadcasters) in Twitch can arbitrarily set their upload rates, which may lead to a significant waste of upload bandwidth with the increasing number of uploaders. In this paper, we propose an effective low-complexity algorithm called *Bubal* to optimize upload bandwidth allocation among massive uploaders. Our objective is to optimize the utility of video uploading from the perspective of CVL platform operators by considering both viewers Quality-of-Experience (QoE) and upload bandwidth cost. To guarantee the effectiveness and fairness of bandwidth allocation, we adopt the optimization framework of *Nash Bargaining Solution* (*NBS*), which can determine the optimal bandwidth budget, upload bitrate and datacenter selection for each uploader jointly. Finally, we conduct extensive trace-driven simulations to evaluate our proposed algorithm and the results show that our algorithm achieves much higher utility than alternative strategies in various conditions.

Keywords: Crowdsourced Video Livecast · Upload bandwidth · Quality-of-Experience (QoE) · Utility maximization · Nash bargaining solution

1 Introduction

In recent years, *Crowdsourced Video Livecast* (*CVL*) flourishes with the prevalence of high-end user devices by leveraging the power of cloud computing

This work was supported by the National Natural Science Foundation of China under Grant U1911201, U2001209, 62072486, 61802452, the Science and Technology Planning Project of Guangdong Province under Grant 2021A0505110008, the Science and Technology Program of Guangzhou under Grant 202007040006, 202002020045, 202103010004.

H. Shen et al. (Eds.): PDCAT 2021, LNCS 13148, pp. 57–68, 2022.
https://doi.org/10.1007/978-3-030-96772-7_6

platforms. A number of worldwide crowdsourced video livecast platforms have emerged, such as Twitch.tv, YouTube Live, Azubu.tv, and Hitbox.tv. As one of the most successful CVL platforms, Twitch.tv has attracted over 200 million concurrent viewers and more than 3 million concurrent broadcasters at its peak hours [2]. What's more, CVL has received research attention from both industry and academia, spanning from measuring real platforms, developing transcoding frameworks to optimizing resources consumed by viewers.

Despite extensive contributions made by previous researchers, there is very limited work focusing on optimizing bandwidth resources allocated to uploaders. However, according to the measurement study [18], 25% of upload bandwidth has been wasted by broadcasters. The reason is that, with an arbitrarily selection of upload bitrates, all uploaders prefer to choose the highest upload bitrates that they can support to maximize the streaming quality of their viewers no matter how many viewers there are, which can cause significant resource wastage.

From the perspective of the CVL platform operators, their goal is to maximize overall utility by maintaining good enough viewers' QoE with reasonable bandwidth cost. However, it is non-trivial to determine the optimal upload bitrate and datacenter selection for the reasons as follows: *First*, we need to balance the upload bitrates of different uploaders to achieve high overall QoE of the platform while minimizing the bandwidth cost. *Second*, since the bandwidth prices and locations of datacenters are different, we need to carefully choose appropriate datacenters for uploaders to upload their videos. *Third*, the viewer population of a particular video stream may fluctuate significantly and rapidly with time. Therefore, the optimal bandwidth and upload bitrates of uploaders should be changed dyanmically with the latest viewer population.

In this paper, to address the above challenges, we attempt to determine an optimal bandwidth budget, upload bitrate and datacenter selection to maximize the overall utility from the perspective of a CVL platform operator. We adopt the *Nash Bargaining Solution* (*NBS*) to ensure the effectiveness and fairness, and design an effective low-complexity algorithm called *Bubal*, which can help CVL platforms control cost and enhance their service quality with a massive number of uploaders.

In summary, our contributions are summarized as follows:

- To the best of our knowledge, we are the first to consider the optimization of upload bandwidth allocation among broadcasters in crowdsourced video livecast systems. We formulate the problem as a constrained utility optimization problem and balance the tradeoff between bandwidth cost and QoE of viewers.
- By exploiting the *Nash bargaining solution* (*NBS*) optimization framework, we design an effective low-complexity algorithm called *Bubal* to solve the optimization problem, which can determine the optimal bandwidth budget, upload bitrate and datacenter selection for each uploader.
- To evaluate the effectiveness of our proposed algorithm, we conduct extensive trace-driven simulations by utilizing the public Twitch live streaming traces. Experimental results show that our proposed algorithm achieves much higher utility than alternative strategies in various conditions.

The rest of this paper is organized as follows. We first introduce the system model in Sect. 3. In Sect. 4, we propose the solution of QoE optimization problem with a given bandwidth budget. In Sect. 4.3, we explore how to solve the utility optimization problem to find the optimal bandwidth budget. We conduct a series of experiments to evaluate the performance of our design in Sect. 5. We discuss the related work in Sect. 2 and conclude the paper in Sect. 6.

2   Related Work

The popularity of Crowdsourced Video Livecast (CVL) has attracted significant attention recently. Related studies can divided into two major categories: i) measurements and pattern analysis of CVL systems, and ii) optimization of transcoding and scheduling.

To understand viewer interactions, *Wang et al.* [15] performed a comprehensive measurement study of the viewer interactions on a popular crowdsourced live broadcasting website in China and further deigned methodologies to predict the popularity of channels. *Yi et al.* [17] for the first time conducted an experiment-based measurement of YouTube's 360 degree live video streaming and concluded the primary design weakness of current CVL systems.

There are quite a few papers focusing on the optimization of the transcoding or scheduling and resource provisioning. *Luo et al.* [9] adopted a novel live video ingest approach, named CrowdSR, to transform a low-resolution video stream into high-resolution video stream for viewers in crowdsourced livecast with super-resolution method. *Zhang et al.* [19] designed a novel framework, CastFlag, to predict the highlights, i.e., key events in livecast and optimize the transcoding task workload. *Ma et al.* [10] conducted a viewer-assisted Crowdsourced Livecast Services (CLS) framework with a fairness-guaranteed task assignment scheme, which was solved by a dynamic programming problem. *Wang et al.* [14] presented an edge-assisted crowdcast framework called DeepCast toward to the heterogeneous and personalized QoE demands of viewers leveraging DRL. Besides, a review study of crowdcast solutions, challenges and opportunities for personalized CVL with intelligent edge technology was provided by *Wang et al.* [13]

Our work differs from previous work in mainly three aspects. *Firstly*, we focus on upload bandwidth allocation problem instead of the optimization on video transcoding or distribution of CVL platforms in previous paper. *Secondly*, we focus on utility optimization, considering bandwidth cost and QoE profits of viewers, jointly. *Thirdly*, this paper provides guidelines, used to empirically set by CVL platforms, for operators to find the optimal bandwidth budget.

3   System Model

In this section, we first introduce our system model for the CVL system. Then, we describe how to formulate the problem as a constrained optimization problem.

3.1 System Overview

In a generic CVL system, there are three major players: $u_i \in \mathcal{U}$ (or *broadcasters*), *CVL platform* with multiple datacenters $d_m \in \mathcal{D}$, and *viewers*. $N = |\mathcal{U}|$ and $M = |\mathcal{D}|$ are total number of elements in uploader and datacenter set, respectively. V_i represents the amount of viewers associated with u_i. A specified workflow is described as follows: the uploader u_i uploads live stream with a bitrate $r_{i,m}$ to a datacenter d_m, and then the CVL platform transcodes the video to multiple bitrates under the uploaded bitrate and delivers video streams to viewers with a suitable bitrates. The goal of our design is to achieve the maximum utility of video uploading by balancing the viewers' QoE and upload bandwidth cost.

3.2 QoE and Bandwidth Cost

The uploaded video is transcoded by the CVL platform based on network conditions and viewers' devices. To evaluate the impact of videos' upload bitrates on viewers' QoE, we define *Opportunity QoE* with the video upload bitrate r_i, which is treated as the upper bound of the actual QoE at the viewers' side[1].

Assume that each viewer needs to be served with the minimum bitrate as r^{min} and similar to the QoE model in [6], the opportunity QoE Q_i^o for all viewers watching the video uploaded by u_i is defined as:

$$Q_i^o = Q(r_i, r^{min}) = \ln\left(1 + \frac{r_i}{r^{min}}\right),$$

where the minimum opportunity QoE for each viewer watching the video uploaded by uploader u_i is defined as $Q_i^{min} = Q(r^{min}, r^{min})$.

In our problem, upload bandwidth cost is incurred when uploaders are uploading videos to datacenters. We define C_m as the bandwidth cost associated with the datacenter d_m. We adopt a pricing model similar to that of Google [1] cloud platform. Let c_m denote the unit price of upload traffic in datacenter d_m, and bandwidth cost associated with datacenter d_m can be defined as $C_m = \sum_{i=1}^{N} r_{i,m} * c_m$. As the perspective of CVL platforms, we define $C = \sum_{m=1}^{M} C_m$ as the total upload bandwidth cost of the CVL platform.

3.3 Problem Formulation

Before the problem formulation, we first introduce some constraints in our model. We denote r_i^{min}, r_i^{max} as the minimum and maximum upload bitrates, respectively. Thereby, we have the following constraints:

$$r_i^{min} \leq r_i = \sum_{m=1}^{M} r_{i,m} \leq r_i^{max}, \forall r_{i,m} \geq 0, \tag{1}$$

$$\sum_{\{m_1=1\}}^{M} \sum_{\{m_2=1, m_2 \neq m_1\}}^{M} r_{i,m_1} * r_{i,m_2} \leq 0, \forall i. \tag{2}$$

---

[1] Transcoded bit rates can not exceed the uploaded bitrate.

In the above constraints, constraint (1) ensures that upload bitrate $r_{i,m}$ would be non-negative and the global upload bitrate r_i of uploader u_i would neither exceed the upper bound nor less than the lower bound. Constraint (2) ensures that the uploader can connect to at most one datacenter at a time. Besides, we assume that each datacenter d_m has the bandwidth of $b_m \in \boldsymbol{b}$, where $\boldsymbol{b} = \{b_m, \forall m\}$ is the total bandwidth of all datacenters. In order to guarantee that the bandwidth requirement of uploaders can not exceed the bandwidth of all the datacenters, we introduce the following constraint:

$$\sum_{i=1}^{N} r_{i,m} \leq b_m, \forall m. \tag{3}$$

Note that our goal is to solve the utility optimization problem with any utility function of aggregated viewers' QoE and bandwidth cost. Then we define the utility optimization problem as:

$$\mathbf{P1}: \operatorname*{argmax}_{r,b} \quad f(\boldsymbol{r}, \boldsymbol{b}) - k * g(\boldsymbol{r}, \boldsymbol{b}),$$

$$\text{s.t. } (1)(2)(3).$$

where k is a tunable parameter representing the weight of upload bandwidth cost. Besides the total bandwidth cost of all the datacenters is defined as:

$$g(\boldsymbol{r}, \boldsymbol{b}) = \sum_{m=1}^{M} C_m.$$

We propose to tackle problem **P1** by solving two subproblems: 1)Optimization of upload bitrates allocation $\boldsymbol{r}$ with a given bandwidth budget; 2)Optimization of utility with vary bandwidth budgets

For the first subproblem, given the total upload bandwidth budget $\boldsymbol{b}$, the major objective of a CVL platform is to maximize the overall QoE of all viewers by determining the upload bitrate and datacenter selection for each uploader, i.e., $\boldsymbol{r} = \{r_{i,m}, \forall i, \forall m\}$, which is indeed a bandwidth allocation problem. Considering both effectiveness and fairness, we employ the *Nash bargaining solution* (*NBS*) in game theory to tackle this problem, which was firstly presented by *Mazumdar et al.* [11] in communication networks. Besides, we introduce the key concepts of *NBS* in our scenario according to the game-theoretical optimization frameworks [16]. The N uploaders can be viewed as the players who are competing for given upload bandwidth $\boldsymbol{b}$ in a CVL system. For each viewer in $\mathcal{V}_i$ associated with uploader u_i, the initial profit is the basic QoE represented as Q_i^b. We need to maximize the profit gain represented as $(Q_i^o - Q_i^b)$. Define the set $G = \{r_{i,j} | \ln(1 + \frac{\sum_{i=1}^{N} r_{i,m}}{r^{min}}) \geq Q_i^b, \forall i \in N, \forall m\}$ and (G, Q_i^b) is a bargaining game by supposing G is nonempty.

Due to the fact that the numbers of viewers associated with different uploaders are distinct, all the players in game have their asynashimmetric weights [4] by adopting the exponentiation of the profit gain, i.e., $(Q_i^o - Q_i^b)^{V_i}$. Intuitively, if an uploader has more viewers, he (or she) should be allocated with more bandwidth resources. Thus, we can define the aggregated viewers' QoE

$$f(\boldsymbol{r}, \boldsymbol{b}) = \prod_{i=1}^{N}(Q_i^o - Q_i^b)^{V_i}$$

as the *Nash* product and with a mathematical derivation, the first subproblem is then formulated as the following *Nash* bargaining problem:

$$\textbf{P2}: \operatorname*{argmin}_{r} \quad -\sum_{i=1}^{N} V_i \cdot \ln(Q_i^o - Q_i^b),$$

$$\text{s.t. } (1)(2)(3).$$

P2 depicts the joint profit in the bargaining game, represented as the product of the profit gains of all the players, which can be maximized by the *Nash* bargaining solution.

4   Upload Bitrate Allocation with Bandwidth Constraints

In this section, we tackle the optimization problem **P2** defined in previous. **P2** is a mixed-integer convex programming (*MICP*) problem, which is a NP-hard problem [8]. Therefore, we relax the problem **P2** into a convex problem **P3**. Then we adopt Lagrangian transformation, dual decomposition, subgradient method and design an effective algorithm to obtain the optimal solution of the problem **P3**. In addition, we also design a heuristic algorithm to obtain the sub-optimal solution for the problem **P2**. With the output of the **P2**, we find the optimal $\boldsymbol{b}$ for maximum overall utility and solve the problem **P1**.

4.1   Problem Relaxation

The first and third constraints in **P2** follow the disciplined convex programming (*DCP*) ruleset [5] while the second constraint violates the *DCP* rules, which ensures that each uploader can connect to at most one datacenter. If we define a binary variable $\boldsymbol{I} \in R^{N*M}$, the second constraint is mathematically equivalent to $\sum_{m=1}^{M} I(i, m) \leq 1, \forall i$, which can be regraded as a binary variable constraint. Therefore, **P2** can be converted to a mixed-integer convex programming (*MICP*) problem with the binary variable constraint [7]. Hence, we relax constraint (2) and formulate **P3** as follows:

$$\textbf{P3}: \operatorname*{argmin}_{r} \quad -\sum_{i=1}^{N} V_i \ln(Q_i^o - Q_i^b),$$

$$\text{s.t. } (1)(3).$$

In the problem **P3**, each uploader may be connected to more than one data-center. However, the upload bitrate for each uploader is aggregated by the upload bitrates over all datacenters, i.e., $r_i = \sum_{m=1}^{M} r_{i,m}$, indicting that the eliminated constraint would not affect the QoE of viewers if the sum r_i is identical.

4.2   UBA Algorithm Design

For the convex problem **P3**, we note that the constraints of the variable r are linear so that we can apply the method of Lagrange multipliers and the dual-based decomposition to solve **P3**. Therefore, we define the Lagrangian function $\mathcal{L}(\cdot)$ associated with **P3** with KKT conditions [5]:

$$
\begin{aligned}
\mathcal{L}(\boldsymbol{r}, \boldsymbol{\alpha}, \boldsymbol{\beta}, \boldsymbol{\kappa}, \boldsymbol{\gamma}) = & -\sum_{i=1}^{N} V_i * ln(Q_i^o - Q_i^b) - \sum_{i=1}^{N}\sum_{m=1}^{M} \alpha_{i,m} * r_{i,m} \\
& + \sum_{i=1}^{N} \beta_i \Big(\sum_{m=1}^{M} r_{i,m} - r_i^{max} \Big) + \sum_{i=1}^{N} \gamma_i \Big(r^{min} - \sum_{m=1}^{M} r_{i,m} \Big) + \sum_{m=1}^{M} \kappa_m \Big(\sum_{i=1}^{N} r_{i,m} - b_m \Big),
\end{aligned}
\tag{4}
$$

where $\boldsymbol{\alpha}, \boldsymbol{\beta}, \boldsymbol{\kappa}, \boldsymbol{\gamma}$ are the dual variables associated with the problem. Let the derivative of Lagrangian function equal to zero and we can obtain

$$
\nabla \mathcal{L}(\boldsymbol{r}^*, \boldsymbol{\alpha}, \boldsymbol{\beta}, \boldsymbol{\kappa}, \boldsymbol{\gamma}) = 0,
\tag{5}
$$

where $\boldsymbol{r}^* = \{r_{i,m}^*, \forall i, \forall m\}$ is the optimal solution of **P3**. Besides, the Lagrange dual function $d(\cdot)$ corresponding to the $\mathcal{L}(\cdot)$ function is defined as follows:

$$
d(\boldsymbol{\alpha}, \boldsymbol{\beta}, \boldsymbol{\kappa}, \boldsymbol{\gamma}) = \inf_{\boldsymbol{r}} \mathcal{L}(\boldsymbol{r}, \boldsymbol{\alpha}, \boldsymbol{\beta}, \boldsymbol{\kappa}, \boldsymbol{\gamma}).
\tag{6}
$$

Note that **P3** is a convex problem and the variable r follows the KKT conditions [5]. Therefore, we can obtain the dual problem corresponding to **P3** without duality gap. The dual problem can be depicted in the following form: Max $d(\boldsymbol{\alpha}, \boldsymbol{\beta}, \boldsymbol{\kappa}, \boldsymbol{\gamma}) = \mathcal{L}(\boldsymbol{r}^*, \boldsymbol{\alpha}, \boldsymbol{\beta}, \boldsymbol{\kappa}, \boldsymbol{\gamma})$, where $d(\cdot)$ is the dual function and $\mathcal{L}(\cdot)$ is the Lagrangian function of **P3**. On the basis of the sub-gradient algorithm, the iterative expressions of $\boldsymbol{\alpha}, \boldsymbol{\beta}, \boldsymbol{\kappa}, \boldsymbol{\gamma}$ and the partial derivatives of $d(\boldsymbol{\alpha}, \boldsymbol{\beta}, \boldsymbol{\kappa}, \boldsymbol{\gamma})$ can be obtain directly, which are omitted for space reasons. The iterative algorithm is terminated when $|d(s+1) - d(s)| \leq \sigma$, where σ is a very small positive scalar and s is the step number. The sub-gradient updating laws guarantee that $\boldsymbol{\alpha}, \boldsymbol{\beta}, \boldsymbol{\kappa}, \boldsymbol{\gamma}$ will converge to the optimal multipliers $\boldsymbol{\alpha}^*, \boldsymbol{\beta}^*, \boldsymbol{\kappa}^*, \boldsymbol{\gamma}^*$ as long as ξ satisfies the *diminishing step size rules* [5].

Based on the above formulation, we design an *Upload Bitrate Allocation* (*UBA*) algorithm for allocating upload bandwidth resource to each uploader, whose details are shown in Algorithm 1. In the *UBA* algorithm, each uploader firstly maximizes the profits of his (or her) viewers by calculating an optimal upload bitrate in each iteration based on the upload bitrates of other uploaders in the previous iteration. When the algorithm converges, all uploaders can obtain stable upload bitrates with a highest overall profit, which maps to the key idea of the *Nash bargaining solution*, i.e., no player can profitably deviate, given the actions of other players and the overall utility is maximized. After the optimal solution $\boldsymbol{r}^*$ of **P3** is obtained, we also design a heuristic algorithm to obtain the sub-optimal solution of **P2**. The details of the heuristic algorithm are shown in line 7–22 in Algorithm 1, whose key is to calculate the sum of bitrates for each uploader firstly and then assign it into datacenters. If the assignment can not be satisfied, we will sacrifice the uploaders with the smallest number of viewers by setting the basic bitrate to these uploaders.

Algorithm 1: Upload Bitrate Allocation Algorithm

Require: $\boldsymbol{b} = \{b_m, \forall m\}$; r^{min}, $r_i^{max}, \forall i$; $V_i, \forall i$; ξ; σ.
Ensure: Optimal bandwidth allocated to uploaders: $\boldsymbol{r}^*$
1: Initialize the Lagrangian multipliers, let $flag = N$, $\varpi = 0.01$;
2: **while** $|d(s+1) - d(s)| > \sigma$ **do**
3:     Update $r_{i,m}, \forall i, \forall m$ based on Eq. (5);
4:     Update step size ξ and iteration round $s \leftarrow s + 1$;
5:     Update $\alpha, \beta, \kappa, \gamma$ based on the partial derivatives of Eq. (6);
6: **end while**
7: **while** Not all uploaders are allocated in a specific datacenter **do**
8:     Initialization: Let $r_{i,m}^{sub} = 0, \forall i, \forall m$;
9:     **for** $i = 1$ to N **do**
10:        **if** $i \leq flag$ **then**
11:            $r_i = \sum_{m=1}^{M} r_{i,m}^*$;
12:        **else**
13:            $r_i = r^{min} + \varpi$;
14:        **end if**
15:        **for** $m = 1$ to M **do**
16:            **if** $r_i \leq (b_m - \sum_{i=1}^{N} r_{i,m}^{sub})$ **then**
17:                $r_{i,m}^{sub} = r_i$; break;
18:            **end if**
19:        **end for**
20:     **end for**
21:     $flag = flag - 1$;
22: **end while**

4.3   Bubal: UBA Algorithm with Optimal Bandwidth Budget

In this subsection, we find the optimal $\boldsymbol{b}$ for maximum overall utility and solve the problem **P1** with the output of the **P2** obtained in last subsection. We assume that all the datacenters have a maximum bandwidth constraint, denoted as $\boldsymbol{b}^{max} = \{b_m^{max}, \forall m\}$. Let $B = |\boldsymbol{b}|$ denote the value of the total bandwidth budget. We can derive the lower and upper bounds of B as $b_l = N * r^{min}$ and $b_{up} = \sum_{i=1}^{N} r_i^{max}$, and we assume $|\boldsymbol{b}^{max}| > b_l$. Note that if we assign B with a specific value, there exist different $\boldsymbol{b} = \{b_b, \forall m\}$ which can ensure $B = |\boldsymbol{b}|$. If the value of B is given, more bandwidth budget should be allocated to the datacenter with smaller unit price of upload traffic. With the Assumption that the datacenters are arranged in an ascending order according to the unit price, i.e., $c_1 \leq c_2 \leq \cdots \leq c_m$, we can determine the unique division $\boldsymbol{b}$ when B is given:

$$\boldsymbol{b} = \{b_1^{max}, ..., b_{i-1}^{max}, B - \sum_{j=1}^{i-1} b_j^{max}, 0, 0, ...\},$$

$$\sum_{j=1}^{i-1} b_j^{max} \leq B \leq \sum_{j=1}^{i} b_j^{max}, \tag{7}$$

where B is in the range of b_l and b_{up}. Besides, assume that $f(\cdot)$ is a concave function and $g(\cdot)$ is a linear function, there exists an optimal value B^* between b_l and b_{up} to maximize the overall utility in **P1**.

Therefore, we design our algorithm called *Bubal* to search the optimal value of B^* and the related b^*. In this algorithm, we iteratively divide the domain space of bandwidth budget in three-fold to obtain the utility with the constraint of bandwidth budget at the fold point and shorten the domain by eliminating the part with lower utility until the space of the domain less than a tiny positive value.

5   Performance Evaluation

In this section, we conduct extensive trace-driven simulations based on the public Twitch living streaming traces.

5.1   Experimental Settings

In our simulation, we discretize time into slots corresponding to a 5-min interval. We retrieve the public Twitch living streaming dataset from [12] to simulate the behaviors of 1000 uploaders in each slot. The unit price for datacenters is set as $[0.02 + 0.02 * m]$ per GB, where m is the index of the datacenter. The minimum and maximum of the upload bitrates for each uploader are set as 0.4 Mbps and 5 Mbps for simplicity. The maximum bandwidth of datacenters is set as $b^{max} = [400, 1000, 600, 2000]$ and we can derive the lower and upper bounds of B^* as $b_l = 400$ and $b_{up} = 5000$. In addition, the weight of bandwidth cost defined in **P1** is initialized as 0.5 and we can increase the value of k to emphasize the importance of bandwidth cost.

In order to evaluate the performance of our proposed algorithm *Bubal*, we mainly select two alternative strategies as baselines:

- *Proportional Allocation (Proportional)* [3], in which the upload bandwidth will be allocated for each uploader based on the proportion of the amount of viewers. If an uploader has a larger proportion of viewers, he (or she) will be allocated with more bandwidth.
- *Average Allocation (Average)*, in which we allocate the upload bandwidth among all uploaders evenly.

Figure 1(a) describes the total number of viewers of 1,000 uploaders over 500 time slots. First, it is obvious that the number of viewers is highly dynamic. Second, there are about 480,000 online viewers of these 1,000 uploaders in the peak time period and the peak-to-valley gap is about 285,000. Figure 1(b) illustrates the CDF of viewers for the uploaders in the time slot 500 and from this figure, nearly 80% uploaders have less than 100 viewers.

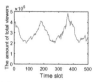 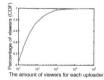 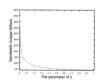

(a) Total viewers of 1000 uploaders over 500 slots.

(b) CDF of viewers of 1000 uploaders in the last slot.

(c) Optimal bandwidth budget with varying k.

(d) QoE gain of 1000 uploaders with varying bandwidth budget.

Fig. 1. Descriptions of the dataset and some experiment results of the bandwidth budget.

5.2 Performance Comparison

We firstly explore the performance of our design compared to alternative strategies. To evaluate our algorithm with different tradeoff requirements between bandwidth cost and viewer QoE, we conduct simulations with three different values of k as 0.5, 0.2, 0.05, the results of which are shown in Fig. 2. When k is higher, it means the CVL platform is more sensitive to bandwidth cost. We find that when $k = 0.5$, which simulates the most cost-sensitive CVL platforms, our proposed *Bubal* achieves the best overall utility and QoE gain compared to the other two baselines while having a slightly higher bandwidth cost. When $k = 0.2$ and $k = 0.05$, which respectively simulate the scenarios that CVL platforms are moderately cost-sensitive and the least cost-sensitive, our proposed *Bubal* still achieves a better overall utility compared to two baselines while having a slightly lower QoE gain but lowest bandwidth cost.

To further explain why *Bubal* always achieves the best overall utility while not always having the highest QoE gain and the lowest bandwidth cost, we show the detailed impact of parameter k (varying from 0 to 1) on bandwidth budget in Fig. 1(c). $k = 0$ means that the bandwidth cost is ignored and all uploaders can be allocated with the maximum upload bitrate. When k increases, the bandwidth budget B^* decreases as CVL platforms care more about the bandwidth cost. As such, three algorithms perform very differently with various bandwidth budgets shown in Fig. 1(d). When the bandwidth budget is low, the slope of QoE gain with *Bubal* is the highest, which means *Bubal* can achieve a high QoE gain benefit. Therefore, as shown in Fig. 2(a), when $k = 0.5$, *Bubal* achieves the best QoE gain while having a slightly higher bandwidth cost. When the bandwidth budget is higher, the slopes of QoE gain with *Proportional* and *Average* are the steepest, successively. Therefore, *Proportional* and *Average* achieve the best QoE gain while having the highest bandwidth cost in Fig. 2(b)/2(c), respectively.

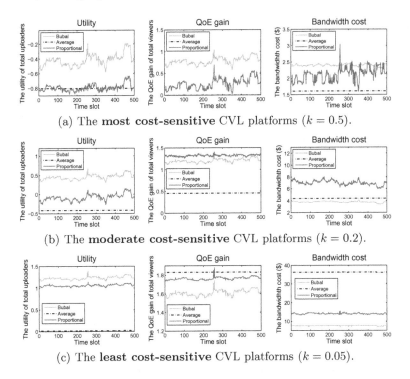

(a) The **most cost-sensitive** CVL platforms ($k = 0.5$).

(b) The **moderate cost-sensitive** CVL platforms ($k = 0.2$).

(c) The **least cost-sensitive** CVL platforms ($k = 0.05$).

Fig. 2. The overall utility, QoE gain and bandwidth cost for different k.

6   Conclusion

In this paper, we focus on utility optimization of upload bandwidth from the perspective of CVL platform operators. We adopt the *Nash Bargaining Solution (NBS)* optimization framework to ensure the effectiveness and fairness and design an effective low-complexity algorithm to determine an optimal bandwidth budget, upload bitrates and datacenter selection. At last, some trace-driven simulations are conducted and the results show that our design can significantly improve the overall utility. In our future work, we plan to study the impact of dynamic network conditions. In addition, we plan to consider more live streaming scenarios and more complicated network structures.

References

1. Google cloud platform pricing. https://cloud.google.com/pricing/, Accessed 2020
2. Twitch revenue and usage statistics. https://www.businessofapps.com/data/twitch-statistics/, Accessed 2020
3. Abdel-Hadi, A., Clancy, C.: A utility proportional fairness approach for resource allocation in 4g-lte. In: 2014 International Conference on Computing, Networking and Communications (ICNC), pp. 1034–1040. IEEE (2014)

4. Boche, H., Schubert, M., Vucic, N., Naik, S.: Non-symmetric nash bargaining solution for resource allocation in wireless networks and connection to interference calculus. In: 2007 15th European on Signal Processing Conference, pp. 1317–1321. IEEE (2007)
5. Boyd, S., Vandenberghe, L.: Convex Optimization. Cambridge University Press, Cambridge (2004)
6. He, J., Wen, Y., Huang, J., Wu, D.: On the cost-qoe tradeoff for cloud-based video streaming under amazon ec2's pricing models. IEEE Trans. Circ. Syst. Video Technol. 24(4), 669–680 (2014)
7. Lubin, M., Yamangil, E., Bent, R., Vielma, J.P.: Extended formulations in mixed-integer convex programming. In: Louveaux, Q., Skutella, M. (eds.) IPCO 2016. LNCS, vol. 9682, pp. 102–113. Springer, Cham (2016). https://doi.org/10.1007/978-3-319-33461-5_9
8. Lubin, M., Zadik, I., Vielma, J.P.: Mixed-integer convex representability. In: Eisenbrand, F., Koenemann, J. (eds.) IPCO 2017. LNCS, vol. 10328, pp. 392–404. Springer, Cham (2017). https://doi.org/10.1007/978-3-319-59250-3_32
9. Luo, Z., et al.: Crowdsr: enabling high-quality video ingest in crowdsourced livecast via super-resolution. In: Lutu, A., Simon, G., Farias, M.C.Q. (eds.) Proceedings of the 31st ACM Workshop on Network and Operating Systems Support for Digital Audio and Video, NOSSDAV 2021, pp. 90–97. ACM (2021)
10. Ma, Y., Xu, C., Chen, X., Xiao, H., Zhong, L., Muntean, G.M.: Fairness-guaranteed transcoding task assignment for viewer-assisted crowdsourced livecast services. In: ICC 2021 - IEEE International Conference on Communications, pp. 1–6 (2021)
11. Mazumdar, R., Mason, L.G., Douligieris, C.: Fairness in network optimal flow control. In: SBT/IEEE International Symposium on Telecommunications, ITS 1990 Symposium Record, pp. 590–596. IEEE (1990)
12. Pires, K., Simon, G.: Dash in twitch: adaptive bitrate streaming in live game streaming platforms. In: Proceedings of the 2014 Workshop on Design, Quality and Deployment of Adaptive Video Streaming, pp. 13–18. ACM (2014)
13. Wang, F., Liu, J., Zhang, C., Sun, L., Hwang, K.: Intelligent edge learning for personalized crowdsourced livecast: challenges, opportunities, and solutions. IEEE Netw. 35(1), 170–176 (2021)
14. Wang, F., et al.: Deepcast: towards personalized qoe for edge-assisted crowdcast with deep reinforcement learning. IEEE/ACM Trans. Netw. 28, 1255–1268 (2020)
15. Wang, X., Tian, Y., Lan, R., Yang, W., Zhang, X.: Beyond the watching: understanding viewer interactions in crowdsourced live video broadcasting services. IEEE Trans. Circ. Syst. Video Technol. 29(11), 3454–3468 (2018)
16. Yaïche, H., Mazumdar, R.R., Rosenberg, C.: A game theoretic framework for bandwidth allocation and pricing in broadband networks. IEEE/ACM Trans. Netw. 8(5), 667–678 (2000)
17. Yi, J., Luo, S., Yan, Z.: A measurement study of youtube 360° live video streaming. In: Proceedings of the 29th ACM Workshop on Network and Operating Systems Support for Digital Audio and Video, pp. 49–54 (2019)
18. Zhang, C., Liu, J., Wang, H.: Towards hybrid cloud-assisted crowdsourced live streaming: measurement and analysis. In: Proceedings of the 26th International Workshop on Network and Operating Systems Support for Digital Audio and Video, p. 1. ACM (2016)
19. Zhang, C., Liu, J., Wang, Z., Sun, L.: Look ahead at the first-mile in livecast with crowdsourced highlight prediction. In: IEEE INFOCOM 2020-IEEE Conference on Computer Communications, pp. 1143–1152. IEEE (2020)

A Batched Jacobi SVD Algorithm on GPUs and Its Application to Quantum Lattice Systems

Rongfeng Huang[1,2], Tianyu Yu[1,2], Shifang Liu[1,2], Xinyin Zhang[1,2], and Yonghua Zhao[1(✉)]

[1] Computer Network Information Center, Chinese Academy of Sciences, Beijing, China
yhzhao@sccas.cn
[2] University of Chinese Academy of Sciences, Beijing, China

Abstract. Batched linear algebra problems are becoming increasingly important in engineering and scientific applications. As the performance of graphics processing units (GPUs) improves rapidly, GPUs are very attractive to solve this class of problems. This paper presents a parallel blocked Jacobi SVD algorithm for many small matrices on GPUs. The parallelism of the Jacobi algorithm is squeezed sufficiently. Our algorithm can be mapped to the GPU memory hierarchy properly due to the blocking structure. Reduction operations used for computing inner products and having low thread utilization are instead by performing the Jacobi rotation on the Gram matrix in parallel. We identify the kernels with sharing data and fuse them to improve memory locality by placing shared data, originally passed via off-chip global memory, into the on-chip shared memory. Numerical results on an NVIDIA Tesla V100 GPU show that our batched SVD routine outperforms state-of-the-art approaches between 2.0× and 4.1× for the examples tested. As one of the applications for our routine, the numerical simulation of quantum lattice systems is tested and achieves a maximum of 54.1× speedups over the CPU implementation running on a 48-core Xeon CPU.

Keywords: Batched execution · SVD · Blocked algorithms · Kernel fusion · GPU

1 Introduction

Batched linear algebra problems are to solve many independent problems simultaneously. When the matrices are large enough to take full advantage of the computing resources of the device, these independent problems are preferred to be solved in serial for better data locality and reuse, thus there is no need

This work is supported by National Key Research and Development Program of China (2017YFB0202202) and Strategic Priority Research Program of Chinese Academy of Sciences (XDC05000000).

H. Shen et al. (Eds.): PDCAT 2021, LNCS 13148, pp. 69–80, 2022.
https://doi.org/10.1007/978-3-030-96772-7_7

for batched routines. However, when matrices are small, such as the matrices of size no more than 512, the workloads of a single matrix cannot saturate the device, especially GPUs. To this end, a lot of matrices should be solved together, and batched routines are required. Up to now there are many batched linear algebra routines, such as batched general matrix-matrix multiplication (GEMM), batched Cholesky factorization, batched lower-upper (LU) factorization, batched singular value decomposition (SVD), to name a few. These routines are widely used in machine learning, computer vision, astrophysics, and other fields [1–4]. The development of routines for batched small matrices computing is relatively easy for multicore CPUs. For example, a combination of the OpenMP and highly optimized LAPACK/BLAS libraries (such as MKL, open-BLAS) usually obtain an optimistic performance, since most of the computation can be performed through the fast CPU cache. However, the development is not intuitive for GPUs due to the lack of large caches.

Batched GEMM may be the most basic operation in dense linear algebra probably because many other batched routines also call it. Many vendors provide the batched GEMM implementation on their devices [5,6] to satisfy the growing demand from different fields. The University of Tennessee also gives an implementation for batched GEMM in open-source package MAGMA both on CPUs and GPUs. There are also a lot of works focusing on batched LAPACK routines on GPUs [7]. For example, Dong et al. [8] presented different implementations of batched Cholesky factorizations. Abdelfattah et al. [9] demonstrated a high-performance routine of batched LU factorization with partial pivoting.

Unlike the Cholesky factorization and LU factorization, the SVD algorithm is iterative, so the computation of all matrices can terminate at the same time barely. After most of the matrices converge, the remaining matrices cannot fully utilize the streaming multiprocessors on GPUs. As a result, it is more challenging to design batched SVD algorithms on GPUs. The cuSOLVER library [10] released by NVIDIA support only batched SVD decompositions for matrices no more than 32×32. Dong et al. [11] presented a method to accelerate the SVD bi-diagonalization stage of a batch of small matrices using GPUs. However, the following SVD diagonalization stage remains unresolved. Badolato et al. [12] used each thread within a warp to compute the SVD of a single matrix. The algorithm implemented in their work was a conventional non-blocked Jacobi algorithm. Boukaram et al. [13] presented batched SVD routines and used these routines for the compression of hierarchical matrices. For the matrices of sizes that were no more than 64×64, whole matrices were loaded up to the register or the shared memory, and thus the good performance was achieved. For the matrices of sizes that were larger than 64×64, because the register and the shared memory cannot hold the entire matrices, the blocked Jacobi SVD algorithm was employed. But the blocked Jacobi rotations in a single matrix were conducted serially, then the GPUs could not be satiated after some matrices terminated early. The batched SVD routines were integrated into the KBLAS library [14].

In this paper, we present an optimized routine for batched SVD decomposition on GPUs and it's applications. We summarize our contributions as follows:

(1) design a parallel blocked Jacobi SVD algorithm, as well as efficient implementations and optimization techniques. In our design, the blocked Jacobi rotations in a single matrix were conducted concurrently. This is the main difference between our work and previous works; (2) replace reduction operations with low thread utilization by performing the Jacobi rotation on the Gram matrix in parallel; (3) show the application of our work by accelerating the quantum lattice simulation.

The remainder of this paper is organized as follows. Section 2 introduces the algorithmic background. In Sect. 3, efficient implementations and optimization techniques are presented. Section 4 provides the experimental results and analysis. Section 5 shows the accelerating of the quantum lattice simulation. Section 6 concludes this paper and outlines the future work.

2   Algorithmic Background

Given a $m \times n$ real matrix A, the SVD decomposition of A is to find a $m \times m$ orthonormal matrix U, a $m \times n$ diagonal matrix Σ, and a $n \times n$ orthonormal matrix V, such that

$$A = U\Sigma V^T \tag{1}$$

The columns of U and V are called the left singular vectors and the right singular vectors respectively. The diagonal entries of Σ are called the singular values and are sorted in decreasing order.

2.1   Jacobi Algorithms

Algorithm 1 describes the canonical one-sided Jacobi SVD algorithm. The algorithm is a repeatedly orthogonalized procedure in sweeps using the Jacobi rotation until all columns are mutually orthogonal up to machine precision. The process of any pair of columns is orthogonalized once is called a sweep, so a sweep includes $n(n-1)/2$ pairs of columns. There are many methods to give all pairs of columns in a sweep. The classical methods include the row-cyclic ordering method and column-cyclic ordering method. Unfortunately, the two methods result in poor parallelism.

One of the superiorities of Jacobi SVD algorithms is parallelism. As long as the picked columns are excluded, step 3 and step 4 can be performed simultaneously. The most common two methods to give all pairs of columns in a sweep that are suitable for parallel calculations are the round-robin method [15] and odd-even method [16]. Despite the parallelism of the round-robin method being superior to the odd-even method, the round-robin method does not converge for some particular matrices [17]. Hence, the odd-even method is adopted because it converges for all matrices [17].

As shown in Algorithm 1, the Jacobi rotation is the core module. Let a_p and a_q be the pth and qth columns of matrix A respectively, then the 2×2 Jacobi rotation matrix $J^{p,q}$ can be achieved by some formulas depending on the inner product of a_p and a_q [15]. The off-norm of a matrix in Algorithm 1 is defined by the Frobenius norm of a new matrix which is equal to the initial matrix except

---

Algorithm 1: Jacobi algorithms

Input: A
Output: U, Σ, V
1   **while** $off(A^T A) > \varepsilon$ **do**
2   **foreach** (p, q) *in* {*All pairs of columns in a sweep*} **do**
3   Calculate the Jacobi rotation matrix $J^{p,q}$
4   Conduct the Jacobi rotation: $[a_p \; a_q] = [a_p \; a_q] \cdot J^{p,q}$ /* BLAS-1
       operation   */
5   **end**
6 **end**
7 Calculate the singular values Σ: $\Sigma = \sqrt{A^T A}$
8 Calculate the left singular vectors U: $U = A\Sigma^{-1}$
9 Calculate the right singular vectors V: $V = \Sigma^{-1} U^T A$
10 Sort the singular values and move the corresponding singular vectors if necessary

---

that the diagonal elements are all zero. In addition, ε is the convergence tolerance. As the Jacobi rotation is a memory-bounded BLAS-1 operation, Algorithm 1 is also memory-bounded.

2.2   Parallel Blocked Jacobi Algorithms

The blocked versions of algorithms accumulate some BLAS-1 or BLAS-2 operations into a BLAS-3 operation. Therefore, the blocked versions are compute-intensive and perform well on a modern machine. In the blocked SVD algorithms, the matrix A is divided into a lot of panels, i.e., $A = [A_1 \; A_2 \; \cdots \; A_K]$. For simplicity, we assume that K is even and the sizes of all panels are equal to NB. The blocked SVD algorithms follow a similar workflow with Algorithm 1 and also iterate sweep by sweep until converge. In each iteration, a pair of panels are picked and the blocked Jacobi rotation is conducted. However, the computation of the blocked Jacobi rotation matrix $BJ^{p,q}$ is more complicated, and iterative algorithms must be used.

In [13], two algorithms are used. One is to compute the SVD decomposition of the Gram matrix, i.e. the inner product of the picked panels. Another is to carry out the QR factorization on the picked panels first, and then apply the SVD decomposition on the upper triangular matrix arising from the QR factorization. The former achieved higher performance than the latter. In this paper, we get the blocked Jacobi rotation matrix by conducting Algorithm 1 on the picked panels directly. However, a trivial design of Algorithm 1 results in poor performance because the calculations of the inner product are reduction operations and can not make good use of GPUs' numerous cores. Our approach is to update the inner product of matrix columns in parallel, and the details are presented in Algorithm 2. In fact, the Gram matrix is the inner product of the columns of the matrix. Except for the initial step (step 4 in Algorithm 2), the costly iterative process (steps 7 to 9 in Algorithm 2) does not visit the picked

---

Algorithm 2: Parallel blocked Jacobi algorithms

   Input: A

   Output: U, Σ, V

1 **while** $off(A^T A) > \varepsilon$ **do**

2   **foreach** (p,q) *in* $\{\textbf{\textit{All pairs of panels in a sweep}}\}$ **do parallel**

       /* Steps 3 to 11 is essentially Algorithm 1   */

3   Initialize $BJ^{p,q}$ as an identity matrix I : $BJ^{p,q} = I$

4   Calculate the Gram matrix $H^{p,q}$: $H^{p,q} = [A_p\ A_q]^T \cdot [A_p\ A_q]$

5   **while** $off(H^{p,q}) > \varepsilon$ **do**

6   **foreach** (p_{in}, q_{in}) *in* $\{\textbf{\textit{All pairs of columns in a sweep}}\}$ **do parallel**

7   Calculate the Jacobi rotation matrix $J^{p_{in}, q_{in}}$

8   Conduct the Jacobi rotation on $H^{p,q}$:

               $H^{p,q}[p_{in} q_{in}] = H^{p,q}[p_{in} q_{in}] \cdot J^{p_{in}, q_{in}}$

               $(H^{p,q}[p_{in} q_{in}])^T = (H^{p,q}[p_{in} q_{in}])^T \cdot J^{p_{in}, q_{in}}$

9   Conduct the Jacobi rotation on $BJ^{p,q}$:

               $BJ^{p,q}[p_{in} q_{in}] = BJ^{p,q}[p_{in} q_{in}] \cdot J^{p_{in}, q_{in}}$

10   **end**

11   **end**

12   Conduct blocked Jacobi rotation on $[A_p\ A_q]$: $[A_p\ A_q] = [A_p\ A_q] \cdot BJ^{p,q}$

       /* BLAS-3 operation   */

13   **end**

14 **end**

15 Calculate Σ, U, and V in a similar way with Algorithm 1

16 Sort the singular values and move the corresponding singular vectors if necessary

---

panels which reside on the global memory. On the other hand, there are no reduction operations from steps 7 to 9. As a result, the performance is greatly improved.

Similar to Algorithm 1, the blocked SVD algorithms are also suited for parallel development. As long as the picked panels are excluded, the blocked Jacobi rotations can be conducted simultaneously. On the other hand, we employ paralleled Algorithm 1 to achieve the blocked Jacobi rotation matrix. Therefore, a parallel blocked Jacobi SVD algorithm (Algorithm 2) enjoying a two-tier parallel can be developed.

3 Design Details

We assumed that all matrices have been stored in the global memory of GPU, and the matrix elements are aligned in a column-major manner. The representative CUDA is used as the programming model of GPUs. However, our ideas are also available for other programming models such as OpenCL and HIP.

3.1   Overall Design

The previous work depended on the independence of the batched execution. For a single matrix, the serial block Jacobi algorithm was used. As a result, the one-dimensional grid was a good choice. Unlike the Cholesky factorization and LU factorization, the Jacobi SVD algorithm is iterative, so the computation of all matrices can terminate at the same time barely. After some matrices terminate early, the remaining matrices cannot utilize the computing resources of GPUs effectively. This problem can be overcome by conducting the parallel block Jacobi algorithm for a single matrix. Therefore, the two-dimensional grid is more favorable. The first dimension of the grid is $n/(2NB)$. The second dimension of the grid is equal to the number of matrices. Then each matrix has a unique ID, and all matrices are factorized concurrently. Because matrices are two-dimensional, the two-dimensional thread block is an appropriate candidate, and the size of the thread block is $(2NB, NB)$. We use a thread block to conduct the blocked Jacobi rotation of a pair of panels and have a 1:2 map between threads and the elements of the Gram matrices.

One of the advantages of CUDA is that users can program on the L1 cache through the on-chip shared memory. The shared memory has the same physical structure and the same bandwidths as the L1 cache, but lower access latency than the L1 cache. It is a pity that the shared memory is a precious resource and the size is no more than 48KB for most GPUs. In our design, the panel size NB is chosen such that the shared memory can hold the Gram matrix which is a $2NB \times 2NB$ matrix. In that way, the costly iterative process (steps 7 to 9 in Algorithm 2) can be performed on the shared memory entirely, so high performance can be achieved. In addition, a column of threads is used to perform steps 7 to 9 in Algorithm 2 for a pair of columns.

Calculating the Gram matrix (step 4 in Algorithm 2) and conducting the blocked Jacobi rotation (step 12 in Algorithm 2) can be fulfilled by batched GEMM routines. There are many excellent batched GEMM routines to use directly. However, in our scenario, the two panels picked are not continuous in memory. Memory copy is inevitable to call existing batched GEMM routines, thereby degrading performance. So new solutions must be proposed.

Our implementation of batched GEMM is similar to the MAGMA but equips a flexible interface. Based on the flexible interface, we just need to shift the pointer to access the picked panels with uncontinuous addresses for performing GEMM and thus avoid unnecessary memory copy. The well-known techniques such as efficient off-chip memory access and double-buffering are used to optimize the efficiency of matrix computations [18].

3.2   Kernel Optimization

For designing batched algorithms on GPUs, higher performance can be delivered by improving data reuse. A common way to improve the reuse is to fuse kernels. Kernel fusion [19] is employed in this paper not only to decrease the associated overload of launching kernels but also to improve memory locality by placing the data shared by multiple kernels, originally passed via off-chip global memory, into the on-chip memory shared memory. We fuse all kernels corresponding to steps 3 to 12 of Algorithm 2 into a single kernel, which brings the following two benefits. First and foremost, different kernels cannot share the register files and the shared memory, so the global memory with the greatest access latency must be used to exchange data. As noted before, the Gram matrix resides on the shared memory. Lunching only a kernel can avoid reading and writing the Gram matrix form and to the global memory. Second, launching kernels is associated with kernel launch overhead. It is advantageous to decrease the number of kernels.

3.3   Convergence Criterion

Since the rates of convergence for different matrices are not equal, keeping track of every matrix is necessary to identify the unconverged matrices. For our batched SVD routine, we exploit the highly optimized batchedGEMM routine from cuBLAS and some auxiliary routines, which are not difficult to develop so the details are omitted for brevity, to calculate the off-norms (step 1 in Algorithm 2). Then, we find the maximum value of the off-norms for all matrices. The algorithm terminates when the maximum value is less than the given tolerance ε. Another convergence criterion i.e. step 5 in Algorithm 2 that is applied within a single thread block can be implemented in a more intelligent way. We use a root thread to calculate the off-norm and broadcast the off-norm to other threads through the shared memory. The iterative process comes to an end when the off-norm is less than the given tolerance ε.

4   Experimental Results and Analysis

4.1   Experimental Setup

We conduct our experiments on a computing platform with a CPU and a GPU. The CPU is an Intel(R) Xeon(R) Gold 6240R CPU whose frequency is 2.4 GHz and has a total of 48 cores. The GPU is an NVIDIA V100-PCIe-32GB GPU. The CUDA version used in this paper is 11.1. Our batched SVD routine is developed in C without any use of low-level instruction sets.

The following two types of synthetic matrices are used to test the performance of our batched SVD routine.

- Type 1: All matrix elements are generated randomly from the uniform distribution $U(0, 1)$.
- Type 2: The matrices are first arranged to upper triangular matrices. What's more, the diagonal elements are equal to n. The remaining matrix elements are generated randomly from the uniform distribution $U(0, 1)$. Matrices in this type are row diagonally dominant.

Figure 1 shows the convergent sweeps of two types of matrices for our batched SVD routine. The sizes of matrices are from 96 to 512. For each size, 200 matrices are tested and the convergent sweeps shown in Fig. 1 are the maximum sweep among the 200 matrices. It is observed that the convergent sweeps of type 1 are larger than the type 2 for all sizes.

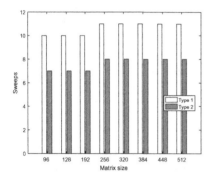 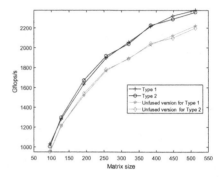

Fig. 1. Convergent sweeps for different types of matrices.

Fig. 2. Performance improvement using kernel fusion.

4.2 Performance Analysis

To verify the impact of kernel fusion, we also develop an unfused version where three kernels are launched for step 4, steps 5 to 11, and step 12 respectively. The Gram matrix and the blocked Jacobi rotation matrix sharing by different kernels are transmitted through the global memory. Figure 2 shows the test results of two versions using 200 matrices that are from type 1 or type 2 and are from the same type. It can be seen that kernel fusion can achieve increments of performance ranging from 6% to 10%. What's more, the benefits of kernel fusion are greater while the matrices become larger. This is because more kernels are launched for larger matrices in the unfused version.

In the following, we compare our routine with kernel fusion with the KBLAS library. There are two batched SVD routines in the KBLAS: the Gram SVD routine and the direct SVD routine. The performance of the Gram SVD routine is higher than the direct SVD routine. Therefore, we compare our routine with the Gram SVD routine. First, we generate matrices with varying amounts for testing. In this test, matrices are all from type 1, and results are shown in Fig. 3(a). Second, 200 matrices mixed with different types based on the ratio of type 1 versus type 2 are generated for testing. The ratios are 2:8 and 8:2. Figure 3(b) presents the results. It is obvious that our routine outperforms the KBLAS for all test cases, scoring speedups ranging from 2.0× up to 4.1×. What's more, the KBLAS gets poor performance for small amounts of matrices but our routine also achieves considerable performance.

In all tests, the singular values, the left singular vectors, and the right singular vectors are both computed. Four quantities err_σ, err_U, err_V and err_D defined in (2) and (3) are used to depict the accuracy of SVD implementations. The σ_i^{ex}

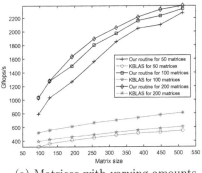

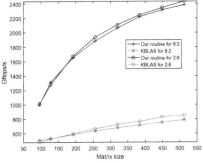

(a) Matrices with varying amounts   (b) Matrices mixed with different types

Fig. 3. Performance comparison of our routine versus the KBLAS.

are the exact singular values. In practice, the exact singular values of random matrices are unavailable, so we use the SVD routines in LAPACK to acquire singular values instead. The $\hat{\Sigma}$, $\hat{U}$ and $\hat{V}$ are the calculated singular values, calculated left singular vectors, and calculated right singular vectors respectively. Table 1 gives the numerical error of our routine and the KBLAS. We can see that our routine is comparable to the KBLAS in the results of err_σ. Nevertheless, our routine is slightly inferior to the KBLAS in the other three quantities. As we can see in Sect 5, the accuracy is sufficient for practical applications.

$$err_\sigma = \max_{1 \le i \le n} \frac{|\sigma_i^{ex} - \hat{\sigma}_i|}{\max(1, \sigma_i^{ex})}, \quad err_D = \frac{\left\| A - \hat{U}\hat{\Sigma}\hat{V} \right\|_F}{\sqrt{n}\, \|A\|_F} \tag{2}$$

$$err_U = \frac{\left\| I - \hat{U}^T\hat{U} \right\|_F}{\sqrt{n}}, \quad err_V = \frac{\left\| I - \hat{V}^T\hat{V} \right\|_F}{\sqrt{n}} \tag{3}$$

5 Application to Quantum Lattice Systems

One of the applications on top of our batched SVD routine presented in this paper is numerical simulations of quantum lattice systems which are very important in modern condensed matter physics. We only show the application of our proposed routine on one-dimensional systems, and multi-dimensional systems can also be applied trivially. For one-dimensional quantum lattice systems, an optimal tensor network is matrix product states (MPS). Reviewing and analyzing MPS algorithms are beyond the scope of this paper. Here we focus on the narrow task of calculating time evolution for one-dimensional quantum lattice systems by the time-evolving block decimation (TEBD) algorithm. We just give a brief description of the TEBD algorithm, and the details can be found in [20].

Table 1. Numerical error of our routine and the KBLAS.

Matrix dimension	Our				KBLAS			
	err_σ	err_U	err_V	err_D	err_σ	err_U	err_V	err_D
96	2.4E–17	1.9E–15	6.4E–14	1.1E–15	3.4E–17	4.3E–16	4.0E–14	4.9E–16
128	7.1E–17	2.1E–15	1.1E–13	2.4E–15	5.8E–17	5.2E–16	4.0E–14	5.2E–16
192	3.4E–17	2.5E–15	1.2E–13	3.0E–15	4.4E–17	6.1E–16	4.0E–14	6.5E–16
256	3.9E–18	2.5E–15	1.1E–13	1.4E–15	3.5E–17	7.2E–16	7.1E–14	7.7E–16
320	5.0E–17	3.2E–15	8.0E–13	2.4E–15	2.8E–17	8.2E–16	4.0E–13	8.7E–16
384	3.6E–17	3.2E–15	5.7E–12	1.9E–15	1.2E–17	9.0E–16	2.3E–12	9.7E–16
448	7.7E–18	3.5E–15	3.8E–13	4.6E–15	1.7E–17	8.8E–16	1.9E–13	9.3E–16
512	8.8E–17	3.8E–15	2.8E–13	3.1E–15	3.9E–17	9.6E–16	1.2E–13	1.0E–15

Table 2. THE SVD routine time ratio of the TEBD algorithm.

Matrix dimension	Percentage
96	70.6%
128	74.1%
256	90.6%
512	95.9%

There are two main steps of the TEBD algorithm. The first step is to contract the two-site-operators and tensors in MPS representation, which results in a non-MPS representation. To recover the MPS representation, each tensor needs to be split into two tensors. To achieve this, the tensors are reshaped to matrices, and the routines of SVD decompositions for matrices are employed. This is the second step.

As a benchmark, we first implement the TEBD algorithm using the TNSPackage [21] with version 3.5.8, which is a highly optimized Fortran 2003 library for tensor network state methods. The one-dimensional quantum lattice system used in this paper is the Heisenberg model. The number of quantum lattices is 100. The physical degree freedom on each site is 2. The initial time step is 0.1, and the time step is decreased to $\frac{1}{5}$ after ten steps walkthrough. The total steps are 50, so the minimum time step is 0.00016. Experimental environments in this section are the same as the Sect. 4. Table 2 shows the running time percentage of SVD routine in the TEBD algorithm implemented by the TNSPackage. We can see that the ratios grow with the increase of matrix dimensions, and the ratio is up to 95.9% when the matrix dimension is equal to 512. Therefore, accelerating the SVD routine is critical for improving the performance of the TEBD algorithm.

In the TEBD algorithm, the splits of tensors are independent, thus the splitting can be conducted simultaneously. For utilizing our proposed batched SVD routine, we first reshape all tensors to matrices and then do SVD decomposition of all matrices simultaneously. Table 3 displays the time in seconds of the TEBD

Table 3. The comparison of the TEBD algorithm for different implementations.

Matrix dimension	TNSPackage	Our	Speedup	Difference
96	27.168	3.700	7.3×	1.6E–13
128	64.320	5.074	12.7×	2.0E–13
256	561.428	17.211	32.6×	2.2E–13
512	4542.161	83.958	54.1×	1.9E–13

algorithm implemented by the TNSPackage and our batched SVD routine. It can be seen that the implementation based on our batched SVD routine outperforms the TNSPackage for all dimensions tested, and the maximum speedup is up to 54.1×. We also compare the numerical difference of the TEBD algorithm implemented by the TNSPackage and our batched SVD routine. The difference is presented in Table 3. In fact, the approximation error of the TEBD algorithm is $O(\delta t)$ introduced by the Trotter-Suzuki decomposition [20]. Obviously, the difference presented in Table 3 is much less, which indicates that our bathed SVD routine is trustworthy.

6   Conclusion

In this paper, we presented a parallel blocked Jacobi algorithm and its efficient implementation for singular value decomposition of many small matrices. Our approach exploits adequately the blocking structure and the parallelism of the blocked Jacobi SVD algorithm thus fitting well into the SIMT GPU architectures. Our implementation needs a CPU only for controlling flow and deliver high performance against state-of-the-art solutions. For illustrating the power of our routine, we further develop an application, the numerical simulation of quantum lattice system, on top of our routine, and achieve a maximum speedup of 54.1× versus its CPU counterpart. In the future, we plan to generalize our methodology for non-uniform workloads.

Acknowledgment. We would like to acknowledge He L. and Dong S. for helpful conversations and insights on numerical simulations of quantum lattice systems.

References

1. Abdelfattah, A., Baboulin, M., Dobrev, V., et al.: High-performance tensor contractions for GPUs. Procedia Comput. Sci. **80**(1), 108–118 (2016)
2. Molero, J.M., Garzón, E.M., García, I., Quintana-Ortí, E.S., Plaza, A.: Efficient implementation of hyperspectral anomaly detection techniques on GPUs and multicore processors. IEEE J. Sel. Topics Appl. Earth Obs. Remote Sens. **7**(6), 2256–2266 (2014)
3. Villa, O., Gawande, N., Tumeo, A.: Accelerating subsurface transport simulation on heterogeneous clusters. In: IEEE International Conference on Cluster Computing, Indianapolis, pp. 1–8. IEEE (2013)

4. Zhang, T., Liu, X., Wang, X., Walid, A.: cuTensor-tubal: efficient primitives for tubal-rank tensor learning operations on GPUs. IEEE Trans. Parallel Distrib. Syst. **31**(3), 595–610 (2020)
5. NVIDIA cuBLAS Homepage. https://docs.nvidia.com/cuda/pdf/cublas_Library.pdf
6. AMD rocBLAS Homepage. https://github.com/ROCmSoftwarePlatform/rocBLAS
7. Abdelfattah, A., Costa, T., Dongarra, J., et al.: A set of batched basic linear algebra subprograms and LAPACK routines. ACM Trans. Math. Softw. **47**(7), 1–23 (2021)
8. Dong, T., Haidar, A., Tomov, S., Dongarra. J.: A fast batched cholesky factorization on a GPU. In: International Conference on Parallel Processing, pp. 432–440. IEEE (2014)
9. Abdelfattah, A., Haidar, A., Tomov, S., Dongarra. J.: Factorization and inversion of a million matrices using GPUs: challenges and countermeasures. In: International Conference on Computational Science, pp. 606–615 (2017)
10. NVIDIA cuSOLVER Homepage. https://docs.nvidia.com/cuda/cusolver/index.html
11. Dong, T., Haidar, A., Tomov, S., Dongarra, J.: Accelerating the SVD bidiagonalization of a batch of small matrices using GPUs. J. Comput. Sci. **26**(5), 237–245 (2018)
12. Badolato, I., Paula, L.D., Farias, R.: Many SVDs on GPU for image mosaic assemble. In: IEEE International Symposium on Computer Architecture and High Performance Computing Workshop, pp. 37–42 (2015)
13. Boukaram, W.H., Turkiyyah, G., Ltaief, H., Keyes, D.E.: Batched QR and SVD algorithms on GPUs with applications in hierarchical matrix compression. Parallel Comput. **74**(5), 19–33 (2018)
14. KBLAS Homepage. https://github.com/ecrc/kblas-gpu, Accessed 30 Nov 2020
15. Brent, P.P., Luk, F.T.: The solution of singular-value and symmetric eigenvalue problems on multiprocessor arrays. SIAM J. Sci. Stat. Comput. **6**(1), 69–84 (1985)
16. Luk, F.T., Park, H.: On parallel Jacobi orderings. SIAM J. Sci. Stat. Comput. **10**(1), 18–26 (1989)
17. Luk, F.T., Park, H.: A proof of convergence for two parallel jacobi SVD algorithms. IEEE Trans. Comput. **38**(6), 806–811 (1989)
18. Rivera, C., Chen, J., Xiong, N., Zhang, J., Song, S.: TSM2X: high-performance tall-and-skinny matrix-matrix multiplication on GPUs. J. Parallel Distrib. Comput. **151**(3), 70–85 (2021)
19. Filipovič, J., Madzin, M., Fousek, J., Matyska, L.: Optimizing CUDA code by kernel fusion: application on BLAS. J. Supercomput. **71**(10), 3934–3957 (2015). https://doi.org/10.1007/s11227-015-1483-z
20. Vidal, G.: Efficient simulation of one-dimensional quantum many-body systems. Phys. Rev. Lett. **93**(4), 40502–40505 (2004)
21. Dong, S., Liu, W., Wang, C., Han, Y., Guo, G., He, L.: TNSPackage: a fortran 2003 library designed for tensor network state methods. Comput. Phys. Commun. **228**(7), 163–177 (2018)

A Molecular Dynamics Based Multi-scale Platelet Aggregation Model and Its High-Throughput Simulation

Zhipeng Xu[1] and Qingsong Zou[2(✉)]

[1] School of Science, Nantong University, Nantong 226019, Jiangsu, China
xuzhp@ntu.edu.cn
[2] School of Computer Science and Engineering and Guangdong Province Key Laboratory of Computational Science, Sun Yat-sen University, Guangzhou 510006, Guangdong, China
mcszqs@mail.sysu.edu.cn

Abstract. In this paper, we develop a multi-scale model to simulate the aggregation of platelets in a low shear-coefficient flow. In this multi-scale model, the Morse potential is used to describe the interaction between the $\alpha IIb\beta3$ receptor and fibrinogen, the dissipative particle dynamics (DPD) is used to simulate fluids on the macro-scale, and the coarse-grained molecular dynamics (CGMD) is used to simulate the fine-scale receptors' biochemical reactions. Moreover, with the assistance of the high-throughput simulations on the heterogeneous cluster, we calibrate the parameters for the Morse potential which are critical in the proper simulation of the aggregation of platelets. With this model, we simulate the long-term behaviour of thrombus formation constructed by many platelets. Our simulating results are consistent with in-vitro experiments on contact areas and detaching forces. Moreover, it reduces the computational cost significantly.

Keywords: Platelet aggregation · High-throughput simulation · Molecular dynamics · Morse potential

1 Introduction

Platelet aggregation is a common phenomenon in the blood flow, which promotes wound repair in general. However, platelet aggregation might also be a crucial factor in triggering thrombosis. For patients suffering from cardiovascular disease or wearing some extracorporeal blood circulation device, abnormal platelet aggregation caused by high blood pressure may cause serious complications. Therefore, understanding the mechanism of platelet aggregation is of great significance for the prevention and treatment of cardiovascular diseases. So far, many medical experiments have been completed to understand the mechanism of platelet aggregation. For instance, some experiments show that platelet aggregation in the vein or aorta with the low-to-medium shear flow is due to fibrinogen

H. Shen et al. (Eds.): PDCAT 2021, LNCS 13148, pp. 81–92, 2022.
https://doi.org/10.1007/978-3-030-96772-7_8

[11, 16, 17] binding distributed in the blood to the $\alpha IIb\beta3$ protein [2]. Some other experiments discover that the initial small clot will attract more platelets to participate, and eventually, they combine to form a large thrombus. Since various factors, including platelet surface proteins, ligands, and shear stress, will participate in the reaction during platelet aggregation, it seems very difficult to discover the mechanism of platelet aggregation only by medical/chemical experiments.

Recently, more and more scientists tried to use numerical simulation to reveal the mechanism of platelet aggregation. Since the process of platelet aggregation usually involves multi-scale physical or chemical behaviors such as the macro-scale fluid flow, and molecular-size reaction occurs among surface proteins, a high-precision simulation requires a multi-scale numerical model that covers at least fluid mechanics and molecular dynamics. Usually, a good simulation model [4–6, 18–21] includes three scales: macro-scale, meso-scale, and micro-scale. With the macro-scale model, we simulate the flow of blood in vessels. Note that the classical fluid dynamics equation such as Navier-Stokes equation and some particle methods [14], such as SPH [10], DPD [1], and SDPD [8, 15], etc., can also be used to characterize the blood flow. With the meso-scale model, we simulate the interaction between the blood fluid and the platelet. The motion of platelets caused by blood flow and the change of flow field due to immersed platelets and thrombi can be calculated in this scale. With the micro-scale model, we simulate the nanometer-level size proteins, which play a critical role in the aggregation of platelets.

It is challenging to simulate all the platelet aggregation process details using full-atom molecular dynamics, but multi-scale models are available. For instance, in [4], Prachi et al. simulate the platelet aggregation with the DPD-CGMD model [20], in which the DPD method is used to solve viscous flow, and the CGMD is used to simulate the movements of the particles in the interior of platelets. With their method, they successfully simulate the aggregation process of two platelets in a blood flow. However, the massive amount of computation limits the application of their model to simulate the aggregation process of more platelets, even on the fastest modern supercomputer.

In this paper, we propose a rigid platelet multi-scale model to simulate the aggregation of more platelets. In our model, each platelet is regarded as a rigid body in the sense that there is no relative movement between the particles/molecules of the same platelet. Of course, this simplified model cannot simulate the process of platelet deformation to produce filopodia. However, our model includes the interaction of the particles/molecules distributed on the membrane of platelets. Since the real platelet aggregation is driven by many $\alpha IIb\beta3$ proteins distributed on the membrane of platelets and the mediation of fibrinogen in the blood, our simplified model can simulate the following main process of platelet aggregation: once there exists two platelets gathers together, the blood flow speed will be slowed down, the consequent increase of shear pressure leads to aggregation of more platelets, and eventually to form an enormous clot.

2   A Rigid Platelet Multi-scale Model

This section introduces basic ingredients to stimulate platelet aggregation with the MD-based rigid platelet multi-scale model.

2.1   DPD Model for Blood Flow

From the microcosmic point of view, calculating the statistical properties for all fluid molecule trajectories is the way to realize the fluid dynamics. However, the enormous of calculations cannot be implemented even on the fastest modern supercomputer. Therefore, the mesoscopic DPD fluid model [12] was established and used in the simulation of biological fluids. Here, the DPD particle represents a cluster of fluid molecules, similar to the renormalization group [7]. Although the details of a single molecule are lost, the physical property of a bunch of DPD particles still can reflect the fluid's motion characteristics [3], even turbulence. Assuming that within the cut-off distance, the ith particle is affected by its surrounding DPD particles, the resultant force and the change in velocity can be written as follows,

$$dv_i = \frac{1}{m_i} \sum_{j \neq i}^{N} \left(\boldsymbol{F}_{ij}^{C} dt + \boldsymbol{F}_{ij}^{D} dt + \boldsymbol{F}_{ij}^{E} dt + \boldsymbol{F}_{ij}^{R} \sqrt{dt} \right). \tag{1}$$

Here, m_i, $\boldsymbol{F}_{ij}^{C}$, $\boldsymbol{F}_{ij}^{D}$, $\boldsymbol{F}_{ij}^{R}$ and $\boldsymbol{F}_{ij}^{E}$ represent the mass of the ith particle, the conservative force, dissipation force, random force and external force of the jth particle on the ith particle, respectively. Detailed representations of the above forces are expressed as below.

$$\begin{aligned} \boldsymbol{F}_{i}^{C} &= a \left(1.0 - \frac{r_{ij}}{r_c} \right) \boldsymbol{e}_{ij}, \\ \boldsymbol{F}_{ij}^{D} &= -\gamma \omega^{D} \left(r_{ij} \right) \left(\boldsymbol{e}_{ij} \cdot \boldsymbol{v}_{ij} \right) \boldsymbol{e}_{ij}, \\ \boldsymbol{F}_{ij}^{R} &= \sigma \omega^{R} \left(r_{ij} \right) \varsigma_{ij} \boldsymbol{e}_{ij}, \\ \omega^{D} \left(r_{ij} \right) &= \left[\omega^{R} \left(r_{ij} \right) \right]^{2} = \left(1.0 - \frac{r_{ij}}{r_c} \right)^{2k}. \end{aligned} \tag{2}$$

The physical meaning of the conservative force $\boldsymbol{F}_{ij}^{C}$ is the compressibility of the fluid. Here r_{ij} is the distance between two particles, r_c represents the cut-off distance, $\boldsymbol{e}_{ij}$ is the unit vector pointing from the ith particle to the jth particle, and the coefficient a is determined by letting the two particles be in the same position (i.e. $r_{ij} = 0$). We may observe that the conservative force is the linear function of the negative correlation with the distance r_{ij}. That is to say, the conservative force attenuates with a larger distance in a linear format. When the particle density increase, the decrease of average distance cause more particles to move in the range of cut-off distance. But the larger repulsive force will promote the density of particles to be stable, which shows compressibility likes spring. Similarly, the small repulsive force corresponding to the low density always attracts other particles to increase the density. The dissipation force $\boldsymbol{F}_{ij}^{D}$ reflects the frictional force between particles that run irregularly in the fluid. Namely, the dissipation force indicates the viscosity of the liquid. The parameter γ is the coefficient of the dissipative force. The magnitude of the dissipative force is related to the relative distance and relative speed between particles. The negative sign of $\boldsymbol{F}_{ij}^{D}$ means the decelerating effect in the direction of relative velocity. The random force $\boldsymbol{F}_{ij}^{R}$ reflects the characteristics of the random Brownian motion of liquid particles. To meet the features of the constant-temperature, constant-volume ensemble (NVT), according to the fluctuation-dissipation theorem, the coefficients of the conservative force, random force, and dissipation force satisfy the following relationship,

$$a = 75k_b T / \left(\rho_f r_c \right), \tag{3}$$

$$\sigma^2 = 2\gamma k_B T, k_B T = 1.0, \tag{4}$$

where ρ_f is the density of DPD particles, and according to Prachi's [4] simulation, the above parameters can be chosen as

$$a = 25.0, \gamma = 67.5, k = 0.25, r_c = 1.7. \tag{5}$$

2.2   CGMD-DPD Model for Fluid-Platelet Interaction

The DPD model at the fluid level only considers the interaction between fluid particles. To present the interaction between fluid particles and particles in the platelet membrane, we need to introduce a platelet interface potential of which the velocity update function can be written as below:

$$dv_i = \frac{1}{m_i} \sum_{j \neq i}^{N} \left(\nabla U_{LJ}\left(r_{ij}\right) dt + \boldsymbol{F}_{ij}^{D} dt + \boldsymbol{F}_{ij}^{R} \sqrt{dt} \right). \tag{6}$$

where, $F_{ij}^{D} = -\gamma \omega^D \left(r_{ij}\right) \left(e_{ij} \cdot v_{ij}\right) e_{ij}, \quad F_{ij}^{R} = \sigma \omega^R \left(r_{ij}\right) \varsigma_{ij} e_{ij}$ and

$$U_{LJ} = 4\epsilon \left[\left(\frac{\sigma}{r_{ij}} \right)^6 - 2 \left(\frac{\sigma}{r_{ij}} \right)^{12} \right].$$

In this model, the particles on the surface of platelets are regarded as a particular part of the fluid during the coupling of fluid and platelets. However, since the pressure from the fluid on the membrane particles can be ignored, there is no conservative force in the above formula. Moreover, the external force is represented by Lenord-Jones potential U_{LJ}, preventing the flow particle from penetrating the membrane [19].

Note that in [4] the L-J potential is replaced by

$$V_{\text{CGMD}} = \sum_{\text{bonds}} k_b \left(r - r_0 \right)^2 + \sum_{L-J} 4\epsilon_{ij} \left[\left(\frac{\sigma_{ij}}{r} \right)^{12} - \left(\frac{\sigma_{ij}}{r} \right)^6 \right], \tag{7}$$

where k_b is the bond energy between two adjacent membrane particles. The bond energy term L-J is used to maintain the structure of the platelet; otherwise, the platelet will shrink to a clump with the minimal energy principle. Since the platelet is assumed to be a rigid body with no deformation for our model, the platelet structure will never change. Therefore, we keep using (6) as our model to simulate the fluid-solid interaction.

2.3 The Morse Potential for Platelet-Platelet Interaction

When two platelets move close to each other, the protein on the surface binds to fibrin to produce an aggregation effect. The attractive force between particles of different platelets drives the aggregation progress. The Morse potential is a common tool to describe the interaction for diatomic molecular in chemical reactions. Prachi and Zhang et al. [19] modified the Morse potential function to simulate fluid and platelet aggregation by calibrating with experimental data. They define

$$E = D_0 \left[e^{-2\alpha(r-r_0)} - 2e^{-\alpha(r-r_0)} \right] + \frac{f^A}{2r_0} (r - r_0)^2 . \tag{8}$$

According to the literature, the CGMD elastic model with harmonic and LJ potentials in Eq. (7) leads to more computational cost. Therefore, we consider building the rigid model that ignores Eq. (7) with original Morse potential to simulate the aggregation. The relationship between the potential energy and the distance for original Morse potential is as follows,

$$E = D_0 \left[e^{-2\alpha(r-r_0)} - 2e^{-\alpha(r-r_0)} \right] . \tag{9}$$

In Eq. 9, D_0 is the coefficient to measure the energy when one molecule moves from the stabilizing point of minimum energy to infinity. r_0 is the equilibrium distance, and alpha is a parameter related to the molecule. When the distance of $r - r_0$ is minimal, the equation will perform a simple harmonic motion at the equilibrium point using Taylor expansion. Hence, two platelets will vibrate near the aggregate balance point when the driven force can be neglected than the Morse force. The parameters D_0, α, and r_0 in Eq. 9 should be specified to make the model computable, which means we should exhaust the parameter space and compare the output metric data with experiment results. In summary, Table 1 lists the equation of each scale for the rigid platelet model, and the contribution of the work is to achieve the detailed parameters for Eq. 9 by using the high-throughput simulation.

3 Parameters Calibration

To determine the parameters multi-scale for platelet aggregation, we need to compare two indicators: contact area and detaching force with medical experimental data. Since molecular dynamics is a multi-body problem, the relationship between the parameters and experimental medical data results is nonlinear. Finding appropriate parameters often takes considerable time and cost.

Table 1. Model of each layer for the rigid platelet model

Layer	Model
Fluid	Eq. 1
Interaction of Fluid-Platelet	Eq. 6
Interaction of Platelet-Platelet	Eq. 9

Here, we use the Hygon DCUs (Deep Computing Units) [22] to accelerate the high-throughput molecular dynamics simulation to achieve model parameters. Figure 1 demonstrates the size of the system as $16\,\mu m \times 16\,\mu m \times 8\,\mu m$, and the system contains 256,000 DPD particles, $23,592 \times 2$ platelets particles. As shown in the figure, each particle (blue point) represents the protein on the membrane, and the bounding of protein and fibrinogen will be described with Morse potential. The max velocity of Poiseuille flow is $0.28\,cm/s$ that driven by a constant force and no-slip boundary conditions [13].

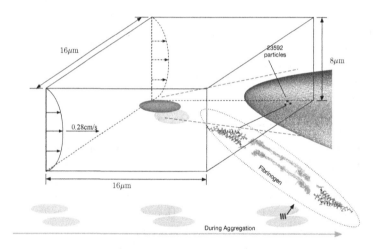

Fig. 1. Profile of the system.

3.1   Contact Area and Detaching Force

When the distance between two platelets is smaller than the critical distance, the protein on the membrane of the platelet will attract the nearest protein to drive the aggregation of two platelets. During the reaction progress, part of the protein detached due to the external force of fluid. Still, part of the proteins will re-aggregate if the driven pressure from the liquid is not too enormous, which is similar to the effect of nylon buckles. Therefore, the contact area calculation can be converted into a particle pair whose distance is less than the sum of the length of the fibrinogen protein and the membrane protein. Some work indicates that the fibrinogen protein length is about 47.5 nm, and the membrane protein is about 20 nm above the cell membrane surface. Therefore, when the distance between two proteins on the surface of two platelets is less than 87.5 nm, namely, 0.5 in the L-J unit, two proteins can be considered as contacted. Consequently, the contact area between two small platelets can be calculated by the following formula,

$$C_a = |C_{AB}| \cdot \frac{S}{N_s}. \tag{10}$$

Here, C_{AB} can be calculated as follows,

$$C_{AB} = \left\{ r_i \mid r_{ij} < T_d, r_{ij} = \|r_i - r_j\|_2 \, r_i \in N_A, r_j \in N_B \right\}. \tag{11}$$

S is the surface area of the membrane; N_s is the number of distance pairs less on the membrane surface, T_d represents the critical distance. $|C_{AB}|$ is the number of distance pairs of the nearest neighbor distance between A and B platelets less than T_d. In the system, $N_s = 23592$, $S \approx 22.696 \, \text{um}^2$ with semi-major axis $a, b = 1.78 \, \text{um}$ and $c = 0.445 \, \text{um}$.

Two platelets will produce an interaction force when they aggregate. When the external force exceeds the critical value, two platelets will separate, so the interaction force can also be called the detaching force. For a single fibrin-$\alpha IIb\beta 3$ protein pair, the interaction force can be measured by atomic force microscopy. Atomic force microscopes use contact currents to image the surface of a sample, which can distinguish single atoms. The detaching force can be obtained by calculating the sum of the Morse force corresponding to all the distance pairs where the distance is less than T_d at the time of contact,

$$F_{\text{detaching}} = \sum_{r_{ij} < T_d} D_0 \left[-2\alpha e^{-2\alpha(r_{ij} - r_0)} + 2\alpha e^{-\alpha(r_{ij} - r_0)} \right]. \tag{12}$$

The result [9] from atomic force microscopy shows that the bonding force between a pair of $\alpha IIb\beta 3$ and fibrinogen is about 10–20 pN. Considering the number of bounded proteins, the detaching force $F_{\text{detaching}}$ between the two platelets is about 9.1 nN–18.2 nN.

3.2 Parameter Calibration with High-Throughput Simulation

During the simulation, we found that DCU acceleration can greatly reduce the calculation time of molecular dynamics than CPU architecture. The benchmark test results show that for a DPD system with the size of 128 mm × 128 mm × 256 mm, including 0.5 billion particles, the calculation speed of the DCU is increased by 13 times compared with CPU parallelism after acceleration. For the case in this manuscript, the 1000-core for one hour of Tianhe-2 has the same efficiency as four nodes with 16 DCU cards for ten minutes in the Kunshan Computing Center. Therefore, the computational cost is reduced to one-tenth, allowing high-throughput molecular dynamics simulation for parameter fitting.

Firstly, we performed coarse-grained searching, where the range of parameter D_0 is 10 to 110 with step 20; α is 0.5 to 2.1 with step 0.2; r_c is 0.6 to 1.0 with

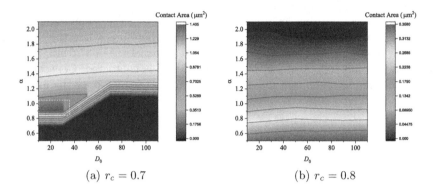

Fig. 2. Contact area phase diagrams of α and D_0.

step 0.1. The coarse-grained results show that when $r_c = 0.7$ or 0.8, platelet aggregation can occur. Figure 2 shows the phase diagrams of the contact area related to D_0 and α. The contact area is represented by color. The blue region represents the infeasible region caused by the penetration of two platelets. When $r_c = 0.8$ (see Fig. 2(b)), the maximum contact area is about $0.36\,\mu m^2$, and when $r_c = 0.7$ (see Fig. 2(a)), the maximum contact area is about $1.405\,\mu m^2$ marked with the white rectangular area, which is much more close to the experiment result.

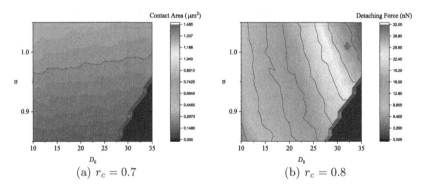

Fig. 3. Contact area and detaching force phase diagrams of α and D_0.

With the coarse-grained parameter simulations, we determined the approximate region for $D_0 \in [10, 35] \times \alpha \in [0.85, 1.1]$. The high precision high-throughput simulation was carried out and displayed in Fig. 3(a) for the white rectangular part, as shown in Fig. 2(a). In the case of fine-grained search, as shown in Fig. 3, we picked up the parameters with maximum contact area (Fig. 3(a)) and the green region that detaching force ranges from 10–20 nN, the parameters of the Morse model were finally determined: $D_0 = 18, \alpha = 0.85, r_0 = 0.7$. With these parameters, the aggregation simulation with Morse potential is in good agreement with the experimental data.

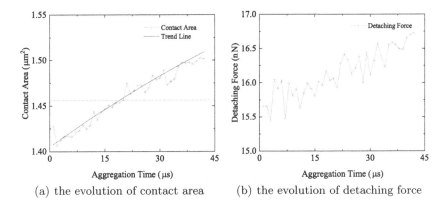

(a) the evolution of contact area   (b) the evolution of detaching force

Fig. 4. The evolutions of platelet contact area and detaching force during the aggregation time.

Figure 4 shows the evolution of platelet contact area and detaching force when $D_0 = 18, \alpha = 0.85, r_0 = 0.7$. When two platelets are very close, they will attract in less than 1 μs. Two platelets slipped driven by the fluid, and the contact area gradually increased and exceeded the lower bound of the contact area after 16 μs. In the aggregation progress, detaching force is always kept in the range of 10 nN–20 nN, as shown in Fig. 4, which is consistent with in-vitro experiments.

Figure 5 shows the contact region of two platelets when $t = 40$ μs. The gray shape represents the projection of the two platelets in the $x - y$ direction, and the red part represents the area where the two platelets aggregate. The contact

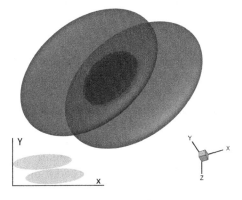

Fig. 5. The contact region for $t = 40$ μs

Table 2. Comparison of literature and in-vitro results.

Parameters	Rigid (our work)	Rigid (Prachi [4])	Deformable (Prachi [4])	In vitro results
Contact area (μm^2)	> 1.4660	0.213 ± 0.001	2.227 ± 0.003	1.4660 − 2.4340
Detaching force (nN)	16.1 ± 0.5	0.844 ± 0.007	17.842 ± 0.027	9.10 − 18.20

region is a round shape due to the regular surface of the rigid body. Table 2 compared Prachi's and our results. In [4], the contact area of rigid platelet is much smaller than non-rigid bodies with the same parameters. But our work of the high-throughput molecular dynamics simulation shows that the model with appropriate potential parameters for a rigid body also can reflect the experiment result.

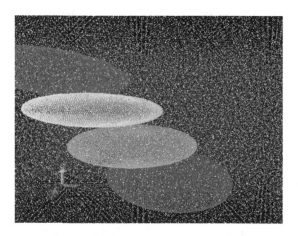

Fig. 6. The contact region for $t = 40\,\mu s$

4   Conclusion

Thrombus is closely related to various diseases. High-precision platelet aggregation simulation helps to understand the formation mechanism of thrombus. Most elastic platelet models based on molecular dynamics are computationally expensive, and it isn't easy to achieve further thrombosis simulation. High-throughput molecular dynamics show that the simulation results of the rigid platelet model are consistent with the actual experimental data. Our rigid platelet model with calibrated parameters is successfully applied to simulate the aggregation of four platelets, as shown in Fig. 6. The simulation of the formation process of thrombosis containing hundreds or thousands of platelets is our next goal.

Acknowledgment. The research was supported in part by NSFC Grant 12071496, Guangdong Provincial NSF Grant 2017B030311001, Guangdong Province Key Laboratory of Computational Science at the Sun Yat-sen University (2020B1212060032), and Nantong Science & Technology Research Plan (No. JC2021133). This work also benefited from resources made available at the National Supercomputer Center in Kunshan.

References

1. Duc, D.-H., Nhan, P.-T., Xijun, F.: An implementation of no-slip boundary conditions in DPD. Comput. Mech. **35**(1), 24–29 (2004)
2. Durrant, T.N., van den Bosch, M.T., Hers, I.: Integrin $\alpha IIb\beta 3$ outside-in signaling. Blood **130**(14), 1607–1619 (2017)
3. Gao, C., Zhang, P., Marom, G., Deng, Y., Bluestein, D.: Reducing the effects of compressibility in DPD-based blood flow simulations through severe stenotic microchannels. J. Comput. Phys. **335**, 812–827 (2017)
4. Gupta, P., Zhang, P., Sheriff, J., Bluestein, D., Deng, Y.: A multiscale model for recruitment aggregation of platelets by correlating with in vitro results. Cell. Mol. Bioeng. **12**(4), 327–343 (2019)
5. Gupta, P., Zhang, P., Sheriff, J., Bluestein, D., Deng, Y.: A multiscale model for multiple platelet aggregation in shear flow. Biomech. Model. Mechanobiol. **20**(3), 1013–1030 (2021). https://doi.org/10.1007/s10237-021-01428-6
6. Han, C., Zhang, P., Bluestein, D., Cong, G., Deng, Y.: Artificial intelligence for accelerating time integrations in multiscale modeling. J. Comput. Phys. **427**, 110053 (2021)
7. Lan, Y.: Bridging steady states with renormalization group analysis. Phys. Rev. E **87**, 012914 (2013)
8. Li, G., Ye, T., Wang, S., Li, X., UI Haq, R.: Numerical design of a highly efficient microfluidic chip for blood plasma separation. **32**(3), 031903 (2020)
9. Litvinov, R.I., Farrell, D.H., Weisel, J.W., Bennett, J.S.: The platelet integrin $\alpha IIb\beta 3$ differentially interacts with fibrin versus fibrinogen. **291**(15), 7858–7867 (2016)
10. Tanaka, N., Takano, T.N.: Microscopic-scale simulation of blood flow using sph method. **02**(04), 555–568 (2005)
11. Vilar, R., Fish, R.J., Casini, A., Neerman-Arbez, M.: Fibrin(ogen) in human disease: both friend and foe. Haematologica **105**(2), 284–296 (2020)
12. Wang, L., Chen, Z., Zhang, J., Zhang, X., Wu, Z.J.: Modeling clot formation of shear-injured platelets in flow by a dissipative particle dynamics method. Bull. Math. Biol. **82**(7), June 2020
13. Willlemsen, S.M., Hoefsloot, H.C.J., Iedema, P.D.: No-slip boundary condition in dissipative particle dynamics. **11**(05), 881–890 (2000)
14. Yamaguchi, T., et al.: Particle-based methods for multiscale modeling of blood flow in the circulation and in devices: challenges and future directions. Ann. Biomed. Eng. **38**(3), 1225–1235 (2010)
15. Ye, T., Phan-Thien, N., Lim, C.T., Peng, L., Shi, H.: Hybrid smoothed dissipative particle dynamics and immersed boundary method for simulation of red blood cells in flows. **95**(6), 063314, June 2017
16. Yesudasan, S., Wang, X., Averett, R.D.: Coarse-grained molecular dynamics simulations of fibrin polymerization: effects of thrombin concentration on fibrin clot structure. J. Mol. Model. **24**(5), 1–14 (2018). https://doi.org/10.1007/s00894-018-3642-7

17. Yesudasan, S., Wang, X., Averett, R.D.: Fibrin polymerization simulation using a reactive dissipative particle dynamics method. Biomech. Model. Mechanobiol. **17**(5), 1389–1403 (2018). https://doi.org/10.1007/s10237-018-1033-8

18. Zhang, N., Zhang, P., Kang, W., Bluestein, D., Deng, Y.: Parameterizing the morse potential for coarse-grained modeling of blood plasma. J. Comput. Phys. **257**, 726–736 (2014)

19. Zhang, P., Gao, C., Zhang, N., Slepian, M.J., Deng, Y., Bluestein, D.: Multiscale particle-based modeling of flowing platelets in blood plasma using dissipative particle dynamics and coarse grained molecular dynamics. Cell. Mol. Bioeng. **7**(4), 552–574 (2014)

20. Zhang, P., Zhang, L., Slepian, M.J., Deng, Y., Bluestein, D.: A multiscale biomechanical model of platelets: correlating with in-vitro results. J. Biomech. **50**, 1–15 (2016)

21. Zhang, P., Zhang, N., Deng, Y., Bluestein, D.: A multiple time stepping algorithm for efficient multiscale modeling of platelets flowing in blood plasma. J. Comput. Phys. **284**, 668–686 (2015)

22. Zhang, Y., Qian, H.: Porting and optimizing g-BLASTN to the ROCm-based supercomputer. In 2020 International Conference on Computer Science and Management Technology (ICCSMT). IEEE, November 2020

Approximation and Polynomial Algorithms for Multi-depot Capacitated Arc Routing Problems

Wei Yu[✉] and Yujie Liao

School of Mathematics, East China University of Science and Technology,
Shanghai 200237, China
yuwei@ecust.edu.cn, y30190191@mail.ecust.edu.cn

Abstract. We study the multi-depot capacitated arc routing problem (MCARP), which generalizes the classical arc routing problem to the more realistic situation with multiple depots. We propose approximation and polynomial algorithms for different variants of the MCARP. First, we present the first constant-factor approximation algorithms for the MCARP and the nonfixed destination variant. Second, for a restricted case of the MCARP with infinite vehicle capacity, called the multi-depot rural postman problem, we devise a $(2 - \frac{1}{2k+1})$-approximation algorithm with k indicating the number of depots. Lastly, we show that the equal-demand MCARP defined on a line graph is polynomially solvable and develop a 2-approximation algorithm for the multi-depot capacitated vehicle routing problem on a line.

Keywords: Approximation algorithm · Multi-depot · Vehicle routing problem · Arc routing problem · Rural postman problem

1 Introduction

Given an undirected graph $G = (V, E)$, which may be a multigraph, with vertex set V and edge set E. Each edge $e \in E$ is associated with a nonnegative cost $c(e)$ and a nonnegative integer demand $d(e)$. There is a fleet of homogeneous vehicles with capacity Q located at a specified vertex $o \in V$, called the depot. The Capacitated Arc Routing Problem (CARP) is to find a set of routes (or closed walks), starting from and ending at the depot, for the vehicles to serve the edges with positive demands such that each vehicle serves a total demand of at most Q (capacity constraint) and the total cost of the routes is minimized. If the demands are defined for the vertices instead of the edges in the CARP, we obtain the Capacitated Vehicle Routing Problem (CVRP).

As noted by Golden and Wong [13], the CVRP can be seen as a special case of the CARP. Because we can split the vertices in the CVRP into two vertices which are connected by a zero-cost edge with a demand equal to the original vertex demand. The CARP occurs frequently in practice applications, including the

© Springer Nature Switzerland AG 2022
H. Shen et al. (Eds.): PDCAT 2021, LNCS 13148, pp. 93–100, 2022.
https://doi.org/10.1007/978-3-030-96772-7_9

inspection of electric power lines [9], distribution service [16], garbage collection [10], school bus routing problem [24], and so on.

A natural extension of the CARP/CVRP is the Multi-Depot Capacitated Arc/Vehicle Routing Problem (MCARP/MCVRP) where there are multiple depots instead of a single depot and the routes are required to start from and end at the same depot (but different routes may use different depots). The motivation to study the MCARP/MCVRP lies not only in their theoretical interest, but also in their wide-spread applications. For the CARP/CVRP, when the service area is large, multiple depots are usually setting up to meet the service requirements [11]. Such depots correspond to vehicle stations, warehouses, dumping places, supply points or relay boxes. For example, the online shopping business usually operates at multiple depots to improve the customers experience and satisfaction in cities [19]. Other applications of the MCARP/MCVRP encompass mail delivery [17], explosive waste recycling [27], police patrolling [7], etc.

One can see that the CARP (resp. CVRP) is NP-hard, since it contains the well-known Rural Postman Problem (resp. Metric Traveling Salesman Problem) as a special case where the vehicle capacity is infinite. In turn, as a generalization of the CARP/CVRP, the MCARP/MCVRP is also NP-hard. Therefore, the existing literature on the MCARP/MCVRP has centered on branch-and-cut approach (e.g. see [12,20]) and meta-heuristics (e.g., see [17,19,23]). However, we address the multi-depot CARP from the point view of approximation algorithms. As far as we know, there are few approximability results on multi-depot variants for the CARP/CVRP. In particular, we have not aware any approximation algorithm for the MCARP.

The research of approximation algorithms for the CARP/CVRP was initiated by Haimovich and Rinnooy Kan [14], who studied the equal-demand CVRP, which is a special case of the CVRP with $d(v) = 1$ for each vertex v. They gave the well-known Iterated Tour Partition heuristic, denoted by $ITP(\alpha)$, where α indicates the approximation ratio of the metric TSP ($\alpha \leq \frac{3}{2}$ due to the results in [5,8]), and proved that $ITP(\alpha)$ achieves an approximation ratio of $1 + (1 - \frac{1}{Q})\alpha$ if the number $n = |V|$ of vertices is a multiple of Q. Later, Haimovich et al. [15] and Altinkemer and Gavish [2] removed the condition that n is a multiple of Q while achieving the same result[1]. For the general CVRP, Altinkemer and Gavish [1] obtained a $(2 + (1 - \frac{2}{Q})\alpha)$-approximation algorithm, called $UITP(\alpha)$, which is an extension of $ITP(\alpha)$ to the general case of unequal demands. A simplified proof of this result can be found in [15]. Recently, Blauth et al. [6] have managed to improve the longstanding ratio for the CVRP to $2 + \alpha - 2\epsilon$ for some absolute constant $\epsilon > 0$. For the equal-demand case, they also devised an improved $(1 + \alpha - \epsilon)$-approximation algorithm.

Besides the results on the CVRP defined on general graphs, there are also approximation algorithms tailored for the CVRP defined on special graphs. Labbe et al. [21] devised a 2-approximation for the CVRP on trees. If the graph is a line, Wu and Lu [26] further improved the ratio to $\frac{5}{3}$. Note that the CVRP on

---

[1] Actually, the versions of $ITP(\alpha)$ in [2,15] are slightly different from that in [14], but we still refer to them as $ITP(\alpha)$.

a half-line (i.e. the depot is located at one of the end point of the line) is already NP-hard [3]. What's worse, the CVRP on a half-line cannot be approximated within ratio $3/2$ unless P = NP [26].

As for the CARP, Jansen [18] showed how to generalize the above $ITP(\alpha)$ and $UITP(\alpha)$ heuristics for the CVRP to obtain approximation algorithms with ratios $1 + (1 - \frac{1}{Q})\alpha_0$ and $2 + (1 - \frac{2}{Q})\alpha_0$ for the CARP with triangle inequality, where α_0 is the approximation ratio for the Rural Postman Problem (due to the results in [4,9], $\alpha_0 \leq \frac{3}{2}$). Wohlk [25] presented an alternative $(2 + (1 - \frac{2}{Q})\alpha_0)$-approximation algorithm for the CARP with triangle inequality. Interestingly, van Bevern [4] proved that any factor β approximation algorithm for the CARP with triangle inequality yields a factor β approximation algorithm for the general CARP (without the triangle inequality). As a result, the (equal-demand) CARP admits an approximation algorithm of ratio $2 + (1 - \frac{2}{Q})\alpha_0$ $(1 + (1 - \frac{1}{Q})\alpha_0)$.

For the multi-depot CVRP, Li and Simchi-Levi [22] developed approximation algorithms with ratios $1 + (2 - \frac{1}{Q})\alpha$ and $2 + (2 - \frac{2}{Q})\alpha$ for the equal-demand case and the general case, respectively. In addition, they also considered the nonfixed destination MCVRP, i.e. a variant of the MCVRP where the vehicles are allowed to depart from one depot but end at another depot, and gave two approximation algorithms with ratios $1 + (1 - \frac{1}{Q})\alpha$ and $2 + (1 - \frac{2}{Q})\alpha$ for the equal-demand case and the general case, respectively.

In this paper, we mainly obtain the following results. First, we present the first approximation algorithms for the MCARP and the nonfixed destination variant, which have constant approximation ratios. Second, for the multi-depot Rural Postman Problem (MRPP), which is a restricted case of the MCARP with infinite vehicle capacity, we devise a better approximation algorithm with ratio $2 - \frac{1}{2k+1}$, where k indicates the number of depots. Lastly, we investigate the MCARP/MCVRP defined on a line graph and show that the equal-demand MCARP on a line is polynomially solvable and propose a 2-approximation algorithm for the MCVRP on a line.

The rest of the paper is organized as follows. We give some notations used throughout the paper in Sect. 2. In Sect. 3 we deal with the approximation algorithms for the nonfixed destination MCARP. Subsequently, we discuss the (fixed destination) MCARP in Sect. 4. Approximation algorithms for the MRPP are presented in Sect. 5. At last, we give approximation and polynomial algorithms for the MCARP/MCVRP defined on a line graph in Sect. 6.

2   Notations

Throughout the paper, we analyze algorithms on different versions of the MCARP/MCVRP. For the MCARP, we denote by Z^* the optimal value. Z_n^* indicates the optimal value of the nonfixed destination MCARP. Z^A denotes the objective value of the solution obtained by some algorithm A.

Let $G = (V, E)$ be the underlying graph with vertex set V and edge set E, $c(e) \geq 0$ indicates the cost (or length) of edge $e \in E$. If $e = (u, v)$, we call u, v the end vertices of e. The nonnegative integer demand of vertex v (edge e) is denoted by $d(v)$ ($d(e)$). The edges with $d(e) > 0$ are called required edges. The set of all required edges is denoted by R. Q is the capacity of the vehicles. For any $u, v \in V$, $c_s(u, v)$ denote the length of the shortest path between u and v. For a subgraph H of G, $V(H)$ and $E(H)$ denote the vertex set and edge (multi)set of H, respectively. The cost of H is defined as $c(H) = \sum_{e \in E(H)} c(e)$. Let $c_R(H)$ be the sum of the costs of the required edges in H. Consequently, the sum of the costs of the non-required edges in H equals $c(H) - c_R(H)$.

3   The Nonfixed Destination MCARP

In this section, we extend the algorithm for the nonfixed destination MCVRP in [22] to solve the nonfixed destination MCARP. Our algorithm, called $NMCARP(\beta)$, also has a simple description by using the result for the CARP (without triangle inequality) in [4]. Here β indicates the approximation ratio for the CARP.

Let $G = (V, E)$ be the original graph for the nonfixed destination MCARP and $D \subseteq V$ is the depot set. $NMCARP(\beta)$ uses a β-approximation algorithm for the CARP as a subroutine and consists of two stages. The first stage is to contract the set D of depots in G into a single depot d to generate a new graph G' and use the β-approximation for the corresponding CARP to derive a solution composed of a series of routes starting from and ending at d. The second stage of the algorithm is to uncontract d back to the original set D of depots, which produces a feasible solution of the original MCARP. The following is the formal description of the algorithm.

Algorithm $NMCARP(\beta)$

Step 1. Obtain a new graph $G' = (V', E')$ from $G = (V, E)$, where $V' = \{d\} \cup (V \setminus D)$ and each edge $(u, v) \in E$ corresponds to an edge $(u', v') \in E'$ with the same cost and demand such that

$$\begin{cases} u' = u, v' = v, & \text{if } u, v \in V \setminus D; \\ u' = u, v' = d, & \text{if } u \in V \setminus D, v \in D; \\ u' = d, v' = v, & \text{if } u \in D, v \in V \setminus D; \\ u' = v' = d, & \text{if } u, v \in D. \end{cases}$$

Note that the last case indicates that (u', v') is a self-loop in G'.

Step 2. Apply a β-approximation algorithm for the CARP defined on G' to generate a solution consisting of l routes $C'_1, \ldots, C'_l$ starting from and ending at the depot d. Moreover, we assume w.l.o.g that each C'_i contains d exactly twice [2].

Step 3. For each C'_i ($i = 1, \ldots, l$), replacing each edge (u', v') of C'_i by the original edge (u, v) corresponding to (u', v'). This will result in a route P_i in G whose both end points are depots in D (but may be different).

---

[2] Otherwise, we can break C'_i into a series of routes containing d exactly twice.

Step 4. Return the routes in $P_1, \ldots, P_l$.

Lemma 1. $Z^{NMCARP(\beta)} \leq \beta Z_n^*$.

Proof. Let $Z^*(G')$ be the optimal value of the CARP defined on G' in Step 2. It can seen that any feasible solution to the nonfixed destination MCVRP induces a feasible solution to the CARP defined on G' of no greater cost after contracting the depots in D into a single depot d. This implies that $Z^*(G') \leq Z_n^*$. By definition, the total cost of the routes $C_1', \ldots, C_l'$ is at most $\beta Z^*(G')$. Observe that in Step 3 the total cost of the routes in $P_1, \ldots, P_l$ is the same as the total cost of the routes $C_1', \ldots, C_l'$. Therefore, $Z^{NMCARP(\beta)} \leq \beta Z^*(G') \leq \beta Z_n^*$.   □

Due to the results in [4,18,25], there exists an approximation algorithm, say $UITP(\alpha_0)$, with ratio $2 + (1 - \frac{2}{Q})\alpha_0$ for the CARP and another approximation algorithm, which we call $ITP(\alpha_0)$, with ratio $1 + (1 - \frac{1}{Q})\alpha_0$ for the equal-demand problem. Recall that α_0 is the approximation ratio for the Rural Postman Problem. Using Lemma 1, this yields the following result.

Theorem 1. *The nonfixed destination MCARP admits a* $(2 + (1 - \frac{2}{Q})\alpha_0)$-*approximation algorithm. If the demands are equal, there is a* $(1 + (1 - \frac{1}{Q})\alpha_0)$-*approximation algorithm.*

Remark 1. One can see that our algorithm has a very simple description, which thanks to the adoption of the β-approximation algorithm for the CARP *without triangle inequality*. In particular, when constructing the graph G' we need not alter the costs and demands of the edges except for contracting the depot set. In contrast, the $UITP_n(\alpha)$ heuristic for the nonfixed destination CVRP, given by Li and Simchi-Levi [22], has to further revise the edge costs by computing the all-pairs shortest path between the vertices in G' and add some dummy edges. Because their algorithm invokes the $UITP(\alpha)$ heuristic for the CVRP, which need the triangle inequality, and G' may not respect the triangle inequality.

4   The (Fixed Destination) MCARP

We now discuss the (fixed destination) MCARP where all the routes are required to start from and end at the same depot.

We give an algorithm, called $MUITP(\alpha_0)$, for the MCARP by modifying the algorithm $NMCARP(\beta)$ as follows. First, we replace the β-approximation algorithm in Step 2 by the above-mentioned algorithm $UITP(\alpha_0)$. Then we modify the solution generated in Step 4 to derive a feasible solution for the MCARP. Let $P_i = d_1^{(i)}, v_1^{(i)}, \ldots, v_r^{(i)}, d_2^{(i)}$ be the ith route with

$$c(P_i) = c_s(d_1^{(i)}, v_1^{(i)}) + \sum_{h=1}^{r-1} c_s(v_h^{(i)}, v_{h+1}^{(i)}) + c_s(v_r^{(i)}, d_2^{(i)}),$$

where $d_1^{(i)}, d_2^{(i)} \in D$ are the depots and $v_h^{(i)} \in V \setminus D$ ($h = 1, \ldots, r$). The modification of P_i ($i = 1, \ldots, l$) to C_i is defined as below: if $d_1^{(i)} = d_2^{(i)}$ then P_i is already feasible and we set $C_i = P_i$, otherwise C_i is replaced by

$$C_i = \begin{cases} d_1^{(i)}, v_1^{(i)}, \ldots, v_r^{(i)}, d_1^{(i)}, & \text{if } c_s(d_1^{(i)}, v_1^{(i)}) + c_s(v_r^{(i)}, d_1^{(i)}) \le c_s(d_2^{(i)}, v_1^{(i)}) + c_s(v_r^{(i)}, d_2^{(i)}); \\ d_2^{(i)}, v_1^{(i)}, \ldots, v_r^{(i)}, d_2^{(i)}, & \text{if } c_s(d_1^{(i)}, v_1^{(i)}) + c_s(v_r^{(i)}, d_1^{(i)}) > c_s(d_2^{(i)}, v_1^{(i)}) + c_s(v_r^{(i)}, d_2^{(i)}). \end{cases}$$

To analyze the performance of the algorithm $MUITP(\alpha_0)$, we define L^* as the cost of the optimal rural postman tour with respect to G' in Step 2. In other words, L^* is the length of the shortest closed walk in G' going through 0 and all required edges. $L(\alpha_0)$ is the cost of an α_0-approximate rural postman tour used by $UITP(\alpha_0)$. Clearly, $L(\alpha_0) \le \alpha_0 L^*$. Moreover, according to $UITP(\alpha_0)$ it holds that $\sum_{i=1}^{l} \sum_{h=1}^{r-1} c_s(v_h^{(i)}, v_{h+1}^{(i)}) \le L(\alpha_0)$.

We proceed to show the following result.

Lemma 2. $Z^{MUITP(\alpha_0)} \le \left(2 + \left(2 - \frac{2}{Q}\right)\alpha_0\right) Z^*$.

Proof. Similarly to the analysis of the $ITP_f(\alpha)$ heuristic for the MCVRP in [22], we can show that $c(C_i) \le c(P_i) + \sum_{h=1}^{r-1} c_s(v_h^{(i)}, v_{h+1}^{(i)})$ and hence

$$Z^{MUITP(\alpha_0)} = \sum_{i=1}^{l} C_i \le \left(2 + \left(1 - \frac{2}{Q}\right)\alpha_0\right) Z_n^* + L(\alpha_0).$$

Since $Z_n^* \le Z^*$ and $L(\alpha_0) \le \alpha_0 L^* \le \alpha_0 Z^*$, the proof of is completed. □

By substituting $ITP(\alpha_0)$ for $UITP(\alpha_0)$ in the above algorithm $MUITP(\alpha_0)$, we can obtain an approximation algorithm for the equal-demand MCARP with ratio $1 + (2 - \frac{1}{Q})\alpha_0$. To sum up, we have the following result for the MCARP.

Theorem 2. There exists a $(2 + (2 - \frac{2}{Q})\alpha_0)$-approximation algorithm for the MCARP. Moreover, for the equal-demand problem there is a $(1 + (2 - \frac{1}{Q})\alpha_0)$-approximation algorithm.

5   The Multi-depot Rural Postman Problem

In this section, we consider the multi-depot Rural Postman Problem (MRPP), which is a restricted case of the MCARP with infinite vehicle capacity, i.e., $Q = +\infty$. Suppose that there are $k = |D|$ depots. Then the MRPP is essentially to find at most k closed walks, each of which starts from and ends at a distinct depot, such that these walks cover all the required edges and the total cost of the walks is minimized.

Theorem 3. There exists a $(2 - \frac{1}{2k+1})$-approximation algorithm for the MRPP.

6   Multi-depot CARP on a Line

In this section, we deal with the MCARP/MCVRP defined on a line graph. We show that the equal-demand MCARP on a line can be solved in $O(n^2)$ time. For the MCVRP on a line, we give the first 2-approximation algorithm.

Theorem 4. *The equal-demand MCARP on a line can be solved in $O(n^2)$ time.*

Theorem 5. *The MCVRP on a line admits a 2-approximation algorithm.*

Acknowledgements. This research is supported by the National Natural Science Foundation of China under grant numbers 11671135, 11871213, 11901255 and the Natural Science Foundation of Shanghai under grant number 19ZR1411800.

References

1. Altinkemer, K., Gavish, B.: Heuristics for unequal weight delivery problems with a fixed error guarantee. Oper. Res. Lett. **6**(4), 149–158 (1987)
2. Altinkemer, K., Gavish, B.: Heuristics for delivery problems with constant error guarantees. Transp. Sci. **6**(4), 294–297 (1990)
3. Archetti, C., Feillet, D., Gendreau, M., Speranza, M.G.: Complexity of the VRP and SDVRP. Transp. Res. Part C Emerg. Technol. **19**, 741–750 (2011)
4. van Bevern, R., Hartung, S., Nichterlein, A., Sorge, M.: Constant-factor approximations for Capacitated Arc Routing without triangle inequality. Oper. Res. Lett. **42**, 290–292 (2014)
5. van Bevern, R., Slugin, V.A.: A historical note on the 3/2-approximation algorithm for the metric traveling salesman problem. Hist. Math. **53**, 118–127 (2020)
6. Blauth, J., Traub, V., Vygen, J.: Improving the approximation ratio for capacitated vehicle routing. In: Singh, M., Williamson, D.P. (eds.) IPCO 2021. LNCS, vol. 12707, pp. 1–14. Springer, Cham (2021). https://doi.org/10.1007/978-3-030-73879-2_1
7. Chen, H., Cheng, T., Shawe-Taylor, J.: A balanced route design for min-max multiple-depot rural postman problem (MMMDRPP): a police patrolling case. Int. J. Geogr. Inf. Sci. **32**(1), 169–190 (2018)
8. Christofides, N.: Worst-case analysis of a new heuristic for the traveling salesman problem. Technical report, Graduate School of Industrial Administration, Carnegie-Mellon University, Pittsburgh (1976)
9. Eiselt, H.A., Gendreau, M., Laporte, G.: Arc routing problems, part II: the rural postman problem. Oper. Res. **43**, 399–414 (1995)
10. Fernandez, E., Fontana, D., Grazia Speranza, M.: On the collaboration uncapacitated arc routing problem. Comput. Oper. Res. **67**, 120–131 (2016)
11. Fernández, E., Rodríguez-Pereira, J.: Multi-depot rural postman problems. TOP **25**(2), 340–372 (2016). https://doi.org/10.1007/s11750-016-0434-z
12. Fernandez, E., Laporte, G., Rodriguez-Pereira, J.: A branch-and-cut algorithm for the multidepot rural postman problem. Transp. Sci. **52**(2), 353–369 (2018)
13. Golden, B.L., Wong, R.T.: Capacitied arc routing problems. Networks **11**(3), 305–315 (1981)
14. Haimovich, M., Rinnooy Kan, A.H.G.: Bounds and heuristics for capacitated routing problems. Math. Oper. Res. **10**(4), 527–542 (1985)

15. Haimovich, M., Rinnooy Kan, A.H.G., Stougie, L.: Analysis of heuristics for vehicle routing problems. In: Golder, B.L., Assad, A.A. (eds.) Vehicle Routing: Methods and Studies, pp. 47–61. Elsevier, Amsterdam (1988)
16. Hertz, A., Laporte, G., Mittaz, M.: A taub search heuristic for the capacitated arc routing problem. Oper. Res. **48**(1), 129–135 (2000)
17. Hu, H., Liu, T., Ning, Z., Zhou, Y., Min, D.: A hybrid genetic algorithm with perturbation for the multi-depot capacitated arc routing problem. J. Appl. Sci. **13**(16), 3239–3244 (2013)
18. Jansen, K.: Bounds for the general capacitated routing problem. Networks **23**, 165–173 (1993)
19. Kansou, A., Yassine, A.: A two ant colony approaches for the multi-depot capacitated arc routing problem. In: International Conference on Computers & Industrial Engineering, Troyes, France, pp. 1040–1045 (2009)
20. Krushinsky, D., Van Woensel, T.: An approach to the asymmetric multi-depot capacitated arc routing problem. Eur. J. Oper. Res. **244**, 100–109 (2015)
21. Labbe, M., Laporte, G., Mercure, H.: Capacitated vehicle routing on trees. Oper. Res. **39**(4), 616–622 (1991)
22. Li, C.-L., Simchi-Levi, D.: Worst-dase analysis of heuristics for multidepot capacitated vehicle routing Problems. ORSA J. Comput. **40**, 790–799 (1992)
23. Liu, T., Jiang, Z., Geng, N.: A genetic local search algorithm for the multi-depot heterogeneous fleet capacitated arc routing problem. Flex. Serv. Manuf. J. **26**(4), 540–564 (2012). https://doi.org/10.1007/s10696-012-9166-z
24. Park, J., Kim, B.I.: The school bus routing problem. Eur. J. Oper. Res. **202**(2), 311–319 (2010)
25. Wohlk, S.: An approximation algorithm for the capacitied arc routing problem. Open Oper. Res. J. **2**, 8–12 (2008)
26. Wu, Y., Lu, X.: Capacitated vehicle routing problem on line with unsplittable demands. J. Comb. Optim. (2020). https://doi.org/10.1007/s10878-020-00565-5
27. Zhao, J., Zhu, F.: A multi-depot vehicle-routing model for the explosive waste recycling. Int. J. Prod. Res. **54**(2), 550–563 (2016)

Zero-Shot Face Swapping with De-identification Adversarial Learning

Huifang Li[1], Yidong Li[1(✉)], Jiaming Liu[2], Zhibin Hong[2], Tianshu Hu[2], and Yan Ren[3]

[1] School of Computer and Information Technology, Beijing Jiaotong University, Beijing 100044, China
{hflili,ydli}@bjtu.edu.cn
[2] Baidu Inc. Baidu Technology Park Building No. 2, Xibeiwang East Road, Beijing 100193, China
{liujiaming03,hongzhibin,hutianshu01}@baidu.com
[3] QI-ANXIN Technology Group Inc., Beijing 100044, China
renyan@qianxin.com

Abstract. In this paper, we propose a Zero-shot Face Swapping Network (ZFSNet) to swap novel identities where no training data is available, which is very practical. In contrast to many existing methods that consist of several stages, the proposed model can generate images containing the unseen identity in a single forward pass without fine-tuning. To achieve it, based on the basic encoder-decoder framework, we propose an additional de-identification (De-ID) module after the encoder to remove the source identity information, which contributes to removing the source identity retaining in the encoding stream and improves the model's generalization capability. Then we introduce an attention component (ASSM) to blend the encoded source feature and the target identity feature adaptively. It amplifies proper local details and helps the decoder attend to the related identity feature. Extensive experiments evaluated on the synthesized and real images demonstrate that the proposed modules are effective in zero-shot face swapping. In addition, we also evaluate our framework on zero-shot facial expression translation to show its versatility and flexibility.

Keywords: Face swapping · Facial expression translation · Adversarial learning

1 Introduction

Image-to-image translation is changing a particular aspect of a given image to the required one, such as changing facial identity, facial expression, hairstyle and

This work is supported by the Fundamental Research Funds for the Central Universities of China 2019YJS032, the Joint Funds of the National Natural Science Foundation of China under Grant No. U1934220, and 2020 Industrial Internet Innovation and Development Project.

H. Shen et al. (Eds.): PDCAT 2021, LNCS 13148, pp. 101–112, 2022.
https://doi.org/10.1007/978-3-030-96772-7_10

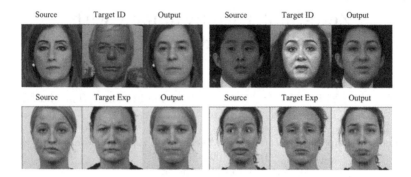

Fig. 1. Visualizations of the image translation results of ZFSNet. The first and second row illustrate the face swapping and facial expression translation results respectively.

gender. It is a popular topic with ubiquitous access to the usage of social media. Face swapping (as shown in the first row of Fig. 1) is a task that transforms the target identity into a source image while keeping the source content like pose, expression, yaw/pitch unchanged. This technique can be widely used for entertainment [10] and data augmentation. With the introduction of generative adversarial networks (GANs) [6], recent years have witnessed great progress in image translation [4,6,7]. However, the success of image translation relies heavily on enormous paired training data, which is unlikely to collect training data for every class in the real world. In order to tackle this situation, we propose a zero-shot face swapping network, which attempts to transfer an unseen target identity to the source face image. It is practical, especially when the target images are difficult to collect.

Recently, existing methods achieve face swapping with deep generative models [6]. For example, Deepfakes [1] firstly leverages the autoencoder network for face swapping and achieves a promising result. However, it requires hundreds or even thousands of examples to train the network and the model could only be applied to a specific identity. Aiming at loosing the one-to-one face swapping constraint, [15] proposes a many-to-many face swapping framework by disentangling identity and content features of faces, and then recombining the content feature with another identity feature. But, it suffers from the limited generalization capability. When tested with unseen identities that are not included in the training data, the model's performance would deteriorate. One explanation of this phenomenon might be that the embedded content features still retain some source identity information, and the redundant source identity could result in an unidentifiable face. To address this problem, [2,14] constrain the content embedding by the standard Gaussian. Specifically, they regularize the content distribution $q_\theta(z|x)$ based on the KL divergence between $q(z|x)$ and $p(z) = N(0, I)$ to force the content embedding to be general and neglect the identity information. Nevertheless, images generated based on this method are usually blurry. A possible cause is that the posterior defined by $q_\theta(z|x)$ is not complex enough [22]. Alternatively, [20] creates a few-shot face reenactment model. It requires a few examples to generalize the model to unseen targets via fine-tuning the trained model, but the time-consuming fine-tuning process restricts its potential application.

In this paper, a general one-stage Zero-shot Face Swapping Network (ZFS-Net) is presented to address the challenging zero-shot face swapping, which requires only one target image and no fine-tuning. The generated image not only has the identity of the unseen targets, but also retains the content (such as pose and expression) of the source image. To achieve it, based on the basic encoder-decoder framework, we propose a novel *De-IDentification (De-ID)* module to destroy the identity-specific features of source images based on an adversarial classifier. As a result, the generated image will not be disturbed by the source identity information. We conduct extensive experiments to validate its effectiveness to destroy the source identity. Then we propose an *Attentive Spatial Style Modulation (ASSM)* module to fuse the source content feature and the target identity adaptively, allowing the decoder to retrieve the appropriate code for each spatial location and pay attention to local details. Extensive experiments are conducted to demonstrate that the proposed modules are effective, and the network can be applied to other image translation tasks, such as facial expression translation (as shown in the second row of Fig. 1).

2   Method

2.1   Overall Framework

As shown in Fig. 2, the basic ZFSNet contains a content encoder Φ_{E_c} to learn content features z_c, an identity encoder Φ_{E_i} to extract the identity information of the target image, and an decoder Φ_D to generate a new image. Then we innovatively introduce a De-IDentification module Φ_{C_l} to disturb the Φ_{E_c} to learn source identity features via the adversarial learning. As a result, there is no stable representation of identity features in z_c and the identity information of source image can not be clearly decoded from z_c. Furthermore, in decoder Φ_D, we propose an Attentive Spatial Style Modulation module to help fuse the source content and the target identity feature adaptively. Therefore, the generated image can contain the identity of the target image and the content of the source image. More details are shown in the following subsections.

2.2   De-identification Module

As mentioned in the previous section, given a source image I_c, a content encoder is employed to extract the face content feature z_c. Intuitively, we expect z_c contains as little identity information as possible while keeping enough content information for the decoder to recover the content of the output face. Inspired by popular adversarial learning method [16], we introduce a de-identification module after the content representation and train the content encoder in an adversarial fashion.

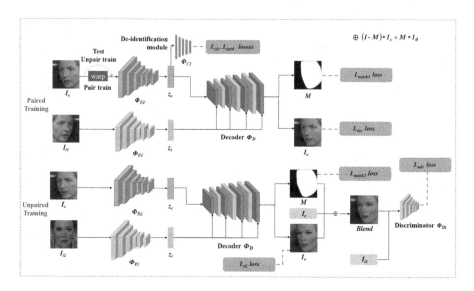

Fig. 2. The framework of our ZFSNet. The model is trained based on a mix-batch training strategy. In paired training, the inputs of the network have the same identity, while in unpaired training, the inputs of the network have different identities.

In this module, we employ a classifier Φ_{C_l} which is a multi-layer perception network (as shown in Table 1), and it takes z_c as input. The learning of Φ_{C_l} and the other sub-networks, i.e. Φ_{E_c}, Φ_{E_i} and Φ_D, are conducted in two iterative steps. In the first step, the parameters of Φ_{E_c} are fixed and the classic cross entropy loss is introduced as follows:

$$L_{cls} = \mathbb{E}[-\log \mathbf{P}(y = \hat{y}|x = z_c))], \tag{1}$$

where $\hat{y}$ is the ground truth identity label of I_c. In this phrase, Φ_{C_l} is trained to extract the identity information from z_c and therefore differentiates the identity of I_c. In the second step, Φ_{C_l} is frozen, and a de-identification loss is imposed. In specific, the de-identification loss L_{deid} is the negative entropy of Φ_{C_l} prediction.

$$L_{deid} = \mathbb{E}[-\mathbf{H}(y|x = \Phi_{Ec}(I_c))]. \tag{2}$$

It should be noted that L_{deid} is jointly imposed with other functional losses to learn Φ_{E_c}. In this manner, the content-related feature in z_c can be effectively encoded by Φ_{E_i} but the identity-related features in z_c is unstable due to L_{deid}, and the identity of the source image can not be learned and captured.

Table 1. Network architecture of the classifier Φ_{C_l}. ID represents the identity number.

Model Φ_{C_l}	BN,	FC (1024), BN, LeakyRelu	FC (1024), BN, LeakyRelu	FC (1024), BN, LeakyRelu	FC (1024), BN, LeakyRelu	FC (512), BN, LeakyRelu	FC (512), BN, LeakyRelu	FC (ID)

2.3   Attentive Spatial Style Modulation Module

The decoder is required to recover the target identity from the identity encoder. Inspired by recent works [8,9], controlling the statistics, a.k.a styles, of feature maps can enable the decoder to yield controllable face synthesis results. However, in [9], features across each spatial location share the same style code. Face editing tasks usually require spatial-aware style modification. Instead of generating global styles, we design an attentive spatial style modulation module to help the decoder retrieve the corresponding style code adaptively.

Concretely, the ASSM module takes a content feature F and an identity feature F_i as inputs, and returns the modulated feature $\tilde{F}$. More concretely, F produces a query map Q, and F_i generates styles V and the corresponding keys K, where Q, K and V are produced by 1×1 convolutions.

Then an attentive matrix A is calculated as

$$A(i,j) = \frac{\exp(\lambda_{at} Q(i)^T \cdot K(j)^T)}{\sum_{\tau \in H' \cdot W'} \exp(\lambda_{at} Q(i)^T \cdot K(\tau)^T)}, \tag{3}$$

where λ_{at} denotes the temperature term to control the sharpness of softmax distribution, i and j are the indices of the row and column in A, which are spatial locations in Q and K respectively. λ_{at} is set to 0.01 as a default setup.

The retrieval style γ is the weighted average of V by multiplying A as

$$\gamma(i) = \sum_{j \in H' \times W'} A(i,j) \cdot V(j). \tag{4}$$

Finally, the modulated feature $\tilde{F}$ are generated by $Norm(Conv(F \otimes \gamma))$, where $Norm(X)$ is the normalization operator, and $\otimes$ refers to element wise product.

Therefore, the modulated feature map $\tilde{F}$ contains both the content of F and the style of F_i, which is achieved by adaptively combining the identity features according to the corresponding semantics in F.

2.4   Mix-Batch Training Strategy

During the training phase, we employ a *Mix-batch Training Strategy*. As shown in Fig. 2, the batch of images is mixed by two different components. One component contains paired images which means I_c and I_{i1} come from the same person, and the output I_o must to be the same as the I_c. This component can help the network quickly learn to generate face images by providing strong reconstruction supervision. Meanwhile, the other component consists of unpaired images that means I_c and I_{i2} have different identities, and the output I_o contains the pose, expression of I_c and the identity of I_{i2}. The unpaired training is essential to enhance the target identity or attribute transfer ability of the model.

When paired images are fed into the network, the output is the reconstruction of I_c as well as its binary face mask M_c. The reconstruction loss are as follows:

$$L_{rec} = SSIM(I_c \cdot M_c, I_o \cdot M)), \quad L_{mask1} = L1(M_c, M), \tag{5}$$

where I_o represents the predicted image, M is the predicted mask, and SSIM refers to the Structural Similarity (SSIM) [19] loss. It is worth mentioning that we just force the network to reconstruct the facial area of the image regardless of the background. Finally, we can simply apply alpha blending by using I_c, I_o and M to get the final face swapping result I_b as $I_b = M \cdot I_o + (1 - M) \cdot I_c$.

As mentioned in Sect. 2.2, we introduce a de-identification classifier Φ_{C_l} in the latent space and train the network Φ_{C_l} and Φ_{E_c} in an adversarial way. The training losses are formulated in Eqs. 1, 2.

For the unpaired branch, to ensure that the generated face in I_o keeps the same identity of I_{i2}, we propose an identity preserving loss L_{id}. We also add a mask reconstruction loss L_{mask2} to guide the network to learn the pose of the source image.

$$L_{id} = L2(f(I_o), f(I_{i2})), \quad L_{mask2} = L1(M_c, M). \tag{6}$$

where $f(\cdot)$ indicates a pre-trained facial identity extractor [5].

The adversarial loss L_{adv} following WGAN-GP [6] is used to learning the parameters of the generator and discriminator. L_{adv} is formulated as Eq. 7, where the first two terms are original critic losses and the last term is a penalty on the gradient norm. $\mathbb{P}_r$ is the real data distribution, $\mathbb{P}_g$ is the generator distribution, $\mathbb{P}_{\tilde{I}}$ is the random interpolation distribution and λ_{gp} is a penalty coefficient.

$$L_{adv} = \mathbb{E}_{I_o \in \mathbb{P}_g}[D(I_o)] - \mathbb{E}_{I_c \in \mathbb{P}_r}[D(I_c)]$$
$$+ \lambda_{gp}\mathbb{E}_{\tilde{I} \in \mathbb{P}_{\tilde{I}}}[(\| \nabla D(\tilde{I})\|_2 - 1)^2]. \tag{7}$$

Finally, we combine these constraints to optimize our network. In the test time, a source image and a target image are fed into the content encoder Φ_{E_c} and the identity encoder Φ_{E_i}, respectively, and the decoder Φ_D equipped with the ASSM module outputs the results.

3   Experiments

3.1   Experiment Setup

Datasets. Our model is trained on the VGGFace2 [3] and FaceForensics++ [17] datasets. To verify the generalization ability of the model over unseen subjects, we choose the last 50 videos of FaceForensics++ as the unseen test set $\mathcal{N}$, meaning that the identities inside are not included in the training data. We also prepare a seen test set $\mathcal{S}$, consisting of 100 subjects with 20 images per subject. The 100 subjects in test set $\mathcal{S}$ are exposed in training and the images are not included in the training. The remaining image sequences of the FaceForensics++ dataset are the training data.

In addition, we validate that our ZFSNet can be applied to other facial translation tasks flexibly. Since face swapping is closely related to facial expression translation, which is a task that changes the source expression of a given image to the target expression, we employ ZFSNet on expression data RaFD [13]. To validate the model, we also prepare the seen test set $\mathcal{S}$ and the unseen test set $\mathcal{N}$ on RaFD. Following [4], we exclude the 'neutral' expression during training and regard the 'neutral' images as the $\mathcal{N}$ test set. The remaining 7 expression categories are retained for training. From the 7 categories, we randomly selected 20 images from each category as a test set $\mathcal{S}$.

Implementation Details. For face swapping, we align and crop the face image with MTCNN [21] and utilize the face recognizer VGGFace2 [3] to extract 256-dim face identity embedding. The cropped image is of size 256×256, and then resized as 128×128.

For facial expression translation, we first train an expression classification model on the RaFD training set based on the VGG19 [18] network and then test the classification accuracy on the set $\mathcal{S}$. The accuracy of the classifier is 99.28%. The expression classification model is used to extract expression embedding.

Metrics. For identity preserving capacity, we compute the **Cosine** similarity of embedding vectors extracted from the widely used face recognition model [5]. The larger value means a higher similarity between the two images. During the experiment, for each subject in the test sets, we firstly find a frontal face image by the Euler angle calculated by Dlib [11] and the frontal face images are used as target images for face swapping. The identity preserving metrics are calculated between the generated image and the frontal target image. To inspect the pose and expression fitting accuracy, we use Dlib [11] to estimate **Euler** angles and **Landmark** position of face images. Then, we compute the root mean square error of Euler angles and the mean distance of the Landmark vectors normalized by the face's binocular distance between the synthesized image and the source image. For these two indicators, a lower value means a smaller difference in pose and expression.

3.2   Ablation Study

The Effectiveness of the Proposed Components. We conduct ablation study to validate the proposed De-ID module and the ASSM module. The configurations are as follows: (1) **Ours** is the proposed network with the De-ID and the ASSM modules. (2) **w/o De-ID** is the network without the De-ID adversarial learning. (3) **w/ KL** refers to the network that constrains the content feature with the KL divergence regularization instead of the proposed De-ID. (4) **w/o ASSM** corresponds to the network without the ASSM module.

Table 2 shows the quantitative results and Fig. 3 visualizes the outputs. We can find that the output images of ZFSNet have the content of the source image and the identity of the target image. On the contrary, when ZFSNet is trained without the De-ID module, the generated images sometimes retains some identity information from source image.

The Impact of the De-ID Module on Content Feature Learning. We further explore whether the De-ID module really prevent the encoder from

Table 2. Quantitative results on $\mathcal{N} - \mathcal{N}$ swapping setting.

Method	Cosine ↑	Euler ↓	Landmark ↓
Our	0.520	18.910	2.877
w/o De-ID module	0.385	20.35	1.631
w/ KL	0.429	31.252	3.324
w/o ASSM	0.481	21.683	2.027

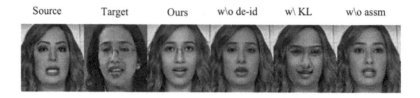

Fig. 3. Results on ablation setups. The source-target images are all from $\mathcal{N}$ set.

extracting identity information. Concretely, we train two models with and without the De-ID module on both face swapping and face expression dataset. Taking z_c of pre-trained models as the input feature, we train classifiers to classify z_c to their corresponding class. Ideally, the more identity related information contained in z_c, the more accurate the classifier will be. Therefore, we expect a significant drop on classification performance or an increase in converged loss when z_c is trained with De-ID.

The training losses of the classifiers are shown in Fig. 4, where each classifier is trained for 2000 iterations, and the weights of ZFSNet are fixed during training. The converged training losses with De-ID module are close to the original training losses with randomly initialized classifiers. Therefore, we can safely draw the conclusion that the De-ID module indeed disturbs the encoder from extracting identity features.

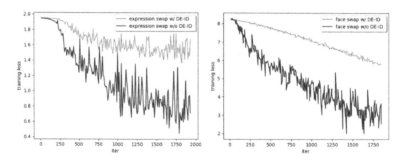

Fig. 4. Training loss of adding and not adding the De-ID module.

3.3   Comparison

We compare our methods with popular face swapping methods Deepfakes [1] and FaceSwap [12]. Deepfakes [1] is an one-to-one swapping model based on the denoising autoencoder. FaceSwap is also a one-to-one swapping model based on the convolutional network by rendering an image with the style of the target image. Our ZFSNet is many-to-many framework for zero-shot face swapping, which requires only one target image and no fine-tuning. Importantly, this comparison is unfair for us, since Deepfakes and FaceSwap need to retrain the face swapping model for each source-target subject pair, and the target identity are used during training. Compared with them, our method can achieve comparable performance or better performance, which proves that our model successfully achieves zero-shot face translation.

Quantitative Comparison. We provide two quantitative comparisons to evaluate our model ZFSNet to validate its zero-shot translation ability. Our ZFSNet is a many-to-many framework and can translate images without fine-tuning. The comparisons are implemented on $\mathcal{N} - \mathcal{N}$ swapping (source and target identities are all from the unseen test set) and $\mathcal{S} - \mathcal{N}$ swapping (source and target identities are from the seen test set and the unseen test set respectively). The results are shown in Tables 3, 4. On $\mathcal{N} - \mathcal{N}$ swapping, our method performs better than Deepfakes and FaceSwap, which is our main concern in this paper. On $\mathcal{S} - \mathcal{N}$ swapping, the performance of our method is comparable to Deepfakes and better than FaceSwap. Our ZFSNet achieves results comparable to or even better than [1,12] without fine-tuning and without using the target image during training. The results illustrates the effectiveness of our method.

Table 3. Quantitative face swapping results on $\mathcal{N} - \mathcal{N}$ swapping setting.

Method	Cosine ↑	Euler ↓	Landmark ↓
Deepfakes [1]	0.506	49.078	4.194
FaceSwap [12]	0.441	29.903	**2.593**
Ours	**0.520**	**18.910**	2.877

Table 4. Quantitative face swapping results on $\mathcal{S} - \mathcal{N}$ swapping setting.

Method	Cosine ↑	Euler ↓	Landmark ↓
Deepfakes [1]	**0.530**	73.137	8.515
FaceSwap [12]	0.446	42.215	**4.453**
Ours	0.515	**29.889**	4.855

Qualitative Comparison. We also visualize the outputs of our method in the Fig. 5. It is obvious that our ZFSNet can preserve the identity of target faces but also retain the content, such as pose, yaw/angle, expression of source faces. It achieves results comparable to Deepfakes and FaceSwap.

| Source | Target | Deepfake [1] | FaceSwap [12] | Ours |

Fig. 5. Quantitative comparison on FaceForensics++ image sequences.

3.4 Facial Expression Translation

We also verifies our ZFSNet on the facial expression translation task. In practice, the facial expression embedding is defined as a kind of identity embedding. We train our model on (RaFD) [13]. The source image and the target expression image are fed into the content encoder and the expression encoder to get content feature z_c and expression feature z_i. Then the decoder decodes z_c and z_i to generate a new expression image I_o.

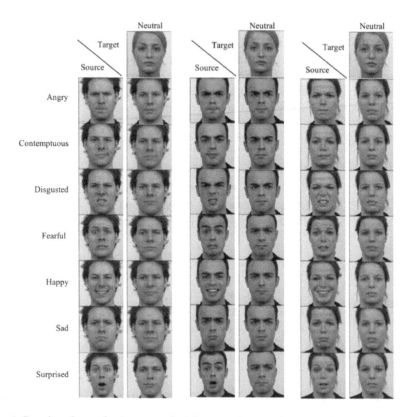

Fig. 6. Results of transferring seven facial expressions to the unseen neutral expression.

To validate the zero-shot expression translation, the source images are selected from the seen 7 expression data and the target image is taken from the unseen neutral expression data. Figure 6 shows the result of translating the expression into the unseen neutral expression. It can be seen that our ZFSNet outputs high quality neutral images, indicating that this model can be flexibly applied to unseen domains.

4   Conclusion

In this paper, we propose a general Zero-shot Face Swapping Network (ZFSNet), which can realize the unseen target face swapping using only one target image. Specifically, we propose a de-identification (De-ID) module to constrain the content encoder and alleviate the identity information retaining problem in the learned content feature. The De-ID module and the content encoder are learned in an adversarial manner. Then we design an attentive spatial style modulation module (ASSM) to combine the content feature and the target identity feature adaptively, guiding the decoder to attend to related local details. Through these improvements, the ZFSNet can successfully generate images containing the specific unseen identity. Moreover, the proposed method is generic and can be easily applied to other attribute translation tasks, such as facial expression translation. Extensive experiments validate the effectiveness of our method. In future work, we will further improve the generalization ability of the model.

References

1. Deepfakes. faceswap (2016). https://github.com/deepfakes/faceswap. Accessed 06 Feb 2019
2. Bao, J., Chen, D., Wen, F., Li, H., Hua, G.: Towards open-set identity preserving face synthesis. In: Proceedings of the IEEE Conference on Computer Vision and Pattern Recognition, pp. 6713–6722 (2018)
3. Cao, Q., Shen, L., Xie, W., Parkhi, O.M., Zisserman, A.: VGGFace2: A dataset for recognising faces across pose and age. In: Proceedings of the IEEE International Conference on Automatic Face & Gesture Recognition, pp. 67–74 (2018)
4. Choi, Y., Choi, M., Kim, M., Ha, J.W., Kim, S., Choo, J.: StarGAN: unified generative adversarial networks for multi-domain image-to-image translation. In: Proceedings of the IEEE Conference on Computer Vision and Pattern Recognition, pp. 8789–8797 (2018)
5. Deng, J., Guo, J., Xue, N., Zafeiriou, S.: ArcFACE: additive angular margin loss for deep face recognition. In: Proceedings of the IEEE Conference on Computer Vision and Pattern Recognition, pp. 4690–4699 (2019)
6. Gulrajani, I., Ahmed, F., Arjovsky, M., Dumoulin, V., Courville, A.C.: Improved training of wasserstein gans. In: Proceedings of the conference on Neural Information Processing Systems, pp. 5767–5777 (2017)
7. Isola, P., Zhu, J.Y., Zhou, T., Efros, A.A.: Image-to-image translation with conditional adversarial networks. In: Proceedings of the IEEE Conference on Computer Vision and Pattern Recognition, pp. 1125–1134 (2017)

8. Karras, T., Laine, S., Aila, T.: A style-based generator architecture for generative adversarial networks. In: Proceedings of the IEEE Conference on Computer Vision and Pattern Recognition, pp. 4401–4410 (2019)

9. Karras, T., Laine, S., Aittala, M., Hellsten, J., Lehtinen, J., Aila, T.: Analyzing and improving the image quality of stylegan. arXiv preprint arXiv:1912.04958 (2019)

10. Kim, H., et al.: Deep video portraits. ACM Trans. Graph. **37**(4), 1–14 (2018)

11. King, D.E.: Dlib-ml: a machine learning toolkit. J. Mach. Learn. Res. **10**, 1755–1758 (2009)

12. Korshunova, I., Shi, W., Dambre, J., Theis, L.: Fast face-swap using convolutional neural networks. In: Proceedings of the IEEE International Conference on Computer Vision, pp. 3677–3685 (2017)

13. Langner, O., Dotsch, R., Bijlstra, G., Wigboldus, D.H., Hawk, S.T., Van Knippenberg, A.: Presentation and validation of the radboud faces database. Cogn. Emot. **24**(8), 1377–1388 (2010)

14. Natsume, R., Yatagawa, T., Morishima, S.: FSNet: an identity-aware generative model for image-based face swapping. In: Proceedings of the Asian Conference on Computer Vision, pp. 117–132 (2018)

15. Natsume, R., Yatagawa, T., Morishima, S.: Rsgan: face swapping and editing using face and hair representation in latent spaces. arXiv preprint arXiv:1804.03447 (2018)

16. Perera, P., Nallapati, R., Xiang, B.: OCGAN: one-class novelty detection using gans with constrained latent representations. In: Proceedings of the IEEE Conference on Computer Vision and Pattern Recognition. pp. 2898–2906 (2019)

17. Rossler, A., Cozzolino, D., Verdoliva, L., Riess, C., Thies, J., Nießner, M.: Faceforensics++: learning to detect manipulated facial images, pp. 1–11 (2019)

18. Simonyan, K., Zisserman, A.: Very deep convolutional networks for large-scale image recognition (2014). arXiv preprint arXiv:1409.1556 3 (2014)

19. Wang, Z., Bovik, A.C., Sheikh, H.R., Simoncelli, E.P.: Image quality assessment: from error visibility to structural similarity. IEEE Trans. Image Peprocessing **13**(4), 600–612 (2004)

20. Zakharov, E., Shysheya, A., Burkov, E., Lempitsky, V.: Few-shot adversarial learning of realistic neural talking head models. In: Proceedings of the IEEE International Conference on Computer Vision, pp. 9459–9468 (2019)

21. Zhang, K., Zhang, Z., Li, Z., Qiao, Y.: Joint face detection and alignment using multitask cascaded convolutional networks. IEEE Signal Process. Lett. **23**(10), 1499–1503 (2016)

22. Zheng, Z., Sun, L.: Disentangling latent space for vae by label relevant/irrelevant dimensions. In: Proceedings of the IEEE Conference on Computer Vision and Pattern Recognition. pp. 12192–12201 (2019)

An User-Driven Active Way to Push ACL in Software-Defined Networking

Haisheng Yu[2,3]([⊠]), Dong Liu[1,3], Wenyong Wang[1,2], Keqiu Li[4], Sai Zou[5], Zhaobin Liu[6], and Yan Liu[1]

[1] Macau University of Science and Technology, Macao, China
[2] University of Electronic Science and Technology of China, Chengdu, China
[3] BII Group, Beijing, China
[4] Tianjin University, Tianjin, China
[5] Guizhou University, Guiyang, China
[6] Dalian Maritime University, Dalian, China
`yuhaisheng1@gmail.com`

Abstract. Compared with the traditional network, Software-Defined Networking (SDN) provides a more convenient network paradigm to build Access Control List (ACL) application. There has been a few studies focusing on ACL application in SDN up to now, but most of the existing work adopts a reactive way to enforce ACL, resulting in new ACL update can not take effect immediately. In this paper, we propose CLACK, an approach for user-driven centralized ACL in SDN. We implement CLACK on both Floodlight and ONOS controller. The experimental results show that CLACK has a better performance than the existing Floodlight firewall application.

Keywords: Access Control List (ACL) · Software-Defined Networking (SDN) · Security · Floodlight · ONOS

1 Introduction

Internet, accommodating a variety of heterogeneous networks and distributed applications [12], has achieved great success and been the enormous power of promoting social and economic development since it is proposed [10]. However, the current Internet environment has changed dramatically as a result of the emerging network services and the network scale expansion, the traditional architecture of Internet has exposed serious deficiencies, such as unexpected delays for data communication [14] and difficulty in the traffic load balance among links [9]. The fundamental reason for that is the tight coupling of control logic and data forwarding in network devices (e.g. router, switch) and the distributed control of network devices [3]. SDN provides an open software programmable model and a diversity of network control functions. It has gained wide recognition and good support from both academia and industry.

Access Control List (ACL) is a network security enhancement. It applies a set of ACL rules to each IP packet and determines whether to forward or drop the

© Springer Nature Switzerland AG 2022
H. Shen et al. (Eds.): PDCAT 2021, LNCS 13148, pp. 113–120, 2022.
https://doi.org/10.1007/978-3-030-96772-7_11

packet based on its header fields. ACL is similar to the stateless firewall or packet filtering firewall which provides basic traffic filtering capabilities [13]. In traditional networks, ACL is often placed in network devices (e.g. router, switch) and can be configured to control both inbound and outbound traffic. Network devices examine each packet and determine whether to forward or drop the packet on the basis of the rules specified in ACL [4]. Unfortunately, the approach has several deficiencies. Firstly, network devices should have appropriate hardware and processing capabilities to enforce ACL, causing a vast expense. What's worse, it is too complicated to design and configure ACL in distributed network devices, not to mention the situation when network security policy changes. The cumbersome maintenance of ACL in complex networks is also prone to error.

The root reason for that lies in the distributed way to enforce ACL in traditional networks. Software-defined Networking (SDN) just provides an convenient network paradigm to solve the problem. SDN separates control logic and forwarding logic in traditional networks, and SDN controller configures networks in a centralized manner rather than distributed configuration [8].

In this paper, we propose CLACK, an approach for user-driven centralized ACL in SDN. CLACK adopts a proactive way to enforce ACL thus to avoid additional delay and save controller's resource, it reacts to new ACL update and network view update in real time to ensure network security. CLACK uses abstract network view to accelerate processing and does match check for new added ACL rule to avoid invalid rule. We implement CLACK on both Floodlight and ONOS controller [2], and CLACK is also integrated into the new version of both controllers.

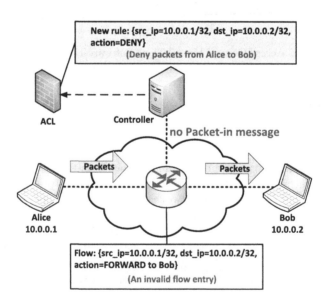

Fig. 1. Network security violation in a reactive way

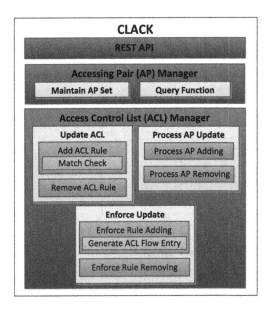

Fig. 2. CLACK architecture

2 Clack Design

2.1 Overview

Figure 2 depicts CLACK's architecture, CLACK provides REST API for users and contains two core modules, *Accessing Pair (AP) Manager and Access Control List (ACL) Manager*. Each module has several submodules in charge of different processing.

In CLACK, each ACL rule contains several match fields and an action field. Packets defined in match fields are forwarded or dropped following the action field. An ACL rule is denoted as:

$$R\{id; nw\_proto; src\_ip; dst\_ip; dst\_port; action\}$$

Each ACL rule has a distinct id. Match fields comprises *nw_proto* (network protocol), *src_ip* (source IP address), *dst_ip* (destination IP address), *dst_port* (TCP or UDP destination port). Match field value may be a wildcard, which can be substituted for all possible field values. *src_ip* and *dst_ip* field use CIDR IP address, which can designate many unique IP addresses. *action* field value is either "ALLOW" or "DENY".

CLACK provides a friendly and centralized user interface through REST API for users to add, remove, and query ACL rules. Users can use CLACK easily by sending an HTTP request containing JSON string, and they don't need to configure distributed switches one by one any more for CLACK does all the work.

CLACK filters IP packets by ACL flow entries exactly reflecting ACL rules in ingress or egress switches. After receiving user's new ACL update request, CLACK updates ACL rules and ACL flow entries immediately.

We will describe CLACK's core modules in the following subsections.

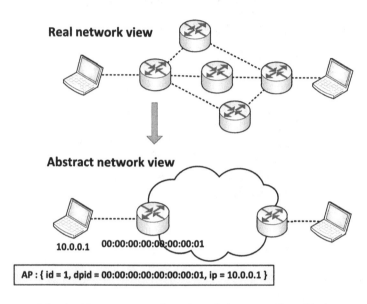

Fig. 3. Abstract network view and Accessing Pair (AP)

2.2 Accessing Pair (AP) Manager

In CLACK, the real network view is transformed to an abstract network view. The abstract network view conceals internal network topology, and it only exposes the interfaces between edge switches and external hosts in the networks, as Fig. 3 depicts.

We use Accessing Pair (AP) to store the interface information in the abstract network view. An AP is denoted as:

$$AP : \{id; dpid; ip\}$$

The fields represent AP id, edge switch's dpid (data path id), and host's IP address, respectively.

AP Manager is a CLACK module, which maintains AP information in real time and provides a query function. AP Manager monitors host update event in the networks and stores all interface information in AP *Set*.

When a new host appears or disappears in the networks, *AP Manager* updates *AP Set* correspondingly and calls *ACL Manager* for further processing which will be described in Sect. 2.3.

AP Manager also provides a query function *getSwitchSet*. Given a CIDR IP address, the function traverses *AP Set* and returns a switch set. Each switch in the set connects with a host whose IP address is contained in the CIDR IP address. This function will be used when generating ACL flow entry.

2.3   Access Control List (ACL) Manager

Access Control List (ACL) Manager is a CLACK module, which updates ACL and processes AP update.

After receiving a new ACL update request, *ACL Manager* verifies its validity and returns an error message if not valid.

If user requests to add a new ACL rule, *ACL Manager* firstly parses user's request JSON string and generates a new ACL rule. It then traverses *ACL Rule Set* to check whether the new ACL rule *matches* another existing rule, the new rule is rejected if a match is found. *ACL Manager* generates a distinct id for each rule passing match check, adds it to *ACL Rule Set* and starts the enforcing stage.

Match check is important because it rejects invalid rules, so as to reduce storage overhead in both switches and controller. Two functions are used in match check, and they give the definition of *match*:

cover(R_{new},R_{old},**field)**: A Boolean function, where R_{new}, R_{old} denote ACL rules and *field* denotes ACL rule's match field. We

$$cover(R_{new}, R_{old}, field) = true \text{ if:}$$

for $field \epsilon \{nw\_proto, dst\_portg\}$, $R_{old}.field$ has a wildcard value, and $R_{new}.field$ has an user-assigned value;

for $field \epsilon \{src\_ip; dst\_ip\}$, $R_{old}.field$ contains all the IP addresses in $R_{new}.field$.

match(R_{new},R_{old}**)**: A Boolean function. We say:

$$match(R_{new}; R_{old}) = true \text{ if:}$$

for $field \epsilon \{nw\_proto, src\_ip, dst\_ip, dst\_port\}$, there is: $R_{new}.field = R_{old}.field$ or $cover(R_{new}, R_{old}.field) = true$.

We say ACL rule R_{new} *matches* R_{old} if all packets filtered by R_{new} is already filtered by R_{old}, and R_{new} will not work at all if added.

If user requests to remove an existing ACL rule, *ACL Manager* firstly parses user's request and gets the rule's id. It then removes the rule from *ACL Rule Set* and starts the enforcing stage.

3   Evaluation

We compare CLACK with the Floodlight firewall application. As is mentioned before, to enforce ACL, CLACK works in a proactive way while Floodlight adopts a reactive way. It means that different events trigger their ACL enforcing process, user's request for CLACK and Packet-in message for Floodlight firewall application; therefore it is unreasonable to compare their performance in general situation. We create a situation that a new ACL update conflicts with ACL flow entry in switches and compare the delay for a new ACL update to take effect, like in Fig. 1.

We build a virtual network in Mininet [1] and run several experiments. For each experiment, we add different numbers of ACL rules in advance and insure that CLACK has to traverse *ACL Rule Set* during update. Then we let host A in the network send ICMP packets to host B using *Ping* command. If host A succeed in *Ping* host B at first, we add a new ACL rule to deny the flow and record the delay until an ACL flow entry drops the flow. If there is already a ACL rule denying the flow and host A fails to *Ping* host B at first, we then remove that ACL rule and record the delay until an regular flow entry forwards the flow.

The delay in the Floodlight firewall application is more than 5000 ms because a flow entry's default idle timeout is set to 5000 ms in Floodlight, no Packet-in messages is sent to the controller as long as the ACL flow entry persists. As a result, new ACL update will not take effect at all until after at least an idle timeout. We regard the delay as 5000 ms uniformly.

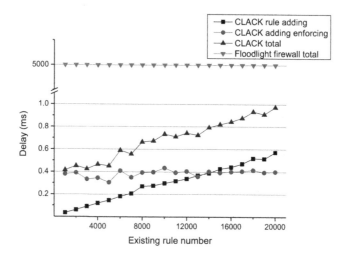

Fig. 4. Add a new ACL rule (single-controller version)

As Fig. 4 shows, in the single-controller version, the delay for rule adding and removing in CLACK goes up linearly as the existing ACL rule number increases because CLACK needs to traverse *ACL Rule Set*. The delay for enforcing ACL update vibrates for reason that CLACK needs to communicate with switches, and the delay depends on the network quality at that time.

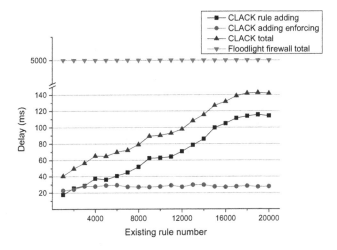

Fig. 5. Add a new ACL rule (multi-controller version)

As Fig. 5 shows, The evaluation result for the multi-controller version is mostly similar with the single-controller version except that the delay for rule removing remains almost unchanging. That is because we use hash tables rather than a single set to store ACL rules, and hash tables is move effective when processing indexing and updating.

The comparison result indicates that CLACK beats the Floodlight firewall application by miles when handling new ACL update requests at the collision situation.

4   Conclusion and Future Work

In this paper, we propose CLACK, an approach for user-driven centralized ACL in SDN. CLACK adopts a proactive way to enforce ACL and reacts to new ACL update and network view update in real time. We implement CLACK on Floodlight and ONOS controller and then conduct a large number of experiments. The experimental results show that CLACK has a better performance than the existing Floodlight firewall application. Dynamic flow tunneling scenario shows that malicious application can evade ACL by simply adding a few flow entries in SDN [11]. The root reason lies in that OpenFlow allows various Set-Field actions that can dynamically change the packet headers [5]. P. Kazemian proposed a real time policy checking tool called *NetPlumber* [6] based on Header Space Analysis [7]. We intent to add security check capability based on HSA in CLACK to prevent attacks from adversaries in the future.

Acknowledgement. This work is supported by Macau Science and Technology Development Fund (Grant No. 0018/2021/A).

References

1. Mininet: An instant virtual network on your laptop. [EB/OL]. http://mininet.org/
2. Onos - a new carrier-grade sdn network operating system designed for high availability, performance, scale-out. [EB/OL]. http://onosproject.org/
3. Casado, M., Foster, N., Guha, A.: Abstractions for software-defined networks. Communications of the ACM (2014)
4. Cisco, I.: Security configuration guide, release 12.2. CISCO, San Jose, CA (2003)
5. Hu, H., Han, W., Ahn, G.J., Zhao, Z.: Flowguard: building robust firewalls for software-defined networks. In: Proceedings of the Third Workshop on Hot Topics in Software Defined Networking, pp. 97–102 (2014)
6. Kazemian, P., Chang, M., Zeng, H., Varghese, G., McKeown, N., Whyte, S.: Real time network policy checking using header space analysis. In: 10th {USENIX} Symposium on Networked Systems Design and Implementation ({NSDI} 13), pp. 99–111 (2013)
7. Kazemian, P., Varghese, G., McKeown, N.: Header space analysis: Static checking for networks. In: 9th {USENIX} Symposium on Networked Systems Design and Implementation ({NSDI} 12), pp. 113–126 (2012)
8. Kim, H., Feamster, N.: Improving network management with software defined networking. IEEE Commun. Mag. $51(2)$, 114–119 (2013)
9. Manoj, N.: Fuzzy controlled routing in a swarm robotic network. IAES Int. J. Robot. Autom.(IJRA) $3(4)$, 272 (2014)
10. Paulus, C.: A brief history of the internet (1997)
11. Porras, P., Shin, S., Yegneswaran, V., Fong, M., Tyson, M., Gu, G.: A security enforcement kernel for openflow networks. In: Proceedings of the First Workshop on Hot Topics in Software Defined Networks, pp. 121–126 (2012)
12. Shrivastav, A.A.: Reorganization of intruder using ad-hoc network and rfid. IAES Int. J. Robot. Autom. (IJRA) $3(4)$, 46–52 (2014)
13. Stallings, W.: Network Security Essentials: Applications and Standards. Applications and Standards, Network Security Essentials (2010)
14. Vasalya, A., Agrawal, R.: Smart telerobotic surveillance system via internet with reduced time delay. Iaes Int. J. Robot. Autom. $2(1)$, 11 (2012)

Photonic Computing and Communication for Neural Network Accelerators

Chengpeng Xia[1]($\boxtimes$), Yawen Chen[1], Haibo Zhang[1], Hao Zhang[1], and Jigang Wu[2]

[1] Department of Computer Science, University of Otago, Dunedin, New Zealand
{chengpeng.xia,hao.zhang}@postgrad.otago.ac.nz
{yawen,haibo}@cs.otago.ac.nz
[2] School of Computers, Guangdong University of Technology, Guangzhou, China

Abstract. Conventional electronic Artificial Neural Networks (ANNs) accelerators focus on architecture design and numerical computation optimization to improve the training speed. Optical technology with low energy consumption and high transmission speed are expected to play an important role in the next generation of computing architectures. To provide a better understanding of optical technology used in ANN acceleration, we present a comprehensive review for the optical implementations of ANNs accelerator in this paper. We propose a classification of existing solutions which are categorized into optical computing acceleration and optical communication acceleration according to optical effects and optical architectures. Moreover, we discuss the challenges for these photonic neural network acceleration approaches to highlight the most promising future research opportunities in this field.

Keywords: Optical neural networks · Optical interconnection networks · Neural network accelerator

1 Introduction

The wide applications of Artificial Intelligence (AI), such as computer vision, speech recognition, and language processing, call for efficient implementation of the model training and inference phases in machine learning [16]. Especially for Artificial Neural Networks (ANNs), due to the seminal work by Hinton et al. on deep learning in 2006, ANNs have reappeared in people's vision [5]. Multiple neural networks have been studied and applied in different fields. However, with large data sets and massively interconnected ANNs, the traditional computer architectures suffer from the efficient inference and prediction due to the limited device computing power.

Photonic architectures with low power consumption, high bandwidth and high transmission speed have been considered as a potential future alternative for electronic architectures. Optical solutions for ANNs computing and communication acceleration emerge as the times require. To this aim, many linear

© Springer Nature Switzerland AG 2022
H. Shen et al. (Eds.): PDCAT 2021, LNCS 13148, pp. 121–128, 2022.
https://doi.org/10.1007/978-3-030-96772-7_12

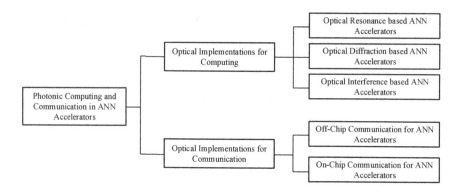

Fig. 1. Classification of photonic implementation in ANN accelerators.

transformations have been demonstrated to be able to performed with passive optics without power consumption and with minimal latency [14]. The feasibility of optical logic gates has also been demonstrated [7]. Hence, optical implementations of neural networks have been investigated to increase the ANN training speed and the energy efficiency [15]. Moreover, optical on/off chip network architectures have been designed, with the aim of increasing model parallelism and data transmission speed.

In this paper we present a survey of approaches for implementing Optical Neural Network (ONN) accelerator. A classification of the existing solutions is proposed which includes two categories: optical implementations for computing and communication. Previous citation focused either on the computing acceleration in neural network or on bottlenecks of photonics technologies, which ignored the contribution of on-chip optical communication to neural networks acceleration. The remainder of this paper is organized as follows: The classification for photonic computing and communication in ANN accelerators is presented in Fig. 1. In Sect. 2, we review the most relevant solutions categorized according to the optical implementations for computing, while in Sect. 3 we describe the optical approaches devised for the communication acceleration of ANN training. Section 4 discusses the challenges and future research opportunities in this field, while Sect. 5 concludes the paper.

2 Optical Implementations for Computing

2.1 Optical Resonance Based Neural Network Accelerators

Inspired by the field of neuroscience in which biological neurons communicate by short pulses. Optical resonance based ANN accelerators have been carefully studied. Since the wavelength specificity of Microring-Ring-Resonator (MRR), a key element of ANN accelerator, the realization of Wavelength Division Multiplexing (WDM) approach is made possible, which is closely tied to the noncoherent architectures of the ONN. In contrast to spatial multiplexing, the WDM channel

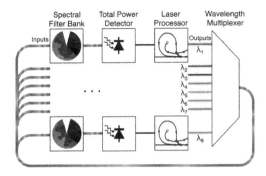

Fig. 2. The Broadcast-and-weight architecture proposed by [17].

can coexist in a single bus waveguide channel without interference, which simplifies the interconnection network of neurons to some extent. An on-chip optical architecture for neural network implementations, named Broadcast-and-Weight (BW) was explored in [17]. As shown in Fig. 2, the BW architecture employs multiple wavelengths to transfer data in parallel with each distinct wavelength outputted to a common bus waveguide. The outputs are multiplexed and distributed to all-neuron connection, in which the broadcast is realized by passively splitting the bus waveguide. The MRR weight bank is an array of reconfigurable filters that can be tuned to drain energy from their resonant wavelength, thereby imprinting the weight coefficient to each corresponding channel.

Inspired by the BW protocol, an photonics convolution accelerator (PCNNA) was proposed for CNNs inference-mode in [11]. PCNNA designed a single-layer multiplexing CNN architecture, which enables the propagation of different neural network layers. The authors argued that as multiple kernels share the same receptive field values per layer, convolution computations for different kernels can be performed in parallel. In the high-level framework, PCNNA is designed to run on two clock cycle domains, the faster domain is used for the operation of the optical network, and the slower domain is used for interfacing with electronic circuits.

2.2   Optical Diffraction Based Neural Network Accelerators

Diffraction effects are usually the main factor limiting the performance of optical devices, while appropriately using the principle of diffraction effect can effectively realize the ONN. Holographic Optical Element (HOE) is one of the research focuses currently in information storage, which is considered to be a great storage tool for weights and directions in the ONN connection [13]. In [19], Zuo et al. presented a Spatial Light Modulator-based (SLM) all-optical ANN, in which optical matrix multiplication is implemented in a clever way. The authors divided the SLM into several regions according to the number of input beams, and each region is a superposition of multiple phase grating stacks, i.e., holograms. The multiplication of ANN is realized by the diffraction of the incident beam in the

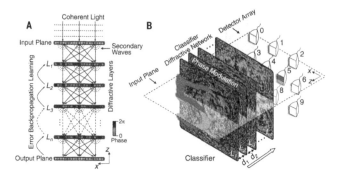

Fig. 3. Diffractive deep neural networks (D^2NN) depicted by [10].

HOEs, in which the weight of the neural network is mapped to the direction of the incident beam. After the diffracted beam passes through a convex lens, it performs a Fourier transform. Finally, beams are focused on the plane in the same direction to realize the accumulation operation.

In addition to holograms, based on the sequentially cascading phase masks, Lin et al. [10] explored a diffraction-based all-optical neural network called D^2NN. As depicted in Fig. 3, in D^2NN, the fully connected neural network is implemented by multiple 3D printed phase masks which are formed as a hierarchical array in order and with interval. Each layer has only one single phase mask representing one layer in the fully connected neural network. The small grids in phase masks denote the neurons, which are loaded as different weight information by different refractive indices and thicknesses in grids. In the same direction of the incident beam, each neuron can be connected to all neurons in the next layer after diffraction, so all neurons can be fully connected in each phase mask. D^2NN changes weight to the neural network by adjusting the phases and changing the light attenuation.

2.3 Optical Interference Based Neural Network Accelerators

Different from diffraction, interference effect usually requires fewer linear light waves, in which waveguides are needed to propagate the light waves. Interference based ANNs implementation mainly relies on the optical device Mach-Ze-Delphi Interferometer (MZI) that is made of two waveguides with directional couplers and phase shifters. MZI has a coherent structure that loads the weight information into the neural network by adjusting the phase and amplitude of the input light. Shen et al. in [15] proposed an all-optical neural network using coherent nanophotonic circuits which became kind of a seminal work for all future interference based ANN accelerator. Singular Value Decomposition (SVD) [9] is used to realize optical matrix multiplication which decomposes the matrix M into $M = U \sum V$ including two unitary matrices U and V and a diagonal matrix $\sum$. MZIs are set up as a cascaded array that is divided into three parts, with each part realizing the matrix U, $\sum$ and V respectively. The cascaded array can be regarded as a fully connected neural network. When the input lights pass through the MZIs, the accelerator applies two parallel coherent light waves at both phase shifters which will cause interference to the input light, so that the matrix multiplication operation in CNN can be well realized in these processes.

3   Optical Implementations for Communication

Existing ANNs have been challenged by the fact that high computational complexity, large amount of computational data, strong demand for memory access, and high demand for system parallelism exist widely in current model training. In the latest ANNs, tens to hundreds of megabytes of parameters are required to execute a single inference pass. Over one billions of operations will generate large amounts of memory access requirements from the processing elements (PE) which makes existing architectures face the challenge of memory wall. In the processing of model training, a large amount of reusable data is usually generated. For example, a huge amount of filter data, input feature map data, and partial sum data are created in the processing of convolution in CNN, in which these data can be regarded as reusable resources.

3.1   Off-Chip Communication for Neural Network Accelerators

Optical interconnection have a deep research history in the field of datacenter. To improve communication performance, prior work shows the benefits of reconfigurable topologies in datacenter networks by adding optical links to the electrical topology [4,12] or by creating all-optical datacenter interconnects [1]. Nevertheless, there are only a limited number of studies on using optical interconnection to optimize the ANN accelerator. In [6] proposed all-optical interconnects for ANN systems named SiP-ML, for strong scaling of ML workloads by leveraging SiP chiplets. Considering the parallelism of ANN algorithm and the singleness and repeatability of communication pattern during entire training, Sip-ML designed two data reuse based topologies at opposite ends of the spectrum. As shown in Fig. 4a, an Optical Circuit Switch (OCS) based topology called SiP-OCS is proposed consisting of Q commercially available optical switches. Each OCS has N ports (the same as the number of GPUs), and each GPU is connected to every OCS in a flat topology. Due to the 10 ms reconfiguration latency, Sip-OCS can last through the entire model training. Meanwhile, Micro-ring resonators embedded in SiP ports are used to build a switch-free topology which completely removes switching elements, named Sip-Ring. MRRs act as spectral filters to select and forward wavelengths, and they enable the reuse of wavelengths across non-overlapping segments of the ring. In contrast to SiP-OCS, SiP-Ring reconfigures wavelengths within each port to achieve logically rich topologies.

Moreover, an Inter/Intra-Chip silicon photonic network for rack-scale computing systems called RSON was presented in [18]. RSON adopts circuit switching for the inter-chip and ONoC because of the relatively high overhead on

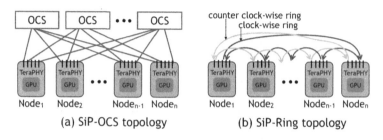

Fig. 4. Two topologies for SiP-ML proposed by [6].

optical path setup/teardown and the difficulty on buffering optical signals. [18] utilized the inter-node interface as the medium to coordinate the request from both local ONoC and optical switch. A channel partition and dynamic path priority control scheme is designed to reduce the control complexity and arbitration overhead.

3.2 On-Chip Communication for Neural Network Accelerators

In [8], the authors considered that electrical interconnection in the existing many-core platform would not be sustainable for handling the massively increasing bandwidth demand of big data driven AI applications. Hence, a rapid topology generation and core mapping of ONoC (REGO) for heterogeneous multi-core architecture was proposed. Based on the genetic algorithm, REGO receives an application task graph including the number of cores and ONoC parameters as inputs, which further includes the available router structure and loss and noise factors of the optical elements. Thus, the REGO can accommodate various router structures and optical elements because it calculates the worst-case OSNR through loss and noise parameters obtained in advance through the parameters of optical.

A fine-grained parallel computing model for ANNs training was depicted in [3] on ONoC, in which the trade-off between computation and communication can be analyzed to support the ANN acceleration. To minimize the total training time, three mapping strategies were designed in each ANN training stage which has the optimal number of cores. The advantages and disadvantages for each mapping strategy are discussed and analyzed in terms of hotspot level, memory requirement, and state transitions.

4   Challenges and Opportunities

In this paper, we reviews the optical approaches to accelerate neural networks from two aspects, i.e., computing and communication. In recent years, with the maturity of ANN theory and the development of silicon optical technology, one of the areas with growing concerns is the implementations of ONN. Nevertheless, there are still some outstanding challenges that limit the inference accuracy, reliability and scalability of ONNs. Hence, we summarize the challenges and opportunities to offer suggestions for future research.

Scalability: The exiting works that have been discussed in this review mainly focus on three approaches to accelerate ANNs model training that are small optical neural network implementation, matrix vector multiplication acceleration and optical network architectures for communication accelerating. The two major issues of the above approaches are area consumption and energy attenuation of the optical devices. The schemes in [14] and [2] described that the optical depth (the number of MZI units traversed through the longest path) for the unitary matrix is limited to $2N - 3$ and N, in an ANN with N number of neurons, respectively. The optical depth increases linearly with the number of neurons increasing which directly translates into additional loss in silicon photonics integrations. Research is thus needed to design new novel architectures for reducing silicon photonic hardware complexity.

Robustness: Robustness also becomes more and more critical due to the scale-up. Specifically, since the phase of each MZI is highly impacted by environmental change, thermal crosstalk and imperfect manufacturing, the phase error is cascaded throughout the computation. Whereas the on-chip thermal crosstalk can be suppressed, the finite encoding precision on phase settings will remain as the fundamental limitation for the ONNs with high computational complexity. The phase errors, in particular, accumulate when the lightwave signal traverses the MZI mesh with an optical depth of $2N + 1$. In addition, such errors propagate through each layer of the network, which ultimately restricts the depth of the neural network. In order to realize robust photonic accelerator, research is needed to achieve effective photonic crosstalk mitigation, phase noise correction, and noise resilient photodetection.

5   Conclusion

In this paper, we provide a comprehensive survey for optical implementation of ANN accelerators, including Photonic computing acceleration and Photonic communication acceleration. For the optical neural networks, we present the current ANN accelerators that are realized by the optical effects. For the optical interconnection, we introduce the existing studies from the perspectives of off-chip communication and on-chip communication for ANN accelerator. Furthermore, we point out the open challenges and the future research opportunities for photonic neural network accelerator, which is expected to provide guidance and insight for future researchers and developers on this research field.

Acknowledgement. This work is supported by the National Natural Science Foundation of China under Grant Nos. 62106052 and 62072118.

References

1. Chen, L., et al.: Enabling wide-spread communications on optical fabric with megaswitch. In: 14th Symposium on Networked Systems Design and Implementation, pp. 577–593 (2017)
2. Clements, W.R., Humphreys, P.C., Metcalf, B.J., Kolthammer, W.S., et al.: Optimal design for universal multiport interferometers. Optica **3**(12), 1460–1465 (2016)
3. Dai, F., Chen, Y., Zhang, H., Huang, Z.: Accelerating fully connected neural network on optical network-on-chip (onoc). arXiv preprint arXiv:2109.14878 (2021)
4. Farrington, N., et al.: Helios: a hybrid electrical/optical switch architecture for modular data centers. In: 2010 ACM SIGCOMM, pp. 339–350 (2010)
5. Hinton, G.E., Osindero, S., Teh, Y.W.: A fast learning algorithm for deep belief nets. Neural Comput. **18**(7), 1527–1554 (2006)
6. Khani, M., et al.: Sip-ml: high-bandwidth optical network interconnects for machine learning training. In: 2021 ACM SIGCOMM, pp. 657–675 (2021)
7. Kim, J.Y., Kang, J.M., Kim, T.Y., Han, S.K.: All-optical multiple logic gates with xor, nor, or, and nand functions using parallel soa-mzi structures: theory and experiment. J. Lightwave Technol. **24**(9), 3392 (2006)
8. Kim, Y.W., Choi, S.H., Han, T.H.: Rapid topology generation and core mapping of optical network-on-chip for heterogeneous computing platform. IEEE Access **9**, 110359–110370 (2021)
9. Lawson, C.L., Hanson, R.J.: Solving least squares problems. SIAM (1995)
10. Lin, X., Rivenson, Y., Yardimci, N.T., Veli, M., et al.: All-optical machine learning using diffractive deep neural networks. Science **361**(6406), 1004–1008 (2018)
11. Mehrabian, A., Al-Kabani, Y., Sorger, V.J., El-Ghazawi, T.: Pcnna: a photonic convolutional neural network accelerator. In: 2018 31st IEEE International System-on-Chip Conference (SOCC), pp. 169–173. IEEE (2018)
12. Mellette, W.M., McGuinness, R., Roy, A., Forencich, A., Papen, G., Snoeren, A.C., Porter, G.: Rotornet: a scalable, low-complexity, optical datacenter network. In: ACM Special Interest Group on Data Communication, pp. 267–280 (2017)
13. Psaltis, D., Brady, D., Wagner, K.: Adaptive optical networks using photorefractive crystals. Appl. Opt. **27**(9), 1752–1759 (1988)
14. Reck, M., Zeilinger, A., Bernstein, H.J., Bertani, P.: Experimental realization of any discrete unitary operator. Phys. Rev. Lett. **73**(1), 58 (1994)
15. Shen, Y., et al.: Deep learning with coherent nanophotonic circuits. Nat. Photonics **11**(7), 441–446 (2017)
16. Silver, D., et al.: Mastering the game of go with deep neural networks and tree search. Nature **529**(7587), 484–489 (2016)
17. Tait, A.N., Nahmias, M.A., Shastri, B.J., Prucnal, P.R.: Broadcast and weight: an integrated network for scalable photonic spike processing. J. Lightwave Technol. **32**(21), 4029–4041 (2014)
18. Yang, P., et al.: Rson: an inter/intra-chip silicon photonic network for rack-scale computing systems. In: 2018 Design, Automation & Test in Europe Conference & Exhibition (DATE), pp. 1369–1374. IEEE (2018)
19. Zuo, Y., Li, B., Zhao, Y., Jiang, Y., Chen, Y.C., Chen, P., et al.: All-optical neural network with nonlinear activation functions. Optica **6**(9), 1132–1137 (2019)

Performance Comparison of Multi-layer Perceptron Training on Electrical and Optical Network-on-Chips

Fei Dai[✉], Yawen Chen, Zhiyi Huang, and Haibo Zhang

University of Otago, Dunedin, New Zealand
{travis,yawen,hzy,haibo}@cs.otago.ac.nz

Abstract. Multi-layer Perceptron (MLP) is a class of Artificial Neural Networks widely used in regression, classification, and prediction. To accelerate the training of MLP, more cores can be used for parallel computing on many-core systems. With the increasing number of cores, interconnection of cores has a pivotal role in accelerating MLP training. Currently, the chip-scale interconnection can either use electrical signals or optical signals for data transmission among cores. The former one is known as Electrical Network-on-Chip (ENoC) and the latter one is known as Optical Network-on-Chip (ONoC). Due to the differences of optical and electrical characteristics, the performance and energy consumption of MLP training on ONoC and ENoC can be very different. Therefore, comparing the performance and energy consumption between ENoC and ONoC for MLP training is worthy of study. In this paper, we first compare the differences between ONoC and ENoC based on a parallel MLP training method. Then, we formulate their performance model by analyzing communication and computation time. Furthermore, the energy model is formulated according to their static energy and dynamic energy consumption. Finally, we conduct extensive simulations to compare the performance and energy consumption between ONoC and ENoC. Results show that compared with ENoC, the MLP training time of ONoC is reduced by 70.12% on average and the energy consumption of ONoC is reduced by 48.36% under batch size 32. However, with a small number of cores in MLP training, ENoC consumes less energy than ONoC.

Keywords: Multi-layer perceptron · Optical network-on-chip · Artificial Neural Networks · Energy consumption

1 Introduction

Multi-layer Perceptron (MLP) is one type of deep learning model that can be applied to classification, recommendation engine, and anomaly detection. However, the training of complex MLP model can be very slow with large data sets. Since the MLP has intrinsic characteristic for parallel computation, more cores can be integrated in many-core systems to accelerate the training of MLP. With

© Springer Nature Switzerland AG 2022
H. Shen et al. (Eds.): PDCAT 2021, LNCS 13148, pp. 129–141, 2022.
https://doi.org/10.1007/978-3-030-96772-7_13

the increasing number of cores integrated into the chip, on-chip interconnection becomes an essential factor to accelerate MLP training which is normally constrained by the communication cost and memory requirements. Electrical Network-on-Chip (ENoC) was first proposed to improve the system performance with communications among cores using electrical signals. However, it has scalability issues due to the hop-by-hop routing via electrical routers, which does not scale well with a large number of cores. Optical Network-on-Chip (ONoC) was proposed as a promising alternative paradigm for ENoC using optical communications among cores. Compared with ENoC, ONoC has many advantages, such as low transmission delay, low power cost, high bandwidth, and large throughput [1]. Moreover, ONoC enables multiple signals transmission in one waveguide using different wavelengths by Wavelength Division Multiplexing (WDM) technology [2]. With these advantages, ONoC has great capability to efficiently perform intensive inter-core communications, and can effectively accelerate the parallel computing of MLP training.

However, ONoC also has some extra overheads such as OE/EO conversion cost, insertion loss caused by the light transmission of the waveguide, and tuning power of micro-ring, which can affect the performance and energy consumption for MLP training. Moreover, the performance of MLP training also depends on different communication patterns in on-chip network, which is dependent on the number of cores, batch size, NN benchmarks, and etc. Up to date, there have been no comparative studies that compare MLP training between ENoC and ONoC regarding the training performance and energy consumption. Only several pieces of work on performance comparison between ENoC and ONoC can be found. The paper [3] compares performance between ENoC and ONoC under different topologies and the report [4] shows performance and energy consumption between ENoC and ONoC by using synthetic traffic. Nevertheless, these studies does not consider the comparisons in scenario of neural network training. Therefore, it is of great importance to investigate the comparison of MLP training efficiency between ONoC and ENoC under different configurations. The research questions include: *1) Does ONoC always outperform ENoC for training MLP training? 2) How much improvement can be achieved for MLP training on ONoC compared with ENoC under different configurations? 3) In what conditions and settings, ENoC consumes less energy than ONoC for the MLP training?* In this paper, we aim to compare the performance and energy consumption of MLP training on ONoC and ENoC under different configurations. We answer the above questions with key contributions summarized as follows:

1. We compare the differences between ONoC and ENoC based on a parallel MLP training method [5]. We formulate their performance by analyzing their communication and computation costs and formulate their energy based on the static and dynamic energy costs.
2. We conduct extensive simulations to compare the MLP performance and energy consumption betwen ONoC and ENoC under different batch sizes using different NN benchmarks. Results show that ONoC outperforms ENoC with an average training time reduction of 70.12% and ONoC is more energy-efficient than ENoC especially when a large number of cores are used.

The remaining part of the paper proceeds as follows: Sect. 2 describes the background of this paper, which includes MLP training, ONoC/ENoC system. Section 3 first illustrates the parallel MLP training on NoC systems, then presents the performance and energy models of ONoC and ENoC. Section 4 compares performance and energy consumption between ONoC and ENoC. Finally, Sect. 5 concludes the paper.

2   Background

2.1   Training of MLP

The training process of MLP consists of forward propagation and backward propagation. We use Z_l to represent the input vector in the layer l (output vector of layer $l - 1$) and W_l to represent the weight matrix at layer l. In the forward propagation, the forward propagation of MLP with n_l neurons at layer l can be defined as $Z_l = f(W_l Z_{l-1} + b_l)$, where $f(*)$ is the activation function, and bias vector is b_l in layer l. In backward propagation, we use the E_l, ΔW_l to represent error vector and gradient of weight in layer l. The error can be calculated as $E_l = (E_{l+1} W_l^T) f'(Z_l)$, where $f'(*)$ is the derivative function of $f(*)$. Then, by using error vector E_l, the gradient of weight can be calculated as $\Delta W_l = Z_l^T E_{l+1}$. Finally, after we obtain the gradient, weights are updated as $W_l = W_l + \sigma \Delta W_l$, where σ is the learning rate.

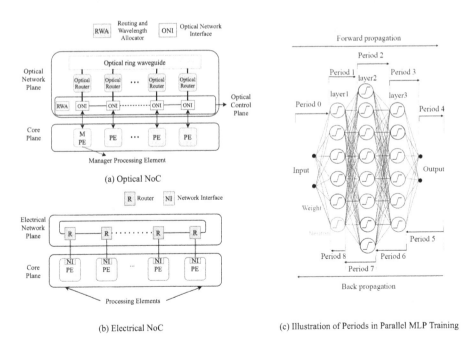

(a) Optical NoC

(b) Electrical NoC

(c) Illustration of Periods in Parallel MLP Training

Fig. 1. Overview of (a) Optical network-on-chip system and (b) Electrical network-on-chip system; (c) Illustration of periods in parallel MLP training.

2.2 Optical and Electrical On-Chip Interconnects

We first illustrate the major differences, advantages, and disadvantages of ONoC and ENoC respectively, then we demonstrate the ONoC and ENoC architectures used in this paper. The main difference between ENoC and ONoC is that they use different transmission media for communications among cores. In ENoC, the communications among cores are conducted through the electrical routers, where the electrical packets from the source go through electrical links and routers until the destination. While the transmission among cores in ONoC is different via optical routers, which can use different wavelengths to communicate in parallel through the waveguide using Wavelength Division Multiplexing (WDM) technology. The merits of optical communication can be summarized as follows: low transmission delay (2–3 cycles between any two points on the chip with a 2 GHz clock), low power cost (roughly independent of the distance), high bandwidth (up to 40 Gb/s per wavelength) and the feasibility of wavelength division multiplexing (64 per waveguide). One of the drawbacks of ONoC is that ONoC requires a large number of optical components, which dissipate a lot of static power. Compared with ONoC, ENoC has good flexibility (a variety of topologies) and it performs well in short distance communication, but ENoC does not scale well resulting in high latency with more cores integrated into the chip.

The overview of ONoC and ENoC architectures used to train the MLP in this paper are shown in Fig. 1(a) and (b) respectively, which are based on ring topology. The ONoC architecture is similar to the one proposed in [6], where the optical network plane has an optical control plane for configuring the optical router (a pair of transmitter and receiver). In the router, the receiver is set with a splitter to split optical signals. As can be seen from Fig. 1(a), the PEs and the optical routers are connected to the optical network interface through vertical links for router configuration and data transmission. Before the communication, Manager Processing Element (MPE) and the Routing Wavelength Allocator (RWA) are used to configure the optical network. After the configuration is finished, the corresponding modulators in transmitters and drop filters in receivers are configured and ready for communications. We assume only one optical waveguide is used in this paper. The ENoC architecture consists of electrical network plane and core plane, as can be seen from Fig. 1(b). The network interface in each PE connects a electric router, and the routers in the electrical network plane concatenate with each other via electrical links by a ring topology. Note that each core in the core plane for ONoC/ENoC has an on-chip distributed memory architecture with its L1 private cache and distributed SRAM connected to the main memory via the memory controller. More details about system parameters will be described in Sect. 4.

3 Methodology on Parallel MLP Training on ONoC and ENoC System

3.1 Parallel MLP Training

We first use an example given in Fig. 1(c) to explain the process of MLP training on ONoC/ENoC system. For parallel computation during MLP training, the neurons in the MLP can be mapped to multiple cores to execute in parallel, where multiple neurons can be mapped onto the same core. As illustrated in Fig. 1(c), one epoch of training is divided into multiple periods based on layers and these periods are executed sequentially. In the initialization process (Period 0), data and MLP instructions in the main memory are loaded to the distributed SRAM of cores. In the subsequent periods, the cores mapped with neurons in the corresponding layer perform computations concurrently and then exchange the outputs with the cores mapped with neurons in the next layer through inter-core communications instead of accessing the main memory.

3.2   Performance Model

As illustrated in Fig. 1(c), one epoch of training is divided into multiple periods based on layers. The FP process is divided into $l + 1$ periods labeled from Period 0 to Period l, and the BP process is divided into another l periods labeled from Period $l + 1$ to Period $2l$. Note that Period 0 is the initialization period, which does not have any computations and communications. To take advantage of data locality, the cores used in the forward propagation will be used in the back propagation. In this way, all MLP parameters and intermediate values are stored in SRAM of the corresponding cores distributively, with these parameters staying in the corresponding SRAM during one epoch of training. Cores used in different layers exchange data by communications on ONoC/ENoC. During the MLP training process, the only difference between ENoC and ONoC is the communication stage, which can result in different training time. Therefore, we first formulate the communication time of ONoC and ENoC separately and then formulate their computation time. Finally, we derive their total MLP training time respectively. Because each epoch of MLP training is repetitive, the formulation below is based on one epoch of MLP training.

Communication Time. We use m to represent the number of cores used in the parallel MLP training and assume the neurons are evenly mapped to the m cores in each period. Let d_i, n_i represent the transferred data volume and neuron number in period i, where $i \in [1, 2l]$. According to the parallel training of FP and BP process, the transferred data volume varies by using different number of cores, as can be calculated by

$$d_i = \begin{cases} 0, & i = 1, l \text{ and } 2l; \\ \frac{n_i va}{m}, & i \in [2, l - 1]; \\ \frac{(n_i n_{2l-i} + n_i) va}{m}, & i \in [l + 1, 2l - 1], \end{cases} \tag{1}$$

where v and a represent the number of batch size and storage size of one parameter, respectively. $d_1, d_l, d_{2l} = 0$ because there is no communication in these periods.

ONoC Communication Time: The communication time of MLP training on ONoC in period i equals the amount of time that the m cores in period i finish exchanging their data d_i with other cores using optical communications. Let s represent the size of flit, then the total number of flits transmitted in period i equals $\lceil \frac{d_i}{s} \rceil$. Assume the number of available wavelengths is λ_{max}. By leveraging the WDM technology, the communications of ONoC in each period can be parallelized by letting multiple cores transmit simultaneously using different wavelengths. For period i that demands communications, all the m cores can transmit concurrently if $m \le \lambda_{max}$; otherwise Time Division Multiplexing (TDM) needs to be used to complete the transmissions from the m cores. The delay of O/E/O conversion, time of flight, de/serialization, and routing and wavelength assignment are represented by Do, Df, Ds, Da, respectively. Let $\varepsilon_1(i)$ be the amount of time required to complete communications in period i for ONoC. We have

$$\varepsilon_1(i) = \left\lceil \frac{m}{\lambda_{max}} \right\rceil \left(\left\lceil \frac{d_i}{s} \right\rceil (Do + Df + Ds) + Da \right). \tag{2}$$

ENoC Communication Time: The communication time of MLP training on ENoC in period i equals the time that the m cores in period i finish exchanging data volume d_i with each other via electrical routers. The communication pattern on ENoC is the same as an all-gather/all-reduce operation among cores. As Bulk synchronous parallel (BSP) model is widely used for evaluating the performance of parallel algorithm in distributed-memory system [7], we use the BSP model to evaluate the performance of all-gather/all-reduce operation during parallel MLP training on ENoC system, with the communication time on ENoC formulated as follows. Each super-step in the BSP model is regarded as one execution period of MLP on ENoC. We denote h_j^i as the number of flits that core j sends or receives during period i, where $i \in [1, 2l]$ and $j \in [1, m]$. Then, the maximum number of flits among all the cores sent or received in period i, denoted as H_i, can be calculated as

$$H_i = \overset{m}{\underset{j=1}{max}}(h_j^i). \tag{3}$$

The process of all the cores exchanging their data with any other cores in each execution period is an all-gather/all-reduce process, in which we use recursive doubling method [8] to execute the all-gather operation. Then, this all-gather/all-reduce process takes $\log_2 m$ sub-steps to finish. The size of data in each core doubles at each sub-step until d_i data volume is fully gathered/reduced. Then, the cost of sending or receiving data volume of d_i in period i is $gH_i \sum_{k=1}^{\log_2 m}(d_i/2^k)$, where g is the bandwidth of the ENoC to transmit data, and k ($k \in [1, \log_2 m]$) is the index of the sub-steps in the all-gather/all-reduce process. Let $\varepsilon_2(i)$ be the amount of time required to complete communications for ENoC in period i. We have

$$\varepsilon_2(i) = gH_i \sum_{k=1}^{\log_2 m} (d_i/2^k) + b_i, \tag{4}$$

where b_i is the latency for barrier synchronization in period i.

Computation Time. The computation time in each period equals the time that the corresponding cores finish processing its computation workload for that period. We use ρ_i to represent the amount of computation for each neuron in period i of the FP process and use σ_i to represent the amount of computation to calculate the gradients and update the weight of one connection based on all training samples. When the batch size (i.e., the number of samples in one training epoch) is larger than one, ρ_i is the amount of computation for each neuron in period i to process all samples in the current training. According to the definition of periods, the neurons in layer i where $i \in [1, l]$ get involved in period i during the FP process, and the neurons in layer $2l - i + 1$ where $i \in [l + 1, 2l]$ get involved in period i during the BP process. Therefore, the corresponding number of neuron n_i in FP process is the same as n_{2l-i+1} in the BP process. Then, the amount of computation for FP process is $\frac{\rho_i n_i}{m}$ where $i \in [1, l]$ and the amount of computation for BP process is $\frac{\sigma_i n_{2l-i+1}(n_{2l-i+1})}{m}$ where $i \in [l + 1, 2l]$.

Let $\tau(i)$ represent the amount of computation time required for each of the m cores in period i and assume all the cores are homogeneous with same computation capacity C. We have

$$\tau(i) = \begin{cases} \frac{\rho_i n_i}{mC}, & i \in [1, l]; \\ \frac{\sigma_i n_i(n_{2l-i+1})}{mC}, & i \in [l + 1, 2l]. \end{cases} \tag{5}$$

Total Training Time. Since we have obtained the communication costs on ONoC and ENoC by Eq. (2) and Eq. (4) and their computation cost by Eq. (5), we can derive the total MLP training time on ONoC and ENoC as follows. The total training time of ONoC, denoted as T_{onoc}, equals the sum of ONoC communication time, computation time, and initialization delay in one epoch of training. Then

$$T_{onoc} = \sum_{i=1}^{2l} (\varepsilon_1(i) + \tau(i)) + \xi, \tag{6}$$

where ξ represents the initialization delay caused by loading input data and MLP instructions from the main memory to the cores in initialization process and other extra main memory access, software overhead, etc.

Similarly, the total training time of ENoC, denoted as T_{enoc}, can be formulated as follows:

$$T_{enoc} = \sum_{i=1}^{2l} (\varepsilon_2(i) + \tau(i)) + \xi. \tag{7}$$

3.3   Energy Model

ENoC Energy Consumption. We use PS and PL to represent the power of switch and power of link. Let E_{stat} be the static energy consumption of ENoC, which can be calculated as

$$E_{stat} = \left(\sum_{i=1}^{n_s} PS_i + \sum_{i=1}^{n_l} PL_i \right) \times T_{enoc}, \tag{8}$$

where n_s is the number of switches and n_l is the number of links used during the MLP training.

We use ES_i and EL_i to represent the energy/bit of the i_{th} switch and link. BS_i and BL_i are used to represent the bits transmitted through the i_{th} switch and link. Let E_{dyn} be the dynamic energy consumption of ENoC, then we have

$$E_{dyn} = \sum_{i=1}^{n_s} (ES_i \times BS_i) + \sum_{i=1}^{n_l} (EL_i \times BL_i). \tag{9}$$

ONoC Energy Consumption. The static energy consumption of ONoC is denoted as OE_{stat}, which is related to the energy costs for micro-ring tuning, laser, and electric-to-optical conversion. So, then static energy consumption of ONoC can be calculated by

$$OE_{stat} = (P_{mt} + P_{laser} + P_{oe}) \times T_{onoc}, \tag{10}$$

where P_{mt}, P_{laser} and P_{oe} represent the powers of micro-ring tuning, laser and electric-to-optical conversion respectively.

The dynamic energy consumption of ONoC is denoted as OE_{dyn}, which is decided by the overall amount of optical flits that traverse through modulator, photo-detector, serializer/deserializer, and waveguide. We use E_m, E_p, E_s and E_w to represent the energy/flit of modulator, photo-detector, serializer/deserializer and waveguide respectively. According to [9], the dynamic energy consumption of ONoC can be calculated as

$$OE_{dyn} = (E_m + E_p + E_s + E_w) \times N_{flits}^3, \tag{11}$$

where N_{flits} is the number of flits.

4   Comparison of MLP Training on ENoC and ONoC

4.1   Simulation Setup

Since the computation part for both ONoC and ENoC are identical, we separate the simulation of computation and communication into the two processes. For the communication level simulation, we build an in-house simulator to simulate the ONoC based on the cost model in Sect. 3.2 while the communication time of ENoC is tested on Garnet standalone mode [10]. To collect computation time and communication traces, we implemented the MLP in C using GNU Scientific Library and BLAS gemm [11] in a machine with an intel i5 3200 CPU and 32 Gb main memory. To get the accurate computation time of each core, we repeat the computation workload of each core a thousand times and then obtain the average time. In this way, we make sure the computation is carried out in the

CPU caches, which matches our simulated architecture. We run the configured workloads with up to 300 threads to generate the communication traces for up to 300 cores. The communication traces are fed into our ONoC and ENoC simulator to obtain the communication time of the simulated ONoC and ENoC systems. Based on the simulated results, we calculate the energy consumption of ONoC and ENoC using the energy model in Sect. 3.3, where the values of ONoC/ENoC energy parameters are retrieved from DSENT [12].

We use the three well-known MLP models [5] for processing fashion-mnist and cifar-10 datasets with high classification accuracy for our simulation, the hyper-parameters for the neural networks can be seen in Table 1. The parameters of the simulated architecture are shown in Table 2, and other ONoC parameters are set as follows: bandwidth/per wavelength 40 Gb/s, waveguide propagation 1.5 dB/cm, waveguide bending 0.005 dB/90°, splitter 0.5 dB, MR pass 0.005 dB/MR, laser efficiency 30%, MR drop 0.5 dB/MR, coupler 1 dB. These parameters are obtained from [5,9,13]. The packet size and flit size for ONoC/ENoC are set as 64 bytes and 16 bytes, respectively. Note that the size of distributed SRAM in Table 2 is the maximum memory requirement for the NN benchmarks under batch size 32 calculated by the worst case. The value of distributed SRAM can be greatly reduced if we adopt state-of-the-art pruning technique for the neural network [14]. If the memory requirement of NN is beyond the memory capacity, the performance will be degraded because additional main memory accesses are required causing extra delay for the training time.

Table 1. Hyper-parameters for Neural network

NN1	784–1000–500–10
NN2	784–1500–784–1000–500–10
NN3	1024–4000–1000–4000–1000–4000–1000–4000–10

Table 2. Parameters of simulated architecture

Core	3.4 *GHz*, 6 *GFLOPS* (64 bit)
Private L1 (I cache/ D cache)	128/128 *KB*
L1 latency	1 *cycle*
Distributed SRAM	42 *M*
Distributed SRAM latency	10 *cycles* (front end/back end)
Memory controller latency	6 *cycles*
Bandwith of main memory	10 *Gb/s*
NoC	Parameters setup
ENoC	2D-Ring, 2 cycles/hop, 2 cycles/routing,
	32 nm, shortest-path routing,
	4 virtual channel router
ONoC	3D-Ring, 1 waveguide, 30 mm length,
	Time of flight & OE/EO: 1 cycle/flit, 64 wavelengths
	De/Serialization: 2 cycles/flit, 10 Gb/s

4.2 Performance Comparison

To better show the performance comparison of ONoC and ENoC, we first compare their computation and communication time by using the NN benchmarks with a list of fixed number of cores (50, 100, 150, 200, 250, 300) under batch size 32. Note that the following results are obtained from one epoch of MLP training including forward and back propagation.

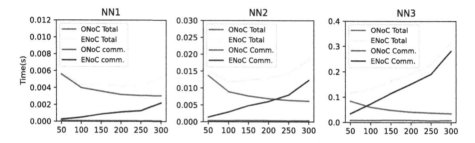

Fig. 2. Performance comparisons of ONoC and ENoC with different number of cores.

From Fig. 2, we can see that the communication time of ONoC during one epoch training almost keeps steady, and the total training time keeps decreasing with the increasing number of cores. However, the communication time of ENoC shows an upward trend with the increasing number of cores and the training time of ENoC (for most of NNs) first decreases and reaches the bottom within the range from 50 to 100 cores, then keeps increasing. The reason for this is that the communication cost on ENoC relates to the number and locations of the communication cores. According to Eq. (4), communication time of ENoC mainly depends on the synchronization time and maximum cost of sending or receiving d_i message in ENoC. The barrier synchronization time of each execution period equals the latency of barrier synchronization for each sub-steps multiplied with the number of sub-steps $\log_2 m$ during the all-gather process. Though data volume to transfer from each core is reducing with the increasing number of cores, the number of sub-steps and synchronization time are increased because more cores need to exchange data with other cores. Therefore, the communication time of ENoC greatly increases with the increasing number of cores. However, the communication time in ONoC depends on the transmission data volume and the number of time slots according to Eq. (1) and Eq. (2). With the increasing number of cores, data volume to transfer from each core is reduced but more time slots are needed to communicate between cores due to limited number of wavelengths. Compared with ENoC, the communication time of ONoC only occupies a very low percentage in the total training time. On average, the MLP training time of ONoC is reduced by 70.12% compared with ENoC.

In conclusion, ONoC outperforms ENoC under different number of cores in MLP training. This effect is more notable when more cores are used for the training (e.g. 300 cores).

4.3   Comparison of Energy Consumption

To show the energy consumption of ONoC and ENoC in a better way, we first compare their static and dynamic energy consumption by using 3 NN benchmarks with a list of number of cores (50, 100, 150, 200, 250, 300) in wavelength number 64 and batch size 32.

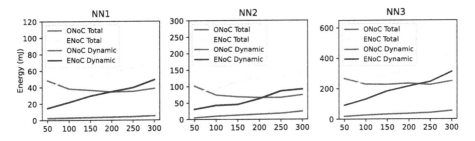

Fig. 3. Energy comparisons of ONoC and ENoC with different number of cores.

Figure 3 shows the energy consumption of 3 NN benchmarks with different number of cores under batch size 32. It can be seen from Fig. 3 that, with the increasing number of cores, the total energy consumption of ONoC is decreasing while its dynamic energy is increasing slowly. However, the energy consumption of ENoC shows a different trend with both total energy and dynamic energy increasing with the increasing number of cores. Besides, we also notice that the total energy consumption of ONoC is larger than ENoC when the number of cores is small (e.g. 50), but is smaller than ENoC with the increasing number of cores. This is because the static power is dominant in ONoC, which is largely dependent on training time according to Eq. (10). However, the dynamic energy consumption is dominated in ENoC, which is mainly related to the communication quantity. From Eqs. (8) and (10), we know that the static energy of both ONoC and ENoC has a linear relationship with the training time. Thus, the static energy consumption of ONoC is decreasing by using more cores in MLP training. Also, as can be seen from Eqs. (9) and (11), the dynamic energy of ENoC is dominated by the electrical components (e.g. switches and links) that flits traverse, while the dynamic energy of ONoC is related to the number of flits that traverse the optical components. When we use more cores in the MLP training on ENoC, the communication requires more electrical components involved which consumes much more dynamic energy resulting in the increasing total energy consumption. When we use a smaller number of cores (e.g. 50), the training time of ENoC and ONoC is more close, but ONoC has a larger static power, which results in larger total energy consumption of ONoC than ENoC. On average, the energy consumption of ONoC is reduced by 48.36% compared with ENoC for the 3 NNs.

In summary, ONoC is more energy-efficient especially when a large number of cores are used for MLP training. ENoC shows better energy efficiency than ONoC when a small number of cores is used for MLP training (e.g. less than 50 in our simulations).

5   Conclusion

In this paper, we first compare the differences of ONoC and ENoC based on a parallel MLP training method. Next, we formulate their performance according to the communication and computation time and formulate their energy consumption based on static and dynamic energy consumption respectively. Then, we conduct simulations to compare performance and energy efficiency of ONoC and ENoC using MLP training. The results show that ONoC outperforms ENoC in MLP training time with 70.12% time reduction on average. Moreover, the energy consumption of ONoC is reduced by 48.36% compared with ENoC under batch size 32. Results also show that, when a smaller number of cores is used in the MLP training, ENoC consumes less energy than ONoC. Our future work can be conducted with extension to other neural networks and other topologies.

References

1. Liu, F., Zhang, H., Chen, Y., Huang, Z., Huaxi, G.: Wavelength-reused hierarchical optical network on chip architecture for manycore processors. IEEE Trans. Sustain. Comput. **4**(2), 231–244 (2017)
2. Yang, W., Chen, Y., Huang, Z., Zhang, H.: Rwadmm: routing and wavelength assignment for distribution-based multiple multicasts in onoc. In 2017 IEEE International Symposium on Parallel and Distributed Processing with Applications and 2017 IEEE International Conference on Ubiquitous Computing and Communications (ISPA/IUCC), pp. 550–557. IEEE (2017)
3. Yahya, M.R., Wu, N., Ali, Z.A., Khizar, Y.: Optical versus electrical: Performance evaluation of network on-chip topologies for uwasn manycore processors. Wirel. Pers. Commun. **116**(2), 963–991 (2021)
4. Okada, R.: Power and performance comparison of electronic 2d-noc and opto-electronic 2d-noc
5. Dai, F., Chen, Y., Zhang, H., Huang, Z.: Accelerating fully connected neural network on optical network-on-chip (onoc). arXiv preprint arXiv:2109.14878 (2021)
6. Liu, F., Zhang, H., Chen, Y., Huang, Z., Gu, H.: Dynamic ring-based multicast with wavelength reuse for Optical Network on Chips. In: IEEE MCSoC (2016)
7. Valiant, L.G.: A bridging model for parallel computation. Commun. ACM **33**(8), 103–111 (1990)
8. Zhuang, X., Liberatore, V.: A recursion-based broadcast paradigm in wormhole routed networks. IEEE Trans. Parallel Distrib. Syst. **16**(11), 1034–1052 (2005)
9. Grani, P., Bartolini, S.: Design options for optical ring interconnect in future client devices. ACM J. Emerg. Technol. Comput. Syst. (JETC) **10**(4), 1–25 (2014)
10. Lowe-Power, J., Mutaal, A.: He gem5 simulator: version 20.0+: a new era for the open-source computer architecture simulator. ArXivorg (2020)

11. Kågström, B., Ling, P., Van Loan, C.: Gemm-based level 3 blas: high-performance model implementations and performance evaluation benchmark. ACM Trans. Math. Softw. (TOMS) **24**(3), 268–302 (1998)
12. Sun, C., et al.: Dsent-a tool connecting emerging photonics with electronics for opto-electronic networks-on-chip modeling. In: 2012 IEEE/ACM Sixth International Symposium on Networks-on-Chip, pp. 201–210. IEEE (2012)
13. Van Laer, A.: The effect of an optical network on-chip on the performance of chip multiprocessors. Ph.D. thesis, UCL (University College London) (2018)
14. Han, S., Mao, H., Dally, W.J.: Deep compression: compressing deep neural networks with pruning, trained quantization and huffman coding. arXiv preprint arXiv:1510.00149 (2015)

The Design and Implementation
of Reconfigurable Quaternary
Logic Processor

Hongjian Wang[1], Youdong Wu[1], Shan Ouyang[2(✉)], Xunlei Chen[2],
Yunfu Shen[2], and Yi Jin[2]

[1] Donghua University, North Renmin Rd. 2999, Shanghai 201620, China
[2] Shanghai University, Shangda Rd. 99,Shanghai 200444, China
ouyangshan@shu.edu.cn

Abstract. We propose a multi-valued processor called *reconfigurable quaternary logic processor* (RQLP), where we use two binary bits to express one quaternary (i.e. 4-valued) bit. The RQLP can be built with massive processor bits. Each processor bit has a unified structure consisting of four column operators which are gathered by an electric potential combiner. The structure of each column operator is composed of a signal selector, working enabler, reconfiguration register, reconfiguration circuit, output enabler, and output generator. The unified structure of each processor bit can be reconfigured into one of 4^{16} types of two-input quaternary logic operators. Compared with modern binary 64-bit processors, the proposed many-bit RQLP can perform much more types of logic operations via hardware, where the massive processor bits on a single RQLP can be divided for parallel processing. We design a general structure of RQLP and provide the prototype circuit for RQLP's processor bit. We implement the RQLP using FPGA and verify it with different quaternary logic operations. Our results demonstrate the effectiveness of RQLP in the aspect of correctness and reconfigurability.

Keywords: Multi-valued logic · Quaternary logic operator ·
Reconfigurable processor · Many-bit processor · FPGA

1 Introduction

In the digital world, although the binary expression and Boolean logic have become the foundation of modern computing, multi-valued or many-valued logic is still a very active field of study [1–3,5–9]. Multi-valued logics differ from binary logic by the fundamental fact that they do not restrict the number of truth values to only two: they allow for a larger set of truth degrees. For example, 4-valued logic or quaternary logic allows four truth degrees which could be represented by four symbols. For binary logic, there are only $2^{(2\times2)} = 16$ types of two-input binary logic operations. For quaternary logic, however, there are $4^{(4\times4)} = 4,294,967,296$ types of two-input quaternary logic operations in total.

© Springer Nature Switzerland AG 2022
H. Shen et al. (Eds.): PDCAT 2021, LNCS 13148, pp. 142–149, 2022.
https://doi.org/10.1007/978-3-030-96772-7_14

It is impossible and unnecessary to design the specific circuit for each of the many types of quaternary logic operators individually.

In this paper, we propose a quaternary processor called *reconfigurable quaternary logic processor* (RQLP), where we use two binary bits to represent the four symbols of a quaternary bit. The RQLP can be built with massive processor bits. Each processor bit has a unified structure, which can be reconfigured into any specific two-input quaternary logic operator. We only have to set different reconfiguration instructions into a processor bit's reconfiguration register in order to realize different logic functions. The main contributions of this paper are summarized as follows:

- We propose a structure of RQLP with massive processor bits. The unified structure of each processor bit consists of four column operators which are gathered by an electric potential combiner. The structure of each column operator is composed of a signal selector, working enabler, reconfiguration register, reconfiguration circuit, output enabler, and output generator. The RQLP has the ability of performing all types of quaternary logic operations.
- We design a prototype circuit for RQLP and its processor bits. Each processor bit is equipped with a reconfiguration register. We use reconfiguration instructions to determine specific logic functions for column operators. The logic function of each processor bit can be changed (or reconfigured) while the RQLP is running, by simply rewriting another reconfiguration instruction into its reconfiguration register.
- We implement a 1-bit RQLP (with only one processor bit) on FPGA device, and verify the effectiveness and reconfigurability of the proposed processor structure and circuit. Based on the 1-bit RQLP, we then realize a many-bit RQLP with 1,696 processor bits.

Compared with conventional binary 64-bit processors, the proposed many-bit RQLP have three merits. Firstly, it can perform much more (almost 4.3 billion) types of logic operations via hardware. Secondly, the massive processor bits on a single RQLP can be divided and assigned to different tasks for parallel processing, where any group of processor bits can be configured into a user-specific operator. Thirdly, the processor bits can be regrouped and reassigned, while the hardware logic function of each processor bit can be reconfigured.

These merits will bring new algorithms and new ways to deal with difficult problems in various fields, where many potential applications can be envisaged. For example, tasks like quaternary logic operations, quaternary symbol transformation and quaternary decision-making, which can only be processed slowly by software in the current binary computers, will be accelerated to finish in one clock cycle on a quaternary logic operator. Currently, we are developing a novel encryption chip that utilizes 4^{16} types of quaternary logic operators to achieve *one-time pad* encrypted real-time communication.

Moreover, the prototype circuit for RQLP and its processor bits can be simplified to implement reconfigurable ternary (i.e. 3-valued) logic processor, or it can be extended to implement reconfigurable n-valued logic processor (where

$n > 4$). We hope RQLP and its construction method will provide new insight into the development of modern processors.

2   Reconfigurable Quaternary Logic Processor

There are various expression methods for n-valued logic. The most common method is one-dimensional n-valued expression. That is, a logic value is expressed by one symbol, where the symbol has n different possible values. For example, a one-symbol set for n-valued logic expression could be $\{0,1,2,...,n-1\}$, where $n = 4$ in the case of quaternary logic expression. However, the values of n-valued logic may be alternatively expressed by multiple symbols, which is a mathematically equivalent information expression form. For example, two binary values could be used for quaternary logic expression, and it is called "2-binary-bit" expression in the rest of this paper. We use 2-binary-bit set $\{00, 01, 10, 11\}$ for quaternary logic expression during the design of RQLP in the rest of this paper. The advantage of adopting this expression form is that it can make full use of existing binary logic devices to make n-valued logic operators in a convenient and inexpensive way.

The design of RQLP starts from a truth table for quaternary logic operation. Conventionally, the truth table for a quaternary logic operation is a 4×4 square table, such as the four examples shown in Table 1 where A and B are two inputs while C is the output. Each A, or B, or C is represented by the 2-binary-bit quaternary logic expression set $\{00, 01, 10, 11\}$.

2.1   General Structure

The RQLP is designed to have massive processor bits, where each processor bit corresponds to a quaternary logic unit that can perform any types of the 4^{16} quaternary logic operations. Inspired by the *decrease-radix design principle* [11] and the *reconfigurable ternary optical processor* [4,10], we design a general structure called *column operator* with four different forms.

Figure 1 shows a schematic diagram of the structure of an m-bit RQLP. Each processor bit includes four column operators, such as ③ and ④, which are connected by an electric potential combiner with four input terminals, such as ⑪. The output terminal of the kth column operator is connected to the kth input terminal of the electric potential combiner, where $k \in \{0,1,2,3\}$. The output of the ith electric potential combiner forms the output signal of the ith processor bit, where $i \in \{0, 1, ..., m-1\}$. In Fig. 1, the output of the kth column operator included in the ith processor bit is denoted as $C_i{}^k$ ($i \in \{0, 1, ..., m-1\}$, and $k \in \{0, 1, 2, 3\}$).

Each of the four column operators mainly includes six components, namely output enabler ⑤, output generator ⑥, A-signal selector ⑦, working enabler ⑧, reconfiguration register ⑨, and reconfiguration circuit ⑩.

The working procedure of the m-bit RQLP is based on the reconfiguration register. A reconfiguration instruction, which can be written into the reconfiguration register by using the line G, determines a specific function for the

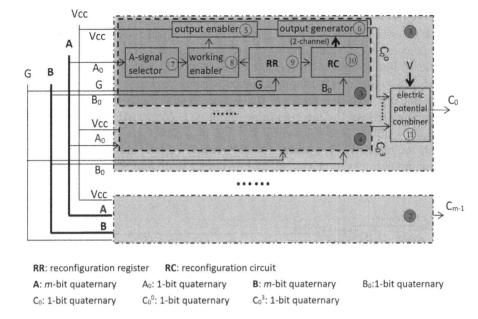

RR: reconfiguration register   RC: reconfiguration circuit

A: m-bit quaternary A_0: 1-bit quaternary   **B**: m-bit quaternary B_0:1-bit quaternary

C_0: 1-bit quaternary C_0^0: 1-bit quaternary C_0^3: 1-bit quaternary

Fig. 1. Schematic diagram of the structure of an m-bit RQLP.

corresponding column operator, that is, to implement one of the 4^{16} types of quaternary logic operations or no operation.

The electric potential combiner of the ith processor bit is designed to combine output signals of all the column operators of that processor bit, and to form a final output signal of that processor bit. Since no matter what value the ith bit of input data **A** is, it will satisfy the selection requirement of one of the four A-signal selectors among the four column operators. Hence, the processor bit can definitely complete the logic operation for any value of the ith bit of the input data **A** and **B**. (Note that the inputs **A** and **B** are m-bit quaternary data.)

The many processor bits can be divided into different groups with flexible group size, where each group can be reconfigured into a specific quaternary logic operator with k ($k \leq m$) processor bits according to user's need, by writing corresponding reconfiguration instructions into the reconfiguration registers. After the task is finished, the many processor bits can be re-grouped and reconfigured.

2.2   Circuit of RQLP's Processor Bit

Based on the general structure, we design a circuit structure of the RQLP's processor bit. An m-bit RQLP (Fig. 1) contains m processor bits, where each processor bit has the same structure (Fig. 2) and working principle. Here, we only give the structure of the ith ($i \in \{0, 1, ..., m-1\}$) processor bit, as shown in Fig. 2. Each processor bit includes four column operators (⑬, ⑭, ⑮, and ⑯) and one electric potential combiner (⑰). The differences among the four column operators only lie in that A-signal selectors (㉑, ㊵, ㊶, and ㊷) have different structures: ㉑ is a NOR gate whose two input terminals are respectively connected to A_i^1 (high bit of the ith line of input data **A**) and A_i^0 (low bit of the ith line of input data **A**); ㊵ is an AND gate with one inverted input terminal, where the inverted input terminal is connected to A_i^1 while the other input terminal is connected to A_i^0; ㊶ is also an AND gate with one inverted input terminal, where the inverted input terminal is connected to A_i^0 while the other input terminal is connected to A_i^1; ㊷ is an AND gate whose two input terminals are respectively connected to A_i^0 and A_i^1. The remaining parts of the four column operators are identical, and we depict them only in the first column operator in Fig. 2.

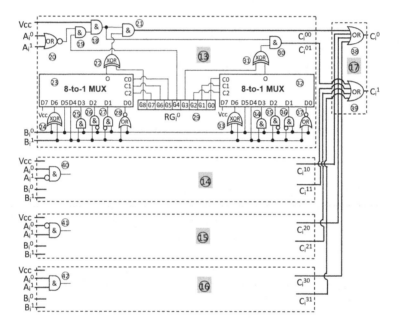

Fig. 2. Schematic diagram of the structure of a RQLP's processor bit. The structure is only for one processor bit where other processor bits are the same.

Now we explain the first column operator in detail. It includes an A-signal selector, a working enabler, a reconfiguration register, a reconfiguration circuit, an output enabler, and an output generator. The A-signal selector is implemented by a NOR gate ㉑ . The working enabler is implemented by an AND gate ⑲ . The reconfiguration register is implemented by a register ㉙ denoted as RG_i^0. (Similarly, RG_i^k is used to denote the reconfiguration register in the kth column operator of the ith processor bit.) The reconfiguration circuit consists of two components. One component is formed by an 8-to-1 multiplexer ㉓; two XOR gates ㉒ and ㉔; an AND gate ㉕ ; two AND gates with inverted input terminal ㉖ and ㉗; and a NOR gate ㉘. Similarly, the other component is formed by an 8-to-1 multiplexer ㉜; two XOR gates ㉛ and ㉝; an AND gate ㉞; two AND gates with inverted input terminal ㉟ and ㊱; and a NOR gate ㊲. The output enabler is implemented by an AND gate ⑱. The output generator is implemented by two AND gates ㉑ and ㉚.

The connections among the parts in the column operator are as shown in Fig. 2. For the two 8-to-1 multiplexers, D0~D7 are eight input signals while C0~C2 are three select lines. Eight input lines of the 8-to-1 multiplexer are respectively connected to one circuit for filtering the input data B_i signal. According to the circuit structure and the working principle of column operators, we can work out the reconfiguration instructions for all 16 possible situations of a column operator. Then, each of the m processor bits can be reconfigured into one bit of quaternary logic operator, so that the entire processor becomes a composite operator having various quaternary logic units.

3   Experiments

To verify the effectiveness of the proposed RQLP, we implement the circuit structure on an embedded Zynq AX7020 FPGA device. We make column operator a module, and we connect four column operator modules according to Fig. 2 to form a RQLP's processor bit. As for resource utilization, it takes 18 LUTs and 36 FFs to implement a processor bit.

Table 1. Truth tables of four tested quaternary logic operations.

C1C0　　A1A0 　 B1B0	Test No.1				Test No.2				Test No.3				Test No.4			
	00	01	10	11	00	01	10	11	00	01	10	11	00	01	10	11
00	00	01	10	11	11	10	01	00	01	10	11	10	01	10		00
01	00	01	10	11	00	11	10	01	10	10	00	01	10	11		10
10	00	01	10	11	01	00	11	10	11	00	00	11	00	01		10
11	00	01	10	11	10	01	00	11	10	01	11	01	00	10		11

We test the processor bit on four quaternary logic operations, whose truth tables are listed in Table 1. Test case No. 1 is a relatively simpler truth table where each column has the same value. Test case No. 2 is a complex truth table where each column and each row all have four different values. Test case No.3 is randomly chosen from all 4^{16} quaternary logic operations. Test case No.4 is also a randomly chosen truth table but with the third column deleted.

Based on the circuit of RQLP's processor bit and the working principle of column operators, we obtain the reconfiguration instructions of the four test cases. Each tested quaternary logic operation has four 9-bit (G8–G0) reconfiguration instructions for the four column operators, forming a 36-bit reconfiguration instruction for the processor bit.

In order to verify the reconfigurability of the proposed RQLP, we test the four quaternary logic operations one-by-one without turning off the FPGA device, so that the processor reconfiguration is done at runtime. For each test case, we firstly input its 36-bit reconfiguration instruction, finishing processor reconfiguration. Then, we input all the 16 A–B combinations one-by-one and check the output results. After the first test case is finished, we continue to test the second one in the same way, without turning the FPGA device off and on again. All the observed outputs of tested cases are consistent with the expected values in Table 1.

The above experiments prove that, for the proposed RQLP, 1) the processor structure and reconfiguration circuit function correctly; 2) the reconfiguration instructions are effective; 3) the processor reconfigurability is valid.

Based on the implemented processor bit, we build a RQLP with massive processor bits. We make 32 processor bits together as a group, where we use a 5:32 address decoder for addressing the 36-bit reconfiguration register of each processor bit. Then, we combine 53 groups using a 6:64 address decoder to form a RQLP with 1,696 processor bits in total. As for resource utilization, this many-bit RQLP takes 31,436 LUTs and 79,938 FFs on the FPGA device.

4   Conclusions and Future Work

In this paper, we have proposed a general structure of RQLP. We have instantiated the general structure, and designed a prototype circuit for processor bit. We have proposed to use reconfiguration instructions to determine specific logic functions for column operators, that is, to implement one of the 4^{16} types of quaternary logic operations. We have implemented a 1-bit RQLP using FPGA and tested it with four carefully selected examples of quaternary logic operations. Based on the 1-bit RQLP, we have also implemented a many-bit RQLP with 1,696 processor bits. Experimental results have verified the effectiveness and reconfigurability of the RQLP structure and circuit.

As a starting work in RQLP, we currently use FPGA to verify the correctness and functionality of our circuit design. In future, we will gradually perform timing and speed evaluation, ISA design, programming model, etc. We will also experimentally compare RQLP with other architectures such as normal CPU or GPU implementations for executing specific applications or benchmarks. The ultimate goal is ASIC chip of multi-valued processor with reconfigurability. On the one hand, we should study how to make the reconfigurable multi-valued processor cooperate seamlessly with current CPUs and GPUs. On the other hand, we need to find more interesting applications that can take full advantage of this new class of processors.

Acknowledgements. The work was supported by the "Fundamental Research Funds for the Central Universities" from Donghua University under grants no. 2232020D-36, the "Shanghai Pujiang Program" from Shanghai Municipal Human Resources and Social Security Bureau under grants no.21PJD001, the "Young Teacher Research Startup Fund" from Donghua University under grants no.112-07-0053079.

References

1. Bhattacharjee, D., Kim, W., Chattopadhyay, A., Waser, R., Rana, V.: Multi-valued and fuzzy logic realization using taox memristive devices. Sci. Rep. **8**(1), 1–10 (2018)
2. Bykovsky, A.Y.: A multiple-valued logic for implementing a random oracle and the position-based cryptography. J. Russ. Laser Res. **40**(2), 173–183 (2019)
3. Homma, N., Saito, K., Aoki, T.: Formal design of multiple-valued arithmetic algorithms over galois fields and its application to cryptographic processor. In: 2012 IEEE 42nd International Symposium on Multiple-Valued Logic, pp. 110–115. IEEE (2012)
4. Jin, Y., Wang, H., Ouyang, S., Zhou, Y., Shen, Y., Peng, J., Liu, X.: Principles, structures, and implementation of reconfigurable ternary optical processors. Sci. China Inf. Sci. **54**(11), 2236–2246 (2011)
5. Kazakova, N., Sokolov, A.: Spectral and nonlinear properties of the complete quaternary code. In: CPITS pp. 76–86 (2020)
6. Novák, V.: A formal theory of intermediate quantifiers. Fuzzy Sets Syst. **159**(10), 1229–1246 (2008)
7. Roy, J.N., Chattopadhyay, T.: All-optical quaternary logic based information processing: challenges and opportunities. In: Design and Architectures for Digital Signal Processing, pp. 81–109. InTech (2013)
8. Stoilos, G., Stamou, G., Pan, J.Z., Tzouvaras, V., Horrocks, I.: Reasoning with very expressive fuzzy description logics. J. Artif. Intell. Res. **30**, 273–320 (2007)
9. Straccia, U.: Reasoning within fuzzy description logics. J. Artif. Intell. Res. **14**, 137–166 (2001)
10. Wang, H., Song, K.: Simulative method for the optical processor reconfiguration on a dynamically reconfigurable optical platform. Appl. Opt. **51**(2), 167–175 (2012)
11. Yan, J., Jin, Y., Zuo, K.: Decrease-radix design principle for carrying/borrowing free multi-valued and application in ternary optical computer. Sci. China Ser. F Inf. Sci. **51**(10), 1415–1426 (2008)

A 3D Dubins Curve Constructing Method Based on Particle Swarm Optimization

Cheng Ji[ID], Chu Wang[ID], Mingyan Song[ID], and Fengmin Wang$^{(\boxtimes)}$[ID]

Beijing Jinghang Research Institute of Computing and Communication,
Beijing 100074, People's Republic of China
casic_wfm@163.com

Abstract. The navigation error of aircraft increases in task. Aircraft has to correct the navigation error under structure constraints to avoid path deviation caused by navigation error. Aircraft path planning with navigation correction under the turning radius constraint is a challenge for traditional path planning methods. In this paper, we propose a 3D Dubins curve constructing method which can draw a smooth path in 3D space for the aircraft, next we extend Dynamic Programming for Navigation Error Correction method by 3D Dubins curves to abtain a feasible path under the constraints of turning radius, and then we improve particle swarm optimization method to compute an almost optimal Dubins curve. Finally our algorithm return a feasible smooth path with approximately the optimal length for the path planning problem with navigation correction under the turning radius constraint.

Keywords: Path planning · Dubins curve · Particle swarm optimization

1 Introduction

Aircraft path planning is a multi-objective optimization problem involving in collision avoiding, complicated landform, structure constraint, risk avoiding and so on. Aircraft path planning is always based on many factors, such as turning radius and climb ability of aircraft. Aircraft path planning has been widely applied in many tasks, such as topographic survey [1], war information reconnaissance [2], electronic interference [3], material placement [4] and so on. The solution of aircraft path planning can be devided into two parts: the first one is to choose the regions of feasible path; the second one is to calculate the aircraft trajectory planning. The regions of feasible path have already been chosen in [5], but the aircraft trajectory planning problem remains to be solved.

For an aircraft trajectory planning strategy, turning radius is an important factor. Many methods aim to compute a feasible aircraft path under the constraint of turning radius, such as the Dubins curve [6] and Clothoid curve [7].

Supported by NNSF of China under Grant No. 11901544.

H. Shen et al. (Eds.): PDCAT 2021, LNCS 13148, pp. 150–160, 2022.
https://doi.org/10.1007/978-3-030-96772-7_15

[8] extended continuous Bezier curves along Z-axis to construct 3D Dubins curve, which is derived from two-dimensional Dubins curve.

In this paper, we propose a novel method to compute the feasible path under the constraint of turning radius in 3D space. We have select feasible navigation error regions based on DyProg [5]. We parameterize a feasible path based on dubins curve under the condition of smoothness and coplanarity. We optimize the parameter by PSO to have the shortest feasible path.

This paper is organized as follows: In Sect. 2, we state the problem of path planning with navigation error correction formally. In Sect. 3, we show that the turning radius constraint is considered in the problem of path planning with navigation error correction, and then we propose the 3D Dubins curve to describe the aircraft path with turning radius and improve PSO to calculate the length of this path. In Sect. 4, we show and analysis the experimental results of the proposed methods on simulated data. In Sect. 5, we conclude our work and show some prospects in future.

2   Problem Formulation

Let A and B be the departure and destination respectively. For a path p from A to B, we continue to use the error correction restriction [5] as the condition restriction of path p, and define $\{p_i\}_{i=1}^n$ as the collection of error correction regions in p. We add a new restriction that turning radius R is no fewer than r.

We consider the problem that how to compute a feasible path such that both the number of error correction regions and the length of the path is minimal.

3   Proposed Methods for Path Planning with Dubins Curve

The feasible path p has been calculated in [5]. In this section, we show the method to compute the feasible path by 3D Dubins curve. In subsection A, we propose a three-dimensional dubins curve to solve the problem of path planning with turning radius. In subsection B, we propose Dynamic Programming for Navigation Error Correction (DyProg) [5] based on 3D Dubins curve to calculate the feasible path. In subsection C, we improve PSO to compute a feasible path with almost minimal length.

As the calculation method is similar, we regard A as p_0 and B as p_{n+1} in the calculation process.

3.1   Smooth Path with Dubins Curve

In this section, we propose a novel method to computing a smooth path from A to B which goes through given error correction regions $\{p_i\}_{i=1}^n$. We construct two-dimensional dubins curve for each adjacent error correction regions. And then, we construct a three-dimensional dubins curve by splicing multiple two-dimensional dubins curves together smoothly.

To construct two-dimensional dubins curves, we need to change three-dimensional parameters to the corresponding two-dimensional parameters. And we need to maintain a linear change in velocity to construct a smooth path. The two-dimensional Dubins curve is smooth, and then we need to keep the velocity in each error correction regions consistent. Define the velocity at p_i is $\overrightarrow{v_i}$, so as to $\overrightarrow{v_{i+1}}$. The Dubins curve is from p_i to p_{i+1}, and $\overrightarrow{v_i}$, $\overrightarrow{v_{i+1}}$ are both in the plane γ:

$$\overrightarrow{p_i p_{i+1}} \cdot (\overrightarrow{v_i} \times \overrightarrow{v_{i+1}}) = 0. \tag{1}$$

We convert 3D space to two-dimensional plane with Gram-Schmidt Orthogonalization to calculate Dubins curve. For each case from p_i to p_{i+1}, we create a two-dimensional coordinate system. We define p_i as the origin point. The following are $\overrightarrow{x}$ and $\overrightarrow{y}$:

$$
\begin{aligned}
\overrightarrow{x} &= \frac{\overrightarrow{p_i p_{i+1}}}{\|\overrightarrow{p_i p_{i+1}}\|} \\
\overrightarrow{y'} &= \overrightarrow{v_i} - (\overrightarrow{v_i} \cdot \overrightarrow{x})\overrightarrow{x} \\
\overrightarrow{y} &= \frac{\overrightarrow{y'}}{|\overrightarrow{y'}|}
\end{aligned}
\tag{2}
$$

We transform the point $Q'(Q'_X, Q'_Y)$ in the two-dimensional plane into the point Q three-dimensional space by the following formula:

$$Q = p_i + Q'_X \cdot \overrightarrow{x} + Q'_Y \cdot \overrightarrow{y} \tag{3}$$

In the two-dimensional plane, p_i is $(0,0)$ and p_{i+1} is $(\|\overrightarrow{p_i p_{i+1}}\|, 0)$. We define the incidence angle of the dubin curve as η and the exit angle as $|\lambda|$. We calculate η and $|\lambda|$ by the following formula:

$$
\begin{aligned}
\eta &= arccos(\frac{\overrightarrow{v_i} \cdot \overrightarrow{p_i p_{i+1}}}{\|\overrightarrow{v_i}\| \|\overrightarrow{p_i p_{i+1}}\|}) \\
\lambda' &= arccos(\frac{\overrightarrow{v_{i+1}} \cdot \overrightarrow{p_i p_{i+1}}}{\|\overrightarrow{v_{i+1}}\| \|\overrightarrow{p_i p_{i+1}}\|}) \\
\lambda &= \lambda' \quad if \quad \overrightarrow{v_{i+1}} \cdot \overrightarrow{y} \geq 0 \\
\lambda &= -\lambda' \quad if \quad \overrightarrow{v_{i+1}} \cdot \overrightarrow{y} < 0 \\
\eta &\in (0, \pi), \lambda \in (-\pi, \pi)
\end{aligned}
\tag{4}
$$

The two-dimensional Dubins curve can be used to obtain a aircraft path that satisfies the constraints of η, λ, $\|\overrightarrow{p_i p_{i+1}}\|$.

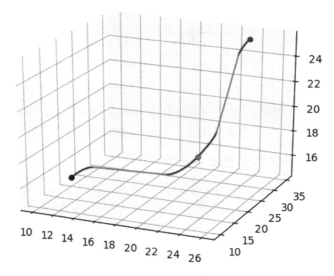

Fig. 1. 3D Dubins curve

In Fig. 1, we show a 3D Dubins curve. We set three error correction regions and give the direction of the velocity of each error correction region, then get a smooth 3D curve through the Dubins curve.

3.2 Dynamic Programming Algorithm with Turning Radius Constraint

We consider improving DyProg to calculate a feasible aircraft path with turning radius. The aircraft cannot change the direction of velocity immediately, so we add a turning radius constraint to this discrete constraint optimization problem. Since the path from p_i to p_j is determined by the directions of $\overrightarrow{v_i}$ and $\overrightarrow{v_j}$, we consider the upper bound of the length of the path from p_i to p_j to calculate the navigation error instead of the Euclidean Distance from p_i to p_j in DyProg.

In our case, the distance between two error correction regions is far shorter than turning radius, define the path in Dubins Set $D = \{LSL, RSR, RSL, LSR\}$, the shortest path in D as the shortest Dubins curve. Redefine the distance between p_i and p_j as $d_{ij} = \frac{\|p_i p_j\|}{R}$, η and λ still as above. The upper bound of the Dubins curve $Dubins_{(max)}$ as follows [9]:

$$
\begin{aligned}
Dubins(max) &= min(D) \\
&\leq min(RSR, LSL) \\
&= |\eta - \lambda| mod(2\pi) + P \\
&\leq 2\pi + P
\end{aligned}
\tag{5}
$$

P in RSR means as follows:

$$P(rsr) = \sqrt{2 + d^2 - 2cos(\eta - \lambda) + 2d(sin\lambda - sin\eta)}$$
$$\leq \sqrt{2 + d^2 - 2 * (-1) + 2d(1 + 1)} \tag{6}$$
$$= d + 2$$

From 5 and 6, we can get

$$Dubins(max) = 2\pi + d + 2$$

Define the length of path from p_i to p_j as len_{ij}:

$$len_{ij} = (2\pi + 2) * R + \|p_i p_j\| \tag{7}$$

We can get the feasible error correction regions by DyProg, but need to consider how to calculate the length of specific aircraft path.

3.3 Improved Partical Swarm Optimization

We describe the velocity $\vec{v_i}$ of each error correction regions p_i by (μ_i, ψ_i) and compute a smooth path from A to B. We calculate the aircraft path with minimal length through optimization $\{(\mu_i, \psi_i)\}_{i=0}^{n+2}$ by PSO [10]. Assuming the direction of velocity the aircraft at each region, we can describe the aircraft path between two error correction regions by Dubins curve to get a complete aircraft path. The aircraft path changes with the direction of velocity the aircraft at each region. We optimize the aircraft path by PSO to get a set of direction of velocity to make the aircraft path as short as possible. Then our problem becomes the Optimization Problem [11]:

$$min(sum(dubins(p_i, p_{i+1}))) \tag{8}$$

Two-dimensional Dubins curve describing aircraft path needs to ensure that the aircraft paths between every two error correction regions are coplanar, so we need to add 1 to 8:

$$min(sum(dubins(p_i, p_{i+1})))$$
$$s.t. \quad \overrightarrow{p_i p_{i+1}} \cdot (\vec{v_i} \times \overrightarrow{v_{i+1}}) = 0(i = 0, 1, 2, ..., n + 2)$$

Then we turn Optimization Problem 8 into:

$$min(sum(dubins(p_i, p_{i+1}) + |\overrightarrow{p_i p_{i+1}} \cdot (\vec{v_i} \times \overrightarrow{v_{i+1}})|)) \tag{9}$$

The problem becomes Optimization Problem 9. Considering the direction of velocity the aircraft at each error correction region pointing to the centre of ball which contains all error correction regions, we can assume the direction of $\vec{v_i}$ in polar coordinates. $\vec{v_i}$ can be defined by (μ_i, ψ_i) as follows:

$$x_i = cos\mu_i sin\psi_i$$
$$y_i = sin\mu_i sin\psi_i$$
$$z_i = cos\psi_i$$

$\overrightarrow{p_ip_{i+1}}$ can be defined as follows:

$$\overrightarrow{p_ip_{i+1}} = (\overrightarrow{p_ip_{i+1}}[x], \overrightarrow{p_ip_{i+1}}[y], \overrightarrow{p_ip_{i+1}}[z])$$

We adjust $\{(\mu_i, \psi_i)\}_{i=0}^{n+2}$ to calculate the aircraft path with minimal length, so we optimize $2n + 4$ parameter by PSO.

Optimization Problem 9 is difficult to accurately guarantee Constraints 1. If coplanarity cannot be guaranteed, we cannot characterize the 3D aircraft path. We propose the improved PSO to solve the problem of non-coplanarity. For each Dubins curve, the coplanar condition is Constraints 1. v_i and v_{i+1} both contain two values. In the ith curve, if we have μ_i, ψ_i and μ_{i+1}, then we calculate ψ_{i+1} by the Constraints 1:

$$\begin{vmatrix} \overrightarrow{p_ip_{i+1}}[x] & \overrightarrow{p_ip_{i+1}}[y] & \overrightarrow{p_ip_{i+1}}[z] \\ cos\mu_i sin\psi_i & sin\mu_i sin\psi_i & cos\psi_i \\ cos\mu_{i+1} sin\psi_{i+1} & sin\mu_{i+1} sin\psi_{i+1} & cos\psi_{i+1} \end{vmatrix} = 0 \qquad (10)$$

For simplicity, define $equ1, equ2, equ3, equ4, equ5, equ6$ as follows:

$$equ1 = \overrightarrow{p_ip_{i+1}}[x] sin\mu_i sin\psi_i cos\psi_{i+1}$$
$$equ2 = \overrightarrow{p_ip_{i+1}}[y] cos\psi_i cos\mu_{i+1} sin\psi_{i+1}$$
$$equ3 = \overrightarrow{p_ip_{i+1}}[z] cos\mu_i sin\psi_i sin\mu_{i+1} sin\psi_{i+1}$$
$$equ4 = \overrightarrow{p_ip_{i+1}}[x] cos\psi_i sin\mu_{i+1} sin\psi_{i+1}$$
$$equ5 = \overrightarrow{p_ip_{i+1}}[y] cos\mu_i sin\psi_i cos\psi_{i+1}$$
$$equ6 = \overrightarrow{p_ip_{i+1}}[z] sin\mu_i sin\psi_i cos\mu_{i+1} sin\psi_{i+1}$$

Constraints 10 equal to:

$$equ1 + equ2 + equ3 - equ4 - equ5 - equ6 = 0$$

For simplicity, define $equ7, equ8, equ9$ as follows:

$$equ7 = cos\mu_i sin\psi_i \overrightarrow{p_ip_{i+1}}[y] - sin\mu_i sin\psi_i \overrightarrow{p_ip_{i+1}}[x]$$
$$equ8 = cos\mu_i sin\psi_i \overrightarrow{p_ip_{i+1}}[z] sin\mu_{i+1} - sin\mu_i sin\psi_i \overrightarrow{p_ip_{i+1}}[z] cos\mu_{i+1}$$
$$equ9 = cos\psi_i \overrightarrow{p_ip_{i+1}}[x] sin\mu_{i+1} - cos\psi_i \overrightarrow{p_ip_{i+1}}[y] cos\mu_{i+1}$$

Then we can repersent ψ_{i+1} with $equ7, equ8, equ9$ as follows:

$$\psi_{i+1} = arctan(\frac{equ1}{equ2 - equ3}) \qquad (11)$$

For the first curve, we assume μ_1, μ_{i+1} and ψ_1, and then ψ_{i+1} can be derived. For the ith curve, we assume μ_i and μ_{i+1}. ψ_i of the p_i region is obtained from the $i-1$th curve, and ψ_{i+1} can be derived. And then our optimization problem become the Optimization Problem 9. The PSO sets two values at p_0 and one value at the other error correction regions, so we can optimize $n+3$ parameter and calculate the other $n+1$ parameter by 11.

Algorithm 1. Improved Partical Swarm Optimization For Track Planning

---

Inputs: $\{p_i\}_{i=0}^{n-1}$, a feasible path p
Outputs: A 3D aircraft path op
Initialization: set PSO parameters, iteration N, particle initial position and velocity, particle initial position fitness
    Step 1: Update and iterate particles:
        while $iterationnumber < N$ **do**
            Update particle speed and position
            Calculating particle fitness $fitness(x)$
            Update particle swarm individual optimal value and population optimal value
        end while
        Go to Step 2.
    Step 2: Calculate 3D Dubins curve:
        for $i = 0$ to $length(p)$ **do**
            $T, Q = dubins(p_i, p_{i+1})$
            Establishing a two-dimensional coordinate system
            $P_i(0,0)$ $P_{i+1}(dis, 0)$
            $V_i(cos\eta_i, sin\lambda_i)$ $V_{i+1}(cos\eta_{i+1}, sin\lambda_{i+1})$
            radius of Dubins curve
            $R_i(sin\eta_i, -cos\lambda_i)$ $R_{i+1}(sin\eta_{i+1}, -cos\lambda_{i+1})$
            $Label1, Label2 = 1$
            if Incident Dubins curve turn left **then**
                $Label1 = -1$
            end if
            if Exit Dubins curve turn left **then**
                $Label2 = -1$
            end if
            circle center of Dubins curve
            $r_i = P_i + Label1 * R_i * R$
            $r_{i+1} = P_{i+1} + Label2 * R_{i+1} * R$
            incident Dubins curve
            $arc_i = r_i + R * (R_i * cos\tau + V_i * sin\tau), \tau \in (\pi, \pi - T)$
            3D incident Dubins curve
            $Arc_i = p_i + arc_i[0] * x_{axis} + arc_i[1] * y_{axis}$
            exit Dubins curve
            $arc_{i+1} = r_{i+1} + R * (R_{i+1} * cos\tau + V_{i+1} * sin\tau), \tau \in (\pi, \pi + Q)$
            3D exit Dubins curve
            $Arc_{i+1} = p_{i+1} + arc_{i+1}[0] * x_{axis} + arc_{i+1}[1] * y_{axis}$
            $\tau = \pi - T, a_1 = Arc_i$
            $\tau = \pi + Q, a_2 = Arc_{i+1}$
            $Str = a_1 a_2$
            $op \cup \{Arc_i, Arc_{i+1}, Str\}$
        end for

return op

fitness(x):   **for** $i = 0$ to $length(p)$ **do**

$\quad\vec{v_i}[x] = cos\mu_i sin\psi_i$

$\quad\vec{v_i}[y] = sin\mu_i sin\psi_i$

$\quad\vec{v_i}[z] = cos\psi_i$

$\quad$calculate ψ by Formula 11

$\quad Fitness+ = dubins(p_i, p_{i+1})$

end for

return Fitness

dubins(p_i, p_{i+1}): $\eta = arccos(\frac{\vec{v_i} \cdot \overrightarrow{p_i p_{i+1}}}{\|\vec{v_i}\|\|\overrightarrow{p_i p_{i+1}}\|})$

$\quad\vec{v_i} = \frac{\vec{v_i}}{\|\vec{v_i}\|}$ as x_{axis} positive direction

$\quad y_{axis} = \vec{v_i} - (x_{axis} \cdot \overrightarrow{p_i p_{i+1}})\overrightarrow{p_i p_{i+1}}$

$\quad y_{axis} = \frac{y_{axis}}{\|y_{axis}\|}$ as y_{axis} positive direction

$\quad|\lambda| = arccos(\frac{\overrightarrow{v_{i+1}} \cdot \overrightarrow{p_i p_{i+1}}}{\|\overrightarrow{v_{i+1}}\|\|\overrightarrow{p_i p_{i+1}}\|})$

$\quad$**if** $\overrightarrow{v_{i+1}} \cdot y_{axis} < 0$ **then**

$\quad\quad\lambda = -|\lambda|$

$\quad$**end if**

$\quad d_{i,i+1} = \frac{\|p_i p_{i+1}\|}{R}$

choose the case of the Dubins curve with η, λ, dis by scheme

calculate the Dubins curve with η, λ, dis and case by formula

---

4   Experiment

In this section, we show the experimental results of our methods on simulated data. In our experiment, we show that Algorithm 1 processes the feasible path into 3D Dubins curve. More details will be shown later in this section. First, let us see the set up of the experiment.

4.1   Experimental Set Up

The datasets of our experiments are simulated and there exists at least one feasible path for each of them. All other error correction regions are generated randomly. In our experiment, we choose two group of simulated parameters: Parameters I and Parameter II. The details of Parameter I are shown as follows:

$$\alpha_1 = 25, \quad \alpha_2 = 15, \quad \delta = 0.001, \quad r = 200$$
$$\beta_1 = 20, \quad \beta_2 = 25, \quad \theta = 30$$

The details of Parameter II are show as follows:

$$\alpha_1 = 20, \quad \alpha_2 = 10, \quad \delta = 0.001, \quad r = 200$$
$$\beta_1 = 15, \quad \beta_2 = 20, \quad \theta = 20$$

From the results of simulations, there are more feasible paths for Parameter I than that for Parameter II if the number of error correction regions is similar. In our experiment, we simulate datasets 1 to 8 whose parameters are shown in Table 1:

Table 1. Parameters of simulated data 1 to 8

No.	Parmeter	Number of error correction regions
1	I	200–400
2	I	400–600
3	I	600–800
4	I	800–1000
5	II	200–400
6	II	400–600
7	II	600–800
8	II	800–1000

In our experiment, our proposed methods are shown as follows:

- DyProg2: DyProg with turning radius constraint.
- IPSO: 3D Dubins curve calculating which is shown in Algorithm 1

In our experiment, the performance of feasible paths is measured by the length of path and running time (RT) in the same hardware environment.

4.2 Experimental Results on Simulated Data

In this section, we calculate the 3D Dubins curve by our methods DyProg2 and IPSO. In DyProg2, we use 7 instead of the Euclidean Distance and then run DyProg. We can get the error correction regions of a feasible path. And then we use the error correction regions to calculate the optimized curve in IPSO. We record the path length before optimization (PLBO, Unit: km), path length after optimization (PLAO, Unit: km), straight path length (SPL, Unit: km), optimization rate (OR), RT of DyProg2 (RTOD, Unit: s) and RT of IPSO (RTOP, Unit: s) in Table 2.

The results of aircraft trajectory planning experiment is shown in Table 2. In Experiment 5, we cannot find a feasible path for the distribution of error correction regions. In the other experiments, DyProg2 and IPSO have a good performance. The optimized length of aircraft path is far less than before optimization. We subtract the SPL from the curved path which contain PLBO and PLAO, and calculate the optimization rate. The optimization rate of Parameter I is up to 85% and the Parameter I is higher than 60%. The RT of DyProg2 is less than 10 s. The RT of PSO is a little longer, but not more than 2 min.

Table 2. Experimental results of RT (Unit: s) on parameters I, II

No.	PLBO	PLAO	SPL	OR	RTOD	RTOP
1	122.17	120.64	120.41	86.67%	0.688	73.203
2	113.49	111.81	111.77	96.61%	2.281	57.719
3	113.32	111.19	111.03	93.01%	6.047	58.719
4	109.27	107.84	107.67	89.48%	8.671	54.234
5	--	--	--	--	--	--
6	118.90	116.22	115.32	75.04%	2.484	84.969
7	129.03	125.94	125.27	82.18%	5.531	90.797
8	113.81	111.99	110.89	62.30%	9.828	85.188

5 Conclusion

In this paper, we consider the problem of aircraft path planning under the constraint of turning radius. In this problem, we propose a 3D Dubins curve, and use this curve to accurately plan the aircraft path. We apply the PSO on optimizing the aircraft path length and obtain an almost optimal aircraft path. In the future, we will try to use different curves to make the feasible paths more suitable for aircraft, and use parallel and distributed computing methods to increase the speed of aircraft path planning.

References

1. Stentz, A.: Optimal and efficient path planning for partially-known environments. In: Proceedings of the 1994 IEEE International Conference on Robotics and Automation, 1994. IEEE (1994)
2. Liu, Yu.Z., Wei, X., et al.: An amphibious vehicle modeling and maneuvering path planning method suitable for military topographic maps. Wuhan Univ. J. Natural Sci. **25**(134(06)), 67–75 (2020)
3. Wang, Y., Wang, S., Tan, M.: Path generation of autonomous approach to a moving ship for unmanned vehicles. IEEE Trans. Industr. Electron. **62**(9), 5619–5629 (2015)
4. Yongwei, L.I., Hongfei, W.: Fuzzy adaptive PID control for six rotor eppo UAV. J. Hebei Univ. Sci. Technol. **38**, 59–65 (2017)
5. Song, M., Ji, C., Wang, C., et al.: A novel dynamic programming based method for path planning with navigation error correction. In: 2020 IEEE 4th Information Technology, Networking, Electronic and Automation Control Conference (ITNEC). IEEE (2020)
6. Dubins, L.E.: On curves of minimal length with a constraint on average curvature and with prescribed initial and terminal positions and tangents. Am. J. Math. **79**(3), 497–516 (1957)
7. Wensen, L.I., Guan, S., Zheng, L., et al.: A smoothing method for tool path with G 2 continuity based on clothoid curves. J. Xi'an Polytechnic Univ. (2019)

8. Cai, W., Zhang, M.: Smooth 3D Dubins curves based mobile data gathering in sparse underwater sensor networks. Sensors **18**(7), 2105 (2018)
9. Shkel, A.M., Lumelsky, V.: Classification of the Dubins set. Robot. Auton. Syst. **34**(4), 179–202 (2001)
10. Innocente, M.S., Sienz, J.: A Study of the Fundamental Parameters of Particle Swarm Optimizers (2021)
11. Gao, H., Li, Y., Zhang, H.: The analysis of alternating minimization method for double sparsity constrained optimization problem. Asia Pacific J. Oper. Res. **37**(4), 2040002 (2020)

Software Systems and Technologies

Towards Conflict-Aware Workload Co-execution on SX-Aurora TSUBASA

Riku Nunokawa[1], Yoichi Shimomura[2], Mulya Agung[3], Ryusuke Egawa[2,4], and Hiroyuki Takizawa[1,2(✉)]

[1] Graduate School of Information Sciences, Tohoku University, Sendai, Japan
nunoriku@hpc.is.tohoku.ac.jp
[2] Cyberscience Center, Tohoku University, Sendai, Japan
{shimomura32,takizawa}@tohoku.ac.jp
[3] Institute of Genetics and Cancer, University of Edinburgh, Edinburgh, UK
mulya.agung@ed.ac.uk
[4] School of Engineering, Tokyo Denki University, Tokyo, Japan
egawa@mail.dendai.ac.jp

Abstract. NEC SX-Aurora TSUBASA is the latest vector supercomputer, consisting of host processors called Vector Hosts (VHs) and vector processors called Vector Engines (VEs). The final goal of this work is to simultaneously use both VHs and VEs to increase the resource utilization and improve the system throughput by co-executing more workloads. However, performance interferences among VH and VE workloads could occur because they share some computing resources and potentially compete to use the same resource at the same time, so-called resource conflicts. As the first step to achieve efficient workload co-execution, this paper experimentally investigates the performance interference between a VH and a VE, when each of the two processors executes a different workload. Our evaluation results clearly demonstrate that some characteristics of a workload such as system call frequency can be used as a good indicator to predict if the workload can affect the performance of another co-executing workload. We believe that this will be helpful to identify a pair of workloads causing frequent resource conflicts, and thus reduce the risk of performance interference between co-executing workloads on an SX-AT system.

Keywords: Workload colocation · SX-Aurora TSUBASA · Performance interference

1 Introduction

Recently, high-performance computing systems often adopt heterogeneous system architectures equipped with different kinds of processors. NEC SX-Aurora TSUBASA (SX-AT) is one of heterogeneous computing systems, which consists of x86 processors and vector processors, called Vector Hosts (VHs) and Vector Engines (VEs), respectively [20]. A VE is physically implemented as a PCI-Express card, which is similar to an accelerator such as a graphics processing

© Springer Nature Switzerland AG 2022
H. Shen et al. (Eds.): PDCAT 2021, LNCS 13148, pp. 163–174, 2022.
https://doi.org/10.1007/978-3-030-96772-7_16

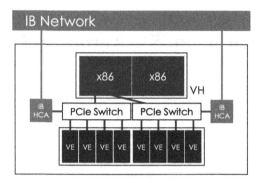

Fig. 1. The hardware configuration of a VI.

unit (GPU). On the other hand, a VH is responsible for executing the operating system (OS) and managing VEs. In one compute node, each VH could manage multiple VEs. Such a node of VHs and VEs is called a Vector Island (VI). The hardware configuration of one VI is illustrated in Fig. 1. Since a VE has a high memory bandwidth of 1.53 TB/s, VEs are expected to achieve high sustained performance at executing memory-intensive scientific computations while using the standard x86 environment provided by the VH [4,9].

Unlike other accelerators such as GPUs, a VE can execute an application as if the whole application is running on the VE. However, when the application running on a VE invokes a system call, the system call is implicitly forwarded to the VH, and processed by the OS running on the VH. In addition to the VH's CPU time for handling system calls, some other computing resources such as the VI's network bandwidth are shared by the VEs. Thus, on a large SX-AT system shared by many users, each VI is exclusively assigned to a job so as to avoid performance interferences among jobs, which could occur by sharing VHs. For example, in the AOBA system installed at Tohoku University Cyberscience Center [17], multiple jobs do not usually share one VI, and one VI might co-execute multiple jobs only if every of the jobs uses only a single VE in the VI. In such an operation policy, a job does not necessarily use all VEs in the assigned VIs, and some of VEs are thus unused during the job execution. Therefore, if multiple jobs are assigned to one VI so that more VHs and VEs are used for the execution, it is possible to increase the utilization of computing resources. However, multiple jobs running on a VI may simultaneously require the same computing resource. This is a so-called resource conflict, and could cause severe performance degradation. For this reason, understanding the performance interference between multiple jobs running on a VI is an important technical issue to achieve high efficiency on SX-AT systems.

This paper first empirically investigates the performance interference between a VH and a VE, when each of the two processors executes a different workload. Then, we discuss workload co-execution with reducing the performance interference due to resource conflicts, in order to improve the resource utilization.

Evaluation results demonstrate that some characteristics of workloads such as system call frequency can be used as a good indicator to identify a pair of workloads causing frequent resource conflicts, and thus reduce the risk of performance degradation while improving the resource utilization.

2   Resource Conflicts on an SX-Aurora TSUBASA System

This section briefly reviews the resource conflicts among VH and VE workloads co-executing in one VI.

When an application is running on a standard x86 Linux system, the application has a user memory space, which is logically different from the kernel memory space used by the OS. On the other hand, when a user memory space is assigned to an application running on a VE, unlike the standard system, the user memory space physically resides on the memory devices attached to the VE. However, even on an SX-AT system, the kernel memory space is located in the VH memory. Namely, when an application is running on a VE, its user memory space is not only logically but also physically isolated from the kernel memory space. System calls on the VE are forwarded to a dedicated process running on the VH, called a VEOS pseudo process, that actually invokes the corresponding system calls on the VH to call the OS kernel. Accordingly, when an application is running on a VE, it internally uses a VH within the VI.

Moreover, if each of a VH and a VE within one VI executes a different application, both of VH and VE workloads share the VH and have their own memory spaces, which are logically and physically isolated from each other. In this case, if the VE workload invokes a system call, the system call request is forwarded to the VEOS process and then the VH workload would be context-switched to the VEOS process so that the VH core can handle the system call from the VE workload. Since the VEOS process spends the CPU time, the VH workload execution would be delayed, degrading the VH performance. If the VH workload cannot immediately be switched to the VEOS process for any reasons, the system call from the VE workload might be delayed, degrading the VE performance. In this way, VH and VE workloads may compete to use the same computing resources such as the VH's CPU time, the VH's memory bandwidth, network and file access. Therefore, the VH and VE workloads can affect their performance each other, referred to as inter-process performance interferences.

Performance interference is expected to occur especially if a workload on either of the VH or the VE intensively uses the shared computing resources. For example, suppose that a memory-intensive workload is running on one of the VH cores. Then, if the memory bandwidth is spent out, the memory access latency of the VEOS process increases and thus the system call from the VE workload is delayed, degrading the VE performance. As in research dealing with performance interference on a single processor [19], in order to maximize the benefits of concurrency while efficiently controlling the overall performance degradation that may occur, it is necessary to clarify the characteristics of the applications that cause conflict through quantitative research. As one kind of major resource conflict, it is known that the total execution time of a workload increases due to access conflicts to the file system [2], which is one of the shared computing resources. If such a root cause of performance interferences is known in advance, it would be possible to schedule jobs so as to avoid resource conflicts among them.

3 Performance Interference by Workload Co-execution

3.1 Evaluation Setup

In this work, we experimentally investigate the effect of co-executing various VH and VE workloads on their performances, and identify the combinations of VH and VE workloads causing severe performance interferences on SX-AT. The execution time of each workload is adjusted to be almost the same. In the evaluation, popular benchmarks of Himeno [5], IOR [1], Intel MPI [6], STREAM [10], b_eff [13], MiniAMR [15], and HPL [12] are first used as VH and VE workloads for general discussions on performance interferences. After that, we further discuss the performance interferences with some tiny benchmark programs that intensively use only particular computing resources, such as the CPU time, memory bandwidth, file I/O, and network. Each benchmark program is compiled for both of a VH and a VE, and executed by using all cores in the processor. The system specifications used in the following evaluations are listed in Table 1.

Table 1. Hardware configuration of NEC SX-Aurora TSUBASA A300-8.

Vector host	Xeon Gold 6126 (12 cores) × 2
Vector engine	Type 10B (8 cores) × 8
Host channel adaptor	Mellanox HDR100 × 2
Operating system	CentOS Linux 8.1.1911
VEOS	veos-2.6.2-1.el8.x86 64
VH compiler	gcc-4.8.5
VE compiler	ncc-3.3.1

3.2 Interference Evaluation Results

We evaluate the changes in execution time when a VH and a VE within one VI co-execute the benchmark programs, expecting that the performance interference will increase the execution time. Figure 2 shows the increase in execution time of each VH benchmark program while changing the combination of VH and VE workloads. On the other hand, Fig. 3 shows the increase in execution time of each

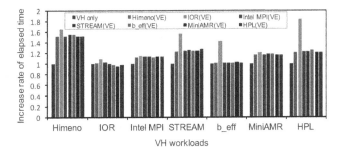

Fig. 2. Increases in elapsed time of VH workloads.

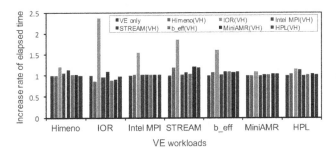

Fig. 3. Increases in elapsed time of VE workloads.

VE benchmark program. The system call frequency of each benchmark program is shown in Fig. 4.

Comparing Figs. 2 and 3, we can see that the VH performance is likely to degrade more significantly than the VE performance when co-executing VH and VE workloads. This is because the VH's computing resources such as the CPU time and memory bandwidth are spent not only by the VH workload but also the VEOS process for handling system calls from the VE workload. Since the Himeno [5] and STREAM [10] benchmarks are memory-intensive workloads, their performances are degraded mainly by sharing the memory bandwidth with the VEOS process. The HPL benchmark is compute-intensive, and thus the performance is degraded by sharing the VH's CPU time with the VEOS process. In comparison with the VH performance, the VE performance degradation is small because the VE computing resources are dedicated to each VE workload, and only the system call overhead increases by co-executing VH and VE workloads. In most scientific computing applications, most of the total execution time is spent for executing kernel loops and hence the system call overhead is not significant. Therefore, these results clearly show that co-execution of VH and VE workloads is a promising approach to improving the resource utilization without critical performance degradation except for some cases.

In Fig. 2, the execution time of every VH workload obviously increases when the IOR benchmark is running on the VE. Similarly, in Fig. 3, the execution time

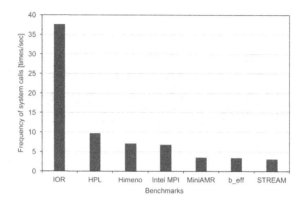

Fig. 4. System call frequency.

of every VE workload increases when the IOR benchmark is running on the VH. Thus, it is clear that the performance interference occurs if the IOR benchmark is running on either of the VH or the VE. This is because the IOR benchmark invokes system calls very frequently for measuring the file I/O performance. As shown in Fig. 4, the IOR benchmark frequently invokes system calls of file I/O operations. Therefore, it is demonstrated that frequent context-switching for handling system calls from the IOR benchmark hinders the co-executing program from consuming the CPU time as well as other shared computing resources.

In addition, VH workloads of MPI applications are generally more sensitive to resource conflicts than VE workloads. One reason for this is that only some of VH cores are spent for executing the VEOS processes and the others are not, resulting in the load imbalance among MPI processes that could lead to a long delay at synchronizations such as MPI collective communications.

The results above suggest that performance interference at co-execution of VH and VE workloads can significantly be affected by the system call frequency. To further analyze the causes of performance interferences, we develop a micro-benchmark program that invokes typical system calls at an arbitrary interval. The program is executed on one processor, either of the VH or the VE, and another benchmark program is co-executed on the other processor. In this work, we have developed tiny benchmark programs to repetitively invoke a pair of system calls at a certain time interval, and evaluate the performance degradation due to the system call overheads. The evaluation results with changing system call frequencies are shown in Figs. 5 and 6. In those figures, *Alone* indicates the execution without co-execution, and thus there is no interference. When we ran the HPL benchmark on the VH side while invoking the read and write system calls on the VE side to exchange 10 KB of data every 100 ms, the performance drop is too large to finish the execution for time measurement. The results clearly indicate that the system call frequency correlates to performance interference. It is because a system call could cause context-switching, switching between kernel and user modes, and access shared computing resources on the VH side via the system call. These results demonstrate that the system call frequency is a good indicator to detect if a workload can degrade the performance of another co-executing workload.

3.3 Avoidance of Performance Interferences

The evaluation results discussed so far have clarified that the system call frequency of a workload can be used to quantify the risk of degrading the performance of co-executing workloads. If a job scheduler knows the system call frequency of each job in advance, the job scheduler might be able to find a combination of jobs that can safely share VIs for co-execution. Since the main purpose of this paper is to experimentally investigate the performance interferences at workload co-execution on an SX-AT system, such a job scheduling mechanism will be discussed in our future work.

Even if a pseudo VEOS process running on the VH core invokes system calls so frequently to cause conflicts, it does not significantly affect the memory access latency nor bandwidth. Figures 7 and 8 show that co-execution of VH and VE workloads (lmbench [11]) does not drastically affect their sustained memory bandwidths, while the overhead of context switching obviously increases with the number of co-running processes and thus the context switching frequency. Those results indicate that, on the VH side, one main factor of causing conflicts is frequent context switching. One major reason for this would be that context

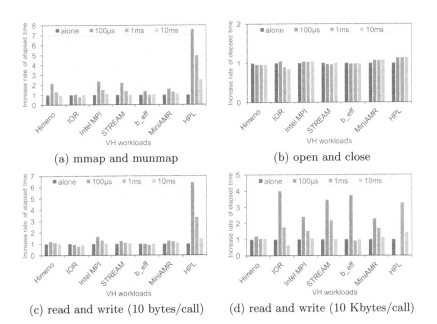

(a) mmap and munmap

(b) open and close

(c) read and write (10 bytes/call)

(d) read and write (10 Kbytes/call)

Fig. 5. Changes in elapsed time of VH workloads when changing system call frequency and type.

170 R. Nunokawa et al.

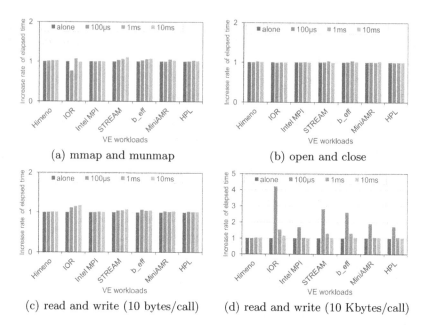

(a) mmap and munmap   (b) open and close

(c) read and write (10 bytes/call)   (d) read and write (10 Kbytes/call)

Fig. 6. Changes in elapsed time of VE workloads when changing system call frequency and type.

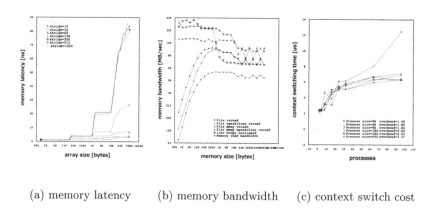

(a) memory latency   (b) memory bandwidth   (c) context switch cost

Fig. 7. VH memory access performance at executing a VH workload alone.

switching could save the context in cache memory by evicting other data and thus increase cache misses. Therefore, it is experimentally shown that VH workloads intensively accessing cached data are prone to be affected by frequent context switching.

One might consider that one approach to avoiding context switching overheads due to the interference is allocating some VH cores to handling the system

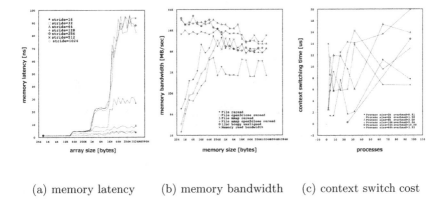

(a) memory latency   (b) memory bandwidth   (c) context switch cost

Fig. 8. VH memory access performance at co-executing VH and VE workloads frequently invoking system calls.

calls forwarded from the VE workloads. However, we have experimentally confirmed that this approach is ineffective for a VI consisting of multiple VEs, such as the configuration in Table 1. Notice that, in our evaluation, the total number of VE cores in the VI is 64 while the total number of VH physical cores is 24. As a result, if all the VE cores are used to execute VE workloads, 64 VEOS processes compete to use 24 VH physical cores, resulting in severe performance degradation. Thus, the degradation is clearly alleviated when the number of VEs managed by the VH becomes smaller, as shown in Fig. 9. In the figure, the vertical axis indicates the increase rate of the execution time at executing the HPL benchmark on the VH side. In this evaluation, a tiny benchmark of calling mmap and munmap is executed on the VE side, by changing the number of VE cores executing the tiny benchmark program in parallel. As shown in Fig. 5(a), this combination of VH and VE workloads cause resource conflicts, resulting in performance degradation. Note that the number of VE workloads running in parallel is changed from 12 to 64 without changing the frequency for each workload to invoke system calls. In Fig. 9, we can see that the performance degradation is clearly mitigated by reducing the number of VE workloads and making some VE cores unused. Consequently, the performance degradation of VH workloads can be restrained by sufficiently reducing the number of VE used cores, simply assuming that every VE workload invokes system calls with the same frequency. However, as this approach also reduces the utilization of VE cores, a way of finding a good trade-off point between performance interference avoidance and resource utilization will be discussed in our future work.

4 Related Work

In Sect. 2, we reviewed that SX-AT adopts a heterogeneous configuration. Therefore, the challenges discussed so far in improving the computational efficiency of

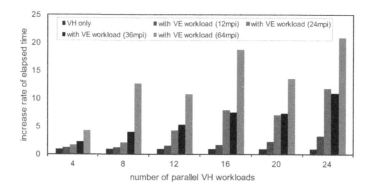

Fig. 9. Increases in elapsed time of a VH workload by increasing the number of VE workloads.

a standard CPU-GPU system might provide interesting insight also for improving the SX-AT efficiency.

A GPU workload running on a standard CPU-GPU system is likely to saturate shared hardware resources, such as memory and network bandwidths due to their massive thread parallelism. Hence, in [7], a platform has been proposed to control the performance trade-off between CPU and GPU workloads. The proposed platform can dynamically determine the GPU concurrency level so as to maximize the system performance with considering both system-wide memory and network conflict information as well as the state of GPU cores.

Another related study introduces a runtime framework for scheduling each of multiple users' OpenCL tasks to its optimal device, either a GPU or a CPU on a CPU-GPU system [18]. The runtime framework uses a performance prediction model based on machine learning at runtime to select optimal devices.

Some algorithms and power prediction models are proposed in [21] for schedulers to co-execute workloads with considering the impact on power consumption as well as other shared resources.

There are many other studies on oversubscription [2], where each CPU is used for the concurrent execution of multiple workloads. However, most of these studies do not assume a heterogeneous computing system consisting of different types of processors. On the other hand, studies on job scheduling and resource allocation for heterogeneous computing systems usually focus on whether a CPU or a GPU is used to execute each job [3], and those existing approaches cannot directly be applied to SX-AT, on which a pseudo process, i.e., VEOS, is running on the VH to control the VE and sharing the VH resources with VH workloads.

Several researchers have evaluated the performance of SX-AT and reported various scientific applications [4,9], VH-VE offload programming [8,16], and I/O performance [14]. However, there is no report that quantitatively evaluates the performance interference when VH and VE workloads coexist. We believe that this study is the first to discuss the concurrent execution of VH and VE workloads through quantitative performance evaluation results.

5 Concluding Remarks

This paper has experimentally investigated the performance interference between a VH and a VE, when each of the two processors executes a different workload. The evaluation results clearly demonstrate that the system call frequency of a workload can be used as a good indicator to predict if the workload can affect the performance of another co-executing workload. It is also worth considering the number of used cores, because performance interference could be restrained if there are some unused VE cores when co-executing VH and VE workloads. These experimental results will be helpful to identify a combination of workloads causing frequent resource conflicts, and thus reduce the risk of performance interference between co-executing workloads on an SX-AT system.

In our future work, we will develop a job scheduling mechanism that uses the experimental findings in this paper to realize conflict-aware workload co-execution on an SX-AT system.

Acknowledgements. The authors would like to thank Associate Professor Masayuki Sato of Tohoku University for his valuable help.

This work is partially supported by MEXT Next Generation High-Performance Computing Infrastructures and Applications R&D Program "R&D of A Quantum-Annealing-Assisted Next Generation HPC Infrastructure and its Applications," and Grant-in-Aid for Scientific Research(B) #21H03449.

References

1. HPC IOR benchmark repository. https://github.com/hpc/ior
2. Aceituno, J.M., Guasque, A., Balbastre, P., Simó, J., Crespo, A.: Hardware resources contention-aware scheduling of hard real-time multiprocessor systems. J. Syst. Architect. **118**, 102223 (2021)
3. Alsubaihi, S., Gaudiot, J.L.: PETRAS: performance, energy and thermal aware resource allocation and scheduling for heterogeneous systems. In: International Workshop on Programming Models and Applications for Multicores and Manycores (2017)
4. Egawa, R., et al.: Exploiting the potentials of the second generation SX-Aurora TSUBASA. In: 2020 IEEE/ACM Performance Modeling, Benchmarking and Simulation of High Performance Computer Systems (PMBS) (2020)
5. Himeno, R.: Himeno benchmark. https://i.riken.jp/en/supercom/documents/himenobmt/
6. Intel Corporation: Introducing Intel MPI benchmarks. https://software.intel.com/content/www/us/en/develop/articles/intel-mpi-benchmarks.html
7. Kayiran, O., et al.: Managing GPU concurrency in heterogeneous architectures. In: IEEE/ACM International Symposium on Microarchitecture (MICRO) (2014)
8. Ke, Y., Agung, M., Takizawa, H.: neoSYCL: a SYCL implementation for SX-Aurora TSUBASA. In: International Conference on High Performance Computing in Asia-Pacific Region, pp. 50–57 (2021)
9. Komatsu, K., et al.: Performance evaluation of a vector supercomputer SX-Aurora TSUBASA. In: The International Conference for High Performance Computing, Networking, Storage, and Analysis, SC 2018, pp. 685–696 (2018)

10. McCalpin, J.D.: STREAM: sustainable memory bandwidth in high performance computers. https://www.cs.virginia.edu/stream/
11. McVoy, L., Staelin, L.: lmbench: portable tools for performance analysis. In: Proceedings of the Annual Conference on USENIX Annual Technical Conference (1996)
12. Petitet, A., Whaley, R.C., Dongarra, J., Cleary, A.: HPL - a portable implementation of the high-performance Linpack benchmark for distributed-memory computers, version 2.3. https://www.netlib.org/benchmark/hpl/
13. Rabenseifner, R., Koniges, A.E.: The parallel communication and i/o bandwidth benchmarks: b_eff and b_eff_io. https://cug.org/5-publications/proceedings_attendee_lists/2001CD/S01_Proceedings/Pages/Authors/Rabenseifner/Rabensei.htm
14. Sasaki, Y., Ishizuka, A., Agung, M., Takizawa, H.: Evaluating i/o acceleration mechanisms of SX-Aurora TSUBASA. In: 2021 IEEE International Parallel and Distributed Processing Symposium Workshops (IPDPSW) (2021)
15. Sasidharan, A., Snir, M.: MiniAMR - a miniapp for adaptive mesh refinement. Technical report (2016)
16. Takizawa, H., Shiotsuki, S., Ebata, N., Egawa, R.: OpenCL-like offloading with metaprogramming for SX-Aurora TSUBASA. Parallel Comput. **102**, 102754 (2021)
17. Tohoku University Cyberscience Center: Supercomputer AOBA (2020). https://www.sc.cc.tohoku.ac.jp/sc20/
18. Wen, Y., O'Boyle, M.F.P.: Merge or separate? Multi-job scheduling for OpenCL kernels on CPU/GPU platforms. In: Proceedings of the General Purpose GPUs, GPGPU-10 (2017)
19. Xiong, Q., Ates, E., Herbordt, M.C., Coskun, A.K.: Tangram: colocating HPC applications with oversubscription. In: IEEE High Performance Extreme Computing Conference (2018)
20. Yamada, Y., Momose, S.: Vector engine processor of NEC's brand-new supercomputer SX-Aurora TSUBASA. In: A Symposium on High Performance Chips (Hot Chips) (2018)
21. Zhu, Q., Wu, B., Shen, X., Shen, L., Wang, Z.: Co-run scheduling with power cap on integrated CPU-GPU systems. In: International Symposium on Parallel and Distributed Processing (2017)

A Learning-Based Scheduler for High Volume Processing in Data Warehouse Using Graph Neural Networks

Vivek Bengre[1], M. Reza HoseinyFarahabady[2(✉)], Mohammad Pivezhandi[1], Albert Y. Zomaya[2], and Ali Jannesari[1]

[1] Department of Computer Science, Laboratory for Software Analytics and Pervasive Parallelism (SwAPP), Iowa State University, Ames, USA
{bvivek2,mpvzhndi,jannesari}@iastate.edu
[2] School of Computer Science, Center for Distributed and High Performance Computing, The University of Sydney, Camperdown, NSW, Australia
{reza.hoseiny,albert.zomaya}@sydney.edu.au

Abstract. The process of extracting, transforming, and loading (also known as ETL) of a high volume of data plays an essential role in data integration strategies in data warehouse systems in recent years. In almost all distributed ETL systems currently use in both industrial and academia context, a simple heuristic-based scheduling policy is employed. Such a heuristic policy tries to process a stream of jobs in the best-effort fashion, however, it can result in under-utilization of computing resources in most practical scenarios. On the other hand, such inefficient resource allocation strategy can result in an unwanted increase in the total completion time of data processing jobs. In this paper, we develop an efficient reinforcement learning technique that uses a Graph Neural Network (GNN) model to combine all submitted tasks graphs into a single graph to simplify the representation of the states within the environment and efficiently make a parallel application for processing of the submitted jobs. Besides, to positively augment the embedding features in each leaf node, we pass messages from leaf to root so the nodes can collaboratively represent actions within the environment. The performance results show up to 15% improvement in job completion time compared to the state-of-the-art machine learning scheduler and up to 20% enhancement compared to a tuned heuristic-based scheduler.

Keywords: Extract Transform Load (ETL) operations · Scheduling policy · Data streaming processing system · Graph neural networks · Job completion time · Reinforcement learning

1 Introduction

The process of extracting, transforming, and loading (also known as ETL) a high volume of data plays an essential role in data integration strategies in data

© Springer Nature Switzerland AG 2022
H. Shen et al. (Eds.): PDCAT 2021, LNCS 13148, pp. 175–186, 2022.
https://doi.org/10.1007/978-3-030-96772-7_17

warehouse systems in recent years. A typical ETL process gathers several types of data from different sources, and then tries to refine and delivers the refined sets to a Data Warehouse (DW) platform (*e.g.*, Amazon Red-shift [1], Azure Data Warehouse Service [2], or Google Big-Query [3]) where the underlying engine allows the end-users to effectively perform the critical business intelligence (BI) activities (such as data predictive analytic). Data processing systems over batch/streaming flows are becoming more and more prominent in the past few years as there is a need to manage apply a set of distributed data mining algorithms over massive data-sets in a petabyte scale.

The range of versatility allows the end-users to submit and run a variety of different algorithms with different load characteristics. In particular, the set of end-users jobs can be scheduled by running a simple scheduling heuristic-based algorithm such as Round Robin (RR), rule based scheduling heuristics, First Come First Serve (FCFS), Shortest Job First (SJF) among others [4,5]. While on a small scale, the achieved performance of such simple scheduling policy can be considered in an acceptable level, the performance degradation caused by applying such simple policies becomes immediately visible on larger clusters that handle various large workloads on their expensive compute applications. As a result, achieving a near optimal solution that can effectively cope with the challenging issues of dedicating an appropriate number of executors to each job or stage when the arrival rate of jobs or data is unknown in prior is highly desirable.

In most distributed ETL frameworks in data warehouse environments, the set of data processing jobs are broken down into smaller sub-tasks which is known as processing stages. Each of these processing stages can be conceptually linked together to form an abstract processing structure (as a graph) that represents the dependencies between the processing stages. Breaking the submitted processing jobs down into smaller stages/fragments makes them more manageable. Moreover, fragmentation makes it possible to run sub tasks in a concurrent/parallel fashion. In most practical scenarios, such smaller tasks are linked together to form an underlying structure for the application that is usually referred to as a Directed Acyclic Graph (DAG). When encoded as DAGs, dedicating jobs to each cluster node is shown to be an NP-hard problem, but we can approximate the solution using graph processing techniques [6]. As such, we use the information present within the job structure to find patterns of efficient execution. Manually traversing all the execution paths to make a decision is not feasible (or extremely slow) for large job sets. Therefore, in this paper, we aim to develop an innovative way to look ahead from the leaf nodes to the root node of the DAG using Graph Neural Networks (GNNs) and decide the order of execution.

Original Contribution

In this paper, we develop an efficient embedding plan to reduce the time of convergence and enhances the amount of the reward in each episode of the reinforcement learning (RL) agents. We employ a Double Deep Q-Networks (DDQN) [7] can tune the parameters of the graph neural networks to set the efficient embedding for the DAGs. For any DQN based algorithm to find an efficient policy (*e.g.*, [8]), it has to explore the state space sufficiently. However, this will make the converging and conforming to a policy take a long time. We use an initial step of the heuristic-based scheduler and reinforcement learning- neural networks agent to assist for efficient policy exploration through the first episode.

Further, we solve the executor limit selection by limiting a stage to one executor and allowing the Agent to select the order. Limiting the number of executors per node allows more executors to be accessible at a given time. We test our model on a simulator built for Apache Spark that also simulates Decima [9]. Our method, Decima, FIFO, and a heuristic-based dynamic partitioning, are compared based on average job completion time, executor usage, and training time.

The main contribution of the current study is summarized as follows.

- We use SageCONV to implement message passing in the reverse direction, which allows us to embed more information in each node for taking actions.
- We make the training process a significant order of magnitude faster by directly representing the Q-values by node feature embedding in the reinforcement learning agent.
- We combine all the DAGs into a single DAG structure to enhance reinforcement learning parallelism and descriptively in-state representation. We train the model by utilizing DDQNs for continuous job arrival.

The rest of this paper is organized as follows. Section 2 highlights the main challenges associated with scheduling of sub-tasks for performing data ETL operations in distributed data processing platforms (such as a data warehouse system). Section 3 presents the details of our proposed scheme. The performance of the proposed solution against famous heuristic-based static and dynamic algorithms is evaluated in Section 4. Finally, Section 5 concludes our work.

2   Problem Statement

The process of data extraction from data sources, transformation, and loading to a central host (commonly known as ETL operations) is among the core strategies and technologies used by enterprises for the data analysis of business information for making business decisions in common Business intelligence (BI) platforms. Business intelligence technologies can handle large amounts of structured/unstructured data to develop and create new strategic business opportunities by easy interpretation of big data sets usually derived from the market in which an enterprise operates (also known as the external data) with data from the internal sources of the business (such as financial and operations data). Such insights can provide enterprises with a competitive market advantage and long-term stability at the broadest level. Common applications of the BI tasks include, but not limited to online analytical processing, data/process/text mining, complex event processing, and predictive/prescriptive analytic. Such applications can empower enterprises to gain insight into new markets or to assess demand and suitability of products and services for different market segments.

Large scale data processing systems can involve a considerable amount of complexity; hence, a significant operational problem can occur when one employs improperly designed data processing systems. Creating an effective scheduling of data processing tasks over limited computing resources across the lifetime of its usage is immensely important in such systems. In particular, an efficient scheduling policy must solve issues such as the decomposition of the original data processing applications to some smaller independent tasks which may be processed in a parallel or distributed manner. Further, thread management, their synchronization and communication can exacerbate the problem as the amount of data becomes larger. Parallel processing of data stream is a very active research topic and there are a myriad of researches that proposed different scheduling strategies to process data streams or real-time data streams [10,11]. The common requirements for all systems are throughput (efficient utilization of available resources) [12]. The average or p-99 response time becomes the target of some previous researches to address. In the rest of this section, we highlight some main challenges when designing a scheduling policy for a large scale data processing application.

Job Scheduling Challenge. Scheduling policies can be grouped to two broad categories of either domain-specific [12,13] or general data processing approaches. The domain-specific policies mostly concentrate on efficient separation of tasks into efficient processing sub-tasks. On the other hand, the general data processing approaches focus on separation of the general jobs into multiple stages and tasks regardless of their intrinsic behavior [11,14,15]. The most commonly used scheduler policies in the industrial projects are those that are designed based on simple heuristic-based [4,5,16] approaches. Authors in [17–20] propose a control-based approach for guaranteeing the Quality-of-Service (QoS) requirements associated with parallel running queries in distributed stream processing engines and event-driven serverless platforms. Such policies usually simplify the scheduling policies by modeling the task properties based on the embedded features of the jobs. These modeling policies can be improved by considering the dependencies among tasks [21], or making them hybrid with the learning mechanisms [22]. However, it has been proven they are inefficient for complex, and high-frequency job arrival [9]. The current trend is to provide a self-intelligible scheduler to enhance resource allocation through time [15,23].

Graph Structure Challenge. Effective handling of task scheduling problems are critically important part of any data processing framework. Because an application can be composed of several partial smaller tasks/operations (also known as the underlying application graph), an optimal scheduler must be optimized accordingly. The goal can be optimizing the utilization of the CPU or memory of the underlying system or to reduce the response time of the tasks (or a combination of both). Having the application graph helps to reduce the model complexity substantially and introduces tools for efficient learning, fast training, and low latency scheduling [24].

Graph Neural Networks. Graph Neural Networks (GNNs) is a deep learning structure that addresses graph-related problems represented via vertices and an edge regarding dependencies. Graph neural networks have a wide variety of applications in Social network recommendations, node classifications, medicinal drug delivery, and protein-protein interaction. The graph embedding is developed to change the nodes and edges representation of the graphs to preserve information while compressing them down to a manageable size. There are multiple ways in which this embedding can be done, but all the procedures use message passing in some way to include the features in the adjacent nodes. Computing the node embedding is based on the user-specified function, and, similarly, edges can have features of their own, and the embedding for each edge is calculated by considering the connected nodes and the node features themselves [24].

Reinforcement Learning. Machine Learning, in essence, is trying to find patterns in data. Very often, optimal data is required by ML algorithms to make the correct prediction. However, data for the optimal solution does not exist in some instances, such as decision-making environments. The optimum has to be found itself without the correct data. Reinforcement learning algorithms provide a way of interacting with the environment to make decisions and classify a decision as good or bad. Reinforcement learning is always goal-directed and is implemented in an active learning model, i.e., the model learns while interacting with the environment.

Reinforcement learning models that make decisions are called agents. An agent has a state, a policy, a value function, and a model. The actions performed by an agent entirely depend on the state it is in, and this state is not to be mistaken by the environmental state. Environment states are generally not completely visible to the Agent; however, there are cases where the environment state is visible in games like Chess. A policy defines agent behavior and maps from state to action, and it is represented by π in the Eqs. 1 and 2. The value function calculates the expected reward by following π for a state s, and the model predicts what the environment does. The model is never perfect but a good approximation of the environment. For reinforcement learning algorithms, the environment is always considered Markovian, i.e., the current time step represents all the time steps before it.

$$\pi(action|state) = P(action|state) \tag{1}$$

$$v_\pi(s) = E\left[\, G_t \mid S_t \,,\ A_t \ \rightarrow \pi(s)\,\right] \tag{2}$$

In Eq. 2 and Eq. 3, G_t represents the total expected reward for state S_t and the action A_t as per policy π. G_t can also be expanded as Eq. 3 to represent the total expected reward. The discount factor γ, shown in Eq. 4, represents the uncertainty with which the reward for the next steps will be computed. The objective of the algorithm is to find the optimal policy π_*.

$$G_t = R_{t+1} + \gamma R_{t+2} + \gamma^2 R_{t+3}... \tag{3}$$

$$\pi_* = max(\sum_{t>0} \gamma^t R^t) \qquad (4)$$

3 Proposed Approach: Design and Analysis

The information present within the structure of the job would help to find efficient patterns of execution. We develop an innovative way to look ahead from the leaf nodes to the root node of the DAG using Graph Neural Networks (GNNs) [6] and decide the order of execution according to an enhanced agglomeration of information. A Double Deep Q-Networks [7] tunes the parameters of the graph neural networks to set efficient embedding for the DAG features. GNNs generalize the conventional deep learning by representing their structure as a set of nodes and edges as their dependencies [25]. The graph neural network can be used to represent the deep neural networks hierarchically to reduce the complexity of training by creating replicated kernels [26–29]. Besides, the stages are limited to one executor, and the Agent decides to dedicate free executors after resources are allocated. To deal with time-consuming convergence in search for an efficient policy on the proposed approach in [8], we propose a hybrid heuristic-based scheduler to assist by executing for the first few episodes. Along with creating a large DAG structure, we also utilize a state representation that helps us to parallelize the training and inference processes.

3.1 Preliminaries

Apache Spark is one of the most widely used open-source computing engines. Spark applications run as independent sets of processes on a cluster, coordinated by the `SparkContext` object, that is in the main program. To run a Spark engine on a cluster, the `SparkContext` object needs to connect to the cluster manager. `SparkContext` object can connect to YARN, Mesos, Kubernetes or Spark's default Standalone manager. Once the nodes are connected to the cluster manager, Spark engine acquires executors on the worker nodes in the cluster, which are processes that run computations and store data for the application. Then, the `SparkContext` object sends the submitted tasks to the executors to be executed.

Spark engine provides a rich selection of APIs and libraries that support Extract Transform Load (ETL) operations, graph computations, streaming jobs, real-time query processing, and Machine Learning capabilities. The model proposed in this paper would be tested based on an accurate simulator built for Apache Spark [9]. The comparison metrics would be average job completion time, executor usage, and training and inference time. Our model would be compared with various heuristic-based schedulers, including First in First out (FIFO), dynamic partitioning algorithms, and the state-of-the-art reinforcement learning-based scheduler named `Decima`. The proposed workflow in this paper is represented in Fig. 1.

Table 1. Notation used in the paper

Entity	Symbol
Discount factor	γ
Action	A_t
Policy function	π
State	S_t

3.2 State Representation

The environment state at any given point contains all the job DAGs that have not been executed. Each job DAG is a sparse matrix of edges and vertices, along with a matrix of features for each node. An environment state can be represented as a collection of sparse matrices with their corresponding feature matrices. The proposed solution in this paper uses something similar to describe the environment state, i.e., it uses one large graph containing all the DAGs present i.e., DAGs that have not been fully executed. A flag is changed to indicate it has completed its execution. The "soft" delete is done to keep the node numbering and positions correct. In the Sect. 3.2, the node numbering for some nodes has been repeated, and these repetitions are representative of the new job arrivals. To identify nodes internally, they've been numbered from 0 to node count where node count is the total number of nodes in the graph. Having this structure allows for adding new jobs quickly by appending them to the existing list. The job features keep changing as new jobs arrive and the cluster state changes. So, it's better to compute the feature matrix just before training or inference. The process of feature calculation is also not expensive as most frameworks provide this information about the node. This aggregated state representation also allows an efficient way to parallelize and compute the embedding in the next step. The final step is to reverse the directions of all the edges in the graph, this is required for the leaf embedding to have influence from the higher nodes.

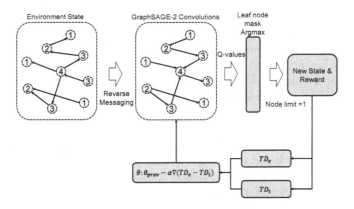

Fig. 1. The workflow and the structure of the proposed solution.

3.3 Graph Embedding

A graph neural network is used to embed each node information as logits. In the case of our solution, the resulting logits are just one number which represents the Q value for selecting a node as its action. The graph neural network takes job dags and the features of each node as input and outputs a Q value for each node. In the graph neural network, we adopted three GraphSAGE [30] layer. In first two layers, the number of input and out features are five while last layer takes five features from the output of second layer as input but it outputs only one feature which is the Q value or logits for each node.

Since the Message Passing path is reversed, the leaf node values calculated will have influence from nodes that are a few generations (in terms of dependency) above it. So, the leaf node value will represent the "path" from the leaf to some parent node. For any node in the graph the embedding is calculated as follows.

$$x_{parent(u)}^l = agg(\{ x_v^{l-1} \ \forall \ v \ \epsilon \ parent(u) \}) \qquad (5)$$

$$x_u^l = \sigma(\ W \ . \ concat(x_u^{l-1}, x_{parent(u)}^l) \ ) \qquad (6)$$

The N or the Neighborhood of a given node automatically changes to the parents/dependants of the node. One round of message passing will not be enough for the leaf nodes to have enough influence from the nodes that are higher up. So, to have a reasonable influence, three rounds of message passing is done. This assures an embedding that will take into account the neighbourhood that spans reasonably away from the leaf nodes. The next step is to train the embedding to give accurate/efficient Q-values per node.

4   Performance Evaluation Results

The proposed approach is based on the Decima spark simulator [9]. We compared the results with FIFO as spark default scheduling, dynamic partitioning scheduler, and Decima. The executor usages, average job completion time, and cumulative distribution of the rewards are three significant evaluated criteria. The jobs are generated randomly based on the TPC-H dataset [31], and the rewards may be increased based on extending the generated job set. The proposed solution includes the same randomness of input jobs, and the evaluation is based on the average ratio for the improvement over multiple runs.

Instead of focusing on matrix factorization, which is a common embedding technique in GCN, we use an inductive method based on node features in Graph-SAGE [30] to learn the embedding features that would generalize to unseen nodes. Our model is based on an aggregation of feature information based on the neighboring nodes, and the back-propagation by stochastic gradient descent is used to train the parameters. The symmetric aggregator function makes the model trainable by ordering the unordered set of vectors as the neighbors of each node. We considered two different aggregator functions, mean and pooling,

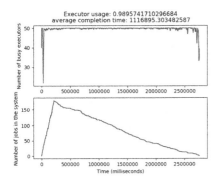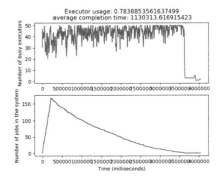

Fig. 2. Performance evaluation of decima executor usage versus dynamic scheduling

Table 2. Parameters for different training stages based on pooling and mean aggregator stages.

Parameter	Pooling	Mean	
Stage	–	1	2
Burning	1000	1000	1000
Learning rate	0.001	0.001	0.001
Episodes	0.001	15	30
Gamma	0.9	0.9	0.9
Assist	90%	100%	0%
Random exploration	10%	0%	100%
Exploration decay	0.9999	0.9998	0.9998

to train the models. Our experimentation in Fig. 3 shows that the pool aggregator requires more training episodes, and the loss value converges considerably slower than the mean aggregator. However, the convergence policy is comparable in terms of the efficiency of scheduling. The parameters are initialized as provided in Table 2.

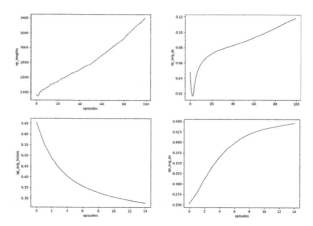

Fig. 3. GraphSAGE with pool aggregator converges fairy fast in the beginning episodes then stabilizes. The left side figure shows the average losses plot, the right side figures represent the average QS value. Top images represent training via pooling aggregator and the down images are stage 1 and stage 2 for mean aggregator.

5   Conclusion

Graphinator successfully reduces the job completion time in high-frequency job arrival cases. Our results show that having a graph neural network computing the Q-value helps execute jobs much more efficiently. Irrespective of the number of parallel nodes assigned, this work also shows that with the assistance of optimized scheduling algorithms, the training time for a model can drastically be reduced. We also show that assigning one executor per stage in a job DAG works well for high-load environments. However, we also observed that the overall response time (makespan) of the jobs is the limiting factor of assigning one node per stage. This limitation can be solved by manually tuning the algorithm for lower loads and increasing the maximum number of executors per stage. The ability to learn of our model helps to efficiently enhance its performance for an extended duration of time with more randomized real-life cluster loads. As future work, the proposed method can be continued to optimize hardware requirements with limited memory, CPU, and storage.

Acknowledgment. We thank the Research IT team *(ResearchIT – RIT)* of Iowa State University for their continuous support in providing access to HPC clusters for conducting the experiments of this research project. Prof. Albert Y. Zomaya acknowledges the support of Australian Research Council Discovery scheme (DP190103710). Dr. MohammadReza HoseinyFarahabady acknowledge the continued support and patronage of *The Center for Distributed and High Performance Computing* in *The University of Sydney, NSW, Australia* for giving access to advanced high-performance computing platforms and industry's leading cloud facilities, machine learning (ML) and analytic infrastructure, the digital IT services and other necessary tools.

References

1. Amazon Redshift: Cloud data warehouse. https://aws.amazon.com/redshift/. Accessed 25 Oct 2021
2. Azure data warehousing architectures. https://docs.microsoft.com/en-us/azure/architecture/data-guide/relational-data/data-warehousing. Accessed 25 Oct 2021
3. BigQuery: Cloud data warehouse. https://cloud.google.com/bigquery. Accessed 25 Oct 2021
4. Isard, M., Budiu, M., Yu, Y., Birrell, A., Fetterly, D.: Dryad: distributed data-parallel programs from sequential building blocks. In: 2007 Proceedings of the 2nd ACM SIGOPS/EuroSys European Conference on Computer Systems, pp. 59–72 (2007)
5. Zaharia, M., et al.: Resilient distributed datasets: a fault-tolerant abstraction for in-memory cluster computing, p. 2 (2012)
6. Scarselli, F., Gori, M., Tsoi, A.C., Hagenbuchner, M., Monfardini, G.: The graph neural network model. IEEE Trans. Neural Netw. **20**(1), 61–80 (2008)
7. Van Hasselt, H., Guez, A., Silver, D.: Deep reinforcement learning with double Q-Learning. In: Proceedings of the AAAI Conference on Artificial Intelligence, vol. 30 (2016)
8. Mnih, V., et al.: Playing Atari with deep reinforcement learning. arXiv preprint arXiv:1312.5602 (2013)
9. Mao, H., Schwarzkopf, M., Venkatakrishnan, S.B., Meng, Z., Alizadeh, M.: Learning scheduling algorithms for data processing clusters. In: Proceedings of the ACM Special Interest Group on Data Communication, pp. 270–288 (2019)
10. Yang, Z., Nguyen, P., Jin, H., Nahrstedt, K.: MIRAS: model-based reinforcement learning for microservice resource allocation over scientific workflows. In: 2019 IEEE 39th International Conference on Distributed Computing Systems (ICDCS), pp. 122–132. IEEE (2019)
11. Peng, Y., Bao, Y., Chen, Y., Wu, C., Guo, C.: Optimus: an efficient dynamic resource scheduler for deep learning clusters. In: Proceedings of the 13th EuroSys Conference, pp. 1–14 (2018)
12. Peng, Y., Bao, Y., Chen, Y., Wu, C., Meng, C., Lin, W.: DL2: a deep learning-driven scheduler for deep learning clusters. arXiv preprint arXiv:1909.06040 (2019)
13. Moritz, P., Nishihara, R., Stoica, I., Jordan, M.I.: SparkNet: training deep networks in Spark. arXiv preprint arXiv:1511.06051 (2015)
14. Mirhoseini, A., et al.: Device placement optimization with reinforcement learning. In: International Conference on Machine Learning, pp. 2430–2439. PMLR (2017)
15. Mao, H., Alizadeh, M., Menache, I., Kandula, S.: Resource management with deep reinforcement learning. In: Proceedings of the 15th ACM Workshop on Hot Topics in Networks, pp. 50–56 (2016)
16. Ghodsi, A., Zaharia, M., Hindman, B., Konwinski, A., Shenker, S., Stoica, I.: Dominant resource fairness: fair allocation of multiple resource types. In: NSDI 2011, pp. 24–24 (2011)
17. Farahabady, M.R.H., Zomaya, A.Y., Tari, Z.: QoS- and contention-aware resource provisioning in a stream processing engine. In: International Conference on Cluster Computing, pp. 137–146 (2017)
18. Wang, Y., Tari, Z., HoseinyFarahabady, M.R., Zomaya, A.Y.: QoS-aware resource allocation for stream processing engines using priority channels. In: International Symposium on Network Computing and Applications (NCA), pp. 1–9 (2017)

19. HoseinyFarahabady, M.R., Zomaya, A.Y., Tari, Z.: A model predictive controller for managing QoS enforcements and microarchitecture-level interferences in a Lambda platform. IEEE Trans. Parallel Distrib. Syst. **29**(7), 1442–1455 (2018)
20. Kim, Y.K., HoseinyFarahabady, M.R., Lee, Y.C., Zomaya, A.Y., Jurdak, R.: Dynamic control of CPU usage in a Lambda platform. In: International Conference on Cluster Computing (CLUSTER), pp. 234–244 (2018)
21. Grandl, R., Kandula, S., Rao, S., Akella, A., Kulkarni, J.: GRAPHENE: packing and dependency-aware scheduling for data-parallel clusters. In: 12th USENIX Symposium on Operating Systems Design and Implementation, OSDI 2016, pp. 81–97 (2016)
22. Kumar, N., Vidyarthi, D.P.: A novel hybrid PSO-GA meta-heuristic for scheduling of DAG with communication on multiprocessor systems. Eng. Comput. **32**(1), 35–47 (2016)
23. Bingqian, D., Chuan, W., Huang, Z.: Learning resource allocation and pricing for cloud profit maximization. Proc. AAAI Conf. Artif. Intell. **33**, 7570–7577 (2019)
24. Zonghan, W., Pan, S., Chen, F., Long, G., Zhang, C., Philip, S.Y.: A comprehensive survey on graph neural networks. IEEE Trans. Neural Netw. Learn. Syst. **32**, 4–24 (2020)
25. Wang, M., et al.: Deep graph library: a graph-centric, highly-performant package for graph neural networks. arXiv preprint arXiv:1909.01315 (2019)
26. Yu, S., Nguyen, P., Abebe, W., Anwar, A., Jannesari, A.: SPATL: salient parameter aggregation and transfer learning for heterogeneous clients in federated learning (2021)
27. Yu, S., Mazaheri, A., Jannesari, A.: Auto graph encoder-decoder for neural network pruning. In: Proceedings of IEEE/CVF International Conference on Computer Vision (ICCV), pp 6362–6372, October 2021 (2021)
28. Yu, S., Mazaheri, A., Jannesari, A.: Auto graph encoder-decoder for model compression and network acceleration. arXiv preprint arXiv:2011.12641 (2020)
29. Liu, H., Simonyan, K., Vinyals, O., Fernando, C., Kavukcuoglu, K.: Hierarchical representations for efficient architecture search. arXiv preprint arXiv:1711.00436 (2017)
30. Hamilton, W.L., Ying, R., Leskovec, J.: Inductive representation learning on large graphs. In: Proceedings of the 31st International Conference on Neural Information Processing Systems, pp. 1025–1035 (2017)
31. TPC-H version 2 and version 3

Adaptive Updates for Erasure-Coded Storage Systems Based on Data Delta and Logging

Bing Wei, Jigang Wu[✉], Xiaosong Su, Qiang Huang, and Yujun Liu

The School of Computer Science and Technology,
Guangdong University of Technology, Guangzhou 510006, China
asjgwucn@outlook.com

Abstract. With the explosive growth of data in modern storage systems, erasure coding is widely used to ensure data reliability because of its low storage cost and high reliability. However, a small update can lead to a *partial update* for erasure-coded storage system, the update of data incurs high I/O latency. This paper proposes an adaptive update approach, named DETOG, which efficiently speeds up the partial update for erasure-coded storage systems. DETOG employs machine learning approaches to classify files into non-write-only and write-only files. For non-write-only files, DETOG uses the data deltas that are the differences between latest data values and original data values, rather than the parity deltas, to reconstruct the lost data. This allows erasure-coded storage systems only need to read the old data for the first update instead of each update. For write-only files, DETOG directly appends the new data to the logs of the data nodes and the parity nodes. This allows erasure-coded storage systems not to read the old data for each update. We implement DETOG on the newly designed prototype storage system to perform performance evaluation. Extensive experimental results on real-world traces show that, DETOG can efficiently improve the I/O throughput.

Keywords: Partial updates · File classifier · Erasure coding · Data delta · Logging

1 Introduction

Modern storage systems continuously expand in scale to cope with the ever-increasing volume of data storage. In large-scale storage systems, it is necessary to ensure both high data availability and data reliability, because failures become more prevalent due to disk crashes, sector errors, or server outages, etc. [10,12,14]. To ensure both high data availability and data reliability, keeping additional redundancy in storage systems is a commonly used approach to enable data recovery once failures occur [7]. Two representatives of redundancy mechanisms are replication and erasure coding (EC) [7]. When replication is applied,

© Springer Nature Switzerland AG 2022
H. Shen et al. (Eds.): PDCAT 2021, LNCS 13148, pp. 187–197, 2022.
https://doi.org/10.1007/978-3-030-96772-7_18

the identical replicas of each data are copied and then distributed across multiple data nodes of storage systems. This can incur substantial storage overhead, especially in the face of the ever-increasing volume of data being stored nowadays. When EC is applied, original data blocks are encoded to generate new parity blocks, such that a subset of data and parity blocks can sufficiently recover all original data blocks. It is known that EC introduces less storage overhead and write bandwidth than replication under the same degree of fault tolerance as replication [16].

Although EC can provide fault tolerance with low redundancy, it can introduces additional performance overhead for small updates. This is because EC needs to maintain the consistency of parity chunks to ensure the correctness of data reconstruction [15]. In EC, two representatives of update mechanisms are re-encoding and delta-based write [5,11,13,16]. In re-encoding, the new parity blocks can be generated by computing a linear combination of the unmodified data blocks and the new data blocks of an EC group [9,14]. Delta-based write computes the new parity blocks based on the change of data blocks instead of summing over all data blocks. It employs the difference between new data and old data to compute the parity deltas, then uses the parity deltas to reconstruct the lost data blocks. In small write scenarios, delta-based write significantly outperforms re-encoding [2,16].

Erasure-coded storage systems usually combine delta-based write and logging to speed up partial updates. Full-logging (FL) saves the disk read overhead of parity chunks by appending all data and parity updates. That is, after the modified data range and parity deltas are respectively sent to the corresponding data and parity nodes, the storage nodes create logs to store the updates [2]. Parity-logging (PL) takes a hybrid of full-overwrite (FO) and FL. It saves the disk read overhead of parity chunks and additionally avoids merging overhead on data chunks introduced in FL, because FO applies in-place updates to both data and parity chunks. However, FL and PL still have to perform a time-consuming write-after-read for each partial update. A speculative partial write scheme for fast parity logging. PARIX performs write-after-write instead of write-after-read to reduce the seek overhead. However, it introduces an extra write for each partial update, in comparison to replication.

In this paper, we focus on how to minimize the I/O overhead of partial updates for erasure-coded storage systems. We propose an adaptive update approach, named DETOG, to solve the problem. DETOG classifies files into non-write-only and write-only using a decision tree (DT) [8]. For non-write-only files, DETOG uses the data deltas that are the differences between latest data values and original data values, rather than the parity deltas, to reconstruct the lost data. This allows DETOG to perform single write instead of write-after-read for the last $n-1$ partial updates, when handling a series of n partial writes to the same data. For write-only files, DETOG performs partial updates using FL. This allows DETOG directly sends the new data to the data nodes and the parity nodes for each update, thereby transforming write-after-read to single write for each partial update. The main contributions of this paper are summarized as follows.

- We propose an adaptive update approach DETOG to speed up partial updates. DETOG uses data deltas instead of parity deltas to bypass the computation of parity deltas and the read of old data. DETOG classify files into non-write-only and write-only using machine learning. When updating non-write-only files for a series of n partial updates to the same data, DETOG performs write-after-read for the first partial update and single write for the last $n-1$ partial updates. When updating write-only files, DETOG performs single write for each partial updates.
- Based on DETOG, we have designed a distributed prototype file system for small-write-intensive workloads. We have implemented DETOG, compared it with the latest work on the proposed storage system through the same real-world I/O trace used in [3]. Extensive experimental results show that DETOG can successfully improve the I/O throughput.

2 Preliminary

We divide file content into blocks and apply EC independently on a per-block basis. We denote an (k, m)-code as an EC approach defined by two parameters k and m. An (k, m)-code encodes k equal-size data blocks to form m parity blocks. Let n denote the number of nodes (or servers) in an erasure-coded storage cluster. We assume $n \geq k+m$, and the collection of $k+m$ data and parity blocks distributed across $k+m$ of the n nodes in the erasure-coded storage cluster. We mainly consider *Maximum Distance Separable* (MDS) codes. It has been proved that MDS codes can achieve the optimal storage efficiency for a given level of fault tolerance [3]. For example, regarding an (k, m)-code, k original data blocks are encoded to generate m parity blocks, and the original data blocks can be reconstructed from any k of the $k+m$ data and parity blocks.

In an EC group, each parity block can be encoded by computing a linear combination of k data blocks. For an (k, m)-code, let $d_j(1 \leq j \leq k)$ denote a data block, $p_i(1 \leq i \leq m)$ denote a parity block, then p_i can be computed by

$$p_i = \gamma_{i1}d_1 + \gamma_{i2}d_2 + \cdots + \gamma_{ik}d_k \tag{1}$$

where $\gamma_{ij}(1 \leq j \leq k, 1 \leq i \leq m)$ denotes an encoding coefficient. All arithmetic operations are performed in the Galois Field $GF(2^w)$ [9]. The re-encoding approach computes the new parity blocks by Eq. (1).

The linearity property of EC provides an alternative to reduce the I/O overhead for computing the new parity blocks, when one or more data blocks are updated. Assume that the data block d_l $(1 \leq l \leq k)$ is updated to d_l' in an EC group, then each parity block in the group must be updated. Each new parity block p_i' $(1 \leq i \leq m)$ can be computed by

$$p_i' = \sum_{j=1, j \neq l}^{k} \gamma_{ij}d_j + \gamma_{il}d_l' = p_i + \gamma_{il}(d_l' - d_l) = p_i + \gamma_{il} \times \Delta d_l = p_i + \Delta p_i \tag{2}$$

where Δd_l is the data delta, Δp_i is the parity delta. Thus, instead of summing over all data blocks, the new parity blocks can be computed by the old parity blocks and the change of the data blocks. The delta-based write approach computes the updated parity blocks by Eq. (2). Furthermore, Eq. (2) can be generalized when only part of a data block is updated, but a subtlety is that a data update may affect different parts of a parity block depending on the erasure code construction

Delta-based write leverages the linearity of EC described in Eq. (2), it introduces smaller I/O overhead than re-encoding for small updates. Three typical delta-based write approaches used in modern EC based storage systems are described as follows.

FO. FO applies in-place updates to both data and parity blocks. It requires an additional disk reads of old parity block at the specific offset.

FL. FL appends all data and parity updates to logs for saving the disk read overhead. That is, after the modified data range and parity deltas are respectively sent to the corresponding data and parity nodes, the storage nodes create logs to store the updates. The logs will be merged with the original blocks when the blocks are read subsequently.

PL. PL can be regarded as a hybrid of FO and FL. It saves the disk read overhead of parity blocks and additionally avoids merging overhead on data blocks introduced in FL. Because data blocks are more likely to be read than parity blocks, merging logs in data blocks can significantly degrade read performance.

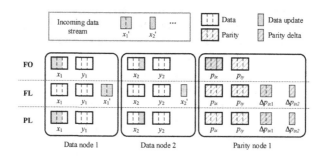

Fig. 1. Illustration on different parity update approaches.

Figure 1 illustrates the differences of the delta-based approaches, using a (2,1)-code as an example. FO performs in-place writes for both data updates and parity deltas; FL appends both data updates and parity deltas according to the incoming order; PL performs in-place writes for data updates and appends parity deltas.

FO introduces extra disk reads for the old parity blocks, in comparison to FL and PL. FL introduces additional disk seeks to the update log for reads, because the data are scattered in the log. PL updates data with in-place manner and uses logging to update parities. It can effectively improve the update performance without affecting data reads.

3   Proposed Approach DETOG

This section presents the proposed approach DETOG, which classifies files into non-write-only and write-only first, then uses different delta-based write approaches to perform updates. In large-scale storage clusters, users are diverse and varying, which results in dynamic features. Machine learning approaches not only accomplish efficient data analysis, but also adapt to dynamic workloads and automatically adjust feature selection. Therefore, we use machine learning approaches to classify files. For non-write-only files, DETOG uses data delta based approach to perform partial updates. For write-only files, DETOG directly appends the new data to the logs of the data nodes and the parity nodes, so as to bypass the read of old data.

3.1   File Classification

In our scenario, both high AUC and low complexity are important. Therefore, we choose DT as the file classifier. Feature extraction dominates the implementation effect of prediction algorithms. The features used in the DT is listed as follows.

File type: file type is strongly related to file classes. For example, a large number of image files that are used to store the checkpoint of applications, are frequently appended, but rarely read. However, some document files are frequently read, but rarely written.

File age: file age is measured by the time interval between current time and the creation time. Intuitively, newer files are more popular.

Recency: the difference between the current access time and the last access time.

File size: file size is related to file classes. In general, for a file, the larger the size, the higher possibility of being frequently appended.

Owner: the owner of a file. There are some file owners who no longer read or write the files after uploading them.

Recent access requests: the number of access requests in a recent configured internal. In general, a higher number means a more high activity of the whole user group.

Access count: the access count of a file in a day.

For a given feature set $\{a_1, a_2, ..., a_n\}$ that has n features, we choose the optimal feature based on the information gain. In general, the larger the information gain, the better the classification. For example, we first choose a_i that has the largest information gain to construct the target set $\{a_i\}$, then remove a_i from the original feature set. Again, we move the optimal feature $\{a_j\}$ from the original feature set to the target set. If $\{a_i, a_j\}$ is superior to the previous target set $\{a_i\}$, which means the effect of the new classification is better than that of the old classification, then the iteration will be repeated accordingly. Otherwise, the process terminates.

3.2 File Updates

Intuitively, PL is the best choice for non-write-only files. However, the old on data nodes have to be read to compute parity deltas in PL. This leads to a time-consuming write-after-read for each partial update. We use data deltas instead of parity deltas to bypass the computation of parity deltas and the read of old data.

Let $p_i^{(r)}$ denote the rth update on parity p_i, and p_i is corresponding to the data d_l in an EC group. Let $d_l^{(0)}$ and $p_i^{(0)}$ denote the original data of d_l and the original parity of p_i, respectively. Assume that d_l is updated r times, then we have $d_l^{(1)}, d_l^{(2)}, \cdots, d_l^{(r)}, p_i^{(1)}, p_i^{(2)}, \cdots, p_i^{(r)}$. According to Eq. (2), we have

$$
\begin{aligned}
p_i^{(r)} &= p_i^{(0)} - \gamma_{il}d_l^{(0)} + \gamma_{il}d_l^{(1)} - \gamma_{il}d_l^{(1)} + \gamma_{il}d_l^{(2)} \\
&\quad - \cdots - \gamma_{il}d_l^{(r-2)} + \gamma_{il}d_l^{(r-1)} - \gamma_{il}d_l^{(r-1)} + \gamma_{il}d_l^{(r)} \\
&= p_i^{(0)} + \gamma_{il}(d_l^{(r)} - d_l^{(0)})
\end{aligned} \tag{3}
$$

the equation illustrates that $p_i^{(r)}$ can be computed by $p_i^{(0)}$, $d_l^{(r)}$, and $d_l^{(0)}$. We propose a new update approach, named data-delta based PL (DDBPL), which is built on PL and Eq. (3).

Figure 2 shows the procedure of DDBPL for non-write-only files, in terms of partial updates. For each partial update, the client first forwards the new data $d_l^{(r)}$ to the data node, then the data node forwards $d_l^{(r)}$ to the parity node. The original data value $d_l^{(0)}$ is read in the 1st partial update, whereas it will no longer be read in subsequent partial updates. In Fig. 2(a) shows the procedure of the 1st partial update. When receiving $d_l^{(1)}$, the data node knows that $d_l^{(0)}$ has not been updated by retrieving its log. Then the data node reads $d_l^{(0)}$ directly. When receiving $d_l^{(1)}$, the parity node appends $d_l^{(1)}$ to its logs, then explicitly request $d_l^{(0)}$ asking the data node. Once receiving the request. The data node appends $d_l^{(1)}$ to its log after sending $d_l^{(0)}$. Once receiving $d_l^{(0)}$, the parity node appends it to the logs and then return success to the parity node.

Figure 2(b) shows the procedure of the rth ($r > 1$) partial update. The data node directly sends the $d_l^{(r)}$ to the parity node. Then the data node in-place writes $d_l^{(r)}$ into the original file. Meanwhile, the parity node appends $d_l^{(r)}$ to its own logs.

In FL, $d_l^{(0)}$ will never be overwritten. Therefore, the data node does not need to send $d_l^{(0)}$ to the parity node. Based on this analysis, we propose a new update approach, named data-delta based FL(DDBFL), which is built on FL and

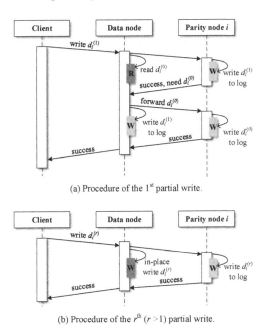

(a) Procedure of the 1st partial write.

(b) Procedure of the rth ($r > 1$) partial write.

Fig. 2. Procedure of DDBPL for non-write-only files, in terms of partial updates.

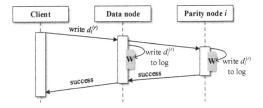

Fig. 3. Procedure of DDBFL for write-only files, in terms of partial updates.

Eq. (3). Figure 3 shows the procedure of DDBFL for write-only files, in terms of partial updates. For each update, the data node and the parity node append $d_l^{(r)}$ ($r \geq 1$) to their own logs.

4   Implementation

Based on DETOG, we implement a prototype of distributed file system named DETFS. DETFS splits file content into fixed-size data blocks, it stores each block at a single data node. DETFS encodes each k consecutive data blocks of a file to generate m parity blocks. The size of a parity block is the same as that of a data block, each parity block is independently stored on a single parity node.

Figure 4 shows the architecture of DETFS. DETFS implements a global master (metadata node) to maintain all file system metadata. The master chooses the node to host a data block or a parity block. When reading a file, the DETFS client first asks the master for the location information of the blocks of the file. It then contacts the data node that holds the target block for data transfer. When writing a file, the DETFS client first asks the master to choose the nodes to host the data block and the corresponding parity blocks. The file classifier is implemented on client. The classifier classifies files into non-write-only and write-only. DETFS uses DDBPL and DDBFL to perform partial updates for non-write-only files and write-only files, respectively. When the utilization of a node (ratio of used disk space at the node to total capacity of the node) reaches a threshold, merging compactions are performed asynchronously to shrink the disk usage of the logs.

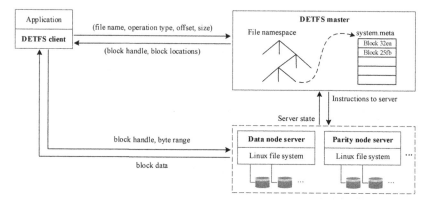

Fig. 4. Architecture of DETFS.

5   Experiments

Our experiments are conducted on 8-node machines, four of which are the data nodes, two of which are the parity nodes, one of which is the client, and the last one is the master. Each machine is configured with two 20-core 2.2 GHz Intel Xeon 4114 CPUs, 128 GB of memory, four 4 TB disks, and the Ubuntu 18.04 LTS operating system. The network is 1-Gigabit Ethernet. The size of each data block or parity block is 64 MB. For an $EC(k, m)$ group, k and m are set to 4 and 2, respectively. This is the same as did as [16]. We evaluate our proposed approach DETOG by comparing with the following four state-of-the-arts: 1) FL [2]; 2) PL [6]; 3) PARIX [16]; and 4) three-way replication (R3) [4]. R3 takes in-place writes for data updates. All approaches are implemented into the DETFS. We evaluate the performance of all approaches using NFS trace set [1]. We randomly sample trace data of each trace in the set using the following steps: 1) extracting distinct files to construct the file set S; 2) constructing the file set S' by randomly sampling on S at 1:100; and 3) extracting the records whose file id belongs to S' from the original data set, so as to construct a new trace sequence according to the timestamp.

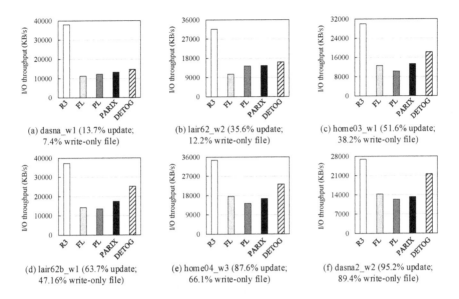

Fig. 5. I/O throughput for all approaches when replaying NFS traces.

5.1 Trace Evaluations

We choose six representative traces with different percentages of overwrites and write-only files to perform performance evaluations. Merging compactions are triggered whenever the utilization of a node (ratio of used space at the node to total capacity of the node) is greater than the threshold value.

Figure 5 shows the I/O throughput for all approaches when replaying NFS traces. R3 always works with the highest I/O throughput for all selected traces. This is because it does not need to perform additional read, parity computation, and data compaction. DETOG performs better than FL, PL, and PARIX for all selected traces, particularly for the traces with the high percentages of updates and write-only file. For example, Fig. 5 (a) shows that DETOG can improve the I/O throughput by 29.55%, 18.71%, and 9.88%, compared with FL, PL, and PARIX, respectively, when the trace $dasna\_w1$ with a update percentage of 13.7% and a write-only file percentage of 7.4% is replayed; whereas Fig. 5 (f) shows that DETOG can improve the I/O throughput by 51.41%, 75.77%, and 62.69%, compared with FL, PL, and PARIX, respectively, when the trace $dasna\_w2$ with a update percentage of 95.2% and a write-only file percentage of 89.4% is replayed. This behavior occurs because DETOG performs a single write for the $r^{(th)}$ ($r \geq 2$) partial updates on the same data for non-write-only files, and a single write for each partial update for write-only files. The higher the overwrite percentage and the write-only file percentage of a trace, the larger the advantage of DETOG.

5.2 Storage Overhead

Figure 6 shows the storage overhead for different approaches replaying NFS traces. R3 always works with the highest storage overhead, and its storage overhead is $3\times$ for all traces. This is because R3 keeps three replicas for every data block, and employs in-place writes instead of log-based writes to perform updates. The storage overhead of FL, PL, PARIX, and DETOG is much lower than that of R3. This demonstrates that EC can significantly reduce storage overhead.

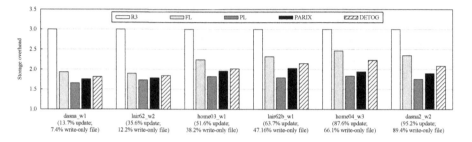

Fig. 6. Storage overhead for different approaches replaying NFS traces.

PL always works with the lowest storage overhead. This is because it updates data block using in-place writes. The storage overhead of PARIX is greater than that of PL. This is because the original data have to be stored on the parity nodes. The storage overhead of DETOG is greater than that of PARIX. This is because DETOG performs logging-based update for the first update on the same data for non-write-only files and performs logging-based update for each update for write-only files. The storage overhead of FL is greater than that of DETOG. This is because FL appends all data and parity updates to logs.

6   Conclusion

We have proposed DETOG, an adaptive update approach to support fast partial updates for erasure-coded storage systems. DETOG classifies files into non-write-only and write-only. For non-write-only files, DETOG uses data deltas rather than parity deltas to bypass the read of old data and the computation of parity deltas. For write-only files, DETOG directly appends the new data to the logs of data nodes and parity nodes, so as to bypass the read of old data. Extensive experimental results show that DETOG has successfully improved the I/O throughput compared with the sate-of-the-art.

Acknowledgment. This work was supported in part by the National Natural Science Foundation of China under Grant No. 62072118, the China Postdoctoral Science Foundation under Grant No. 2021M690733, and the Key-Area Research and Development Program of Guangdong Province under Grant 2019B010121001.

References

1. Harvard NFS traces. http://iotta.snia.org/traces/nfs/3378. Accessed August 2021
2. Aguilera, M.K., Janakiraman, R., Xu, L.: Using erasure codes efficiently for storage in a distributed system. In: 2005 International Conference on Dependable Systems and Networks, pp. 336–345 (2005)
3. Chan, J.C., Ding, Q., Lee, P.P., Chan, H.H.: Parity logging with reserved space: towards efficient updates and recovery in erasure-coded clustered storage. In: 12th USENIX Conference on File and Storage Technologies, pp. 163–176 (2014)
4. Ghemawat, S., Gobioff, H., Leung, S.T.: The Google file system. In: Proceedings of the 19th ACM Symposium on Operating Systems Principles, pp. 29–43 (2003)
5. Hu, Y., Cheng, L., Yao, Q., Lee, P.P., Wang, W., Chen, W.: Exploiting combined locality for wide-stripe erasure coding in distributed storage. In: 19th USENIX Conference on File and Storage Technologies, pp. 233–248 (2021)
6. Jin, C., Feng, D., Jiang, H., Tian, L.: RAID6L: a log-assisted raid6 storage architecture with improved write performance. In: 2011 IEEE 27th Symposium on Mass Storage Systems and Technologies, pp. 1–6. IEEE (2011)
7. Kadekodi, S., Rashmi, K., Ganger, G.R.: Cluster storage systems gotta have HeART: improving storage efficiency by exploiting disk-reliability heterogeneity. In: 17th USENIX Conference on File and Storage Technologies, pp. 345–358 (2019)
8. Myles, A.J., Feudale, R.N., Liu, Y., Woody, N.A., Brown, S.D.: An introduction to decision tree modeling. J. Chemometr. J. Chemome. Soc. 18(6), 275–285 (2004)
9. Plank, J.S., Greenan, K.M., Miller, E.L.: Screaming fast Galois field arithmetic using Intel SIMD instructions. In: 11th USENIX Conference on File and Storage Technologies, pp. 299–306 (2013)
10. Shen, Z., Lee, P.P.: Cross-rack-aware updates in erasure-coded data centers: design and evaluation. IEEE Trans. Parallel Distrib. Syst. 31(10), 2315–2328 (2020)
11. Silberstein, M., Ganesh, L., Wang, Y., Alvisi, L., Dahlin, M.: Lazy means smart: reducing repair bandwidth costs in erasure-coded distributed storage. In: Proceedings of International Conference on Systems and Storage, pp. 1–7 (2014)
12. Subedi, P., Huang, P., Young, B., He, X.: FINGER: a novel erasure coding scheme using fine granularity blocks to improve Hadoop write and update performance. In: 2015 IEEE International Conference on Networking, Architecture and Storage, pp. 255–264. IEEE (2015)
13. Xia, M., Saxena, M., Blaum, M., Pease, D.A.: A tale of two erasure codes in HDFS. In: 13th USENIX Conference on File and Storage Technologies, pp. 213–226 (2015)
14. Xu, B., Huang, J., Qin, X., Cao, Q.: Traffic-aware erasure-coded archival schemes for in-memory stores. IEEE Trans. Parallel Distrib. Syst. 31(12), 2938–2953 (2020)
15. Ye, L., Feng, D., Hu, Y., Wei, X.: Hybrid codes: flexible erasure codes with optimized recovery performance. ACM Trans. Storage 16(4), 1–26 (2020)
16. Zhang, Y., Li, H., Liu, S., Xu, J., Xue, G.: PBS: an efficient erasure-coded block storage system based on speculative partial writes. ACM Trans. Storage 16(1), 1–25 (2020)

Matching Program Implementations and Heterogeneous Computing Systems

Martin Sandrieser$^{(\boxtimes)}$ and Siegfried Benkner

Research Group Scientific Computing, Faculty of Computer Science,
University of Vienna, Vienna, Austria
{martin.sandrieser,siegfried.benkner}@univie.ac.at

Abstract. High performance computing (HPC) systems have become highly parallel aggregations of heterogeneous system elements. Different kinds of processors, memory regions, interconnects and software resources constitute the modern HPC computing platform. This makes software development and efficient program execution a challenging task. Previously, we have developed a platform description framework for describing multiple aspects of computing platforms. It enables tools and users to better cope with the complexities of heterogeneous platforms in a programming model and system independent way.

In this paper we present how our platform model can be used to describe program implementation variants that utilize different parallel programming models. We show that by matching platform models of program implementations to descriptions of a concrete heterogeneous system we can increase overall resource utilization. In addition, we show that our model featuring control relationships brings significant performance gains for finding platform patterns within a commonly used heterogeneous compute cluster configuration.

Keywords: Modeling · Platform · Heterogeneous computing

1 Introduction

Software development and efficient program execution for highly parallel computing systems has always been challenging. With the spread of heterogeneous computing paradigms those challenges got aggravated. Users and tools now have to cope with different kinds of hardware resources and diverse programming environments available within a single system. Achieving high computational performance while maintaining productivity is very demanding. Therefore, methods and tools are required to better support programming of heterogeneous systems.

Previously we have developed an XML-based platform description language (PDL) as well as a generic platform model [13]. The main goal of these *platform description facilities* is to enable programmers to describe – in a machine-readable way – hardware- and software-properties that are *relevant* for application tuning, tool support and portability of software. They provide a holistic

© Springer Nature Switzerland AG 2022
H. Shen et al. (Eds.): PDCAT 2021, LNCS 13148, pp. 198–209, 2022.
https://doi.org/10.1007/978-3-030-96772-7_19

view about the computing *platform* which we define as a set of hardware- *and* software resources.

Our platform description facilities also enable to describe generic platform patterns. *Platform patterns* describe how processing- and memory resources interact. Such interactions are usually only defined implicitly by programming models and not available in a machine-readable form. Multiple programming models may adhere to high-level platform patterns. In addition to high-level interactions of resources, our modeling approach also allows to capture low-level hardware and software information such as memory-sizes, locality and CPU-properties. By supporting both aspects, high-level resource interactions and low-level entity properties, we aim at providing descriptor facilities that are usable for a variety of use-cases at different layers of abstraction.

In this paper we make the following contributions:

– We introduce our platform description framework which is based on a generic platform model.
– We use our platform modeling framework to model characteristics of program implementation variants developed with MPI [11], OpenMP [10], Nvidia CUDA [12] and AMD HIP [7].
– We show that by matching platform descriptors of program implementation variants and of a target system we can increase resource utilization. Utilizing our modeling framework we generate optimized program execution configurations that improve benchmark application performance by up to 2.9x.
– We show that our hierarchical modeling approach based on control relationships results in more efficient graph search for finding platform patterns compared to an approach that does not use a hierarchical model.

This paper is structured as follows. In Sect. 2 we present context and related work. In Sect. 3 we introduce our platform description framework. Sect. 4 shows how our approach is used to improve resource utilization on a highly heterogeneous system. In Sect. 5 we evaluate our modeling approach with respect to the applicability of a graph algorithm. Section 6 summarizes our findings.

2   Context and Related Work

Using higher level models that capture aspects of the computing environment is a common method in all software development domains. Especially in the context of high performance computing (HPC) we observe a wide variety of platform abstractions to improve programmer productivity. In many cases utilized abstractions focus on locality information and are tightly coupled with specific programming languages or runtime systems.

A prominent example is the X10 [4] programming language. X10 introduces the concept of *place* which describes a locality boundary for data and computational tasks. How such *places* are mapped to concrete resources of an execution environment can be influenced externally with low programmer interaction.

This methodology highly increases programmer productivity and code portability. Therefore, there exist multiple similar approaches to improve portability through adaptable locality abstractions e.g., Chapel [3], HPX [8], Charm++ [9].

The memory hierarchy is a key factor for achieving high computational performance. Hence, the projects Sequoia [6], HPT [16] and Legion [1] utilize tree-based models of a system's memory organization. Also, these projects use changeable mappings of abstract descriptors to concrete hardware resources to improve code portability.

The previously mentioned approaches all combine abstract platform modeling and mapping with specific programming languages or runtime systems. Our approach does not include a specific programming environment. In fact, in addition to locality information, we aim at describing the properties and resource interactions of the programming approach itself. This serves to support the interoperability of software in heterogeneous environments where multiple programming models are combined within one system or application.

In this paper, we use our modeling approach to support the selection of program implementation variants. Implementation variants achieve the same computational task but are implemented in different flavors, often with different programming models and resource requirements. Such a programming methodology is common in heterogeneous environments where programs need to be adapted to a diverse set of hardware resources. However, in many cases the resource requirements of *implementation variants* are only defined implicitly with string-based identifiers. Our approach aims at providing more detailed, machine processable structural information on *how* an implementation variant utilizes resources.

3 Platform Descriptors

Describing *relevant* properties of the computing platform in a structured and machine-readable way is a challenging task. Description facilities have to be generic and adaptable to support a wide variety of use-cases ranging from high-level platform patterns to low-level hardware specific information.

Our platform descriptor facilities utilize a generic platform model. This model is based on a hierarchical aggregation of processing units, memory regions and interconnect entities. We represent this model as an undirected graph with different node and edge types. The nodes in this graph are of type *processing unit* (PU) or *memory region* (MR). Edges between nodes represent *control relationships* between *processing units* or *interconnects*. An *Interconnect* describes communication and data-transfer within the platform. In addition, we define a *control relationship* as the possibility for *offloading* computational tasks from one processing unit to another [13]. Due to this hierarchical control relation between PUs, we further introduce three different PU-types: *Master*, *Hybrid* and *Worker*. Master PUs may delegate work to other processing units and at least one master must exist within a platform. Worker PUs execute work delegated by other PUs but cannot offload work. Hybrid PUs may act as both, master or worker. Figure 1 depicts an example *platform graph* with 5 processing units and a single

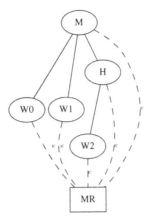

Fig. 1. Example platform graph with master (M), hybrid (H) and worker (W0, W1, W2) processing units. One memory region (MR) is accessible for all processing units. This memory *interconnect* is depicted as dashed edges. The *control* edges are shown as solid lines.

shared memory region. The PUs form a hierarchy with one intermediate level (H). The shared memory access is modeled by *interconnect* edges between the PUs and the memory region (MR).

3.1   Programming Models

What distinguishes our approach from other approaches that focus on hardware description (e.g., [2]) is the capability to express *logical* relationships between system entities which are usually defined implicitly by the programming environment. Hence, in our approach multiple platform descriptions for the same physical hardware may exist depending on *how* system resources are utilized. Moreover, platform descriptions may combine multiple platform models within one graph. For example, this situation arises for hybrid programs that combine multiple programming models. This is a common scenario for clusters of shared-memory machines (e.g., MPI+OpenMP) or machines equipped with accelerators (e.g., OpenMP+OpenCL).

3.2   Abstraction Levels

To be applicable for a wide variety of use-cases, platform description facilities should enable system modeling at different levels of abstraction. Our model has been designed to support coarse grained and fine grained modeling of software and hardware characteristics. Therefore, in addition to the structural graph-based model, we support the attachment of arbitrary descriptor *properties* to all system entities. This support has been realized via a generic key-value scheme. We distinguish between the following descriptor abstraction levels:

- **High-Level:** Generic platform patterns which capture entity interactions found in multiple programming environments. We have pre-specified generic patterns often found in the HPC domain such as *Threading, Message-Passing* or *Accelerator* (see Fig. 2).
- **Mid-Level:** Platform descriptors that may comprise abstract higher-level patterns but make further refinements regarding entity quantities and their connectivity. For example, a high-level *thread* pattern might be present at several sub-parts of a complex platform that features multiple shared memory regions (i.e., a cluster of shared-memory machines).
- **Low-Level:** Platform descriptors that include mappings of the abstract platform entities (processing units, memory regions and interconnects) to concrete hardware and software resources of a computing system.

A major motivation for our approach is that the same modeling facilities can be used at all levels of the computing platform. This aims at improving the interoperability between programming approaches, supporting portability and performance optimization.

3.3 Programming Support

We have implemented our platform modeling framework as a C++ programming library. This library supports the import and export of platform descriptors to/from an XML-based storage format. In addition, it provides functionality to work with high-level platform models, store and query entity properties and automatic creation of platform descriptions for concrete target systems.

4 Case Study: Improving System Utilization

In this section we investigate a common performance tuning problem occurring in heterogeneous systems and show how our approach can improve application throughput and resource utilization.

Problem: We consider a highly heterogeneous compute cluster. Each of the compute nodes has different hardware characteristics and therefore efficient program execution requires the utilization of different programming models and/or configuration parameters on each machine. Finding good configurations usually requires the manual examination of program implementation variants (i.e., for each available programming model) and low-level hardware details. This process is often time consuming and requires a high degree of expert knowledge.

Our approach provides means to describe programming model characteristics as well as low-level platform details. By comparing descriptors of a program's *required* platform and descriptors of the concrete execution environment, efficient program mapping configurations can be created automatically. This approach alleviates users from time-consuming application tuning steps and improves portability.

In what follows we show a concrete example for a highly challenging heterogeneous system configuration. We generate program execution configurations that can utilize all available resources of the heterogeneous platform and therefore increase application throughput.

Execution Environment: The heterogeneous compute cluster *Exa* is comprised out of 4 compute nodes (exa01-04) that are connected via 4X QDR Infiniband and an Ethernet network. Exa01 features 4 Intel Xeon 6138 2.0 GHz (4 × 20cores) with 4 NUMA domains and 192 GB RAM. Exa02 is comprised of 2 AMD Epyc 7501 2.0 GHz (2 × 32cores) with 8 NUMA domains and 96 GB RAM. The nodes exa03 and exa04 each feature 2 Intel Xeon 6130 2.1 GHz (2 × 16cores) with 2 NUMA domains and 96 GB RAM. Exa03 is further equipped with one Nvidia Tesla V100 32 GB GPU. The node exa04 features one AMD Radeon Instinct MI25 16 GB GPU. With the complex memory configurations, different kinds of processors and GPU accelerators, this system poses great challenges for executing applications that aim at using all available resources.

We automatically created a platform description for the whole system in the following way. As input we use hardware locality information gathered from the Hwloc [2] library, Cmake-based library discovery and Nvidia/AMD GPU management libraries. For each NUMA domain we model one memory region (MR). Per NUMA memory region we then use one CPU-core as *master* processing unit and the remaining cores as *worker* entities. We insert *control relationship* edges between master and worker PUs. Processing units and memory regions are connected via shared memory *interconnect* edges. Those edges also store relative distances between PUs and NUMA domain MRs as edge properties. In addition, the GPUs in exa03 and exa04 are modeled as *worker* PUs with one distinct memory region. There is one CPU-core acting as master for one GPU worker. Subsequently, we insert *interconnect* edges between the GPU memory region and the related master and worker PUs. To express the availability of a message-passing library on the target system, we insert *message* interconnect edges between master processing units.

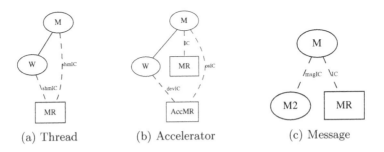

(a) Thread   (b) Accelerator   (c) Message

Fig. 2. Platform patterns used in program implementation variant descriptions.

Application: We investigate the execution of the XSBench Monte Carlo neutron transport application benchmark [15]. This application is available in a variety of different programming models and is therefore suitable to run on all available resources of the *Exa* machine. We use implementations that utilize the following programming models: OpenMP, CUDA, HIP and MPI. Each program implementation variant is compiled into a separate binary executable. In addition to the intra-process parallelism of the application, multiple processes can be combined via an MPI [11] coordination layer. This may result in complex execution configurations featuring different programming models (e.g., MPI+OpenMP+X) within one application run. To utilize our approach for generating suitable mappings to the target environment, we model each application variant.

For the OpenMP programming model, we create a model that utilizes a *Thread* pattern. As depicted in Fig. 2a, this pattern has one master PU and one worker PU connected to a shared memory region. For the CUDA and HIP implementation variants we model an *Accelerator* pattern. Fig. 2b shows this pattern with one master PU and one worker PU with one additional distinct worker memory region (AccMR). The worker refers to a CUDA/HIP device. To distinguish between the CUDA and HIP programming environments, we further annotate the accelerator entities with key/value properties. For implementation variants featuring message-passing, we use a *Message* pattern (Fig. 2c) consisting of a message interconnect between master processing units.

Mapping: We use an execution configuration generator that produces MPI rankfiles equipped with additional information on executable filenames and thread counts. For finding suitable mappings, we search for platform patterns *message, thread* and *accelerator* defined by the requirement descriptors that model the application implementation variants. We search for these platforms within the concrete execution environment description of the *Exa* system. Since all descriptors utilize the graph-based model described in Sect. 3, we can rely on the wide-spread VF2 [5] (sub-)graph isomorphism algorithm. The generator records all concrete system entities from the target description that are capable of forming a specific platform pattern. It maps message interconnect participants to MPI ranks, worker PUs of the thread model to thread groups and worker entities of the *accelerator* pattern to GPUs.

Results: We have conducted experiments on the Exa system with 4 reference configurations OpenMP (OMP), CUDA, HIP, MPI+OMP. The reference configurations were executed on exa01 (OMP), exa03 (CUDA), exa04 (HIP) and nodes exa01-04 (MPI+OMP). Reference configurations were run with default settings with resource selection as specified by the original application. We compare the reference against two auto-generated execution configurations created by our approach. These versions utilize all compute nodes exa01-04. All programs were run on CentOS 7.8.2003, Kernel 3.10 and have been compiled with GCC 8.3.0 with -O3 flags. For the GPUs we used NVCC/CUDA 11.3 and HIP 4.1.0 with Clang 12. In addition, OpenMPI 4.0.5 with UCX 1.8.1 was used. All distributed (MPI) application versions execute the full amount of work (no work sharing across ranks) and use MPI for coordination and performance data reporting. Hence, we show total lookups measured by all ranks. We use XSBench V20 with benchmark size *large* and *event-based* simulation. For the GPU-based variants we

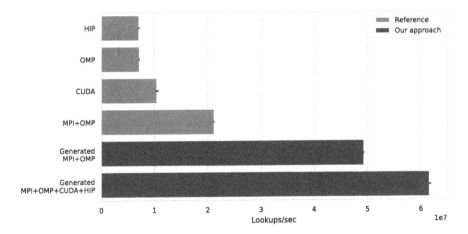

Fig. 3. XSBench performance for different program execution configurations. Using our modeling framework, we can automatically generate execution configurations that utilize all available resources and improve performance.

include device data-transfer in the timing. All results are mean values gathered from 10 repeated application runs.

Figure 3 shows the application performance of different execution configurations. We observe that since the threading pattern in the target platform description is built around NUMA domains our generated MPI+OMP configuration outperforms the reference version that does not consider the NUMA organization. The highest overall performance is achieved by our generated configuration MPI+OMP+CUDA+HIP that uses all available program variants. This version considers NUMA-based mapping and selects the CUDA and HIP implementations for compute nodes exa03 and exa04.

5   Model Performance Evaluation

Introducing a platform model that includes the logical relationships of how processing units are utilized is an uncommon approach. Many existing projects follow a platform model that is predetermined by the physical hardware organization. This usually results in tree-like hierarchies that often resemble a system's memory hierarchy. Our approach also provides memory locality information, but achieves this through a more generic graph structure with memory-associated interconnect edges.

To evaluate our platform model, we have performed experimental evaluations that aim at answering the following question:

Does the hierarchical platform model featuring control relationships and different processing unit classes bring an advantage for finding platform patterns?

Therefore, we evaluate the search performance of the VF2 [5] algorithm for finding platform patterns. We compare our hierarchical platform model against a reference modeling approach that does not utilize control relationships and different processing unit classes.

Experimental Setup: Our implementation uses the Boost Graph Library (BGL) [14] from Boost Version 1.74.0. For matching of platform patterns in larger platform graphs, we use the *VF2* [5] (sub-)graph isomorphism algorithm implementation from BGL. All examples have been compiled with GCC 8.3.0 and -O3 optimization flag.

We search for small platform pattern graphs within larger platform graphs. These larger graphs resemble a commonly used HPC system configuration which is based on shared-memory multi-processor systems with multiple NUMA domains. This model represents a commonly used multi-socket compute node where each processor features multiple CPU cores. Compute nodes are further connected to a larger cluster via a networking fabric. For all experiments, we have modeled a generic cluster of shared-memory compute nodes in the following way: 16 processing units (PU) have two shared-memory interconnect relations with two distinct memory regions (MR). One MR is local and the other MR is remote to each group of PUs. This distance is stored as an edge property with the interconnect in the graph representation. Each of the compute nodes in the system features 2×16 general-purpose PUs that represent CPU cores and two distinct MRs representing NUMA domains. For experiment configurations that feature accelerators, we assume that 10% of the compute nodes are equipped with one accelerator per NUMA domain. We evaluate the platform pattern search performance for platform graphs representing systems with up to 100 compute nodes.

We consider a common HPC use-case of hybrid parallel programs that use message-passing for communication and combine the message-passing model with another parallel programming environment (i.e., MPI+X). For the message-passing layer, we model a topology of participating processes in a Cartesian grid. Hence, we insert *message* interconnect edges in the platform graph in such a way that a 3-dimensional processing unit topology is constructed. The resulting platform graph structure resembles a commonly used 3D-torus interconnect network topology. In the example, this kind of messaging interconnect exists between general-purpose *master* processing units.

We have conducted the experiments on a server machine running CentOS 7.8.2003, Kernel 3.10, which was equipped with two Intel Xeon Gold 6130 16-core 2.10 GHz processors and 96 GB RAM. All results are based on the mean from 10 repeated runs. Error bars in plots show the 95% confidence interval.

For the pattern search, we check vertex equivalence by comparing vertex types (Master, Hybrid, Worker, Memory). For edge equivalence we compare edge types (Control, Interconnect) and sub-types (e.g., Message, Shared-Memory).

Thread: As described in Sect. 4, this platform pattern features one master PU and one worker PU which share a memory region (MR). Since the concrete system under investigation features 2×16 CPU-cores and two NUMA domains, we model one master PU and 15 worker PUs which have access to two MRs, one for

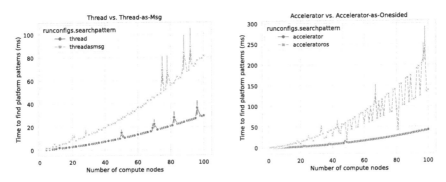

Fig. 4. Pattern search performance with and without control relationships

each NUMA domain. The master PUs are connected via messaging interconnect edges in a 3D-torus fashion.

For the alternative modeling approach that is used as comparison, we omit control relationships and therefore also do not use the worker PUs. However, to still capture a *threading* relation between processing units, we insert message interconnects between one PU that takes a coordinative role and the remaining 15 PUs in the same NUMA domain. All the PUs are modeled as master PUs but only the coordinative master is participating in the inter-NUMA 3D-torus messaging interconnect. Since there is no further differentiation between message interconnects, there is a semantic gap in the reference model. The reference also matches for PU interactions that span across remote NUMA domains. Hence, we observe that the control relationships provide more utility for locality modeling.

We observe that the control relationship approach for modeling of the thread patterns brings significant performance advantages. As shown in Fig. 4, for all cluster sizes of up to 100 compute-nodes featuring 3200 CPU-cores, the mean time to find all thread patterns with control relationships is well below 40ms. For the reference thread pattern that omits control relationships mean search times are higher in all cases.

Accelerator: Due to the increase of heterogeneous computing, this pattern became more and more important in recent years. The accelerator pattern models the offloading of computational tasks to often specialized compute units that feature distinct memory regions. We model this pattern by introducing a control relationship between a master and a worker PU.

As the reference modeling approach that does not use control relationships, we use a onesided model. The structural difference of this model is that the control relationship is again replaced by a message interconnect and no worker PUs are used. Similar to the thread model we use the coordination master PU for the inter-NUMA torus messaging interconnect.

The experimental results show that finding the reference pattern without control relationships has much higher performance variations and lower performance compared to when control relationships are used. As shown in Fig. 4, the average search times for the reference can reach around 250 ms whereas our approach does not go beyond 50 ms.

6   Conclusion

Utilizing heterogeneous computing systems is a challenging task. Users have to consider a diverse set of hardware and software resources. This makes software development and application tuning time-consuming and error-prone. Methods and tools are needed that improve productivity and performance.

In this paper we utilized a platform description framework that supports tools and users to better cope with heterogeneous systems. Our approach is based on a hierarchical platform model that enables to capture major characteristics of hardware and software in a structured way. In addition to low-level system properties, our framework enables to describe high-level structural platform patterns which are usually implicitly defined by the programming environment.

We have shown that our approach can support the automatic generation of optimized program execution configurations in a highly heterogeneous environment. By automatically combining different program implementation variants, each developed with a different programming model, we could increase resource utilization of a highly heterogeneous cluster. We achieved this by describing software implementations as well as the target execution environment with the same platform modeling framework. We then used a common graph algorithm to determine which implementation variant should be mapped to which sub-parts of the target machine. This approach alleviates users from time-consuming optimization tasks that usually require expert knowledge about software implementations and the hardware execution environment. Using our approach, we could improve the performance of a hybrid benchmark application by up to 2.9×.

In addition, we did show the applicability of our approach for modeling a 100-node heterogeneous compute cluster with complex NUMA memory setup, 3200 CPU-cores and GPU accelerators. We could show that our model is well suited for finding high-level platform patterns in the 100-node cluster model. In addition, we did show that our hierarchical platform model brings significant search performance improvements compared to a reference approach that omits hierarchical control relationships between processing units.

In the future we will perform the automatic generation of platform descriptors from program execution runs. In addition, we will investigate the use of platform models for task-based runtime systems to facilitate dynamic adaptation of programs.

References

1. Bauer, M., Treichler, S., Slaughter, E., Aiken, A.: Legion: expressing locality and independence with logical regions. In: International Conference on High Performance Computing, Networking, Storage and Analysis, SC 2012, pp. 1–11. IEEE (2012)

2. Broquedis, F., et al.: hwloc: a generic framework for managing hardware affinities in HPC applications. In: 2010 18th Euromicro Conference on Parallel, Distributed and Network-Based Processing, pp. 180–186 (February 2010). ISSN 2377-5750. https://doi.org/10.1109/PDP.2010.67
3. Chamberlain, B., Callahan, D., Zima, H.: Parallel programmability and the Chapel language. Int. J. High Perform. Comput. Appl. **21**(3), 291–312 (2007). https://doi.org/10.1177/1094342007078442
4. Charles, P., et al.: X10: an object-oriented approach to non-uniform cluster computing. ACM SIGPLAN Not. **40**(10), 519–538 (2005). https://doi.org/10.1145/1103845.1094852
5. Cordella, L.P., Foggia, P., Sansone, C., Vento, M.: A (sub)graph isomorphism algorithm for matching large graphs. IEEE Trans. Pattern Anal. Mach. Intell. **26**(10), 1367–1372 (2004). https://doi.org/10.1109/TPAMI.2004.75
6. Fatahalian, K., et al.: Sequoia: programming the memory hierarchy. In: Proceedings of the 2006 ACM/IEEE Conference on Supercomputing, SC 2006, p. 83-es (November 2006). https://doi.org/10.1109/SC.2006.55
7. HIP: HIP Programming Guide - ROCm Documentation 1.0.0 documentation. https://rocmdocs.amd.com/en/latest/Programming_Guides/HIP-GUIDE.html
8. Kaiser, H., Heller, T., Adelstein-Lelbach, B., Serio, A., Fey, D.: HPX: a task based programming model in a global address space. In: Proceedings of the 8th International Conference on Partitioned Global Address Space Programming Models, PGAS 2014, pp. 1–11. ACM, New York (October 2014)
9. Kalé, L., Krishnan, S.: CHARM++: a portable concurrent object oriented system based on C++. In: Paepcke, A. (ed.) Proceedings of OOPSLA 1993, pp. 91–108. ACM Press (September 1993)
10. Menon, R., Dagum, L.: OpenMP: an industry-standard API for shared-memory programming. Comput. Sci. Eng. **5**, 46–55 (1998). https://doi.org/10.1109/99.660313
11. MPIForum: MPI: A Message-passing Interface Standard, Version 3.1; June 4, 2015 (2015). https://www.mpi-forum.org/docs/mpi-3.1/mpi31-report.pdf
12. Nvidia: CUDA C++ Programming Guide (2020). https://docs.nvidia.com/cuda/pdf/CUDA_C_Programming_Guide.pdf
13. Sandrieser, M., Benkner, S., Pllana, S.: Using explicit platform descriptions to support programming of heterogeneous many-core systems. Parallel Comput. **38**(1–2), 52–65 (2012)
14. Siek, J., Lee, L., Lumsdaine, A.: The Boost Graph Library: User Guide and Reference Manual. Addison-Wesley (2002)
15. Tramm, J.R., Siegel, A.R., Islam, T., Schulz, M.: XSBench - the development and verification of a performance abstraction for Monte Carlo reactor analysis. In: The Role of Reactor Physics toward a Sustainable Future, PHYSOR 2014, Kyoto (2014). https://www.mcs.anl.gov/papers/P5064-0114.pdf
16. Yan, Y., Zhao, J., Guo, Y., Sarkar, V.: Hierarchical place trees: a portable abstraction for task parallelism and data movement. In: Gao, G.R., Pollock, L.L., Cavazos, J., Li, X. (eds.) LCPC 2009. LNCS, vol. 5898, pp. 172–187. Springer, Heidelberg (2010). https://doi.org/10.1007/978-3-642-13374-9_12

FastDCF: A Partial Index Based Distributed and Scalable Near-Miss Code Clone Detection Approach for Very Large Code Repositories

Liming Yang[1], Yi Ren[1(✉)], Jianbo Guan[1(✉)], Bao Li[1], Jun Ma[1], Peng Han[2], and Yusong Tan[1]

[1] National University of Defense Technology, Changsha, China
{ylm19,renyi,guanjb}@nudt.edu.cn
[2] CS&S Information System Engineering Co., Ltd., Beijing, China

Abstract. Despite a number of techniques have been proposed over the years to detect clones for improving software maintenance, reusability or security, there is still a lack of language agnostic approaches with code granularity flexibility for near-miss clone detection in big code in scale. However, it is challenging to detect near-miss clones in big code since it requires more computing and memory resources as the scale of the source code increases. In this paper, we present Fast-DCF, a fast and scalable distributed clone finder, which is partial index based and optimized with multithreading strategy. Furthermore, it overcomes single node CPU and memory resource limitation with MapReduce and HDFS by scalable distributed parallelization, which further improves the efficiency. It cannot only detect Type-1 and Type-2 clones but also can discover the most computationally expensive Type-3 clones for large repositories. Meanwhile, it works for both function and file granularities. And it supports many different programming languages. Experimental results show that FastDCF detects clones in 250 million lines of code within 24 min, which is more efficient compared to existing clone detection techniques, with recall and precision comparable to state-of-the-art approaches. With BigCloneBench, a recent and widely used benchmark, FastDCF achieves both high recall and precision, which is competitive with other existing tools.

Keywords: Clone detection · Distributed algorithm · Large scale code analysis · Efficiency and scalability · Language agnostic · Multiple granularities

1 Introduction

Code clones are source code fragments that are identical or similar to each other, which widely exist in different software projects [1]. Code clones can be categorized according to the level of similarity [22], i.e., Type-1 are exact clones, Type-2 are parameterized clones, Type-3 are clones with further modifications (like inserting or deleting statements) based on Type-1/2, and Type-4 are clones that are not syntactically similar but semantically similar. Code fragments that are not exactly identical but share certain level of similarity are known as near-miss clones [14].

© Springer Nature Switzerland AG 2022
H. Shen et al. (Eds.): PDCAT 2021, LNCS 13148, pp. 210–222, 2022.
https://doi.org/10.1007/978-3-030-96772-7_20

Code cloning can be helpful if it is properly used, but it is also regarded as a bad programming since it can raise maintenance costs [15], reduce code quality [16], and even propagate software vulnerabilities [3, 6]. Many researchers have proposed code clone detection to address these clone-related problems.

In the big data era, large scale software is widely deployed in mission critical systems. Studying clones in big code is a useful way to improve the code quality and to facilitate inter-project maintenance. Therefore, it is necessary to extend clone detection to large scale systems. However, as code size grows, the detection turns much more expensive since the number of code fragment comparisons to detect clones drastically increases. For instance, the time complexity of one-to-one code segment matching is $O(n^2)$, which makes 25 million comparisons for only 5 thousand segments. Thus, enormous computation resources and memory are required. Furthermore, near-miss clones are the most common clones in software systems and the most needed in code clone detection [20]. However, near-miss clone detection is particularly expensive because numerous differences (i.e., insertion, deletion or modification of source code lines or tokens) between code segments need to be examined. Detecting near-miss clones in large scale systems is a challenging task.

A number of tools have been proposed to address this problem [2, 7, 22–25]. However, non-distributed techniques still take hours or even days to detect inter-project clones on 250 million lines of code (MLOC) [22, 23] because of limited computation and memory resources in single node. Distribution is an effective way to solve this problem. However, existing distributed approaches have some problems. Benjamin et al. present an index-based clone detection approach [25]. It is both incremental and scalable to very large codebases. But it only supports Type-1 and Type-2 clone detection. IBFET [2] is a MapReduce based tool which utilizes an index-based features extraction technique to detect code clones. But IBFET is non-distributed in preprocessing stage, and this will become a bottleneck when processing large code. Furthermore, since inter-projects often contains code written in diverse programming languages, which makes it necessary to support multi-language code detection to work with codes cross large repositories. And it is also important to be flexible to support different granularities of detection. For example, function-level detection is suitable for vulnerable detection based on clone detection [6] while file-level detection is handy for license violation checking. Therefore, it is necessary for a clone detection approach to support for many different languages and multiple granularities.

In this paper, we present FastDCF, an efficient and effective distributed clone detection approach that can detect clones in inter-project/intra-project big code with flexibility in both programming language and code processing granularity:

Efficiency and Scalability: In order to break the limitation of computation and memory resources, we design FastDCF as a fully distributed approach. This makes FastDCF can work efficiently and scalably on a massive code base. To further improve the efficiency of our approach, we use partial token indexing to reduce the number of required comparisons.

Type-1/2/3 Clone Detection: To detect near-miss clones, FastDCF use a simple and fast bag-of-tokens strategy which is resilient to Type-3 changes to compare code blocks. Therefore, FastDCF can detect Type-1/2/3 clones.

Language Agnostic and Multiple Granularities: By our designed parser, FastDCF transforms source code into their lower-case equivalent. This allows FastDCF support many languages such as C, C++, Java, Python, and C Sharp, and support code granularities at both file and function levels.

We evaluate FastDCF in terms of efficiency, scalability, recall, precision, language support and multi-granularity detection. The experimental results show that FastDCF significantly outperforms existing typical tools, including IBFET [2], DCCFinder [24], SourcererCC [22], CloneWorks [23] and so on. It takes only a few minutes for FastDCF to detect clones on 250 MLOC. FastDCF is 10 times faster than CloneWorks on 250 MLOC and 60 times faster than SourcererCC on 75 MLOC. According to available literature and the test results, FastDCF is the fastest approach which has been implemented to detect near-miss clones for large scale systems.

The rest of this paper is organized as follows. Section 2 summarizes existing approaches concerning code clone detection. Section 3 discusses several key issues for designing a fast and scalable distributed code detection tool and presents the design of FastDCF. Section 4 describes our implementation. Section 5 demonstrates comprehensive experimental evaluations and the results between our approaches and the most competitive existing tools with large scale real-world code. The paper concludes with discussion in Sect. 6.

2 Related Work

There are many approaches on large scale code clone detection, and we can divide them into two categories: non-distributed and distributed scalable clone detection.

Non-distributed Scalable Clone Detection. Nicad is a text-based single node processing approach [7], which uses longest common subsequence algorithm to compare lines of source code. It can detect Type-1, Type-2 and Type-3 clones. SourcererCC [22] and CloneWorks [23] are also non-distributed approaches. They use effective token-based single node methods. Though these approaches improve the efficiency of clone detection on large scale code, there are bottlenecks in these approaches since the resources of single node are limited.

Distributed Scalable Clone Detection. With the development of hardware capabilities and virtualization technology, distributed and parallel processing optimization for clone detection is emerging. DCCFinder [24] is the first distributed clone detection tool which run CCFinder [4] in parallel. In order to be analyzed with CCFinder, the target must be partitioned into small pieces. Every node loads two pieces to detect clones between them. Hummel *et al.* use an index-based strategy to enlarge the scale of clone detection and to provide real-time cloning information for very large software [25]. However, they can only detect Type-1 and Type-2 clones. IBFET is an index-based method that uses hash algorithms to extract features from source code and these features are saved by HBase [2]. IBFET can scale clone detection to billions of LOC at file level granularity. However, IBFET is not a fully distributed clone detection tool since it only optimizes feature-based index creation and code clone detection and retrieval by parallelization, with core steps such as preprocessing and normalization, and feature extraction not parallelized. This significantly affects the overall efficiency of it and these non-distributed core steps will turn to be bottlenecks, if the code is very large.

3 Design

3.1 Preliminary Concepts and Definition

In this section, we introduce concepts and definition regarding code clones or appear in our approach.

Code block is a continuous segment of source code, which can be a function or a sequence of statements in a source file. *A clone pair* is a pair of code blocks that are similar and detected as clones. *A clone group* is a set of similar code blocks and consists of a number of clone pairs. *Clones* are made up of clone pairs or groups. *Query code block* is the code block which is used to query index and get potential clones. *Candidates* are code blocks returned by *query code blocks'* query index. They are potential clones of *query code blocks. Zipf's law* is an assertion. It claims that f, the frequencies of specific events, is inversely proportional to their rank r in probability [11].

3.2 Efficiency and Scalability Limitation of Existing Techniques: Experiments and Analysis

Due to single node capacity limitation of main memory and CPU, the scalability of non-distributed tools is usually prohibited when the size of code reaches a threshold. SourcererCC is the first approach proposed and implemented to detect clones in MLOC. To illustrate this dilemma, we evaluate SourcererCC [22] with *bcb_reduced* dataset, the data size of which is 10 MLOC. The experimental environment is set according to [22]. The tests are carried out in a workstation with 4 Intel Xeon Platinum 8269CY cores and 16G RAM (8G are set as available). Figure 1 shows the CPU usage and memory usage changes over the time.

From Fig. 1(a), we can see that the CPU usage rate shows a fluctuating increase in the start, and it finally reaches the usage rate of almost 100% shortly after the start. This suggests that SourcererCC contains mainly CPU intensive tasks and has a large demand for computing resources when processing large scale code. As shown in Fig. 1(b), the memory usage increases in a more fluctuating way in the begging. Then it reaches nearly 52% of the upper limit we set. This is because the big code data are usually loaded from and kept in the memory. The larger the amount of code, the more memory is required. From Fig. 1(the screenshots of the running system), we can see memory and CPU usage are always close to upper limit since detecting clones in big code requires much computation and memory resources.

3.3 Design Goals and Our Approaches

We want to design an approach that can detect clones in inter-project/intra-project big code with flexibility in both programming language and code processing granularity.

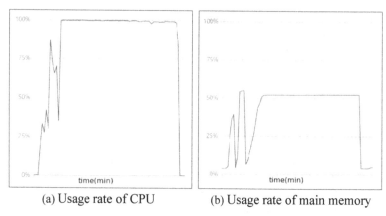

(a) Usage rate of CPU   (b) Usage rate of main memory

Fig. 1. SourcererCC: the usage rate of CPU and main memory

From Fig. 1, we can know detecting clones in big code requires much computation and memory resources. In order to address this problem, we propose I^2nOPT, an intra/inter-node optimized method which combines distributed parallelization and token-based partial indexing. And by building our parser with flexible source code parsing techniques, we allow our approach can support multi language and granularity code clone detection.

3.3.1 I^2nOPT: Combination of Distributed Parallel Optimization and Token-Based Partial Indexing

We propose a fast and scalable approach combined both distributed parallel optimization and token-based partial indexing. We use distribution as inter-node optimization to breaks the boundary of single node resource limitation and use token-based partial indexing as intra-node optimization to further improve the efficiency and scalability of our approach. Another benefit of using token-based partial indexing is that it can detect near-miss clones.

Inter-node Optimization. Generally speaking, clone detection is divided into two stages, preprocessing stage and clone detection stage, both of which require a lot of computing and memory resources. We parallelize FastDCF in both preprocessing stage and clone detection stage. Multi-threading is used in each stage. Codebase in our design consists of many projects which are collected and maintained by administrators. User code is the project which is submitted by users and is used to find clones between user code and codebase. Sub-codebase is a part of codebase, which is used for parallelization.

Distributed preprocessing stage is the first parallelization stage. We divide the job into smaller tasks and assigns them to each node. The big codebase is split into a number of smaller sub-codebases and the preprocessing is executed independently in a mapper for each sub-codebase.

In clone detection stage, source code has been split into many small fragments. In order to detect all clones between two projects, each node loads a preprocessed sub-codebase and keeps it in memory. Then the user code is streamed into the main memory to node and detect clones between user code and loaded sub-codebase. User code is not stored in the memory. This is repeated until all of the potential clones are identified. This way makes our approach faster since it makes full use of the distributed CPU and memory resources.

Intra-node Optimization. When detecting clones between a loaded sub-codebase and user code, token-based partial index [22, 23] is accepted. In traditional token-based approaches, the source code is converted into code blocks made up of tokens and each code block are compared with another to detect clone pairs. The time complexity is $O(n^2)$ and is not desirable in large scale clone detection. Thus, we use partial index into FastDCF to reduce the number of comparisons and to save the computational overhead. We state it in the form of the following property formally:

Property 1: *Code block A consist of t_1 tokens and B consist of t_2 tokens, each in predefined order. Denote a sub-block of A as S_A and a sub-block of B as S_B. If $|A \cap B| \geq i$, i is the given threshold, then any sub-blocks S_A which consists of t_1-i+1 and SB which consists of t_2-i+1 tokens will have at least one token overlapped.*

To illustrate this property, let us consider two code blocks $A = \{T1, T2, T3, T4, T5\}$ and $B = \{T6, T7, T3, T4, T5\}$ with 5 tokens ($t = 5$) each. If two blocks have more than 4 common tokens, they are considered as clones ($i = 4$). Then if we want to find out if A and B are clones, according to this property, we only need to check if any of their sub-blocks consisting of $t-i+1 = 2$ tokens have shared tokens. In this example, they do not because they have no common tokens in their sub-blocks (marked in bold). We could have most certainly figured out that A and B are not clones because even if the remaining tokens are all the same, the number of shared tokens will not reach the threshold. In other words, this property can help us deduce if two blocks will not be clones by comparing only their sub-blocks instead of comparing all the tokens of A and B. Tokens in sub-blocks are used as partial index in our approach. Furthermore, software vocabulary exhibit very similar characteristics to natural languages corpus and also follow Zipf's law [11]. That means the frequency of tokens decreases very rapidly with rank, and a few popular tokens prevail in most of the code blocks and rare tokens are shared by a few code blocks. According to this law, we sort code blocks from low to high frequency and take first $f-t+i$ tokens as sub-blocks.

Near-Miss Clone Detection. Near-miss clones are common clones in real projects, and it is necessary to detect near-miss clones when designing a clone detection tool. FastDCF is token based. And compared to existing token-based tools, FastDCF can detect near-miss clones in that it supports bag-of-tokens model. The model is similar to bag-of-words model. It computes similarity by common tokens. It can detect near-miss clones as long as two code blocks share enough tokens to exceed a given threshold. While other token-based approaches use token sequences as a unit of match [4], which is more difficult to detect near-miss clones.

3.3.2   Flexible Source Code Parsing

In addition to fast and scalable clone detection, we hope our approach is convenient and user friendly, and can be applied to different scenarios. We hope FastDCF is language agnostic and support multiple-granularities detection. In order to achieve this goal, we need a flexible parser to convert the source code of different languages into intermediate representation in any granularity we want. Therefore, we aim to build our parser by using TXL [9]. TXL is a functional programming language specifically designed for expressing source transformation tasks. We use it in FastDCF to extract code blocks from source code at different granularities. Thus, FastDCF is language agnostic and can detect clones at both file level and function level.

4 FastDCF Implementation

We implement FastDCF in Java with about 3000 lines of code. As shown in Fig. 2, Fast-DCF fulfills the fast and effective detection of big code in four stages: data submitting, codebase splitting, preprocessing and clone detection. The output of the previous step becomes the input of the next step and it yields the final detection by elaborate steps. We use HDFS [21] and MapReduce [5] as the distributed computing framework of our parallelization.

Data Submitting. In data submitting stage, the administrator uploads the codebase and the user submits the code for clone detection. In order to improve the disk space usage, we package a number of small files into one big file in SequenceFile format.

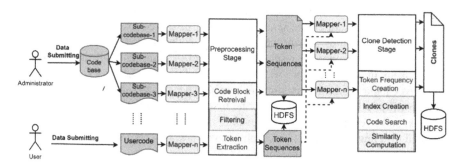

Fig. 2. Implementation of FastDCF

Codebase Splitting. The whole codebase is too large to fit into the memory. In order to solve this problem, we break the codebase into smaller sub-codebases and the size of each sub-codebase is suitable for the memory capacity of each node.

Preprocessing. Preprocessing stage converts data blocks (the sub-codebase or the user code) into token sequences. Each node loads a sub-codebase as an input. Then it performs code block retrieval, filtering and token extraction. The code block retrieval module retrieves code blocks from given sub-codebase by using the robust parser. Filtering module filters code blocks which do not satisfy required size. In token extraction module, tokens are extracted with operator and separator filtered and assembled into token sequences. Finally, the preprocessed token sequences are written back into HDFS.

Clone Detection. In clone detection stage, clones between the codebase and the user code are to be detected. Each node loads a sub-codebase and all user code. By counting the frequency of each token in sub-codebase via token frequency creation module, local token frequency is produced. Then index creation module creates partial index for each sub-codebase. In code search module, tokens in sub-block from the user code are used to query the index info and to generate candidates. Finally, FastDCF computes the similarity by using Jaccard approach [22] and outputs the detection results.

5 Evaluation

FastDCF is evaluated in four aspects: 1) we evaluate the scalability and efficiency of FastDCF using inputs of varying sizes in terms of lines of code and compare it with other start-of-art tools. 2) we measure FastDCF's recall BigCloneBench [27], and we also measure the precision. 3) we verify the effectiveness of our distributed optimization by comparing the efficiency before and after using distribution 4) we show the ability of FastDCF to detect clone at file-level and function-level. We rented a total of 23 instance ESC machines. Each machine has a quad-core CPU, 16 G memory and 60 G hard disk. The Hadoop version is 2.7.7, and Ubuntu16.04 is used as the operating system. We limit each task to use up to 10 G of memory. We evaluate distributed tools on multiple machines and non-distributed tools on a single machine.

5.1 Execution Time and Scalability

Table 1. Execution time for varying input sizes

	FastDCF	CloneWorks	Nicad	SourcererCC
1M	42 s	22 s	1 min 1 s	1 min 18 s
10M	5 min 41 s	4 min 16 s	2 h 4 min 12 s	29 min 18 s
30M	7 min 36 s	18 min 7 s	Internal	49 min 19 s
75M	9 min 42 s	52 min 19 s	–	9 h 47 min 15 s
150M	15 min 7 s	1 h 54 min 35 s	–	–
250M	23 min 19 s	4 h 3 min 24 s	–	–

Comparing with Non-distributed Methods. We compare FastDCF's execution time and scalability against three clone detection tools, including CloneWorks [23], SourcererCC [22] and Nicad [7], which are representative and pioneer work in clone detection for big code. We chose them because they perform well in large-scale detection [2]. Nicad is a popular tool that support Type-3 detection. SourcererCC is the first tool designed for large scale clone detection. CloneWorks optimizes the implementation details on the basis of SourcererCC and the efficiency is improved. Files were randomly selected form IJaDataset [12] to build inputs of different size, ranging from 1 MLOC to 250 MLOC. Experimental results are shown in Table 1.

From Table 1, we can see that FastDCF is able to scale with reasonable execution time when the input size increases. Its execution time decreases from 1 MLOC 2 250 MLOC. In contrast, Nicad is able to scale to the 10 MLOC input, but it cannot scale to a dataset of 30 MLOC or more. According to the description in [8], due to the limitation of its internal data structure, it cannot handle large computation of clone pairs, which prevents its scaling up when the code size turns larger. CloneWorks can scale better than Nicad and SourcererCC. But it spends more time than FastDCF when the input is larger than 10 MLOC. When the size is less than 10 MLOC, the effect of FastDCF's distributed strategy is not obvious and its execution speed is slightly inferior to CloneWorks. The reason is that parallelization brings extra delay. However, as the size of the input becomes larger, FastDCF's lead over other tools becomes obvious. When the size of the input reaches 250 MLOC, the efficiency of FastDCF is 8 times that of CloneWorks.

Comparing with Distributed Methods. We also compare FastDCF with representative distributed methods, including the technique of Hummel et al. [25] and IBFET. Table 2 shows the comparison results of clone detection with other index-based distributed clone detection techniques. We use Linux 2.6 as the dataset, which contains about 11 MLOC. Hummel's method can only detect Type-1 and Type-2 clones and they spend much more time than IBFET and FastDCF. IBFET can support Type-1, Type-2 and Type-3 clones. However, FastDCF has an obvious advantage over IBFET on execution time. FastDCF performs best in three tools because of its subtle distributed design which is based on partial index.

Table 2. Clone detection execution time comparison

Techniques	Linux-Kernel	Clone types
Hummel	47 min 29 s	T-1, T-2
IBFET	20 min 40 s	T-1, T-2, T-3
FastDCF	7 min 45 s	T-1, T-2, T-3

5.2 Distributed Parallelization

In order to measure the performance speedup through distributed parallelization in Fast-DCF, we conduct two experiments. In the first experiment, the number of nodes is kept constant and the size of the data grows. In the second experiment, input size is kept constant while the number of nodes grows.

Figure 3 illustrates the results of the first experiment. The number of nodes is fixed at 23. The value represented by the y-axis is the ratio of the time required for distributed methods to the time required for non-distributed methods and x-axis's value means input size, which is from 1M to 250M. When the code size is less than or equal to 10M, the performance of distributed approach is worse than non-distributed approach (except 10M preprocessing). This is mainly due to the extra communication overhead of distrusted nodes. When the code size grows, the effect of parallelization optimization turns obvious.

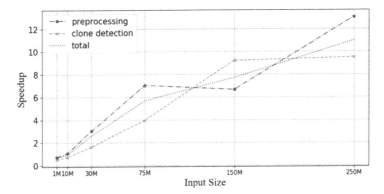

Fig. 3. Different size of the data

Figure 4 shows the results of the second experiment. The code size is 250 MLOC. The value of x-axis is the number of nodes that varies from 1 to 23. The value represented by the y-axis is ratio of multiple nodes to a single node and time. When the number of nodes increases, the average time spent on preprocessing and clone detection decreases. And the optimization effect of the preprocessing is even better than that of clone detection. And the speedup of the preprocessing and the clone detection are both nearly linear.

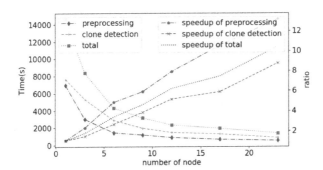

Fig. 4. Different number of the nodes

5.3 Precision and Recall

BigCloneBench is a big clone benchmark of manually validated clone pairs in the inter-project software repository IJaDatset [12]. In order to measure the recall in more detail, we further divide the Type-3 and Type-4 clones into four categories based on their syntactical similarity: Very Strongly Type-3 (VST3) clones have a syntactical similarity between 90% and 100%, Strongly Type-3 (ST3) in 70%–90%, Moderately Type-3 (MT3) in 50%–70% and Weakly Type-3/Type-4 (WT3/4) in 0–50%. The more details are explained in [27]. MT3 and WT3/4 are not belong to near miss clones, therefore they are not in consideration of our work.

It can be seen from Table 3 that FastDCF has perfect detection of Type-1 and near-perfect Type-2 detection. This means that FastDCF has strong ability to detect Type-1 and Type-2 clones. FastDCF has excellent Type-3 recall for the VST3 category. Fast-DCF's Type-3 recall is slightly lower for the ST3 recall. Though Nicad can detect more clones, as we see previously in Sect. 5, the execution time of Nicad for larger inputs and its scalability constrains at the 100 MLOC input are not as good. CloneWorks and SourcererCC are both competitive Type-3 clone detectors.

Table 3. BigCloneBench recall and precision results

	Type-1	Type-2	VST3	ST3	Precision
FastDCF	100	99	93	67	94
CloneWorks	100	99	94	62	93
Nicad	100	100	100	95	80
SourcererCC	100	98	93	61	86

Precision. Measuring clone detection precision remains an open problem since there is no standard benchmark or methodology. We estimate the precision of the tools by manually validating a random sample of their outputs, which is the typical accepted approach. We randomly selected 100 clones, which is a statistically significant sample. The results are show in Table 3. FastDCF has the best precision of 94%, which is slightly better than CloneWorks. Nicad and SourcererCC also have good precision but is lower than that of FastDCF.

5.4 Multi-granularity Detection

FastDCF can detect clones at different granularities. The function-level detection is validated in the experiments in previous sections. We use Linux-kernel 5.10 to measure the function of file level granularity detection. The results show that FastDCF is capable to input codes in the format of files. And the file level clones can be detected. For instance, FastDCF detects the clone pair of "linux-master/arch/x86/um/ptrace_32.c" and "linux-master/arch/x86/um/ptrace_64.c" which is similar in content.

6 Conclusion

In this paper, we propose FastDCF, a fast and scalable near-miss clone detection technique, which exploits distribution strategy over MapReduce framework to scale the detection to large scale and uses partial indexing and multi-threading to improve the scalability and efficiency. We measure the efficiency and scalability with 250 MLOC of IJaDataset. Experimental results show that outperforms existing work in scale. Fast-DCF's recall and precision are comparable to the state-of-the-art clone detection tools. And it achieves the goal of multi-language support and multiple code granularities. To the best of our knowledge, FastDCF is the most efficient tool which has been implemented to detect near-miss clone. For the future work, we plan to apply our approach to vulnerability detection for large scale software such as OS distributions, Web servers, data-intensive large systems and so on.

Acknowledgement. The work in this paper is supported by the Natural Science Foundation of China (Under Grant NO.: 61872444 and U19A2060) and the National Key Research and Development Program of China (2018YFB1003602).

References

1. Lopes, C.V., et al.: DéjàVu: a map of code duplicates on GitHub. Proc. ACM Program. Lang. **1**, 1–28 (2017)
2. Akram, J., Mumtaz, M., Luo, P.: IBFET: index-based features extraction technique for scalable code clone detection at file level granularity. Softw. Pract. Exp. **50**(1), 22–46 (2020)
3. Baker, B.S.: On finding duplication and near-duplication in large software systems. In: Proceedings of 2nd Working Conference on Reverse Engineering, pp. 86–95 (1995)
4. Kamiya, T., Kusumoto, S., Inoue, K.: CCFinder: a multilinguistic token-based code clone detection system for large scale source code. IEEE Trans. Softw. Eng. **28**, 654–670 (2002)
5. Dean, J., Ghemawat, S.: MapReduce: a flexible data processing tool. Commun. ACM **53**, 72–77 (2010)
6. Kim, S., Woo, S., Lee, H., Oh, H.: VUDDY: a scalable approach for vulnerable code clone discovery. In: IEEE Symposium on Security and Privacy (SP) (2017)
7. Cordy, J.R., Roy, C.K.: The NiCad clone detector. In: IEEE 19th International Conference on Program Comprehension, pp. 219–220 (2011)
8. Chen, K., Liu, P., Zhang, Y.: Achieving accuracy and scalability simultaneously in detecting application clones on Android markets. In: Proceedings of the 36th International Conference on Software Engineering, pp. 175–186 (2014)
9. The TXL Programming Language. https://www.txl.ca/. Accessed 21 Apr 2020
10. Roy, C.K., Cordy, J.R.: A mutation/injection-based automatic framework for evaluating code clone detection tools. In: Software Testing, Verification and Validation Workshops, ICSTW 2009, pp. 157–166 (2009)
11. Hindle, A., Barr, E.T., Su, Z., Gabel, M., Devanbu, P.: On the naturalness of software. In: 34th International Conference on Software Engineering (ICSE), pp. 837–847 (2012)
12. Ambient Software Evoluton Group, IJaDataset 2.0 (January 2013). http://secold.org/projects/seclone. Accessed 21 Oct 2019
13. Roy, C.K., Cordy, J.R., Koschke, R.: Comparison and evaluation of code clone detection techniques and tools: a qualitative approach. Sci. Comput. Program. **74**, 470–495 (2009)
14. Zibran, M.F., Saha, R.K., Asaduzzaman, M., Roy, C.K.: Analyzing and forecasting near-miss clones in evolving software: an empirical study. In: IEEE International Conference on Engineering of Complex Computer Systems (2011)

15. Mayrand, J., Leblanc, C., Merlo, E.M.: Experiment on the automatic detection of function clones in a software system using metrics. In: International Conference on Software Maintenance (1996)
16. Lavoie, T., Eilers-Smith, M., Merlo, E.: Challenging cloning related problems with GPU-based algorithms. In: International Workshop on Software Clones (2010)
17. Pham, N.H., Nguyen, T.T., Nguyen, H.A., Nguyen, T.N.: Detection of recurring software vulnerabilities. In: IEEE/ACM International Conference on Automated Software Engineering (2010)
18. Li, H., Kwon, H., Kwon, J., Lee, H.: CLORIFI: software vulnerability discovery using code clone verification. Concurr. Comput. Pract. Exp. **28**, 1900–1917 (2016)
19. Saha, R.K., Roy, C.K., Schneider, K.A., Perry, D.E.: Understanding the evolution of Type-3 clones: an exploratory study. In: 2013 10th IEEE Working Conference on Mining Software Repositories (MSR) (2013)
20. Wang, P., Svajlenko, J., Wu, Y., Xu, Y., Roy, C.K.: CCAligner: a token based large-gap clone detector. In: IEEE/ACM 40th International Conference on Software Engineering (ICSE), pp. 1066–1077 (2018)
21. Honnutagi, P.S.: The Hadoop distributed file system. Int. J. Comput. Sci. Inf. Technol. **5**, 6238–6243 (2014)
22. Sajnani, H., Saini, V., Svajlenko, J., Roy, C.K., Lopes, C.V.: SourcererCC: scaling code clone detection to big code. In: Proceedings of the 38th International Conference on Software Engineering, pp. 1157–1168 (2015)
23. Svajlenko, J., Roy, C.K.: CloneWorks: a fast and flexible large-scale near-miss clone detection tool. In: IEEE/ACM International Conference on Software Engineering Companion (2017)
24. Livieri, S., Higo, Y., Matushita, M., Inoue, K.: Very-large scale code clone analysis and visualization of open source programs using distributed CCFinder: D-CCFinder. In: 29th International Conference on Software Engineering, ICSE 2007, pp. 106–115 (2007)
25. Hummel, B., Juergens, E., Heinemann, L., Conradt, M.: Index-based code clone detection: incremental, distributed, scalable. In: 2010 IEEE International Conference on Software Maintenance, pp. 1–9 (2010)
26. Roy, C.K., Cordy, J.R.: Near-miss function clones in open source software: an empirical study. J. Softw. Maint. Evol. Res. Pract. **22**, 165–189 (2012)
27. Svajlenko, J., Islam, J.F., Keivanloo, I., Roy, C.K., Mia, M.M.: Towards a big data curated benchmark of inter-project code clones. In: IEEE International Conference on Software Maintenance and Evolution, pp. 476–480 (2014)
28. Jang, J., Agrawal, A., Brumley, D.: ReDeBug: finding unpatched code clones in entire OS distributions. In: IEEE Symposium on Security and Privacy, pp. 48–62 (2012)

Towards Optimal Fast Matrix Multiplication on CPU-GPU Platforms

Senhao Shao, Yizhuo Wang$^{(\boxtimes)}$, Weixing Ji, and Jianhua Gao

School of Computer Science and Technology, Beijing Institute of Technology, Beijing
100081, China
frankwyz@bit.edu.cn

Abstract. Increasing computing power has become available through the use of GPUs, bringing new opportunities to accelerate fast matrix multiplication using GPUs. Although researchers have proposed several optimization schemes for the Strassen algorithm on the GPU, they have not fully utilized the computing resources of CPU. In this paper, we propose a CPU-GPU heterogeneous implementation for the Winograd algorithm based on task graph scheduling. It uses work-stealing scheduler to achieve balanced load. We also propose two recursive task graph extension strategies: homogeneous and heterogeneous extension. We invoke different execution strategies in different recursive levels and design a predictor based on the random forest regression model to make a decision. Finally, the experimental evaluations are performed on a CPU-GPU heterogeneous platform. It shows that the improved Winograd algorithm achieves an average speedup of 1.6x, 1.5x and 1.4x against to cuBLAS, Winograd on CPU, and Winograd on GPU for matrices with matrix dimension greater than 5000, respectively.

Keywords: Winograd algorithm · Matrix multiplication · Random forest regression · CPU-GPU heterogeneous architecture

1 Introduction

Matrix multiplication is an important linear algebra operation with a myriad of applications in image processing, scientific computing, etc. Fast matrix multiplication algorithms have lower time complexity than standard matrix multiplication with $O(n^3)$ time complexity. In 1969, Volker Strassen proposed the first fast matrix multiplication with a time complexity of $O(n^{2.81})$, which is named Strassen algorithm [19]. It is a divide-and-conquer algorithm that decomposes matrix multiplication, reorganizes the calculation based on block matrix multiplication, and completes the calculation through 7 recursive matrix multiplications and 18 matrix additions. Its proposal has led to more research on fast

This work is supported by the National Natural Science Foundation of China (Grant Nos. 61972033).

matrix multiplication, resulting in faster methods, such as the Coppersmith-Winograd algorithm.

Heterogeneous computing system usually consists of one or multiple CPUs with a set of computing cores, and a GPU. In the system, the CPU is a latency-optimized general purpose processor that is best for executing a wide variety of tasks quickly, while the GPU is a throughput-optimized specialized processor that is designed to accelerate a number of specific tasks that demonstrate a high degree of parallelism. At present, the CPU-GPU heterogeneous computing is mainly divided into two cases: (1) The CPU is only responsible for task scheduling and not involved in calculation; (2) Both CPU and GPU are responsible for calculation. Most of the existing Strassen algorithms are implemented on GPU or CPU, and the computing resources of both computing units cannot be fully utilized at the same time. Our implementation based on the collaborative computing of the CPU and GPU can fully tap the computing performance of the CPU and GPU.

In this paper, we propose a CPU-GPU heterogeneous implementation for the Winograd algorithm based on task graph scheduling. We also propose two recursive task graph extension strategies: homogeneous and heterogeneous extension. We invoke different execution strategies in different recursive levels. In our implementation, a predictor based on the random forest regression model is applied to find the approximate optimal extension strategy for a given matrix. The input of the runtime system is the task graph generated according to the extension strategy, and the runtime system uses work-stealing scheduler to achieve balanced load. Finally, we perform the experimental evaluations on a CPU-GPU heterogeneous platform consisting of Intel i9-10920X CPU and GTX 3090 GPU. It shows that the proposed Winograd algorithm achieves an average speedup of 1.6x, 1.5x and 1.4x against to cuBLAS, Winograd on CPU, and Winograd on GPU for matrices with matrix dimension greater than 5000, respectively.

2   Related Work

In order to reduce the time complexity of matrix multiplication, some researchers have conducted a myriad of researches [13,18]. Pan constructed a fast linear non-commutative algorithm for matrix multiplication by using the trilinear operations with a time complexity of $O(n^{2.7951})$ [16]. Bini et al. proposed an approximate algorithm with a time complexity of $O(n^{2.7799})$ [3]. Strassen achieved the time complexity of $O(n^{2.4785})$ by using the laser method [20]. Subsequently Coppersmith and Winograd adopted the laser method to reduce the time complexity to $O(n^{2.376})$ [4]. Francois Le Gall proposed a method based on convex optimization to reduce the time complexity to $O(n^{2.3728639})$ [13]. However, the current research has only theoretical significance.

Although fast matrix multiplications have lower complexity, they have numerical stability problems. Some researchers have studied the numerical stability problem of fast matrix multiplications, and found that a limit on the number of recursion levels will not affect the numerical stability of the algorithm [6,8].

Therefore, after some levels of recursion, the subsequent implementation relies on the standard general matrix multiplication.

With the improvement of the performance of multi-core processors, fast matrix multiplications based on multi-threaded architecture have an extensively research [5,11]. Huang et al. used the BLIS software framework to implement the Strassen algorithm, which effectively avoided the additional intermediate matrix storage [9]. Ballard et al. developed an automatic code generation tool that can automatically generate sequential and shared-memory implementations of each fast algorithm [2].

The fast matrix multiplications based on the GPU architecture have been widely implemented as the computing performance of the GPU improves. Li et al. implemented the Strassen and Winograd algorithms based on NVIDIA C1060 GPU [14]. Lai et al. implemented the Strassen algorithm and proposed to determine the cut-off point based on the experience-driven model [12]. Ray et al. compared Strassen's algorithm and classical matrix multiplication on CPU and GPU respectively [17]. Huang et al. proposed the novel Strassen primitive under the GPU architecture, which effectively reused the shared memory and registers to avoid additional memory space overhead [10].

Although fast matrix multiplications have been extensively optimized based on CPU or GPU, the implementations have failed to effectively utilize the computing resources of CPU and GPU.

3   Method

3.1   Overall Framework

As shown in Fig. 1, the overall framework includes the runtime system and task graph generation transforming the recursive Winograd algorithm into a non-recursive task graph. First, we perform feature calculations based on the input matrix, use the offline training model to obtain the optimal extension strategy, and finally generate a task graph based on the extension strategy. The task graph can be abstracted into a directed acyclic graph. In the task graph, each circle represents a task node, representing matrix operation, and the flow between nodes represents the dependency between tasks. The runtime system schedules tasks based on the task graph. Current task scheduling algorithms can be classified into two main groups: static scheduling and dynamic scheduling. Static scheduling is the mechanism, where the decision is made before the task is executed, while the dynamic scheduling algorithm allocates resources at runtime. In our implementation, we adopt the dynamic scheduling algorithm based on work stealing, and its process is shown in Fig. 2. The CPU and GPU, called worker, have a ready queue of ready tasks respectively. Initially, we assign tasks to the CPU and GPU based on the Round-Robin scheduling algorithm. At runtime, the worker firstly check the ready queue. If the queue is not empty, it will remove the head of the queue and execute it. When a task is completed, it may cause some tasks to become ready. If there exist such tasks, the tasks will be placed at the end of the ready queue of the current worker. When the worker runs out of the ready tasks, it will perform the stealing operation from another worker, and the tail of the stolen ready queue will be inserted into the tail of the current ready queue.

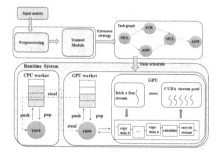

Fig. 1. The framework of the heterogeneous implementation of fast matrix multiplication.

```
void task_schedule() {
    while(run) {
        if(!task_queue.empty()) {
            task = task_queue.pop();
            task();//run task
        } else {
            this->work_steal();
        }
    }
}
void work_steal() {
    victim = runtime->choise_victim();
    task = victim->stole();
    if(task != NULL)
        task_queue.push(task);
    else
        yield();
}
Task* stole() {
    if(stolable)
        return task_queue.pop();
    else
        return NULL;
}
```

Fig. 2. Task scheduling process based on work stealing.

The analysis method of offline trace is applied to evaluate the heterogeneous load of the work stealing scheduling method. It is mainly divided into two parts: grabbing task runtime trace and visualization using the bokeh library. After all the tasks are completed, the trace information captured through the heterogeneous runtime system that manages the running environment and records the running time of each task is written to the trace file. The running time includes the start time and finish time of the task. The format of the trace is divided into two parts. The first part is in the format of "running device 0 - running device 1", accounting for the first line independently. The second part is the specific execution trace of the task in the format of "running device - start time - finish time", which takes up from the second line to the last line. As shown in Fig. 3, it is an example of the heterogeneous load visualization using the bokeh library. The horizontal axis represents the time, and the vertical axis represents the device name. The area covered in red indicates that the device is performing

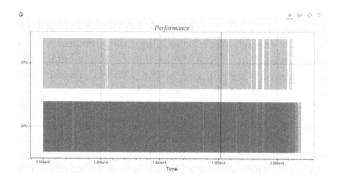

Fig. 3. Offline trace visualization of the heterogeneous system load.

tasks, and the blank gap is either used for data transmission or idle. It can be seen from the figure that the load of CPU and GPU is basically balanced.

3.2 Winograd

Table 1. The 18-variables Winograd algorithm

ID	Task	ID	Task
1	$S_3 = A_{11} - A_{21}$	12	$P_1 = A_{11} * B_{11}$
2	$T_3 = B_{22} - B_{12}$	13	$U_2 = P_1 + P_6$
3	$P_7 = S_3 * T_3$	14	$U_3 = U_2 + P_7$
4	$S_1 = A_{21} + A_{22}$	15	$U_4 = U_2 + P_5$
5	$T_1 = B_{12} - B_{11}$	16	$U_7 = U_3 + P_5$
6	$P_5 = S_1 * T_1$	17	$U_5 = U_4 + P_3$
7	$S_2 = S_1 - A_{11}$	18	$T_4 = T_2 - B_{21}$
8	$T_2 = B_{22} - T_1$	19	$P_4 = A_{22} * T_4$
9	$P_6 = S_2 * T_2$	20	$U_6 = U_3 - P_4$
10	$S_4 = A_{12} - S_2$	21	$P_2 = A_{12} * B_{21}$
11	$P_3 = S_4 * B_{22}$	22	$U_1 = P_1 + P_2$

The Winograd algorithm is a variant of Strassen algorithm. Its computing sequence is shown in Table 1. Considering the computing sequence as a set of tasks, a single level Winograd algorithm can be abstracted into the task graph based on the dependency between variables, as shown in Fig. 4(a). Because 18 additional intermediate matrices are needed, this algorithm is called 18-variables Winograd algorithm. In order to facilitate synchronization between tasks in a heterogeneous environment, we add an empty task named "Join" to the task graph. For the convenience of analysis, assume that the matrix multiplication involves a square matrix, that is, $m = k = n$. Assuming that the extra storage used by the above algorithm is denoted as $E(m, k, n)$. The expression is as follows:

$$E(m, k, n) = 4 \cdot \frac{m}{2} \frac{k}{2} + 4 \cdot \frac{k}{2} \frac{n}{2} + 3 \cdot \frac{m}{2} \frac{n}{2} + E(\frac{m}{2}, \frac{k}{2}, \frac{n}{2}) \tag{1}$$

$$E(m, k, n) = \sum_{i=1}^{\log m} \frac{1}{4^i}(4 \cdot mk + 4 \cdot kn + 3 \cdot mn) \tag{2}$$

With the continuous recursion of the algorithm, more intermediate storage will be introduced. Because of the obvious advantages of the algorithm for large-scale matrix, the storage space consumption is severe. Lai et al. implemented the Winograd algorithm with the number of intermediate matrices of 2, optimizing

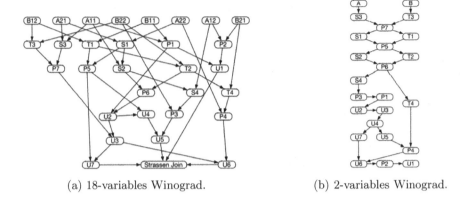

(a) 18-variables Winograd.   (b) 2-variables Winograd.

Fig. 4. The task graph of the Winograd algorithm with 18 and 2 additional intermediate matrices.

the number of the intermediate storage [12]. The task graph is shown in Fig. 4(b).
The sequence of the computation is shown in Table 2.

Table 2. The 2-variables Winograd algorithm

ID	Task		ID	Task	
1	$S_3 = A_{11} - A_{21}$	X	12	$P_1 = A_{11} * B_{11}$	X
2	$T_3 = B_{22} - B_{12}$	Y	13	$U_2 = P_1 + P_6$	C_{12}
3	$P_7 = S_3 * T_3$	C_{21}	14	$U_3 = U_2 + P_7$	C_{21}
4	$S_1 = A_{21} + A_{22}$	X	15	$U_4 = U_2 + P_5$	C_{12}
5	$T_1 = B_{12} - B_{11}$	Y	16	$U_7 = U_3 + P_5$	C_{22}
6	$P_5 = S_1 * T_1$	C_{22}	17	$U_5 = U_4 + P_3$	C_{12}
7	$S_2 = S_1 - A_{11}$	X	18	$T_4 = T_2 - B_{21}$	Y
8	$T_2 = B_{22} - T_1$	Y	19	$P_4 = A_{22} * T_4$	C_{11}
9	$P_6 = S_2 * T_2$	C_{12}	20	$U_6 = U_3 - P_4$	C_{21}
10	$S_4 = A_{12} - S_2$	X	21	$P_2 = A_{12} * B_{21}$	C_{11}
11	$P_3 = S_4 * B_{22}$	C_{11}	22	$U_1 = P_1 + P_2$	C_{11}

It is assumed that the additional storage of the algorithm is denoted as
$R(m, k, n)$, which is as follows:

$$R(m, k, n) = \frac{m}{2} max(\frac{k}{2}, \frac{n}{2}) + \frac{k}{2}\frac{n}{2} + R(\frac{m}{2}, \frac{k}{2}, \frac{n}{2}) \tag{3}$$

$$R(m, k, n) = \sum_{i=1}^{\log m} \frac{1}{4^i}(m \cdot max(k, n) + kn) \tag{4}$$

Compared with the 18-variables algorithm, the algorithm introduces fewer intermediate matrices, reducing the overall storage.

4   Regression Model Predictor

4.1   "Depth First" and "Breadth First"

In the field of parallel computing, researchers have carried out breadth-first and depth-first parallel strategies to avoid communication problems. Depth-first and breadth-first are alternative ways for processors to process subproblems in the recursive problems. At a depth-first step, subproblems are executed in sequence, while at a breadth-first step, subproblems are executed in parallel.

Although the breadth-first strategy reduces the amount of communication between subproblems and exposes higher parallelism, the extra memory consumption is required compared to the depth-first strategy. In the shared-memory environment, the interleaving strategies of the depth-first and breadth-first will affect the memory consumption of fast matrix multiplication algorithm, cache access mode, the number of execution threads and the size of base problem. All of these will lead to the performance difference. In the heterogeneous environment, we can speculate that different interleaving strategies can lead to different performance of fast matrix multiplication. Because the number of threads adopted in this paper is fixed, it is different from the implementation in homogeneous environment. Since the 2-variables Winograd algorithm has more dependencies and most of the tasks are executed in sequence, the execution is similar to the depth-first, so the depth-first strategy in this paper corresponds to the 2-variables Winograd algorithm, while the breadth-first strategy corresponds to the 18-variables Winograd algorithm.

4.2   Strategy Sequence

Recursive task graph extension includes the homogeneous extension and heterogeneous extension. The homogeneous extension means that the task graph generated by each recursion is same, which is reflected in the Winograd algorithm with 18 variables or 2 variables in each recursion. The heterogeneous extension means that the algorithm used for each recursion is distinct. The strategy sequence is applied to describe the task graph generation.

The strategy sequence is a string consisting of the character B and D. Each character represents a recursive extension strategy, where D represents a depth-first strategy that is the 2-variables Winograd algorithm, and B represents a breadth-first strategy that is the 18-variables Winograd algorithm. The length of the sequence determines the cutoff point for fast matrix multiplication. The task graph of the homogeneous extension strategy sequence "BB" and the heterogeneous extension strategy sequence "BD" are shown in Fig. 5.

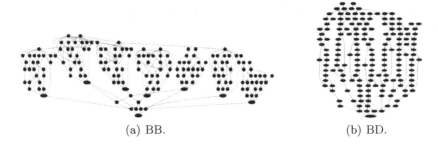

(a) BB.   (b) BD.

Fig. 5. The task graph of the homogeneous extension strategy sequence "BB" and the heterogeneous extension strategy sequence "BD"

4.3   Details of the Implementation

Recursive task graph extension can be divided into the homogeneous extension and heterogeneous extension. Due to the complexity and diversity of extension strategies for the same matrix, a predictor based on the random forest regression algorithm is applied to find the approximate optimal extension strategy by predicting the performance. Suppose that for a given matrix M, the set of extension strategies is $\{SEQ_1, SEQ_2,...,SEQ_n\}$. The performance is in the case of $G(M, SEQ_i)$, $i = 1, 2, ..., n$. The predictor can return an approximately optimal extension strategy based on the predicted performance:

$$Seq = argmax(G(M, SEQ_1), G(M, SEQ_2), ..., G(M, SEQ_n)) \tag{5}$$

As shown in the Fig. 6, the prediction consists of two phases. The first is the offline training phase, which focuses on generating performance data on a heterogeneous runtime system using a series of extension strategies based on a given dataset. Then, the random forest regression algorithm is used for training based on the performance data, and the selected series of features (matrix size, extension strategy, recursion depth, number of temporary matrices, maximum size of temporary matrices, and minimum size of temporary matrices). The second stage is the online decision phase, where a series of features are generated according to the extension strategy for a given matrix, and the trained model is applied to predict the performance, and finally the extension strategy with the optimal prediction performance is selected as the output.

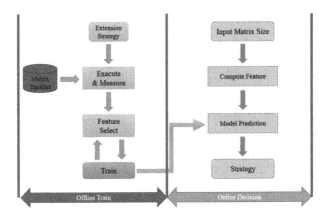

Fig. 6. Regression model predictor based on random forest regression algorithm.

5   Experiment

5.1   Experimental Setup

All experiments are conducted on a heterogeneous platform consisting of a GTX 3090 GPU and Intel i9-10920X CPU. The CPU is running at 3.5 GHz with 12 cores and 256 GB of memory. The GPU has 10,496 cuda cores with a 24 GB GDDR6X memory configuration. Our software environment is based on Ubuntu OS, GCC 9.0 and cuda 11.0.

5.2   Performance Evaluation

In order to evaluate the performance of heterogeneous fast matrix multiplication quantitatively, GFLOPS is used to measure the strengths and weaknesses of each implementation. The expression for computing GFLOPS is shown below:

$$GFLOPS = \frac{2n^3}{seconds} \times 10^{-9} \tag{6}$$

5.3   Heterogeneous Implementation

In order to evaluate the effectiveness of the heterogeneous implementation, a series of experiments are conducted. We select a total of 113 matrices at intervals of 64 between matrix sizes from 1024 to 8192 and extension strategies of "BDB", "BD", "B", "BB", "BDDB", "D", "BBD", "DBD". As shown in Fig. 7, it shows that the improved Winograd algorithm achieves an average speedup of 1.6x, 1.5x and 1.4x against to cuBLAS, Winograd on CPU, and Winograd on GPU [12] for matrices with matrix dimension greater than 5000, respectively, and the performance of the "BB" and "BD" extension strategies drops suddenly in a matrix size of 5200. Based on the analysis of the trace information, we find that the decrease in speedup is due to the overhead involved in a large-scale submatrix multiplication task executed by CPU.

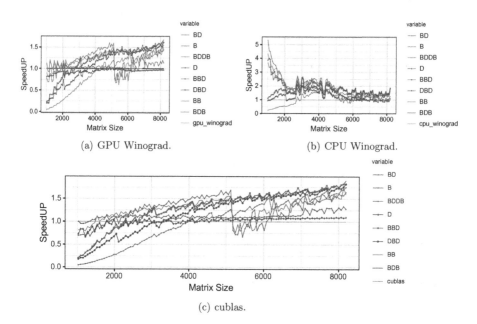

(a) GPU Winograd.   (b) CPU Winograd.

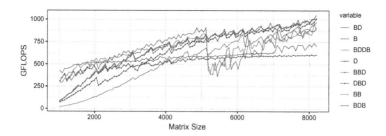

(c) cublas.

Fig. 7. The speedup ratio of each extension strategy relative to cuBLAS, GPU-Winograd and CPU-Winograd implementation.

5.4   Extension Strategy

Different recursive extension strategies correspond to different algorithm implementations. We conduct experimental evaluations for extension strategies, and analyze the impact of different extension strategies on performance. We take a total of 113 matrices selected from a matrix range of 1024–8192 with an interval of 64 as an example, and select some extension strategies for performance statistics.

Fig. 8. The performance comparison between different extension strategies.

It can be seen from the Fig. 8 that the extension strategies corresponding to the best performance of different matrices are distinct. The extension strategies of "B", "BB", "D" and "BD" have shown the optimal performance when the matrix size is less than 2000. The performance of "BDB", "DBD", etc. improves as the matrix size increases. The extension strategies of "BDB", "DBD", and "BBD" show better performance than other strategies for the relatively large matrices. Therefore, different execution strategies in different recursive levels have a significant impact on the performance.

5.5 Regression Model Predictor

The performance predictor based on the random forest regression can predict the performance of a given matrix. In order to distinguish from the training dataset, we take 103 matrices with an interval of 70 between 1023 and 8193 as an example to illustrate the effectiveness of the predictor. As shown in Fig. 9, the red circle solid line represents the best performance predicted by the predictor for each matrix. The blue triangle solid line represents the performance of the actual optimal extension strategy for each matrix.

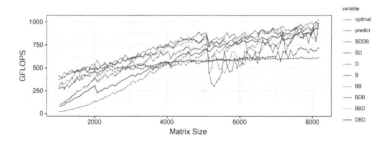

Fig. 9. The comparison between the predicted performance of the model and the actual performance of each extension strategy. (Color figure online)

In order to measure the correctness of the predictions, we use the root mean square error (RMSE), the maximum, the minimum, and the mean absolute error (MAE) for evaluation, as follows:

$$RMSE = \sqrt{\frac{1}{m}\sum_{i=1}^{m}(y_i - \overline{y_i})^2} \tag{7}$$

$$MAE = \frac{1}{m}\sum_{i=1}^{m}|y_i - \overline{y_i}| \tag{8}$$

In the above formula, y_i is the performance of the actual optimal extension strategy for the $i - th$ matrix, $\overline{y_i}$ is the performance predicted by model in milliseconds. The evaluation results are shown in Table 3. From the table, it shows that the performance predicted by model is similar to that of the actual optimal strategy, the maximum error is less than 100 ms, and the minimum error is less than 0.1ms. As shown in Fig. 10, we take two matrices as examples to evaluate the rationality of the extension strategy predicted by model. The maximum and minimum errors of the matrix with a scale of 4733 are 26.278 ms and 0.2217 ms, and the maximum and minimum errors of the matrix with a scale of 8163 are 120.039 ms and 5.015 ms. It can be seen that the performance of the extension strategy predicted by model for matrices is similar to the performance of the actual extension strategy. The optimal strategies predicted by model are "BD", and "BBD", respectively, which are also consistent with the actual optimal extension strategies. Moreover, in the online decision-making stage, the preprocessing time for predicting the optimal extension strategy is about 6 milliseconds. The proportion of preprocessing overhead decreases as the matrix size increases. Therefore, the random forest regression model designed in this paper has feasibility in selecting the optimal extension strategy by predicting performance.

Table 3. The evaluation results.

Evaluation index	Milliseconds
Root mean squard error	20.087428
Mean absolute error	12.618624
Max absolute error	93.297792
Min absolute error	0.004760

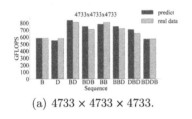

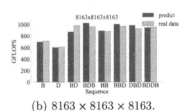

(a) 4733 × 4733 × 4733.   (b) 8163 × 8163 × 8163.

Fig. 10. The performance of the extension strategies predicted by model.

6   Conclusion

In this paper, a CPU-GPU heterogeneous Winograd algorithm is implemented. We propose two recursive task graph extension strategies: homogeneous and heterogeneous extension, invoke different execution strategies in different recursive levels and design a predictor based on the random forest regression model to make a decision. In our implementation, we firstly perform feature calculations based on the input matrix, then invoke the trained model to obtain the optimal extension strategy, and generate task graph based on the extension strategy. The input of the runtime system is the task graph, and the runtime system uses work-stealing scheduler to achieve balanced load. Overall, our method achieved higher performance than GPU-based approaches, including CUBLAS, and CPU-based approach.

References

1. Ballard, G., Demmel, J., Holtz, O., Lipshitz, B., Schwartz, O.: Communication-optimal parallel algorithm for Strassen's matrix multiplication. In: Proceedings of the Twenty-Fourth Annual ACM Symposium on Parallelism in Algorithms and Architectures, pp. 193–204 (2012)
2. Benson, A.R., Ballard, G.: A framework for practical parallel fast matrix multiplication. ACM SIGPLAN Not. **50**(8), 42–53 (2015)
3. Bini, D., et al.: O (n2. 7799) complexity for nxn approximate matrix multiplication (1979)
4. Coppersmith, D., Winograd, S.: Matrix multiplication via arithmetic progressions. In: Proceedings of the Nineteenth Annual ACM Symposium on Theory of Computing, pp. 1–6 (1987)
5. D'Alberto, P., Nicolau, A.: Adaptive Winograd's matrix multiplications. ACM Trans. Math. Softw. (TOMS) **36**(1), 1–23 (2009)
6. Demmel, J., Dumitriu, I., Holtz, O., Kleinberg, R.: Fast matrix multiplication is stable. Numer. Math. **106**(2), 199–224 (2007)
7. Demmel, J., et al.: Communication-optimal parallel recursive rectangular matrix multiplication. In: 2013 IEEE 27th International Symposium on Parallel and Distributed Processing, pp. 261–272. IEEE (2013)
8. D'Alberto, P., et al.: The better accuracy of Strassen-Winograd algorithms (Fast-MMW). Adv. Linear Algebra Matrix Theory **4**(01), 9 (2014)
9. Huang, J., Smith, T.M., Henry, G.M., van de Geijn, R.A.: Implementing Strassen's algorithm with BLIS. arXiv preprint arXiv:1605.01078 (2016)
10. Huang, J., Yu, C.D., Geijn, R.A.v.d.: Strassen's algorithm reloaded on GPUs. ACM Trans. Math. Softw. (TOMS) **46**(1), 1–22 (2020)
11. Kumar, B., Huang, C.H., Sadayappan, P., Johnson, R.W.: A tensor product formulation of Strassen's matrix multiplication algorithm with memory reduction. Sci. Program. **4**(4), 275–289 (1995)
12. Lai, P.W., Arafat, H., Elango, V., Sadayappan, P.: Accelerating Strassen-Winograd's matrix multiplication algorithm on GPUs. In: 20th Annual International Conference on High Performance Computing, pp. 139–148. IEEE (2013)
13. Le Gall, F.: Powers of tensors and fast matrix multiplication. In: Proceedings of the 39th International Symposium on Symbolic and Algebraic Computation, pp. 296–303 (2014)
14. Li, J., Ranka, S., Sahni, S.: Strassen's matrix multiplication on GPUs. In: 2011 IEEE 17th International Conference on Parallel and Distributed Systems, pp. 157–164. IEEE (2011)
15. Lipshitz, B., Ballard, G., Demmel, J., Schwartz, O.: Communication-avoiding parallel Strassen: implementation and performance. In: SC 2012: Proceedings of the International Conference on High Performance Computing, Networking, Storage and Analysis, pp. 1–11. IEEE (2012)

16. Pan, V.Y.: Strassen's algorithm is not optimal trilinear technique of aggregating, uniting and canceling for constructing fast algorithms for matrix operations. In: 19th Annual Symposium on Foundations of Computer Science (SFCS 1978), pp. 166–176. IEEE (1978)
17. Ray, U., Hazra, T.K., Ray, U.K.: Matrix multiplication using Strassen's algorithm on CPU & GPU. Int. J. Comput. Sci. Eng. **4**(10), 98–105 (2016)
18. Stothers, A.J.: On the complexity of matrix multiplication (2010)
19. Strassen, V.: Gaussian elimination is not optimal. Numer. Math. **13**(4), 354–356 (1969)
20. Strassen, V.: The asymptotic spectrum of tensors and the exponent of matrix multiplication. In: 27th Annual Symposium on Foundations of Computer Science (SFCS 1986), pp. 49–54. IEEE (1986)

Temperature Matrix-Based Data Placement Using Improved Hungarian Algorithm in Edge Computing Environments

Yuying Zhao[1,2], Pengwei Wang[1,2(✉)], Hengdi Huang[1], and Zhaohui Zhang[1]

[1] School of Computer Science and Technology, Donghua University, Shanghai 201620, China
wangpengwei@dhu.edu.cn

[2] Engineering Research Center of Digitalized Textile and Fashion Technology, Ministry of Education, Shanghai 201620, China

Abstract. The scale of data shows an explosive growth trend, with wide use of cloud storage. However, there are problems such as network latency and power costs. The emergence of edge computing brings data close to the edge of the network, making edge computing a good supplement to cloud computing. The spatiotemporal characteristics of data have been largely ignored in studies of data placement and storage optimization. To address this, we propose a temperature matrix-based data placement method using an improved Hungarian algorithm (TEMPLIH). A temperature matrix reflects the influence of data characteristics on its placement. A replica selection algorithm based on a temperature matrix (RSA-TM) can meet latency requirements. An improved Hungarian algorithm (IHA-RM) is proposed on the basis of replica selection, which satisfies the balance among the multiple goals of latency, cost, and load balancing. Compared with commonly used data placement strategies, experiments show that TEMPLIH can effectively reduce the cost of data placement while meeting user access latency requirements and maintaining a reasonable load balance between edge servers.

Keywords: Edge computing · Data placement · Data temperature · Hungarian algorithm · Load balancing

1 Introduction

Cloud computing has developed rapidly. However, with the advent of artificial intelligence and 5G, applications continue to appear and amounts of data increase, placing high demands on network latency. Hence, edge computing is in great demand because it places computing at or near the physical location of the data source, enabling faster and more reliable service.

From the perspective of application providers, centralized cloud computing adapts with difficulty to accommodate frequent data interaction. It has become increasingly powerless in terms of network latency, broadband load, and data management costs. Hence, they seek to reduce their operating costs while meeting the service requirements of users, and data caching in the edge computing environment is the object of much

© Springer Nature Switzerland AG 2022
H. Shen et al. (Eds.): PDCAT 2021, LNCS 13148, pp. 237–248, 2022.
https://doi.org/10.1007/978-3-030-96772-7_22

research. Although researchers have done much optimization work, they have focused on improving the optimization algorithm itself in terms of latency, cost, and service quality. In fact, with increasing amounts of data, there is a huge space for exploration, especially in terms of regional temporal and spatial characteristics. Whether in social networks or streaming media, there are obvious differences between individuals and regions.

Therefore, in this study, we propose a concept of data temperature that considers the temporal and spatial characteristics to model and calculate data. To be precise, it is based on the temperature matrix to obtain a data replica placement scheme that satisfies the latency. Finally, the improved Hungarian algorithm based on the cost matrix reduces the cost of data placement while ensuring reasonable load balancing.

This study makes three main contributions:

- We propose the concept of data temperature and its calculation model. On this basis, we construct a data temperature matrix, which can be used to optimize the placement of data;
- To meet the user's latency needs and improve the user experience, we propose a data replica matrix selection algorithm based on a temperature matrix (RSA-TM), which can obtain a replica placement solution that meets latency requirements;
- We propose an improved Hungarian algorithm (IHA-RM) based on the data replica matrix, which can satisfy user latency needs, and guarantees the load balance and cost-effectiveness of data placement.

The remainder of this paper is organized as follows. Section 2 discusses related work. Section 3 provides related definitions and the calculation model of the problem. Section 4 discusses the design of the algorithm. Section 5 compares our algorithm with some classic algorithms. Section 6 presents our conclusions.

2   Related Work

As the quantity of data increases, so does the number of users. The reasonable placement of data must not only meet the increasingly high service-quality requirements of users, but also take into account the constraints of system storage space and computing power in the context of large-scale data storage in a real-world environment. Current research on strategy optimization of data placement focuses on cost optimization, latency optimization, and load balancing in the cloud computing environment.

Cloud computing has an on-demand usage model. Service providers hope to reduce operating costs while meeting user service requirements. Wang et al. [1] proposed a multi-cloud storage architecture. A multi-objective optimization problem was defined to minimize total cost and maximize data availability. This can be solved by a method based on non-dominated sorting genetic algorithm II (NSGA-II) and a set of non-dominated solutions called a Pareto optimality set. Wang et al. [2] proposed an adaptive data placement architecture that can adjust according to time-varying data access patterns and topics to minimize the total cost and maximize data availability. Wang et al. [3] proposed a method based on an ant colony algorithm for data hosting in a multi-cloud environment, constrained by optimization objectives such as cost and availability.

With the development of the network and the emergence of various applications, service providers cannot just reduce costs and ignore increasing latency requirements of users. Wang et al. [4] analyze the geographical distribution characteristics of data centers through a clustering algorithm, and propose an effective data initialization strategy, then they use a genetic algorithm to further optimize the cost-effectiveness and minimal latency. Rao et al. [5] studied the problem of minimizing the total cost while ensuring the quality of service for different locations and times, modeling it as constrained mixed integer programming problem.

The load balance of the system is another important factor affecting performance [6]. Pujol et al. [7] proposed an algorithm to locate connected user data in the same service while maintaining load balance, with the aim to maintain a better online social environment. Tran and Zhang [8] proposed a framework based on evolutionary algorithms to place data to minimize and balance the server load, and to optimize storage efficiency. Chen et al. [9] proposed a method to explore the potential social relationships of users in social networks while balancing the workload between servers to minimize the traffic between them.

The emergence of edge services can effectively provide real-time, high-bandwidth, and low-latency access to applications. There has been much research on content placement in a combined edge environment. Cao et al. [10] presents a method combined NSGA-II with multi-group method which has better ability of global search to help users determine cloud and edge services to store and access data object. Xu et al. [11] studied the service caching problem in MEC's cellular network. An online algorithm was proposed for the random online service caching of edge computing to minimize computational latency under the constraint of long-term energy consumption.

While there is a lack of research on data placement based on the edge environment. Most such research has addressed the optimization of algorithms, without considering the temporal and spatial characteristics of the data. We propose temperature matrix-based data placement using an improved Hungarian algorithm (TEMPLIH), combining temperature, replica, and cost matrices. While ensuring user latency, we can reduce storage costs as much as possible while balancing loads through the improved Hungarian algorithm.

3 System Model and Problem Definition

We introduce the system structure of edge data placement; define the three matrices, including the temperature matrix, data replica matrix, and cost matrix; and define the optimization objectives and constraints.

3.1 System Framework

We define a dataset $D, D = \{d_1, d_2, d_3, \ldots d_m\}$ as a data block of a user's requests for data. The user area, $R = \{r_1, r_2, r_3, \ldots r_N\}$, is the access area formed by the user set, and is used for latency calculation. The edge server, $S = \{s_1, s_2, s_3, \ldots s_K\}$, includes a number of edge server sets in each area provided by each service provider to store data blocks that meet latency requirements. Each edge server is associated with a set of attributes $<P_e^s, P_e^b, P_e^o, l_e>$, where P_e^s is the storage price, P_e^b is the bandwidth price, P_e^o is the obtained operation price, and l_e is the storage capacity. The relationship between edge server, user area and data is shown in Fig. 1.

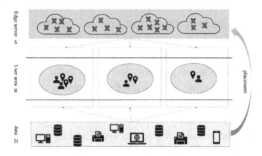

Fig. 1. Framework of data placement in edge environment.

3.2 Data Temperature and Calculation

Since the popularity of data access differs across regions, data have their own attributes according to the degree of access to them in different regions [12]. This degree of preference must consider the changes in data attributes and spatial characteristics during a certain period of time. Spatiotemporal data refers to geographic entities whose spatial elements or attributes change over time. We propose the concept of data temperature based on the attributes of the data and the regional characteristics of the data distribution. On this basis, we define that each data block contains a set of attributes $<d_c, d_t, d_d, d_f>$, where d_c is the number of clicks, d_t is the number of comments, d_d is the number of downloads of the video, and d_f is a user-favorited video. The importance x_i of each data block d_i is evaluated and calculated by the number of clicks and views, numbers, downloads, and favorites. The number of views, comments, and downloads accounts for 0.8, while the number of favorites accounts for 0.2; i.e.,

$$x_i = 0.8(d_c + d_t + d_d) + 0.2d_f. \tag{1}$$

The relative weight w_i of data block d_i is determined by the ratio of the importance of x_i to that of all other data,

$$w_i = \frac{x_i}{\sum_i^{m-1} x_i}. \tag{2}$$

According to the change characteristics of data temperature, H is the temperature value of the current data, w is the relative importance, H_0 is the initial temperature, and k is the attenuation coefficient. Heat is positively correlated with importance and timeliness, and negatively correlated with time.

$$H(t) = w * H_0 * e^{-kt} \tag{3}$$

The data temperature matrix T_{mn} is defined to store the temperature values of data in different regions, i.e., the temperature value $h_{m,n}$ of data m in area n,

$$T_{mn} = \begin{pmatrix} h_{1,1} & \cdots & h_{1,n} \\ \vdots & \ddots & \vdots \\ h_{m,1} & \cdots & h_{m,n} \end{pmatrix}. \tag{4}$$

In addition, because the number of edge servers differs by region, their computing power, storage cost, and operational cost also differ. We define a regional server matrix to record servers by region.

$$R_{nk} = \begin{cases} 1 & \text{Server } k \text{ is in area } n \\ 0 & \text{Server } k \text{ is not in area } n \end{cases} \tag{5}$$

3.3 Network Latency

Satisfying the user's access latency requirements is important in the optimization of data placement strategies. We take time latency as a constraint to ensure that users can access the data they want within an acceptable time. We guarantee that the maximum response time of each request is 200 ms [13]. We use geographic distance as a rough measure of network latency, which we express as a linear function of distance. The correlation between latency and geographic distance can be obtained through network latency data collection, and the round-trip time (RTT) [14, 15] is used to calculate the data access latency,

$$l_m = \max_{d \in S(t)} \{5 + 0.02D(d)\}. \tag{6}$$

where $D(d)$ is the distance between the user and the data center, $\widehat{D}$ is the maximum acceptable time latency, and the average access latency is as follows.

$$\overline{a}(\sum_{i=1}^{M} l_i) \leq \widehat{D} \tag{7}$$

3.4 System Cost

To reduce the average access latency, the number of data copies must be appropriately increased, which will increase the cost. The cost of the service provider and the average latency in responding to user requests are conflicting considerations. To place more copies of content on edge nodes can reduce the average latency in responding to file requests, but it will increase the resource usage of edge nodes. We consider the three main parts of resource usage costs, i.e., the costs of data calculation, bandwidth, and storage.

At time t, the storage cost of data d_i is the total cost of storage for a placement plan, including storage, network, and operation, is

$$\widehat{P}_C = \sum_{e \in S(t)} z_i P_e^s + \sum_{e \in S(t)} z_i P_e^b + \sum_{e \in S(t)} d_c P_e^o \tag{8}$$

3.5 Load Balancing

With the explosive growth of data requiring storage and processing, to maintain a good system balance is of practical significance. If the server stores a group of active users, a large number of visits will be accepted. At this time, a longer response time will diminish the user experience. By maintaining a good load balance of the storage system, system performance and response speed can be improved. The load of a data placement scheme is

$$L = \sqrt{\frac{1}{K} \sum_{i=1}^{M} (U_m - U_K)^2} \tag{9}$$

where K is the total number of servers, M is the number of servers where data is placed, U_m is the server utilization, and U_K is the total server utilization. The smaller the value of L, the more balanced the load.

3.6 Problem Definition

The optimization goal is to perform reasonable data placement for any given data object and to give its placement plan in the edge environment, so that its cost and load at the edge can reach a relatively balanced state. Therefore, the entire optimization problem can be defined as follows.

$$minC = \sum_{m=1,n=1,k=1}^{M,N,K} E_{mnk} \widehat{P}_C \tag{10}$$

$$minL = \sqrt{\frac{1}{K} \sum_{i=1}^{M} (U_m - U_K)^2} \tag{11}$$

$$\overline{a}(\sum_{i=1}^{M} l_i) \leq \widehat{D} \tag{12}$$

4 Algorithm Design

TEMPLIH consists of a data replica selection algorithm based on a temperature matrix (RSA-TM), and the improved Hungarian algorithm based on a replica matrix (IHA-RM).

RSA-TM considers the characteristics of the data and obtains the data temperature matrix, which can screen suitable data and reduce unnecessary resource consumption. When the latency condition is met, placement is stopped and the data placement area is recorded. Otherwise, we select areas to place the data in descending order according to the data temperature matrix, and stop placing it when the latency requirement is met. The time complexity in calculating the temperature matrix is $O(MN)$. We define a data replica matrix based on the temperature matrix. The placement area where data m satisfies the latency in area n is recorded as 1, and otherwise it is 0, i.e.,

$$L_{mn} = \begin{cases} 1 & \text{Data } m \text{ is placed in area } n \\ 0 & \text{Data } m \text{ is not placed in area } n \end{cases} . \tag{13}$$

Algorithm 1 Data replica matrix selection algorithm based on temperature matrix (RSA-TM)
Input: Data D; User area R; Server S; The capacity of the data block stored by the server Cap_m
Output: Data replica matrix L_{mn}
1:   $L_{mn} \leftarrow \emptyset$
2:   **for** data block $d_m \in D$ **do**
3:       **for** area $r_n \in R$ **do**
4:          $T_{mn} \leftarrow$ Calculate the temperature matrix by formula (3)
5:          $M \leftarrow$ Regional temperature is sorted by T_{mn}
6:       **end for**
7:       **for** area $r_n \in M$ **do**
8:          $\overline{ave} \leftarrow$ Calculate the latency by formula (6)
9:          **if** $\overline{ave} \leq 200$ and $Cap_m < l_e$ **then**
10:            $Rindex \leftarrow$ Storage area location
11:          **else**
12:            $index \leftarrow$ Select the area according to temperature
13:          **end if**
14:       **end for**
15: **end for**
16: **Return** L_{mn}

When meeting user access latency, to obtain a data placement solution at the least cost while ensuring load balance, we propose an improved Hungarian algorithm based on the replica matrix (IHA-RM). The data server placement matrix D_{mk} expresses the placement relationship between data m and area server k,

$$D_{mk} = \begin{cases} 1 & \text{Data } m \text{ is placed on server } k \\ 0 & \text{Data } m \text{ is not placed on server } k \end{cases}. \tag{14}$$

We combine the regional server matrix R_{nk} and data server placement matrix D_{mk} to get the placement cost of the data on the server in each region according to the cost calculation formula. The cost matrix $P_N = [p_1, p_2, p_3, ..., p_N]$ represents the placement cost of the data block on the server in each region, i.e., the data placement cost matrix P of data block m and server k under the N areas is collected, the cost of the server storage data block is recorded as $C_{k,m}$, and

$$P_n = \begin{pmatrix} C_{1,1} & \cdots & C_{1,m} \\ \vdots & \ddots & \vdots \\ C_{k,1} & \cdots & C_{k,m} \end{pmatrix}. \tag{15}$$

In our scenario, the data and servers in each area are often not equal. Therefore, we compare the numbers of data blocks and computing resources in each area. If these are equal, the standard Hungarian algorithm can be used to solve the problem. If they are unequal, we must determine the numbers of servers and data blocks. If the number of servers exceeds the number of data blocks, we add the number of virtual data blocks (add 0) to create as many dimensions as the number of servers, and then use the standard Hungarian algorithm. If there are more data blocks than there are servers, the cost matrix is split, according to the dimension of the number of servers, into a small matrix of the number of data blocks divided by the number of servers. If the number of data blocks in the last sub-matrix is less than the number of servers, the number of virtual data blocks (add 0) is added to make it consistent with the number of servers. After completing the matrix, we use the traditional Hungarian algorithm to determine the data placement plan. The time complexity of calculating the data server matrix and cost matrix is $O(NMK)$.

Algorithm 2 Improved Hungarian algorithm based on replica matrix (IHA-RM)

Input: Data replica matrix L_{mn}; regional server matrix R_{nk} ; Number of regional servers $Rnum_k$; Number of area data blocks $Dnum_k$

Output: Load L, cost C

1:   $E_{mnk} \leftarrow \emptyset$, $Load \leftarrow \inf$, $C \leftarrow \inf$, $P_N \leftarrow \emptyset$
2:   **for** each area $r_n \in R$ **do**
3:       $D_{mk} \leftarrow R_{nk}$ Server dimension and L_{mn} data dimension
4:       $P_N \leftarrow$ Calculate the cost matrix by formula (8)
5:       **for** each cost matrix $p_n \in P_N$ **do**
6:           **if** $Dnum_k = Rnum_k$ **then**
7:               $Sindex \leftarrow$ Use the Hungarian algorithm to select the lowest cost and record
8:               the placement location
9:           **else if** $Dnum_k < Rnum_k$ **then**
10:               $p_n \leftarrow$ add virtual data block 0 in $Rnum_k$ dimension
11:               $Sindex \leftarrow$ Use the Hungarian algorithm to select the lowest cost and
12:               record the placement location
13:           **else if** $Dnum_k > Rnum_k$ **then**
14:               $r = Dnum_k / Rnum_k$
15:               $R \leftarrow$ Divide p_n into the set of r matrices with $Rnum_k$ as the dimension
16:               **for** each matrix $R_i \in R$ **do**
17:                   **if** $Dnum_k < Rnum_k$ **then**
18:                       $R_i \leftarrow$ add virtual data block 0 in $Rnum_k$ dimension
19:                   **else**
20:                       $Sindex \leftarrow$ Use the Hungarian algorithm to select the lowest cost
21:                       and record the placement location
22:                   **end if**
23:               **end for**
24:           **end if**
25:       **end for**
26:   **end for**
27:   $L \leftarrow$ Calculate the load by formula (9)
28:   $C \leftarrow$ Calculate the cost by formula (8)
29:   **Return** L, C

---

5   Experimental Evaluation

We introduce simulation experiment settings and give multiple benchmark algorithms for comparison. Experimental evaluation shows that our algorithm can balance the cost and load balance goals of data placement under the premise of satisfying latency requirements.

5.1   Experiment Setup

We introduce the video dataset, edge server information, and parameter settings. The dataset is a YouTube popular video dataset with 40,726 items, including the number of views, shares, comments, and likes.

Regional edge server information was obtained from the websites of major cloud service providers, including storage price ($/GB), bandwidth price ($/GB), get operation price ($/10k times), and latitude and longitude of the edge server.

The experiment was run on a computer with an Intel Core i7-7500U at 2.7 GHz, with 8 GB memory and Windows 10.

5.2   Experimental Results and Analysis

We compared the cost and load rate of TEMPLIH with those of several other algorithms for data placement with the same experimental data.

- **Random:** The distribution relationship between the data and server is obtained from the replica matrix, and the data block is randomly placed on the regional edge server.
- **Latency-based** [16]: The data are placed on the regional edge server with the lowest total network latency. We calculate the data placement considering cost and load balancing.
- **Cost-based** [5]: According to the replica matrix, we can obtain the distribution relationship between the data and server. We place the data block on the edge server with the lowest cost.
- **Load Balance** [8]: After the data replica matrix that meets the latency requirement is known, the data blocks are sequentially placed in the edge server.

The algorithm performance was evaluated by changing the number of data blocks from 6000 to 13000. The data block size was fixed at 0.6 GB, the number of servers was 425, and the server capacity was 600 GB. Figures 3 and 2 describe the cost and load rate, respectively, of the data placement schemes obtained by the five algorithms. It can be seen that the load rate of our algorithm is similar to that of the load balance algorithm, but its total average cost is 18.9% less.

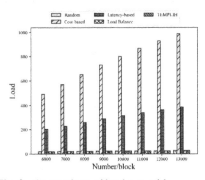
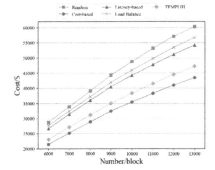

Fig. 2. Comparison of load rate with changing of data blocks.

Fig. 3. Comparison of cost with changing of data blocks.

The data block size was changed to 1.2 GB, with 10,000 fixed data blocks. The number of servers and their capacities were consistent with the above experiment. Figure 5 shows the cost changes of the placement schemes obtained by the five algorithms. It can be seen that the data block size was too large, the data resources tended to be saturated, and the cost was reduced. Figure 4 compares the load rates of the five algorithms. As the size of the data block increases, the distribution of blocks becomes more dispersed, so the load rate decreases when the number of servers and their capacities are unchanged. The load will be more balanced. Our TEMPLIH algorithm is less effective in cost than the data solution obtained by the Cost algorithm. However, Fig. 4 demonstrates that the load rate of the cost-based algorithm is 32.8 times that of our proposed algorithm in terms of load conditions. It is worth noting that the load balancing of the algorithm based on cost is much worse than the TEMPLIH algorithm.

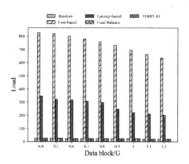 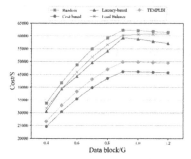

Fig. 4. Comparison of load rate with changing data block size.

Fig. 5. Comparison of cost with changing data block size.

Changing the range of server capacity from 400 GB to 650 GB, there were 10,000 data blocks of size 0.6 GB, and the number of servers remained unchanged. Figures 6 and 7 show the changes in load rate and the cost of data placement, respectively, for the five algorithms when the server capacity changed. It can be seen that the load rate increases with the server capacity. This is because the increase in server capacity enables better placement options for data blocks when resources are relatively abundant. Combined with Figs. 6 and 7, with the increase of server capacity. The load rate of the algorithm we proposed is similar to that of the load balancing algorithm. Figure 7 shows that our proposed method (TEMPLIH) performs better than the load balancing algorithm in terms of cost, and our algorithm saves 16.8% in total average cost.

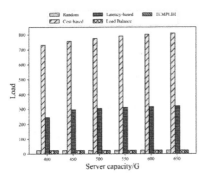

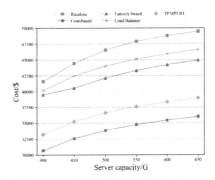

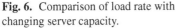

Fig. 6. Comparison of load rate with changing server capacity.

Fig. 7. Comparison of cost with changing server capacity.

6 Conclusion and Future Work

In the current environment where the scale of data and the number of terminals continue to expand, demands on network latency continue to increase. In the edge environment, the edge server can take advantage of its own lightweight, real-time computing capabilities, and closer proximity to users to place data reasonably, which can effectively improve user experience. However, how to use data characteristics and quickly weigh the relationship between various indicators is a problem that remains to be solved in the field of data placement. Our proposed TEMPLIH can optimize the cost and load balance of data in the edge environment under the premise of meeting the latency requirements. Specifically, the RSA-TM and the IHA-RM are adopted. Experiments have proved that with respect to optimization effects, the TEMPLIH strategy, which considers the data temperature matrix is better than the traditional multi-cloud data storage strategy. In future work, we will consider data characteristics for collaborative application research on data placement and task scheduling.

Acknowledgement. This work was partially supported by the National Natural Science Foundation of China (NSFC) under Grant 61602109, DHU Distinguished Young Professor Program under Grant LZB2019003, Shanghai Science and Technology Innovation Action Plan under Grant 19511101802, Fundamental Research Funds for the Central Universities.

References

1. Wang, P., Zhao, C., Liu, W., Chen, Z., Zhang, Z.: Optimizing data placement for cost effective and high available multi-cloud storage. Comput. Inform. **39**(1–2), 51–82 (2020). https://doi.org/10.31577/cai_2020_1-2_51
2. Wang, P., Zhao, C., Wei, Y., Wang, D., Zhang, Z.: An adaptive data placement architecture in multicloud environments. Sci. Program. **2020**(1), 1–12 (2020). https://doi.org/10.1155/2020/1704258

3. Wang, P., Zhao, C., Zhang, Z.: An ant colony algorithm-based approach for cost-effective data hosting with high availability in multi-cloud environments. In: 2018 15th International Conference on Networking, Sensing and Control (ICNSC), pp. 1–6. IEEE (2018). https://doi.org/10.1109/ICNSC.2018.8361288

4. Wang, P., Chen, Z., Zhou, M., Zhang, Z., et al.: Cost-effective and latency-minimized data placement strategy for spatial crowdsourcing in multi-cloud environment. IEEE Trans. Cloud Comput. 1 (2021). https://doi.org/10.1109/TCC.2021.3119862

5. Rao, L., Liu, X., Xie, L., Liu, W.: Minimizing electricity cost: optimization of distributed internet data centers in a multi-electricity-market environment. In: 2010 Proceedings IEEE INFOCOM, pp. 1–9. IEEE (2010). https://doi.org/10.1109/INFOCOM.2010.5461933

6. Kumar, A., Kalra, M.: Load balancing in cloud data center using modified active monitoring load balancer. In: 2016 International Conference on Advances in Computing, Communication, & Automation (ICACCA) (Spring), pp. 1–5. IEEE (2016). https://doi.org/10.1109/ICACCA.2016.7578903

7. Pujol, J.M., Erramilli, V., Siganos, G., Yang, X., et al.: The little engine(s) that could: scaling online social networks. IEEE/ACM Trans. Netw. **20**(4), 1162–1175 (2012). https://doi.org/10.1109/TNET.2012.2188815

8. Tran, D.A., Zhang, T.: S-PUT: An EA-based framework for socially aware data partitioning. Comput. Netw. **75**(24), 504–518 (2014). https://doi.org/10.1016/j.comnet.2014.08.026

9. Chen, H., Jin, H., Wu, S.: Minimizing inter-server communications by exploiting self-similarity in online social networks. IEEE Trans. Parallel Distrib. Syst. **27**(4), 1116–1130 (2016). https://doi.org/10.1109/TPDS.2015.2427155

10. Cao, E., Wang, P., Yan, C., Jiang, C.: A Cloudedge-combined data placement strategy based on user access regions. In: 6th International Conference on Big Data and Information Analytics (BigDIA 2020), Shenzhen, China, pp. 243–250 (2020). https://doi.org/10.1109/BigDIA51454.2020.00046

11. Xu, J., Chen, L., Zhou, P.: Joint service caching and task offloading for mobile edge computing in dense networks. In: IEEE Conference on Computer Communications, pp. 207–215. IEEE (2018). https://doi.org/10.1109/INFOCOM.2018.8485977

12. Wang, P., Wei, Y., Zhang, Z.: Optimizing data placement in multi-cloud environments considering data temperature. In: the 7th International Conference on Artificial Intelligence and Security, pp. 167–179. ICAIS (2021). https://doi.org/10.1007/978-3-030-78612-0_14

13. Khalajzadeh, H., Dong, Y., Grundy, J., Yang, Y.: Improving cloud-based online social network data placement and replication. In: IEEE International Conference on Cloud Computing, pp. 678–685. IEEE (2016). https://doi.org/10.1109/CLOUD.2016.0095

14. Wu, Z., Butkiewicz, M., Perkins, D., Katz-Bassett, E., Madhyastha, H.V.: SPANStore: cost-effective geo-replicated storage spanning multiple cloud services. In: Proceedings of the Twenty-Fourth ACM Symposium on Operating Systems Principles, pp. 292–308. ACM (2013). https://doi.org/10.1145/2517349.2522730

15. Wu, Y., Wu, C., Li, B., Zhang, L., Lau, F.: Scaling social media applications into geo-distributed clouds. IEEE/ACM Trans. Netw. **23**(3), 689–702 (2015). https://doi.org/10.1109/TNET.2014.2308254

16. Li, X., Wu, J., Tang, S., Lu, S.: Let's stay together: towards traffic aware virtual machine placement in data centers. In: IEEE Conference on Computer Communications, pp. 1842–1850. IEEE (2014). https://doi.org/10.1109/INFOCOM.2014.6848123

Realtime Physics Simulation of Large Virtual Space with Docker Containers

Seiji Saito and Satoshi Fujita$^{(\boxtimes)}$

Graduate School of Advanced Science and Engineering, Hiroshima University,
Kagamiyama 1-4-1, Higashi-Hiroshima 739-8527, Japan
fujita@hiroshima-u.ac.jp

Abstract. In this paper, we propose a way of distributed processing of realtime physics simulations for 3D video games with a large virtual space. The basic idea of the proposed method is to divide a given virtual space into multiple subspaces, and to simulate each subspace with a physics simulator running on a container of virtual environment by assuming that subspaces are sufficiently independent so that each simulation is not affected by the others. In the prototype system we have implemented, the configuration of objects in the subspace allocated to a client is exchanged among hosts every few frames through WebSocket. According to the experiments conducted with the prototype system, it is confirmed that we could achieve a sufficiently high processing speed and high frame rate by bounding the number of objects in each subspace, even if the entire virtual space contains a huge number of virtual objects exceeding 10,000.

Keywords: Edge computing · Virtual world · Physics simulation · Docker container · Cloud game

1 Introduction

A Japanese novelist Reki Kawahara wrote a light novel called *Sword Art Online* in 2002, which depicts various conflicts of characters playing a VRMMORPG (Virtual Reality Massively Multiplayer Online Role-Playing Game) called Sword Art Online, launched in 2022 (in the novel). This virtual online game allows more than 10,000 players to simultaneously log in to the system, and the scenery of the virtual world including the shape of monsters and the face of other players dynamically changes in realtime according to: the movement of the location and the gaze of the player (e.g., through walking or flying), interfering with the virtual world (e.g., engagement in battles), and other miscellaneous game events.

From a technical point of view, realtime rendering of high-resolution videos such as 4K or 8K quality is becoming a reality with the rapid progress in GPU technology. A typical example is *Detroit: Become Human*, which is a game software for PlayStation 4 released by Sony Interactive Entertainment (SIE) in 2018. On the other hand, in recent years, specific game software called VR games have

© Springer Nature Switzerland AG 2022
H. Shen et al. (Eds.): PDCAT 2021, LNCS 13148, pp. 249–260, 2022.
https://doi.org/10.1007/978-3-030-96772-7_23

become widely popular, especially in game genres such as shooting, action, simulation and strategy, so that realistic artificial images which can be mistaken for photographs are being developed through head-mounted display (HMD) of game players. Based on the above technological trends, this paper focuses on another important issue in VRMMORPG: *the scalability issue related to the complexity of the virtual space and the number of players.* The basic idea of our proposed method is to divide the entire virtual space into several subspaces, and assign each subspace to a separate machine for processing, in order to keep the peak load of each physical server as low as possible.

If objects in the virtual space and the gaze of the player are both stationary, we can generate a high resolution still image within a short time by using a sophisticated rendering engine provided on the server, and even when the player's gaze dynamically changes, the rendering results for each gaze can be combined to generate a realistic video stream. Therefore, the remaining problem is *how to keep track of the position and state of virtual objects in the virtual space as they are updated by external events.* In this paper, we consider this challenging issue and propose a method for calculating the position and state of virtual objects without exceeding the processing capacity. Such physics simulations are generally conducted by using physics engines such as PhysX[1], Open Dynamics Engine, and Newton Game Dynamics. It should be worth noting here that in the physics simulation for video games, the accuracy can be often sacrificed to some extent since a high responsiveness is much more important than the accuracy. In fact, it is common to treat only limited number of objects relevant to the player as the target of physics simulations and regard the rest as static images, since the changes in the distant scene on the human retina are usually very small, even if any. However, there could exist some situations in which the details of moving images which becomes visible as a result of player's actions have a significant impact on the player's impression; e.g., the reader could imagine the *ears of wheat rustling in the wind* and the *changes in the scene of a snowstorm caused by changes in temperature.* With those observations, we thought that it would be of great significance to study the basis for realizing such physics simulations in a scalable manner with as little loss of accuracy as possible.

In this paper, we focus on PhysX as the concrete real-time physics engine, and investigate the way of decentralizing physics simulations using a container-based virtual environment. We implemented a prototype system consisting of one server application and one or more client applications. Each application is assigned a specific machine, where each client is executed on a Docker container to allow for live migration of clients depending on the change of the load of physical machines. The partitioning of a large virtual space into subspaces is realized by using the coordinates in the virtual space, which could dynamically change according to the load of the clients. In order to properly conduct such a subspace processing, the server should designate the information on the subspace in a rigid manner, and should send it to the clients in a reliable and timely manner. To this end, we introduce a specific data format called O-data (object data) and

---

[1] https://github.com/NVIDIAGameWorks/PhysX.

use WebSocket to send network commands written as a text data. With the prototype system, we conducted experiments to evaluate the performance of the proposed method. The result of experiments shows that although it reduces the load of the physics simulation, the aggregation of the simulation results becomes a bottleneck so that the host could not keep a high frame rate such as 90 fps.

The remainder of this paper is organized as follows. Section 2 overviews related work. Section 3 describes the proposed method. Section 4 summarizes results of evaluations. Finally, Sect. 5 concludes the paper with future work.

2   Related Work

The design of scalable Cloud Gaming Platform (CGP) has been a main concern in realizing an efficient handling of requests issued by a huge number of game players in real-time. Many existing works on CGP explore an effective way of assigning tasks to virtual machines (VMs) and assigning resources to each VM [3,5,8–10,12,18–20]. Avino et al. [1] measured the amount of CPU utilizations by Docker containers while executing the game server of a multiplayer game, to evaluate the suitability of container architecture for Multi-access Edge Computing. In the experiments, they used Minecraft Pocket Edition[2] (version 0.10.5) as the container of game server and employed an emulator called Genymotion[3], which emulates an Android client, to test the behavior of mobile clients. In addition, to realize a rigorous verification, they installed FRep[4] of Android application on each emulator. The evaluation results show that for game services, the overhead due to Docker increases as the number of servers increases.

Messaoudi et al. [13] evaluated the performance of Unity 3D, which is one of the most popular game engines, in MEC environments. Their main question was whether the computation of the game engine can be properly offloaded to edge servers, and they considered this question by dividing the game engine into several modules. The conclusion of the paper can be summarized as follows: 1) there is a high correlation between CPU and GPU consumptions, and in many cases GPU was the main cause of performance limitation; 2) the frame rates of device-friendly games were generally higher than 60 fps; 3) some modules related to rendering were mostly in standby mode, and the CPU consumption associated with those modules was not significant; and 4) in many games, the rendering process accounted for 70% of the CPU load, but in a certain class of games with complex scripts, the non-graphical components accounted for most of the CPU utilization.

Messaoudi proposed a game system called Offload 3D FPS [14] based on the Unity 3D. A scene in the game system is a projection of dynamic foreground onto a static background or a static layout, and it classifies game objects (GOs) processed by the game engine into several types. Different types of GOs are placed in the game world and controlled by modules in different manners, so that the game player

---

[2] MinecraftPocketEdition. http://www.pocketmine.net/.
[3] Genymotion. https://www.genymotion.com.
[4] FRep. http://strai.x0.com/frep/.

explores the virtual world through interactions with them. Offload 3D FPS tries to offload modules controlling GOs to meet the performance requirements.

Gaming Anywhere [6] is an open source cloud gaming platform developed by a group in Taiwan. It runs on several platforms including Windows and macOS, and can be easily customized by replacing several components with others. This architecture has two basic flows called data flow and control flow. The data flow is used to stream audio-video (A/V) frames from the server to clients, whereas the control flow is used to send user actions from clients to the server. In this system, every game selected by the users runs on the game server, and agents of the users run along with the selected game on the same server. The agent can be a standalone process or a module (in the form of a shared object or DLL) injected into the selected game depending on the game type and implementation. Since the server of Gaming Anywhere delivers encoded A/V frames using standard RTSP and RTP protocols, clients can watch the game play by simply accessing the corresponding URL using a standard VLC-enabled multimedia player.

A fog-based architecture proposed by Kannan *et al.* [7] uses Gaming Anywhere as the underlying platform. In this architecture, the game server is realized as a Docker container, and is created from the source code of Gaming Anywhere and other necessary packages and libraries, More specifically, after selecting the target of task offload, it deploys the docker container created from a docker image to the selected fog node. The deployed container acts as a dedicated game server which contains necessary game resources such as video/audio encoders, decoders, and realtime streaming capabilities.

Simiscuka *et al.* [16] proposed a social VR-IoT (Virtual Reality Internet of Things) environment in which IoT devices are shared and controlled on a virtual platform. This environment includes a synchronization scheme called VRITESS (VR-IoT Environment Synchronization Scheme) which allows VR headsets to be used to control real-world IoT objects. VRITESS updates real objects according to instructions given in the virtual world, and vice versa. Results of experiments show that the local network testbed exhibits lower latency than the cloud testbed, and experiments conducted on communication protocols implemented in the cloud testbed indicate that MQTT protocol has lower latency and less data traffic than REST-based protocols.

3   Prototype System

3.1   Overview

In this section, we describe an overview of the prototype system which uses Docker containers the virtual environment for executing physics operations, and PhysX as the physics operation simulator. We also use glut to visualize the results of physics operations, and WebSocketpp for the communication between (virtual) machines.

The prototype system consists of one server application and one or more client applications. See Fig. 1 for illustration. Each application is assigned a specific machine, where each client is not executed directly on the physical machine

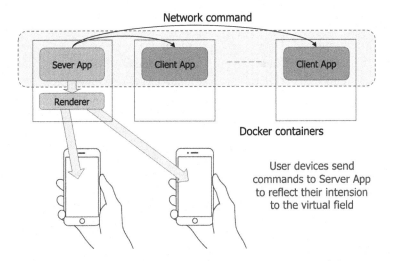

Fig. 1. Prototype system consisting of server and client applications.

but on a Docker container (this configuration is intended to allow for live migration of clients depending on the change of the load of physical machines). The program is written as a console application in C++, and the server application and the client application have the same structure as a program. Thus, when the application starts on a machine, we need to select the execution mode, i.e., whether to run as a server or a client, in addition to the URI of WebSocket connection. If it is invoked as a server application, it immediately builds the PhysX_Scene corresponding to the entire virtual space and starts the glut rendering of the space, and if it is invoked as a client application, it transits to the waiting state to accept requests from the server. It then builds the PhysX_Scene corresponding to an assigned subspace according to instructions received from the server application.

3.2   Partitioning into Subspaces and Assigning to Clients

In the proposed method, a large-scale virtual space is divided into several subspaces to reduce the machine load in physics simulation. In the following explanation, the number of clients and the number of subspaces are both fixed to two, and clients and subspaces are distinguished with name A or B. In the prototype system, the server is responsible for the entire space, and each client is responsible for each subspace. The partitioning of the whole space into subspaces is realized by using the coordinates in the PhysX_Scene, e.g., whether or not the value of x-coordinate exceeds 0. It is also possible to change the boundary of the partition according to the load of the clients.

A client conducts the processing of an assigned subspace, which means the physics simulation of objects whose coordinates are contained in the subspace. In order to properly conduct such a subspace processing, the server should designate

Table 1. Network commands.

Command	Data	Explanation
Init	None	Initialization of PhysX_Scene
Object	O-data	Update of PhysX_Objects
Input	Input keydata	Process the input keydata
Return	None	Return O-data to the server

the information on the subspace in a rigid manner, and should send it to the client in a reliable and timely manner. In other words, we should determine the way of representing the subspace information and the way of transferring the represented information. In the prototype system, we introduce a specific data format called **O-data** (object data) for the former, and for the latter, we use WebSocket to send **network commands** written as a text data (see Table 1 for illustration). In summary, the allocation (and updates) of a subspace to a client is realized in the following two steps: 1) the server creates an O-data for each subspace and packs it into a network command; and 2) the server sends a created network command to each client through WebSocket. The result of physics operations is collected to the server by returning another O-data to the server from the client.

3.3   Distributed Simulation of the Virtual Space

After assigning a subspace to a client, a physics simulation using PhysX is actually conducted on each client, which is almost the same as when the entire space is simulated on a single machine. The server, on the other hand, does not conduct such a physics simulation, but only maintains the position and angle of the PhysX_Objectin the entire virtual space (note that to generate the game view, the rendering of the virtual space should also be conducted by glut, while it could be turned off).

Before starting the physics simulation, each client receives O-data from the server through network commands to reflect objects in the assigned subspace to the scene. Since the O-data contains all objects which should exist in that scene in a mixed manner, so that some objects in the O-data already exist in the scene and others do not, we should conduct the matching of object IDs, in such a way that if an object with the same ID already exists in the scene, the information on the object should be updated with the O-data, and otherwise, we should add a new object to the scene. Such an addition of objects can be done while running the physics simulation. However, if the added object intersects with an existing object, it would lead the physics simulation to a wrong result. Thus, to avoid such an intersect, the prototype system takes an approach such that when a new object is added to the scene, it is added at a position which is slightly higher than the position designated in the O-data, which is based on an intuition such

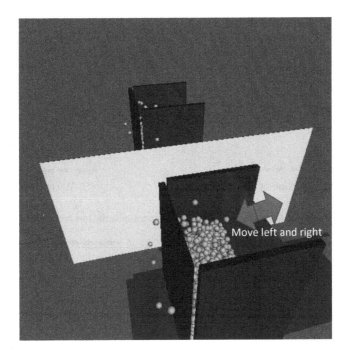

Fig. 2. Virtual space to be simulated.

Table 2. Specifications of machines.

Name	CPU	RAM	GPU
Host	Intel Core i3-7100	8 GB	NA
Client A	Intel Core i7-7700	16 GB	GeForce GTX 1070 Ti
Client B	Intel Core i7-7700K	16 GB	GeForce GTX 1080

that objects being simulated are less likely to be in a high position due to the effect of gravity.

4 Evaluation

4.1 Setup

To evaluate the performance of the proposed method, we conducted experiments using the prototype system. In the experiments, we use one host machine and two client machines, which are referred to as Host, Client A, and Client B, respectively. The specifications of those machines are summarized in Table 2. In the experiments, we conducted simulations of a virtual space (i.e., PhysX_Scene) illustrated in Fig. 2, which consists of two subspaces isolated by a big green wall and several small walls enclosing a large number of PhysX_Objects. When it is

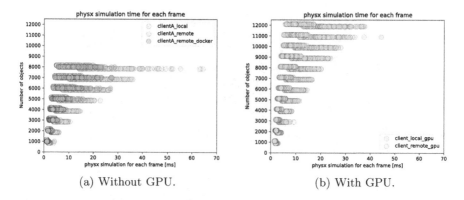

(a) Without GPU.   (b) With GPU.

Fig. 3. Scatter plot of the execution time of physics simulation conducted on Client A.

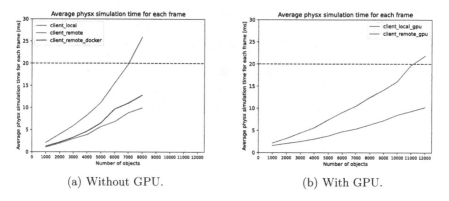

(a) Without GPU.   (b) With GPU.

Fig. 4. Average execution time of physics simulation conducted on Client A. (Color figure online)

simulated with two clients, the subspace in front of the green wall is assigned to Client A, the other subspace is assigned to Client B, and during the simulation, one of enclosing walls in each subspace moves left and right to stir up PhysX_Objects inside, to intentionally cause collisions of objects so as to keep the load for the physics simulation sufficiently high.

In the following, to clarify the effect of GPU and Docker virtualization in the physics simulation, we also evaluate the performance *without GPU* and when the application is directly executed on the target machine *without Docker*. In addition, to clarify the effect of decentralization, we evaluate the performance on a single machine, which is indicated as "local" in the figures of the experimental results.

4.2   Effect of Decentralization for Reducing the Simulation Time

At first, we evaluate the effect of decentralization in terms of the reduction of the simulation time. Figure 3 summarizes the distribution of the simulation time per

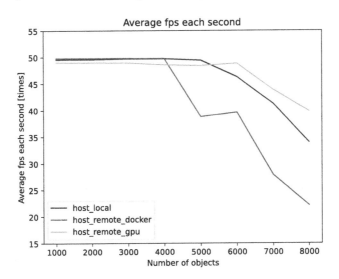

Fig. 5. The number of frame updates per second (fps) observed by the host.

frame conducted by Client A for each number of objects, where we evaluated 150 frames for a fixed number of objects. The simulation time was measured with a C++ library called chrono, and we did not conduct rendering since our objective is to evaluate the performance of the physics simulation. For reference, this figure includes the results without distributed processing (i.e., local) and with Docker (i.e., docker). The difference between figures (a) and (b) is whether GPU is used or not. From these results, it can be seen that the simulation time of most frames is within the target time of 20 ms with the decentralization, while it is often not within 20 ms when the simulation is conducted on a single machine (i.e., local). Figure 4 shows the average simulation time for each number of objects. From this figure, we can observe that the average simulation time increases almost in proportion to the number of objects, indicating a reduction in the simulation time due to decentralization and an increase in the simulation time due to the use of Docker. In addition, we can find that the use of GPU certainly reduces the average simulation time. Note that in this figure, the target time of 20 ms (corresponding to 100 fps) is indicated by a horizontal blue dashed line.

To properly evaluate the effect of decentralization in a *consecutive* task such as real-time physics simulation, it is not enough to look at the average simulation time per frame, but it is also necessary to evaluate the number of frames to be processed per fixed time including the time required for communicating with the host; i.e., the throughput. To this end, we count the number of updates per second, where the timing of update is when the reflection of O-data to the host is completed. The results are shown in Fig. 5. This figure summarizes the number of frame updates per second (fps) which are measured 60 times for a fixed number of objects, where (a) shows the scatter plot of fps values and (b) is the average fps value for each number of objects. From these figures, it can be

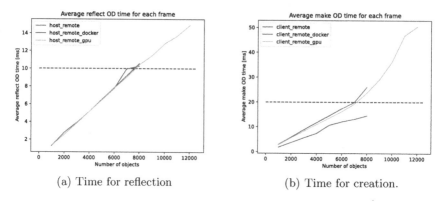

(a) Time for reflection   (b) Time for creation.

Fig. 6. Average processing time for O-data.

found that the fps value is more stable in the case with single machine than in the case with distributed processing. In particular, in the distributed processing, the variation of fps values increases with the increase in the number of objects. The reason for this phenomena will be discussed later.

4.3   Overhead of Decentralization

Finally, to evaluate the overhead associated with the decentralization, we measured the time required for creating/reflecting O-data, respectively. The former is the time required to create O-data on Client A, and the latter is the time required to reflect O-data received from Client A on the host. Note that since a half of objects are processed on Client A in our setup, the number of objects to be reflected is half of the number of objects present on the host. The average time for reflecting O-data is shown in Fig. 6(a), which includes the results with Docker and GPU for comparison. In all cases, the time required to reflect O-data is proportional to the number of objects; e.g., when there are 10000 objects, the average time required to reflect O-data is about 12 ms.

Figure 6(b) shows the average time taken to create O-data on Client A. From this figure, we can see that the creation time is the shortest when Docker is used, followed by GPU without Docker. For example, the creation time for 8000 objects is about 13 ms when Docker is used, although it takes about 20 ms in other cases, which equals to the time length for one frame. This indicates that although the physics simulation itself becomes faster as the number of objects allocated to the client decreases, our current implementation could not achieve sufficient throughput due to the bottleneck of returning the simulation results to the host, which is a reason of the badness of the proposed method illustrated in the last subsection.

5   Concluding Remarks

This paper proposes a distributed processing method for the physics simulation of a large virtual space. By using PhysX as a physics simulator and Docker containers as a virtual machine environment, we realized a prototype system which does not depend on specific platforms. As a result of experiments conducted using the prototype system, it is confirmed that although the distributed processing certainly reduces the load of the physics simulation, the aggregation of the simulation results to the host becomes a bottleneck so that the host could not maintain a sufficiently high frame rate such as 100 fps.

Our future work includes the optimization of the creation and reflection of O-data, investigation of methods for dealing with cases in which the subspace is not explicitly separated and objects come and go across boundaries, and automatic scaling due to increases or decreases in the load. We plan to use orchestration tools such as Kubertenes for dynamic partitioning of tasks and migration between physical computers.

References

1. Avino, G., Malinverno, M., Malandrino, F., Casetti, C., Chiasserini, C.F.: Characterizing docker overhead in mobile edge computing scenarios. In: Proceedings of the Workshop on Hot Topics in Container Networking and Networked Systems (HotConNet), pp. 30–35 (2017)
2. Erez, T., Tassa, Y., Todorov, E.: Simulation tools for model-based robotics: comparison of bullet, Havok, MuJoCo, ODE and PhysX. In: Proceedings of the IEEE International Conference on Robotics and Automation (ICRA) (2015)
3. Finkel, D., Claypool, M., Jaffe, S., Nguyen, T., Stephen, B.: Assignment of games to servers in the OnLive cloud game system. In: Proceedings of the Annual Workshop on Network and Systems Support for Games (NetGames 2014) (2014)
4. He, H., Zheng, J., Li, Z.: Comparing realistic particle simulation using discrete element method and physics engine. In: Proceedings of the Geo-Congress (2020)
5. Hong, H.-J., Chen, D.-Y., Huang, C.-Y., Chen, K.-T., Hsu, C.-H.: QoE-aware virtual machine placement for cloud games, In: Proceedings of the Annual Workshop on Network and Systems Support for Games (NetGames 2013), pp. 1–2 (2013)
6. Huang, C.-Y., Chen, K.-T., Chen, D.-Y., Hsu, H.-J., Hsu, C.-H.: GamingAnywhere: the first open source cloud gaming system. ACM Trans. Multimedia Comput. Commun. Appl. 10(1s), 1–25 (2014)
7. Kannan, M.: Enhancing cloud gaming user experience through docker containers in fog nodes. M.Sc. thesis, National College of Ireland (2019)
8. Li, Y., Tang, X., Cai, W.: Play request dispatching for efficient virtual machine usage in cloud gaming. IEEE Trans. Circuits Syst. Video Technol. 25(12), 2052–2063 (2015)
9. Lin, Y., Shen, H.: Leveraging fog to extend cloud gaming for thin-client MMOG with high quality of experience. In: Proceedings of the 35th ICDCS, pp. 734–735. IEEE (2015)
10. Lin, Y., Shen, H.: CloudFog: leveraging fog to extend cloud gaming for thin-client MMOG with high quality of service. IEEE Trans. Parallel Distrib. Syst. 28(2), 431–445 (2017)

11. Lu, Z., Sankaranarayanan, G., Deo, D., Chen, D., De, S.: Towards physics-based interactive simulation of electrocautery procedures using PhysX. In: Proceedings of the IEEE Haptics Symposium (2010)
12. Marzolla, M., Ferretti, S., D'Angelo, G.: Dynamic resource provisioning for cloud-based gaming infrastructures. ACM Comput. Entertainment **10**(3), 4:1-4:20 (2012)
13. Messaoudi, F., Ksentini, A., Simon, G., Bertin, P.: Performance analysis of game engines on mobile and fixed devices. ACM Trans. Web **9**(4) (2016). Article no. 39
14. Messaoudi, F.: User equipment based-computation offloading for real-time applications in the context of Cloud and edge networks. Ph.D thesis, Université Rennes 1 (2019)
15. Pugalendhi, A.: Cloud gaming system in docker container image. M.Sc. thesis, National College of Ireland (2018)
16. Simiscuka, A.A., Markande, T.M., Muntean, G.-M.: Real-virtual world device synchronization in a cloud-enabled social virtual reality IoT network. IEEE Access **7**, 106588–106599 (2019)
17. Soltesz, S., Pötzl, H., Fiuczynski, M.E., Bavier, A., Peterson, L.: Container-based operating system virtualization: a scalable, high-performance alternative to hypervisors. In: Proceedings of the 2nd ACM SIGOPS/EuroSys European Conference on Computer Systems (EuroSys 2007), pp. 275–287 (2007)
18. Süselbeck, R., Schiele, G., Becker, C.: Peer-to-peer support for low latency massively multiplayer online games in the cloud. In: Proceedings of the 8th Annual Workshop on Network and Systems Support for Games (NetGames 2009), pp. 1–2 (2009)
19. Tian, H., Wu, D., He, J., Xu, Y., Chen, M.: On achieving cost-effective adaptive cloud gaming in geo-distributed data centers. IEEE Trans. Circuits Syst. Video Technol. **25**(12), 2064–2077 (2015)
20. Wang, S., Liu, Y., Dey, S.: Wireless network aware cloud scheduler for scalable cloud mobile gaming. In: Proceedings of the IEEE International Conference on Communications (ICC), pp. 2081–2086 (2012)
21. Xavier, M.G., Neves, M.V., Rossi, F.D., Ferreto, T.C., Lange, T., De Rose, C.A.F.: Performance evaluation of container-based virtualization for high performance computing environments. In: Proceedings of the 21st Euromicro International Conference on Parallel, Distributed, and Network-Based Processing (2013)

A Deep Reinforcement Learning-Based Approach to the Scheduling of Multiple Workflows on Non-dedicated Edge Servers

Yongqiang Gao[1,2,3(✉)] and Ke Feng[2,3]

[1] Engineering Research Center of Ecological Big Data, Ministry of Education, Hohhot 010021, China
[2] Inner Mongolia Engineering Laboratory for Cloud Computing and Service Software, Hohhot 010021, China
[3] College of Computer Science, Inner Mongolia University, Hohhot 010021, China
gaoyongqiang@imu.edu.cn, 31909051@mail.imu.edu.cn

Abstract. Prompted by the remarkable progress in mobile communication technologies, more and more users are starting to execute their workflow applications on the mobile edge computing environment. Scheduling multiple parallel workflows on a non-dedicated edge server is a great challenge because of different users' requirements. In this paper, we propose an approach based on Deep Reinforcement Learning (DRL) to schedule multiple workflows on an edge server with multiple heterogeneous CPUs to minimise the violation rate of service level agreement of workflows. The effectiveness of our proposed approach is evaluated by simulation experiments based on a set of real-world scientific workflows. The results show that our approach performs better than the current state-of-the-art approaches applied to similar problems.

Keywords: Edge server · Scientific workflows · Multiple workflows scheduling · Resource allocation · Deep reinforcement learning

1 Introduction

Due to the rapid development of scientific computing, scientific workflow application has become an extensive data application, requiring large-scale infrastructure to execute reasonably. The inherent resources of mobile devices cannot meet their regular operation; therefore, scheduling workflows on heterogeneous

Supported in part by the National Natural Science Foundation of China under Grant 61662052, in part by the Natural Science Foundation of Inner Mongolia Autonomous Region under Grant 2021MS06002, in part by he Science and Technology Planning Project of Inner Mongolia Autonomous Region under Grant 2021GG0155, and in part by the Major Research Plan of Inner Mongolia Natural Science Foundation under Grant 2019ZD15.

© Springer Nature Switzerland AG 2022
H. Shen et al. (Eds.): PDCAT 2021, LNCS 13148, pp. 261–272, 2022.
https://doi.org/10.1007/978-3-030-96772-7_24

resources has become an urgent problem to be solved. Previous studies usually schedule the scientific workflow generated by the application to the cloud computing platform with powerful computing resources [1]. However, the cloud computing platform is too far away from users. It will increase communication costs and energy consumption, obviously fatal to some applications requiring low latency. Therefore, edge computing can solve this problem as a complementary computing platform between mobile devices and remote cloud. In this distributed architecture, the large-scale services initially handled by the central node are cut into smaller parts and distributed to the edge nodes closer to users for processing, which significantly reduces the delay and energy consumption. Existing studies usually focus on offloading single or multiple workflows on the edge server [2], and there is little literature on multiple workflows scheduling on the non-dedicated edge server. In this paper, we propose a multiple workflows scheduling algorithm based on DRL to assign workflow tasks to appropriate CPUs on the non-dedicated edge server to reduce the violation rate of service level agreement of workflows and improve the QoS of the edge server. The contributions of this paper are as follows:

- We investigate the scheduling problem of multiple workflows on the non-dedicated edge server with multiple heterogeneous CPUs to minimize the violation rate of service level agreement of workflows.
- We formulate the scheduling problem into a constrained optimization model and propose a novel PRDDQN algorithm based on DRL to solve the problem. The proposed PRDDQN utilizes a new sample storage structure to optimize the sampling process.
- We evaluate the effectiveness of our approach by simulation experiments conducted on real-world scientific workflows. The results show that, compared with other alternatives, our approach has better performance.

The rest of this paper is organized as follows. The related works are summarized in Sect. 2. Section 3 describes the models and problem formulation. Section 4 describes the proposed PRDDQN algorithm in detail. The experimental results are presented in Sect. 5. Finally, and the conclusion is drawn in Sect. 6.

2   Related Work

As we all know, the workflow scheduling problem is an NP-hard problem [3], so it is difficult to find an optimal solution for the problem. Typically there are two kinds of methods to solve this problem: heuristic algorithm and meta-heuristic algorithm. For heuristic algorithm, Yuan *et al.* [4] proposed a DBL algorithm with deadline constraints. The algorithm divides the nodes of the same layer into the same group from the bottom to the top based on the deep reverse layering of nodes and then uses the reverse layering to transform the deadline of workflow into the time interval of activity to optimize the cost locally. In addition, there are many heuristic algorithms to optimize different objectives, such as accuracy, reliability, *etc* [5–8]. For the meta-heuristic algorithm, Gao *et al.* [9] proposed a new Pareto-based multi-objective workflow scheduling algorithm HGAABC. It combines the development capability in ABC [10] with the exploration capability in GA [11] and maps each task to the instance series of the corresponding virtual machine type according to the pay-per-use pricing model to reduce the cost of the virtual machine and make-span of workflow. Rizvi et al. [12] proposed a scheduling method HBDCWS, which minimizes the scheduling time and cost of the workflow by allocating budget and deadline for workflow in advance. Unlike these studies, we proposed an approach based on DRL to schedule multiple workflows to minimize the violation rate of service level agreement of workflows.

Some literature has recently studied how to use machine learning algorithms to schedule workflow applications in a cloud computing environment. Tong et al. [13] proposed a new artificial intelligence algorithm - deep Q-learning scheduling algorithm, which combines the advantages of Q-learning algorithm and deep neural network, the target is to minimize the make-span of the workflow and maximize load balancing. Dong et al. [14] developed an Actor-Critic algorithm and designed a new P-Network model to predict the queuing order of tasks and reduce the average execution time in the workflow. Wang et al. [15] proposed a multi-agent DQN algorithm in which the optimized target cost and total execution time of the workflow are regarded as a Markov game between two agents, the Nash equilibrium of two optimization objectives is obtained finally. Different from these studies, we focus on the scheduling problem of multiple workflows on non-dedicated edge severs.

3   Problem Modeling

3.1   System Model

Assuming there are many users in a particular area, and there is a base station with a non-dedicated edge server in this geographic area. In this paper, we consider a non-dedicated edge server with multiple heterogeneous processor resources represented by $CPUS = \{CPU_1, CPU_2, \ldots, CPU_l\}$. This non-dedicated edge server includes a workflow scheduler. At different times, these users can submit tasks associated with the workflow to the workflow scheduler by cellular mobile network or WIFI. Next, workflows are sent to the proposed PRD-DQN algorithm, which is used to find the optimal placement for each workflow task. Finally, the results are collected and then returned to the corresponding user. Figure 1 shows the proposed system architecture in this paper.

3.2   Workflow Model

We utilize $WF = \{wf_1, wf_2, \ldots, wf_m\}$ to denote a system that is composed of multiple scientific workflows. A scientific workflow which submitted by a user can be represented as a Directed Acyclic Graph (DAG) $G = (T, D)$, where $T = \{t_{m,0}, t_{m,1}, \ldots, t_{m,n}\}$ is a set of different tasks of the workflow m represented by vertices and $D = \{d_{m,i,j} | t_{m,i}, t_{m,j} \in T\}$ is a set of dependencies between

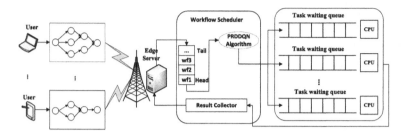

Fig. 1. System architecture.

tasks $t_{m,i}$ and $t_{m,j}$ represented by directed edges. A dependency $d_{m,i,j}$ indicates a constraint between tasks $t_{m,i}$ and $t_{m,j}$, which means that task $t_{m,j}$ can start to execute only after task $t_{m,i}$ completed its execution on the corresponding CPU and transferred all data to task $t_{m,j}$. Therefore, task $t_{m,i}$ can be called the predecessor of task $t_{m,j}$, and task $t_{m,j}$ is called the successor of task $t_{m,i}$. A task without any predecessor, we call it the entry task t_{entry}. Similarly, we call the task exit task t_{exit} which has no successor. For a task $t_{m,i}$, it may have multiple predecessors or successors, defined as $pr(t_{m,i})$ and $su(t_{m,i})$. We can think that task $t_{m,i}$ is ready only when all the predecessors of task $t_{m,i}$ have been completed. In addition, each edge $d_{m,i,j}$ has a weight, representing the data transferred from task $t_{m,i}$ to task $t_{m,j}$. However, its transmission time is too short, so that it can be ignored in this paper. Each task $t_{m,i}$ has its length, also called workload, which can be expressed as $LD_{m,i}$. When each user submits a workflow, they specify a deadline for the workflow to be represented as $Deadline_m$, and the edge server must observe. Otherwise, it will cause the violation of the service level agreement of workflow, which will reduce the QoS of the edge server.

3.3 Scheduling Model

The completion time of each workflow is called make-span, denoted by MS_m. Because t_{exit} is the last task in the workflow to be executed, make-span is equivalent to the completion time of t_{exit}. MS_m can be calculated as

$$MS_m = CT_{m,t_{exit},k} \tag{1}$$

where $CT_{m,t_{exit},k}$ is the completion time of the last task in the workflow.

A task can only be scheduled to one CPU, and the CPU release its resources until the completion of this task. When task $t_{m,i}$ is scheduled to the cpu_k, its run-time can be calculated as

$$RT_{m,i,k} = \frac{LD_{m,i}}{PP_k} \tag{2}$$

where PP_k represents the processing performance of cpu_k in terms of Million Instruction Per Second (MIPS). The earliest start time of task $t_{m,i}$ can be calculated as

$$ST_{m,i,k} = \begin{cases} 0, & if \quad t_{m,i} = t_{entry} \\ \max(\max_{t_{\hat{m},q} \in SC(k)} CT_{\hat{m},q,k}, \quad \max_{t_{m,p} \in pr(t_{m,i})} CT_{m,p,\hat{k}}), \\ & otherwise \end{cases} \quad (3)$$

where $SC(k)$ represents a collection of all tasks scheduled on cpu_k. $CT_{\hat{m},q,k}$ is the completion time of task $t_{\hat{m},q}$ on cpu_k and $CT_{m,p,\hat{k}}$ is the completion time of the direct precursor task of task $t_{m,i}$. Therefore, the completion time of task $t_{m,i}$ $CT_{m,i,k}$ can be calculated as

$$CT_{m,i,k} = ST_{m,i,k} + RT_{m,i,k} \quad (4)$$

Our target is to schedule multiple workflows to appropriate CPUs to minimize the violation rate of service level agreement of workflows. That is to say, make every workflow complete before its deadline as much as possible. Therefore, the scheduling problem can be formulated as

$$Minimize \quad VSLA = \sum_{m \in WF} \frac{V_m}{SIZE(WF)} \quad (5)$$

$$Subject\ to \quad \sum_{k=1}^{SIZE(CPU)} \sum_{s=1}^{SIZE(TQ)} x_{m,i,s,k} = 1 \quad (6)$$
$$\forall m \in WF, \forall i \in T_m$$

$$\sum_{m=1}^{SIZE(WF)} \sum_{i=1}^{SIZE(T_m)} x_{m,i,s,k} = 1 \quad (7)$$
$$\forall k \in CPU, \forall s \in TQ$$

$$ST_{m,i,k} \geq \max_{t_{m,p} \in pr(t_{m,i})} ST_{m,p,\hat{k}} + RT_{m,p,\hat{k}} \quad (8)$$

$$ST_{m,i,k} + RT_{m,i,k} \leq \min_{t_{m,q} \in su(t_{m,i})} ST_{m,q,\hat{k}} \quad (9)$$

$$x_{m,i,s,k} \in \{0,1\} \quad (10)$$

Constraints (10) define the value ranges of decision variables $x_{m,i,s,k}$, where $x_{m,i,s,k}$ represents whether the ith task of workflow m is assigned to the sth location in waiting queue of CPU_k. T_m represents the set of all tasks of workflow m, CPU represents the set of processors, WF represents the workflow set to be scheduled, and TQ represents the queue of the task queue. The constraint (6) ensures that each task can only appear in the task queue once. The constraint (7) ensures that each position in the task queue can only be occupied by one task. Constraints (8) and (9) are constraints on the dependencies between tasks in the workflow. In (5), $VSLA$ represents the violation rate of service level agreements for all scheduled workflows, V_m represents whether the workflow m violates the service level agreement, and the value of V_m can be calculated in the following way: when the total execution time of wf_m exceeds the $Deadline_m$, V_m is 1; otherwise, V_m is 0.

4   The Prioritized Replay Double DQN Algorithm

Multiple workflows scheduling problem is an NP-hard problem, so we propose an algorithm PRDDQN based on DRL to find the approximate optimal solution.

4.1   Algorithm Theory

The parameter updating method of neural network of traditional DQN algorithm may lead to an overestimation problem in which Q-value is super significant. Therefore, we introduce another neural network to eliminate the influence of some maximum errors.

$$Q(S_t, A_t) \leftarrow R_{t+1} + \gamma Q(S_{t+1}, \max_a Q(S_{t+1}, a; \omega), \omega^-) \tag{11}$$

In addition, the PRDDQN algorithm uses an experience replay mechanism. In the process of interaction between the agent and environment, the data obtained by the agent will be put into replay memory. When the parameters of the neural network need to be updated, mini-batch sampling data will be taken from replay memory to train the neural network. Similar to the PRDDQN algorithm, the DQN algorithm also uses an experience replay mechanism, but its sampling method is random sampling. It has an apparent defect: some random samples have little effect on the training of the neural network; therefore, there is no need to extract such samples. In order to solve this shortcoming, the proposed PRDDQN algorithm uses a new storage structure called *sumtree*, which is a binary tree structure. Each leaf node of *sumtree* stores the priority P of each sample, and each non-leaf node has only two branches. The value of this node is the sum of the two branches, so the top node of *sumtree* is the sum of all P of leaf nodes. When sampling, we divide the sum of P at the top node by the number of samples to be sampled into several intervals and then randomly select a number in each interval. According to the number, we find the sample for this sampling. Through *sumtree*, the PRDDQN algorithm can sample the data that are really worth learning.

4.2   Algorithm Framework

The pseudo-code of the PRDDQN algorithm is presented in Algorithm 1. The main steps of the algorithm are as follows: firstly, initializing the variables and

---

Algorithm 1: Framework of PRDDQN algorithm

Input: budget T, mini-batch m, decay factor γ, exploration rate ε, replay interval I and replay capacity N, exponents α and β, the number of leaf nodes of *sumtree* R, Q target network parameter update frequency C

Output: scheduling scheme A

1 Initialize action-value function Q with random weights ω, initialize target action-value function $\hat{Q}$ with random weights $\omega^- = \omega$;

2 Initialize structure of *sumtree*, initialize the priority P_j of R leaf nodes of *sumtree* is 1;

3 Initialize the agent and environment, including workflows and CPUs;

4 **for** $t=1$ to T **do**

5   The agent observes current state S_t, obtains its eigenvector ϕ_t;

6   With probability ε select a random action a_t, otherwise select
$a_t = \arg\max_a Q(\phi(S_t), a; \omega)$;

7   The agent take action a_t and get reward r_t according to (12) and get whether it is in the termination state $final_t$;

8      $S_t = S_{t+1}$;

9   Store transition $(\phi_t, a_t, r_t, \gamma_t, final_t, \phi_{t+1})$ in *sumtree* with maximal priority $P_t = \max_{i<t} P_i$;

10   **if** $t \bmod I = 0$ **then**

11   **for** $j=1$ to m **do**

12   Take samples $(\phi_j, a_j, r_j, \gamma_j, final_j, \phi_{j+1})$ from *sumtree* based on probability $P(j) = \frac{P_j^\alpha}{\sum_i P_j^\alpha}$;

13   Compute importance-sampling weight $\omega_j = (N \times P(j))^{-\beta} \div \max_i \omega_i$;

14   Set $y_j = \begin{cases} r_j, & if\ final_j = true \\ r_j + \gamma_j * Q(\phi_j, \arg\max_{a'} Q(\phi_j, a; \omega), \omega^-) \\ & if\ final_j = false \end{cases}$;

15   Perform a gradient descent step on $\frac{1}{m} \sum_{j=1}^m \omega_j (y_j - Q(\phi_j, a_j; \omega))^2$ with respect to the network parameters ω;

16   Compute TD-error $\delta_j = y_j - Q(\phi_j, a_j; \omega)$;

17   Update transition priority $P_j = |\delta_j|$;

18   **end**

19   Every C steps reset $\hat{Q} = Q$

20   **end**

21   **if** *all the tasks have been scheduled* **then**

22   break;

23   **else**

24   Return to step (6)

25   **end**

26 **end**

27 **end**

28 Return the collection of actions A;

---

the experience replay memory *sumtree*. Then the sample is sampled from replay memory according to the sampling probability. The TD-error of all samples is updated by calculating the target Q value and the loss function. Finally, after reaching a certain number of training times, the Q network parameters are synchronized to the target Q network. In summary, the most significant difference between PRDDQN and the traditional DQN algorithm is to add a priority to the stored samples. The larger the priority value of the sample, the more climbing space for improvement of the prediction accuracy of the sample, which means the more the sample needs to be learned. At the same time, the parameter update method of the Q target network is improved to reduce the error caused by the overestimation of the Q-value.

5   Experiments, Results and Discussion

This section introduces the experimental settings and then evaluates our proposed algorithm compared with several representative algorithms. Finally, the experimental results are analyzed and discussed.

5.1   Experiments Setup

In order to verify the effectiveness of our approach, we build a simulation platform to simulate the non-dedicated edge server environment. The edge server is equipped with seven heterogeneous CPUs, as shown in Table 1. The platform is developed in Python 2.0 language and compiled with Python compiler Pycharm. In our experiments, we utilized five types of workflows from the Pegasus project.

Table 1. Processing performance of CPUs

CPU	Processing performance (MIPS)
CPU 1	5.66
CPU 2	8
CPU 3	1
CPU 4	2.83
CPU 5	2.45
CPU 6	4
CPU 7	0.07

The performance of the proposed PRDDQN algorithm is compared to that of a HBDCWS algorithm proposed in [12], a DBL algorithm proposed in [4] and a DQN algorithm proposed in [15]. DQN algorithm and PRDDQN algorithm are both DRL-based algorithms, so their neural networks need to be trained.

This paper uses a three-layer, fully connected neural network structure to construct the estimated Q value network and the target Q value network. The input is a vector that length is 8. The size of the network hidden layer is 20 and 7, respectively. The former layer uses the Relu activation function, and the latter layer uses the linear activation function. The reward function is set as follows:

$$r = 1 - \frac{V_i - V_b}{V_w - V_b} \qquad (12)$$

where V_b is the number of workflows violating the service level agreement obtained by scheduling all workflows to the CPU with the best performance, and V_w is the number of workflows violating the service level agreement obtained by scheduling all workflows to the CPU with the worst performance.

5.2   Results and Discussion

Firstly, we analyze the effect of the new storage structure used by the PRDDQN algorithm during the neural network training. In this experiment, the number of tasks for Cybershake workflow, Sipht workflow, Inspiral workflow, Montage workflow, and Epigenomics workflow is set to 30, 29, 30, 25, and 24. The rewards obtained by the DQN algorithm and PRDDQN algorithm after the training are expressed in Fig. 2.

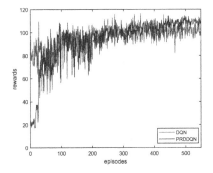
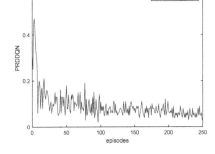

Fig. 2. Reward curve of DQN algorithm and PRDDQN algorithm.

Fig. 3. Violation rate curve of PRD-DQN algorithm.

As seen in Fig. 2, after more than 500 steps of training, the reward value of both algorithms finally stabilized to about 110, but the reward value curve of the DQN algorithm fluctuated wildly and could not converge stably until the end. In the beginning, the reward value obtained by the PRDDQN algorithm was relatively small, but it has increased significantly after training to about 40 steps, which indicates that the PRDDQN algorithm has been adjusting the priority of samples through training in the early step. The priority of samples has almost been adjusted in about 40 steps, and then only accurate, valuable data are extracted during sampling, so the reward obtained will be significantly improved; the DQN algorithm always adopts the method of random sampling, which is disturbed by useless sampling data, so it fluctuates wildly. In a word, the PRDDQN algorithm gets rewards faster and more stable. The curve of service level agreement violation rate of workflows based on PRDDQN is shown in Fig. 3.

Next, we compare the CPU utilization of four algorithms under five types of workflows with 138 tasks. The Gantt chart of scheduling results are displayed in Fig. 4.

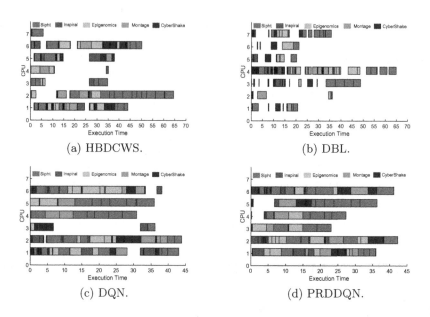

(a) HBDCWS.   (b) DBL.

(c) DQN.   (d) PRDDQN.

Fig. 4. Gantt chart of four scheduling algorithms.

From Fig. 4, we can see that the tasks scheduled by the DBL algorithm and HBDCWS algorithm are relatively scattered, and almost every CPU has a long idle time. Although the tasks scheduled by the DQN algorithm are relatively centralized, CPUs still have a long idle time. In contrast, the tasks scheduled by the PRDDQN algorithm are not only concentrated but also almost have no idle time once CPUs start running, which significantly increases the utilization of CPU resources. Moreover, compared with HBDCWS and DBL algorithms, the DQN algorithm and PRDDQN algorithm will no longer schedule tasks on CPU 7 after training for specific steps; this is because the processing performance of CPU 7 is relatively poor. Once a task is scheduled to this CPU, the waiting time of other tasks will increase significantly, which will affect the overall scheduling time; it can be verified by the scheduling time of DBL and HBDCWS algorithms.

Finally, we compare the violation rate of service level agreement of four algorithms under the different scales of workflows. In this experiment, five workflows have four sizes: 138, 497, 995, and 2069 tasks. Figure 5 shows the comparison of

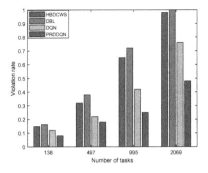

Fig. 5. The violation rate of service level agreement under different scale of workflows.

the violation rate of the service level agreement of four scheduling algorithms with the different number of tasks.

It can be seen that with the increase of the number of tasks, the violation rates of the four algorithms are increasing. When the number of tasks is small, there is little difference in the violation rates of the four algorithms. However, when the number of tasks gradually increases, the violation rates of the DBL algorithm and HBDCWS algorithm increase sharply, while the violation rates of the DQN algorithm and PRDDQN algorithm are also increasing, but they are far less than the other two algorithms. Especially when the number of tasks is 2069, the violation rate of the PRDDQN algorithm is only half of that of the DBL algorithm. The DQN algorithm has too many samples in the replay memory, so the training effect is not good, increasing the violation rate. However, due to the size limitation of the experience replay memory, its violation rate will not increase too much. The PRDDQN algorithm can select functional samples for training, so with the increase of the number of tasks, the violation rate of the PRDDQN algorithm will not increase significantly; it also shows that our algorithm has better performance in reducing the violation rate of workflows.

6   Conclusion

In this paper, we propose a DRL algorithm PRDDQN to solve multiple workflows scheduling problems. Because the research target of this paper is only the violation rate of service level agreement of workflows, we intend not to be limited to single objective scheduling in future research and consider other factors to improve the QoS of the non-dedicated edge server such as security of workflows. Moreover, policy iteration based methods such as DDPG or A3C will also be considered to solve the multiple workflows scheduling problems.

References

1. Arabnejad, V., Bubendorfer, K., Ng, B.: Dynamic multi-workflow scheduling: a deadline and cost-aware approach for commercial clouds. Future Gener. Comput. Syst. **100**, 98–108 (2019)
2. Chen, X., Zhang, H., Wu, C., Mao, S., Ji, Y., Bennis, M.: Optimized computation offloading performance in virtual edge computing systems via deep reinforcement learning. IEEE Internet Things J. **6**, 4005–4018 (2018)
3. Yu, J., Buyya, R., Ramamohanarao, K.: Workflow scheduling algorithms for grid computing. In: Xhafa, F., Abraham, A. (eds.) Metaheuristics for Scheduling in Distributed Computing Environments. SCI, vol. 146, pp. 173–214. Springer, Heidelberg (2008). https://doi.org/10.1007/978-3-540-69277-5_7
4. Yuan, Y., Li, X., Wang, Q., Zhang, Y.: Bottom level based heuristic for workflow scheduling in grids. Chin. J. Comput.-Chin. Ed. **31**(2), 282 (2008)
5. Jia, L., Zhang, X., Zhang, H.: Heuristic task scheduling algorithm for distributed systems. Comput. Eng. Appl. **53**(12), 63–69 (2017)
6. Li, J.F., Liu, D.Y., Yu, Q.Y.: Grid workflow based on planning and dynamic scheduling. J. Jilin Univ. (Eng. Technol. Ed.) **37**(2), 407–412 (2007)
7. Luo, Z.-y., Wang, P., You, B., Su, J.,: Optimization scheduling of workflow's accuracy based on reverse reduction under constraint time. J. Beijing Univ. Posts Telecommun. **40**(1), 99 (2017)
8. Yan, C., Zhi-gang, H., Li, X., Xiao, P.: Reliable scheduling algorithm for time-constrained grid workflow. J. Chin. Comput. Syst. **33**(7), 1528–1532 (2012)
9. Gao, Y., Zhang, S., Zhou, J.: A hybrid algorithm for multi-objective scientific workflow scheduling in IaaS cloud. IEEE Access **7**, 125783–125795 (2019)
10. Liang, Y.-C., Chen, A.H.-L., Nien, Y.-H.: Artificial bee colony for workflow scheduling. In: 2014 IEEE Congress on Evolutionary Computation (CEC), pp. 558–564. IEEE (2014)
11. Rehman, A., Hussain, S.S., ur Rehman, Z., Zia, S., Shamshirband, S.: Multi-objective approach of energy efficient workflow scheduling in cloud environments. Concurr. Comput. Pract. Exp. **31**(8), e4949 (2019)
12. Rizvi, N., Ramesh, D.: HBDCWS: heuristic-based budget and deadline constrained workflow scheduling approach for heterogeneous clouds. Soft Comput. **24**(24), 18971–18990 (2020). https://doi.org/10.1007/s00500-020-05127-9
13. Tong, Z., Chen, H., Deng, X., Li, K., Li, K.: A scheduling scheme in the cloud computing environment using deep q-learning. Inf. Sci. **512**, 1170–1191 (2020)
14. Dong, T., Xue, F., Xiao, C., Zhang, J.: Workflow scheduling based on deep reinforcement learning in the cloud environment. J. Ambient Intell. Humaniz. Comput. **12**(12), 10823–10835 (2021). https://doi.org/10.1007/s12652-020-02884-1
15. Wang, Y., et al.: Multi-objective workflow scheduling with deep-q-network-based multi-agent reinforcement learning. IEEE Access **7**, 39974–39982 (2019)

A MVCC Approach to Parallelizing Interoperability of Consortium Blockchain

Weiyi Lin[1,2], Qiang Qu[1,3(✉)], Li Ning[1], Jianping Fan[1,2], and Qingshan Jiang[1]

[1] Shenzhen Institute of Advanced Technology, Chinese Academy of Sciences,
Shenzhen, China
{wy.lin,qiang,li.ning,jp.fan,qs.jiang}@siat.ac.cn
[2] University of Chinese Academy of Sciences, Beijing, China
[3] Huawei Cloud Blockchain Lab, Shenzhen, China

Abstract. Driven in part of the rapid growth of consortium blockchain applications, blockchain interoperability becomes extremely essential to exchange transactional data among decentralized applications. To ensure the data integrity of transactions, the state-of-the-art studies of the blockchain interoperability apply data locks, which however severely decrease system efficiency. To boost interoperability performance, this paper proposes a novel approach based on multi-version concurrency control to parallelize interoperable transactions, which aims high transaction processing throughput while ensuring data integrity. The experimental evaluation with the Smallbank benchmark shows that the proposed method achieves up to 4x performance increase (in terms of processed transactions per second, TPS) compared with the existing methods, and moreover, it decreases the average latency with 58%.

Keywords: Blockchain interoperability · MVCC · Data parallel · Transaction integrity

1 Introduction

With the advent of Bitcoin [1], blockchain technology has been used in many fields such as finance [20], health [11], supply chain [18], and government affairs [21] due to its features of decentralization, immutability, and traceability for building low cost and high security trust among multiparties [12]. Consortium blockchains (e.g., Hyperledger Fabric [10]), superior in performance and consortium management, are widely applied as the underlying platforms for various decentralized applications. The development of consortium blockchains calls for the demand of transaction exchanges among the decentralized applications, which is the blockchain interoperability [6,22,23,25].

Many studies have been proposed on the realization of blockchain interoperability, such as Notary [22], Sidechains/Relays [23,24], and Hash-locking [25,26]. The focus of these methods is mainly on how to build trust between blockchains. Besides, based on the solutions above, data locks are usually applied to ensure the data integrity of blockchain interoperability [8,9]. Since consortium blockchain

© Springer Nature Switzerland AG 2022
H. Shen et al. (Eds.): PDCAT 2021, LNCS 13148, pp. 273–285, 2022.
https://doi.org/10.1007/978-3-030-96772-7_25

systems do not directly provide locking interfaces, data locks are implemented with smart contracts, called contract locks. One flaw of contract locks is that users need to ensure the data integrity of blockchain interoperability by themselves [8,9]. Interoperable parties need to lock transactional data according to a consistent paradigm, which is agreed by all smart contracts. Otherwise, other transactions can access these data directly by their paradigm on another contract, failing the lock. Additionally, since contract locks are entirely implemented by users, the data integrity of the interoperability would be easily destroyed by a single mistake. Therefore, the traditional methods are challenged, which cannot guarantee data integrity via the system automatically but relying on the manual control of users.

Another challenge of contract locks is the performance. Due to the blocks of read and write caused by data locks, this kind of the methods severely decreases interoperability performance [30]. Unlike the performance of blockchains having received much attention [13–17], few are on boosting the interoperability performance. Thus transaction exchanges among blockchain applications are essential in practice. Boosting the interoperability performance while ensuring data integrity has therefore become a critical issue.

To tackle these challenges, we propose an approach based on Multi-Version Concurrency Control (MVCC) [27], which is a lockless scheme that aims to reduce read and write blocks. Our MVCC-based approach parallelizes the interoperability of consortium blockchain while ensuring data integrity through the system automatically. In summary, this paper has the following contribution:

1. To propose a novel MVCC approach for interoperability. In order to ensure transaction integrity and parallel interoperability, we optimize the underlying storage, reconstruct the PutState and GetState methods of consortium blockchains, and introduce the corresponding interoperable transaction interfaces.
2. To implement the proposed approach on Hyperledger Fabric and present transaction integrity analysis to prove its effectiveness.
3. To provide experimental evaluation that shows that the proposed method achieves up to 4x performance increase compared with the existing methods, and moreover, it decreases the average latency with 58%.

2   Background

2.1   Hyperledger Fabric

Hyperledger Fabric (HLF) [10], an open-source project under the Linux Foundation, is an enterprise-level consortium blockchain platform. A shared, distributed state called *world state*, is updated constantly through the submission of transactions on HLF. The *world state* is maintained as a versioned key-value store on HLF currently supports LevelDB [3] and CouchDB [4]. A transaction containing multiple operations defined in a smart contract(*chaincode* in Fabric) will be considered a successful submission after execution and validation. In the validation phase, one node compares the version of each key-value read in the execution phase with the version in the current *world state*, and then judges whether it is consistent. If they are all consistent, each key updated by the transaction would be synchronized to the *world state* and can be read by other transactions. Otherwise, the transaction fails, and the changes would not be applied. The distributed ledger maintains the complete history of all the transactions (successful and failed) in the network, which are grouped into blocks.

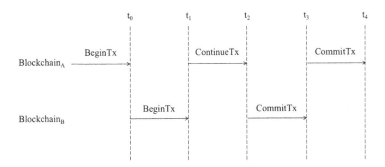

Fig. 1. The interoperable transaction processing

Through the mechanism above, the data integrity of a single blockchain transaction can be guaranteed because all changes are simultaneously submitted. However, in the interoperability scenario, an interoperable transaction is composed of multiple transactions spanning blocks on the two related blockchains as shown in Fig. 1. Temporary data submitted earlier may be accessed by other transactions without data locks, leading to the destruction of transaction integrity.

2.2 Related Work

The research studies on blockchain interoperability can be categorized into *Notary*, *Sidechains/Relays*, and *Hash-locking* [6,22–26]. The notary scheme [22] uses a centralized organization to replace the technical trust guarantee, that is, by selecting a trusted third party as an intermediary. Differently, sidechains/relays do not rely on third parties to verify the correctness of the transactions [23,24]. Instead, one blockchain reads and verifies data from another by itself. Hash-locking [25,26], which is limited to asset swap scenarios, is based on smart contracts. The atomicity of transactions is ensured by cleverly combining time locks and hash locks. These studies only consider building trust between blockchains but overlook the data integrity of blockchain interoperability.

Based on the solutions above, contract locks [8,9], implementing data locks on smart contracts, are usually applied to guarantee the data integrity of blockchain interoperability. However, this kind of guarantee relies on the manual control of users. Additionally, the read-write blocking caused by data locks greatly reduces performance.

Multi-Version Concurrency Control (MVCC) [27] is also relevant to this work. It is a concurrency control scheme that can be implemented without locks [28,30,33]. MVCC aims to solve the starvation of reading and writing operations caused by read-write locks. It is used in some of the most widely deployed disk-oriented DBMSs today, including Oracle (since 1984 [5]), Postgres (since 1985 [7]), and MySQL InnoDB engine (since 2001). In MVCC, each item of data retains multiple version copies. And each transaction can see a snapshot of the database to operate on its visible data version at a specific moment. Other transactions cannot see any changes in the transaction before the transaction is completed. HLF has adopted MVCC, providing the latest version of the *world state* comparison, but it only takes effect in a single blockchain scenario. In other words, a transaction can read the latest version of a state, even if the interoperable transaction to update it has not yet been submitted, thereby destroying the integrity.

3   Problem Statement

Our problem is defined over two blockchains, $Blockchain_A$ and $Blockchain_B$. Table 1 lists the notations used throughout the paper.

Table 1. The summary of notations

Notation	Definition
t_i	Block submission time, having $t_i > t_j$ if $i > j$
k_i	A state key
v_j	The transaction state version, v_j is a newer version than v_{j-1}
$tsid$	Transaction serial ID
t_n	The transaction that updates the current state, n is its $tsid$
$s_{v_j,t_n}^{k_i}$	The leaf node of MVM-DAG
MVM-DAG	The Multi-Version Merkle Directed Acyclic Graph we proposed
$active\_list$	The active transaction list while the *snapshot* is generated
WS	The write set of transaction
P_w	The probability of write operations

Definition 1 (Cross-chain Transaction). A complete interoperable transaction on one blockchain side is denoted by a *cross-chain* transaction.

A *cross-chain* transaction is composed of multiple sub-transactions to interact with the other blockchain. The following transaction operation interfaces need to be implemented:

- *BeginTx* starts a *cross-chain* transaction on one blockchain.
- *ContinueTx* continues the *cross-chain* transaction after the execution of the other blockchain.

- *CommitTx* commits all operations of a *cross-chain* transaction.
- *RollbackTx* rolls back all operations of the *cross-chain* transaction.

As shown in Fig. 1, blockchain submits only the validated transactions in a block at t_i while applying operations to *world state*. Thus, for a *cross-chain* transaction that operates across blocks, the temporary data generated by the sub-transactions before the final submission should be invisible to other transactions. Otherwise the integrity would be destroyed as shown in *Example 1*.

Example 1. In an interoperable transaction, the account on blockchain A first deducts the transfer amount, and then blockchain B should increase the corresponding account balance. If the execution on B fails, the A system must roll back. At the same time, there is another contract on A to grant a subsidy based on the account balance. The contract is executed after A deducts the money, and the corresponding account receives the subsidy. Then A rolls back that account due to the transaction execution failure on the B system. Thus, the account can obtain subsidies through system loopholes.

It is the dirty read on invisible temporal data that cause the problem in *Example* 1. Contract locks tackle that by blocking invisible versions of data via data locks. However, it also decreases the efficiency as *Example* 2.

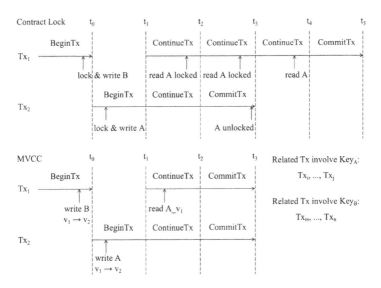

Fig. 2. A read-write blocking case

Example 2. Figure 2 illustrates two *cross-chain* transactions on an identical blockchain. Tx_1 writes(puts) the state of $k_B(Key_B)$ first, and reads(gets) the state of $k_A(Key_A)$. Then Tx_2 writes the state of k_A. Meanwhile, related transactions involving $k_A(k_B)$ include $Tx_i, ..., Tx_j(Tx_m, ..., Tx_n)$.

In the contract lock scheme, Tx_1 cannot read the state of k_A until t_3 because Tx_2 holds a lock on k_A in advance. Finally, Tx_1 completes the read of k_A after Tx_2 is submitted, submits at t_5. Since Tx_1 writes k_B and holds a lock on it, Tx_m, ..., Tx_n, can all be blocked due to the inability to access k_B. Moreover, Tx_m, ..., Tx_n can block more transactions shortly afterward, dragging down overall performance. On the contrary, in MVCC, Tx_1 can read the state of k_A without blocking. Therefore, it would not block other data-related transactions.

We aim to find a MVCC approach for the blockchain interoperability satisfying: (1) **integrity ensured:** each transaction obtains its visible version and blocks the invisible version; (2) **data locks removed:** to achieve good performance via reducing read-write blocking caused by data locks.

4   Multi-version Merkle Directed Acyclic Graph

The original MVCC on HLF only supports the latest version match while not making full use of the historical data of the blockchain, as discussed in Sect. 2. That inspired us to utilize these data to realize the traceability of the state versions. Thus, we transform the Merkle Tree into a Multi-Version Merkle Directed Acyclic Graph (MVM-DAG) to store and trace these versions of data.

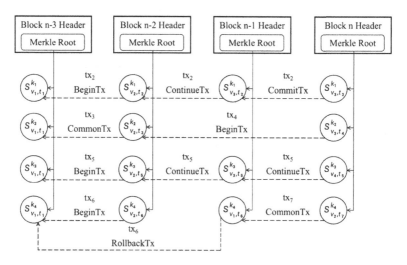

Fig. 3. Multi-Version Merkle Directed Acyclic Graph, MVM-DAG

Figure 3 is a MVM-DAG example. Each block in the blockchain contains a Merkle tree keeping the historical state data. Each leaf has a pointer to its previous state to effectively support state traceability. The leaf can be expressed as $s^{k_i}_{v_j,t_n} = \{value, point(s^{k_i}_{v_j-1,t_m})\}$.

A transaction can access its visible versions of states according to $tsid$ via the structure proposed above. Thus, the system effectively avoids the accumulation of reading requests caused by write locks. Since it is hard to keep a uniform transaction number between blockchains, the ID of a *cross-chain* transaction is determined by its first transaction on a chain. For example, tx_2 is a *cross-chain* transaction with *tsid* t_2 determined by *BeginTx*. During its execution, k_1 is updated to v_2 and v_3, which are temporary data until the block n is submitted. Note that they are not visible or accessible to other transactions.

5   Algorithms

We implement MVCC to parallelize interoperability by MVM-DAG. We re-implement the *PutState* and *GetState* for HLF, making each transaction operates on its visible versions of states, blocking invisible ones. Further, we provide *cross-chain* transactions with specific operation interfaces.

5.1   Operations on States

Each transaction, in the beginning, generates a *snapshot*, which is used for subsequent version matching of its operating state. Such *snapshot* includes *tsid* of the transaction, *active_list*, and the write set (WS), which supports rollback. Accordingly, we re-implement *PutState* and *GetState* as Algorithm 1.

Algorithm 1. Operations on States

1: **procedure** GETSTATE(TC, k) ▷ TC, Transaction Context
2:     $RV \leftarrow TC.Get(\text{``snapshot''})$ ▷ k, key of state s
3:     **if** $s.version > RV.active\_list.max\_id$ **then**   ▷ max_id, the max *tsid*
4:         **while** $s.version > RV.active\_list.max\_id$ **do**
5:             $s \leftarrow s.roll\_ptr$
6:         **end while**
7:     **end if**
8:     **if** $s.version < RV.active\_list.min\_id$ **then**
9:         **return** $s.value$
10:     **end if**
11:     **if** $s.version = RV.ts\_id$ **then**
12:         **return** $s.value$
13:     **end if**
14:     **if** $s.version \in RV.active\_list.tx\_list$ **then**
15:         **return** $s.roll\_ptr.value$
16:     **else return** $s.value$
17:     **end if**
18: **end procedure**
19: **procedure** PUTSTATE(SD, TC, k, v, WS) ▷ SD, State Database
20:     $s \leftarrow SD.Get(k)$ ▷ WS, Write Set
21:     $new\_s \leftarrow state\{\}$ ▷ new_s, the new state to be written
22:     $RV \leftarrow TC.Get(\text{``snapshot''})$
23:     $new\_s.version \leftarrow RV.tsid$
24:     $new\_s.value \leftarrow v$
25:     $new\_s.roll_ptr \leftarrow s$
26:     $WS.Append(new\_s)$
27: **end procedure**

GetState is to return the visible state version to the caller transaction. As Algorithm 1, we get the state s with its latest version from the *world state*. If $s.version > active\_list.max\_id$, it means that other transactions have updated this state after *snapshot* generation. This version should be invisible for the caller transaction. Execute the same process to judge its previous version via pointer $roll\_ptr$ until $s.version <= active\_list.max\_id$. Next, supposing $s.version < active\_list.min\_id$, it indicates that the transaction updating this state has been submitted. Thus, this version state is visible and can be returned. Then, if $s.version = RV.tsid$, the transaction updating this state is the caller itself. This version state is visible and can be returned. Last, if $s.version$ is in $active\_list.tx\_list$, it means that the transaction updating this state has not been committed. This version state is invisible. Execute the same process to judge its previous version via pointer $roll\_ptr$. Otherwise, $s.version$ is not in $active\_list.tx\_list$, it turns out the transaction updating this state is committed. This version state is visible and can be returned.

PutState is to put a new version state to the world state while the state is writable. As Algorithm 1, we get state s with its latest version from the *world state*. If the state does not exist, create a new state object directly, including the updated *value* and *version*. If the state exists, judge whether the transaction updating this state has been committed as GetState does. The state cannot be updated if that transaction has not been committed. If not, a new state object is created, including the updated *value* and a pointer $roll\_ptr$ to the current state object, and the state is updated.

5.2   Interoperable Transaction Operation Interfaces

Algorithm 2. Interoperable Transaction Operation Interfaces

```
 1: procedure BEGINTX(AL, TSN, TC)                           ▷ AL, Active tx List
 2:     tsid ← GenerateTsid(TSN)                  ▷ TSN Transaction Serial Number
 3:     AL.tx_list.Append(tsid)                        ▷ TC, Transaction Context
 4:     RV_tsid ← Createsnapshot(AL, tsid)
 5:     TC.Put("snapshot", RV)
 6: end procedure
 7: procedure CONTINUETX(tid, TC)                 ▷ tid, tsid of the previous phase
 8:     tsid ← GetCCTxid(tid)
 9:     RV ← GetRVByid(tsid)
10:     TC.Put("snapshot", RV)
11: end procedure
12: procedure COMMITTX(tid)
13:     tsid ← GetCCTxid(tid)
14:     AL.tx_list.Remove(tsid)
15: end procedure
16: procedure ROLLBACKTX(tid)
17:     tsid ← GetCCTxid(tid)
18:     RV ← GetRVByid(tsid)
19:     WS ← []                                                  ▷ WS, Write Set
20:     for s ∈ RV.write_set do
21:         while s.version == RV.tsid do
```

22:              $s \leftarrow s.roll\_ptr$
23:          **end while**
24:          $new\_s \leftarrow state\{value : s.value, roll\_ptr : s, version : RV.tsid\}$
25:          $WS.Append(new\_s)$
26:      **end for**
27:      **return** WS
28: **end procedure**

For a *cross-chain* transaction, the specific operation interfaces of each stage are as Algorithm 2. *BeginTx* generates the *tsid* and adds it to the list of currently active transactions, according to the block and location of the transaction. Then it generates a *snapshot* and stores it in the transaction context. *ContinueTx* inherits the *tsid* and *snapshot* of the *cross-chain* transaction, continuing the remaining operations. *CommitTx* inherits the *tsid* and *snapshot* of the *cross-chain* transaction, commits all updated states, and removes the transaction from the active transaction list of the system. *RollbackTx* inherits the *tsid* and *snapshot* of the *cross-chain* transaction, rolls back all updated states. The specific operation is to read the write set from the *snapshot*, obtain all versions of states before being changed by the *cross-chain* transaction, update states using the previous versions, and remove it from the active transaction list.

6   Evaluation

Setup: We implemented the approach on two independent blockchains. Each includes two organizations and three ordering nodes, and each organization includes two nodes. All nodes are built on the configuration in Table 2. Since the approach only focuses on the effectiveness and performance of interoperability, the experiments are on the *Notary*, skipping the identity verification step.

Table 2. Experiment environment

	Configuration
Operating system	Ubuntu 16.04 LTS
Platform	HLF 2.2
CPU	Intel(R) Xeon(R) CPU E5-2630v4 @ 2.20 GHz
Memory	24G
Network bandwidth	1 Gbit/s
Consensus	Raft

SmallBank [32] is used as the experimental data that simulates a typical asset transfer scenario. The data set provides six types of transactions for manipulating these data, including five updates and one query. In one run, we repeatedly

Table 3. Isolation of concurrency control methods

Methods	Dirty read	Fuzzy read	Phantom read
Write lock	☑	☑	☑
Read check	☐	☑	☑
Read-write lock	☐	☐	☑
MVCC	☐	☐	☐

trigger these six types of transactions randomly. One of the five update transactions is selected with the probability P_w, and the read-only transaction is selected with $1 - P_w$. In each transaction, the account to be accessed is selected according to the Zipfian distribution. The value of s determines the skewness of accounts access, the conflict probability of transactions. The accessing is evenly distributed when $s = 0$.

Based on the experimental data of SmallBank, this experiment compares the contract locks and MVCC scheme. We provide several implementation schemes for contract locks, including *Write Lock*, *Read Check*, and *Read-Write Lock* for the integrity analysis.

Integrity Analysis: Ensuring the transaction integrity is to ensure the *atomicity*, *consistency*, *isolation*, and *durability* (ACID) characteristic of the transaction [31].

- *atomicity*: All methods in Table 3 can ensure that the data updated during the transaction execution is locked. After the execution, the blockchain system decides to commit the update or roll back the data state. Therefore, they all can ensure the atomicity of the transaction.
- *consistency*: The blockchain system can ensure data consistency after the transaction execution. First, a transaction would not be tampered with once submitted, so the content is consistent. At the same time, by comparing the Merkle root, which is stored in the header of each block, it can be ensured that the database state after each node executes the block is consistent.
- *isolation*: Transaction isolation mainly refers to solving several data reading problems, including dirty read, unrepeatable read, and phantom read. Table 3 lists the ability above of the MVCC and several data lock methods. The method we proposed can deal with all the problems above.
- *durability*: The blockchain system can ensure that the data can not be tampered with once it is submitted. At the same time, in the case of accidental data loss, it also provides disaster recovery capabilities.

Findings: We implement a read-write lock as a contract lock at the chaincode layer of HLF. A lock check must be performed once data is read or written. We evaluate the interoperability performance using SmallBank. Figures 4 and 5 show the changes in transaction throughput and latency, respectively, under different P_w and s.

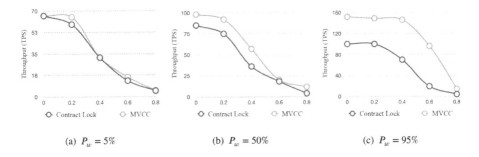

(a) $P_w = 5\%$ (b) $P_w = 50\%$ (c) $P_w = 95\%$

Fig. 4. Transaction throughput of MVCC and contract lock methods

The value of s determines the conflict probability of transactions. As s rises, resource competition intensifies, leading to more conflicts, and transaction throughput drops rapidly. P_w determines the number of read-only transactions. In the $P_w = 5\%$, $P_w = 50\%$, and $P_w = 95\%$ three cases, MVCC performs better than Contract Lock. In MVCC, read operations would not block write operations because of no data locks. Thus, the optimization of MVCC is mainly in the read operation. So, when $P_w = 5\%$, the performance is equivalent. However, when $P_w = 50\%$ and $s > 0.4$, the throughput can reach 1.5x Contract Lock. Additionally, when $P_w = 95\%$, the performance improvement is significant. When $s > 0.6$, the throughput can reach 4x, and the delay is 42% of the other one.

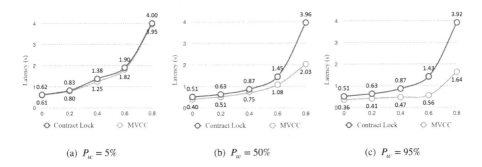

(a) $P_w = 5\%$ (b) $P_w = 50\%$ (c) $P_w = 95\%$

Fig. 5. Transaction latency of MVCC and contract lock methods

7   Conclusion

This paper overviewed the challenges of contract locks for data integrity and performance. To solve the issues of the existing methods, we proposed a MVCC approach for blockchain interoperability and implemented it on HLF. Experiments with data integrity analysis demonstrated the effectiveness and efficiency of the proposed approach. The findings show that the proposed approach achieved up to 4x performance increase compared with the existing methods, and decreased the average latency with 58%.

Acknowledgments. This work was partially supported by National Key Research and Development Project of China (Grant No. 2019YFB2102500), National Natural Science Foundation of China (No. 61902385), Shenzhen Key Basic Research Project (JCYJ20200109115422828), Huawei Cloud Research Project (YBN2020085125) and National Archives Technology Project (2020-X-10).

References

1. (2021). https://bitcoin.org/bitcoin.pdf
2. (2021). https://github.com/ethereum/wiki/wiki/White-Paper
3. Dean, J., Ghemawat, S.: (2021). https://github.com/google/leveldb/
4. Apache CouchDB (2021). https://couchdb.apache.org/
5. Oracle Timeline (2021). http://oracle.com.edgesuite.net/timeline/oracle/
6. Buterin, V.: Chain interoperability. R3 Research Paper (2016)
7. Stonebraker, M., Rowe, L.A.: The design of POSTGRES. SIGMOD (1986)
8. Zakhary, V., Agrawal, D., El Abbadi, A.: Atomic commitment across blockchains. Proc. VLDB Endowment **13**(9)
9. He, Y., Zhang, C., Wu, B., et al.: A cross-chain trusted reputation scheme for a shared charging platform based on blockchain. IEEE Internet Things J. (2021)
10. Androulaki, E., et al.: Hyperledger fabric: a distributed operating system for permissioned blockchains. In: Proceedings of the Thirteenth EuroSys Conference (2018)
11. Warnat-Herresthal, S., et al.: Swarm learning for decentralized and confidential clinical machine learning. Nature **594**(7862), 265–270 (2021)
12. Muzammal, M., Qu, Q., Nasrulin, B.: Renovating blockchain with distributed databases: an open source system. Future Gener. Comput. Syst. **90**, 105–117 (2019)
13. Thakkar, P., Senthil Nathan, N.: Performance benchmarking & optimizing hyperledger fabric blockchain platform (2018)
14. Qu, Q., Nurgaliev, I., Muzammal, M., et al.: On spatio-temporal blockchain query processing. Future Gener. Comput. Syst. **98**, 208–218 (2019)
15. Sharma, A., Schuhknecht, F.M., Agrawal, D., et al.: Blurring the lines between blockchains and database systems: the case of hyperledger fabric. In: SIGMOD, pp. 105–122 (2019)
16. Ruan, P., Loghin, D., Ta, Q.T., et al.: A transactional perspective on execute-order-validate blockchains. In: SIGMOD, pp. 543–557 (2020)
17. Nurgaliev, I., Muzammal, M., Qu, Q.: Enabling blockchain for efficient spatio-temporal query processing. In: Hacid, H., Cellary, W., Wang, H., Paik, H.-Y., Zhou, R. (eds.) WISE 2018. LNCS, vol. 11233, pp. 36–51. Springer, Cham (2018). https://doi.org/10.1007/978-3-030-02922-7_3

18. Saberi, S., et al.: Blockchain technology and its relationships to sustainable supply chain management (2018)
19. Chacko, J.A., Mayer, R., Jacobsen, H.A.: Why do my blockchain transactions fail? A study of hyperledger fabric. In: SIGMOD, pp. 221–234 (2021)
20. Zhang, L., et al.: The challenges and countermeasures of blockchain in finance and economics. Syst. Res. Behav. Sci. **37**(4), 691–698 (2020)
21. Batubara, F.R., Ubacht, J., Janssen, M.: Challenges of blockchain technology adoption for e-government: a systematic literature review (2018)
22. Thomas, S., Schwartz, E.: A protocol for interledger payments (2015). https:// interledger.org/interledger.pdf
23. Kwon, J., Buchman, E.: A network of distributed ledgers. Cosmos 1–41 (2018)
24. Polkadot, W.G.: Vision for a heterogeneous multi-chain framework. https://github. com/polkadot-io/polkadotpaper/raw/master/PolkaDotPaper.pdf
25. Herlihy, M.: Atomic cross-chain swaps. arXiv e-prints arXiv: 1801.09515 (2018)
26. Herlihy, M., Liskov, B., Shrira, L.: Cross-chain deals and adversarial commerce. VLDB J. 1–19 (2021). https://doi.org/10.1007/s00778-021-00686-1
27. Reed, D.P.: Naming and synchronization in a decentralized computer system. Massachusetts Institute of Technology (1978)
28. Larson, P.Å., Blanas, S., Diaconu, C., et al.: High-performance concurrency control mechanisms for main-memory databases. Proc. VLDB Endowment **5**(4) (2011)
29. Qu, Q., et al.: Graph-based knowledge representation model and pattern retrieval. In: 2008 Fifth International Conference on Fuzzy Systems and Knowledge Discovery, vol. 5. IEEE (2008)
30. Wang, T., Kimura, H.: Mostly-optimistic concurrency control for highly contended dynamic workloads on a thousand cores. Proc. VLDB Endowment **10**(2), 49–60 (2016)
31. Herlihy, M.P., Wing, J.M.: Linearizability: a correctness condition for concurrent objects. ACM Trans. Program. Lang. Syst. (TOPLAS) **12**(3), 463–492 (1990)
32. Cahill, M.J.: Serializable isolation for snapshot databases (2009)
33. Yu, X., Bezerra, G., Pavlo, A., et al.: Staring into the Abyss: an evaluation of concurrency control with one thousand cores. Proc. VLDB Endowment **8**(3) (2014)

An Effective and Reliable Cross-Blockchain Data Migration Approach

Mengqiu Zhang[1,2], Qiang Qu[1,3(✉)], Li Ning[1], Jianping Fan[1,2], and Ruijie Yang[3]

[1] Shenzhen Institute of Advanced Technology, Chinese Academy of Sciences, Shenzhen, China
{zhangmq,qiang,li.ning,jp.fan}@siat.ac.cn
[2] University of Chinese Academy of Sciences, Beijing, China
[3] Huawei Cloud Blockchain Lab, Shenzhen, China
yangruijie1@huawei.com

Abstract. As blockchain is widely applied, various decentralized applications would inevitably encounter data migration problems, for reasons, such as the multilevel blockchain scenarios, the exhaustion of blockchain disk space and the swap of the rapidly evolving blockchain engines. In order to proceed the applications smoothly, it is necessary to migrate original blockchain data to a new blockchain instance, which is the cross-blockchain data migration. However, ensuring the reliability of data provenance and the data consistency, and balancing migration efficiency and historical state granularity, introduce unique challenges over cross-blockchain data migration. This paper proposes an effective and reliable cross-blockchain data migration approach to coping with these challenges. To ensure the reliability, a collective mechanism of controlling, executing and storing procedures is proposed to assort migration transactions between blockchains. Furthermore, we propose two migration schemes in order to adapt decentralized application scenarios. Extensive experiments are conducted to demonstrate the effectiveness of the proposed approach.

Keywords: Blockchain · Data migration · Cross-blockchain · Distributed transactions · Decentralized applications

1 Introduction

Since 2008, the Blockchain technology introduced by Satoshi Nakamoto in "Bitcoin: A Peer-to-Peer Electronic Cash System" [1] has been paid enormous attention due to the growing demands of decentralized applications for trust purpose. The emergence of Ethereum [2] enables blockchain applicable in wide fields because of the leverage of smart contract. Meanwhile, a line of blockchain engines and platforms are proposed in order to satisfy particular features. With

© Springer Nature Switzerland AG 2022
H. Shen et al. (Eds.): PDCAT 2021, LNCS 13148, pp. 286–294, 2022.
https://doi.org/10.1007/978-3-030-96772-7_26

the fast development of blockchain, we have witnessed the technology being broadly used in the applications of product tracing, privacy protection, supply chain, finance, health, and decentralized file storage [3,4]. The increasing volume of blockchain-based applications shows that people are recently keen to set up blockchain systems, which presents a underlying requirement of cross-blockchain data migration due to the limitation of blockchain data storage, the scenarios of multi-level blockchains, and the swap need of the rapidly evolving blockchain engines [5].

With the changes in technology, policy and market circumstances, blockchain applications have encountered a series of new problems. For instance, the distributed consistent storage of blockchain raises huge consumption of space and blockchain services suffer considerable pressure from the unprecedented growth of decentralized transactions [6]. On the other hand, to ensure the competitiveness and safety of blockchain-based applications, we often need to replace underlying blockchain engines to adapt new application requirements, e.g., the latest version of Hyperledger Fabric. Hereby, cross-blockchain data migration is necessary to copy the data from the original blockchain to a new instance. However, how to ensure the reliability, data consistency while realizing the efficiency of the migration remains challenging to the traditional data migration methods in centralized systems [7].

Thus, the paper proposes an effective and reliable cross-blockchain data migration approach. A collective mechanism of contrailing, executing and storing procedures is proposed with the following three procedures to assort the migration transactions. In general, a controlling procedure provides services for cross-blockchain data migration including registration of blockchain that requires data migration. An executing procedure provides solo and aggregate migration methods in the process of cross-blockchain data migration. The storing procedure is used to store configuration files and data migration records. This approach with the three modules can effectively implement cross-blockchain data migration, and the experiments show the effectiveness and reliability.

The rest of this paper is organized as follows. Section 2 discusses the related work of data migration. Section 3 presents the proposed approach with the collective mechanism design and its three main modules. The detailed experiments and the application usage of the proposed methods are discussed in Sect. 4. Section 5 concludes the paper.

2   Related Work

We classify the literature into the data migration in the traditional centralized systems and the blockchain decentralized systems [8,11,14], respectively.

In the traditional centralized systems, Research on data migration is carried out on moving data stored on devices in a network from one configuration to another. For instance, Haller [10] mentioned the importance of data migration to maintain system competitiveness and proposed a general migration architecture. Sujit Biswas et al. [11] proposed a blockchain data migration method for the medical field, which supports the migration of medical records from traditional databases to the blockchain. These methods are based on traditional databases, and they do not consider the complexity of data structures of distributed applications in the migration methods. These methods are thus hard to be directly adapted to the cross-blockchain migration problem.

In blockchain decentralized systems, a limited number of methods have been proposed for data migration due to the short research history of blockchain. However, few study realized the importance of the cross-blockchain data management, e.g., blockchain interoperability and data migration. For the blockchain interoperability, Wang H et.al. [9] introduced a blockchain router that empowers blockchains to connect and communicate cross chains, and Herlihy M et al. [14] introduced several commonly used cross-chain transaction methods. They described novel safety and liveness properties, along with two alternative protocols for implementing cross-chain deals in a system of independent blockchain ledgers. These methods are able to support interoperation between blockchains, but they cannot be directly applied for cross-blockchain data migration because of the lack of consideration on historical data status, consistency and thoughput. For the cross-blockchain data migration, VeChain [12] introduced a method of swapping original tokens and newly-issued tokens, and Bandara et al. [13] introduced a set of blockchain migration scenarios and data fidelity levels and then identified several patterns to achieve those migration scenarios under varying data fidelity levels. These methods are designed for particular systems and they are lack of generalization for effective cross-blockchain data migration.

3   The Proposed Migration Approach

Our purpose is to conduct effective and reliable cross-blockchain data migration when various decentralized applications encounter data migration problems. To achieve this goal, the approach provides a collective mechanism of controlling, executing and storing procedures to assort migration transactions between blockchains. Blockchain information needs to be recorded before migration for ensuring that the data source and migration process are reliable. Two migration schemes are proposed to adapt decentralized application scenarios. Furthermore, we apply configuration parameters, migration records, and other information to support recovery after migration interruption. Table 1 lists the notations used throughout the paper.

Table 1. The summary of notations

Notation	Definition
$name_{from}$, $name_{to}$	User-defined chain names during registration
$solo$, $aggr$	Solo and aggregate migration mode.
CFG	Configuration parameter, logfile path etc.
$timeout$	Timeout threshold of migration event
$blockout$	Threshold of traversed blocks in a migration event
$routineMax$	Maximum number of coroutines during migration event

Figure 1 overviews the proposed cross-blockchain data migration approach. The approach with a collective mechanism of controlling, executing and storing procedures provides custom parameter configuration to support personalized migration for various application scenarios. The architecture ensures the reliability of data sources and the consistency of transactions while balancing migration efficiency and historical state granularity.

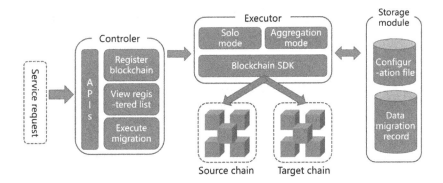

Fig. 1. The cross-blockchain data migration method architecture

3.1 Preparing for the Migration

Before data migration, blockchain information needs to be registered to ensure that data sources are trusted. In order to ensure data source reliability, consistency and invariance of migration transactions, two to three steps are necessary to implement data migration: registering a blockchain, viewing a registered list (optional), and executing the migration. Registration means recording information about the source and target blockchain before migration, including the user-defined *name* (blockchain name), *channel* (channel name), *type* (Blockchain Type), *config* (configuration file path) and *certs* (Certificate file path). Viewing registered list is to query the list of successfully registered blockchains. Executing migration selects the migration mode and operating parameters in terms of the configuration of input to migrate data from the $name_{from}$ to the $name_{to}$.

3.2 Cross-Chain Data Migration Process

In a specific migration, the cost, migration duration, and data consistency need to be considered. In order to balance efficiency and historical status granularity, the data migration approach we proposed supports two execution modes: *solo* and *aggr*.

Figure 2 shows the solo *solo* and aggregation *aggr* migration mode . N represents the number of transactions in the block, and M represents the number of key-value pairs (K-V) included in the block. In the solo mode, information of each transaction on the source chain can be written into the replication chain separately. In the aggregation mode, X represents the number of blocks aggregated at a time. M represents the number of K-V pairs remaining after the repeated K-V pairs are removed from the transaction set in X blocks. This mode supports the deduplication of the read-write set of X blocks on the source chain and then aggregates them into a transaction to be written to the target new blockchain instance.

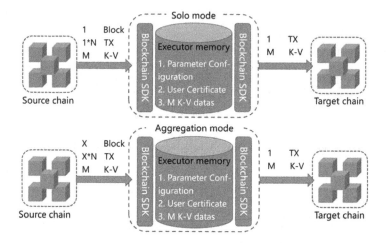

Fig. 2. The schematic of solo pattern

Algorithm 1 shows the execution of cross-blockchain data migration.

Algorithm 1. cross-blockchain Data Migration

Require: $name_{from}$, $name_{to}$
1: $chain_{from}, chain_{to} \leftarrow init(name_{from}, name_{to})$
2: $h_{point} \leftarrow getBreakpoint(name_{from}, name_{to})$
3: $h_{end} \leftarrow chain_{from}.GetBlockHeight()$
4: $CFG \leftarrow GetConfig()$
5: **if** $mode == solo$ **then**
6:     **for** $h_{point} \rightarrow h_{end}$ **do**
7:         $block \leftarrow chain_{from}.GetBlock(h_{point})$
8:         $TX \leftarrow unmarshal(block)$
9:         **for** $i = 1 \rightarrow i = len(TX)$ **do**
10:             $chain_{to}.InputTX(tx_i)$
11:         **end for**
12:         $h_{point} + +$
13:     **end for**

14: **else if** $mode == aggr$ **then**
15:     **for** $h_{point} \rightarrow h_{end}$ **do**
16:         **while** $MEETCONDITION$ **do**
17:     ▷ The number of blocks obtained reaches $blockout$ or the time it takes to execute reaches $timeout$
18:             $block \leftarrow chain_{from}.GetBlock(h_{point})$
19:             $TX \leftarrow unmarshal(block), TXset \leftarrow append(TX)$
20:             $h_{point} + +$
21:         **end while**
22:         $tx \leftarrow aggrTX(TXset)$
23:         $chain_{to}.InputTX(tx)$
24:     **end for**
25: **end if**

In this approach, we first initialize blockchain that needs data migration to ensure the reliability of the data source, then get the starting and ending block height of the source blockchain for data migration by using $getBreakpoint$ and $GetBlockHeight$ functions. If the migration mode is $solo$ in the CFG, executing procedure would unmarshal the blocks of the source blockchain to obtain transactions and ordinally write them into the target blockchain. Elsewhen the migration mode is $aggr$, executing procedure would traverse blocks in the source blockchain until the number of blocks obtained reaches $blockout$ or the time it takes to execute reaches $timeout$, then the algorithm removes duplicate keys from transaction set TX and aggregates them into a transaction. Finally, it writes the transaction to the target blockchain and repeats the process until the cross-blockchain data migration is completed.

To support the complete execution of the data migration process and the function of resuming broken migration. The configuration and data migration record should be stored. The configuration contains parameters such as working $mode$, $logpath$, and running parameters including $timeout$, $blockout$, and $routineMax$ in the aggregation mode.

4   Experimental Results

To verify the effectiveness of the cross-blockchain data migration method and test the effect of different configuration parameters on the migration results, sets of experiments are carried out: comparative experiments of the solo and the aggregation migration mode, and parameter studies of the approach.

4.1   Comparison Study of *solo* and *aggr*

A dataset including 1000 transactions is used to perform five groups of cross-blockchain data migration tests based on the $solo$ and $aggregate$ mode, where configuration of $aggregate$ is: $timeout = 50$, $blockout = 50$, and $routineMax = 50$.

Table 2. Data migration tests for the *solo* model and the *aggr* model

Sequence	Solo migration mode					Aggregate migration mode				
	Migration result				Time	Migration result				Time
1	☑Full	☐ Part	☐ Failure		2017 s	☑Full	☐ Part	☐ Failure		13 s
2	☑Full	☐ Part	☐ Failure		2070 s	☑Full	☐ Part	☐ Failure		13 s
3	☑Full	☐ Part	☐ Failure		2053 s	☑Full	☐ Part	☐ Failure		10 s
4	☑Full	☐ Part	☐ Failure		2032 s	☑Full	☐ Part	☐ Failure		7 s
5	☑Full	☐ Part	☐ Failure		2049 s	☑Full	☐ Part	☐ Failure		13 s

As Table 2 shows, both the *solo* and *aggregate* modes effectively complete
full-blockchain data migration. The average migration duration in *solo* is 2044 s,
while *aggregate* is 11 s. Both modes ensure that the world states of the target
blockchain and the source chain are entirely consistent. The solo mode additionally ensures that the historical states of the target and source chain are
consistent.

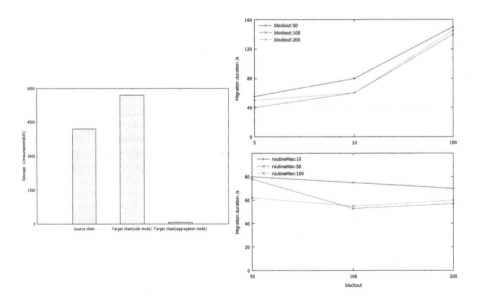

Fig. 3. Comparison of storage consumption and migration duration

Figure 3 shows the storage consumption of the source and target blockchain
in the two migration modes. The storage consumption of the target blockchain
in *solo* is slightly higher than that of the source blockchain because more block
header data is contained. However, in *aggregation*, the storage consumption of
the target blockchain is much lower due to the fewer transactions and blocks.
The advantage of the *solo* mode is that it can simultaneously make the world

state and historical state of the target new blockchain completely consistent with the source blockchain. Furthermore, the *aggregation* mode achieves higher efficiency but less storage consumption.

4.2 Configuration Parameter Study for Aggregation

The *timeout* is fixed to 10 s, and 9 sets of data migration experiments are performed using the data set containing 100,000 transactions.

Each set of experiments successfully completes the total amount of data migration. The migration efficiency is shown in the upper right corner of Fig. 3. On the one hand, the migration duration decreases as *routineMax* increases. On the other hand, when *blockout* is small, the migration duration decreases as the number of aggregation blocks increases. When *blockout* is large, the block processing time is greater than the transaction submission time. The migration duration will increase as the number of aggregation blocks increases.

Then we test the comparison of migration duration while *blockout* and *timeout* is different, *routineMax* is fixed to 50. The migration efficiency is shown in the lower right corner of Fig. 3. Since the production of the last block during migration often fails to meet the "maximum number of transactions" condition, it is necessary to wait for the timeout to meet the *timeout* condition to produce blocks, and the migration duration will increase with the increase of *timeout*.

5 Conclusion

In this paper, we proposed an effective and reliable approach to coping with scenarios where historical data on a blockchain needs to be migrated to a new blockchain engine. A collective mechanism with various methods were presented in order to achieve the reliability of the migration process. In addition, we discussed two migration methods, the *solo* and *aggr* modes, and analyzed the pros and cons of them. We demonstrated the effectiveness of the proposed method given extensive experiments under different configuration parameters.

Acknowledgments. This work was partially supported by National Key Research and Development Project of China (Grant No. 2019YFB2102500), National Natural Science Foundation of China (No. 61902385), Shenzhen Key Basic Research Project (JCYJ20200109115422828), Huawei Cloud Research Project (YBN2020085125) and National Archives Technology Project (2020-X-10).

References

1. Nakamoto, S.: Bitcoin: a peer-to-peer electronic cash system. Decentralized Bus. Rev. 21260 (2008)
2. Wood, G.: Ethereum: a secure decentralised generalised transaction ledger. Ethereum Project Yellow Paper **2014**(151), 1–32 (2014)

3. Nasrulin, B., Muzammal, M., Qu, Q.: ChainMOB: mobility analytics on blockchain. In: 2018 19th IEEE International Conference on Mobile Data Management (MDM). IEEE, pp. 292–293 (2018)
4. Muzammal, M., Qu, Q., Nasrulin, B.: Renovating blockchain with distributed databases: an open source system. Future Gener. Comput. Syst. **90**, 105–117 (2019)
5. Xie, J., Yu, F.R., Huang, T., et al.: A survey on the scalability of blockchain systems. IEEE Netw. **33**(5), 166–173 (2019)
6. Kanza, Y.: Technical perspective: revealing every story of data in blockchain systems. ACM SIGMOD Record **49**(1), 69 (2020)
7. Das, S., Nishimura, S., Agrawal, D., et al.: Albatross: lightweight elasticity in shared storage databases for the cloud using live data migration. Proc. VLDB Endowment **4**(8), 494–505 (2011)
8. Carreira, P., Galhardas, H.: Efficient development of data migration transformations. In: Proceedings of the ACM SIGMOD International Conference on Management of Data, pp. 915–916 (2004)
9. Wang, H., Cen, Y., Li, X.: Blockchain router: a cross-chain communication protocol. In: Proceedings of the 6th International Conference on Informatics, Environment, Energy and Applications, pp. 94–97 (2017)
10. Haller, K.: Towards the industrialization of data migration: concepts and patterns for standard software implementation projects. In: van Eck, P., Gordijn, J., Wieringa, R. (eds.) CAiSE 2009. LNCS, vol. 5565, pp. 63–78. Springer, Heidelberg (2009). https://doi.org/10.1007/978-3-642-02144-2_10
11. Biswas, S., Sharif, K., Li, F., et al.: Blockchain for e-health-care systems: easier said than done. Computer **53**(7), 57–67 (2020)
12. VeChain: 'VeChainThor wallet manual including token swap and X node migration, July 2018. https://cdn.vechain.com/vechainthor wallet manual en v1.0.pdf
13. Bandara, H.M.N.D., Xu, X., Weber, I.: Patterns for blockchain data migration. In: Proceedings of the European Conference on Pattern Languages of Programs 2020, pp. 1–19 (2020)
14. Herlihy, M., Liskov, B., Shrira, L.: Cross-chain deals and adversarial commerce. VLDB J. 1–19 (2021). https://doi.org/10.1007/s00778-021-00686-1

Algorithm for the Facility Location Problem with Origin and Destination

Fengmin Wang$^{(\boxtimes)}$, Chu Wang, Na Li , and Wenxing Kang

Beijing Jinghang Research Institute of Computing and Communication,
Beijing 100074, People's Republic of China

Abstract. The Uncapacitated Facility Location Problem with Origin and Destination (FLPWOD) is an extension of the Uncapacitated Facility Location Problem (UFLP), where each unit of demand has its own origin and destination, and must be shipped from its origin via a location at which a transit station is built, to its destination. As in the UFLP, facilities can be opened at any of the predefined locations with given fixed costs. In classical location models, the clients have to be assigned to the open facilities, and the assignment cost is the distance between a client and an open facility. In the FLPWOD, the demands with origins and destinations have to be assigned to the open facilities, and the assignment cost is the length of a tour form the origin to the destination through an open facility. LP-rounding approximation algorithm is developed with the first constant approximation ratio 4.

Keywords: Facility location · Origin and destination · LP-rounding · Approximation algorithm

1 Introduction

The Uncapacitated Facility Location Problem with Origin and Destination (FLPWOD)is an extension of the Uncapacitated Facility Location Problem (UFLP), which has been extensively investigated in the field of combinatorial optimization over the past three decades [2,5,9]. The UFLP consists of locating uncapacitated facilities among a set of candidate sites and of allocating clients to open facilities in such a way that the sum of location and allocation costs is minimized. More precise, in the UFLP, the inputs are a facility set F, a client set C, a nonnegative facility opening cost for every facility in F, and a nonnegative service cost for connecting each pair of a facility in F and a client in C. The connection cost is often assumed to be metric. The objective is to open (locate) some facilities in F, and connect (allocate) each client in C to one of the open facilities, in such a way that the sum of opening and connection costs is minimized. In this model, each client is serviced separately. However, in several applications, visits to clients may be combined, such as in the bike sharing systems (see, e.g. [12,14,16]). The FLPWOD corresponds to the case

Supported by NNSF of China under Grant No. 11901544.

H. Shen et al. (Eds.): PDCAT 2021, LNCS 13148, pp. 295–302, 2022.
https://doi.org/10.1007/978-3-030-96772-7_27

where depots must be located and two clients can be serviced together from a given depot. Such applications arise naturally in container transportation, in petroleum delivery, and in bulk garbage collection.

1.1 Related Work

We briefly review here the studies related to the facility location problem. Shmoys et al. [13] developed the first constant factor approximation algorithm for the metric uncapacitated facility location problem. They used the LP-rounding technique to obtain the approximate ratio 3.16. The ratio was improved later by Chudak and Shmoys [3] who provided a randomized rounding based 1.736-approximation algorithm. Currently, Li [7] gives the best approximation ratio of 1.488. On the hardness side, Guha and Khuller [4] presents that it is hard to approximate uncapacitated facility location problem within a factor of 1.463. For the capacitated version, An et al. [1] consider the metric capacitated facility location problem, and present a constant factor approximation algorithm based on LP-rounding. Furthermore, the (randomized) LP-rounding techniques have been successfully used to design several algorithms for the facility location problem and its variants (see [8,10,15] and reference therein). Nezhad et al. [11] investigated the facility location problem with point and area destinations in fuzzy environment.

1.2 Our Contribution

The main contributions of this paper are summarized as follows.

- We firstly introduce the FLPWOD which generalizes the classic facility location problem.
- We present LP-rounding approximation algorithm with the ratio 4.
- Our algorithm obtain the first constant approximation ratio for the FLPWOD.

1.3 Organization

The remainder of this paper is organized as follows. We state the FLPWOD, give its model and algorithm in Sect. 2, and theoretical analysis are conducted to show how the LP-rounding approximation algorithm dealing with the FLPWOD problem. Section 3 is devoted to conclusions and future works.

2 Uncapacitated Facility Location Problem with Origin And Destination

2.1 Problem Statement

Consider a set of locations $N = \{1, \ldots, n\}$, the travel costs between them, $c_{st} \geq 0$, $s, t = 1, \ldots, n$, are assumed symmetric and satisfy the triangle inequality.

There is a facility set $F \subseteq N$, and a origin and destination demand pair set $D = \{(i,j) : i,j \in N\}$. In the uncapacitated facility location problem with origin and destination (FLPWOD), we should select some facilities to open, and assign each demand pair to exactly one open facility; for each demand pair $(i,j) \in D$, there is a positive integral demand d_{ij} that must be shipped to its assigned facility. For each location $k \in F$, the non-negative cost of opening a facility at k is f_k. The cost of assigning demand pair (i,j) to an open facility at k is $c_{ijk} = c_{ik} + c_{kj}$ per unit of demand shipped. The objective of the FLPWOD is to minimize the sum of the fixed facility location costs and of the assignment costs. The general solution structure of the FLPWOD addressed in this study is represented in Fig. 1.

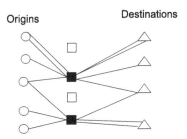

Fig. 1. Solution structure of the FLPWOD.

We introduce the following two decision variables: y_k and x_{ijk}. If a facility is open at location k, $y_k = 1$, if not, $y_k = 0$; and if the origin and destination demand pair (i,j) is assigned to facility k, $x_{ijk} = 1$, if not, $x_{ijk} = 0$. The model is as follows.

$$\min \sum_{k \in F} f_k y_k + \sum_{(i,j) \in D} \sum_{k \in F} d_{ij} c_{ijk} x_{ijk}$$

$$\text{s. t.} \sum_{k \in F} x_{ijk} = 1, \quad \forall (i,j) \in D, \tag{1}$$

$$x_{ijk} \leq y_k, \quad \forall (i,j) \in D, k \in F,$$

$$x_{ijk}, y_k \in \{0,1\}, \quad \forall (i,j) \in D, k \in F.$$

The first constraint guarantees that any origin and destination demand pair $(i,j) \in D$ should be assigned to only one transit station $k \in F$. The second constraints indicate that if the demand pair $(i,j) \in D$ is assigned to the transit station $k \in F$, then the facility k must be open.

Relax the $0-1$ constraints of the above integer program (1), we have the following linear relaxation program.

$$\min \sum_{k \in F} f_k y_k + \sum_{(i,j) \in D} \sum_{k \in F} d_{ij} c_{ijk} x_{ijk}$$

$$\text{s. t.} \sum_{k \in F} x_{ijk} = 1, \quad \forall (i,j) \in D, \tag{2}$$

$$x_{ijk} \le y_k, \quad \forall (i,j) \in D, k \in F,$$

$$x_{ijk}, y_k \ge 0, \quad \forall (i,j) \in D, k \in F.$$

2.2 Algorithm

Our algorithm is a slight adaptation of the approximation algorithm for the uncapacitated facility location problem by Shmoys et al. [13], where we think of the origin destination pair as an imaginary client in the facility location problem. The major contribution of this paper is to show that the LP-rounding algorithm of Shmoys et al. [13] can be easily adapted to solve the FLPWOD. We present the following definition used in our algorithm.

Definition 1. *For each demand pair* $(i,j) \in D$, *given* g_{ij}. *A feasible solution* (x, y) *to the linear program (2) is said to be g-close, if it satisfies the property*

$$x_{ijk} > 0 \Rightarrow c_{ijk} \le g_{ij}.$$

We can see from the above definition that if a fractional solution to the linear program (2) is g-close, then whenever a demand (i,j) is fractionally assigned to a (partially opened) facility k, the cost c_{ijk} associated with that assignment is not too big. In our algorithm, based on solving the linear relaxation of the integer program (1), we apply the filtering and rounding technique to obtain a new g-close fractional solution. We then show how to round the g-close fractional solution to a $3g$-close integer solution.

We now give the details of the rounding algorithm.

Algorithm 1. *We run the following steps.*

Step 1. Solve the linear program (2). Denote the feasible fractional solution by (x, y).

Step 2. (Filtering and rounding) Let α *be a fixed value in the interval* $(0,1)$. *For each demand pair* $(i,j) \in D$, *we sort the connection costs* c_{ijk} *over all facilities* $k \in F$, *in nondecreasing order; add the associated values* x_{ijk} *in this order, note* k^* *to be the first facility for which this running sum is at least* α, *we set* $c_{ij}(\alpha) = c_{ijk^*}$. *For each demand pair* $(i,j) \in D$, *let* $\alpha_{ij} = \sum_{k \in F: c_{ijk} \le c_{ij}(\alpha)} x_{ijk}$. *We then round the fractional solution* (x, y) *to obtain* $(\bar{x}, \bar{y})$ *as follows. For each demand pair* $(i,j) \in D$, *and each facility* $k \in F$, *we set*

$$\bar{x}_{ijk} = \begin{cases} x_{ijk}/\alpha_{ij}, & \text{if } c_{ijk} \le c_{ij}(\alpha), \\ 0, & \text{otherwise}, \end{cases} \qquad \bar{y}_k = \min\{1, y_k/\alpha\}.$$

For each demand pair $(i,j) \in D$, *let* $g_{ij} = c_{ij}(\alpha)$, *then* $(\bar{x}, \bar{y})$ *is a g-close solution.*

Step 3. (Clustering and rounding)

Step 3.1 (Construct clustering) The algorithm maintains a feasible fractional solution $(\hat{x}, \hat{y})$; initially, we set $(\hat{x}, \hat{y}) = (\bar{x}, \bar{y})$. Let D^c denote the set of demand pairs that are selected as the center of the cluster, U denote the set of demand pairs that have not been cluster. At the beginning of the algorithm, set $D^c := \emptyset$, $C := \emptyset$, $U := D$.

Consider each demand pair $(i, j) \in U$, for the given values g_{ij}, find $(i^c, j^c) := \arg\min_{(i,j) \in U} g_{ij}$. If there are more than one $(i, j) \in U$, such that g_{ij} is the smallest, then (i^c, j^c) is one of them. Let $F^{(i^c, j^c)} := \{k \in F : \hat{x}_{i^c j^c k} > 0\}$. $S^{(i^c, j^c)} := \{(i, j) : \exists k \in F^{(i^c, j^c)}, \hat{x}_{ijk} > 0\}$. Denote the cluster centered at (i^c, j^c) as $C^{(i^c, j^c)} := F^{(i^c, j^c)} \cup S^{(i^c, j^c)}$. Update $D^c := D^c \cup \{(i^c, j^c)\}$, $C := C \cup \{C^{(i^c, j^c)}\}$, $U := U - S^{(i^c, j^c)}$.

Iterate over the above clustering process, until $U = \emptyset$. Go to Step 3.2.

Step 3.2 (Rounding)

For each demand pair $(i^c, j^c) \in D^c$, denote $k^c := \arg\min_{k \in F^{(i^c, j^c)}} f_k$, open k^c, assign the demand pairs in $S^{(i^c, j^c)}$ to the facility k^c. We have

$$\hat{y}_k = \begin{cases} 1, & k = k^c, \\ 0, & k \in F^{(i^c, j^c)} - \{k^c\}, \end{cases} \qquad \hat{x}_{ijk} = \begin{cases} 1, & (i,j) \in S^{(i^c, j^c)}, k = k^c, \\ 0, & (i,j) \in S^{(i^c, j^c)}, k \neq k^c. \end{cases}$$

So far we obtain a 3g-close solution $(\hat{x}, \hat{y})$ (See the proof of Lemma 3).

The fractional solution obtained by Step 2 denoted by $(\bar{x}, \bar{y})$ is feasible. By the definition of $\bar{x}$, we have

$$\sum_{k \in F} \bar{x}_{ijk} = \sum_{k \in F : c_{ijk} \le c_{ij}(\alpha)} (x_{ijk}/\alpha_{ij}) + \sum_{k \in F : c_{ijk} > c_{ij}(\alpha)} 0$$

$$= \sum_{k \in F : c_{ijk} \le c_{ij}(\alpha)} x_{ijk} / \sum_{k \in F : c_{ijk} \le c_{ij}(\alpha)} x_{ijk}$$

$$= 1.$$

Thus the first condition of program (2) hold. Furthermore, $\bar{x}_{ijk} \le 1$. Since (x, y) is feasible, we have $x_{ijk} \le y_k$. If $c_{ijk} \le c_{ij}(\alpha)$, $\bar{x}_{ijk} = x_{ijk}/\alpha_{ij} \le y_k/\alpha_{ij}$. By the definition of $c_{ij}(\alpha)$, we have $\alpha_{ij} \ge \alpha$. So $y_k/\alpha_{ij} \le y_k/\alpha$. Thus $\bar{x}_{ijk} \le \bar{y}_k$. If $c_{ijk} > c_{ij}(\alpha)$, $\bar{x}_{ijk} = 0 \le \bar{y}_k$. The second condition of program (2) hold as well. The feasibility of the solution $(\hat{x}, \hat{y})$ is clearly visible. The algorithm only assigns demand $(i, j) \in D$ to an opened facility, and when we set any variable $\hat{y}_k$ to 0, we also set each variable $\hat{x}_{ijk}$ to 0.

2.3 Analysis

We present the following lemma which is important in analyzing the assignment cost.

Lemma 1. *For each demand pair $(i, j) \in D$, $c_{ij}(\alpha) \le \frac{1}{1-\alpha} \sum_{k \in F} c_{ijk} x_{ijk}$.*

Proof. Let $K = \{k : c_{ijk} \geq c_{ij}(\alpha)\}$, then by the definition of $c_{ij}(\alpha)$, we have $\sum_{k \in F-K} x_{ijk} < \alpha$, which together with the fact that $\sum_{k \in F} x_{ijk} = 1$, imply that $\sum_{k \in K} x_{ijk} \geq 1 - \alpha$. Hence, $\sum_{k \in F} c_{ijk} x_{ijk} \geq \sum_{k \in K} c_{ijk} x_{ijk} \geq (1-\alpha) c_{ij}(\alpha)$, i.e., $c_{ij}(\alpha) \leq \frac{1}{1-\alpha} \sum_{k \in F} c_{ijk} x_{ijk}$. □

We now analyze the approximation factor of Algorithm 1, i.e., analyze the relationship between the cost of the solution obtained from Algorithm 1 and the cost of the optimal solution denoted by OPT. In order to bound the total cost of the solution $(\hat{x}, \hat{y})$, we provide the following lemmas to bound the facility cost and the assignment cost respectively.

Lemma 2. *The facility cost of the feasible integer solution $(\hat{x}, \hat{y})$ is no more than $\frac{1}{\alpha}$ times of the facility cost of the feasible fractional solution (x, y), i.e.,*

$$\sum_{k \in F} f_k \hat{y}_k \leq \frac{1}{\alpha} \sum_{k \in F} f_k y_k.$$

Proof. By step 3.2 in Algorithm 1, $f_{k^c} = \min_{k \in F^{(i^c, j^c)}} f_k$. Since the minimum of a set of numbers is never more than their weighted average, and $\sum_{k \in F^{(i^c, j^c)}} \bar{x}_{ijk} = 1$, we obtain $f_{k^c} \leq \sum_{k \in F^{(i^c, j^c)}} f_k \bar{x}_{ijk}$. We have present at the end of Subsect. 2.2 that $\bar{x}_{ijk} \leq \bar{y}_k$, so $f_{k^c} \leq \sum_{k \in F^{(i^c, j^c)}} f_k \bar{y}_k$. This inequality implies that the facility cost of $\hat{y}$ never increases throughout the execution of the algorithm, hence $\sum_{k \in F} f_k \hat{y}_k \leq \sum_{k \in F} f_k \bar{y}_k$. By the definition of $\bar{y}$, we know that $\bar{y}_k \leq \frac{1}{\alpha} y_k$. Finally, we obtain that $\sum_{k \in F} f_k \hat{y}_k \leq \frac{1}{\alpha} \sum_{k \in F} f_k y_k$. □

Lemma 3. *The assignment cost of the feasible integer solution $(\hat{x}, \hat{y})$ is no more than $\frac{3}{1-\alpha}$ times of the assignment cost of the feasible fractional solution (x, y), i.e.,*

$$\sum_{k \in F} \sum_{(i,j) \in D} d_{ij} c_{ijk} \hat{x}_{ijk} \leq \frac{3}{1-\alpha} \sum_{k \in F} \sum_{(i,j) \in D} d_{ij} c_{ijk} x_{ijk}.$$

Proof. Consider the demand pair in the cluster $C^{(i^c, j^c)}$. According to Step 3 in Algorithm 1, there are the following case.

Case 1. If $(i, j) = (i^c, j^c)$, then $c_{ijk^c} = c_{i^c j^c k^c} \leq g_{i^c j^c}$.

Case 2. If $(i, j) \neq (i^c, j^c)$, then there must exist $k \in F^{(i^c, j^c)}$ such that $\hat{x}_{ijk} > 0$. We have $c_{ijk} \leq g_{ij}$. If $k = k^c$, then $c_{ijk^c} \leq g_{ij}$. If $k \neq k^c$, then $\hat{x}_{i^c j^c k} > 0$. We have $c_{i^c j^c k} \leq g_{i^c j^c}$. By the triangle inequality, we have the following inequalities. When $i \neq i^c, j \neq j^c$,

$$c_{ijk^c} = c_{ik^c} + c_{k^c j} \leq c_{ik} + c_{i^c k} + c_{i^c k^c} + c_{kj} + c_{kj^c} + c_{k^c j^c}$$
$$= c_{ijk} + c_{i^c j^c k} + c_{i^c j^c k^c} \leq g_{ij} + 2g_{i^c j^c} \leq 3g_{ij}.$$

When $i = i^c, j \neq j^c$,

$$c_{ijk^c} = c_{i^cjk^c} = c_{i^ck^c} + c_{k^cj} \leq c_{i^ck^c} + c_{kj} + c_{kj^c} + c_{k^cj^c} \leq c_{i^cj^ck^c} + c_{ijk}$$
$$+ c_{i^cj^ck} \leq g_{ij} + 2g_{i^cj^c} \leq 3g_{ij}.$$

When $i \neq i^c, j = j^c$,

$$c_{ijk^c} = c_{ij^ck^c} = c_{ik^c} + c_{k^cj^c} \leq c_{ik^c} + c_{i^ck} + c_{i^ck^c} + c_{k^cj^c} \leq c_{ijk} + c_{i^cj^ck}$$
$$+ c_{i^cj^ck^c} \leq g_{ij} + 2g_{i^cj^c} \leq 3g_{ij}.$$

Since for each demand pair $(i, j) \in D$, $g_{ij} = c_{ij}(\alpha)$, and by Lemma 1, $c_{ij}(\alpha) \leq \frac{1}{1-\alpha} \sum_{k \in F} c_{ijk} x_{ijk}$, we obtain that $c_{ijk^c} \leq \frac{3}{1-\alpha} \sum_{k \in F} c_{ijk} x_{ijk}$. Add all the demand pairs in the cluster $\mathcal{C}$, we obtain

$$\sum_{k \in F} \sum_{(i,j) \in D} d_{ij} c_{ijk} \hat{x}_{ijk} \leq \frac{3}{1-\alpha} \sum_{k \in F} \sum_{(i,j) \in D} d_{ij} c_{ijk} x_{ijk}.$$

$\square$

Theorem 4. *The total cost of the feasible integer solution $(\hat{x}, \hat{y})$ is no more than 4 times of the OPT, i.e.,*

$$\sum_{k \in F} f_k \hat{y}_k + \sum_{k \in F} \sum_{(i,j) \in D} d_{ij} c_{ijk} \hat{x}_{ijk} \leq 4OPT.$$

Proof. By Lemma 2 and Lemma 3, we have that

$$\sum_{k \in F} f_k \hat{y}_k + \sum_{k \in F} \sum_{(i,j) \in D} d_{ij} c_{ijk} \hat{x}_{ijk}$$
$$\leq \frac{1}{\alpha} \sum_{k \in F} f_k y_k + \frac{3}{1-\alpha} \sum_{k \in F} \sum_{(i,j) \in D} d_{ij} c_{ijk} x_{ijk}$$
$$\leq \max\{\frac{1}{\alpha}, \frac{3}{1-\alpha}\}(\sum_{k \in F} f_k y_k + \sum_{k \in F} \sum_{(i,j) \in D} d_{ij} c_{ijk} x_{ijk})$$
$$\leq \max\{\frac{1}{\alpha}, \frac{3}{1-\alpha}\}OPT.$$

Set $\alpha = 1/4$, we obtain the theorem. $\square$

3   Conclusion

In this paper, we introduce the uncapacitated facility location problem with origin and destination, where each unit of demand has its own origin and destination, and must be shipped from its origin via a location at which a transit station is built, to its destination. An LP-rounding approximation algorithm is developed with the ratio 4, which is a good reference for other methods to improve the approximation ratio. And for further research in the future, one can present experiment and analysis about the algorithm. There are several other directions for future research, such as considering the capacitated facility location problem with origin and destination, the k-level facility location problem with origin and destination.

References

1. An, H.C., Singh, M., Svensson, O.: LP-based algorithms for capacitated facility location. In: Proceedings of IEEE, Symposium on Foundations of Computer Science. IEEE Computer Society, pp. 256–265 (2014)
2. Comuejols, G., Nemhauser, G.L., Wolsey, L.A.: The uncapacitated facility location problem. In: Mirchandani, P.B., Francis, R.L. (eds.) Discrete Location Theory. Wiley, New York, pp. 119–171 (1990)
3. Chudak, F.A., Shmoys, D.B.: Improved approximation algorithms for the uncapacitated facility location problem. SIAM J. Comput. **33**, 1–25 (2003)
4. Guha, S., Khuller, S.: Greedy strikes back: improved facility location algorithms. J. Algorithms **31**(1), 228–248 (1999)
5. Hh, A., Zo, B.: An improved scatter search algorithm for the uncapacitated facility location problem. Comput. Ind. Eng. **135**, 855–867 (2019)
6. Klincewicz, J.G.: Enumeration and search procedures for a Hub location problem with economies of scale. Ann. Oper. Res. **110**, 107–122 (2002)
7. Li, S.: A 1.488 Approximation algorithm for the uncapacitated facility location problem. In: Proceedings of the ICALP, Part II, pp. 77–88 (2011)
8. Li, Y., Du, D., Xiu, N., Xu, D.: Improved approximation algorithms for the facility location problems with linear/submodular penalties. Algorithmica **73**(2), 460–482 (2015)
9. Labbe, M., Louveaux, F.V.: Location problems. In: DelPAmico, M., Maffioli, F., Martello, S. (eds.) Annotated Bibliographies in Combinatorial Optimization. Wiley, Chiehester, UK, pp. 261–281 (1997)
10. Lv, W., Wu, C.: An LP-rounding based algorithm for a capacitated uniform facility location problem with penalties. J. Comb. Optim. **41**(4), 888–904 (2021). https://doi.org/10.1007/s10878-021-00726-0
11. Nezhad, N.A.T., Moradi, S., Karamali, G.: Fuzzy facility location problem with point and rectangular destinations. Int. J. Math. Oper. Res. **18**(1), 21–44 (2021)
12. Quilliot, A., Sarbinowski, A.: Facility location models for vehicle sharing systems. In: Computer Science Information Systems. IEEE (2016)
13. Shmoys, D.B., Tardös, É., Aardal, K.I.: Approximation algorithms for facility location problems. In: Proceedings of the Twenty-Ninth Annual ACM Symposium on Theory of Computing, pp. 265–274 (1997)
14. Wang, F., Hu, X., Wu, C.: 2-level station location for bike sharing. In: Zhang, Z., Li, W., Du, D.Z. (eds.) Algorithmic Aspects in Information and Management. AAIM 2020 (2020)
15. Xu, G., Xu, J.: An LP rounding algorithm for approximating uncapacitated facility location problem with penalty. Inf. Process. Lett. **94**, 119–123 (2005)
16. Zhang, J., Pan, X., Li, M., Yu, P.S.: Bicycle-sharing systems expansion: station re-deployment through crowd planning. In: ACM SIGSPATIAL International Conference on Advances in Geographic Information Systems ACM, vol. 2 (2016)

Reinforcement Learning-Based Auto-scaling Algorithm for Elastic Cloud Workflow Service

Jian-bin Lu, Yang Yu[✉], and Mao-lin Pan

School of Computer Science and Engineering, Sun Yat-sen University, Guangzhou 510006, China
yuy@mail.sysu.edu.cn

Abstract. Deploying a workflow engine as a service on a container cloud environment can improve its service quality and reliability, but auto-scaling of the elastic cloud workflow service doesn't attract much study attention. Current auto-scaling algorithms oriented to common microservices consider little about the characteristics of a long time and high cost of starting up workflow service, which can easily cause problems such as untimely scaling and excessive scaling. Given this, based on reinforcement learning and semi-Markov decision process (SMDP) modeling, an auto-scaling algorithm for elastic cloud workflow engine is proposed, which enables the cloud workflow service to scale in time, appropriately allocating resources and ensuring service availability. Simulation comparison experiments show that the algorithm automatically scales instances in advance and adapts to changes in traffic through the reinforcement learning SMDP strategy, so that it reduces the violation rate in Service Level Agreements (SLA), and improves the availability of the cloud workflow service.

Keywords: Workflow · Cloud computing · Auto scaling · Reinforcement learning

1 Introduction

With the increase of globalization, business process management (BPM) is expected to help modern enterprises be both competitively agile and cost-efficient. And due to the development of cloud computing, BPM is located as a service that offers a dedicated business process in a cloud-based manner, so-called BPM as a service (BPMaaS) [1]. Current researches on cloud workflow services focus on the application and architecture design of cloud workflow services to improve the efficiency of the cloud environment but pay little attention to the elasticity of cloud workflow services [2]. To improve the elasticity of BPMaaS, it is significant to auto-scale the cloud workflow engine services, one of the cores of BPMaaS. However, compared with the general cloud services, the cloud workflow engine service has a larger granularity, takes longer to start, and consumes more resources [3], and auto-scaling such a service has to face more challenges.

Considering the stochasticity and uncertainty in the cloud environment, solutions based on Reinforcement Learning (RL) are purposed to solve the auto-scaling problems [4]. The auto-scaling problems are usually modeled as Markov decision processes

© Springer Nature Switzerland AG 2022
H. Shen et al. (Eds.): PDCAT 2021, LNCS 13148, pp. 303–310, 2022.
https://doi.org/10.1007/978-3-030-96772-7_28

(MDP) problems. In cloud auto-scaling problems, the RL agent learns how to allocate appropriate resources in a pay-per-use manner. However, due to the characteristics of cloud workflow services, the observation of rewards and states is not as intuitive as ordinary microservices and it is necessary to auto-scale the BPMS proactively. Applying ordinary RL methods will cause untimely scaling, over-allocation of resources, and oscillation.

In addressing these challenges, this paper purposes an automatic scaling algorithm for elastic cloud workflow services based on load prediction and reinforcement learning considering the features of cloud workflow service scaling. The algorithm models the automatic scaling problem of cloud workflow services as SMDP and combines reinforcement learning and load prediction algorithms to perform automatic scaling operations on cloud workflow services. And it can auto-scale the services in advance with the changes in traffic load and allocate resources rationally so that it can provide stable service.

2 Problem Description

This section will analyze the auto-scaling problem of cloud workflow services from the perspectives of auto-scaling and reinforcement learning.

The auto-scaling problems for cloud applications are commonly abstracted as a MAPE (Monitoring, Analysis, Planning, and Execution) control loop [5]. And because of the longtime startup and the high resource consumption, the cloud workflow engine service should be scaled proactively. And oscillation should be prevented as it results in resource wastage and more SLA violations.

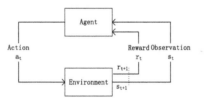

Fig. 1. MDP interaction process between an agent and the environment.

SMDP has proven to be a successful approach to help make the best decisions in the stochastic environment and it is feasible to model the auto-scaling problem of cloud workflow engines as an SMDP problem [6]. We apply reinforcement learning to the automatic scaling problem of cloud workflow services. We will describe the problem modeling as an SMDP, as is depicted in Fig. 1. An SMDP is defined as a 5-tuple $(S, \psi, P.(\cdot, \cdot), R.(\cdot, \cdot), \gamma)$, where:

S represents the environmental state space. The indicators of the last several time intervals are combined as a state.

Ψ represents the decision sequence space. A decision sequence comprises a scale action and the number of time intervals it stays (i.e. $\langle +1, 0, 0, 0 \rangle$).

$P_a(s, s')$ represents the probability that action a in state s at time t will lead to state s' at time $t + 1$.

$R_a(s, s')$ represents the (expected) immediate reward received after transitioning from state s to state s' due to action a.

γ is the discount factor. It represents the difference in importance between future and immediate rewards.

The auto-scaling problem of cloud workflow engine services is complex, requiring more monitoring indicators to achieve more precise control. And the state-action space in such problems is relatively large. It costs a lot of resources to maintain such a space. Also, it may cause oscillation because of its explore policies and frequent actions.

3   RL-Based Auto-scaling Algorithm for Elastic Cloud Workflow Service

The objective of the proposed algorithm is to auto-scale the cloud workflow engine service to attain maximum resource utilization, minimal response time, and maximum throughput. The system architecture and the algorithm are introduced in this section.

3.1   System Design

The proposed algorithm is implemented on Kubernetes, an open-source system for the management of containerized applications [7]. And the architecture and its components are presented in Fig. 2. The major components of the architecture are explained subsequently.

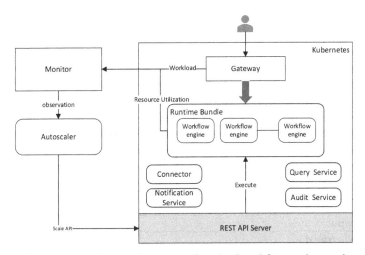

Fig. 2. System architecture for auto-scaling cloud workflow engine services.

Monitor. The system collects indicators such as the amount of workload to be processed, resource utilization, and the number of database interactions, and uses the indicators as observations to be processed by the RL agent.

Autoscaler. The system calculates the best scaling action based on the performance, utilization, and load information sent by the monitor.

The overview of the proposed system is stated as follows: The autoscaler takes scale action of the cloud workflow engine containers through the interface provided by the Kubernetes cluster, and the scaling action will be adopted at regular intervals. The indicator monitor obtains workload, resource utilization, and other performance indicators from Kubernetes and the cloud workflow engine container, and submits these performance indicators to the autoscaler for calculation and processing. The autoscaler obtains the feedback indicator from the indicator monitor at the next time point after the operation is performed, and performs the reward calculation of the previous state and the state of the next state. The autoscaler uses the SARSA algorithm to learn the auto-scaling strategy, which can predict future reward estimates from the current state.

3.2 Algorithm Design

In the SMDP problem, the optimal Q-function satisfies Eq. 1.

$$Q^*(s, a) = \sum_{s' \in \chi} P_a(s, s') \int_0^\infty \int_0^t e^{-\beta \tau} ds dF_{ss'}(t|a)$$

$$+ \sum_{y \in X} P_a(s, s') \int_0^\infty e^{-\beta \tau} \max_{a' \in A} Q^*(s', a') dF_{ss'}(t|a) \tag{1}$$

Here, $F_{ss'}(\cdot|a)$ represents the distribution that the time until the transition from s to s' occurs. Equation 1 leads SARSA for SMDP to update the function $Q(\cdot, \cdot)$ as expressed in Eq. 2.

$$Q'(S_t, \psi_t) \leftarrow Q(S_t, \psi_t) + \alpha \left[\frac{1-e^{-\beta \tau}}{\beta} r_t + e^{-\beta \tau} Q(S_{t+1}, \psi_{t+1}) - Q(S_t, \psi_t) \right] \tag{2}$$

Here, $\frac{1-e^{-\beta \tau}}{\beta} r_t$ is cumulative reward and $e^{-\beta \tau}$ is the discount factor that means the difference in importance between future and immediate rewards. The proposed algorithm is described in Algorithm 1.

Algorithm 1: RL-based Auto-scaling Algorithm for Elastic Cloud Workflow Engine Services

Input: S

1 **while** *true* **do**
2   select Ψ from S using the policy derived from Algorithm 2
3      $R_{total} = 0$
4   **for** $a \in \Psi$ **do**
5   take action a
6   get s, r from monitor
7          $R_{total} = R + R_{total}$
8   combine s into new state S'
9   select Ψ' from S' using the policy derived from Q
10   update $Q(S, \Psi)$

We combine the indicators that the monitor gains, i.e. CPU utilization and workload, into a state s. Then we take state s in the past τ time intervals as the state of RL S, as described in Eq. 3.

$$S = \langle s_0, a_0, s_1, a_1, \ldots, s_{\tau-1}, a_{\tau-1}, s_\tau \rangle \tag{3}$$

Inspired by Deep RL, we use a neural network approximation function to estimate Q-value. We combine the ϵ-greedy policy and time series forecasting algorithm, propose an ϵ-workload-predict method, as is described in Algorithm 2.

Algorithm 2: ϵ-workload-predict policy

    Initialize: $\epsilon = 1$
    Input: S
    Output: Ψ

---

1   **if** $rand(0,1) < \epsilon$ **then**
2   **return** $argmax_{\Psi_I} Q(S, \Psi_i)$
3   **else**
4   **return** $rand(\Psi)$ for $\Psi_{i,0} = \dfrac{workload_{pred}}{load_{max}} - ins_{cur}$

For rewards, we set penalties for SLA violation and rewards for saving resources, as the first part of the reward function in Eq. 4.

$$r = \frac{1 - e^{-\rho \frac{t_{res}}{RTTH}}}{1 - \sigma} - \theta \; \Delta ins \tag{4}$$

Autoscaler calculates the reward and receives the next state S'. Then it takes the action sequence ψ' through the neural network and ϵ-workload-prediction and updates the Q value through Eq. 2.

4 Experiment

To evaluate the performance of RL-based autoscaling algorithm for cloud workflow engine service, the design of the experiment is introduced in this section, and then the experimental results are given and analyzed.

4.1 Experiment Design

To study the advantages and disadvantages of the proposed algorithm, the experiment separately tested and compared the performance of static threshold algorithm, SARSA algorithm modeled as MDP, and proposed algorithm in auto-scaling of runtime bundle containers of Activiti Cloud. The environment of this experiment is a Kubernetes cluster deployed on 3 local servers. Each server is configured with Intel(R) Xeon(R) CPU E5-2609 v3 @ 1.90 GHz, 32 GB memory. The official reference version of Activiti Cloud was deployed in the experiment, which offers a set of cloud-native building blocks designed to run on distributed infrastructures [8].

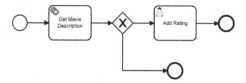

Fig. 3. A process definition for ranking movies.

Activiti Cloud separates the creation of the process definition, and parses it out, and stores it in the database when deploying the cloud workflow engine. And it takes a similar time to process different requests of creating processes of various definitions. The process definition used in the experiment is as shown in Fig. 3. We send different types of requests such as creating processes and finishing tasks to test the elasticity of the system.

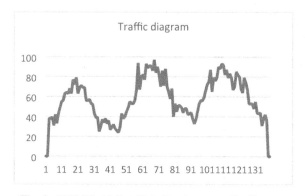

Fig. 4. 1998 World Cup Web Site Access traffic diagram.

To simulate the actual traffic more realistically, this article uses part of the access traffic of the 1998 World Cup as the data set of the access traffic, as is shown in Fig. 4. For convenience, we intercept the part of the diagram from June 1st to June 4th.

4.2 Experiment Result

This section evaluates the static threshold algorithm, the SARSA algorithm, and the algorithm in this article from the aspects of CPU utilization, resource usage, and SLA violation rate. SLA violation stipulates that response time exceeds 1s.

As is depicted in Fig. 5(a), the static threshold algorithm is unable to handle traffic peaks in time. MDP-based SARSA algorithm would cause oscillation. The proposed algorithm can automatically scale cloud workflow engine service in time with changes in traffic and mitigate oscillation. And Fig. 5(b) and Table 1 show that the static threshold algorithm is unable to cope with changes in traffic, resulting in high response time and SLA violation rate. MDP-based SARSA can scale in time with load changes to a certain extent. But due to the oscillation it causes, its average response time is also high. The proposed algorithm can scale cloud workflow engine service in time and SLA violation rate and average response time are reduced.

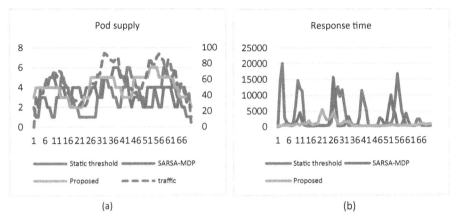

(a)   (b)

Fig. 5. (a) Pod supply comparisons with Static threshold, SARSA-MDP algorithm. (b) Response time comparisons.

Table 1. Comparison of SLA violation rate, average response time, and average pod supply.

Algorithm	SLA violation rate/%	Average response time/ms	Average pod supply
Static threshold	45	3443	3.01
MDP-based SARSA	28	1534	3.70
Proposed	17	937	4.01

As is depicted in the above figures and tables, compared with the other algorithms, the proposed algorithm can scale cloud workflow engine service in time. It reduces the SLA violation rate and improves the availability of cloud workflow engine services. And the proposed algorithm allocates a little more resources, but the SLA violation rate reduces by 39% and the average response time reduces by 39%.

5   Conclusion

To improve the elasticity of cloud workflow engine service, allocate resources appropriately and achieve high availability, we design a cloud workflow engine auto-scaling algorithm based on reinforcement learning considering the characteristics of cloud workflow engine service. We model the auto-scaling problem of cloud workflow engine service as an SMDP problem, use ϵ-workload-predict policy for strategy exploration, and use SMDP-based SARSA algorithm to learn appropriate scaling policy. As is shown in experiments, the proposed algorithm can scale cloud workflow engine service automatically with changes in traffic load. It reduces the SLA violation rate and improves the availability of cloud workflow engine services.

Although the proposed algorithm can solve the elasticity problem of cloud workflow engine service to a certain extent, there are still some improvements in the research of the thesis. Firstly, the convergence speed of reinforcement learning is relatively slow, and it may be difficult to cope with sudden changes in traffic load in practical applications. To ensure the high availability of cloud workflow engine service, methods such as parallel learning can be used to speed up the convergence. Secondly, due to the cache mechanism of cloud workflow engine service, CPU and other resource utilization in the initial stage are relatively high. How to effectively start a cloud workflow engine in advance is also a future research direction. Last but not the least, we choose Activiti Cloud as a cloud workflow engine service for experiments and it is still to be verified and tested to improve on auto-scaling of other workflow engines.

Acknowledgements. This work is Supported by the NSFC-Guangdong Joint Fund Project under Grant No. U20A6003;the National Natural Science Foundation of China (NSFC) under Grant No. 61972427; the Research Foundation of Science and Technology Plan Project in Guangdong Province under Grant No. 2020A0505100030.

References

1. Baeyens, T.: BPM in the cloud. In: Daniel, F., Wang, J., Weber, B. (eds.) BPM 2013. LNCS, vol. 8094, pp. 10–16. Springer, Heidelberg (2013). https://doi.org/10.1007/978-3-642-40176-3_3
2. Schulte, S., Janiesch, C., Venugopal, S., Weber, I., Hoenisch, P.: Elastic business process management: state of the art and open challenges for BPM in the cloud. Fut. Gener. Comput. Syst. **46**, 36–50 (2015)
3. Garí, Y., Monge, D.A., Pacini, E., Mateos, C., Garino, C.G.: Reinforcement learning-based application autoscaling in the cloud: a survey. Eng. Appl. Artif. Intell. **102**, 104288 (2021)
4. Van, M.: The Logic of Adaptive Behavior: Knowledge Representation and Algorithms for Adaptive Sequential Decision Making under Uncertainty in First-Order and Relational Domains. IOS Press (2009)
5. Qu, C., Calheiros, R.N., Buyya, R.: Auto-scaling web applications in clouds: a taxonomy and survey. ACM Comput. Surv. (CSUR) **51**, 1–33 (2018)
6. Bradtke, S.J., Duff, M.O.: Reinforcement learning methods for continuous-time Markov decision. In: Advances in Neural Information Processing Systems, vol. 7, p. 393 (1995)
7. Kubernetes. https://kubernetes.io/. Accessed 11 Jun 2021
8. Activiti.org. https://www.activiti.org/. Accessed 11 Jun 2021

Optimal Energy Efficiency Strategy of mm Wave Cooperative Communication Small Cell Based on SWITP

Taoshen Li[1]($\boxtimes$) and Mingyu Lu[2]

[1] China-ASEAN International Join Laboratory of Integrate Transport, Nanning University,
8 Longting Road, Nanning, People's Republic of China
`19920091@gxu.edu.cn`

[2] School of Computer, Electronics and Information, Guangxi University, 100 Daxue Road,
Nanning, People's Republic of China

Abstract. Aiming at the optimization problem in the stage of simultaneous wireless information and power transfer (SWITP), an optimal energy efficiency strategy of millimeter-wave cooperative communication small cell based on SWITP was proposed to maximize the link energy efficiency, in which the receiver of user equipment devices worked in the power splitting mode. Under the constraints of minimum link transmission rate and minimum energy harvested, the strategy maximized the link energy efficiency of the system by jointly optimizing the transmitting power control and the power splitting factor. Since the original problem is a non-convex fractional programming problem and the NP-hard, the strategy transformed the original problem into a tractable convex optimization problem which is easy to solve by Dinkelbach method, and then Lagrange dual method was used to solve the problem. Finally, a cross-iteration algorithm was designed to get the optimal solution. Simulation results show that the proposed strategy is more effective and superior than the traditional power control method and the maximum transmit power method.

Keywords: Millimeter-wave cooperative communication · Simultaneous wireless information and power transfer (SWITP) · Energy harvesting · Energy efficiency · Spectral efficiency · Power beacon

1 Introduction

The 5G wireless communications has brought new challenges to traditional energy-constrained wireless networks. Energy harvesting (EH) technology can harvest energy from the radio frequency (RF) and use it for subsequent wireless communication, which can prolong the lifetime of equipment and improve the performance of wireless network. The simultaneous wireless information and power transfer (SWITP) is an effective way to solve the problem of energy limitation in wireless communication networks, and can realize information transmission and energy harvesting at the same time [1]. The device-to-device (D2D) technology is a direct communication model between two peer-to-peer user nodes, which can reduce the resource consumption and delay of access and

© Springer Nature Switzerland AG 2022
H. Shen et al. (Eds.): PDCAT 2021, LNCS 13148, pp. 311–323, 2022.
https://doi.org/10.1007/978-3-030-96772-7_29

backhaul network, alleviate the data pressure of the core network of the communication system, and improve the spectrum utilization and system capacity. The millimeter-wave (mm Wave) band mainly includes 30–300 Ghz, and it has rich spectrum resources, high transmission rate and few interference sources. Obviously, the application of D2D and mm Wave can improve the performance of wireless network by improving spectrum efficiency and system throughput.

The Energy harvesting (EH) of RF signal can provide continuous and stable energy for mobile devices, so as to ensure D2D sustainable communication. Therefore, the application of SWITP technology to D2D communication is a potential solution. [2] and [3] studied a D2D network with wireless power and information transmission (WPIT) function. Based on SWIPT, [4] proposed a D2D communication EH heterogeneous cellular network. [5] presented a novel D2D-aware caching policy for high-rate D2D mm Wave communication. [6] proposed an energy-efficient multicast scheduling scheme that can utilize D2D communications. [7] solved the average energy efficiency of EH-based D2D communication heterogeneous networks.

In 5G network, the deployment of ultra dense cells can greatly reduce the propagation loss of wireless energy transmission (WET). [8] focused on the design and optimization of SWITP network with 5G new frequency. [9] proposed a low-power multi-antenna mm Wave receiver architecture. [10] implemented SWITP in mm Wave network by power splitting (PS) method. [11] designed a wireless Ad-hoc network with power beacon (PB) aided mm Wave. [12] studied the feasibility of using mm Wave for WET in a large-scale network composed of PB and energy collector. [13] used non-orthogonal multiple access (NOMA) to improve spectral efficiency in mm Wave massive multiple-input multiple-output (MIMO) systems.

Most of the existing researches on energy harvesting technology using mm Wave only consider harvesting mm Wave energy from RF signal energy sources (such as base station, AP and PB), and does not consider the case of SWITP based on the receiving end. However, in D2D communication, the transmitter and receiver are a paired device pair, which should not be considered separately. Moreover, the deployment of multi antenna system also means greater energy consumption. Aiming at the green communication demand, this paper apples energy harvesting technology in D2D and mm Wave communication, establishes a new small cell network model of user equipment devices (UEs) and mm Wave cooperative communication for high-low frequency hybrid networking, and proposes an optimal energy efficiency strategy based on mm Wave cooperative communication small cell under SWIPT to maximize the link energy efficiency. Finally, the feasibility and effectiveness of the proposed scheme are illustrated by simulation and comparison experiments.

2   System Model

2.1 Network Model

Consider the cellular cell of 5G high and low frequency hybrid network as shown in Fig. 1. Within the base station (BS), there are multiple mm Wave small cells suitable for transmission using mm Wave technology. BS works in the Sub-6 GHz spectrum range and provides additional signal services for other mm wave small cells. Since the mm Wave cell uses mm Wave communication and works in different frequency bands with the macro cell, the interference between the macro cell and the mm Wave cell can be avoided. In addition, because mm Wave has the characteristics of directional transmission, high path loss and sensitivity to blocking, the interference between mm Wave cells and the interference between indoor and outdoor mm Wave cells can be almost ignored.

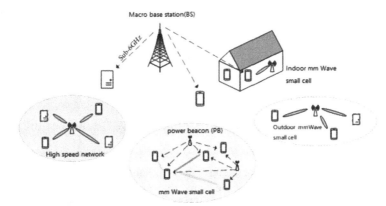

Fig. 1. 5G high-low frequency hybrid networking cellular cell

Assuming that the UEs in the mm Wave cell work in the WPCN mode, the system working time slot is shown in Fig. 2. In a WPCN cycle, all UEs in a small cell first obtain energy from the RF signal radiated by PB through energy harvesting technology, and then use SWIPT to realize simultaneous transmission of energy and information in the downlink phase.

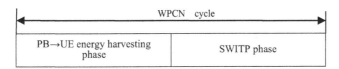

Fig. 2. Structure of full-duplex relay

2.2 System Model

In the SWITP phase, the mm Wave small cell system model is shown in Fig. 3.

In Fig. 3, K pairs of energy limited transmitters (TX) and receivers (RX) are represented by $\Phi_{TX} = \{1, 2, \cdots, K\}$ and $\Phi_{RX} = \{1, 2, \cdots, K\}$ respectively. In consideration of computing power and resource saving, it is assumed that all energy limited devices are equipped with a single antenna. Assuming that each RX adopts SWITP technology. From the mm Wave signal transmitted by the corresponding TX, each RX harvests a

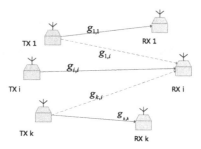

Fig. 3. Illustration of the UE paired system model

certain amount of energy from the received signal through the power splitting method. The signal received by the i-th RX can be expressed as:

$$y_i = h_{(i,i)}L(\sqrt{r_{(i,i)}} \cdot x_i + \sum_{j \in \Phi, j \neq i} h_{(j,i)}L(\sqrt{r_{(j,i)}} \cdot x_j + n_A \tag{1}$$

Where, $h_{(i,i)}$ denotes the quasi-static fading of the i-th channel link, and $L(r_{(i,i)}^{1/2})$ denotes the path loss factor; x_i is the mark of the signal transmitted from TX_i. The second part of the formula represents the common channel interference caused by other TX to RX_i except $TX_{i \cdot n_A} \sim \mathcal{CN}(0, \sigma_A^2)$ denotes the additive white Gaussian noise produced by the antenna in the RF signal receiving stage, and its variance is σ_A^2 and the mean value is 0.

Assuming that the PS structure is shown in Fig. 4 and each RX divides the received signal into two power streams by PS method, the power stream of information decoding at RX_i is as follows:

$$y_i^{ID} = \sqrt{\rho_i} \cdot y_i + n_0 = \sqrt{\rho_i} \cdot \left(h_{(i,i)}L(\sqrt{r_{(i,i)}} \cdot x_i + \sum_{j \in \Phi, j \neq i} h_{(j,i)}L(\sqrt{r_{(j,i)}} \cdot x_j + n_A \right) + n_0 \tag{2}$$

Where, $0 < \rho_i < 1$ represents the power split ratio and $n_0 \sim \mathcal{CN}(0, \sigma_0^2)$ denotes the additive white Gaussian noise produced by information decoding circuit, and its variance is σ_0^2 and the mean value is 0.

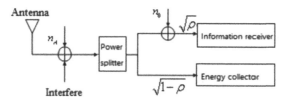

Fig. 4. The RX structure of power splitter

The signal-to-noise ratio of RX_i is

$$SINR_i = \frac{\rho_i P_i |h_{(i,i)}|^2 L(r_{(i,i)})}{\rho_i \left(\sum_{j \in \Phi_{TX}, j \neq i} P_j |h_{(j,i)}|^2 L(r_{(j,i)}) + \sigma_A^2 \right) + \sigma_0^2} \tag{3}$$

Where, P_i denotes the transmission power of TX_i, and P_j denotes the transmission power of other TX with common channel interference. According to Shannon theory, the unit bandwidth throughput of i-th pair of UEs can be expressed as:

$$R_i = \log_2(1 + SINR_i) = \log_2 \left(1 + \frac{\rho_i P_i |h_{(i,i)}|^2 L(r_{(i,i)})}{\rho_i \left(\sum_{j \in \Phi_{TX}, j \neq i} P_j |h_{(j,i)}|^2 L(r_{(j,i)}) + \sigma_A^2 \right) + \sigma_0^2} \right) \tag{4}$$

Similarly, the power flow for energy harvesting can be expressed as:

$$y_i^{EH} = \sqrt{1-\rho_i} \cdot y_i = \sqrt{1-\rho_i} \cdot \left(h_{(i,i)} L(\sqrt{r_{(i,i)}}) \cdot x_i + \sum_{j \in \Phi, j \neq i} h_{(j,i)} L(\sqrt{r_{(j,i)}}) \cdot x_j + n_A \right) \tag{5}$$

Since the energy carried by the noise n_A and n_0 is too small to activate the energy collection circuit, it can be ignored. Therefore, the energy harvested at RX_i is:

$$E_i = (1 - \rho_i) \eta \left(P_i |h_{(i,i)}|^2 L(r_{(i,i)}) + \sum_{j \in \Phi_{TX}, j \neq i} P_j |h_{(j,i)}|^2 L(r_{(j,i)}) \right) \tag{6}$$

According to the linear power consumption model [14], the total power consumption of the i-th pair of UEs is:

$$P_i^{tot} = \xi P_i + 2 P_{cir} \tag{7}$$

Where, $\xi \in [1, \infty)$ denotes the efficiency of power amplifier, and P_{cir} is the static circuit power consumed by the filter, digital to analog converter and other modules.

The energy efficiency on the i-th pair of UEs is defined as:

$$EE_i = \frac{R_i}{P_i^{tot}} \tag{8}$$

3   Problem Description and Solution Strategy

Under the joint constraints of minimum rate and minimum energy harvesting, the strategy proposed in this paper takes the energy efficiency of all UEs as the optimization goal, and optimizes the transmission power control and power shunt factor to transmit more bits per unit power. Therefore, the mathematical model of the optimization problem P1 can be expressed as follows:

$$
\begin{aligned}
\max_{P_i,\rho_i} &\ \sum_{i\in\mathcal{K}} EE_i \\
\text{s.t. } &C1:\ E_i \geq E_{min},\ \forall i \in \mathcal{K} \\
&C2:\ P_i \leq P_{max},\ \forall i \in \mathcal{K} \\
&C3:\ 0 < \rho_i < 1,\ \forall i \in \mathcal{K} \\
&C4:\ R_i \geq R_{th},\ \forall i \in \mathcal{K}
\end{aligned}
\tag{9}
$$

Where, $\mathcal{K} = \{1, \ldots, k\}$ is the set index of UE pair; E_{min} is the minimum EH constraint on RX; P_{max} denotes the maximum allowable transmission power on TX; R_{th} denotes the minimum rate threshold on UE link.

In order to express the solution process of the optimal value conveniently, let $N_A = \sigma_A^2$, $N_0 = \sigma_0^2$, $g_{i,i} = |h_{(i,i)}|^2 L(r_{(i,i)})$, $I_{j,i} = \sum_{j\in\Phi_{TX},j\neq i} P_j |h_{(j,i)}|^2 L(r_{(j,i)})$. Then, P1 can be rewritten as

$$
\begin{aligned}
\max_{P_i,\rho_i} &\ \sum_{i\in\mathcal{K}} \frac{\log_2\left(1+\frac{\rho_i P_i g_{i,i}}{\rho_i(I_{j,i}+N_A)+N_0}\right)}{\xi P_i + 2P_{cir}} \\
\text{s.t. } &C1:\ (1-\rho_i)\eta\left(P_i g_{i,i}+I_{j,i}\right) \geq E_{min},\ \forall i \in \mathcal{K} \\
&C2:\ P_i \leq P_{max},\ \forall i \in \mathcal{K} \\
&C3:\ 0 < \rho_i < 1,\ \forall i \in \mathcal{K} \\
&C4:\ \log_2\left(1 + \frac{\rho_i P_i g_{i,i}}{\rho_i(I_{j,i}+N_A)+N_0}\right) \geq R_{th},\ \forall i \in \mathcal{K}
\end{aligned}
\tag{10}
$$

Obviously, the optimization problem P2 is a nonlinear planning problem, and is difficult to find an accurate solution. According to Dinkelbach method, this problem can be transformed into an equivalent convex subtraction problem.

Assuming q^*_{ee} is the optimal value of the problem, it is defined as follows:

$$
q^*_{ee} = \max_{P_i,\rho_i} \sum_{i\in\mathcal{K}} \frac{\log_2\left(1 + \frac{\rho_i^* P_i^* g_{i,i}}{\rho_i^*(I_{j,i}+N_A)+N_0}\right)}{\xi P_i^* + 2P_{cir}}
\tag{12}
$$

Where, P_i^* and ρ_i^* are the optimal transmission power and power split ratio when the energy efficiency of the i-th pair of UEs reaches the optimal value. method, the equivalent subtractive objective function can be obtained by Dinkelbach method. Therefore, the original optimization problem P2 can be rewritten as:

$$
\begin{aligned}
\max_{P_i,\rho_i} &\ \sum_{i\in\mathcal{K}} \left\{\log_2\left(1 + \frac{\rho_i P_i g_{i,i}}{\rho_i(I_{j,i}+N_A)+N_0}\right) - q_{ee}(\xi P_i + 2P_{cir})\right\} \\
\text{s.t. } &C1:\ (1-\rho_i)\eta\left(P_i g_{i,i}+I_{j,i}\right) \geq E_{min},\ \forall i \in \mathcal{K} \\
&C2:\ P_i \leq P_{max},\ \forall i \in \mathcal{K} \\
&C3:\ 0 < \rho_i < 1,\ \forall i \in \mathcal{K} \\
&C4:\ \log_2\left(1 + \frac{\rho_i P_i g_{i,i}}{\rho_i(I_{j,i}+N_0)}\right) \geq R_{th},\ \forall i \in \mathcal{K}
\end{aligned}
\tag{13}
$$

The rewritten problem P2 is a convex optimization problem, which can be solved by common convex optimization methods (such as Lagrange dual method). The Lagrange function of Eq. (13) is

$$
\begin{aligned}
\mathcal{L}&(P_i, \rho_i, \lambda_{1,i}, \lambda_{2,i}, \lambda_{3,i}, \lambda_{4,i}) \\
&= \sum_{i \in \mathcal{K}} \left(\log_2 \left(1 + \frac{\rho_i P_i g_{i,i}}{\rho_i (I_{j,i} + N_A) + N_0} \right) - q_{ee}(\xi P_i + 2P_{cir}) \right) \\
&\quad + \sum_{i \in \mathcal{K}} \lambda_{1,i} \big((1 - \rho_i) \eta \big(P_i g_{i,i} + I_{j,i} \big) - E_{\min} \big) \\
&\quad + \sum_{i \in \mathcal{K}} \lambda_{2,i}(P_i - P_{\max}) + \sum_{i \in \mathcal{K}} \lambda_{3,i}(\rho_i - 1) \\
&\quad + \sum_{i \in \mathcal{K}} \lambda_{4,i} \left(\log_2 \left(1 + \frac{\rho_i P_i g_{i,i}}{\rho_i (I_{j,i} + N_A) + N_0} \right) - R_{th} \right)
\end{aligned}
\tag{14}
$$

Where, $\{\lambda_1, \lambda_2, \lambda_3, \lambda_4\} \geq 0$ respectively represent the Lagrange multipliers of C1–C4, and the dual function of Lagrange function (14) is:

$$
\min_{\lambda_{1,i}, \lambda_{2,i}, \lambda_{3,i}, \lambda_{4,i}} \; \max_{P_i, \rho_i} \; \mathcal{L}(P_i, \rho_i, \lambda_{1,i}, \lambda_{2,i}, \lambda_{3,i}, \lambda_{4,i})
\tag{15}
$$

The P_i and ρ_i can be obtained by Karush Kuhn Tucker (KKT) condition:

$$
P_i = \left(\frac{(1 + \lambda_{4,i}) \log_2 e}{(q_{ee}\xi + \lambda_{2,i} - \lambda_{1,i}(1 - \rho_i)\eta g_{i,i})} - \frac{N_0 + \rho_i(I_{j,i} + N_A)}{\rho_i g_{i,i}} \right)^+
\tag{16}
$$

$$
\rho_i = \left\{ \frac{-N_0(2A_0 + P_i g_{i,i})}{2A_0(A_0 + P_i g_{i,i})} + \frac{\sqrt{N_0 P_i g_{i,i} \left(N_0 P_i g_{i,i} + \frac{4A_0(A_0 + P_i g_{i,i})(1 + \lambda_{4,i}) \log_2 e}{\lambda_{1,i}\eta(P_i g_{i,i} + I_{j,i}) + \lambda_{3,i}} \right)}}{2A_0(A_0 + P_i g_{i,i})} \right\}^+
\tag{17}
$$

Where, $A_0 = I_{j,i} + N_A$, $\{x\}^+ = \max\{1, x\}$. The Lagrange multipliers $\lambda_{1,i}, \lambda_{2,i}, \lambda_{3,i}$ and $\lambda_{4,i}$ can be updated iteratively by gradient descent method. That is

$$
\lambda_{1,i} = \left[\lambda_{1,i} - \alpha \big((1 - \rho_i)\eta \big(P_i g_{i,i} + I_{j,i} \big) - E_{\min} \big) \right]^+, \; \forall i \in \mathcal{K}
\tag{18}
$$

$$
\lambda_{2,i} = \left[\lambda_{2,i} - \alpha (P_i - P_{\max}) \right]^+, \; \forall i \in \mathcal{K}
\tag{19}
$$

$$
\lambda_{3,i} = \left[\lambda_{3,i} - \alpha (\rho_i - 1) \right]^+, \; \forall i \in \mathcal{K}
\tag{20}
$$

$$
\lambda_{4,i} = \left\{ \lambda_{4,i} - \alpha \left[\log_2 \left(1 + \frac{\rho_i P_i g_{i,i}}{\rho_i (I_{j,i} + N_A) + N_0} \right) - R_{th} \right] \right\}^+, \; \forall i \in \mathcal{K}
\tag{21}
$$

Where, α is the step size to ensure convergence.

According to the above analysis, a cross iterative algorithm to solve the overall optimization problem is described as follows:

Algorithm 1: Cross iterative algorithm of transmit power control and power splitting factor

Input: energy conversion rate η, path loss factor α_L and α_N, Gaussian white noise power N_0 and N_A, circuit static power consumption P_{cir}, amplifier efficiency ξ, threshold P_{max}, E_{min}, R_{th}, maximum number of iterations T, convergence threshold ε, step size of iteration α.

Output: optimal $P_i^*, \rho_i^*, q_{ee}^*$

    Initialize $P_i, \rho_i, q_{ee}, \lambda_{1,i}, \lambda_{2,i}, \lambda_{3,i}, \lambda_{4,i}$ and n(number of loop iterations)

    while $(n<T)$ {

        Calculate the P_i according to formula (16);

        Calculate the ρ_i according to formula (17);

$$\text{if}\left(\left| \log_2\left(1 + \frac{\rho_i P_i g_{i,i}}{\rho_i\left(I_{j,i} + N_A\right) + N_0} \right) - q_{ee}\left(\xi P_i + 2P_{cir}\right) \right| < \varepsilon \right) \{$$

        $q_{ee}^* \leftarrow q_{ee}$;

        $P_i^* \leftarrow P_i$;

        $\rho_i^* \leftarrow \rho_i$;

        break;

    }

    else {

        Update $\lambda_{1,i}, \lambda_{2,i}, \lambda_{3,i}, \lambda_{4,i}$ according to formulas (18),(19),(20) and (21)

        $n=n+1$;

    }

    }

    Return $P_i^*, \rho_i^*, q_{ee}^*$.

---

4   Experimental Results and Analysis

4.1   Experimental Environment and Parameter Setting

In order to illustrate the feasibility and effectiveness of our strategy, this section will evaluate, analyze and verify the proposed strategy through simulation experiments. The parameters of simulation experiments are set by mmwave channel and power consumption model mentioned in [7] and [16].The experimental parameters are set as follows: maximum transmit power of TX $P_{max} = 23$ dBm, energy conversion efficiency $\eta = 0.7$, circuit static power consumption $P_{cir} = 50$ mW, path loss factor $\alpha_L = 2$, $\alpha_N = 4$, amplifier efficiency $\xi = 1/0.38$, Gaussian white noise power $N_0 = -70$ dBm, $N_A = -100$ dBm, minimum collected energy threshold $E_{min} = -14$ dBm, throughput threshold $R_{th} = 5$bit/s/H.

In the simulation scenario, TX-RX links are randomly deployed in an area. The distances between each expected TX-RX link and interference link are 40 m and 80 m respectively. In the following comparative experimental analysis, each simulation experimental value is the average value of the experimental data generated after 100 times of independent execution of the algorithm.

4.2   Performance Analysis and Comparison of Algorithms

In order to compare and analyze the performance of the proposed strategy, we take the traditional transmission power control algorithm as the comparison algorithm. The traditional transmit power control algorithm with the most energy efficiency does not consider the dynamic joint optimization of the PS of SWITP technology. Therefore, referring to the comparison method in [7], we designed the power control algorithm of equally divided PS of SWITP (PC-E scheme) to compare with our strategy.

The first experiment is to analyze the relationship between the maximum transmission power threshold and energy efficiency. In the experiment, the threshold P_{max} is set to 50 mW, 100 mW, 150 mW, 200 mW and 250 mW respectively. The experimental comparison results are shown in Fig. 5. With the increase of P_{max}, the energy efficiency of the links of the two schemes also increases. This is because within an appropriate range, with the increase of the P_{max}, the allowable transmission power on TX becomes larger and larger, which increases the transmission throughput and improves the link energy efficiency. However, when P_{max} reaches 200 mW, although the increase of TX transmission power can bring greater throughput, the energy consumption of the link also increases, resulting in a downward trend of link energy efficiency with the increase. Therefore, it is very important to select an appropriate maximum transmission power threshold. From the simulation results, to obtain better performance, the setting of AA needs to consider the trade-off between throughput and energy consumption. In the later simulation experiment, P_{max} is set to 200 mW.

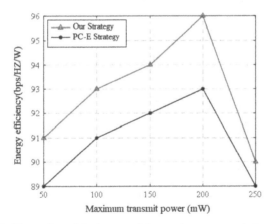

Fig. 5. Illustration of the impact of the maximum transmission power

The second experiment is to compare and analyze the impact of the minimum energy collection threshold on energy efficiency. In the experiment, the threshold E_{min} is set to − 20 dBm, −18 dBm, −16 dBm, −14 dBm and −12 dBm respectively. The experimental results are shown in Fig. 6. The experimental results show that the link energy efficiency decreases with the increase of the minimum energy collection threshold. This is because according to the first law of thermodynamics, when the signal power transmitted on TX remains unchanged, if the energy collection power becomes larger, the power used for information transmission becomes smaller, resulting in smaller throughput.

From the experimental comparison results of Fig. 5 and Fig. 6, it can be seen that our strategy are better than the traditional power control scheme in energy efficiency performance. In order to further verify the effectiveness of our scheme, the third and fourth experiments draw on the comparison method of [17] and add a benchmark scheme of dynamic PS with maximum transmission power (expressed by PS-max) as the comparison scheme.

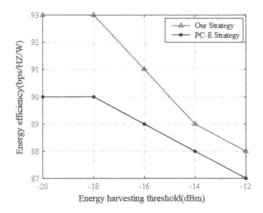

Fig. 6. Illustration of the impact of the energy harvesting threshold

The third experiment is to compare the effects of different TX-RX link distances on link energy efficiency under the three schemes. The experimental results are shown in Fig. 7. It can be seen from the experimental comparison results that the energy efficiency of the three schemes decreases gradually with the increase of TX-RX link distance. This is because the path loss between TX-RX increases with the increase of the distance between them, and the channel gain decreases, resulting in the decrease of energy efficiency. However, from the comparison results of three experiments, the performance of the scheme in this paper is still better than the other two comparison schemes. This is because the dynamic optimization scheme using joint transmit power and power diversion factor can obtain an optimal swipt power diversion factor, so as to achieve the optimal trade-off between link throughput and energy consumption.

The fourth experiment is to compare and analyze the influence of interference link distance on energy efficiency. In the experiment, the distances of interference links are 60 m, 70 m, 80 m, 90 m and 100 m respectively. The experimental results are shown in Fig. 8. It can be seen from the experimental comparison results that the energy efficiency of the three schemes is improved with the increase of the interference link distance. This is because with the increase of interference link distance, the SINR of TX-RX link increases, and the link throughput also increases according to Shannon's theorem. Therefore, when the link energy consumption is fixed, the more bits transmitted, the greater the link energy efficiency. Under the same interference link distance, the performance of our scheme is better than the other two comparison schemes. This is

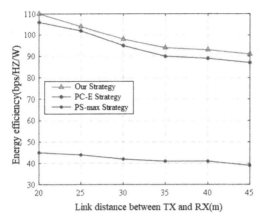

Fig. 7. Illustration of the impact of the distance of TX-RX

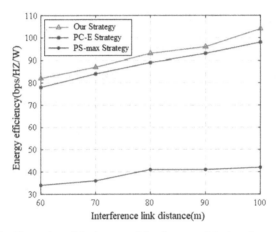

Fig. 8. Illustration of the impact of the distance of the interference link

because the our scheme can better meet the balance of link throughput and energy consumption, so as to maximize energy efficiency.

5   Conclusions

This paper studies the energy efficiency optimization of mm Wave cooperative small cell under SWITP. Firstly, the system model of energy-limited UE pairing in mm Wave small cell is constructed, and a SWITP-based optimal energy efficiency strategy of mm Wave cooperative communication small cell is proposed to maximize the link energy efficiency. In order to achieve the goal of green communication, under the joint constraints of minimum link transmission rate and minimum energy harvesting, the strategy maximizes the energy efficiency of the system link by optimizing the transmission power control and power diversion factor. As the original problem is a nonconvex fractional programming problem, the strategy uses Dinkelbach method to transform the objective function into a convex optimization problem, and then uses Lagrange dual method to solve it. The simulation results show that the proposed strategy is better than the traditional power control method and maximum transmit power method in optimizing the energy efficiency performance of the system.

Acknowledgment. These works are supported by the Guangxi science and technology plan project of China (No. AD20297125).

References

1. Clerckx, B., Zhang, R., Schober, R., Ng, D.W.K., Kim, D.I., Vincent Poor, H.: Guest editorial wireless transmission of information and power—part II. IEEE J. Sel. Areas Commun. **37**(2), 249–252 (2019)
2. Deng, N., Haenggi, M.: The energy and rate meta distributions in wirelessly powered D2D networks. IEEE J. Sel. Areas Commun. **37**(2), 269–282 (2019)
3. Luo, Y., Hong, P., Su, R., et al.: Resource allocation for energy harvesting-powered D2D communication underlaying cellular networks. IEEE Trans. Veh. Technol. **66**(11), 10486–10498 (2017)
4. Yang, H.H., Lee, J., Quek, T.Q.S.: Heterogeneous cellular network with energy harvesting-based D2D communication. IEEE Trans. Wirel. Commun. **15**(2), 1406–1419 (2016)
5. Giatsoglou, N., Ntontin, K., Kartsakli, E., Antonopoulos, A., Verikoukis, C.: D2D-aware device caching in mmWave-cellular networks. IEEE J. Sel. Areas Commun. **35**(9), 2025–2037 (2017)
6. Niu, Y.Y., Liu, Y.L., Chen, X., Zhong, Z., Han, Z.: Device-to-device communications enabled energy efficient multicast scheduling in mmWave small cells. IEEE Trans. Commun. **66**(3), 1093–1109 (2018)
7. Kuang, Z., Liu, G., Li, G., et al.: Energy efficient resource allocation algorithm in energy harvesting-based D2D heterogeneous networks. IEEE Internet Things J. **6**(1), 557–567 (2019)
8. Zhai, D., Zhang, R., Jianbo, D., Ding, F.Z., Richard, Y.: Simultaneous wireless information and power transfer at 5G new frequencies: Channel measurement and network design. IEEE J. Sel. Areas Commun. **37**(1), 171–186 (2019)
9. Khan, T.A., Alkhateeb, A., Heath, R.W.: Millimeter wave energy harvesting. IEEE Trans. Wirel. Commun. **15**(9), 6048–6062 (2016)
10. Tu, L.T., Di Renzo, M.: Analysis of millimeter wave cellular networks with simultaneous wireless information and power transfer. In: 2017 International Conference on Recent Advances in Signal Processing, Telecommunications & Computing, Da Nang, Vietnam, IEEE Press (2017)
11. Zhou, X., Guo, J., Durrani, S., et al.: Power beacon-assisted millimeter wave ad hoc networks. IEEE Trans. Wirel. Commun. **66**(2), 830–844 (2017)
12. Khan, T.A., Heath, R.W.: Wireless power transfer in millimeter wave tactical networks. IEEE Sig. Process Lett. **24**(9), 1284–1287 (2017)
13. Dai, L., Wang, B., Peng, M., Chen, S.: Hybrid precoding-based millimeter-wave massive MIMO-NOMA with simultaneous wireless information and power transfer. IEEE J. Sel. Areas Commun. **37**(1), 131–141 (2019). https://doi.org/10.1109/JSAC.2018.2872364
14. Wang, X., Jin, T., Hu, L., et al.: Energy-Efficient power allocation and Q-learning-based relay selection for relay-aided D2D communication. IEEE Trans. Veh. Technol. **69**(6), 6452–6462 (2020)

15. Yang, L., Xiong, K., Fan, P., Ding, Z., Zhong, Z., Letaief, K.B.: Global energy efficiency in secure MISO SWIPT systems with non-linear power-splitting EH model. IEEE J. Sel. Areas Commun. **37**(1), 216–232 (2019)
16. Lee, K., Hong, J.-P., Seo, H., Choi, W.: Learning-based resource management in device-to-device communications with energy harvesting requirements. IEEE Trans. Commun. **68**(1), 402–413 (2020)
17. Ding, H., Zhang, H., Tian, J., et al.: Energy efficient user association and power control for dense heterogeneous networks. In: 2018 International Conference on Computing, Networking and Communications, Maui, HI, USA. IEEE Press (2018)

Low Latency Execution Guarantee Under Uncertainty in Serverless Platforms

M. Reza HoseinyFarahabady[1]([✉]), Javid Taheri[2], Albert Y. Zomaya[1], and Zahir Tari[3]

[1] School of Computer Science, Center for Distributed and High Performance Computing, The University of Sydney, Sydney, NSW, Australia
{reza.hoseiny,albert.zomaya}@sydney.edu.au
[2] Department of Mathematics and Computer Science, Karlstad University, Karlstad, Sweden
javid.taheri@kau.se
[3] School of Computing Technologies, RMIT University, Victoria, Australia
zahir.tari@rmit.edu.au

Abstract. Serverless computing recently emerged as a new run-time paradigm to disentangle the client from the burden of provisioning physical computing resources, leaving such difficulty on the service provider's side. However, an unsolved problem in such an environment is how to cope with the challenges of executing several co-running applications while fulfilling the requested Quality of Service (QoS) level requested by all application owners. In practice, developing an efficient mechanism to reach the requested performance level (such as p-99 latency and throughput) is limited to the awareness (resource availability, performance interference among consolidation workloads, etc.) of the controller about the dynamics of the underlying platforms. In this paper, we develop an adaptive feedback controller for coping with the buffer instability of serverless platforms when several collocated applications are run in a shared environment. The goal is to support a low-latency execution by managing the arrival event rate of each application when shared resource contention causes a significant throughput degradation among workloads with different priorities. The key component of the proposed architecture is a continues management of server-side internal buffers for each application to provide a low-latency feedback control mechanism based on the requested QoS level of each application (*e.g.*, buffer information) and the worker nodes throughput. The empirical results confirm the response stability for high priority workloads when a dynamic condition is caused by low priority applications. We evaluate the performance of the proposed solution with respect to the response time and the QoS violation rate for high priority applications in a serverless platform with four worker nodes set up in our in-house virtualized cluster. We compare the proposed architecture against the default resource management policy in Apache OpenWhisk which is extensively used in commercial serverless platforms. The results show that our approach achieves a very low overhead (less than 0.7%) while it can improve the p-99 latency of high pri-

© Springer Nature Switzerland AG 2022
H. Shen et al. (Eds.): PDCAT 2021, LNCS 13148, pp. 324–335, 2022.
https://doi.org/10.1007/978-3-030-96772-7_30

ority applications by 64%, on average, in the presence of dynamic high traffic conditions.

Keywords: Dynamic controller of computer systems · Serverless computing · Virtualized platforms · Quality of Service (QoS)

1   Introduction

Serverless computing, also known as function-as-a-service (FaaS) or lambda services, has increasingly become popular in recent years due to their unique flexibility of paying per usage business model. The new paradigm enables the business owners to design and develop complex data-intensive applications by breaking it into more manageable functional units. The FaaS paradigm can also be exploited to execute a wide range of applications including, but not limited to, web services, information exchange systems, machine learning, data mining, and image and text processing [1–4].

Adaptive micro-service computing in the form of event streaming is the current trend of the FaaS (serverless) paradigm. However, extensive empirical evaluations have revealed that the resource management policies adapted by almost all commercial products can lead to long delays in the internal buffers of high priority applications (hence a degraded performance), particularly when a significant contention among consolidated workloads occurs across a shared environment (*e.g.*, see [3,5–7]). When the buffering of unprocessed events becomes higher than a predefined threshold, the FaaS platform suffers from a high latency delay, and therefore a degraded performance perceived by the application end-users [4,8,9].

Based on our observations using several real workload bench-markings, the following inefficiencies are deemed as the main limiting factors for a proper deployment of a low-latency computation. First, the lack of a congestion control mechanism to stabilize the throughput of the underlying hardware can lead to a high level of instability in the latency of computation for some (if not all) applications that share a physical machine. Second, open-loop mechanisms – currently employed by almost all commercial products– introduce a significant delay and fluctuated utilization level of computing resources, particularly when there is an abrupt change in the arrival rate of some applications. Third, an inaccurate estimation of arrival rate or the degraded performance among collocated applications (usually due to a random disturbance of the input variables) can significantly degrade the level of performance isolation among consolidated workloads inside a working node, and therefore leads to a critical level of QoS violation incidents for high priority applications. In such contexts, it is vital to improve the operational efficiency of the underlying platform to respond to the application requests as requested by application owners. In practical scenarios, a feedback controller can be effectively employed by the service provider to provision the right amount of computing resources to each serverless application during the run-time.

Most existing FaaS/serverless platforms are unaware of the time-line target value and the quality of service (QoS) requirements perceived by end-users. In fact, such platforms merely aim to enhance the average or a specific percentile of the query response time or the average resource utilization of the underlying devices. As a result, the transit delay in the response time of each application, which is usually caused by the waiting time in the internal buffer of each functional unit, may significantly exceed a desired threshold value set by an application owner (*i.e.*, a QoS violation incident occurs). Supporting the desired QoS enforcement level is challenging, since real-time events may arrive in a burst manner at any arbitrary rate (*e.g.*, due to a varying market demand or traffic status for a data science application in a financial context). Furthermore, the degree of shared resource contention among consolidated workloads may change over the course of their execution; this makes the problem of allocating computing resources to guarantee the QoS requirements even more challenging. To address such barriers, the main aim of this research work is to design a "feedback control" mechanism to support applications' QoS enforcement levels in FaaS platforms. Most of the existing open-source FaaS platforms, such as Dask [10] and Apache OpenWhisk [11], only aim to support fast processing of event-driven applications on-the-fly; they usually update the results of running processing units in a timely fashion, once the corresponding events are triggered within a predefined interval.

In this paper, we consider soft real-time serverless applications (such as those found in the finance sector) in which a processing delay may degrade the level of QoS achievement from end-users' perspectives, but may yield loss of revenue for the service provider. If enough information about the worst-case execution time (WCET) or worst-case resource requirement (WCRR) of each submitted application is available, then the results of classic schedulability theory can be properly employed to decide if a given deadline constraint can be fulfilled or not. In such a case, a priority-based or a deadline-based scheduling policy can be used to provide an implementation to guarantee the timing constraint during the course of execution. Because in most practical cases, such information about the worst-case values cannot be derived in the compile time, the platform may encounter under utilization of computing resources. Our aim, in this paper, is to control the level of delay in the internal buffer of each functional unit to be lower than a specific threshold (even in the presence of burst traffic), while the resource requirement of each submitted task is *unknown in prior* and may *vary* during the execution time (*i.e.*, due to changes in the external load of each functional unit).

The rest of this paper is organized as follows. Section 2 highlights the main challenges associated with fulfilling the timing constraints of application tasks in FaaS platforms with shared resources when there is uncertainty in the actual resource consumption and the execution time of each functional unit. Section 3 presents the details of our proposed feedback control scheme. The performance of the predictive model controlling scheme is evaluated in Sect. 4. Finally, Sect. 5 concludes our work.

2   Problem Statement

In this section, the overall structure of the target platform and its execution plan is presented. We discuss the performance optimization challenge in a FaaS platform as a resource allocation problem that needs to be adjusted dynamically in response to external events, while meeting quality of service (QoS) constraints. We also give a high-level description of the proposed feedback control approach for supporting the desired QoS performance of each submitted application.

2.1   FaaS Platform and Application Structure

An overall architecture of FaaS platforms can be described as follows. The FaaS paradigm enables application developers to represent the software architecture of a complex application by breaking it down into manageable functional units (FU) [12]. Each functional unit responds to a series of events that might be triggered by external or internal event sources. We assume that the underlying platform runs a set of event-driven CPU-intensive applications, denoted by $\Lambda = \{A_1, A_2 \cdots \}$. Each serverless application, A_j, can be modeled as a set of FUs, denoted by $\Lambda_A = \{F_1, F_2 \cdots \}$; each FU might be triggered by a set of predefined events. The set of all event sources that a particular F_j needs to trigger is shown by $\mathcal{E}_{F_j} = \{e_1, e_2 \cdots \}$. The main responsibility of a FaaS platform is to invoke the corresponding FUs once triggering event occur [13]. The service provider can also select to pack and execute several FUs, that possibly might belong to different QoS classes, into a single physical machine. We further assume that there are m physical machine that the controller can decide to deploy a copy of a FU to be executed in the next controlling interval.

2.2   Quality of Service Semantic

In this paper, we assume that the service provide of a FaaS platform can specify a certain number of level of service agreements (SLA) as quality of service (QoS) classes, where each QoS class identifies a commitment between the service provider and application owners as an agreed run-time performance target. In most event-driven applications, the response time of service after the corresponding event is triggered can be considered as the main performance metric for a QoS class. The SLA target for such a metric is usually represented as the 99th percentile of application response time. We assume that the SLA contract defines exactly q different QoS classes, shown by $\{Q_1 \cdots Q_q\}$ from which an application owner can choose the requested performance target and get billed accordingly. Each QoS class Q_j stipulates two values of $< \mathcal{R}_j^*, \mathcal{P}_{j,\Delta t} >$, where $\mathcal{R}_j^*$ denotes an upper bound for the attained response time to be fulfilled by the service provider during the course of execution, and $\mathcal{P}_{j,\Delta t}$ represents an upper-bound for the percentage of QoS violation that is accepted by the end-user within an interval of length Δt (such semantic is similarly defined and used by authors in [14]).

One of the key challenges in guaranteeing absolute service delay in a FaaS platform is to find a resource allocation solution to achieve the desired delay for submitted applications belonging to different QoS classes, even in the presence of varying load conditions that are unknown in priori [15]. Another challenge in the context of resource management problem is how to bridge the levels of abstraction (such as functional units, delay, internal buffer, stability conditions, and the arrival rate) to formulate and solve an optimal control problem. The main contribution of this paper is that we formulate and solve such resource management problems in a dynamic environment by employing the design principles of *control theory*. Using a feedback loop, it can provide the aforementioned delay guarantee for a FaaS platform with multiple QoS levels when the underlying system exhibits dynamic behavior. Furthermore, we employed the result of *queuing theory* to predict the the statistical properties of the internal buffers of each software component.

3   Design Approach

In this section, we formally introduce the steps to design a feedback controller to support the desired QoS enforcement bounds in the presence of dynamic workload in a serverless platform.

3.1   Main Components

The architecture of the proposed feedback controller can be described as follows. It consists of a rate estimator to predict the future rate of arrival events for each FU, a system model to represent the behavior of complex dynamical systems (here to estimate the length of unprocessed events in the internal buffer of each FU), an optimization component, and a target FaaS platform that consists of serverless working nodes to execute the submitted scripts (Fig. 1).

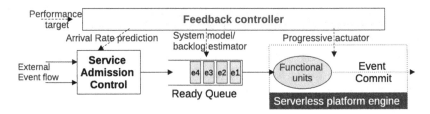

Fig. 1. An overall structure of the proposed feedback controller running across a FaaS/serverless platform with multiple worker nodes

The feedback controller is designed based on the principles of model predictive control (MPC) theory that is used to control the underlying system components while satisfying a set of predefined performance constraints. It relies on dynamic system models that is obtained by system identification techniques based on empirical results. One of the biggest advantages of using MPC in nonlinear systems is that it produces a robust near-optimal solution against erroneous values in the prediction or system models. Such a robustness is achieved by optimizing the target system variables over a finite time-horizon, while keeping the future system states into account [16]. The controller only applies one step of the control action, and then repeatedly optimizes the entire process in the next interval by considering the current and future states of the involving components. The actuator employs the Linux's built-in control groups, cgroup. It is a resource allocation mechanism that limits the amount of resources available to each FU in the next controlling interval.

3.2   Monitoring and System Model

The monitor component is invoked at each sampling interval τ to compute the average arrival rate, the number of unprocessed events in the internal buffer of each FU, and their service time during the last sampling period. Such information is used by the optimizer to estimate the arrival rate for each FU, and to compute the new process budget in the forthcoming interval. We employ a classical autoregressive moving average (ARMA) model to predict the arrival rate of incoming events to each FU, denoted by $\lambda_{j,\tau}$ as a linear function of the past observations and the forecast errors at prior H intervals. The ARMA model with parameters $\mathcal{K}$, ϕ and θ can be formally defined as follows.

$$\lambda_{j,\tau} = \mathcal{K}_j + \sum_{h=1}^{H} \phi_{j,\tau-h}\lambda_{j,\tau-h} + \sum_{h=1}^{H} \theta_{j,\tau-h}\epsilon_{j,\tau-h} \qquad (1)$$

Here, ϵ_t is an uncorrelated innovation process with mean zero representing the past errors, $\lambda_{j,\tau-h}$ are the past observations of arrival rate [17], and $H \geq 1$ is the order of the ARMA predictor. A higher order ARMA model is more accurate, while it requires more complex computation as the number of submitted applications in a given host.

To design an effective feedback control system, it is essential to predict the system performance dynamics when the incoming workload changes. We developed a simple model to capture the relation between the "queue size" and the "delay" perceived by each service. Such a model can be used by the optimizer module to bound the number of unprocessed events in the internal buffer of each application. We employed the Allen-Cunneen formula of $G/G/N$ queue [18] to estimate the average response time experienced by each event right before its processing by the corresponding FU, as stated below.

$$\mathsf{W}_m = \frac{\mathsf{P}_{cb,m}}{\mu m(1-\rho)} \left(\frac{\mathsf{C}_s^2 + \mathsf{C}_d^2}{2} \right) \qquad (2)$$

Here, W_m represents the waiting time experienced by each unprocessed event when both the arrival and the service time follows a general distribution; m is the number of concurrently running instance of the corresponding FU; ρ represents the monitored utilization of the computing resource; C_d and C_s represent the coefficient of variation for inter-arrival and the service time, respectively; and $P_{cb,m}$ represents the probability that all m instances are fully utilized and no more events can be processed at this interval.

3.3 Optimizer

Once a new FaaS script is submitted, the optimizer component decides a working node to run the submitted script. The optimizer calculates the amount of performance degradation to be experienced by previously allocated applications in such a host, and then chooses the one that minimizes such degradation among all possible allocation decisions. It also ensures that the total capacity of processors does not exceed the computing requests in any working node.

At each sampling interval τ, the controller compares the sampled delay of submitted applications, denoted by $y_{j,\tau}$, to the desired absolute delay of the corresponding QoS class, denoted by $\mathcal{R}_j^*$. Based on the error value, denoted by $(e_{j,\tau} = |\mathcal{R}_j^* - y_{j,\tau}|)$, the optimizer computes the computing budget (i.e., the CPU share) to be allocated to each F_j. Such value is used by the progressive actuator to (re)allocate the process budget of each running process in the target host.

Although the main goal of the optimizer is to reach the desired response time for applications in different QoS classes, the controller must provide a robust solution, too. That is, it should be able to effectively handle changes in the incoming workload, as the arrival traffic rate of each application is usually unknown and could change over time. Because of such robustness requirement, we selected the model predictive control approach to determine the appropriate values for the amount of CPU-shares for each FU. In particular, the MPC optimization module performs a series of actions at every controlling interval, denoted by $\tau \in \{T_1, T_1 + \Delta T \cdots\}$, which are highlighted as follows.

- The monitoring module gathers a sample of non-processed events in the internal buffer for every FU to estimate an upper-bound for the queuing delay of each application within the next controlling intervals.
- The optimizer calculates the required processor share to be allocated to every F_j such that its response time in the future T_{ref} intervals brings the performance error of the output response, $e_{j,\tau+T_{ref}}$, to zero.
- In case the entire computing resource demand exceeds the available capacity of such resources, the optimizer performs a cost-benefit analysis (CBA) to determine the near optimal allocation of computing resources to minimize the rate of QoS violation incidents across the entire platform.
- Once the optimizer resolves a possible allocation of processing capacity to each FU, the progressive actuator applies one step of the updating action to the current CPU share of FUs by considering the the response speed factor (T_{ref}). Having a value greater than one for T_{ref} guarantees a robust performance output even in the presence of errors in the workload prediction or the system performance model.

– Finally, in the next controlling interval, the entire cycle of monitoring (as a feedback loop), modeling, and optimization is repeated.

3.4   Cost-Benefit Analysis (CBA)

To optimally exploit the cost-effectiveness of available computing resources, we develop a model to promptly adjust the resource allocation in response to fluctuating workloads, based on the estimation of total demand, queuing delay, and the projected QoS violation rate of each application. Such a process is able to allocate more computing resources prior to the occurrence of a high volume or high resource-demanding workload. In a virtualized environment, however, the computing resources can be dynamically provisioned and managed by leveraging the estimation of resources requested by different QoS classes in the forthcoming intervals (*e.g.*, by exploring characteristics of the traffic patterns of each application using Eq. (1)). We developed a simple CBA method to significantly reduce the operational costs without compromising the level of quality of service. Such factors are impacted by how a serverless platform manages available computing resources in presence of high incoming traffic, and therefore having a set of appropriate tools to optimize such a process is an important differentiator. In the following section, we present the proposed mechanism by modeling the resource allocation burden as a profit maximization problem. We also developed a dynamic programming method to find solutions in reasonable amounts of time.

We use notation $\mathcal{C}_\tau^\Sigma$ to denote the sum of requested CPU cap demanded by all submitted applications at interval τ. In the same manner, we use notation $\mathcal{C}_{j,\tau}$ to denote the processing demand requested by a specific FU F_j at τ. Moreover, let $\mathcal{U}^*$ denote the maximum processing capacity available in the entire FaaS platform (which depends on the number of working host). Our assumption to employ the CBA during the given interval is that $\mathcal{C}_\tau \geq \mathcal{U}^*$. The CBA is stated as a *reward* function, denoted by R, to be maximized when only a partial fulfillment of requested resource capacity of FU F_j is possible. The reward function is formulated as follows.

$$\mathrm{R}_{j,\tau}(r) = (\mathcal{C}_{j,\tau} - r_{j,\tau}) \times \mathcal{I}_{q_j} \tag{3}$$

Here, $r_{j,\tau}$ is the partial fulfillment of F_j resource request. In Eq. (3), notation $\mathcal{I}_{q_j}$ denotes a constant factor represent the importance of F_j compared to other FUs that might belong to different QoS classes. The objective function to maximize the total contribution received by the service provider is formulated as follows.

$$\max_{r,\tau} \sum_{F_j \in \lambda} \mathrm{R}_{j,\tau}(r) \tag{4}$$

subject to the obvious constraints of resource availability at any given time. We developed a dynamic programming approach to find a near-optimal solution for the above-mentioned optimization problem. In particular, we only allowed the values of partial resource allocation to be taken from a certain bracket, that is

$r_{j,\tau} \in \mathcal{D} = \{5\%, 10\%, \cdots, 100\%\} \times \mathcal{U}_m^*$ in every working machine m. Then we can develop the Bellman equation of sub-optimization problem as follows.

$$V_\omega(\mathsf{R}_\omega) = \max_{0 \leq r_\omega \leq \mathsf{R}_\omega} V_{\omega+1}(\mathsf{R}_\omega - r_\omega) + \mathsf{R}_{j,\tau}(r_\omega) \qquad (5)$$

where $V_\omega(.)$ denotes the optimal reward of allocating R_ω resources among all not-yet-allocated FUs.

4   Performance Evaluation

To evaluate the performance of the proposed controlling mechanism, we implement the proposed solution as a proxy tier into the latest version of Apache Open-Whisk (version 20.11) running in our in-house cluster consisting four nodes, each equipped with an Intel i7-7700 CPU with 8 cores, and 64 GB main memory. The proposed approach is evaluated against the default policy of Open-Whisk. The application test cases are chosen from a set of functional workloads from Cloud-Suite [19] in the category of web services (WS). We conducted experiments with different load traffic patterns by varying the number of HTTP requests per second, and the probability distribution that the incoming traffic is drawn from (i.e., Poisson and Weibull distributions). The average number of triggered events per FU varies in the range of $\lambda_j \in [1000, 5000]$ requests per minute.

Each class is defined by a set-point value for the 99-th percentile response time over a period of one second. Our configuration for the set-point values for each QoS class merely allows the available capacity of computing resources to fulfill the response time of highest priority application requests (Q_1). By continues monitoring of the actual response time of applications in each QoS class, we can evaluate the ability of the controller to identify the total amount of QoS violation rates due to the dynamic workload incurred by low priority applications.

4.1   Result Summary

Plots in Fig. 2 show the rate of QoS violation incidents for applications in different priority classes as we increase the total number of applications from 64 to 512. This performance metric reflects how well the proposed controller can satisfy the requested service level agreement compared to the results obtained by applying the default policy of Open-Whisk. Result shows that the default policy evenly allocates the computing capacity in a round-robin fashion, that in turn, causes a significant QoS violation rate for applications in high priority classes (Q_1 and Q_2). By contrast, our proposed controller can dynamically identify and prevent a high violation rate for Q_1 and Q_2 applications. On average, the enhancement of QoS violation rate for Q_1 and Q_2 applications using the proposed controller is 64% and 51%, respectively.

Plots in Fig. 3 show the attained processor utilization of FUs belonging to different QoS classes as the total number of applications in each QoS class is

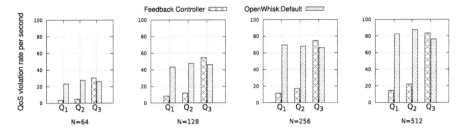

Fig. 2. The QoS violation rate experienced by applications in different QoS classes. The target response time of each QoS class is set to a value such that the available resources can only satisfy the demands from high priority applications. The total number of submitted applications varies from 64 to 512.

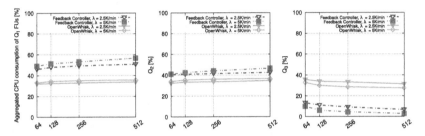

Fig. 3. Aggregated processor utilization of applications belonging to different QoS classes as the number of applications in each QoS classes increases.

increased. Results confirm that the aggregated processor utilization for applications in Q_1 and Q_2 are significantly enhanced by applying the proposed feedback controller compared to the results of default policy in Open-Whisk. The normalized value of such improvements is 36% and 24% for Q_1 and Q_2 applications, respectively. The reason for such improvements is that the proposed controller uses the CBA to allocate higher amount of available processor capacity to Q_1 and Q_2 FUs, while preventing a host to perform near its saturation point. Results also confirm that the utilized processor capacities are mostly consumed to effectively fulfill the target performance of high priority applications. Improving such a parameter can significantly enhance the service provider revenue by decreasing the wasted utilization of computing resources, as well as improving the end-users satisfaction level.

4.2 Computational Overhead

We measure the overhead time incurred by performing different steps of monitoring, predicting and solving the optimization problem using dynamic programming approach. Table 1 lists such an overhead when the total number of applications reaches to $N = 512$. Results shows that the fraction of such overhead remains below 0.7% of the controlling interval length (1 s).

Table 1. Computational overhead when total number of applications increases.

N	Overhead [Sec.]
64	0.07
128	0.17
512	0.68

5   Conclusion

Serverless technology is a recent computing paradigm that allows developers for enjoying automatic scaling and high availability for running scripts without the burden of infrastructure management. Developing a QoS aware resource allocation mechanism for serverless computing platform has drawn significant attention in recent years. In this paper, we developed a QoS-aware resource controller that can guarantee the response time of event-driven applications, while mitigating the performance isolation problem experienced by high priority applications in a platform with shared resources. The experimental results using an in-house Open-Whisk cluster with four nodes confirm the effectiveness of the proposed solution when coping with modern workloads inspired by web services applications. In particular, the proposed solution can reduce the overall QoS violation rate for high priority applications by 64% on average.

Acknowledgment. Prof. Albert Y. Zomaya acknowledges the support of Australian Research Council Discovery scheme (DP190103710). Prof. Javid Taheri would like to acknowledge the support of the Knowledge Foundation of Sweden through the AIDA project. Prof. Zahir Tari would like to acknowledge the support of the Australian Research Council (grant DP200100005). Dr. MohammadReza HoseinyFarahabady acknowledge the continued support and patronage of *The Center for Distributed and High Performance Computing* in *The University of Sydney, NSW, Australia* for giving access to advanced high-performance computing platforms and industry's leading cloud facilities, machine learning (ML) and analytic infrastructure, the digital IT services and other necessary tools.

References

1. Menascé, D.A., Almeida, V.A.F., Riedi, R., Ribeiro, F., et al.: Hierarchical and multiscale approach to analyze e-business workloads. Perform. Eval. **54**, 33–57 (2003)
2. Poccia, D.: AWS Lambda in Action: event-driven serverless applications. Simon and Schuster (2016)
3. Sbarski, P., Kroonenburg, S.: Serverless architectures on AWS: with examples using Aws Lambda. Simon and Schuster (2017)
4. Kim, Y.K., HoseinyFarahabady, M.R., Lee, Y.C., Zomaya, A.Y.: Automated fine-grained CPU cap control in serverless computing platform. IEEE Trans. Parallel Distrib. Syst. **31**(10), 2289–2301 (2020)

5. Schad, J., Dittrich, J., et al.: Runtime measurements in the cloud: observing, analyzing, and reducing variance. Proc. VLDB Endow. **3**, 460–471 (2010)
6. Wang, H., et al.: A-DRM: architecture-aware distributed RA of Virt. Clusters. In: ACM SIGPLAN/SIGOPS on Virtual Execution Environments, pp. 93–106 (2015)
7. Shuai, Y., Petrovic, G., Herfet, T.: OLAC: an open-loop controller for low-latency adaptive video streaming. In: 2015 IEEE International Conference on Communications (ICC), pp. 6874–6879 (2015)
8. Taheri, J., Zomaya, A.Y., Kassler, A.: A black-box throughput predictor for VMs in cloud environments. In: European Conference on Service-Oriented and Cloud Computing, pp. 18–33. Springer (2016). https://doi.org/10.1007/978-3-319-44482-6_2
9. Al-Dulaimy, A., Taheri, J., Kassler, A., HoseinyFarahabady, M.R., Deng, S., Zomaya, A.: MULTISCALER: a multi-loop auto-scaling approach for cloud-based applications. IEEE Trans. Cloud Comput. (2020)
10. NumFOCUS. Dask: Advanced Parallelism for Analytics, Enabling Performance. https://dask.org/ (2021)
11. Apache Org. OpenWhisk: Open Source Serverless Cloud Platform. https://openwhisk.incubator.apache.org (2021)
12. Kim, Y.K., HoseinyFarahabady, M.R., Lee, Y.C., Zomaya, A.Y., Jurdak, R.: Dynamic control of CPU usage in a lambda platform. In: 2018 IEEE International Conference on Cluster Computing (CLUSTER), pp. 234–244 (2018)
13. HoseinyFarahabady, M.R., Zomaya, A.Y., Tari, Z.: MPC for managing QoS enforcements & microarchitecture-level interferences in a lambda platform. IEEE Trans. Parall. Distrib. Syst. **29**(7), 1442–1455 (2018)
14. Hoseinyfarahabady, M.R., Tari, Z., Zomaya, A.Y.: Disk throughput controller for cloud data-centers. In: International Conference on Parallel and Distributed Computing, Applications and Technologies, pp. 404–409 (2019)
15. HoseinyFarahabady, M.R., Taheri, J., Tari, Z., Zomaya, A.Y.: A dynamic resource controller for a lambda architecture. In: 2017 46th International Conference on Parallel Processing (ICPP), pp. 332–341 (2017)
16. Rawlings, J., Mayne, D.Q., Diehl, M.M.: Model predictive control: theory, computation, and design. Nob Hill Publishing, Madison, Wisconsin (2017)
17. Box, G., et al.: Time Series: Forecasting & Control. Wiley (2008)
18. Allen: Probability, Statistics, Queueing Theory. Academic Press, Cambridge (1990)
19. Ferdman, M., Adileh, A., et al.: Clearing the clouds: a study of emerging scale-out workloads on modern hardware. In: Architectural Support for Programming Languages & Operating Systems, ASPLOS, pp. 37–48. ACM (2012)

High Resolution Patient-Specific Blood Flow Simulation in a Full-Size Aneurysmal Aorta Based on a Parallel Two-Level Method

Jie Zhou[1], Jing Li[1], Shanlin Qin[2(✉)], and Rongliang Chen[2(✉)]

[1] School of Mathematics and Statistics, Changsha University of Science
and Technology, Changsha 410014, China
[2] Shenzhen Institutes of Advanced Technology, Chinese Academy of Sciences,
Shenzhen 518055, China
{sl.qin,rl.chen}@siat.ac.cn

Abstract. An accurate and efficient blood flow simulation in patient-specific arteries is instructive for the diagnose and treatment of various vascular diseases, which is, however, computationally challenging because of the complicated geometry of the artery and the turbulence in the blood flow. In this work, we introduce a parallel scalable two-level additive Schwarz method for fast solving the Navier-Stokes equations in a patient-specific full-size aorta with aneurysms. Distributions of the hemodynamics, such as the pressure, velocity, and wall shear stress, are presented and analyzed. The algorithm is studied with a focus on its robustness against different values of model parameters and parallel scalability. The results show that the proposed method is robust to solve large and complicated simulation problems with over 25 million unstructured elements using over 5000 processors on a supercomputer.

Keywords: Aortic aneurysm · Blood flow simulation · Parallel computing · Newton-Krylov-Schwarz · Two-level additive Schwarz method

1 Introduction

Blood flow simulation has been used to investigate the hemodynamics of vascular diseases, such as stenosis, dissection, and aneurysm. However, an accurate and efficient description of the flow field is computationally challenging due to the complexity of the geometry and the large scale of the problem, which requires the development of robust and efficient parallel numerical methods [16].

This work is financially supported by the NSFC (Grant No. 11801543 and 12071461) and the Shenzhen grant (Grant No. JCYJ20190806165805433 and RCYX20200714114735074). Jing Li is supported by Hunan Provincial Natural Science Foundation of China (2021JJ30697) and the Scientific Research Project of the Hunan Provincial office of Education (20A022).

© Springer Nature Switzerland AG 2022
H. Shen et al. (Eds.): PDCAT 2021, LNCS 13148, pp. 336–348, 2022.
https://doi.org/10.1007/978-3-030-96772-7_31

The Newton-Krylov method is a powerful method for solving nonlinear systems, which adopts a Newton-type method for handling the nonlinear equations and a Krylov subspace method for solving the linear system at each Newton step to get the Newton search direction. However, the Krylov method, whose convergence rate is dependent on the condition number of the matrix, always fails to converge or converges very slow for large or complicated problems as considered in this paper. One efficient method to accelerate the Krylov subspace method is the preconditioner. That is to design a preconditioner to reduce the condition number of the matrix before applying the Krylov subspace method. Many precondition techniques have been studied for the blood flow simulations, such as the dual threshold incomplete LU factorization and the incomplete block-LU factorization [2]. A Newton-Krylov method preconditioned with additive Schwarz methods, which is called Newton-Krylov-Schwarz (NKS), is studied recently for the blood flow simulation in the cerebral artery [9] and abdominal aorta [12].

The performance of the NKS method depends largely on the effect of the preconditioner, especially when using a large number of processor cores. In this work, we introduce a two-level Schwarz preconditioner for the NKS method and simulate the blood flow of a full-size aorta with aneurysms. The two-level Schwarz preconditioner has been applied in solving many problems, such as the fluid-structure interaction [6], the multigroup neutron diffusion [7], the elastic crack analysis [4] and the porous media [8]. Most of these works adopt a pair of nested meshes since the interpolation and restriction matrices between the coarse and fine meshes can be easily obtained. However, the nested meshes are difficult to generate, especially for a computational domain with complex structures [3]. Therefore, we consider the non-nested meshes, where the coarse and fine meshes are independently generated and the interpolation is achieved by using the radial basis function. This method has been used to solve the linear system [1], the Poisson equation [13], the coupled PDE system [15] and so on.

In our previous work, the two-level overlapping Schwarz algorithm has been used to simulate the blood flow in a cerebral artery with stenoses and achieves a good strong scalability [3]. In this work, we use it to simulate the blood flow in a full-size aorta with aneurysms and further study the performance of the algorithm. Especially, the performance of the algorithm is comprehensively studied by testing the strong and weak scalability, and investigating the influence of subdomain overlapping size, and the level of fill-ins of the incomplete factorization that is used as the subdomain solver. We also report the robustness of the algorithm against different values of the model parameters, such as the viscosity, resistance, and compliance, which may be different among various diseases.

The rest of this paper is organized as follows. In Sect. 2, we introduce the 3D artery geometry and the mesh that used in the simulation, and followed by a detailed introduction of the two-level NKS method. In Sect. 3, we present some results of the hemodynamics of the aneurysmal aorta and study the numerical performance of the algorithm with respect to its robustness and scalability. Some concluding remarks are drawn in Sect. 4.

2 Methodology

2.1 Image Segmentation and Mesh Generation

As shown in Fig. 1, the geometry of a full-size aorta, from the ascending aorta to the iliac arteries, is reconstructed from the CT image by using the software Mimics (Materialise, Leuven, Belgium). The geometry has 1 inlet at the ascending aorta and 13 outlets at the major branch vessels, including the common carotid artery, the brachiocephalic artery, the left subclavian artery, the common hepatic artery, the splenic artery, the superior mesenteric artery, the left and right renal arteries, and the left and right common iliac arteries. There are three aneurysms located in the aortic arch and the right and left common iliac arteries, marked as dashed squares 1, 2, and 3 in the left of Fig. 1, respectively.

A coarse mesh of 68,506 and a fine mesh of 13,902,281 tetrahedral elements are generated independently to cover the geometry by using a commercial software ICEM (ANSYS, Canonsburg, Pennsylvania), as shown in the enlarged views in the right of Fig. 1. It can be seen that the size of the elements in the coarse mesh (red) is larger than that in the fine mesh (blue) and the nodal points are not nested since they are independently generated. The mesh is critical to the accuracy of the numerical results, and its generation includes the following main steps: (1) import the geometry into ICEM and create parts for the wall, the inlet, and the outlets to assign different boundary conditions; (2) set a global mesh size for the overall meshing and adjust local mesh size for different parts; and (3) create an unstructured mesh of tetrahedral elements to cover the whole domain and export it after a check of the mesh quality. The mesh is partitioned into non-overlapping subdomains by ParMETIS, which ensures the number of elements in each processor is roughly balanced.

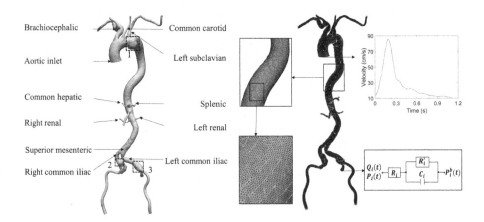

Fig. 1. The geometry, meshes and boundary conditions of the aorta with major branch vessels and aneurysms. (Color figure online)

2.2 Governing Equation and Boundary Conditions

The blood flow is considered as an incompressible Newtonian fluid and governed by the following Navier-Stokes equations [11],

$$\begin{cases} \rho\big(\dfrac{\partial \boldsymbol{u}}{\partial t} + (\boldsymbol{u} \cdot \nabla)\boldsymbol{u}\big) + \nabla p - \mu \Delta \mathbf{u} = 0 \; in & \Omega \times (0,T], \\ \nabla \cdot \boldsymbol{u} \qquad\qquad\qquad\qquad = 0 \; in & \Omega \times (0,T], \end{cases} \tag{1}$$

where ρ and μ are the density and the dynamic viscosity of the blood, $\boldsymbol{u}$ and p are the velocity vector and the pressure to be solved, respectively.

The Dirichlet and non-slip boundary conditions are imposed on the inlet Γ_I and wall Γ_W as follows,

$$\begin{cases} \boldsymbol{u} = \boldsymbol{v_I}, \, on & \Gamma_I \times (0,T], \\ \boldsymbol{u} = 0, \;\; on & \Gamma_W \times (0,T], \end{cases}$$

where $\boldsymbol{v_I}$ is a pulsatile velocity waveform obtained from the patient-specific clinical measurement in the ascending aorta, as shown in Fig. 1.

A three-element Windkessel model is applied at each outlet to account for the impact of the downstream vasculature, which is governed by the following equation [5],

$$P_i(t) + R_i' C_i \frac{dP_i(t)}{dt} = (R_i + R_i')Q_i(t) + P_i^b(t) + R_i R_i' C_i \frac{dQ_i(t)}{dt},$$

where R_i, R_i', C_i, $P_i(t)$ and $Q_i(t)$ are the resistances, the compliance, the pressure and the flow rate at the ith outlet respectively, as shown in Fig. 1. $P_i^b(t)$ is the pressure at the downstream vasculature. As given in [3], the analytic solution of this equation is

$$P_i(t) = R_i Q_i(t) + \big(P_i(0) - R_i Q_i(0)\big)e^{-t/\tau_i} + \int_0^t \frac{e^{-(t-s)/\tau}}{C_i} Q_i(s)ds,$$

where $\tau_i = R_i' C_i$; $P_i(0)$ and $Q_i(0)$ are the initial pressure and flow rate at the ith outlet. Here, the distal pressure $P_i^b(t)$ is assumed to be 0.

During the calculation, a total resistance R_T and total compliance C_T will be introduced, whose values are manually adjusted so that the obtained diastolic and systolic pressures at the inlet match the clinically measured values. Then, R_T and C_T are split to each outlet for the values of R_i and C_i by the radius of the vessels.

2.3 Newton-Krylov-Schwarz Method with a Two-Level Preconditioner

For the full discretization of Eq. (1), we adopt a stabilized P_1-P_1 finite element method in space and an implicit backward Euler method in time [3]. After the discretization, we obtain a large, sparse, and nonlinear algebraic system at each time step, which is denoted as

$$\mathcal{F}(\chi) = 0, \tag{2}$$

where χ includes all the velocity and pressure at each mesh point.

To solve Eq. (2), the NKS method is adopted, which updates the solution through the following iterative method

$$\chi_{k+1} = \chi_k + \tau_k S_k,$$

where τ_k is a step length calculated from a line search method and S_k is the Newton correction obtained by inexactly solving the Jacobian system at each Newton step in the sense

$$\| J_k M_k^{-1} M_k S_k + \mathcal{F}(\chi_k) \| < \epsilon_l \mathcal{F}(\chi_k),$$

where ϵ_l is a given relative tolerance to control the "exactness" of the solution of the Jacobian system and M_k is a two-level Schwarz preconditioner defined as

$$M^{-1} = I_H^h B_c^{-1} (I_H^h)^T + \sum_{l=1}^{N_p} (R_l^0)^T B_l^{-1} R_l^\delta \left(I - J_k I_H^h B_c^{-1} (I_H^h)^T \right).$$

where I_H^h is an interpolation operator from the coarse mesh to the fine mesh. B_l^{-1} is a fine-level subdomain preconditioner for the Jacobian matrix J_k. B_c^{-1} is a coarse-level preconditioner for the inverse of the coarse-level Jacobian matrix. N_p is the number of subdomains, which also equals the number of processors used in parallel computing. δ is the overlapping size extended from the nonoverlapping subdomains Ω_l ($l = 1, 2, \ldots, N_p$) to the overlapping subdomains Ω_l^δ. R_l^0 and R_l^δ are the restriction operators that map the global vectors in Ω to those in Ω_l and Ω_l^δ respectively. Notably, it is difficult to directly solve the problem on the fine mesh, but much easier on the coarse mesh, which can then be interpolated to the fine mesh by using a radial interpolation basis function, as described in [3].

3   Results and Discussion

In this section, we will present some numerical results of the hemodynamics in a full-size patient-specific aorta with a focus on the performance of the proposed algorithm, carried out on the Tianhe 2A supercomputer at the National Supercomputer Center in Guangzhou, China.

3.1   Simulation Results and Discussion

For the simulation, the values of the total resistance R_T and total compliance are chosen as 1012.27 dyn $\cdot$ s/cm^5 and 1.026146×10^{-2} cm^5/dyn, with which, the simulated pressure matches with the patient's pressure. Figure 2 shows the spatial distributions of the pressure, streamline of the velocity, and wall shear stress (WSS) in the aorta during a systolic period. It can be seen that the pressure gradually decreases along the artery from the proximal to the distal ends, and the range of the pressure matches with that reported in [10]. The streamline of the velocity shows that physiologically reasonable values of the velocity are obtained with relatively lower velocity in the aneurysmal region compared to other regions. Some secondary flows are developed at the aneurysmal regions 1 and 2 that are marked in Fig. 1. Similar results are reported in [17].

The distribution of the WSS shows that relatively lower WSS can be observed in the aneurysm compared to the other regions, as has been shown in [12]. It is reported that the WSS shifts to a low level during the growing period of the aneurysm, and the rupture usually occurs at these sites [19]. The features of the hemodynamics in the aneurysmal regions should consequently have an impact on the aneurysm development and rupture, which should be studied more extensively.

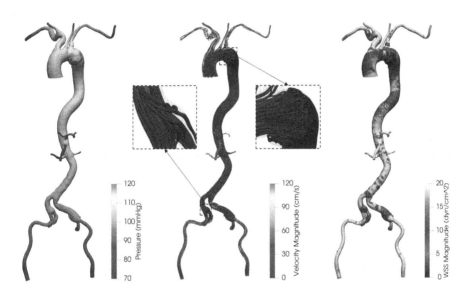

Fig. 2. Spatial distributions of the pressure, streamline of the velocity and WSS at the period of systole

3.2   Robustness and Scalability

In this subsection, we show the robustness and parallel scalability of the proposed NKS method for the simulation of the hemodynamics in the whole aorta. The algorithm has several important parameters, such as the time-step size Δt, the viscosity μ, the overlapping size δ, the ILU fill-in level, and the resistance and compliance, which affect the performance of the method.

For all the numerical tests in this subsection, the stopping criteria for the linear and nonlinear solvers are set to be 10^{-6} (relative error). In all tables, "Newton", "GMRES", and "Time (s)" refer to the average number of Newton iterations per time step, the average number of GMRES iterations per Newton iteration, and the average compute time in seconds per time step, respectively. In the two-level method, the coarse-level problem is solved by the GMRES method preconditioned with a one-level Schwarz preconditioner and we use the maximum number of iterations ("Coarse Its") as the stopping condition for the coarse-level GMRES. For each test, we only change one parameter to see the performance of the algorithm. In the two-level method, we use a mesh with 6.85×10^4 elements as the coarse mesh, and all the tests are carried out on two meshes (mesh1 with 3.26×10^6 elements and mesh2 with 1.39×10^7 elements) for comparison.

Table 1 shows the influence of the time-step size Δt on the performance of the algorithm, and four time-step sizes 5×10^{-4}, 1×10^{-3}, 2×10^{-3} and 4×10^{-3} are tested. All tests are performed on two different meshes, namely the mesh1 with 3.26×10^6 elements and the mesh2 with 1.39×10^7 elements. Results show that, in general, with the increase of the time-step size, the number of Newton and GMRES iterations and the compute time increase, which means that the solver becomes more difficult to converge. For example, when the time-step size increases to 4×10^{-3}, the GMRES iterations are almost tripled for the coarse mesh case (mesh1) and diverge for the fine mesh case (mesh2). The main reason is that the initial guess of Newton's method becomes too far from the exact solution for the large time-step size case, which slows down the convergence or even diverges. Table 1 also shows that the fine mesh case is more difficult to solve than the coarse mesh case, and at the same time, our algorithm shows good robustness with respect to the mesh refinement since both the linear and nonlinear iterations increase a little bit after a threefold increase in the problem size, which shows that the proposed algorithm has the potential to solve even larger problems. In the rest of the paper, we use 1×10^{-3} as the default time-step size.

Table 1. The impact of the time-step size Δt on the performance of the solver. The mesh1 and mesh2 are carried out with 120 and 480 processors (same setups are used for the rest test cases), respectively. Here NC means "Not Converge".

Δt	Mesh1: 3.26×10^6			Mesh2: 1.39×10^7		
	Newton	GMRES	Time(s)	Newton	GMRES	Time(s)
5×10^{-4}	2.20	5.09	21.67	2.60	7.92	28.26
1×10^{-3}	2.30	5.23	22.65	2.40	6.13	25.42
2×10^{-3}	3.10	6.48	30.29	3.20	8.00	34.91
4×10^{-3}	3.10	17.31	34.92	NC	–	–

In Table 2, we show the impact of the accuracy of the coarse-level solution on the performance of the proposed two-level method. The accuracy of the coarse problem is controlled by "Coarse Its", where larger "Coarse Its" corresponds to a more accurate coarse-level solution. From the results, we see that with the increase of the "Coarse Its", the number of Newton iterations doesn't change, and the number of GMRES iterations decreases, which means that the two-level preconditioner becomes stronger with the increase of "Coarse Its". But at the same time, the time spent on the coarse-level will increase when "Coarse Its" increases, which makes the total compute time increase if "Coarse Its" reaches a certain value. Therefore, the optimal choice of "Coarse Its" is 40 in terms of computing time for this test case and we will use 40 as the default value for "Coarse its" for all the rest tests.

Table 2. The impact of the stopping condition for the coarse-level GMRES on the performance of the solver

	Mesh1: 3.26×10^6			Mesh2: 1.39×10^7		
Coarse Its	Newton	GMRES	Time(s)	Newton	GMRES	Time(s)
30	2.30	6.37	22.91	2.40	6.13	25.50
40	2.30	5.23	22.65	2.40	6.13	25.42
50	2.30	5.20	22.70	2.40	6.13	25.44
60	2.30	5.09	22.73	2.40	6.13	25.60

The viscosity μ is an important parameter in blood flow simulation. Table 3 shows that the two-level method performs a robust convergence for a wide range of μ. We observe that as the viscosity increases, the number of Newton iteration gradually stabilizes at a constant, the number of GMRES iteration shows a small variation, and the computation time gradually stabilizes. Moreover, the effect of the viscosity μ is similar for both meshes, which indicates that the proposed algorithm is robust with respect to the viscosity.

Table 3. The impact of the viscosity μ on the performance of the solver

	Mesh1: 3.26×10^6			Mesh2: 1.39×10^7		
μ	Newton	GMRES	Time(s)	Newton	GMRES	Time(s)
0.01	2.85	5.89	27.69	2.50	6.68	26.87
0.04	2.35	5.26	23.03	2.40	6.42	25.76
0.07	2.25	5.36	22.12	2.40	6.54	26.29
0.10	2.25	5.20	22.11	2.40	6.86	26.42

In Table 4, the two-level preconditioner also shows a robust performance to the resistance R and the compliance C. The total resistance R and the total compliance C are critical parameters for the Windkessel model, which are generally determined by the clinical conditions of the patient. The results show that the number of Newton and GMRES iterations are almost stable with small variations leading to a slight fluctuation of the computation time. Overall, the proposed algorithm is robust to both the resistance R and the compliance C.

For the two-level Schwarz preconditioner, the fill-in level of the incomplete LU (ILU) [14] is another parameter to affect the performance of the algorithm,

Table 4. The impact of the resistance R and compliance C on the performance of the solver

	Mesh1: 3.26×10^6			Mesh2: 1.39×10^7		
$R(dyn \cdot s/cm^5)$	Newton	GMRES	Time(s)	Newton	GMRES	Time(s)
5.06×10^2	2.45	5.33	23.90	2.40	6.51	25.69
1.012×10^3	2.30	5.23	22.65	2.40	6.13	25.42
2.024×10^3	2.30	5.76	22.69	2.40	7.04	26.13
$C(cm^5/dyn)$	Newton	GMRES	Time(s)	Newton	GMRES	Time(s)
5.131×10^{-3}	2.35	5.36	23.14	2.40	6.29	25.54
1.026×10^{-2}	2.30	5.23	22.65	2.40	6.13	25.42
2.052×10^{-2}	2.35	5.23	23.02	2.40	6.04	25.47

which is tested and summarized in Table 5. N_p is the number of processors used for solving the problem. We use different levels of fill-in with different subdomain solvers to test the robustness of the proposed algorithm. We fix the overlapping size at 2, the coarse ILU level at 1, and test on the meshes with 1.39×10^7 and 2.60×10^7 elements. We conclude that the algorithm is stable as the fill-in level of ILU increases. The results show that the numbers of Newton and GMRES iterations are almost stable and the compute time increases with the increase of the fill-in levels. This means that we can use very small fill-in levels in our simulation, which is unlike the one-level method that usually needs large fill-in levels.

Table 5. The effect of the ILU fill-in levels on the performance of the algorithm

	Mesh1: 1.39×10^7				Mesh2: 2.60×10^7			
Subsolve	N_p	Newton	GMRES	Time(s)	N_p	Newton	GMRES	Time(s)
ILU(0)	720	2.40	6.38	17.54	1440	2.50	8.28	19.29
ILU(1)	720	2.40	5.67	18.04	1440	2.50	8.88	20.34
ILU(2)	720	2.40	5.75	19.89	1440	2.50	8.76	23.42
ILU(3)	720	2.40	6.58	23.90	1440	2.60	8.77	27.54

Table 6 studies the impact of the subdomain overlapping size on the proposed algorithm. The overlapping size is used to control the amount of information exchanged between subdomains. For the one-level method, with the increase of the number of subdomains (equal to the number of processors for the parallel computing), the preconditioner becomes weaker and therefore usually needs a large overlapping size as reported in [6]. For the proposed two-level method, the results show that the numbers of Newton and GMRES methods are not sensitive to the overlapping size, which means that we can use a very small overlapping size in the simulation. Overlapping always means repeat works. Therefore, in the design of the parallel algorithm, we hope to use small overlapping to save time. The theory of the two-level domain decomposition method also suggests that the convergence rate is independent of the overlapping size which is consistent with our results [18].

Table 6. The effect of the overlapping size δ on the performance of the solver

Overlap(δ)	Mesh1: 1.39×10^7				Mesh2: 2.60×10^7			
	N_p	Newton	GMRES	Time(s)	N_p	Newton	GMRES	Time(s)
0	720	2.40	7.67	18.27	1440	2.20	12.27	18.90
1	720	2.40	7.08	18.39	1440	2.20	10.71	17.88
2	720	2.40	6.58	18.38	1440	2.20	9.24	17.56
3	720	2.40	6.17	18.49	1440	2.20	9.86	18.96

To understand the parallel scalability of the two-level preconditioner, we test the weak scalability and strong scalability of the algorithm. For the weak scalability, the number of linear iterations and the computing time should theoretically stabilize at a constant when the number of processor cores and the problem size increase at the same rate to keep the same subproblem size for each processor. Results are shown in Table 7. Four meshes with 3.26×10^6, 6.70×10^6, 1.39×10^7 and 2.60×10^7 elements, are used in the tests, and they are solved with 180, 360, 720, and 1440 processor cores, respectively. The results in Table 7 show that the numbers of Newton and GMRES iterations stay close to a constant when the number of mesh elements and the number of processor cores increases proportionally, and the computing time per time step does not change a lot. Our results indicate that the proposed algorithm is weakly scalable.

Table 7. The weak scalability results tested on four different meshes

Mesh	N_p	Newton	GMRES	Time(s)
3.26×10^6	180	2.35	5.28	16.11
6.70×10^6	360	2.30	7.42	17.60
1.39×10^7	720	2.20	5.86	16.21
2.60×10^7	1440	2.25	7.09	17.53

For the strong scalability, we only test two meshes with 1.39×10^7 and 2.60×10^7 elements. The results of the strong scalability in Table 8 show that the number of Newton iterations remains almost constant for both meshes as the number of processors increases and the number of GMRES iterations increases slowly at first and then fast when the number of processors reaches 2880. For the coarse mesh, when the number of processors increases from 360 to 2880, the increase in the number of GMRES iterations is slow, and the rate of computing time reduction is relatively uniform. For the fine mesh, when the number of the processor increases from 2880 to 5760, the number of GMRES increases by 4 times, which results in a quick drop in the parallel efficiency. The main reason for the low efficiency is that the problem size is too small for 5760 processors, which makes the ratio of the computing time and the communication time between processors too small. Communication is the main bottleneck for achieving high parallel efficiency. One way to increase the parallel efficiency is to increase the problem size.

We define the speed up and the parallel efficiency as speedup $= t_m/t_n$ and efficiency $= (t_m \times N_{pm})/(t_n \times N_{pn})$, where t_m and t_n are the average computing time per time step under the usage of N_{pm} and N_{pn} processor cores, and $N_{pm} \leq N_{pn}$. The parallel efficiency of the two-level algorithm is 45% when the number of processor cores reaches 2880 for the coarse mesh with 1.39×10^7 elements, and 35% when processor cores reaches 5760 for the fine mesh with 2.60×10^7 elements. Overall, the proposed algorithm is robust and scalable for the solution of large-scale problems.

Table 8. Strong scalability results tested on two different meshes

Mesh	N_p	Newton	GMRES	Time(s)	Speedup	Ideal	Efficiency
1.39×10^7	360	2.40	5.54	42.35	1.00	1.00	100%
	720	2.40	6.63	24.45	1.73	2.00	87%
	1440	2.40	9.13	15.87	2.67	4.00	67%
	2880	2.30	17.09	11.69	3.62	8.00	45%
2.60×10^7	720	2.50	8.16	55.60	1.00	1.00	100%
	1440	2.60	10.50	36.60	1.52	2.00	76%
	2880	2.40	22.13	22.67	2.45	4.00	61%
	5760	2.40	80.54	20.18	2.76	8.00	35%

4   Conclusion

In this work, a parallel NKS algorithm with a two-level preconditioner is used to simulate the blood flow in a full-size aorta with aneurysms. A large nonlinear system is obtained from the discretization of the Navier-Stokes equations by using a stabilized finite element method in space and an implicit backward Euler method in time. The system is then solved by the NKS algorithm with a two-level Schwarz preconditioner, which is constructed by a radial interpolation basis function between the non-nested meshes. Numerical tests show that the algorithm is robust to the viscosity, the overlapping size, and the fill-in level and demonstrate good strong and weak scalability with up to 5000 processor cores.

References

1. Antonietti, P.F., Houston, P., Hu, X., Sarti, M., Verani, M.: Multigrid algorithms for hp-version interior penalty discontinuous Galerkin methods on polygonal and polyhedral meshes. Calcolo **54**(4), 1169–1198 (2017)
2. Badia, S., Quaini, A., Quarteroni, A.: Modular vs. non-modular preconditioners for fluid-structure systems with large added-mass effect. Comput. Methods Appl. Mech. Eng. **197**(49–50), 4216–4232 (2008)
3. Chen, R., et al.: A parallel non-nested two-level domain decomposition method for simulating blood flows in cerebral artery of stroke patient. Int. J. Numer. Methods Biomed. Eng. **36**(11), e3392 (2020)
4. Chen, X., Cai, X.C.: Effective two-level domain decomposition preconditioners for elastic crack problems modeled by extended finite element method. Commun. Comput. Phys. **28**(4), 1561–1584 (2020)
5. Grinberg, L., Karniadakis, G.E.: Outflow boundary conditions for arterial networks with multiple outlets. Ann. Biomed. Eng. **36**(9), 1496–1514 (2008)
6. Kong, F., Cai, X.C.: A scalable nonlinear fluid-structure interaction solver based on a Schwarz preconditioner with isogeometric unstructured coarse spaces in 3D. J. Comput. Phys. **340**, 498–518 (2017)
7. Kong, F., et al.: A fully coupled two-level Schwarz preconditioner based on smoothed aggregation for the transient multigroup neutron diffusion equations. Numer. Linear Algebra Appl. **25**(3), e2126 (2018)
8. Luo, L., Liu, L., Cai, X.C., Keyes, D.E.: Fully implicit hybrid two-level domain decomposition algorithms for two-phase flows in porous media on 3D unstructured grids. J. Comput. Phys. **409**, 109312 (2020)
9. Luo, L., Shiu, W.S., Chen, R., Cai, X.C.: A nonlinear elimination preconditioned inexact Newton method for blood flow problems in human artery with stenosis. J. Comput. Phys. **399**, 108926 (2019)
10. Meidert, A.S., Nold, J.S., Hornung, R., Paulus, A.C., Zwißler, B., Czerner, S.: The impact of continuous non-invasive arterial blood pressure monitoring on blood pressure stability during general anaesthesia in orthopaedic patients. Eur. J. Anaesthesiol. **34**(11), 716–722 (2017)
11. Morris, P.D., et al.: Computational fluid dynamics modelling in cardiovascular medicine. Heart **102**(1), 18–28 (2016)
12. Qin, S., et al.: Efficient parallel simulation of hemodynamics in patient-specific abdominal aorta with aneurysm. Comput. Biol. Med. **136**, 104652 (2021)
13. Radhakrishnan, A., Xu, M., Shahane, S., Vanka, S.P.: A non-nested multilevel method for meshless solution of the Poisson equation in heat transfer and fluid flow. arXiv preprint arXiv:2104.13758 (2021)
14. Saad, Y.: Iterative Methods for Sparse Linear Systems. SIAM (2003)
15. Salvador, M., Dede', L., Quarteroni, A.: An intergrid transfer operator using radial basis functions with application to cardiac electromechanics. Comput. Mech. **66**(2), 491–511 (2020). https://doi.org/10.1007/s00466-020-01861-x
16. Shang, Y.: A parallel two-level finite element variational multiscale method for the Navier-Stokes equations. Nonlin. Anal. Theory Methods Appl. **84**, 103–116 (2013)
17. Sheidaei, A., Hunley, S., Zeinali-Davarani, S., Raguin, L., Baek, S.: Simulation of abdominal aortic aneurysm growth with updating hemodynamic loads using a realistic geometry. Med. Eng. Phys. **33**(1), 80–88 (2011)

18. Toselli, A., Widlund, O.: Domain Decomposition Methods-Algorithms and Theory. Springer, Heidelberg (2004). https://doi.org/10.1007/b137868
19. Wang, Y., Leng, X., Zhou, X., Li, W., Siddiqui, A.H., Xiang, J.: Hemodynamics in a middle cerebral artery aneurysm before its growth and fatal rupture: case study and review of the literature. World Neurosurg. **119**, e395–e402 (2018)

Optimizing Data Locality by Executor Allocation in Reduce Stage for Spark Framework

Zhongming Fu[1][(✉)] , Mengsi He[1] , Zhuo Tang[2] , and Yang Zhang[3]

[1] College of Computer Science and Technology, University of South China,
Hengyang, China
fuzhongming@hnu.edu.cn
[2] College of Information Science and Engineering,
Hunan University, Changsha, China
[3] Science and Technology on Parallel and Distributed Laboratory (PDL),
National University of Defense Technology, Changsha, China

Abstract. Data locality is a key factor influencing the performance of Spark systems. As the execution container of tasks, the executors started on which nodes can directly affect the locality level achieved by the tasks. This paper tries to improve the data locality by executor allocation in reduce stage for Spark framework. Firstly, we calculate the network distance matrix of executors and formulate an optimal executor allocation problem to minimize the total communication distance. Then, an approximation algorithm is proposed and the approximate factor is proved to be 2. Finally, we evaluate the performance of our algorithm in a practical Spark cluster by using several representative benchmarks: sort, pageRank and LDA. Experimental results show that the proposed algorithm can help to improve the data locality and application/job performance obviously.

Keywords: Communication distance · Data locality · Executor allocation · Spark

1 Introduction

Apache Spark becomes the popular parallel computing framework for massive data processing. A typical Spark application contains one or more jobs, and a job usually consists of many stages. Since these stages are executed sequentially, the intermediate output of the former stage is used as the input of the later stage. When the tasks of a stage run in parallel on different nodes, the data communication is required during the job execution. In the map (i.e., shuffleMap) stage, each task reads a data block to process and outputs the intermediate data to local disks. In the reduce (i.e., result) stage, each task fetches part of the intermediate data from all the previous tasks for processing. This is a many-to-many communication mode. The resulting large amount of network traffic in

© Springer Nature Switzerland AG 2022
H. Shen et al. (Eds.): PDCAT 2021, LNCS 13148, pp. 349–357, 2022.
https://doi.org/10.1007/978-3-030-96772-7_32

these two stages can extend execution time and congest the cluster network, thereby hindering the system [1].

For improving performance, data locality is a key factor considered by the task scheduling of Spark stages [2]. The task scheduling determines the executor on which node the task runs and the data locality refers to scheduling computation/task close to data. In particular, in the map stage, the task scheduler uses the delay scheduling algorithm [3] that assigns the map task to the node which stores the data block, thus to avoid copying data remotely. In the reduce stage, the task scheduler assigns the reduce task to one of the nodes that holds more intermediate data to the task, thus to minimize the data transmission volume.

However, as the execution container of tasks, the executors can limit the nodes available for the task scheduling, which affects the locality level achieved by the tasks. On the one hand, if the executor is not started on the node in which a data block is located in the map stage, the map task is almost impossible to retrieve data locally. On the other hand, if the executors are started on the node away from each other in the reduce stage, the reducer has to span a long network distances to get data. In the Spark framework, *spreadOut* and *noSpreadOut* are two algorithms provided to decide the executors start up. Unfortunately, none of them fully consider the locality factor.

In this paper, we improve the data locality of tasks from the view of executor allocation considering the reduce stage for Spark applications. As the number of reduce stages in general is much greater than that of map stages, the reduce stage has an important impact on the entire application/job performance. The main contributions of this paper are summarized as below.

- We calculate the network distance matrix of executors, and formulate an executor allocation problem to minimize the total communication distance. This problem proved to be an NP-Hard problem.
- We propose an optimal executor allocation approximation algorithm, and prove that the approximate factor of the algorithm is 2.
- We implement our algorithm in Spark-3.0.1 and evaluate its performance on representative benchmarks. The experiment results explain that the proposed algorithm can decrease the task execution time for better data locality.

The rest of this paper is organized as follows. Section 2 reviews related research. Section 3 presents the proposed executor allocation algorithm. Experiments and performance evaluation are given in Sect. 4. Section 5 concludes this paper.

2   Related Work

A lot of research has been done to optimize the cross-node/rack data communication problem in MapReduce-type frameworks, which can be categorized as follows:

Task Scheduling. In the design of MapReduce, Dean et al. [4] took the locality of map tasks into account to save bandwidth consumption. The priority of tasks scheduled to nodes is classified into three levels: *node-local*, i.e., the task and its data block are on the same node; *rack-local*, i.e., the task and its data block are on different nodes but on the same rack; and *off-rack*, i.e., the task and its data block are on different racks but on a cluster. Further, using the time-for-space strategy, Zaharia et al. [3] proposed the delay scheduling algorithm. If there is no task can obtain data locally on the request node, it will wait for a small amount of time and in the hope of obtaining better locality from subsequent nodes. In a cluster that quickly releases resources, the delay scheduling could achieve a higher proportion of node-local tasks while preserving fairness.

Besides the map stage, the data locality for reducers also affects the job performance. Tang et al. [5] presented a minimum transmission cost reduce task scheduler (MTCRS). It decides the appropriate launching locations for reduce tasks according to the waiting time of each reduce task and the transmission cost set, which is computed by the sizes and the locations of intermediate data partitions.

Data Pre-fetching. From another angle, Sun et al. [6] designed a high performance scheduling optimizer (HPSO), a prefetching service based task scheduler to improve data locality for MapReduce jobs. Their idea is to predict the most appropriate nodes to which future map tasks should be assigned and then preload the input data to memory without any delaying on running normal tasks. Nevertheless, the method may incur additional overhead and could not help to alleviate the network traffic of cluster.

As our early work [7], we optimized the task locality in the map stage by the executor allocation in Spark framework. In this paper, we focuses on the executor allocation in the reduce stage, with the purpose of providing tasks with the possibility of better locality when scheduling the reduce tasks.

3 Executor Allocation Algorithm

This section first formulates the optimal executor allocation problem, and then presents the approximation algorithm for the problem.

3.1 Optimal Executor Allocation Problem

When a Spark application is submitted to the cluster and to be executed, the master registers with the resource manager and applies for the resources to start a group of executors. An executor is the container of executing tasks, which actually is a collection of computing resources (i.e., cpu and memory). A task can be scheduled to run on a node requiring to have idle executors.

In the initial state of allocating executor for an application, some particular data structures are defined as follows:

(1) E: A set of executors allowed to be started on the nodes, the number is m. The element e_i^l represents the ith executor that can be started on the lth node if marked. In the Spark system, the number of executors allowed to

start on each node can be calculated based on the free resources of the node, formalized as:

$$exe\_num_i = \min\{[\frac{free\_cpu_i}{cpu\_conf}], [\frac{free\_memory_i}{memory\_conf}]\}, \qquad (1)$$

where exe_num_i indicates the number of executors allowed to be started on node N_i, and cpu_conf and $memory\_conf$ are the CPUs and memory capacity configured by the executor respectively.

(2) D: A matrix of $m \times m$ represents the communication distance between two executors of E, represented as:

$$D = \begin{bmatrix} d_{00} & d_{01} & \cdots & d_{0(m-1)} \\ d_{10} & d_{11} & \cdots & d_{1(m-1)} \\ \vdots & \vdots & \ddots & \vdots \\ d_{(m-1)0} & d_{(m-1)1} & \cdots & d_{(m-1)(m-1)} \end{bmatrix},$$

where d_{ij} represents the communication distance between executor e_i and e_j.

The communication distance depends on the network latency and bandwidth. To capture the data locality, we divide the proximity level (PL) of two executors into three levels: (1) two executors are on the same node, then PL is equal to 0; (2) two executors are on different nodes of the same rack, then PL is equal to 1; (3) two executors are on different nodes of different racks, then PL is equal to 2. Then the distance d_{ij} can be further calculated as:

$$d_{ij} = \begin{cases} 0, if\ \mathrm{PL} = 0 \\ 2 \times \left(\frac{1}{band_{NS}} + latency_{NS}\right), if\ \mathrm{PL} = 1 \\ 2 \times \left(\frac{1}{band_{NS}} + latency_{NS}\right) + 2 \times \left(\frac{1}{band_{SS}} + latency_{SS}\right), if\ \mathrm{PL} = 2 \end{cases}, \tag{2}$$

where $band_{NS}$ is the network bandwidth from node to switch, $band_{SS}$ is the network bandwidth from switch to switch, $latency_{NS}$ is the network delay from node to switch, and $latency_{SS}$ is the network delay from switch to switch.

In this model, our purpose is to start the required executors on nodes close to each other. Assuming that the number of executors required by the application is k, so the optimal executor allocation problem can be described as selecting a subset $E^{'} \in E$ to minimize the total communication distance between two executors. This problem can be formalized as follows by using Integer Programming:

$$min \sum_{i=0}^{m-1} \sum_{j=0}^{m-1} d_{ij} \times (x_i \times x_j),$$

$$subject\ to\ \sum_{i=0}^{m-1} x_i = k, x_i \in \{0,1\}, 0 \le i < m-1, \qquad (3)$$

where x_i is a binary variable, whose value is 1 means that the executor e_i is selected, and value is 0 means that the executor is not selected.

Theorem 1. *The optimal executor allocation problem (abbreviated as the OEA problem) is NP-Hard.*

Proof. The k-clique problem in graph theory can be shown to reducible to the *OEA* problem. That is, for any instance of the k-clique, an instance of *OEA* can be created in polynomial time such that solving the instance of *OEA* solves the instance of k-clique as well. According to the NP completeness of the k-clique problem, the *OEA* problem can be proved to be NP-Hard [8].

3.2 Approximation Algorithm

Algorithm 1 describes the approximation algorithm for the optimal executor allocation problem. Firstly, the algorithm selects k nearest executors (including e_j itself) for each executor e_i. For executor e_i, the set of its k nearest executors is represented as $S(e_i)$, and the sum of communication distances from executor e_i to other $k-1$ executors is calculated and represented as $C(e_i)$. Then, find the smallest $C(e_v)$ among all executors, and assign the executor set $S(e_v)$ to $MinSet$. Thirdly, calculate the total communication distance between two executors of $MinSet$ and represent it as $MinCost$. Finally, return to $MinSet$.

Algorithm 1: Approximation Algorithm

Input:
> The set of executors allowed to start: E;
> The communication distance matrix: D;
> The number of executors required: k;

Output:
> The executors selected to start.

1 **begin**
2 | for each executor e_i of E, find k executors nearest (including e_i itself) to e_i, represented as $S(e_i)$;
3 | calculate the sum of communication distances from executor e_i to other $k-1$ executors:
4 | $C(e_i) = \sum_{e_j \in S(e_i)} d_{ij}$;
5 | find the smallest $C(e_v)$ and the executor set is represented as $MinSet$;
6 | calculate the total communication distances between executors of $MinSet$, represented as $MinCost$;
7 | **return** $MinSet$.
8 **end**

The algorithm takes $O(m)$ time to find the nearest k executors by using the optimal algorithm. For m executors, the time it takes is $m \times O(m)$. Therefore, the time complexity of Algorithm 1 is $O(m^2)$, where m is the number of executors allowed to start.

Theorem 2. *The approximate factor of the approximation algorithm to the optimal executor allocation problem is 2.*

Proof. The solution of the approximation algorithm for the optimal executor allocation is $MinSet$, and the sum of the communication distances between executors is $MinCost$. Let $MinSet^*$ be the optimal solution, and the sum of the communication distances between executors of $MinSet^*$ is $MinCost^*$. Then for $MinCost^*$, there is:

$$MinCost^* = \frac{1}{2} \sum_{e_i \in MinSet^*} \sum_{e_j \in MinSet^*} d_{ij} \leq \frac{1}{2} \sum_{e_i \in MinSet^*} \sum_{e_j \in MinSet} d_{ij}$$

$$= \frac{1}{2} \sum_{e_i \in MinSet^*} C(e_i) \geq \frac{1}{2} \sum_{e_i \in MinSet^*} MinCost = \frac{k}{2} \times MinCost.$$

$$(4)$$

For $MinCost$, there is:

$$MinCost = \frac{1}{2} \sum_{e_i \in MinSet} \sum_{e_j \in MinSet} d_{ij}. \tag{5}$$

Let C_{e_v} gets the minimum total communication distances $MinCost$. According to the triangular inequality [9], there is:

$$\sum_{e_i \in MinSet} \sum_{e_j \in MinSet} d_{ij} \leq \sum_{e_i \in MinSet} \sum_{e_j \in MinSet} (d_{iv} + d_{vj})$$

$$= \sum_{e_i \in MinSet} \sum_{e_j \in MinSet} d_{iv} + \sum_{e_i \in MinSet} \sum_{e_j \in MinSet} d_{vj}$$

$$= \sum_{e_i \in MinSet} \left(\sum_{e_j \in MinSet} d_{vi} \right) + \sum_{e_i \in MinSet} \left(\sum_{e_j \in MinSet} d_{jv} \right)$$

$$= k \times \left(\sum_{e_i \in MinSet} d_{iv} \right) + k \times \left(\sum_{e_j \in MinSet} d_{jv} \right)$$

$$= k \times MinCost + k \times MinCost. \tag{6}$$

Therefore, for $MinCost$, there is:

$$\frac{1}{2} \times 2k \times MinCost = k \times MinCost. \tag{7}$$

The approximate factor of our solution $MinSet$ is:

$$\sigma = \frac{MinCost}{MinCost^*} = \frac{k \times MinCost}{\frac{k}{2} \times MinCost} = 2. \tag{8}$$

Therefore, the approximation algorithm for the optimal executor allocation problem is a 2-approximate algorithm.

4   Experimental Evaluation

We evaluate the performance in a data center with the KVM technology used to build virtual machines. Each VM is equipped with 4 virtual cores, 8 GB RAM and 64GB disk space. We then deploy the Spark-3.0.1 cluster in the data center that contains 18 nodes (each server starts 2 VMs).

4.1   Performance

(1) Micro-benchmark

Sort is a frequently used application with the function of making data objects in order. The experiment uses 30GB data set of *Wikipedia entries* as input data. This application contains a job with two stages: map stage and reduce stage, each stage has 80 tasks. To evaluate the performance under different numbers of executors, the required number of executors is set to 30, 40, and 50 respectively in the procedure.

Figure 1(a) reveals the performance comparison of the three executor allocation methods, where the proposed approximation algorithm is marked as *OTCD*. It illustrates that the job execution time of *OTCD* lower than *spreadOut*, *noSpreadOut*. In particular, when the required number of executors is 50 (i.e., Executor_50), compared with other two methods, *OTCD* decreases the execution time by 32.8% and 24.5%, respectively.

Figure 1(b) shows the comparison of the reduce stage time under different methods. In this stage, the reduce tasks take a lot of time to obtain the intermediate data from previous tasks. Because the reduce stage is considered in our optimization of data locality through executor allocation, it can be seen that comparing Fig. 1(a), *OTCD* has a significant performance improvement in the reduce stage. In particular, when the required number of executors is 40 (i.e., Executor_40), by comparison with *spreadOut* and *noSpreadOut*, *OTCD* reduces the execution time by 37.1% and 28.2% respectively.

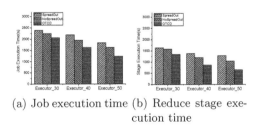

(a) Job execution time (b) Reduce stage execution time

Fig. 1. Performance comparison of different methods under Sort.

(2) Macro-benchmark

To evaluate the performance under more complex applications, we select two popular machine learning algorithms pageRank and LDA from the Spark examples for testing. Since these two applications contain one or more jobs, in which a job usually contains a lot of stages, the application execution time is used.

PageRank is a widely recognized iterative algorithm for ranking web pages according to their importance. The experiment uses 10GB data set of *WT10g* as input data, and set the parameter *numIterations* to 10 in the procedure. In the application execution, it consists of 1 job and 13 stages.

From the experimental result of Fig. 2(a), it can be seen that compared with *spreadOut* and *noSpreadOut*, *OTCD* has the shortest application execution time. In particular, when the number of executors required is 40 (i.e., Executor_40), *OTCD* reduces the application time by 41.2% and 24.6% respectively.

LDA is a document generation model in natural language processing, which identifies the hidden subjects in a large-scale documents. The experiment runs on 20GB *arXiv Bulk Data data set* and the procedure sets the parameter *maxIterations* to 20. This application is concretely executed as 26 jobs and 90 stages totally.

The experimental results illustrate that *OTCD* has a greater performance advantage than other two methods, as shown in Fig. 2(b). In particular, when the number of executors required is 50 (i.e., Executor_50), *OTCD* decreases the application time by 72.7% and 43.2% compared with *spreadOut* and *noSpread-Out*, respectively. As we can see for the application with many jobs and stages, optimizing the data locality by executor allocation in multiple reduce stages can bring a more substantial performance improvement.

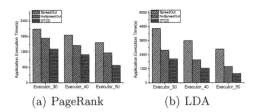

(a) PageRank   (b) LDA

Fig. 2. Performance comparison under macro-benchmark.

5   Conclusion

This paper has optimized the data locality by executor allocation for Spark framework. We propose an optimal executor allocation approximation algorithm, and the experimental results show that it can improve the data locality for lower data communication. As our future work, we intend to consider the input data distribution of each stage in the executor allocation.

Acknowledgment. The work is supported by the Doctoral Research Startup Foundation of University of South China (No. 200XQD083).

References

1. Shabeera, T.P., Kumar, S.D.M.: A novel approach for improving data locality of mapreduce applications in cloud environment through intelligent data placement. Int. J. Serv. Technol. Manag. **26**(4), 323–340 (2020)
2. Cheng, L., et al.: Network-aware locality scheduling for distributed data operators in data centers. IEEE Trans. Parallel Distributed Syst. **32**(6), 1494–1510 (2021)
3. Zaharia, M., Borthakur, D., Sarma, J.S., Elmeleegy, K., Shenker, S., Stoica, I.: Delay scheduling: a simple technique for achieving locality and fairness in cluster scheduling. In: European Conference on Computer Systems, pp. 265–278 (2010)
4. Dean, J., Ghemawat, S.: Mapreduce: simplified data processing on large clusters. Commun. ACM **51**, 107–113 (2008)
5. Xia, T., Wang, L., Geng, Z.: A reduce task scheduler for mapreduce with minimum transmission cost based on sampling evaluation. Int. J. Database Theory Appl. **8**, 1–10 (2015)
6. Sun, Mingming, Zhuang, Hang, Zhou, Xuehai, Lu, Kun, Li, Changlong: HPSO: prefetching based scheduling to improve data locality for mapreduce clusters. In: Sun, Xian-he, et al. (eds.) ICA3PP 2014. LNCS, vol. 8631, pp. 82–95. Springer, Cham (2014). https://doi.org/10.1007/978-3-319-11194-0_7
7. Fu, Z., Tang, Z., Yang, L., Liu, C.: An optimal locality-aware task scheduling algorithm based on bipartite graph modelling for spark applications. IEEE Trans. Parallel Distrib. Syst. **31**(10), 2406–2420 (2020)
8. Garey, M.R., Johnson, D.S.: Computers and Intractability: A Guide to the Theory of np-Completeness. W.H. Freeman & Co., San Francisco (1979)
9. Alicherry, M., Lakshman, T.V.: Optimizing data access latencies in cloud systems by intelligent virtual machine placement. In: 2013 Proceedings IEEE INFOCOM (2013)

TEFRED: A Temperature and Energy Cognizant Fault-Tolerant Real-Time Scheduler Based on Deadline Partitioning for Heterogeneous Platforms

Yanshul Sharma, Zinea Das, and Sanjay Moulik[⊠]

Indian Institute of Information Technology Guwahati, Guwahati, India
{yanshul.sharma,zinea.das,sanjay}@iiitg.ac.in

Abstract. Energy consumption and peak temperatures on MPSoCs are growing exponentially as transistor density increases, rendering systems unstable. Thus, in modern real-time systems, fault-tolerance is an essential design feature. This paper proposes TEFRED, a heuristic scheduling strategy that addresses the problem of controlling energy and peak temperature levels simultaneously on systems with two types of cores while remaining resistant to transient faults. Our experimental results demonstrate that TEFRED can save considerable energy and lower core peak temperatures compared to a state-of-the-art energy-efficient fault-tolerant scheduler.

Keywords: Heterogeneous · Fault-tolerant · Temperature · Energy

1 Introduction

Real-time systems are widely employed in high-risk sectors such as automobiles, aviation, and even medicine. The applications executing in such systems tend to have high demand, which led to the deployment of such systems from single to multicore platforms a decade ago. In homogenous multicore platforms, general-purpose cores cannot deliver the degree of efficacy afforded by heterogeneous multicore platforms. This is because heterogeneous architectures are made up of various types of cores, each of which is suited for a particular set of activities. Due to this reason, every task will need a different duration to finish on other cores. Hence, the preparation of task schedules is more challenging on heterogeneous multicore platforms.

As real-time systems are prone to failure, fault-tolerance is essential for such systems. Faults can be permanent, transient, or intermittent. We focus on transient faults in this paper, which have risen exponentially over time as transistor density, frequency, temperature, and other factors have increased. *Standby-sparing* is a commonly used technique for fault-tolerance. Each task has two copies: the primary copy runs on the primary core, while the backup copy runs only if the first copy fails (as determined by an acceptance test).

© Springer Nature Switzerland AG 2022
H. Shen et al. (Eds.): PDCAT 2021, LNCS 13148, pp. 358–366, 2022.
https://doi.org/10.1007/978-3-030-96772-7_33

The power density of MPSoCs has increased dramatically as the level of amalgamation on the chips has increased. In [14], the authors presented an energy cognizant scheduling strategy for tasks given as Directed Acyclic Graphs (DAGs) on a heterogeneous platform with two types of cores that can handle at most one transient fault per task and one permanent processor fault at the same time. The authors have suggested work for energy management and fault-tolerance while preserving service-level in mixed-criticality multicore systems in [15]. They utilized the task replication technique to handle failures and a variety of execution modes to keep the service quality high. In [4], the system chooses temporal redundancy and/or spatial redundancy approaches to achieve their aim. The slacks in task execution times are used to reduce energy usage. The rise in power density of SoCs is closely connected to their rising temperatures, which plays a crucial role in degrading the regular operation of these systems, rendering them unreliable. Interconnect latency rises by roughly 5% for every 10 °C increase in temperature, while MOS-current driving capability drops by around 4% [13]. Due to timing breaches, this results in transient faults. The authors presented a MILP framework for separate scheduling activities on a heterogeneous platform in [18]. A MILP solver requires an exponential amount of time to solve problems with more granularity. As a result, they devised a two-stage heuristic that included task allocation to clusters and task replication, followed by task assignment to cores and frequency selection while preserving reliability and temperature restrictions. In [8], the authors looked at the power consumption of tasks on a heterogeneous platform, as well as the removal or decrease of waiting times for tasks that shared the same successor task. In [16], two heuristic techniques were devised: the leakage-aware workload stabilizing strategy and the temperature management strategy. They employed the variable-sized bin packing approach for task partitioning to ensure adequate resource usage under energy and temperature restrictions.

Although numerous studies address the challenge of energy-efficient scheduling for fault-tolerant real-time systems on homogeneous multicore architecture, just a few use heterogeneous multicore architecture. Furthermore, no previous research has combined thermal control and energy efficiency for fault-tolerant real-time systems. Hence, we propose a heuristic-based scheduler named TEFRED, which performs thermal and power management in fault-tolerant heterogeneous multicore platforms with two types of cores. As we would like to think, the proposed strategy fits precisely to the platforms that have cores with different micro-architectures but have identical ISA, like Helio X20 ® or big.LITTLE ®.

2   Specifications

System Model: We have contemplated a set of n periodic tasks $\Gamma = \{\tau_1, \tau_2, \ldots, \tau_n\}$ to be scheduled on a heterogeneous processing platform Π which uses two types of cores: $\{\Pi^{LP}$ for power efficiency, and $\Pi^{HP}\}$ for performance. Each of the core type comprises of r cores, where j^{th} core of type Π^m is denoted as Π_j^m. It may be noted that we already have such processing platforms in market. Each occurrence of a periodic task τ_i is associated with a tuple $< exec_i^{LP}, exec_i^{HP} >$ (execution requirements on respective core types at maximum frequency), deadline/period d_i, a tuple $< tss_i^{LP}, tss_i^{HP} >$ (steady-state temperatures on respective core types), a tuple $< u_i^{LP}, u_i^{HP} >$ (utilization w.r.t. LP and HP cores). The steady-state temperature of a task on a core is defined as the maximum temperature attained by the core when the same task is run on it for an infinitely long time, possibly with multiple instances. We assume implicit task deadlines. Every task set is characterized by a parameter called Utilization Factor (UF), which gives a measure of resource utilization corresponding to the given task set.

Power Model: We have used the analytical core energy model given in [10]. For our system, the dynamic power consumption $P \propto fv^2$; where f is the operating frequency and v is the supply voltage. Again, the supply voltage is linearly proportional to the operating frequency. Hence, $P = cf^3$; where c is the constant of proportionality. For efficient power management, we have employed Dynamic Power Management (DPM). This energy-saving mechanism minimizes static power consumption by switching the core to sleep mode when it is idle.

Thermal and Fault Model: The thermal model used in our work is based on [12]. For an interval $[t_0, t_e]$ in which τ_i is executing on the core Π_j^m, if the core temperature is Γ_0 at time t_0, the temperature Γ_e at the end of the interval at time t_e is given by: $\Gamma_e^m = tss_i^{\Pi_j^m} + (\Gamma_0 - tss_i^{\Pi_j^m})e^{-B(t_e-t_0)}$, where B is a constant depending upon power consumption in the system.

We have used the standby-sparing system, where each task has two copies, primary and backup. The primary copy of a task is scheduled on the LP core, while the backup copy is scheduled on the HP cores. Whenever a primary copy completes its execution, acceptance or sanity tests [6] is done to check if any transient fault occurred. If yes, then the backup copy is executed on the HP core. Otherwise, the backup copy is deallocated from the HP core. This system works on the assumption that each task can undergo fault at most once, and there can be at most q transient faults per frame, where a frame is a group of time-slots into which the execution in a system can be divided.

Algorithm 1: TEFRED

Input: Set of tasks Γ, Set of cores Π, Number of transient faults q
Output: Energy and Temperature aware Fault-Tolerant Schedule
1 Let $\{\tau_1, \tau_2, \ldots, \tau_n\}$ be set of ready tasks
2 Compute average steady-state temperature, $tss_{avg} = \sum_{i=1}^{n}(tss_i^{LP})/n$
3 **while** *true* **do**
4   Using *deadline-partitioning*, compute next frame (say k^{th}) R_k
5   Compute shares required by each task on LP and HP cores at R_k
6      $core^{LP}$=ASSIGN-TO-LP-CORES (Γ, tss_{avg})
7      $core^{HP}$=ASSIGN-TO-HP-CORES (Γ)

---

3   Proposed Scheduling Scheme

TEFRED works in three phases to prepare a schedule for a set of real-time periodic tasks Γ on a heterogeneous platform Π comprising of two types of cores. In the first phase, it uses *deadline partitioning* to compute the set of frames [11]. The second phase assigns tasks to the power-efficient cores while controlling the excessive rise in its peak temperature using an efficient temperature-aware heuristic. The third phase creates a heuristic schedule for tasks in the backup cores by slot reservation for possible transient faults.

TEFRED (Algorithm 1): It starts by computing the next frame using a mechanism called *deadline partitioning* [11]. Then within the ensuing frame, it computes the shares of each task τ_i on both *LP* and *HP* cores using the following equation: $shr_i^m = \lceil u_i^m \times |R_k| \rceil$, where m is one of $\{HP, LP\}$, $u_i^m = exec_i^m/d_i$ and $|R_k|$ denotes the size of the ensuing frame R_k. It calls Algorithm 2 to get the task schedule on the power-efficient cores. Finally, it calls Algorithm 3 to get the reserved slots in case of faults.

Algorithm 2: ASSIGN-TO-LP-CORES

   Input: Set of tasks Γ, tss_{avg}^{LP}
   Output: Task schedule on LP core $(core^{LP})$
1 Set $L_{hot} = \emptyset$, $L_{cool} = \emptyset$ and $core^{LP} = \emptyset$
2 **for** *each task Γ_i* **do**
3   **if** $(tss_i^{LP} > tss_{avg}^{LP})$ **then** Add Γ_i to L_{hot}
4   **else** Add Γ_i to L_{hot} sorted in non-increasing order of tss_i^{LP}
5 **while** $L_{hot} \neq \phi$ *and $L_{cool} \neq \phi$* **do**
6   Extract task Γ_i from the front of L_{hot} and add it to the end of $core^{LP}$
7   Extract task Γ_i from the front of L_{cool} and add it to the end of $core^{LP}$
8 **if** $(L_{hot} = \phi)$ **then** Add all tasks from front of L_{cool} to the end of $core^{LP}$
9 **else** Add all tasks from front of L_{hot} to the end of $core^{LP}$
10 Schedule $core^{LP}$ onto LP cores using McNaughtons's wrap around rule

---

ASSIGN-TO-LP-CORES (Algorithm 2): Firstly, it initializes empty lists L_{hot}, L_{cool} and $core^{LP}$. Consider each task τ_i in the task set Γ and assign it either to L_{hot} or L_{cool} on the basis of the thumb rule that if its steady-state temperature (tss_i^{LP}) is greater than the average steady-state temperature of the task set (tss_{avg}), then assign it to the hot list L_{hot}, else assign it to the cool list L_{cool}. The hot list must contain tasks in the non-increasing order of tss_i^{LP}, and the cool list must contain tasks in the non-decreasing order of tss_i^{LP}. Once these two lists are formed, extract the hottest task and the coolest task from the hot list and cool list alternatively and assign them to the third list $core^{LP}$. At last, McNaughtons's wrap-around rule [9] is applied on $core^{LP}$ to schedule the tasks on available LP cores. McNaughton's wrap-around rule helps to prepare an optimal schedule for tasks on a homogeneous multicore platform. Since we are assigning primary copies of tasks on the same core type, i.e., LP, we have used the wrap-around rule to prepare the final schedule.

ASSIGN-TO-HP-CORES (Algorithm 3): In the considered platform, there are equal number of LP and HP cores, which makes the platform suitable for *backup-overloading* [5] technique. Since for each task, we have two shares, i.e., on LP cores and HP cores in a frame, when a task has been allotted to the core Π_j^{LP} for a certain time interval, the exact proportionate workload for the task has to be allotted on the corresponding Π_j^{HP}. For each core, Π_j^{HP} in Π^{HP}, the algorithm creates a list *eList* of all tasks in non-increasing order of their shares on the core Π_j^{HP}. Then it finds the sum of the first q shares from *eList* and calls this sum *backup_slots*. Finally, it assigns this contiguous series of slots as late as possible in the current frame to cancel their execution on the HP core if the corresponding primary copies are successfully executed on the LP core. The algorithm overlaps q tasks in the *backup_slots*, thus following the non-work-conserving strategy of backup overloading. Since we have reserved backup slots equivalent to the sum of q tasks having the highest shares, the HP core will utilize all of these slots only in the worst case. In most cases, some slots in these *backup_slots* will remain idle when the corresponding tasks in the LP core have been successfully executed.

Algorithm 3: ASSIGN-TO-HP-CORES

Input: Set of tasks Γ, Number of transient faults q
Output: Reserved slot schedule on HP core

1   **for** $j = 1 : r$ *in* Π^{HP} **do**
2   Create list *eList* of all tasks in non-increasing order of their share on Π_j^{HP}.
3   Initialize *backup_slots* $= 0$
4   **for** $i = 1 : q$ *in eList* **do**
5         $backup\_slots = backup\_slots + exec_i^{HP}$
6   Reserve *backup_slots* number of slots as late in the frame as possible

7   **return** reserved slot schedule on HP core

---

4   Experimental Set Up and Results

We have implemented the *TEFRED* algorithm and compared it against the following two algorithms based on homogeneous multicore platforms: i. A homogeneous version of *TEFRED* named *TEFRED-HM*, and ii. An energy-efficient fault-tolerant scheduler named *FEED-O* [1]. We will use *TEFRED-HET* to refer to our proposed strategy for heterogeneous platforms from now onwards. To the best of our knowledge, no work focusing on fault-tolerance coupled with temperature and energy management has been done yet. As temperature is also an essential aspect of our work, we have compared the performance of *TEFRED-HET* against *TEFRED-HM*, which focuses on fault-tolerance, energy, and temperature; and *FEED-O*, which focuses on fault-tolerance and energy.

Table 1. Task specifications for benchmark programs

Program	Execution requirement (in ms)	Steady state temperature (in °C)	Program	Execution requirement (in ms)	Steady state temperature (in °C)
Bodytrack	3824	85	Canneal	1007	80
Dedup	6455	91	Fluidanimate	4090	81
Freqmine	11082	84	Stream	6156	68
Swaptions	4535	76	Blackscholes	1203	85

All our simulations have been run for a total execution time of 100000 time slots with task sets having pre-specified *utilization factors* or *system workload*. For each set of input parameters, the average of the 50 simulations has been considered the outcome. The PARSEC [2] benchmark suite (with a large input set) has been used by us to substantiate efficiencies of the algorithms over different real-life scenarios that may arise Table 1. For all the experiments, we have taken $n = 20$ by selecting tasks from the 8 benchmark applications (with some tasks repeated in the set to form the taskset of size 20). We received periodic performance traces from Gem5 [3] simulator for an 8-core based heterogeneous chip-multiprocessor (considering 32 nm CMOS technology), where each of the faster 4 Out-of-Order cores can operate at a frequency of 3.0 GHz, and each of the 4 smaller In-Order cores can have a frequency of 1.8 GHz. We have used *DPM* for efficient energy consumption. Note that, for each of our cores (both in-order and out-of-order), we have considered Alpha 21364 ISA. For complete periodic performance-power-thermal analysis, we integrated gem5 [3], McPAT-monolithic [7], and HotSpot 6.0 [17] simulators are adopted.

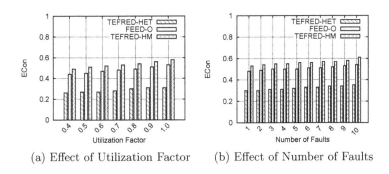

(a) Effect of Utilization Factor   (b) Effect of Number of Faults

Fig. 1. Effect on energy consumption

Experimental Results: We have performed a set of extensive simulation-based experiments to gauge the efficiency of the algorithms.

Experiment 1: We varied *UF* from 0.4 to 1.0, and the number of transient faults to be handled by the system per frame was fixed at 10. Figure 1a shows that with the increase in *UF*, *ECon* values increase. It is because with the increase in *UF* (based on only the primary cores), the idle time of the HP cores with DPM capability decrease, which leads to higher energy consumption. However, *TEFRED-HET* can outperform *TEFRED-HM* and *FEED-O* because the latter algorithms are oblivious to the heterogeneity of the cores and choose the cores for backup-overloading randomly. In contrast, *TEFRED-HET* compensates *ECon* by assigning all tasks to the *LP* cores. It can be observed from Fig. 1a that the values of ECon vary from 0.26 to 0.31, 0.44 to 0.53, and 0.49 to 0.58 for *TEFRED-HET*, *FEED-O*, and *TEFRED-HM* with the variation in UF values, respectively.

Experiment 2: We varied the number of faults q from 1 to 10 at $UF = 0.6$. It can be observed from Fig. 1b that q is directly proportional to *ECon* because the number of backup slots on the *backup cores* increase with q. Also, each failed task running on a *HP* core requires higher energy consumption than the same on *LP* core. Hence, the *ECon* values are quite lesser for *TEFRED-HET* as compared to *TEFRED-HM* and *FEED-O*. It can be observed from Fig. 1b that the values of *ECon* vary from 0.3 to 0.35, 0.48 to 0.54, and 0.53 to 0.61 for *TEFRED-HET*, *FEED-O*, and *TEFRED-HM* with the variation in q values, respectively.

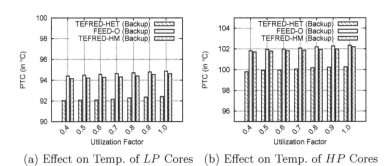

(a) Effect on Temp. of *LP* Cores   (b) Effect on Temp. of *HP* Cores

Fig. 2. Effect on temperature of cores

Experiment 3: In this experiment, we have used the settings of *Experiment 1*. From Fig. 2, we observe that the PTC values of primary and backup cores increase with *UF*. It is because as the workload of the core increases with an increase in *UF*, the core gets lesser time to cool down and hence showcases higher peak temperatures. The temperature-aware heuristic strategy in *TEFRED-HET* and *TEFRED-HM* achieves efficient PTC values because they schedule hot and cool tasks alternatively. However, task-to-core assignments are more efficient in *TEFRED-HET* with respect to *TEFRED-HM*. As *TEFRED-HM* also chooses random cores for task-assignment, it leads to lesser efficient scheduling and higher temperature on cores.

5   Conclusion

In this paper, we propose a *fault-tolerant* heuristic scheduling mechanism, *TEFRED-HET*, which successfully schedules tasks meeting their implicit deadlines. It outperforms *TEFRED-HM* which is a homogeneous version of *TEFRED-HET* and a state-of-the-art fault-tolerant energy-aware scheduler for homogeneous platforms named *FEED-O*. The proposed algorithm adopts the *DPM* technique for minimization of static energy consumption and reserves only necessary backup slots for a known number of maximum possible transient faults. *TEFRED-HET* also utilizes the difference in steady-state temperatures of the tasks to achieve the remarkable reduction in peak temperatures of the system.

References

1. Bansal, S., Bansal, R.K., Arora, K.: Energy efficient backup overloading schemes for fault tolerant scheduling of real-time tasks. J. Syst. Architect. **113**, 101901 (2021)
2. Bienia, C., Kumar, S., Singh, J.P., Li, K.: The PARSEC benchmark suite: characterization and architectural implications. In: International Conference on Parallel Architectures and Compilation Techniques, pp. 72–81 (2008)
3. Binkert, N., et al.: The gem5 simulator. ACM SIGARCH Comput. Archit. News **39**(2), 1–7 (2011)
4. Chatterjee, N., Paul, S., Chattopadhyay, S.: Task mapping and scheduling for network-on-chip based multi-core platform with transient faults. J. Syst. Architect. **83**, 34–56 (2018)
5. Ghosh, S., Melhem, R., Mosse, D.: Fault-tolerant scheduling on a hard real-time multiprocessor system. In: International Parallel Processing Symposium, pp. 775–782. IEEE (1994)
6. Koren, I., Krishna, C.M.: Fault-Tolerant Systems. Elsevier, Cambridge (2010)
7. Li, S., Ahn, J.H., Strong, R.D., Brockman, J.B., Tullsen, D.M., Jouppi, N.P.: McPAT: an integrated power, area, and timing modeling framework for multicore and manycore architectures. In: IEEE/ACM International Symposium on Microarchitecture, pp. 469–480 (2009)
8. Li, T., Zhang, T., Yu, G., Song, J., Fan, J.: Minimizing temperature and energy of real-time applications with precedence constraints on heterogeneous MPSoC systems. J. Syst. Architect. **98**, 79–91 (2019)
9. McNaughton, R.: Scheduling with deadlines and loss functions. Manage. Sci. **6**(1), 1–12 (1959)
10. Moulik, S., Devaraj, R., Sarkar, A.: HEALERS: a heterogeneous energy-aware low-overhead real-time scheduler. IET Comput. Digit. Tech. **13**(6), 470–480 (2019)
11. Moulik, S., Sarkar, A., Kapoor, H.K.: Energy aware frame based fair scheduling. Sustain. Comput. Inform. Syst. **18**, 66–77 (2018)
12. Moulik, S., Sarkar, A., Kapoor, H.K.: TARTS: a temperature-aware real-time deadline-partitioned fair scheduler. J. Syst. Architect. **112**, 101847 (2021)
13. Narayanan, V., Xie, Y.: Reliability concerns in embedded system designs. Computer **39**(1), 118–120 (2006)

14. Roy, A., Aydin, H., Zhu, D.: Energy-efficient fault tolerance for real-time tasks with precedence constraints on heterogeneous multicore systems. In: International Green and Sustainable Computing Conference, pp. 1–8. IEEE (2019)
15. Safari, S., Ansari, M., Ershadi, G., Hessabi, S.: On the scheduling of energy-aware fault-tolerant mixed-criticality multicore systems with service guarantee exploration. IEEE Trans. Parallel Distrib. Syst. **30**(10), 2338–2354 (2019)
16. Sha, S., Wen, W., Chaparro-Baquero, G.A., Quan, G.: Thermal-constrained energy efficient real-time scheduling on multi-core platforms. Parallel Comput. **85**, 231–242 (2019)
17. Stan, M.R., Zhang, R., Skadron, K.: Hotspot 6.0: Validation, acceleration and extension (2015)
18. Zhou, J., et al.: Reliability and temperature constrained task scheduling for makespan minimization on heterogeneous multi-core platforms. J. Syst. Softw. **133**, 1–16 (2017)

Algorithms and Applications

Social Recommendation via Graph Attentive Aggregation

Yuanwei Liufu and Hong Shen$^{(\boxtimes)}$

Sun Yat-sen University, GuangZhou, China
liufyw@mail2.sysu.edu.cn, shenh3@mail.sysu.edu.cn

Abstract. Recommender systems play an important role in helping users discover items of interest from a large resource collection in various online services. Although deep graph neural network-based collaborative filtering methods have achieved promising performance in recommender systems, they are still some weaknesses. Firstly, existing graph neural network methods only take user-item interactions into account neglecting direct user-user interactions which can be obtained from social networks. Secondly, they treat the observed data uniformly without considering fine-grained differences in importance or relevance in the user-item interactions. In this paper, we propose a novel graph neural network social graph attentive aggregation (SGA) which is suitable for parallel training to boost efficiency which is the common bottleneck for neural network deployed machine learning models. This model obtains user-user collaborative information from social networks and utilizes self-attention mechanism to model the differentiation of importance in the user-item interactions. We conduct experiments on two real-world datasets and the results demonstrate that our method is effective and can be trained in parallel efficiently.

Keywords: Recommendation system · Social recommendation · Graph neural network · Parallel computing

1 Introduction

Recommender systems have been studied to resolve the issue of information overload in various fields during the past decades, such as products-to-customer recommendation in e-commerce platforms and people-to-people recommendation in social networks, etc. Collaborative filtering (CF), which assumes that two users with similar behaviors may show similar interests in items, is a class of widely-used personalized recommender systems based on the user-item interaction data such as purchases and clicks.

Thanks to the strong capability of Graph Neural Networks (GNNs) [5] in representing graph data, there is an increasing number of studies utilizing GNNs [8,23,25] to learn representations in CF, yielding promising performance gains. Our model is mainly based on Neural Graph Collaborative Filtering (NGCF) [23] which regards user-item interactions as a bipartite graph structure and use graph aggregation techniques to capture collaborative information.

© Springer Nature Switzerland AG 2022
H. Shen et al. (Eds.): PDCAT 2021, LNCS 13148, pp. 369–382, 2022.
https://doi.org/10.1007/978-3-030-96772-7_34

Despite the effectiveness of NGCF, we argue that traditional CF models often suffer from the sparsity problem [1] so as NGCF. For example, users usually give feedbacks on a very small proportion of items with the same preference intensity level. And thus there's no sufficient data to build the models. An easy way to solve this problem is to take into consideration more information.

Besides user-item interactions, social recommender system take social relations among users (user-user interactions) into account to model user' preferences. As shown in social theories, people are easily influenced by their friends in the same social community. And thus people in social neighbors tend to have similar preference [2,7,8] We notice that considering direct user-user interaction in CF obtained from social relation among users can bring a great amount of semantic information and collaborative information in the recommender system.

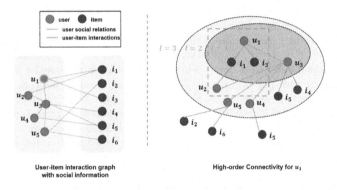

Fig. 1. An example of the proposed graph model and the high-order connectivity with social information

The graph structure with direct user-user interaction information is illustrated in Fig. 1. The user to be analyzed in this recommender system is u_1 that is highlighted with double circle in the left sub-figure. The right sub-figure shows the hierarchical structure expanded from u_1 where l is the distance of the node to u_1. In the right sub-figure, the collaborative information is related to the distance of node. For example the distance between u_1 and i_1 is 1 ($u_1 \rightarrow i_1$) while the distance between u_1 and i_4 is 2 ($u_1 \rightarrow u_3 \rightarrow i_4$), thus we can assume that u_1 is more likely to choose i_1 than i_4. And the distance between u_1 and u_3 is less than the distance between u_1 and u_2, which indicates that the preferences of u_1 is more similar to u_3 than u_2. From the right sub-figure, we can easily notice that without considering the social relation information, a large amount of collaborative information will be lost (only nodes framed with purple dotted lines will be left in Fig. 1). We believe that the introduction of social relations among users brings more expressive power to the model.

Unlike many GNN based social recommendations utilizing complex neural model, we use a simple yet effective way to model the interaction by encoding both items and users in the same vector space. And we also verify through experiment that our model can be easily trained in parallel.

Moreover, we argued that it's unreasonable to make the assumption that the weights of interacted items are same. For example, more attention should be paid to the baby products than the other products when someone has bought a diapers, as there might be a newly born baby in his family. Self-attention mechanisms [21] which is able to assign learnable importances for neighbors during embedding aggregation.

To summarize, the main contributions of this paper include:

- We show that social relation is important to be considered in Graph Neural Network for CF and propose a novel graph neural network with graph aggregation techniques.
- We propose a new GNN layer of social graph attentive aggregation (SGA) with self-attention mechanism to capture fine-grained modeling of user-item interaction and user-user interaction.
- We demonstrate that our model can obtain promising result on various real-world datasets and be efficiently trained in parallel.

2 Related Work

In this section, we mainly take a view of existing work on Graph-based CF (i.e. social recommendation and attention mechanism).

2.1 Graph-Based CF

This line of studies often regard users and items as nodes and interactions between them as the edges and thus build the bipartite user-item interaction graph. Then a variety of graph-based methods are used to get the embeddings of users and items. With the embedding information, we can utilize interaction modeling methods to reconstruct the historical interactions or predict the future interactions.

Owing to the popularity of GNNs nowadays, a great number of studies on graph-based recommender system has been proposed. GC-MC [3] may be the first research with GNNs. It utilizes a GAE [15] framework with GCN as encoder and bilinear decoder for the matrix completion task which regards the recommendation task as a link prediction problem in bipartite graphs. However, it mainly focuses on user ratings predicting task which requires ratings as side-information. And it's very time-consuming and thus not suitable for using in CF with large-scale datasets. The closest work to ours is NGCF done by Wang *et al.* [23]. The NGCF model use GCN to obtain high-order collaborative information in the user-item bipartite graph. However, as we discuss above, it neglect the social relation among users which contain a lot of collaborative information. Moreover, attention mechanism and the order information of user-item interactions could be considered to improve model expression.

2.2   Social Recommendation

Thanks to the popularity of social platforms, the exploitation of social relation information has drawn a lot of attention of reseachers. Considering user-user interaction, social recommendation tend to be a promising method to alleviate the data sparsity issue which often occurs in the former CF model. The general idea of social recommendation is that similar users would have similar preferences and thus have similar latent embeddings. Early proposed models are mainly based on matrix factorization. SR2 [17] obtains social embedding by regularizing latent user factors to force the connected user in social relation graph close to each other. SBPR [27] is based on BP [20] that considers social pair-wise information and it tends to assign higher ratings to the items that his friends may prefer. There are also some studies to consider other side-information in social network to construct the model. For example, TrustSVD [9], ContextMF [13], PTPMF [24] consider trust influence, social context and the strength of social ties, respectively. However, all the models discussed above were only based on shallow models which only considerate one-hop relations in social network. Instead of only considering the direct social relation of the users, our model differs from these works in using GNN to capturing the high-order social information.

2.3   Attention

To enable fine-grained modeling of user-item interactions and user-user interactions, our model relies on the neural attention mechanism, which have been widely applied in the domains of natural language processing [21] and computer vision [19]. For recommender systems, several studies attempt to employ attention-based memory networks to capture complex and fine-grained user-item interactions in CF [6]. Additional side information such as texts [29] and heterogeneous relations [28] can also be integrated into the memory network. However, they only still center around user-item interactions. In contrast, our model also considers direct user-user interactions which captures fine-grained high-order contexts. And the methods above mostly considerate one-hop semantic information only while our layerwise aggregation model can capture multi-hop semantic information.

3   Methodology

In this section, we will introduce our social graph attentive aggregation (SGA) model for social recommendation via graph attentive aggregation in detail. An overview of the proposed framework is demonstrated in Fig. 2. It consists of three components: (1) pre-trained embedding layer, which parameterizes each user and item into low-dimension dense vector preserving their interaction information. (2) multiple graph aggregation layers, which can aggregate both social relations among users and interactions between users and items. (3) preference prediction, which integrate the user and item embedding and output their proximity score to make proper recommendation.

3.1   Pre-trained Embedding Layer

Many neural-based recommendation systems based on collaborative filtering parameterize each user and item into latent embeddings [11,12,20]. In these models, users and items are represented by dense low-dimension vectors that encode items similarity and user preferences. By learning the representation of users and items in advance, we can use simple operations to get the preference score. The interaction matrix is usually used to train the embeddings, which is a $0, 1$ matrix R where R_{ij} indicates the ith user is related to the jth item, i.e., user has some interaction with the item. Since we refine the embeddings by aggregating information from user-item interaction graph and user social user graph, it's useful to utilize the embeddings of users and items trained by previous methods that have been proved efficient and effective to get better performance. In our experiments we use the initial interaction matrix as the pre-trained embeddings.

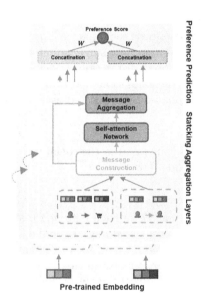

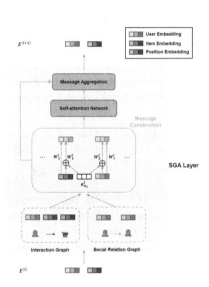

Fig. 2. Multiple SGA layers   **Fig. 3.** A single SGA layer

3.2   Graph Attentive Aggregation Layer

We will start by introducing the building blocks of a single graph attentive aggregation layer (Fig. 3), as the single layer is utilized throughout the framework and model how information flows and aggregates in social recommendation graph. The ultimate model can therefore be built by stacking multiple graph attentive aggregation layer followed by a point-wise non-linearity, through which we can explore high-order interactions among users and items.

First-Order Aggregation. In graph theory, the connected nodes in graph are likely to share the same property [14]. By incorporating and aggregating node features in learning algorithm, graph neural network could explicitly learn the topological structure of each nodes' neighborhood (the first-order proximity) as well as the distribution of node features in the neighborhood [10]. Traditionally, many previous graph aggregation based recommender systems treat data as bipartite graph [23]. The user preferences can be inferred by interacted items, and the collaborative similarity of items is measured by the users who consume them. From a graph aggregation prospective, user's embedding could only propagate to items, vice versa.

However, intuitively the social relations can influence users' behaviors. Some people may choose some items they've never bought before after friends' strong recommendation, which motivates the consideration of feature aggregation among users when we describe users in a graph aggregation way. We build upon this basis to perform graph aggregation operation on each connected users and user-item interactions. In a composite graph including user social relations and user-item interactions, we can simultaneously encode each node's first-order proximity with different types of node, i.e. user and item, into single latent space by aggregating the neighborhood information without distinction. Specifically, in each layer all user nodes will be updated by their adjacent nodes including user and items nodes, while all item nodes are updated by connected user nodes as there no relations among item nodes.

Message Construction. For a connected node pair (u, v) in the social recommendation graph, we define the message from node v to u as:

$$\mathbf{M}_{(u,v)} = f(\mathbf{e}_u, \mathbf{e}_v), \tag{1}$$

where $\mathbf{M} \in \mathbf{R}^{N \times N \times d}$ is the message embedding matrix for each pair (u, v), and $f(\cdot)$ is the message encoding function, which takes two embeddings, $\mathbf{e}_u$ and $\mathbf{e}_v$, as inputs and outputs a embedding of the same dimension. It can be implemented by simple element-wise multiplication or Multi Layer Perceptron (MLP) or any other transformation. Here our implementation of $f(\cdot)$ is the same as the model in [23]:

$$\mathbf{M}_{(u,v)} = \frac{1}{\sqrt{|\mathcal{N}_u| |\mathcal{N}_v|}} \Big(\mathbf{W}_1 \mathbf{e}_v + \mathbf{W}_2 (\mathbf{e}_u \odot \mathbf{e}_v) \Big), u \neq v, \tag{2}$$

where $\mathbf{W}_1, \mathbf{W}_2 \in \mathbb{R}^{d' \times d}$ are two trainable linear transformations that are used to extract features for later aggregation. The term $\mathbf{e}_v \odot \mathbf{e}_v$ is used to encode the interaction on each dimension, where $\odot$ denotes the element-wise product. This term is more expressive to encode node pair affinity, followed by a fully connected layer. The term $\mathbf{W}_1 \mathbf{e}_v$ could retain the initial information from neighborhoods, acting like skip-connection [11] to some extents. It can improve model's capacity while avoiding the twisting of data, thus promote the generalization performance of the model.

After the joint transformation for pair (u, v), we use the graph Laplacian normalization factor $1/\sqrt{|\mathcal{N}_u| |\mathcal{N}_v|}$ to normalize the messages, where $|\mathcal{N}_u|$ and

$|\mathcal{N}_v|$ denotes the number of first-order neighbors of the node u and v, respectively. Without this Laplacian normalizing factor, the high-degree nodes will receive superabundant messages in the graph aggregation process, which breaks the balance of message aggregation and reduce the utility of the model.

Self-attention Layer. Self-attention is a special case of attention mechanism and has been successfully applied in graph-structure data to assign different importances to the neighborhoods of each node [22]. In the social recommendation graph, the self-attention layer is used to capture user's global dependencies on users in social relations and on items in interactions graph without regard to their distances by applying multiple aggregation.

For each node u, a shared self-attention operation $f \colon \mathbb{R}^d \times \mathbb{R}^d \to \mathbb{R}$ is performed on all the message embeddings $\mathbf{M}_{(u,v)}$ where $v \in \mathcal{N}(u)$, and outputs the attention coefficients that indicate the importance of the messages from its neighborhoods. Specifically, we first apply a shared linear transformation parametrized by a weight matrix $\mathbf{W}_a \in \mathbb{R}^{d \times d}$ to the message embeddings.

$$\mathbf{c}_{(u,v)} = f(\mathbf{M}_{(u,u)}\mathbf{W}_a, \mathbf{M}_{(u,v)}\mathbf{W}_a). \tag{3}$$

Note that we take the self-connection of u into consideration, which can be calculated by the first term in Eq. (2), as the weight matrix $\mathbf{W}_1$ is enough to represent the self-connection aggregation.

$$\mathbf{M}_{(u,u)} = \mathbf{W}_1 \mathbf{e}_u. \tag{4}$$

As we model the graph aggregation process layerwise and high-oder global dependencies could be computed by stacking aggregation layer, it's neither effective nor efficient to compute the messages and attention coefficients of all nodes with attention mechanism. Therefore, we use masked attention to preserve the first order graph structure—only compute $\mathbf{c}_{(u,v)}$ where v is u' first order neighbors.

In our experiments, the attention operation f is a simple feedforward neural network with a non-linearity activation LeakyReLU that takes the concatenation of two embeddings as inputs and outputs a single score, followed by the softmax function to nomalize the masked attention coefficients.

$$\mathbf{c}_{(u,v)} = \text{Softmax}\left(\text{LeakeyReLU}\left((\mathbf{M}_{uu}\mathbf{W}_a)(\mathbf{M}_{uv}\mathbf{W}_a)^T\right)\right). \tag{5}$$

Message Aggregation. Next we will introduce how to refine u's embedding by aggregating the messages from u's first-order neighbors. To formally describe u's representation $e_u^{(l+1)}$ after the $(l+1)^{th}$ aggregations, we use the following function as:

$$e_u^{(l+1)} = \sigma\left(\mathbf{W}_{agg} \cdot f_{agg}\left(\mathbf{M}^{(l)}, u, \mathcal{N}(u), \mathbf{c}\right) + \mathbf{b}\right), \tag{6}$$

where $\mathbf{M}^{(l)}$ denotes the message matrix in the lth aggregation, $\mathcal{N}$ and $\mathbf{c}$ denotes the set of u's neighbors and attention coefficient matrix for each connected pair, respectively. After the aggregation, we apply a single layer network parameterized by the weight $\mathbf{W}_{agg}$ and the bias $\mathbf{b}$, followed by non-linear activation function $\sigma(\cdot)$, e.g. LeakyReLU [18].

We implemented the aggregator as weighted sum pooling with self-connection, i.e.

$$f_{agg}\left(\mathbf{M}^{(l)}, u, \mathcal{N}(u), \mathbf{c}\right) = \mathbf{m}_{(u,u)} + \sum_{v \in \mathcal{N}_u, v \neq u} \mathbf{c}_{(u,v)} \mathbf{m}_{(u,v)}. \tag{7}$$

As stated previously, we take the self-connection for each node's aggregation that acts like skip-connection to retain the information of original features. Through the attentive aggregation, we can refines a user's (or an item's) embedding by considering both connected users and connected items, explicitly exploiting both the social relations and user-item dependencies.

3.3 Preference Prediction

After stacking L aggregation layers according to the complexity of the data, we obtain multiple representations for node u, namely $\{\mathbf{e}_u^{(1)}, \mathbf{e}_u^{(2)}, \cdots, \mathbf{e}_u^{(L)}\}$. Each representation captures the dependencies between u and its direct neighborhoods (i.e. social influences among users and user preferences for items).

In order to promote the model performance, we apply skip connections to concatenate the multiple representations for each node. Finally, a shared fully-connected layer is used in case of sparsity and the curse of dimensionality. As such, we not only enrich the pre-trained embeddings with several aggregation layers but also allow controlling the aggregation level by changing L, thus could promote the generalization performance regardless of graph complexity. Typically, we use the average degree of nodes in the social recommendation graph as the reference for selecting L.

Next we will build our recommender system to learn the model parameters. With the representations of all users and items, we can conduct the simple inner product to estimate the user's preference for the target item. For the loss function, we choose the pairwise BPR loss [20] to optimize the model:

$$Loss = \sum_{(u,i,j) \in (O)} -\ln \sigma(\hat{y}_{ui} - \hat{y}_{uj}) + \lambda \|\Theta\|_2^2 \tag{8}$$

where $\mathcal{O} = \{(u,i,j)|(u,i) \in A^+, (u,j) \in A^-\}$ denotes the pairwise training data while $\hat{y}_{ui}$ denotes user u's preference for item i, A^+ is the set of connected pairs in the composite social recommendation graph, A^- indicates the pair without connection that is usually obtained by sampling. $\lambda \|\Theta\|_2^2$ is the L_2 regularization term to control the capacity of the model.

4   Experiment

In this section, we detail our experimental setup. We describe the experimental datasets in Sect. 4.1. Baselines and evaluation metrics are given in Sect. 4.2 and

Sect. 4.3, respectively. Training and parameter settings are in Sect. 4.4. Finally, we report our experimental results by comparing the overallperformance and efficiency of the proposed model and the baseline models in Sect. 4.5.

4.1 Dataset

We conduct experiments on the two real-world datasets: Last.FM and Gowalla, the detail information of which are described as follows.

- **Last.fm** [4]: It contains music artist listening records of 2K users from Last.fm online music systems[1]. The artists are viewed as items in this dataset. In order to ensure the dataset quality, we use the 10-core setting, i.e., only retaining users and items with at least ten interactions.
- **Gowalla** [16]: It is a location-based social network datasets where users can share their locations by checking-in. In this dataset, we treat locations as items and predict the user-location interaction. We use the datasets published by wang et al. [23] in our experiments.

4.2 Baselines

To demonstrate the effectiveness of the proposed model, we compare our model with the following baseline methods.

- **MF** [20]: It is a matrix factorization methods based on the implict feedback of user-item interactions. The method is optimized with Bayesian personalized ranking(BPR) loss, which can be viewed as a maximum posterior estimator derived from the Bayesian formulation of the problem.
- **GC-MC** [3]: It is a collaborative filtering method based on Graph convolution network [14]. The method views the user-item interactions as a bipartite graph and use a graph auto-encoder framework to learn the representations of users and items.
- **HOP-Rec** [26]: It is a unified method of factorization and graph models that captures high-order information within a user-item interaction matrix. The high-order information is obtained with random walks on the graph and is used to enrich the user-item interaction data.
- **NGCF** [23]: It is a graph-based collaborative filtering methods that learns embeddings of users and items by leveraging high-order connectivities in the user-item interaction bipartite graph.

4.3 Evaluation Metrics

To evaluate the performance of the proposed model, we adopt precision@k, recall@k and ndcg@k as evaluation metrics which are detailed as follows:

---

[1] http://www.lastfm.com/.

Precision@k is the fraction of top-k retrieved items that are relevant to user's preference, i.e., items appearing in the test set of the user. It can be calculated by:

$$\text{Precision@}K = \frac{d}{k}, \tag{9}$$

where d is the number of relevant items in the top-k retrieved items.

Recall@k is the fraction of items that are relevant to user's preference that are successfully retrieved in top-k results, which can be calculated by:

$$\text{Recall@K} = \frac{d}{n}, \tag{10}$$

where n is the total number of relevant items of the user.

Ndcg@k is a widely used measure in retrieval task performance evaluation. The main idea is that highly relevant items should appear earlier in the retrieved results, i.e., lower ranks. It assign each items a graded relevance and penalize high relevant items appearing latter in the retrieved results. The range of ndcg@k is [0, 1] with higher value representing better performance.

In our experiment we set $k = 20$ and report the average metrics for all users in the test set.

4.4   Parameter Settings

In our experiments, the number of hidden layers is set to 3 with the number of hidden units in each layer set to 64 and we fix the size of embeddings of users and items to 64 as well. The model is implemented using tensorflow.

4.5   Experiment Results

We compare performance of different methods by performing item retrieval task, whose goal is to retrieval the most relevant items given a user. Specifically, given a user, we calculate the relevance scores with items that do not appear in the training set of the user and rank them accordingly. Then we calculate the evaluation metrics described in Sect. 4.3.

Table 1. Overall performance (k = 20).

Method	Last.fm			Gowalla		
	Precision	Recall	ndcg	Precision	Recall	ndcg
MF	0.0492	0.2265	0.2598	0.3987	0.1291	0.1878
GC-MC	0.0531	0.2368	0.2577	0.0431	0.1395	0.1960
HOP-Rec	0.0587	0.2401	0.2601	**0.0512**	0.1399	0.2128
NGCF	0.0668	0.2457	0.2687	0.0478	0.1547	0.2237
Ours	**0.0712**	**0.2497**	**0.2723**	0.0489	**0.1601**	**0.2294**

The overall performance of the proposed model and the baselines are given in Table 1, from which we obtain the following results:

- Compared with MF, GC-MC, which treats the user-item interactions as bipartite graph and aggregates feature of neighbors to lean embeddings of users and items, achieves better results. HOP-Rec and NGCF, which considers higher order interactions between entities, also gets better performance. The result indicates that the complex relations between users and items can be better captured by aggregating features of higher order neighbors.
- The proposed model achieved best performance on Last.fm dataset and has the best performance in terms of recall@k and ndcg@k on Gowalla dataset. The results indicate the effectiveness of the proposed attentive layer. This can be explained that our proposed model is not only able to capture high order relations of entities, but also capture the relative importance of the neighbors with the attention mechanism.

4.6   Parallel Efficiency Evaluation

To evaluate the parallel efficiency of the proposed model, we compare our model with our baseline model MGCF and GraphRec [8] which also take social relation into account. We utilize KaHip as our choice of graph partitioning method and launch the experiment on 1 machine with 8 Nvidia GTX 2080Tis. We set the parameter as Sect. 4.3 and evaluate the speedup-ratio on the datasets proposed in Sect. 4.1. The result is shown in Fig. 4.

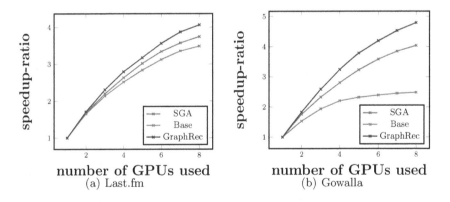

Fig. 4. The Speedup ratio with different GPUs used.

In Last.fm dataset, social edges are limited, so all three models perform similarly. However, when the number of social relations increase in Gowalla datase, the speedup ratio of GraphRec drops sharply. It proves that our SGA model achieve better performance than other GNN-based social recommendation model while maintaining similar parallel efficiency with the model without considering social relations.

5 Conclusion and Future Work

In this paper, we proposed a social graph attentive aggregation (SGA) network for social recommendation. Our model combines the strength of NGCF for leveraging high-order collaborative information from user-item bipartite graph and the social networks for utilizing direct user-user interaction information to alleviate the data sparsity issue. Moreover, we also utilized attention mechanism to enable fine-grained modeling. The experimental results showed that our model is effective and suitable for parallel training for efficiency speed up.

For future work, we will take more side information other than social networks into consideration. For example, if two items were put in the same shopping cart, we can assume that these two items are related and can be modeled as an edge in user-item graphs to further alleviate the sparsity problem. Moreover, we will explore effective parallelization strategies to further boost the efficiency of our model.

Acknowledgement. This work is supported by Key-Area Research and Development Plan of Guangdong Province #2020B010164003.

References

1. Adomavicius, G., Tuzhilin, A.: Toward the next generation of recommender systems: a survey of the state-of-the-art and possible extensions. IEEE Trans. Knowl. Data Eng. **6**, 734–749 (2005)
2. Bakshy, E., Rosenn, I., Marlow, C., Adamic, L.: The role of social networks in information diffusion. In: Proceedings of the 21st International Conference on World Wide Web, pp. 519–528. ACM (2012)
3. Berg, R.V.D., Kipf, T.N., Welling, M.: Graph convolutional matrix completion. arXiv preprint arXiv:1706.02263 (2017)
4. Cantador, I., Brusilovsky, P., Kuflik, T.: 2nd workshop on information heterogeneity and fusion in recommender systems (hetrec 2011). In: Proceedings of the 5th ACM Conference on Recommender Systems. RecSys 2011, ACM, New York, NY, USA (2011)
5. Defferrard, M., Bresson, X., Vandergheynst, P.: Convolutional neural networks on graphs with fast localized spectral filtering. In: Advances in Neural Information Processing Systems, pp. 3844–3852 (2016)
6. Ebesu, T., Shen, B., Fang, Y.: Collaborative memory network for recommendation systems. In: The 41st International ACM SIGIR Conference on Research & Development in Information Retrieval, pp. 515–524. ACM (2018)
7. Fan, W., Derr, T., Ma, Y., Wang, J., Tang, J., Li, Q.: Deep adversarial social recommendation. arXiv preprint arXiv:1905.13160 (2019)
8. Fan, W., et al.: Graph neural networks for social recommendation. In: The World Wide Web Conference, pp. 417–426. ACM (2019)
9. Guo, G., Zhang, J., Yorke-Smith, N.: TrustSVD: collaborative filtering with both the explicit and implicit influence of user trust and of item ratings. In: Twenty-Ninth AAAI Conference on Artificial Intelligence (2015)
10. Hamilton, W., Ying, Z., Leskovec, J.: Inductive representation learning on large graphs. In: Advances in Neural Information Processing Systems, pp. 1024–1034 (2017)

11. He, K., Zhang, X., Ren, S., Sun, J.: Deep residual learning for image recognition. In: Proceedings of the IEEE Conference on Computer Vision and Pattern Recognition, pp. 770–778 (2016)
12. He, X., Liao, L., Zhang, H., Nie, L., Hu, X., Chua, T.S.: Neural collaborative filtering. In: Proceedings of the 26th International Conference on World Wide Web, pp. 173–182. International World Wide Web Conferences Steering Committee (2017)
13. Jiang, M., Cui, P., Wang, F., Zhu, W., Yang, S.: Scalable recommendation with social contextual information. IEEE Trans. Knowl. Data Eng. **26**(11), 2789–2802 (2014)
14. Kipf, T.N., Welling, M.: Semi-supervised classification with graph convolutional networks. arXiv preprint arXiv:1609.02907 (2016)
15. Kipf, T.N., Welling, M.: Variational graph auto-encoders. arXiv preprint arXiv:1611.07308 (2016)
16. Liang, D., Charlin, L., McInerney, J., Blei, D.M.: Modeling user exposure in recommendation. In: Proceedings of the 25th International Conference on World Wide Web, pp. 951–961. International World Wide Web Conferences Steering Committee (2016)
17. Ma, H., Zhou, D., Liu, C., Lyu, M.R., King, I.: Recommender systems with social regularization. In: Proceedings of the Fourth ACM International Conference on Web Search and Data Mining, pp. 287–296. ACM (2011)
18. Maas, A.L., Hannun, A.Y., Ng, A.Y.: Rectifier nonlinearities improve neural network acoustic models. In: Proceedings ICML, vol. 30, p. 3 (2013)
19. Mnih, V., Heess, N., Graves, A., et al.: Recurrent models of visual attention. In: Advances in Neural Information Processing Systems, pp. 2204–2212 (2014)
20. Rendle, S., Freudenthaler, C., Gantner, Z., Schmidt-Thieme, L.: BPR: Bayesian personalized ranking from implicit feedback. In: Proceedings of the Twenty-Fifth Conference on Uncertainty in Artificial Intelligence, pp. 452–461. AUAI Press (2009)
21. Vaswani, A., et al.: Attention is all you need. In: Advances in Neural Information Processing Systems, pp. 5998–6008 (2017)
22. Veličković, P., Cucurull, G., Casanova, A., Romero, A., Lio, P., Bengio, Y.: Graph attention networks. arXiv preprint arXiv:1710.10903 (2017)
23. Wang, X., He, X., Wang, M., Feng, F., Chua, T.S.: Neural graph collaborative filtering. arXiv preprint arXiv:1905.08108 (2019)
24. Wang, X., Hoi, S.C., Ester, M., Bu, J., Chen, C.: Learning personalized preference of strong and weak ties for social recommendation. In: Proceedings of the 26th International Conference on World Wide Web, pp. 1601–1610. International World Wide Web Conferences Steering Committee (2017)
25. Wu, L., Sun, P., Hong, R., Fu, Y., Wang, X., Wang, M.: SocialGCN: an efficient graph convolutional network based model for social recommendation. arXiv preprint arXiv:1811.02815 (2018)
26. Yang, J.H., Chen, C.M., Wang, C.J., Tsai, M.F.: HOP-rec: high-order proximity for implicit recommendation. In: Proceedings of the 12th ACM Conference on Recommender Systems, pp. 140–144. ACM (2018)
27. Zhao, T., McAuley, J., King, I.: Leveraging social connections to improve personalized ranking for collaborative filtering. In: Proceedings of the 23rd ACM International Conference on Conference on Information and Knowledge Management, pp. 261–270. ACM (2014)

28. Zhou, X., Liu, D., Lian, J., Xie, X.: Collaborative metric learning with memory network for multi-relational recommender systems. arXiv preprint arXiv:1906.09882 (2019)
29. Zhou, X., Mascolo, C., Zhao, Z.: Topic-enhanced memory networks for personalised point-of-interest recommendation. arXiv preprint arXiv:1905.13127 (2019)

MACSQ: Massively Accelerated DeepQ Learning on GPUs Using On-the-fly State Construction

Marcel Köster$^{(\boxtimes)}$, Julian Groß, and Antonio Krüger

German Research Center for Artificial Intelligence (DFKI),
Saarland Informatics Campus, Campus D3.2, 66123 Saarbrücken, Germany
{marcel.koester,julian.gross,antonio.krueger}@dfki.de

Abstract. The current trend of using artificial neural networks to solve computationally intensive problems is omnipresent. In this scope, *DeepQ* learning is a common choice for agent-based problems. DeepQ combines the concept of Q-Learning with (deep) neural networks to learn different Q-values/matrices based on environmental conditions. Unfortunately, DeepQ learning requires hundreds of thousands of iterations/Q-samples that must be generated and learned for large-scale problems. Gathering data sets for such challenging tasks is extremely time consuming and requires large data-storage containers. Consequently, a common solution is the automatic generation of input samples for agent-based DeepQ networks. However, a usual workflow is to create the samples separately from the training process in either a (set of) pre-processing step(s) or interleaved with the training process. This requires the input Q-samples to be materialized in order to be fed into the training step of the attached neural network. In this paper, we propose a new GPU-focussed method for on-the-fly generation of training samples tightly coupled with the training process itself. This allows us to skip the materialization process of all samples (e.g. avoid dumping them disk), as they are (re)constructed when needed. Our method significantly outperforms usual workflows that generate the input samples on the CPU in terms of runtime performance and memory/storage consumption.

Keywords: Massively-parallel processing · Neural networks · Q-learning · Graphics processing units · GPUs · State construction

1 Introduction

Neural network and DeepQ learning become more and more prominent [19]. Due to advancements in parallel GPU-based processing over the past years, applying DeepQ learning to large-scale problems becomes feasible. However, a severe limitation is always the dataset processing in general. Either researches have to deal with large binary-based datasets in data storages or they favor automatic sample generation. Although even combinations of both approaches are also common choices, we focus on purely automatic generation of training samples in this paper.

This work has been developed in the project APPaM (01IW20006), which is partly funded by the German ministry of education and research (BMBF).

© Springer Nature Switzerland AG 2022
H. Shen et al. (Eds.): PDCAT 2021, LNCS 13148, pp. 383–395, 2022.
https://doi.org/10.1007/978-3-030-96772-7_35

In this context, we have to randomly generate a large number of *states* used for training. A *state* thereby contains all environment information in which the agent(s) live(s) in. It also includes the exact state of all agents in order to represent them as precise as necessary for the overall problem domain description. Given a set of generated states, a single Q-matrix is trained for each of them. After training these matrices, they act as desired outputs for an attached neural network. The inputs of this network are then given by the different states. This allows for learning computational rules to infer Q-based decisions on environmental conditions defined by the input states.

Since these states must be generated prior to learning, a common choice is the generation on the CPU side. This allows to conveniently model the state-generation code in an arbitrary programming language. It is often possible to use straight-forward parallelization principles on the CPU-side to improve performance of the state-generation logic. Although this seems to be a perfect choice at first sight, large-scale problems require hundreds of thousands of states to achieve high learning accuracy. This often causes scalability issues on the CPU side and/or storage problems when saving all generated samples to a storage device for learning.

In this paper, we propose a new high-level method and a set of GPU-driven algorithms to accelerate DeepQ learning. In particular, our approach enables automatic (re-)generation of states on GPU devices without any further CPU intervention. This helps to significantly outperform CPU-based sample generation on the one hand and to reduce the required memory consumption in already GPU-specialized learning pipelines on the other hand.

2   Related Work

As outlined in the introduction, DeepQ learning is a state-of-the-art of often-chosen method. For this reason, it also a well-researched topic in general covered by hundreds of applications. Although it is widely applied, the usual way to train these networks is by generating sample input states on the CPU [19]. For example, Mnih et al. [18,19] evaluated different games using CPU-created samples. Also, papers reasoning about improving precision and convergences mainly take CPU-generated samples into account [3,6,22]. In contrast to these mainly CPU-driven methods in terms of state generation, the work by Liang et al. [14] takes GPU-acceleration into account. In this paper, like in many others [17], CPU-evolved samples are passed to the GPUs for performing multiple training epochs [23]. To overcome runtime and memory limitations of these approaches we generate samples on-the-fly on the GPUs which also improves training performance.

Recent work has shown significant performance improvements when using GPUs in the context of massively parallel simulations. A well known example is the work by Groß et al. [4,5] accelerating parallel neighborhood lookups in large-scale 3D particle simulations (e.g. general [12] and fluid simulations [11]). However, GPU acceleration is not particularly limited to particles in general. There have been great advancements in the domain of purely GPU-optimized simulation methods for arbitrary domains [7,9]. This makes GPUs more applicable to general purpose simulations targeting many parallel states.

A prominent optimization technique to leverage the parallel performance of GPUs, is the use of proper memory-access patterns [1,13,21]. This task becomes particularly challenging in our domain while processing multiple states in parallel. Previous work by Köster et al. [10] evaluates various possibilities to design suitable data-structure layouts in this context. We follow their advises and use the same techniques to realize all of our memory-access patterns.

Most similar to our approach in terms of tracking states, is the work by Köster et al. [8]. The authors target the setting in which is it often beneficial to *not* remember states by storing them but to efficiently reconstruct them when needed. Our new method is based on the same principle but with a different purpose, which requires major adjustments of this approach to be used in our domain. In terms of parallel learning, our method borrows architectural concepts from the one by Amin et al. [2]. In contrast to their approach, our algorithms focus on multiple network adjustments using many states per GPU. However, we also perform parallel feed-forward steps while adjusting the matrix and bias weights using parallel reductions.

3   MACSQ

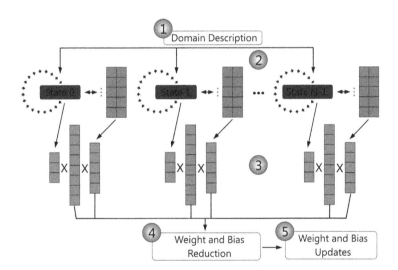

Fig. 1. A single update step of our processing pipeline. First, we need a given domain description (step 1). Afterwards, we instantiate different states by iteratively sampling for valid solutions (green, step 2). The actual Q-matrices for each state are maintained in shared memory (blue, step 2) which are also iteratively built. Next, we feed the state description and their Q-matrices into the same neural network in parallel, which we want to train (yellow, step 3). Finally, we perform a parallel reduction of all matrix weights and bias vectors (step 4) in order to realize the network updates (step 5). (Color figure online)

As outlined in the introduction, we focus on the automatic generation of states on the GPU. For this purpose, we leverage the high-level architectural design of state reconstruction by Köster et al. [8] (see Sect. 2). The main idea in this scope is to avoid storing states in memory/on a storage device, if they are not needed for the current operation. However, this implies that they have to be re-computed (reconstructed) later on in order to use them again. Figure 1 shows a single step of our approach while taking the nature of GPUs into account.

We assume a given domain description (model) that can be imperatively executed in the context of multiple states on a GPU (see also Sect. 4). This description is then used to spawn multiple states that are created using a *random-number generator (RNG)*. Thereby, the RNG is maintained and managed in the background without being tied to the domain description. This gives us the ability to reconstruct the *same states* by using previously stored RNG-states, which will be recovered for reconstruction. In order to improve performance, we maintain all Q-matrices for each state in shared memory. This significantly reduces the number of expensive global-memory accesses, since Q learning requires many updates to the Q-matrix values.

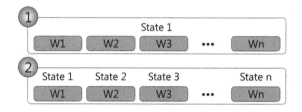

Fig. 2. Traditional processing approach (1): Each state is processed by a single thread group on the GPU. Our concept inspired by [10] (2): Each state is processed by a single warp. Since a thread group contains multiple warps in our case, we process multiple states per thread group.

To ensure scalability, while keeping the overhead for the GPU warp schedulers as low as possible, we spawn many large thread groups covering as much as threads as possible on each GPU device (see also Sect. 5). Within each group, we use a single warp per state, rather than using the whole group to process a single state (see Fig. 2). This approach has already been successfully used in previous work [10] to handle thousands of states efficiently in parallel. The concept is suitable for *small-scale* (in terms of a few number of agents and environment properties that must be tracked), as well as *large-scale*, domain descriptions. In the case of small-scale descriptions, many parallel threads working on a single state can easily become idle. This causes loss of occupancy, and thus, often significant performance bottlenecks. In contrast to this problem, large-scale domain descriptions would require many threads to improve the overall throughput. However, these domains usually require more samples in general, which implies more threads working on the different states at the same time. Using the method presented here, ensures scalability in the context of small-scale and large-scale problems by using a compromise in the number of threads per state.

Algorithm 1 shows our GPU-friendly state-initialization algorithm that is applied to each state. As mentioned above, we assign a single warp per state. Consequently, we have to compute a globally unique state index per warp first. Note that the algorithm contains a divergent branch as one of its first instructions: If the currently computed warp-wide state index exceeds the current number of states, all threads in this warp leave the current group. This case occurs in the presence of a number of states that is not dividable by the total number of warps in all thread groups. Note further, that this is a not a performance issue. If all threads in a warp leave the thread group, the warp dispatcher can activate another warp, which implicitly realizes the concept of *thread compaction* on a warp level [10].

Algorithm 1: High-Level State-Initialization Algorithm

```
/* Compute the state index for each warp in each group         */
```
1 stateIdx := gridIdx · $\frac{\text{groupDim}}{\text{warpSize}}$ + warpIdx;
2 **if** *stateIdx ¿= numStates* **then**
3 | **return**;
4 **end**
5 random := **LoadRNG**(stateIdx);
6 validInitialization := 0;
7 **while** *validInitialization* $\neq 1$ **do**
8 | initialized := **DomainDescription.InitState**(stateIdx, random);
9 | validInitialization := **Warp.AllReduceAdd**(initialized);
10 **end**
11 **StoreRNG**(stateIdx, random);

From an algorithmic point of view, we use an RNG-based iterative initialization approach: We use the current domain description to perform a parallel initialization using all threads of a single warp (referred to as *lanes*, lines 7–10). Each thread invocation returns a lane-local result whether the initialization has been valid, in terms of domain-specific constraints. After each initialization attempt, we perform a warp-wide reduction to verify that all lanes have returned a successful initialization result. This process is repeated until a single attempt has been successful iote that the domain-description implementation needs to take care of initializing all state-dependent properties/agent states using the lanes of a single warp.

Our main algorithm to compute all Q-matrices is presented in Algorithm 2. In analogy to Algorithm 1, we have to query and verify the current state index of each warp. Next, we allocate a sufficient amount of shared memory per thread group to store all Q-matrices for each state (each warp, line 5). Each warp computes its unique sub-view into shared-memory in order to address the associated Q-matrix elements (line 6). Afterwards, each warp initializing its Q-matrix by either loading pre-training Q-values, or zeroing them (in the case of a new training process, line 7).

The following lines of the algorithm use a `GetFromFirstLane` function. Its purpose is to execute the passed function invocation in the first lane of each warp only. All other lanes do not perform an operation while the function invocation is evaluated. Subsequently, all lanes participate in a divergent-free warp-shuffle operation in which each lane gets the value from the first lane. Using this efficient approach, allows us to broadcast the single result value from the function invocation to all other threads in the warp.

Algorithm 2: Massively-Parallel Q-Determination Algorithm

    /* Compute the state index for each warp in each group   */

1 stateIdx := gridIdx $\cdot \frac{\text{groupDim}}{\text{warpSize}}$ + warpIdx;

2 **if** *stateIdx ¿= numStates* **then**

3 | **return**;

4 **end**

    /* Initialize the Q-matrix for all active warps in this group   */

5 sharedQ := **SharedMemory** $\left[\text{qDim.X} \cdot \text{qDim.Y} \cdot \frac{\text{groupDim}}{\text{warpSize}} \right]$;

6 qViewPerState := **SubView**(sharedQ, qDim.X $\cdot$ qDim.Y $\cdot$ warpIdx);

7 **LoadOrInitQView**(stateIdx, qViewPerState);

8 random := **LoadRNG**(stateIdx);

    /* Build or update the Q-matrix   */

9 numSourcePossibilities := **GetFromFirstLane**(

10   **DomainDescription.GetNumSourcePossibilities**(stateIdx, random));

    /* Perform the specified number of Q-tries   */

11 **for** $i := 1$ *to* #*Q-S* **do**

        /* Determine the current source possibility for all threads in

           this warp   */

12   source := **GetFromFirstLane**(

13   **NextRandom**(random 0, numSourcePossibilities));

        /* Get a target possibility for this thread (if any)   */

14   (hasTarget, target) := **DomainDescription.TryGetTarget**(

15   stateIdx, source, random);

        /* Determine the reward for this thread (if any)   */

16   (hasReward, reward) := **DomainDescription.TryGetReward**(

17   stateIdx, source, hasTarget, target);

        /* Get the Q-matrix data   */

18   currentQ := qViewPerState[source, target];

19   nextQ := qViewPerState[source, **SelectQTarget**(target)];

        /* Compute the updated Q-value using α and γ */

20   newQ = **UpdateQ**(reward, currentQ, nextQ);

        /* Wait for all threads and propagate changes   */

21   **Warp.Barrier**;

        /* Update the Q-matrix after reading all data   */

22   **if** *hasReward* **then**

23 | qViewPerState[source, target] := newQ;

24   **end**

        /* Wait for all threads and propagate changes   */

25   **Warp.Barrier**;

26 **end**

    /* Store the state of the current RNG   */

27 **StoreRNG**(stateIdx, random);

    /* Export Q-matrix values to the neural network input   */

28 **ExportToNeuralNetworkOutput**(stateIdx, qViewPerState);

The primary idea here is to perform (at least) a specified number of Q-samples per state (#Q-S, lines 11–26, see also Sect. 5). At least here refers to the fact that each lane in a warp gets the same Q-source value (lines 12–13) for sampling in each iteration, which can result in a number of warpSize·#Q-S samples in sum. Then, all lanes try to determine a valid Q-target value within the Q-dimensions according to the domain-specific constraints (lines 14–15). As this operation can fail for each target possibility, this function returns a tuple consisting of a success value `hasTarget` and the actual Q-target reference `target` (if any). A prerequisite at this point is the fact that the domain-description logic has to ensure that different lanes will be assigned to different targets. Otherwise, this results in race conditions during Q-matrix updates later on. Although this might sound quite sophisticated to achieve in general, it turns out to be straight forward in most cases in practice based on our experience. A common use case is to select between different target values in a certain range. By subdividing this range into several sections based on the warp size, the different target-value intervals can be directly assigned to the different lanes.

The remaining steps are to determine the reward (lines 16–17) and to perform the computation of the `newQ` value based on current α and γ settings (lines 18–20). Before issuing any Q-matrix value updates, we have to wait for all lanes in the warp. This is important since the computation of the `newQ` values involves reading data from the current Q-matrix. Removing this barrier would lead to read-write race conditions. If a reward could be determined for the current lane in lines 16–17, the `newQ` value can be updated in shared memory. Note that we also need an additional barrier after the Q-matrix updates to avoid reading outdated information in the next iteration. Finally, we store the current (state-dependent) RNG state and export the Q-matrix for each state from shared memory to a location a global memory for training purposes.

4   Implementation Details

We have used C# in combination with the ILGPU-compiler[1] to implement our system. ILGPU is used to compile parts of our application written in managed code to executable GPU code that can be run on our NVIDIA GPUs. Note we perform all memory allocations prior to launching any GPU kernel in order to avoid unnecessary latencies and blocking operations. Furthermore, we completely avoid using floating-point-based atomic operations to have deterministic and reproducible results [20] in the context of reduction operations. However, given different group sizes targeting different GPUs [1,15,20,21], the results may still vary. This is not an issue in general, as a fixed group size using our implementation on a particular GPU architecture (e.g. NVIDIA Ampere [21]) always yields the same results. Furthermore, we use an *Xorshift*-based random-number generator to compute new random numbers on-the-fly on the GPU [16].

5   Evaluation

The whole evaluation section is based on a simple, yet challenging, agent-based simulation/optimization problem (see Fig. 3). It is build around an assignment problem from the field of manufacturing, which requires different agents to be assigned to different working stations. The agents can move between the stations

---

[1] www.ilgpu.net.

by taking a pre-defined movement-time-matrix into account. Thereby, the overall purpose is to assemble products that have to pass all stations in order to be completed. If a product reaches a station, a single work step needs to be performed on the product using an agent (if any). After completing a single work step, the product is passed to the next station (until it reaches the final station). Note that only a single agent can be assigned to a station at a time; although multiple agents might stand in front of the station. Moreover, only a single product is allowed to be on a station at any point in time.

Fig. 3. A sample production line with 10 stations (black lines), 5 products (purple) and 4 agents (in front of their stations, green). Agents can move freely between the stations. (Color figure online)

In order to evaluate different computational workloads and simulate multiple use cases, we have to differentiate between scenarios and states. A scenario refers to a given number of stations and agents, whereas a single state lives within its parent scenario definition and contains an actual description of all product/station/agent states. Based on this differentiation, Fig. 3 shows a sample state within a scenario of 10 stations and 4 agents.

Changing a scenario configuration, also influences the size of the hidden layers used for implementing the assignment logic[2]. Table 1 presents the evaluated scenario configurations, as well as their neural network settings. Note that we do not use any convolutional networks for these simple scenarios while taking common pitfalls into account [3]. These configurations have been selected because they refer to existing use cases from reality. Note that these configurations do not contain any products since product placement and agent assignment remain state dependent rather than scenario dependent.

Table 1. The used evaluation scenarios (1–3) with different station and agent setups. The Q-dimension is always equal to the squared number of stations in all cases. Note that the neural network configuration is chosen in a way that the input dimension (size of the input layer) is equal to the number of stations + agents. The output dimension (size of the output layer) is equal to the corresponding Q-dimension (as we learn whole Q-matrices) and the size of the hidden layer (like the number of samples) has been determined using an offline auto-tuning process. #Q-S refers to the number of samples to compute the Q-matrix in each state and #N-S refers to the total number of training states.

Scenario	#Stations	#Agents	Q-Dimension	#Q-S	Network	#N-S
1	10	4	10×10	20K	$14 \times 64 \times 100$	192K
2	12	4	12×12	28K	$16 \times 72 \times 144$	512K
3	16	6	16×16	50K	$24 \times 128 \times 256$	1792K

---

[2] For the sake of simplicity, we use a single hidden layer for all evaluation scenarios.

Table 2. Thread group configurations for the used GPUs, their number of states per thread group and the number of dispatched states in parallel. Note that this number is twice as large compared to the maximum number of parallel states per GPU to maximize occupancy.

	GTX 1080 Ti	RTX 3090
Group size	**1024**	**768**
States per group	**32**	**24**
#Parallel states	$28 \times 2 \times 32 = \mathbf{1792}$	$82 \times 2 \times 24 = \mathbf{3936}$
#Dispatched states	$1792 \times 2 = \mathbf{3584}$	$3936 \times 2 = \mathbf{7872}$

We use two different GPUs from NVIDIA, a GTX 1080 Ti and an RTX 3090, and compare these results to a pure profiling-tuned C#-based sample-generation engine running an AMD Ryzen 3950X. As discussed in Sect. 3, we process multiple states per GPU thread group. Table 2 depicts the used group sizes in order to achieve maximum occupancy on our evaluation GPUs. Note that the number of dispatched states in parallel is also referred to as the *batch size (BS)* in the remainder of this section.

As presented in the introduction, a common approach is to generate all samples used for learning on the CPU to the actual training step. Table 3 shows runtime measurements for our three evaluation scenarios (see Table 1) using a purely CPU-based state-generation step. As expected, the runtime grows significantly with the complexity of the scenario. However, the runtime is primarily dominated by the number of samples #N-S and not by the required number of Q-learning samples #Q-S. This is due to the fact, that the Q-matrices are maintained in the L1/L2 caches.

Table 3. Runtime in seconds for generating all samples (#N-S) on our evaluation CPU for learning purposes.

Scenario	#N-S	Ryzen 3950X (16 Cores, 32 Threads)
1	192K	**48.75 s**
2	512K	**160.37 s**
3	1792K	**1,717.51 s**

Using our purely-GPU-based method, results in considerable runtime improvements (see Table 4). Since we make excessive use of the L1 caches to maintain our Q-matrices (in shared memory), the overall runtime is primarily dominated by the number of training samples #N-S (similar to the CPU version). However, in this evaluation table we differentiate between two types A and B. In the first case (type A), we generate a single batch (achieving maximum occupancy on the device) only. Type B covers the case in which we have to generate all states on the GPU.

Table 4. Runtime measurements in seconds on the evaluation GPUs. Type A: generation of a single batch only (BS, see also Table 2). Type B: iterative generation of all states #N-S in GPU memory.

Scenario	Type	GTX 1080 Ti	σ	BS	RTX 3090	σ	BS
1	A	**0.005 s**	0	3584	**0.004 s**	0	7872
*	B	**2.911 s**	0.032	–	**1.172 s**	0.053	–
2	A	**0.080 s**	0	3584	**0.007 s**	0	7872
*	B	**11.906 s**	0.206	–	**4.831 s**	0.024	–
3	A	**0.516 s**	0.024	3584	**0.349 s**	0.015	7872
*	B	**261.832 s**	0.563	–	**85.386 s**	0.451	–

Comparing the runtime of our GPU-based method with the CPU implementation reveals speedups from 6.5× to 16.75× on the GTX 1080 Ti and from 20× to 41× on the RTX 3090. Note that speedup decreases the more samples are generated at once in these simple evaluation scenarios. This is due to the fact that the maximum occupancy has already been reached using our computed batch sizes. Note that the speedup will not decrease any further since the parallel processing capabilities ouf our GPU devices beat our CPU by orders of magnitude. This is particularly helpful when dealing with larger scenarios and problem domains yielding even higher speedup factors. If the actual network-training step is performed on the GPU, the CPU samples need to be copied to the GPU devices. Moreover, if all training samples do not fit into global GPU memory, we need to "page-in" and "page-out" subsets of them. This makes the CPU-version even slower.

Consider the total memory consumption of our states (including their Q-matrices) shown in Table 5. Since our new approach is also capable of reconstructing "old" (already seen) states, it is possible to limit the number of states that must be held in memory at any point in time. Limiting this number to be equal to the batch size, allows us to reduce the memory consumption on our benchmarks by factors of 53× up to 500× (see Table 5). Although this is not required given our simple evaluation scenarios (as all samples fit into main memory), this still shows great improvement possibilities in large-scale applications.

Table 5. The memory consumption of a single state in bytes. The GPU columns present the total memory consumption in MB when processing a batch-size number of states in parallel. The right-most column (All States) depicts the memory consumption in MB when materializing all training states #N-S in memory. ote that a single entry in the Q-matrix is implemented using a 32-bit float.

Scenario	State size	GTX 1080 Ti	RTX 3090	All states
1	414 B	**1.42 MB**	**3.11 MB**	**75.81 MB**
2	592 B	**2.02 MB**	**4.44 MB**	**289.06 MB**
3	1046 B	**3.57 MB**	**7.85 MB**	**1787.60 MB**

A common strategy is using a certain number of samples per training epoch, which can be regenerated on-the-fly, as discussed above (see Table 6). However, this imposes an additional runtime overhead. On our benchmarks, the measured slowdown of regenerating samples (type A), rather than maintaining all of them in main memory (type B), lies between 4× and 5×. We do not believe that this is a severe limitation as "paging-in" and "paging-out" states in large-scale applications will result in even larger overheads.

Table 6. Neural-network training setups using multiple epochs. A given number of randomly chosen samples (out of the set of all training samples #N-S) is used per epoch. Type A: using on-the-fly state reconstruction with the help of multiples of the batch size. Type B: generating all states on the GPU prior to the training step.

Scenario	Epochs	#Samples	Type	GTX 1080 Ti	RTX 3090
1	900	960	A	**12.8 s**	**4.9 s**
*	*	*	B	**2.9 s**	**1.2 s**
2	1000	2560	A	**57.6 s**	**22.9 s**
*	*	0	B	**11.9 s**	**4.8 s**
3	1500	6000	A	**1,296.7 s**	**399.4 s**
*	*	0	B	**261.8 s**	**85.4 s**

6   Conclusion

In this paper, we presented a new approach to on-the-fly sample generation and training for agent-based DeepQ networks. It is entirely GPU based and does not require a CPU interop, which makes it a great choice for asynchronous processing.

The evaluation sections describes the significant speedups and memory size reduction using our method. Compared to CPU-based sample generation, our GPU-designed algorithms help to achieve runtime improvements by 6.5× (on an older GPU architecture) and up to 41× on a recent GPU device using our simple evaluation scenarios. Larger-scale real-world scenarios will yield substantially higher improvements. It is also possible to trade runtime performance against memory consumption. Accepting a slowdown of up to 5× on the one hand, we are able to reduce the memory consumption by up to 500× on the other hand. We argue to trade the memory consumption for the runtime performance, since large-scale applications require billions of samples that have to be paged-in and out of GPU memory. This causes even worse runtime slowdowns.

Analyzing further scenarios in detail will reveal even more optimization potential. Hence, we would like to improve our method to take additional domain-dependent factors into account.

Acknowledgment. The authors would like to thank Nurten Öksüz for her suggestions and feedback regarding our paper.

References

1. AMD: AMD Vega Instruction Set Architecture (2019)
2. Amin, M.A., Kashif, M., Umer, M., Rehman, A., Waheed, F., Rehman, H.U.: Parallel backpropagation neural network training techniques using graphics processing unit. Int. J. Adv. Comput. Sci. Appl. (2019)
3. Fu, J., Kumar, A., Soh, M., Levine, S.: Diagnosing Bottlenecks in Deep Q-learning Algorithms (2019)
4. Groß, J., Köster, M., Krüger, A.: Fast and efficient nearest neighbor search for particle simulations. In: Proceedings of the Conference on Computer Graphics & Visual Computing (CGCV-2019). The Eurographics Association (2019)
5. Groß, J., Köster, M., Krüger, A.: CLAWS : Computational load balancing for accelerated neighbor processing on GPUs using warp scheduling. In: Proceedings of the Conference on Computer Graphics and Visual Computing (CGCV-2020). The Eurographics Association (2020)
6. Hasselt, H.V., Guez, A., Silver, D.: Deep reinforcement learning with double Q-learning. In: Proceedings of the Thirtieth AAAI Conference on Artificial Intelligence. AAAI Press (2016)
7. Köster, M., Groß, J., Krüger, A.: FANG: fast and efficient successor-state generation for heuristic optimization on GPUs. In: Wen, S., Zomaya, A., Yang, L.T. (eds.) ICA3PP 2019. LNCS, vol. 11944, pp. 223–241. Springer, Cham (2020). https://doi.org/10.1007/978-3-030-38991-8_15
8. Park, J.H., Shen, H., Sung, Y., Tian, H. (eds.): PDCAT 2018. CCIS, vol. 931. Springer, Singapore (2019). https://doi.org/10.1007/978-981-13-5907-1
9. Köster, M., Groß, J., Krüger, A.: High-performance simulations on GPUs using adaptive time steps. In: Qiu, M. (ed.) ICA3PP 2020. LNCS, vol. 12452, pp. 369–385. Springer, Cham (2020). https://doi.org/10.1007/978-3-030-60245-1_26
10. Köster, M., Groß, J., Krüger, A.: Massively parallel rule-based interpreter execution on GPUs using thread compaction. Int. J. Parallel Program. 48(4), 675–691 (2020)
11. Köster, M., Krüger, A.: Adaptive Position-Based Fluids: Improving Performance of Fluid Simulations for Real-Time Applications. Int. J. Comput. Graph. Animation (2016)
12. Köster, M., Krüger, A.: Screen space particle selection. In: Proceedings of the Conference on Computer Graphics and Visual Computing (CGCV-2018). The Eurographics Association (2018)
13. Köster, M., Leißa, R., Hack, S., Membarth, R., Slusallek, P.: Code Refinement of Stencil Codes. Parallel Process. Lett. (PPL) 24, 1441003 (2014)
14. Liang, J., Makoviychuk, V., Handa, A., Chentanez, N., Macklin, M., Fox, D.: GPU-accelerated robotic simulation for distributed reinforcement learning (2018)
15. Lustig, D., Sahasrabuddhe, S., Giroux, O.: A formal analysis of the NVIDIA PTX memory consistency model. In: Proceedings of the Twenty-Fourth International Conference on Architectural Support for Programming Languages and Operating Systems (2019)
16. Marsaglia, G.: Xorshift RNGs. J. Statist. Software, Articles 8 (2003)
17. Mnih, V., et al.: Asynchronous methods for deep reinforcement learning. In: Proceedings of The 33rd International Conference on Machine Learning. Proceedings of Machine Learning Research, PMLR (2016)
18. Mnih, V., et al.: Playing Atari with Deep Reinforcement Learning (2013)
19. Mnih, V., et al.: Human-level control through deep reinforcement learning. Nature 518, 529–533 (2015)
20. NVIDIA: faster parallel reductions on Kepler (2014)

21. NVIDIA: CUDA C Programming Guide v11.5 (2021)
22. Gama, J., Camacho, R., Brazdil, P.B., Jorge, A.M., Torgo, L. (eds.): ECML 2005. LNCS (LNAI), vol. 3720. Springer, Heidelberg (2005). https://doi.org/10.1007/11564096
23. Stooke, A., Abbeel, P.: Accelerated methods for deep reinforcement learning (2019)

Model-Based Multi-agent Policy Optimization with Dynamic Dependence Modeling

Biyang Hu, Chao Yu$^{(\boxtimes)}$, and Zifan Wu

School of Computer Science and Engineering, Sun Yat-Sen University,
Guangzhou 510006, China
{huby25,wuzf5}@mail2.sysu.edu.cn, yuchao3@mail.sysu.edu.cn

Abstract. This paper explores the combination of model-based methods and multi-agent reinforcement learning (MARL) for more efficient coordination among multiple agents. A decentralized model-based MARL method, Policy Optimization with Dynamic Dependence Modeling (POD2M), is proposed to dynamically determine the importance of other agents' information during the model building process. In POD2M, the agents adapt their mutual dependence during building their own dynamic models in order to make a trade-off between an individual-learning process and a coordinated-learning process. Once the dynamic models have been built, the policies are then trained based on one-step model predictive rollouts. Empirical experiments on both cooperative and competitive scenarios indicate that our method can achieve higher sample efficiency against the compared model-free MARL algorithms, and outperforms the centralized method in large domains.

Keywords: Multi-agent reinforcement learning · Model-based policy optimization · Dynamic dependence

1 Introduction

Reinforcement learning (RL) has made exciting progress in a variety of domains, such as Atari games [1], Go [2] and recently Android System [3]. RL algorithms can be divided into two categories: model-based methods and model-free methods. Model-based methods build a predictive dynamic model of the true environment such that the agent can learn the policy with the simulation samples to reduce the sample complexity [4]. In contrast, model-free methods learn the policies directly from the experience data. While model-free methods have been proved as a general solution for learning complex tasks [5–8], these algorithms suffer from the cost of sample efficiency. Especially in some scenarios such as medical and military fields, collecting enough experience data to train a model-free RL agent can be very difficult. In contrast, model-based methods can guarantee high sample efficiency of learning. However, the accuracy of model estimation

© Springer Nature Switzerland AG 2022
H. Shen et al. (Eds.): PDCAT 2021, LNCS 13148, pp. 396–411, 2022.
https://doi.org/10.1007/978-3-030-96772-7_36

acts as an essential bottleneck to policy quality, generally resulting in inferior performance of model-based methods compared to their model-free counterparts. Recently, several studies have proposed various model-based methods [9–11] that can achieve higher sample efficiency and similar asymptotic performance compared to model-free RL methods in single agent learning environments.

In contrast to single-agent RL, Multi-agent RL (MARL) has been extensively applied to various scenarios including multi-robot systems [12,13], real-time strategic games [14,15] and autonomous driving [16,17]. The main challenge of MARL is that an agent is required to interact with other agents and the environment feedback depends on the joint actions of all the agents. The coexistence of other agents and the concurrent update of multiple agents' policies cause the non-stationarity issue from the perspective of each learning agent. This issue is further exaggerated in model-based MARL, where agents not only need to reason about other agents' behaviors in a dynamic environment, but also need to build a model that is able to correctly capture the transition of this environment. An intuitive solution [18] is to build a centralized dynamic model to approximate the transition process with the inputs of all the agents' observations. However, this kind of centralized method may lead to poor performance in complex problems due to the exponential increase of complexity in the number of agents.

This paper focuses on how to learn a decentralized dynamic model for each agent to approximate the transition process with the information of others only when it is necessary. In multi-agent systems, the mutual dependence among the agents and necessity of coordination can dynamically change over time. For example, at a certain time-step, the multi-agent system can be in a loosely coupled state [19], in which an agent has weak dependence with others for coordination, so that it is enough to use its own information to build its local dynamic model. In order to consider the dynamic mutual dependence of agents when building their local dynamic models, we propose a novel model-based MARL method called Policy Optimization with Dynamic Dependence Modeling (POD2M), in which each agent's policy is optimized by using simulation experiences from its local dynamic model that dynamically incorporates other agents' information during the model estimation process. The main feature of our proposed method is to dynamically adapt mutual independence during building their local dynamic models so that the agents can make a trade-off between an individual-agent learning process and a coordinated learning process. Moreover, when considering the information of others in the coordinated process, the input dimension of our method increases linearly with the number of the agents, which addresses the exponential complexity issue in the centralized approach. We validate our method in both cooperative scenarios and competitive scenarios using the particle environment [20]. The results reveal that our method can converge efficiently and derive higher sample efficiency than model-free algorithms. The final asymptotic performance shows that our method can achieve a comparable result against the centralized model-based MARL method in small-scale domains and much better performance in larger domains.

The rest of the paper is organized as follows. Section 2 discusses the related work, followed by a background introduction of RL and model-based learning in Sect. 3. Section 4 provides a detailed description of our method and Sect. 5 reports experimental studies. At last, Sect. 6 concludes the paper.

2   Related Work

Model-based RL has two main challenges: model building and model using. For model building, the most common methods [21, 22] include building deterministic models or probabilistic models. It depends on whether the transition of state is determined in the specific application environment. For model using, the agent policy can be learned by exploiting the model prediction experiences. The typical Dyna-Q algorithm [23] provides a model-based training framework with both model-predicted and environment-returned experiences. Shooting methods [24] utilize the model to predict the state transition process with fixed step size and compute the accumulated reward during the predicted steps to help select the action. Methods based on model-based value function expansion [25] and policy search with back-propagation through paths [26] integrate both model-free and model-based processes into the policy optimization. The previous work of theoretical analysis [4] provided a monotonic improvement guarantee by enforcing a distance constraint between the learning policy and the data collecting policy. On this foundation, subsequent work [27, 28] makes a deduction to derive a return discrepancy bound with the branched rollout and constructs a policy optimization framework based on the experiences generated by the dynamic model. Other algorithms learn the dynamic model in the latent space, such as Dreamer [10], which constructs a close-loop training scheme and verifies that the learned model can predict the transition states accurately in a long period of rollouts. MuZero [11] extends the model-based methods with monte-carlo tree search and derives an end-to-end strategy to update the set of networks.

In terms of MARL, the framework of centralized training with decentralized execution (CTDE) is commonly used as the basis of the coordination among multiple agents. Decentralized policies are learned in a centralized manner so that they can share information such as parameters without restriction during training. Algorithms based on CTDE [20] use a centralized value function by considering all the agents as a single one to solve the non-stationary problem during the training process. Although CTDE algorithms can solve many multi-agent problems, they must search in the joint observation-action space which grows exponentially with the number of agents. On this foundation, a method [29] with attention mechanism is applied to solve the credit-assignment challenges and further improves the performance of CTDE framework. In addition to CTDE, another typical type of decentralized training algorithms [30] decomposes the centralized value function to a number of respective value functions and guarantees a positive growth of total returns but they are also constrained by the number of agents. Some other algorithms [31] utilize the reward shaping mechanism to promote coordination and distribute each agent an intrinsic reward representing their individual goal. This kind of reward shaping methods requires a total state to train the intrinsic reward distributor which is impossible for some application scenarios. Last but not the least, the role-based algorithms [32] believe that each agent performs different roles and the action space can be segmented according to the role, which is not always feasible in some multi-agent cases.

For the model-based MARL problem, there is relatively limited work in the literature to our knowledge. A common solution is to build a centralized prediction dynamic model [18,33] to deal with the non-stationary problem. The method of centralized model predict the transition process considering all the agents and each agent trains the policy based on the CTDE framework. Obviously, the centralized model encounters the dimension explosion problem with the growth of the number of agents. Some decentralized methods, e.g., [34], provide a general framework and return discrepancy bounds of model-based MARL. However, these methods require each agent to model its opponents or partners and precisely predict their actions which may cost tremendous computation consumption.

3   Preliminaries

In this section, we first introduce the MARL problems, and then the traditional methods of model-based RL including the model building and the model training therein.

3.1   MARL

We consider the framework of Markov Games, which is a multi-agent extension of Markov Decision Processes (MDP). $\mathcal{S}$ is the state space in the games. $\mathcal{A}^i$ is the action space of agent $i \in 1, ..., n$ and $\mathcal{A} = \prod_{i=1}^{n} \mathcal{A}^i$ is the joint action space. $\mathcal{R}^i : \mathcal{S} \times \mathcal{A} \to \mathbb{R}$ is the reward function of agent i. In cooperative scenarios, each agent i observe a reward $r = R(s, \mathbf{a})$ shared by all agents. $\mathcal{T} : \mathcal{S} \times \mathcal{A} \to \mathcal{S}$ defines the probability distribution over possible next states. $\gamma \in [0, 1]$ is the discount factor. At each time step, agent i receives a partially observable variant o^i which contains partial information from the global state $\mathcal{S}$. Agent i uses its policy $\pi^i(a_t^i|o_t^i)$ to demonstrate the probability of taking action a_t^i at the observation o_t^i at time step t. The agents aim to find the optimal policy π_*^i that maximizes their expected discounted returns denoted by the objective function as $\eta : \pi_*^i = \arg\max_{\pi^i} \eta\left[\pi^i\right] = \mathbb{E}_{a^1 \sim \pi^1, ..., a^n \sim \pi^n, s \sim \mathcal{T}}\left[\sum_{t=0}^{\infty} \gamma_t r_t^i\left(s_t, a_t^1, ..., a_t^n\right)\right]$.

Policy gradient methods [23] aims to estimate the gradient of an agent's expected returns with respect to the parameter θ of policy π_θ. This gradient of the objective function is given as follows:

$$\nabla_\theta J\left(\pi_\theta\right) = \nabla_\theta \log\left(\pi_\theta\left(a_t|s_t\right)\right) \sum_{t'=t}^{\infty} \gamma^{t'-t} r_{t'}\left(s_{t'}, a_{t'}\right). \tag{1}$$

The term $\sum_{t'=t}^{\infty} \gamma^{t'-t} r_{t'}(s_{t'}, a_{t'})$ can lead to high variance. To this end, the Actor-Critic (AC) [35] framework uses a critic Q-function $Q_\phi(s_t, a_t) = \mathbb{E}\left[\sum_{t'=t}^{\infty} \gamma^{t'-t} r_{t'}(s_{t'}, a_{t'})\right]$ to approximate the expected discounted returns. The approximated Q-function with respect to parameter ϕ is learned by minimizing the regression loss as follows:

$$\mathcal{L}_Q(\phi) = \mathbb{E}_{(s,a,r,s') \sim \mathcal{D}} \delta_\phi(s, a, s')$$
$$\delta_\phi(s, a, s') = \left(r(s,a) + \gamma \mathbb{E}_{a' \sim \pi(s')}\left[Q_{\overline{\phi}}(s', a')\right] - Q_\phi(s,a) \right)^2, \tag{2}$$

where δ_ϕ is the TD-error, $Q_{\overline{\phi}}$ is the target Q-function that is updated with several intervals and $\mathcal{D}$ is the replay buffer storing the past experiences. Once a critic is updated by minimizing the TD-error, the actor π_θ can be improved by maximizing the action-value function for actions produced by the policy.

3.2   Model-Based RL

Model-based RL learns a forward dynamic model to approximate the true transition function $\mathcal{S} \times \mathcal{A} \rightarrow \mathcal{S}$ and reward function $\mathcal{S} \times \mathcal{A} \rightarrow \mathbb{R}$ of the environment. The dynamic model is trained on the true environment dataset $\mathcal{D}_{env} = \{(s_t, a_t, s_{t+1}, r_t, d_t)\}_{t=0}^N$, where r_t is the sampled reward and d_t is the termination indicator denoting the end of the episode.

There are two methods to build the learned dynamic model: deterministic methods and probabilistic methods. For deterministic models, the standard way is to train the model to minimize the Mean Squared Error (MSE) between the predictive states and the true states as follows:

$$\mathcal{L}_{MSE} = \sum_{t=1}^N \|\hat{p}(s_t, a_t) - s_{t+1}\|_2^2, \tag{3}$$

where $\hat{p}(s_t, a_t)$ is the deterministic next state predicted by the dynamic model with the inputs of current state and current action.

For probabilistic models, Gaussian probabilistic method is commonly used to predict a distribution over next states: $\hat{s}_{t+1} \sim \mathcal{N}(\mu(s_t, a_t), \sigma(s_t, a_t))$ and optimizes the Negative Log Likelihood (NLL) by:

$$\mathcal{L}_{NLL} = \sum_{t=1}^N [\mu(s_t, a_t) - s_{t+1}^T \sigma^{-1}(s_t, a_t)[\mu(s_t, a_t) - s_{t+1}] + \log \det \sigma(s_t, a_t)]. \tag{4}$$

In order to consider uncertainty over model predictions, model-based RL methods usually use the ensembles of learned models [36] rather than a single model. Each model $\hat{p}^j$ in the ensemble is trained on its own copy of the dataset $\mathcal{D}_{env}^j$ independently. The final prediction for an ensemble of M models is then given by:

$$\hat{s}_{t+1} = \frac{1}{M} \sum_{j=1}^M \hat{p}^j(s_t, a_t). \tag{5}$$

In the following sections, we denote the model ensemble for agent i as $\hat{p}^i$ for simplicity.

4   The POD2M Method

We propose a model-based MARL method named Policy Optimization with Dynamic Dependence Modeling (POD2M). POD2M has two key components including the model-based policy optimization and the dynamic dependence modeling among multiple agents. In POD2M, each agent learns a dynamic model and uses the data collected from the model rollouts to learn a policy. The overall framework of our proposed POD2M method, including the structure of the critic network, the computation graph of the policy optimization and the prediction process of the dynamic model, is given in Fig. 1.

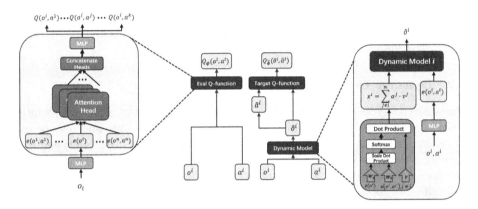

Fig. 1. The overall framework of our proposed method. The computation graph of the model-based TD-error is placed in the middle. The critic network, as shown in the left, uses the attention mechanism to adapt the dynamic dependence of other agents. In order to optimize the policy, the dynamic model is used to derive the values of target Q-function. Note that the attention module in critic network is shared with dynamic model during the process of policy optimization since they both need to consider the information of other agents.

4.1   Model-Based Policy Optimization

Policy optimization with dynamic models learns an accurate critic Q-function Q_{ϕ^i} with parameter ϕ^i for each agent. Denoting the policy of agent i as π_{θ^i} with parameter θ^i and the transition function of the true environment as $p\left(o^i_{t+1}|o^i_t, a^i_t\right)$, the traditional TD-learning can be seen as an optimization problem:

$$\arg\min_{\phi^i} \mathbb{E}_{\substack{o^i_t \sim \mathcal{D} \\ o^i_{t+1} \sim p\left(o^i_{t+1}|o^i_t, \pi^i_\theta(o^i_t)\right)}} \left[\delta_{\phi^i}\left(o^i_t, \pi_{\theta^i}(o^i_t), o^i_{t+1}\right)\right]. \tag{6}$$

Computing the gradient of TD-error δ_{ϕ^i} requires considering the effect of action $a_t^i = \pi_{\theta^i}(o_t^i)$ on the transition to the subsequent state o_{t+1}^i, and this equals to back-propagating through the true environment dynamics $p\left(o_{t+1}^i | o_t^i, a_t^i\right)$. In POD2M, agent i learns a decentralized model $\hat{p}^i\left(\hat{o}_{t+1}^i | o_t^i, a_t^i\right)$ to approximate its own state transitions and uses the learned model to derive predicted rollouts.

In Eq. (2), the approximate Q-function of subsequent state o_{t+1}^i is used to optimize the critic network. In order to incorporate the model estimations, we take advantage of the dynamic model to make one-step predictions and sample $\hat{o}_{t+1}^i$ from $\hat{p}^i\left(\cdot | o_t^i, \pi_{\theta^i}(o_t^i)\right)$, leading to the following model-based TD-error:

$$\hat{\delta}_{\phi^i}(o_t^i, \pi_{\theta^i}(o_t^i), \hat{o}_{t+1}^i) = \left[r(o_t^i, a_t^i) + \gamma Q_{\bar{\phi}^i}\left(\hat{o}_{t+1}^i, \pi_{\theta^i}(\hat{o}_{t+1}^i)\right) - Q_{\phi^i}(o_t^i, a_t^i)\right]^2. \quad (7)$$

In this one-step policy optimization method, the agents only need to learn the transition model rather than reward model or opponents' policy models. However, some commonly used model-based RL methods [27,28,37] require not only predicted transition function but also predicted reward function and opponents' polices. These methods may take compound bias into policy optimization, potentially resulting in bad performance and high variance.

4.2 Dynamic Dependence Modeling

There are many ways for an agent to take the information of other agents into consideration, such as communication [38], social influence [39], and opponents modeling [40]. Dynamically assigning importance weights to other agents enables each agent to selectively consider the information of other agents. We apply the attention mechanism [41] in our method for dynamic dependence modeling and thus efficient critic learning. Taking agent i's observation o^i, action a^i and the information of other agents (o^{-i}, a^{-i}) as input, the critic Q-function can be written as follows:

$$Q_{\phi^i}(o^i, a^i, o^{-i}, a^{-i}) = Q_{\phi^i}(e^i(o^i, a^i), x^i)$$
$$x^i = \sum_{j \neq i} \alpha^j v^j, \quad (8)$$

where e^i is a one-layer MLP embedding function, x^i is the contribution from other agents, v^j is agent j's values, and α^j is the attention weight of agent j. Since the attention mechanism requires the same embedding space among selectors, keys and values, the embedding function e^i is used to map (o^i, a^i) to the same dimension with x^i, i.e., the weighted sum of other agents' values. The attention weight α^j is derived by comparing embedding e^j with e^i and mapping the similarity value between the two embeddings into a softmax: $softmax\left(\dfrac{W_q W_k^T}{\sqrt{d_{w_k}}}\right)$ [41], where W_q transforms e^i into a "query" and W_k transforms e^j into a "key".

Multiple attention heads are used in our experiments, and each head maintains a separate tuple of parameters (W_k, W_q, V). The vector x^i is then constructed simply by concatenating the contribution from others.

The learning of the dynamic models utilizes the same attention component in the critic learning. In this way, each agent is able to selectively take other agents' information into account when predicting its own state transition. The dynamic model for agent i can be written as:

$$\hat{o}^i_{t+1} = \hat{p}^i(\cdot|e^i(o^i_t, a^i_t), x^i_t). \tag{9}$$

The counterfactual advantage trick [42] defined below is employed to solve the credit assignment problem:

$$A^i = Q_{\phi^i}(o, (a^i, a^{-i})) - \mathbb{E}_{a' \sim \mathcal{A}^i} Q_{\phi^i}(o, (a', a^{-i})), \tag{10}$$

where o is the concatenated observations of all the agents, a^{-i} is the joint action of all the agents except agent i and a' is every possible action that agent i can take. The gradient of the objective function in Eq. (1) then can be given by:
$\nabla_{\theta^i} J\left(\pi_{\theta^i}\right) = \nabla_{\theta^i} \log\left(\pi_{\theta^i}\left(a^i|o^i\right)\right) A^i.$

Algorithm 1. Policy Optimization with Dynamic Dependence Modeling (POD2M)

Initialize: policy π_{θ^i}, Q-function Q_{ϕ^i}, dynamic model $\hat{p}^i$, ,target policy $\pi_{\overline{\theta}^i}$, target Q-function $Q_{\overline{\phi}^i}$, environment buffer $\mathcal{D}_{env}$

1: **for** each episode **do**
2:      **for** m trajectories **do**
3:          Collect transitions $\left(o^i, a^i, o'^i, r^i\right)$ acting according to the policy π_{θ^i}
4:          $\mathcal{D}_{env} \leftarrow \mathcal{D}_{env} \cup \left(o^i, a^i, o'^i, r^i\right)$
5:      **end for**
6:      **for** model training steps **do**
7:          Train model $\hat{p}^i$ on $\mathcal{D}_{env}$
8:      **end for**
9:      **for** policy optimization steps **do**
10:         Extract local information $\left(o^i, a^i, r^i\right) \sim \mathcal{D}_{env}$
11:         Compute the encoding representation $e(o^i, a^i)$ and weighted sum x^i of other agents
12:         $\hat{y} \leftarrow r\left(o^i, a^i\right) + \gamma Q_{\overline{\phi}^i}(e^i(\hat{o}^i, \pi_{\overline{\theta}^i}(\hat{o}^i)), \hat{x}^i)$ where $\hat{o}^i \sim \hat{p}^i\left(\cdot|o^i, a^i\right)$
13:         $\hat{\delta}_{\phi^i}(o^i, \pi_{\theta^i}(o^i), \hat{o}^i) \leftarrow \left(\hat{y} - Q_{\phi^i}(e^i(o^i, \pi_{\theta^i}(o^i), x^i))\right)^2$
14:         $\phi^i \leftarrow \phi^i - \alpha_Q \nabla_{\phi^i} \hat{\delta}_{\phi^i}$
15:         $\overline{\phi}^i \leftarrow \tau\phi^i + (1 - \tau)\overline{\phi}^i$
16:         **if** t mod d=0 **then**
17:             $\theta^i \leftarrow \theta^i + \alpha_\pi \nabla_{\theta^i} \log\left(\pi_{\theta^i}(a^i|o^i)\right) A^i(o^i, a^i)$
18:             $\overline{\theta}^i \leftarrow \tau\phi^i + (1 - \tau)\overline{\theta}^i$
19:         **end if**
20:      **end for**
21: **end for**

The overall algorithm of our proposed POD2M method is present in Algorithm 1. For simplicity, the algorithm is described in the perspective of agent i and we use o^i to represent the current local observation and $\hat{o}^i$ to represent the model predicted subsequent observation. For the interaction with the true environment (line 2 to 5), the sampled trajectories are used to train the dynamic model and policy optimization. The training method of the dynamic model (line 6 to 8) for agent i can be written as

$$\mathcal{L}_{model} = \sum_{t=1}^{N} \left\| \hat{p}^i \left(e^i(o_t^i, a_t^i), x_t^i \right) - o_{t+1}^i \right\|_2^2 . \tag{11}$$

RL agent use both true trajectories and predicted rollouts to update its critic and policy networks (line 9 to 19).

5   Experiments

5.1   Setup

We evaluate our method in the two-dimensional Multi-agent Particle Environment (MPE) [20] that consists of X agents and Y landmarks. There are multiple environments including cooperative scenarios (all agents maximize a shared return) and competitive scenarios (agents have conflicting aims) in MPE. The agents have continuous observation spaces (information including the location and speed) and discrete action spaces (move up, down, left, right and stay). Here we focus on three scenarios, i.e., the Spread, Tag and Adversary as introduced in Fig. 2.

We first introduce the model-based policy optimization method in multi-agent systems with centralized dynamic model, denoted as Policy Optimization with Centralized Modeling (POCM). We regard POCM as an essential method to compare to our proposed POD2M. The main idea of POCM method is to consider the multiple agents as a single agent. The multi-agent systems have only one single dynamic model to approximate the transition function of the true environment. Since this model serves for all the agents and performs a centralized role in the system, it can be considered as a centralized model and formulated as follows:

$$\left(\hat{o}_{t+1}^1, ..., \hat{o}_{t+1}^n \right) = \hat{p} \left(o_t^1, a_t^1, ..., o_t^n, a_t^n \right) . \tag{12}$$

The centralized model for the multi-agent systems can be constructed by considering the local observations of all the agents as the input, and the concatenation of all the predicted local observations as the output. In competitive scenarios, the single opponent agent uses the model-based deterministic policy gradient method [37] to update its policy.

An ensemble of 8 neural networks of 3 hidden layers with 256 neurons is used for the dynamic models that learn the transition between the current and next states for agent i as $\hat{o}_{t+1}^i = o_t^i + \hat{p}(o_t^i, a_t^i)$. We employ multi-layer perceptrons for the actor (3 layers, 64 neurons for each agent) and the critic (3 layers, 128 neurons for each agent). All the neural networks are trained with Adam optimizer with learning rate of 0.001 and weight decay of 0.0001. As we describe in the section of our method, we employ the attention component for both critic networks and dynamic models with 4 attention heads and respective "quer","key" and "value" parameters. We use the same dimension of inputs between critic networks and the attention component by utilizing the state embedding function $e^i(o^i_t)$ and state-action embedding function $e^i(o^i_t, a^i_t)$, which are used to encode the information for the attention component, with 1 layer and 128 neurons. We employ a delay in the policy updates d of 2 and a soft-update ratio τ of 0.01 for target networks. We employ a discounted factor γ of 0.95. Moreover, we employ categorical sampling for action selections and set norm gradient clipping to 10 by default for all the experiments.

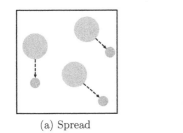 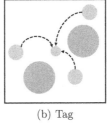 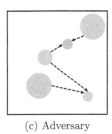

(a) Spread   (b) Tag   (c) Adversary

Fig. 2. (a) Spread: a cooperative scenario including 3 agents and 3 landmarks and these agents should learn to reach the landmarks respectively while avoiding collisions and repeated overlays. (b) Tag: a competitive scenario including 3 good agents (red), 1 opponent (green) and random obstacles (grey). The good agents learn to cooperate to pursue and capture their opponent while the opponent agent, possessing faster speed, learns to avoid being caught by the good agents. (c) Adversary: a competitive scenario including 2 good agents (blue), 1 opponent agent (red), 1 goal landmark (green) and 1 fake landmark (grey). The opponent agent can only observe the position of good agents and aim to find out the good landmark to overlay while the 2 good agents learn to confuse their opponent and reach the goal landmarks respectively. (Color figure online)

5.2   Results

Cooperative Scenario. To make a full comparison between POD2M and model-free methods, Value-Decomposition Networks (VDN) [30], Multi-Actor-Attention-Critic (MAAC) [29] and Counterfactual Multi-Agent (COMA) [42] are implemented in the fully cooperative scenario, i.e. Spread, though they are originally applied to the SMAC [43] tasks. As shown in Fig. 3, in the Spread domain, the average reward achieves nearly -5.5 when all the agents are able to reach their landmarks respectively. In contrast to traditional model-free algorithms, the convergence of model-based methods are much faster. This reveals

that POD2M can achieve higher sample efficiency than model-free MARL methods. The centralized method POCM can also achieve high learning performance
in this domain due to its relatively small scale and thus accurate estimation of
the centralized model.

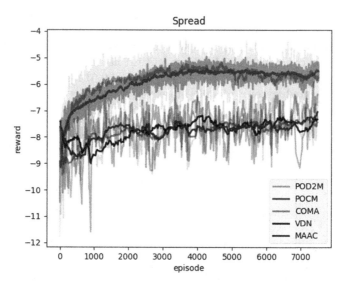

Fig. 3. The reward curve of POD2M against traditional model-free MARL algorithms
and POCM method in the cooperative scenario for 7500 episodes.

Competitive Scenarios. Tag is a competitive scenario where three good agents
learn their own policies and get the rewards respectively instead of a shared
return. Hence, it is hard to use the rewards of the three good agents to represent
the performance of the method in this scenario. We evaluate the coordinated
behaviors of the three good agents by the learning curve of the opponent agent
pursued and chased by the good agents. The Adversary domain is also a competitive scenario that two good agents receive their rewards respectively. Since
the goals of the two agents is relatively unified, we use the sum of their rewards
to assess the learning results of this scenario. In these competitive scenarios, the
dynamic models for the good agents are constructed by considering the whole
agents' information including the information of their opponent. The opponent
agent uses its own information to build the dynamic model and utilizes the same
policy optimization method as the good agents.

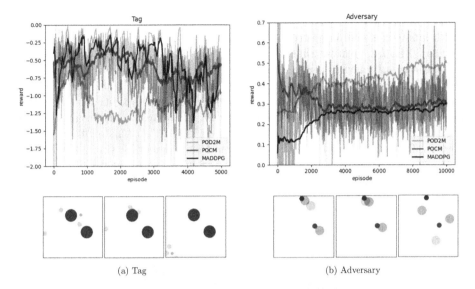

(a) Tag   (b) Adversary

Fig. 4. (a) The reward curve of the opponent agent pursed by the good agents. The less reward the opponent agent receives, the better learning performance the good agents have achieved. (b) The average return of the 2 cooperative agents. Higher rewards indicate better learning performance.

Note that in the Tag and Adversary scenarios, we only compare POD2M with POCM and Multi-Agent Deep Deterministic Policy Gradient (MADDPG) [20]. The methods mentioned in Spread, such as COMA, VDN and MAAC, are tested in the fully cooperative SMAC tasks and thus not suitable for competitive scenarios. POCM method constructs a centralized model for all the agents in the environment to approximate the transition function. In other words, the centralized model includes the information of both the good agents and opponent agent.

In Fig. 4 (a), we can see that the reward of the opponent agent shows an upward trend in the early stage, because the opponent agent learns to avoid being caught. After a few episodes, the good agents have learned the coordinated behaviors to purse and capture their opponent so that the reward of the opponent falls. However, the good agents using the POD2M method can learn more quickly to capture the opponent agent, compared to the MADDPG and POCM methods. In Fig. 4 (b), POD2M still performs best among the three methods. It is a bit surprising to observe that, in this domain, the performance of POCM is rather poor, suggesting the limits of building centralized model in competitive domains.

Larger Scale Scenario. POD2M takes the mutual dependence of other agents into consideration by using the soft limits instead of the total inputs of local observations and actions. We extend the POD2M method to a larger scale domain to evaluate its scalability. We employ Spread with 6 cooperative agents and 6 landmarks compared to the 3 particles scenario mentioned above.

From Fig. 5, we can see that POD2M can still keep high sample efficiency and achieve a steady asymptotic performance. The model-free algorithms combine the information of all the agents as the inputs of their critic Q-functions. Due to the exponential growth of the dimension, the expression capacity decreases significantly, which makes policy learning difficult. Unlike in the small scale domain in Fig. 3, where POCM performs similarly with POD2M, in this relatively larger domain, POCM cannot converge to the same level of POD2M, since POCM uses the combination of local observations and actions to estimate the joint model and thus encounters the same scalability problem as the model-free methods.

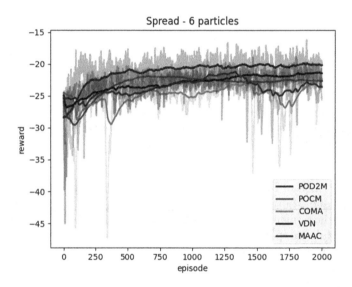

Fig. 5. The larger scale performances among model-based and model-free algorithms

6 Conclusion

In this paper, we investigated model-based MARL problems and designed a method utilizing the dynamic dependence among agents and model-based policy optimization for more efficient model estimation and policy learning. In multi-agent systems, the agents need to dynamically adapt their dependence when building their own dynamic models in order to make a trade-off between the individual-agent learning process and the coordinated learning process. We validate our method in both cooperative scenarios and competitive scenarios using the particle environment. The results reveal that our method can converge efficiently and derive higher sample efficiency than the model-free algorithms. The final asymptotic performance shows that our method can achieve a comparable result against the centralized model-based MARL method in small-scale domains and much better performance in larger domains. In the future, we plan to provide theoretical analysis of our proposed method, and evaluate it in other more complex domains.

Acknowledgement. This work is supported by the National Natural Science Foundation of China under Grant 62076259.

References

1. Mnih, V., et al.: Human-level control through deep reinforcement learning. Nature **518**(7540), 529–533 (2015)
2. Silver, D., et al.: Mastering the game of go with deep neural networks and tree search. Nature **529**(7587), 484–489 (2016)
3. Toyama, D., et al.: Androidenv: a reinforcement learning platform for android. arXiv preprint arXiv:2105.13231 (2021)
4. Luo, Y., Xu, H., Li, Y., Tian, Y., Darrell, T., Ma, T.: Algorithmic framework for model-based deep reinforcement learning with theoretical guarantees. arXiv preprint arXiv:1807.03858 (2018)
5. Silver, D., Lever, G., Heess, N., Degris, T., Wierstra, D., Riedmiller, M.: Deterministic policy gradient algorithms. In International Conference on Machine Learning, pp. 387–395. PMLR (2014)
6. Schulman, J., Levine, S., Abbeel, P., Jordan, M., Moritz, P.: Trust region policy optimization. In: International Conference on Machine Learning, pp. 1889–1897. PMLR (2015)
7. Schulman, J., Wolski, F., Dhariwal, P., Radford, A., Klimov, O.: Proximal policy optimization algorithms. arXiv preprint arXiv:1707.06347 (2017)
8. Haarnoja, T., Zhou, A., Abbeel, P., Levine, S.: Soft actor-critic: off-policy maximum entropy deep reinforcement learning with a stochastic actor. In: International Conference on Machine Learning, pp. 1861–1870. PMLR (2018)
9. Moerland, T.M., Broekens, J., Jonker, C.M.: Model-based reinforcement learning: a survey. arXiv preprint arXiv:2006.16712 (2020)
10. Hafner, D., et al.: Learning latent dynamics for planning from pixels. In: International Conference on Machine Learning, pp. 2555–2565. PMLR (2019)
11. Schrittwieser, J., et al.: Mastering atari, go, chess and shogi by planning with a learned model. Nature **588**(7839), 604–609 (2020)
12. Todorov, E., Erez, T., Tassa, Y.: Mujoco: a physics engine for model-based control. In: 2012 IEEE/RSJ International Conference on Intelligent Robots and Systems, pp. 5026–5033. IEEE (2012)
13. Chao, Yu., Dong, Y., Li, Y., Chen, Y.: Distributed multi-agent deep reinforcement learning for cooperative multi-robot pursuit. J. Eng. **2020**(13), 499–504 (2020)
14. Vinyals, O., et al.: Starcraft II: a new challenge for reinforcement learning. arXiv preprint arXiv:1708.04782 (2017)
15. Wu, Z., Yu, C., Ye, D., Zhang, J., Piao, H., Zhuo, H.H.: Coordinated proximal policy optimization. arXiv preprint arXiv:2111.04051 (2021)
16. Wang, R.E., et al.: Model-based reinforcement learning for decentralized multiagent rendezvous. In Conference on Robot Learning (CoRL), pp. 711–725 (2020)
17. Chao, Yu., et al.: Distributed multiagent coordinated learning for autonomous driving in highways based on dynamic coordination graphs. IEEE Trans. Intell. Transp. Syst. **21**(2), 735–748 (2019)

18. Willemsen, D., Coppola, M., Che de Croon, G.: Mambpo: sample-efficient multi-robot reinforcement learning using learned world models. arXiv preprint arXiv:2103.03662 (2021)

19. Chao, Yu., Zhang, M., Ren, F., Tan, G.: Multiagent learning of coordination in loosely coupled multiagent systems. IEEE Trans. Cybernet. **45**(12), 2853–2867 (2015)

20. Lowe, R., Wu, Y., Tamar, A., Harb, J., Abbeel, P., Mordatch, I.: Multi-agent actor-critic for mixed cooperative-competitive environments. In: Advances in Neural Information Processing Systems, pp. 6382–6393 (2017)

21. Nagabandi, A., Kahn, G., Fearing, R.S., Levine, S.: Neural network dynamics for model-based deep reinforcement learning with model-free fine-tuning. In: 2018 IEEE International Conference on Robotics and Automation (ICRA), pp. 7559–7566. IEEE (2018)

22. Chua, K., Calandra, R., McAllister, R., Levine, S.: Deep reinforcement learning in a handful of trials using probabilistic dynamics models. In: Advances in Neural Information Processing Systems, pp. 4759–4770 (2018)

23. Sutton, R.S.: Integrated architectures for learning, planning, and reacting based on approximating dynamic programming. In: Machine Learning Proceedings 1990, pp. 216–224. Elsevier (1990)

24. Wang, T., Ba, J.: Exploring model-based planning with policy networks. arXiv preprint arXiv:1906.08649 (2019)

25. Feinberg, V., Wan, A., Stoica, I., Jordan, M.I., Gonzalez, J.E., Levine, S.: Model-based value estimation for efficient model-free reinforcement learning. arXiv preprint arXiv:1803.00101 (2018)

26. Clavera, I., Fu, V., Abbeel, P.: Model-augmented actor-critic: Backpropagating through paths. In: International Conference on Learning Representations (2020)

27. Janner, M., Fu, J., Zhang, M., Levine, S.: When to trust your model: model-based policy optimization. In: Advances in Neural Information Processing Systems, pp. 12498–12509 (2019)

28. Rajeswaran, A., Mordatch, I., Kumar, V.: A game theoretic framework for model based reinforcement learning. In: International Conference on Machine Learning, pp. 7953–7963. PMLR (2020)

29. Iqbal, S., Sha, F.: Actor-attention-critic for multi-agent reinforcement learning. In: International Conference on Machine Learning, pp. 2961–2970. PMLR (2019)

30. Sunehag, P., et al.: Value-decomposition networks for cooperative multi-agent learning. arXiv preprint arXiv:1706.05296 (2017)

31. Du, Y., Han, L., Fang, M., Liu, J., Dai, T., Tao, D.: Liir: learning individual intrinsic reward in multi-agent reinforcement learning. In: Advances in Neural Information Processing Systems, pp. 4403–4414 (2019)

32. Wang, T., Dong, H., Lesser, V., Zhang, C.: Roma: multi-agent reinforcement learning with emergent roles. In: International Conference on Machine Learning, pp. 9876–9886 (2020)

33. Park, Y.J., Cho, Y.S., Kim, S.B.: Multi-agent reinforcement learning with approximate model learning for competitive games. PLoS ONE **14**(9), e0222215 (2019)

34. Zhang, W., Wang, X., Shen, J., Zhou, M.: Model-based multi-agent policy optimization with adaptive opponent-wise rollouts. arXiv preprint arXiv:2105.03363 (2021)

35. Konda, V.R., Tsitsiklis, J.N.: Actor-critic algorithms. In: Advances in Neural Information Processing Systems, pp. 1008–1014 (2000)

36. Kurutach, T., Clavera, I., Duan, Y., Tamar, A., Abbeel, P.: Model-ensemble trust-region policy optimization. In: International Conference on Learning Representations (2018)

37. D'Oro, P., Jaśkowski, W.: How to learn a useful critic? Model-based action-gradient-estimator policy optimization. In: Advances in Neural Information Processing Systems, pp. 313–324 (2020)

38. Sukhbaatar, S., Fergus, R., et al.: Learning multiagent communication with back-propagation. In: Advances in Neural Information Processing Systems, pp. 2244–2252 (2016)

39. Wang, T., Wang, J., Wu, Y., Zhang, C.: Influence-based multi-agent exploration. In: International Conference on Learning Representations (2019)

40. He, H., Boyd-Graber, J., Kwok, K., Daumé III, H.: Opponent modeling in deep reinforcement learning. In: International Conference on Machine Learning, pp. 1804–1813. PMLR (2016)

41. Vaswani, A., et al.:. Attention is all you need. In: Advances in Neural Information Processing Systems, pp. 5998–6008 (2017)

42. Foerster, J., Farquhar, G., Afouras, T., Nardelli, N., Whiteson, S.: Counterfactual multi-agent policy gradients. In: Proceedings of the AAAI Conference on Artificial Intelligence, vol. 32, pp. 2974–2982 (2018)

43. Samvelyan, M., et al.: The starcraft multi-agent challenge. In: International Conference on Autonomous Agents and Multiagent Systems (AAMAS), pp. 2186–2188 (2019)

Multi-index Federated Aggregation Algorithm Based on Trusted Verification

Zhenshan Bao, Wei Bai, and Wenbo Zhang[✉]

The Faculty of Information Technology, Beijing University of Technology, Beijing 100124, China
zhangwenbo@bjut.edu.cn

Abstract. Movited by the modern phenomenon of distributed data collected by edge devices at scale, federated learning can use the large amounts of training data from diverse users for better representation and generalization. To improve flexibility and scalability, we propose a new federated optimization algorithm, named as Multi-index federated aggregation algorithm based on trusted verfication(TVFedmul). TVFedmul is optimized based on Fedavg algorithm, which overcomes a series of problems caused by the original aggregation algorithm, which only takes the single index of data quantity as a reference factor to measure the aggregation weight of each client. The improved aggregation algorithm is based on multi-index measurement, which can reflect the comprehensive ability of clients more comprehensively, so as to make overall judgment. Further, we introduces hyperparameter α, which can be changed to determine the importance of the indexes. Finally, via extensive experimentation, the efficiency and effectiveness of the proposed algorithm is verified.

Keywords: Federated learning · Aggregation algorithm · Distributed learning

1 Introduction

With the growing prevalence of edge devices, designing communication-efficient techniques for learning using client data is an increasingly important area in distributed machine learning. AI-based solutions rely intrinsically on appropriate algorithms, but even more so on large training datasets [1]. Federated learning has emerged as an important paradigm in modern large-scale machine learning [2]. In federated learning, the training data remains distributed over a large number of clients [3]. Data is typically generated at different scenarios, which can lead to significant differences in the distribution of data across data partitions [4]. A federated learning system is often composed of servers and clients, with an architecture that is similar to parameter servers [5]. The main objective of federated learning is to fit a model to data generated from network devices without continuous transfer of the massive amount of collected data from edge of the network to back-end servers for processing [6, 7].

Federated averaging (Fedavg) [8] has emerged due to its simplicity and low communication cost. In each iteration, the algorithm selects a number of clients with a ratio

© Springer Nature Switzerland AG 2022
H. Shen et al. (Eds.): PDCAT 2021, LNCS 13148, pp. 412–420, 2022.
https://doi.org/10.1007/978-3-030-96772-7_37

of ρ, and performs the stochastic gradient decent and loss function on the local private data. The key challenges for Fedavg are 1) The update mode of Fedavg with reference to single data quantity may cause clients to overstate the quantity of data in order to make their local model occupy a large proportion in aggregation. 2) Fedavg increases the insecurity of the system. 3) In the training process, the noise data will downgrade the model. On the contrary, if the dataset with small data amount is of good quality and more representative [9, 10], it also makes its own contribution to the model. 4) When the data is heterogeneous (non-iid), fedavg may result in unstable and slow convergence.

To address the above, in this study, we propose a new algorithm TVFedmul. The contributions of our work can be summarized as follows.

1) TVFedmul take the data quantity, as well as data quality, into the contribution to federal learning model.
2) TVFedmul increases the security and fairness of the federated system to a certain extent.
3) TVFedmul make the federated system more flexible and scalable.
4) The customized federated learning is realized and the practicability of the algorithm is improved.

2 Related Work

Recently we have witnessed significant progress in developing novel methods that address different challenges in federated learning. Zhang et al. [11] proposed an asynchronous approach with "soft" averaging, which only consider the data center setting, and do not consider datasets that are unbalanced and non-iid, properties that are essential to the federated learning setting. Chen et al. [12] proposed FedSA, a novel federated learning algorithm that accelerates convergence and resists performance degradation caused by non-iid data and staleness. Despite the attention on performance degradation with non-iid data in recent works [13], none of them provide the theoretical guarantees. Zhou et al. [14] proposed methods that dynamically change learning rates, including learning rate decay and adaptive learning rates. Xie et al. [15] proposed an algorithm that uses a mixed hyperparameter to balance the robustness-efficiency trade-offs. However, this method, in general, only evaluate equally sized local data, thus failed to generalize into more practical situations where most real-world data are different in size. Alireza Fallah et al. [16] considered the heterogeneous case in federated learning, and studied a personalized variant of the classic federated learning formulation in which the goal is to find a proper initialization model for the users that can be quickly adapted to the local data of each user after the training phase. Li et al. [17] proposed a q-FFL, a novel optimization objective inspired by fair resource allocation in wireless networks that encourages fairer accuracy distributions across devices in federated learning. However, none of the federated learning algorithms studied the effect of the quality of the privacy data owned by the clients.

3   TVFedmul

3.1   Weight Calculation

Data Quantity Proportion

We denote data quantity ratio as Q_1, which is fixed during each round of aggregation because the number of data of each client is determined.

Assume that there are k clients, each client $i \in [1, k]$ has its own local private data D_i containing n_k data samples. $\sum_{i=1}^{k} n_k$ represents the total number of data owned by each client, denoted as n. Then the data quantity ratio Q_1^i of client i is calculated as follows Eq. (1).

$$Q_1^i = \frac{n_i}{n}, i \in (1, 2 \cdots k) \tag{1}$$

Data Quality Proportion

We denote data quality ratio as Q_2. In federated learning, the update effect is the most intuitive reflection of the data quality. Therefore, the TVFedmul algorithm introduces verification nodes to verify the model update effect of each client.

The verification node can obtain the model update information of each client. Therefore, the verification node should be an honest node with high comprehensive capability. In TVFedmul, the honesty and comprehensive ability of each client are measured by their performance on the public data set. The verification nodes of this round are selected from the first λ clients with the highest model verification scores in the previous round. The clients selected as the verification node of this round will not participate in the training of this round, but will validate and score the updated model from other clients with their local data set. It can be seen that the verification nodes change dynamically in each round, and so does the public data set, which increases the generalization ability of the model to a certain extent. To prevent clients with high-quality data from being selected as validation nodes that do not participate in model updates, thus breaking the overall model iteration efficiency, the first λ nodes in the even number position are selected as the verification nodes according to the score from high to low.

Assume that there are k clients, m verification nodes. S_{ij} represents the test accuracy of the model update for the ith client on the jth verification node. Then the final score S_i is calculated as follows:

$$S_i = \frac{1}{m} \sum_{j=1}^{m} S_{ij} \tag{2}$$

where $\sum_{i=1}^{k} S_i$ represents the total score of each client, as S. Then the ratio of data quality to Q_2^i is calculated as follows:

$$Q_2^i = \frac{S_i}{S}, i \in (1, 2 \cdots k) \tag{3}$$

3.2 Aggregation

The objective function is $\min\limits_{\omega \in R^d} f(\omega)$, Then the $f(\omega)$ is calculated as follows:

$$f(\omega) \stackrel{def}{=} \frac{1}{n} \sum_{i=1}^{n} f_i(\omega) \tag{4}$$

$$f_i(\omega) = L(x_i, y_i; \omega) \tag{5}$$

where $L(x_i, y_i; \omega)$ represents the result of the loss of sample (x_i, y_i) as predicted on the given parameter ω.

Assume D_k is the data set owned by the k-th client, n_k represents the size of clients. The average loss of the samples for client k is:

$$F_k(\omega) = \frac{1}{n_k} \sum_{i \in P_k} f_i(\omega) \tag{6}$$

The gradient of the k client in the t iteration is $g_k = \nabla F_k(\omega_t)g_k$, learning rate is η. Then the calculation of local update for this round is as follows:

$$\omega_{t+1}^k \leftarrow \omega_t^k - \eta \nabla F_k(\omega^k) \tag{7}$$

After each client completes the local update, the results are uploaded to the verification nodes. Then they uploads to the aggregation server that calculates the update weight of each client in the round and performs the aggregation.

The aggregation weight Q_t^i of the client k in the round t is:

$$Q_t^i = \alpha \frac{n_i}{n} + (1 - \alpha) \frac{1}{m} \frac{\sum_{j=1}^{m} S_{ij}}{S} \tag{8}$$

Here, α is a hyperparameter that can be changed according to the specific federated learning task, used to adjust the two influencing factors.

The score of the local model on the public test set reflects the data quality of the clients to some extent. $\frac{S_i}{S}$ is used as one of the reference factors together with $\frac{n_k}{n}$ to determine the contribution of clients to the global model. Compared with the fedavg algorithm, the integrated metrics make the evaluation of the clients more rigorous and comprehensive, more conducive to the aggregate server to make a judgment as a whole. In addition, because of many iterations, the local model of each client has a different percentage Q_2^i for each round, as a result, the comprehensive weight of each client in each round of model aggregation is different, and the variable weight truly reflects the contribution of each client to the global model of updating.

The global parameter of round t aggregation is:

$$\omega_{t+1} \leftarrow \sum_{k=1}^{k} Q_t^k \omega_{t+1}^k \tag{9}$$

where ω_{t+1}^k comes from Eq. (7).

The total loss function of round t model is:

$$f_t(\omega) = \sum_{k=1}^{k} Q_t^k F_k(\omega) \tag{10}$$

Where $F_k(\omega)$ comes from Eq. (6).

4 System Model

Figure 1 shows the architecture of TVFedmul algorithm. The algorithm consists of distributed training stage, model verification stage and model aggregation stage.

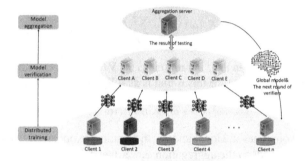

Fig. 1. The architecture of TVFedmul

5 Experimental Validation

5.1 Datasets

In this section, we empirically evaluate the proposed algorithm in iid and non-iid. The training set is partitioned onto n = 100 devices. We conduct experiments on benchmark: MNIST (http://yann.lecun.com/exdb/mnist/). When it is used to non-iid, each client can only own a part of the data sets of categories. First, the MNIST is sorted in descending order with labels 0 to 9, and then the images are sliced to make the image labels in each slice the same, that is, the same number. Divide it into 200 pieces, each containing 300 images. Distributed to 100 clients to simulate the private data owned by each client that is assigned only two possible data sets: 600 images containing only one kind of label and 300 images each containing two kinds of label. During the federal training, clients do not share data with each other. They can only access the data assigned to them, and can only access the numbers with two different labels, which well simulates the data distribution in the non-iid.

5.2 Experimental

Non-IID

In order to verify the influence of the proportion of clients, two algorithms were used to conduct experiments. Among them, in Fedavg, a total of 200 rounds of training, ρ were set at 0.1, 0.3, 0.5 and 0.7 respectively, as shown in Fig. 2. In TVFedmul, a total of 260 rounds of training, α were set at 0.5, ρ were set at 0.1, 0.3, 0.5, 0.7, respectively, as shown in Fig. 3. It can be seen from the results that, the more clients participate in the training, the faster convergence rate of the model, and the higher accuracy.

In order to verify the influence of the two factors in the TVFedmul, α were taken for comparison experiment, the proportions of data quantity were 0.1, 0.3, 0.5, 0.7 and 0.9, and the proportions of data quality were 0.9, 0.7, 0.5, 0.3 and 0.1. The experiment round was 260. The results are shown in Fig. 4. It can be seen from the results that when α is different, the convergence trend of the model is almost the same, but the convergence rate and the final accuracy are different. When $\alpha = 0.1$, the convergence effect of the model is the best, when $\alpha = 0.9$, it is the worst, and with the increase of α, the convergence effect of the model is better and better.

In order to further verify the effectiveness, two algorithms under the same experimental conditions were compared, as shown in Fig. 5. Among them, the training rounds are 240, ρ is 0.7, α is 0.1. It can be seen from the results that the model convergence speed of the improved algorithm is faster, and the final model accuracy reaches 94.59%, which is 2.53% higher than that of the Fedavg (92.06%). The Fig. 6. shows the loss of training.

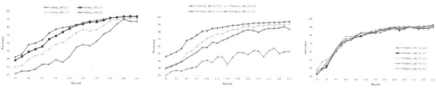

Fig. 2. Fedavg-noniid-ρ **Fig. 3.** TVFedmul-noniid-ρ **Fig. 4.** TVFedmul-noniid-α

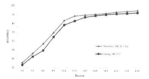

Fig. 5. TVFedmul & Fedavg-noniid

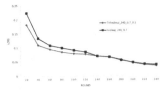

Fig. 6. The training loss of TVFedmul & Fedavg-noniid

IID

The same experiment is carried out in the iid.

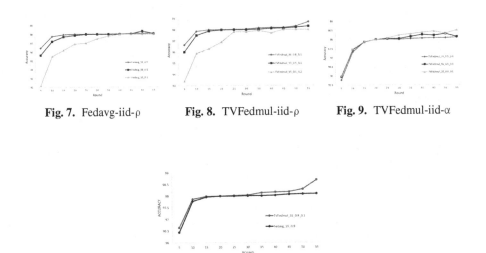

Fig. 7. Fedavg-iid-ρ   **Fig. 8.** TVFedmul-iid-ρ   **Fig. 9.** TVFedmul-iid-α

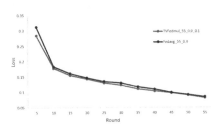

Fig. 10. TVFedmul & Fedavg-iid

Fig. 11. The training loss of TVFedmul & Fedavg-iid

As shown in Fig. 7 and Fig. 8 different values of the parameters are verified by using Fedavg algorithm and TVFedmul algorithm, which are 0.1, 0.5 and 0.9 respectively. The experimental results are consistent, that is, the convergence rate and training accuracy of the model are improved with the increase of the number of clients.

As shown in Fig. 9, the convergence effect of the model with hyperparameters of 0.1, 0.5 and 0.9 is shown, again confirming that data quality has a greater impact on the federated system, two factors should be considered in model aggregation. As shown in Fig. 10, TVFedmul is superior to Fedavg in iid, and the training accuracy of the model is improved from 98.1% to 98.69%. The Fig. 11. shows the loss of training.

6 Conclusion

In this work, we propose TVFedmul, which takes data quantity and data quality into consideration that calculate the aggregation weight more rigorous and comprehensive, speeds up the convergence rate and improves the accuracy of the global model. With the introduction of the data quantity, the comprehensive weight of the clients is adjusted according to the actual training effect, which improves the flexibility of the system. In addition, the way of multi-index aggregation to some extent increases the cost of evil node, and protects the fairness and security of the system. Finally, the introduction of super-parameter realizes customized federated learning.

References

1. Warnat-Herresthal, S., Schultze, H., Shastry, K.L., et al.: Swarm Learning for decentralized and confidential clinical machine learning. Nature **594**(7862), 265–270 (2021)
2. Jenny, H., Mehryar, M., Theertha, S.A.: FedBoost: communication-efficient algorithms for federated learning. In: International Conference on Machine Learning, pp. 3931–3941 (2020)
3. Karimireddy, S.P., Kale, S., Mohri, M., et al.: SCAFFOLD: stochastic controlled averaging for on-device federated learning. ArXiv (2019)
4. Kevin, H., Amar, P., Onur, M., et al.: The Non-IID data quagmire of decentralized machine learning. In: International Conference on Machine Learning, pp. 4337–4348 (2020)
5. Reisizadeh, A., Mokhtari, A., Hassani, H., et al.: FedPAQ: a communication-efficient federated learning method with periodic averaging and quantization. In: International Conference on Artificial Intelligence and Statistics, vol. 108, pp. 2021–2030 (2020)
6. Lingjuan, L., Jiangshan, Y., Karthik, N., et al.: Towards fair and privacy-preserving federated deep models. IEEE Trans. Parallel Distribut. Syst. **31**, 2524–2541 (2020)
7. Acar, D.A., Zhao, Y., Navarro, R.M., et al.: Federated learning based on dynamic regularization. In: International Conference on Learning Representations (2021)
8. McMahan, H.B., Moore, E., Ramage, D., et al.: Communication-efficient learning of deep networks from decentralized data. In: International Conference on Artificial Intelligence and Statistics, vol. 54, pp. 1273–1282 (2017)
9. Nishio, T., Yonetani, R.: Client selection for federated learning with heterogeneous resources in mobile edge. In: IEEE International Conference on Communications, pp. 1–7 (2019)
10. Li, L., Xu, W., Chen, T., et al.: RSA: byzantine-robust stochastic aggregation methods for distributed learning fron heterogeneous datasets. In: Proceeding of the AAAI Conference on Artificial Intelligence, vol. 33, pp. 1544–1551 (2019)
11. Zhang, S.X., Choromanska, A., LeCun, Y.: Deep learning with elastic averaging SGD. In: NIPS, vol. 28 (2015)
12. Chen, M., Mao, B.C., Ma, T.Y.: A staleness-aware asynchronous Federated Learning algorithm with non-IID data. Fut. Generation Comput. Syst. **120**, 1–12 (2021)

13. Li, X., Huang, K., Yang, W., et al.: On the convergence of FedAvg on Non-IID data. Arxiv (2020)
14. Wei, D., Yi, Z., Nanqing, D., et al.: Toward understanding the impact of stalenessn in distributed machine learning. In: International Conference on Learning Representations (2019)
15. Xie, C., Koyejo, O., Guptal, I.: Asynchronous federated optimization. ArXiv (2019)
16. Fallah, A., Mokhtari, A., Ozdaglar, A.: Personalized federated learning: a meta-learning approach. ArXiv (2020)
17. Li, T., Sanjabi, M., Smith, V.: Fair resource allocation in federated learning. ArXiv (2020)

Few-Shot Generative Learning by Modeling Stereoscopic Priors

Yuehui Wang, Qing Wang, and Dongyu Zhang$^{(\boxtimes)}$

Sun Yat-sen University, Guangzhou, China
wangyh83@mail2.sysu.edu.cn, zhangdy27@mail.sysu.edu.cn

Abstract. Few-shot image generation, which aims to generate images from only a few images for a new category, has attracted some research interest in recent years. However, existing few-shot generation methods only focus on 2D images, ignoring 3D information. In this work, we propose a few-shot generative network which leverages 3D priors to improve the diversity and quality of generated images. Inspired by classic graphics rendering pipelines, we unravel the image generation process into three factors: shape, viewpoint and texture. This disentangled representation enables us to make the most of both 3D and 2D information in few-shot generation. To be specific, by changing the viewpoint and extracting textures from different real images, we can generate various new images even in data-scarce settings. Extensive experiments show the effectiveness of our method.

Keywords: Computer vision · Few-shot image generation · Generative adversarial network · Data augmentation

1 Introduction

The challenge of learning new concept from very few examples, often called *few-shot learning* or *low-shot learning*, is a long-standing problem. Some recent works [9,11] explore the ability of few-shot generation under specific circumstances. To be more concrete, [11] proposes a meta-learning based method of generating personalized talking head images. [9] presents a framework to learn a generative model from a single natural image. However, they only focus on the information brought by 2D image dataset, we consider to use 3D priors to guide image generation.

In this paper, we explore image generation in few-shot settings and simultaneously care for 3D information: shape, viewpoint and texture. First, the *shape* of the objects in the generated images depends on the category of our 2D image dataset (*e.g.*, car, chair and table). Second, by changing the *viewpoint* of the

Supplementary Information The online version contains supplementary material available at https://doi.org/10.1007/978-3-030-96772-7_38.

H. Shen et al. (Eds.): PDCAT 2021, LNCS 13148, pp. 421–429, 2022.
https://doi.org/10.1007/978-3-030-96772-7_38

camera in the process of rendering 3D priors, we can get a variety of 2.5D samples (*e.g.*, depth images). After that, we extract the *texture* of an arbitrarily sampled image from the 2D image dataset. Finally, we recombine these three factors, with our novel generative model *Few-shot Generative Network with 3D priors (FGN-3D)*, to generate new images.

Fig. 1. Qualitative results. When given a real 3D prior (with determined *shape* and *viewpoint*) and a texture image, our model successfully apply the texture to the prior and generate realistic images without mode collapse nor mode confusion.

The few-shot learning ability of our proposed method is obtained through two stages: (a) meta-learning and (b) fine-tuning. Meta-learning is performed on *base classes* where a large training set of 3D collections and corresponding 2D real images is available. In the course of meta-learning, our system simulates few-shot learning tasks and learns to transform 2.5D samples (*e.g.*, depth images) into realistic RGB images. After that, we fine tune our models, with high-capacity generator and discriminator pre-trained via meta-learning, on *novel classes* where the training data is scarce. The proposed network quickly learns to generate realistic images of novel classes, which are unseen during meta-learning, after a few training steps. Note that during the whole training process, the 3D priors and the 2D real images do *not* need to be from the same class, *i.e.*, our model is class-agnostic. Figure 1 shows some qualitative results produced by our model, where the desired texture is applied to the specified 3D prior, regardless of their classes.

Summarizing the contributions of this paper, we:

- Propose a two-stage training model (FGN-3D) which introduces 3D priors into image generation in few-shot scenarios.
- Demonstrate that our model produces the state-of-the-art results compared to extended baselines while retaining good generalization performance.

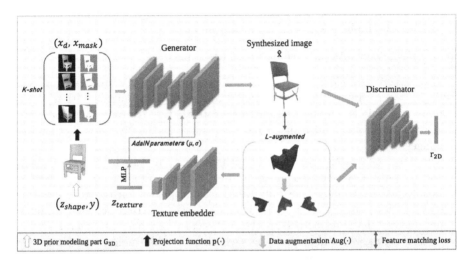

Fig. 2. Overview of the proposed FGN-3D model. To generate image $\hat{x}$, we first extract k depth and mask pairs from a 3D prior (from modeling in meta-learning stage or sampling in fine-tuning stage), after that we encode l augmented texture images into $Z_{texture}$. Finally we recombine them and choose the one with the lowest feature matching loss as the output.

2   Method

2.1   Architecture and Notation

First we'd like to introduce the necessary notations. Let $\mathbb{I}$ denote the 2D RGB image space $\mathbb{R}^{H \times W \times 3}$, $\mathbb{V}$ the 3D prior space $\mathbb{R}^{V \times V \times V}$ and $\mathbb{C} = \{0, \dots, L\}$ the discrete label space. Our training dataset S consists of 3D collections $\{v_i\}_i^N$ and real 2D RGB images $\{x_j\}_j^M$, i.e., $S = \{\{v_i\}_i^N, \{x_j\}_j^M\}$. Note that we use i and j to accentuate *no* pair relationship between 3D and 2D data. For few-shot learning, we separate the label space $\mathbb{C}$ into $\mathbb{C}_{base}$ where large number of training data are available and $\mathbb{C}_{novel}$ which is underrepresented.

Then we introduce the network architectures of different modules in the framework. In the meta-learning stage of our approach, the proposed FGN-3D framework is split into two parts: (a) 3D priors modeling part and (b) 2D image generation part. Figure 2 shows an overview of the proposed FGN-3D framework. Specifically, for 3D priors modeling part, two networks are trained:

- The *3D priors generator* G_{3D} takes a latent code z_{shape} sampled from a normal distribution, a class label $y \in \mathbb{C}_{base}$ and outputs a 3D instance $\hat{v}$, *i.e.*, $\hat{v} = G_{3D}(z_{shape}, y)$.
- The *3D priors discriminator* D_{3D} takes a 3D instance v, a class label $y \in \mathbb{C}_{base}$ and outputs a single scalar r_{3D}, *i.e.*, $r_{3D} = D_{3D}(v, y)$, which indicates whether the input v is a real instance from class y.

For 2D image generation, three networks are trained:

- The *texture embedder* E maps a real image x into a vector $z_{texture}$, *i.e.*, $z_{texture} = E(Aug(x); \phi)$. Here, $Aug(\cdot)$ represents data augmentation operations and ϕ is the model parameters. Note that E is designed to be class-agnostic to leverage all training data and increase the diversity of generated images.
- The *image generator* G_{2D} takes a depth image x_d, texture latent code $z_{texture}$ and outputs a synthesized image $\hat{x}$, *i.e.*, $\hat{x} = G_{2D}(x_d, z_{texture}; \psi)$. Here x_d is obtained by employing a fully differentiable projection function p with a specific viewpoint vp on a 3D prior v: $x_d = p(v, vp)$. Here, ψ denotes model parameters that are learned in the meta-learning stage. In general, during meta-learning, we aim to learn ψ such that G_{2D} are able to maximize the similarity between its outputs and the real image.
- The *image discriminator* D_{2D} takes a 2D image x, a class label $y \in \mathbb{C}_{base}$ and outputs a single scalar r_{2D}, *i.e.*, $r_{2D} = D_{2D}(x, y; \varphi)$. which indicates whether the input x is a real image from class y.

For each training stage, we first train the two parts separately to ensure that G_{3D} is able to generate realistic 3D priors and that G_{2D} is able to generate corresponding RGB images given the depth map x_d. After that we train them jointly to improve the diversity and quality of the generated images.

2.2   Meta-Learning on Base Classes

3D Priors Modeling. We base our 3D priors generator G_{3D} and discriminator D_{3D} on the 3D-GAN architecture proposed by [10]. However, vanilla 3D-GAN suffers model collapse and unstable training process when extended to multi-class generation setting. To address these problems, the Wasserstein distance [2] and spectral normalization [6] are used. Besides, following the advice of [7], we feed the conditional information y into the discriminator by projection instead of concatenation. Specifically, the loss function of modeling 3D priors is:

$$\min_{G_{3D}} \max_{D_{3D}} \mathcal{L}_{3D} = \mathbb{E}_v [D_{3D}(v, y)]$$
$$- \mathbb{E}_{z_{shapep}} [D_{3D}(G_{3D}(z_{shape}, y), y)]. \tag{1}$$

2D Image Generation. The training process of 2D image generation part is done by simulating episodes of K-shot learning. In each episode, we randomly sample a 3D instance $\hat{v}$ from G_{3D} and a real image x from training dataset. Then, K depth images $\{x_{d1}, x_{d2}, \ldots, x_{dk}\}$ are obtained by changing the viewpoint in the projection function $p(\hat{v}, vp)$. Additionally, we can also get K corresponding image masks $\{x_{mask1}, x_{mask2}, \ldots, x_{mask}\}$ with a simple threshold, which will later be used to regularize the synthesized image. To increase the diversity of generated images, we produce L augmented real images: $\{x_1, x_2, \ldots, x_l\} = Aug(x)$ before feeding them into the texture embedder E.

Here we use CycleGAN-like [12] architecture. We employ two generators and two discriminators: forward (from depth to real RGB) generator G_{fw} and discriminator D_{fw}, backward (from real RGB to depth) generator G_{bw} and discriminator D_{bw}. We train these four networks jointly with adversarial losses and cycle-consistency losses. More formally, when training forward, the adversarial loss is given by:

$$\mathcal{L}_{fw} = \mathbb{E}_x [\log(D_{fw}(x))] + \mathbb{E}_{(x_d, \{x_1, \ldots, x_l\})} [\log(1 - D_{fw}(\hat{x})], \tag{2}$$

where

$$\hat{x} = G_{fw}(x_d, E(\{x_1, \ldots, x_l\})). \tag{3}$$

When training backward:

$$\mathcal{L}_{bw} = \mathbb{E}_{x_d} [\log(D_{bw}(x_d))] + \mathbb{E}_x [\log(1 - D_{bw}(G_{bw}(x)))]. \tag{4}$$

Cycle-consistency losses are also used to enforce the bijective relationship between the two domains in the forward and backward phase:

$$\mathcal{L}_{fw}^{cyc} = \mathbb{E}_x [\|G_{fw}(G_{bw}(x)) - x\|_1^1], \tag{5}$$

and

$$\mathcal{L}_{bw}^{cyc} = \mathbb{E}_{(x_d, \{x_1, \ldots, x_l\})} [\|G_{bw}(\hat{x}) - x_d\|_1^1]. \tag{6}$$

Additionally the feature matching loss [4] is employed to make sure our generated $\hat{x}$ share the same texture as the input real image x in general. Removing the last layer from D_{fw}, we construct a feature extractor D'_{fw} which is then used to extract features from $\hat{x}$ and $\{x_1, \ldots, x_l\}$:

$$\mathcal{L}_{FM} = \mathbb{E}_{(\hat{x}, \{x_1, \ldots, x_l\})} [\|D'_{fw}(\hat{x}) - \sum_l \frac{D'_{fw}(x_l)}{L}\|_1^1]. \tag{7}$$

At this point, we write the full loss of the 2D image generation process as

$$\mathcal{L}_{2D} = \mathcal{L}_{fw} + \mathcal{L}_{bw} + \mathcal{L}_{fw}^{cyc} + \mathcal{L}_{bw}^{cyc} + \lambda_{fm}\mathcal{L}_{FM}, \tag{8}$$

where λ_{fm} shows the weight of feature matching loss.

Full Model. Our full objective in this stage is as follows:

$$\min_{(G_{3D},G_{fw},G_{bw})} \max_{(D_{fw},D_{bw})} \mathcal{L}_{3D} + \mathcal{L}_{2D}. \tag{9}$$

2.3   Fine-Tuning on Novel Classes

Once the meta-learning has finished, the forward generator G_{fw} is able to generate RGB image for novel class, which is unseen during meta-learning stage, conditioned on the depth images projected from 3D priors. In this stage, the fine-tuning loss of image generation is:

$$\mathcal{L}_{2D}^{finetune} = \mathbb{E}[\log(D_{2D}(x))] + \mathbb{E}[\log(1 - D_{2D}(\hat{x})], \tag{10}$$

where

$$\hat{x} = G_{2D}(p(v,vp), E(\{x_1,\ldots,x_l\})). \tag{11}$$

The full objective in this stage is:

$$\min_{G_{2D}} \max_{D_{2D}} \mathcal{L}_{2D}^{finetune} + \lambda_{fm}\mathcal{L}_{FM}. \tag{12}$$

3   Experiment

3.1   Experimental Setting

Baselines. We compare our method against five popular GAN variants: DCGAN [8], LSGAN [5], WGAN-GP [2] and VON [13]. Since the vanilla baselines are class-specific, we extend them to support multi-class generation for fair comparison. Detail extensions are as follows:

- *3D-free GAN variants:* We simply extend them into conditional generation based on class labels, *i.e.*, c-DCGAN, c-LSGAN and c-WGAN-GP.
- *extended-VON:* We introduce multi-class generation setting (conditional 3D-GAN) and texture extraction ability (texture encoder) into VON.

Note that they require much more training data than our method in the paper they originally proposed.

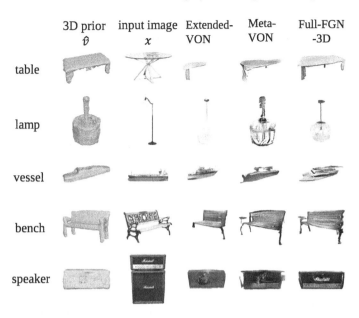

Fig. 3. Quantitative comparison between meta-VON and our method with $T = 20$ on novel classes, where T represents the number of samples used for fine-tuning.

Datasets

- *3D collections:* We use ShapeNet [1] models for 3D priors modeling. Specifically, we choose the five largest classes (car, chair, airplane, sofa and rifle) as our base classes $\mathbb{C}_{base}$. For each one of them, we limit the number of CAD models to 500. The next five largest classes (table, lamp, vessel, bench, speaker) are novel classes $\mathbb{C}_{novel}$, where there are at most 20 models for each one of them.
- *2D images:* There are 500 images for each class in $\mathbb{C}_{base}$, where cars and chairs are all crawled from Google, for the rest three classes (airplane, sofa and rifle), 250 images are from Google and 250 are renderings from corresponding classes in ShapeNet. Similar to 3D collections settings, each class in $\mathbb{C}_{novel}$ holds 20 images at most.

Metrics. We calculate Fréchet Inception Distance (FID) [3] to evaluate distribution matching between generated images and real images, lower FID values mean better image quality and diversity.

Table 1. Quantitative comparisons with FID, smaller numbers are better. Here '-' represents severe model collapse. Note that even in base class, where other baselines use all the training data and we use only part of them, our model also shows SOTA performance.

Methods\Classes	Car	Chair	Airplane	Sofa	Rifle	Table	Lamp	Vessel	Bench	Speaker	mFID ↓
c-DCGAN	153.2	245.0	258.8	201.5	186.5	–	–	–	–	–	209.0
c-LSGAN	175.6	235.4	224.6	177.6	137.3	–	–	–	–	–	190.1
c-WGAN-GP	143.1	174.1	217.6	156.9	110.9	–	–	–	–	–	160.5
extended-VON	81.3	**58.8**	96.1	58.9	89.8	219.7	240.5	223.3	281.3	266.6	161.6
FGN-3D (ours)	**77.2**	64.7	**90.2**	**55.6**	**86.2**	**89.0**	**102.4**	**111.8**	**98.6**	**106.4**	**88.2**

3.2 Main Results

We provide both quantitative and qualitative evaluation on baselines and our model. Please refer to our supplementary material for more training details and additional results.

Qualitative Evaluation. Figure 1 demonstrates some images generated by the proposed model, when given a 3D prior and a texture image (regardless of their classes). Note that our method applies texture information well without mode collapse or mode confusion, which are often observed in other baselines. Figure 3 shows more examples on novel classes with $T = 20$, where T represents the number of samples used in fine-tuning stage. Note that the diversity and quality of generated images are both improved with our method.

Quantitative Evaluation. Table 1 reports quantitative results of our model and all baselines on both base classes and novel classes. Averaged FID is reported and our model (FGN-3D) outperforms all baselines both on base classes and novel classes, obtaining state-of-the-art results (Table 2).

Table 2. Analysis on benefits of introducing two-stage training strategy and making full use of 3D information for few-shot generation.

Methods\Classes	Table	Lamp	Vessel	Bench	Speaker
meta-VON	93.4	105.0	133.3	144.9	106.9
meta-FGN-3D	95.5	118.9	115.1	102.3	116.8
full-FGN-3D	**89.0**	**102.4**	**111.8**	**98.6**	**106.4**

4   Conclusion

In this paper, we propose a two-stage model based on GANs (FGN-3D), which introduces 3D priors into image generation in few-shot scenarios. Empirical evidence has been provided that by fully utilizing 3D structure information, our model outperforms all extended baselines fewer samples (20 at most) on novelty.

References

1. Chang, A.X., et al.: Shapenet: an information-rich 3d model repository. arXiv preprint arXiv:1512.03012 (2015)
2. Gulrajani, I., Ahmed, F., Arjovsky, M., Dumoulin, V., Courville, A.C.: Improved training of wasserstein gans. In: NeurIPS (2017)
3. Heusel, M., Ramsauer, H., Unterthiner, T., Nessler, B., Hochreiter, S.: Gans trained by a two time-scale update rule converge to a local nash equilibrium. In: NeurIPS (2017)
4. Liu, M.Y., et al.: Few-shot unsupervised image-to-image translation. In: ICCV (2019)
5. Mao, X., Li, Q., Xie, H., Lau, R.Y., Wang, Z., Paul Smolley, S.: Least squares generative adversarial networks. In: ICCV (2017)
6. Miyato, T., Kataoka, T., Koyama, M., Yoshida, Y.: Spectral normalization for generative adversarial networks. In: ICLR (2018)
7. Miyato, T., Koyama, M.: cGANs with projection discriminator. In: ICLR (2018)
8. Radford, A., Metz, L., Chintala, S.: Unsupervised representation learning with deep convolutional generative adversarial networks. arXiv preprint arXiv:1511.06434 (2015)
9. Shaham, T.R., Dekel, T., Michaeli, T.: Singan: learning a generative model from a single natural image. In: ICCV (2019)
10. Wu, J., Zhang, C., Xue, T., Freeman, W.T., Tenenbaum, J.B.: Learning a probabilistic latent space of object shapes via 3d generative-adversarial modeling. In: NeurIPS (2016)
11. Zakharov, E., Shysheya, A., Burkov, E., Lempitsky, V.: Few-shot adversarial learning of realistic neural talking head models. In: ICCV (2019)
12. Zhu, J.Y., Park, T., Isola, P., Efros, A.A.: Unpaired image-to-image translation using cycle-consistent adversarial networks. In: ICCV (2017)
13. Zhu, J.Y., et al.: Visual object networks: image generation with disentangled 3D representations. In: NeurIPS (2018)

Distributed Fair k-Center Clustering Problems with Outliers

Fan Yuan[1], Luhong Diao[1], Donglei Du[2], and Lei Liu[1($\boxtimes$)]

[1] Department of Operations Research and Information Engineering,
Beijing University of Technology, Beijing 100124, People's Republic of China
yuanfan@emails.bjut.edu.cn, {diaoluhong,liuliu_leilei}@bjut.edu.cn
[2] Faculty of Management, University of New Brunswick,
Fredericton, NB E3B 5A3, Canada
ddu@unb.ca

Abstract. Big data clustering is a fundamental problem with a vast number of applications. Due to the increasing size of data, interests in clustering problems in distributed computation models have increased. On the other hand, because important decision making is being automated with the help of algorithms, therefore, fairness in algorithms has become an especially important research topic. In this work, we design new distributed algorithms for the fair k-center problem with outliers. Our main contributions are: (1) In the fair k-center problem with outliers setting we give a 4-approximation ratio algorithm. (2) In the distributed fair k-center problem with outliers setting we give a 18-approximation ratio algorithm.

Keywords: Clustering problem · Approximate algorithm · Fair k-center problem with outliers · Distributed fair k-center problem with outliers

1 Introduction

Clustering problem is an important problem in the area of machine learning, where we want to compute a small summary of the data. For example, if the input data is enormous, we do not want to run our machine learning algorithm on the whole input but on a small representative subset. How to select such a representative summary is quite important. It is well known that if the input is biased, then the machine learning algorithms trained on this data will exhibit the same bias. This is a classic example of selection bias but as exhibited by algorithms themselves. Currently used algorithms for data summarization have been shown to be biased with respect to attributes such as gender, race, and age (see, e.g., [24]), and this motivates the fair data summarization problem. Recently, the fair k-center problem was shown to be useful in computing fair summary [22]. In this paper, we study the distributed fair k-center clustering with outliers on massive data in machine learning area. Our main results are distributed algorithms for fair k-center problem with outliers.

© Springer Nature Switzerland AG 2022
H. Shen et al. (Eds.): PDCAT 2021, LNCS 13148, pp. 430–440, 2022.
https://doi.org/10.1007/978-3-030-96772-7_39

Fair k-center models: we are given a set V of n points, the number of groups be m, target summary size be k, and we want to select a summary S such that S contains k_j points belonging to group j, where $k = \sum_{j=1}^{m} k_j$. And we want to minimize $\max_{i \in V} d(i, S)$, where d denotes the distance function. For k-center, there are simple greedy algorithms with an approximation ratio of 2 [16, 19], and getting better than 2-approximation is NP-hard [18]. The NP-hardness result also applies to the more general fair k-center. The best algorithm known for fair k-center is a 3-approximation algorithm that runs in time $O(n^2 \cdot \log n)$ [15]. For fair k-center problems the latest result is Chiplunkar et al. [9] who give a 3-approximation algorithm for the fair k-center problems and a 17-approximation algorithm for the distributed fair k-center problems.

The k-center problem is popular for clustering datasets which are not subject to noise since the objective is sensitive to error in the data because the worst case (maximum) distance of a point to the centers is used for the objective. In the case where data can be noisy [1–3], previous work has considered the k-centers with outliers problem [4]. In this problem, the objective is the same, but additionally one may discard a set of z points from the input. These z points are the outliers and are ignored in the objective. Here, the best known algorithm is a 3-approximation [4].

Once datasets become large, known algorithms for these two problems become ineffective. Due to this, there have been several works on distributed computing [5–8]. The work of [7] was the first to consider k-center clustering in the distributed setting. Their work gave an $O(1)$-round $O(1)$-approximate MapReduce algorithm.

As far as we know, there is no article that studies fair k-center problem with outliers in a distributed or non-distributed setting. In addition, the problem with outliers is far more difficult than the problem without outliers and more suitable for practical applications, so we studied this problem and gave the corresponding algorithm analysis.

1.1 Our Contribution

In this work, we consider a fair k-center problem with outliers and a distributed fair k-center problem with outliers. We have given the corresponding constant approximation ratio algorithms for the above two problems.

1.2 Organization

We first cover preliminary definitions and basic properties in Sect. 3. Then, the algorithm and its analysis are proposed in Sect. 4. We give two main results for different setting respectively. Finally, we conclude the paper in Sect. 5.

2 Related Work

Fair clustering has been studied under another notion of fairness, where each cluster must be balanced with respect to all the groups (no over-or-under-representation of any group) [14], and this line of work also has received a lot of attention in a short span of time [11–13, 20, 25].

The k-median clustering problem with fairness constraints was first considered by [17] and with more general matroid constraints was studied by [23]. The work of Chen et al. [15] and Kale [21] also actually apply for matroid constraints. There has been a lot of work done on fairness, and we refer the reader to the overview in [22].

3   Preliminaries

In the fair k-center problem we are given a set V of n points, a distance function $d : V \times V \longrightarrow \mathbb{R}_{\geq 0}$, and an integer k. Each point belongs to one of m groups, say $\{1, ..., m\}$. Let $g : V \to \{1, ..., m\}$ denote this group assignment function. Further, for each group j, we are given a capacity k_j. Let $k = \sum_{j=1}^{m} k_j$. For points $i, j \in V$, assume $d(i, i) = 0$, $d(i, j) = d(j, i)$, and that the distances obey the triangle inequality: for each triple $i, j, l \in V$, we have $d(i, j) + d(j, l) \geq d(i, l)$. For a point $i \in V$ and a set $S \subseteq V$, we use $d(i, S) = \min_{j \in S} d(i, j)$ to define the distance between a point and a set. For the convenience of proofs and narratives, we use $B(v, r, V) = \{u : u \in V, d(u, v) \leq r\}$ to denote the ball around a point v with radius r. In the fair k-center problem, the goal is to choose a set of centers with size k such that $\max_{i \in V} d(i, S)$ is minimized.

In the k-center problem with outliers, the goal is to choose a set $S \subseteq V$ with k points and a set Z of z points such that $\max_{i \in V \setminus Z} d(i, S)$ is minimized. Note that in this problem the algorithm simply needs to choose the center point set S, because the z points to be deleted are the z points farthest from the center point set S.

4   Problems and Algorithms

4.1   Fair k-center Problem with Outliers

First we introduce a widely used algorithm for the k-center problem with outliers in this section. The k-center problem with outliers is more challenging than the version without outliers because one has to also determine which points to discard, which can drastically change which centers should be chosen. Intuitively, the right algorithmic strategy is to choose centers such that there are many points around then. This idea was formalized in the algorithm of Charikar er al. [4], a well-known and influential algorithm for this problem in the single machine setting.

Theorem 4.1 ([4]). *Algorithm 1 is a 3-approximation algorithm for the k-center problem with outliers, And the number of points deleted by the algorithm is no more than $| z |$.*

Algorithm 1. Outliers $(V, k, r, 3r)$

1: set V, integer k, and radius r.
2: Step 1: $V' = V$, $P = \emptyset$
3: Step 2: **While** $| P | \le k$ **do**:
4: Step 3:   For $\forall v \in V'$ compute $B(v, r, V')$.
5: Step 4:   Let $v_{max} = argmax_{v \in V'} | B(v, r, V') |$.
6: Step 5: $P \leftarrow P \bigcup \{v_{max}\}$.
7: Step 6:   compute $B(v_{max}, 3r, V')$.
8: Step 7: $V' \leftarrow V' \backslash B(v_{max}, 3r, V')$.
9: Step 8: **Output** P.

Algorithm 1 summarizes the approach of Charikar er al. [4]. It takes as input the set of points V, the desired number of centers k and a parameter r. The parameter r is a 'guess' of the optimal solution's value. The algorithm's performance is best when $r = OPT$ where OPT denotes the optimal k-center objective value after discarding z points. The value of r can be determined by doing a binary search on possible values of r between the minimum and maximum distances of any two points.

For each point $v \in V$, the set $B(v, r, V')$ contains points with distance r from v in V. The algorithm adds the points v_{max} to the solution set which covers the largest number of points among all $B(v, r, V')$. The idea here is to add points which have many points nearby. Then the algorithm removes all points from the universe which are within distance $3r$ from v_{max} and continues until k points are found. Further, it can be shown that when $r = OPT$, after selecting the k centers, there are at most z outliers remaining in V'. Algorithm 1 is a 3-approximation algorithm, and easy to use and understand. Our algorithm for the fair k-center problem with outliers is based on Algorithm 1. So we first introduce this algorithm.

Next we introduce two algorithms GetReps() and HittingSet() to handle the fair constrains in our problem. These two algorithms are the two sub-algorithms in the paper [9], and they are used to deal with fairness constraints. GetReps() takes as input a set V of points with radius r, a group assignment function g, and a subset $P \subseteq V$. For each $p \in P$, initialize $N_p = p$. GetReps() includes in N_p one point, from each group, which is within distance r from p whenever such a point exists. Informally, if P is a good but infeasible set of centers, then GetReps() finds representatives N_p of the groups in the neighbor of each $p \in P$. Thus with a loss at most r, we can construct a feasible solution from N_p.

The algorithm HittingSet() finds a feasible solution from a collection of sets of representatives. Algorithm HittingSet() takes as input a collection $N = (N_1, ..., N_K)$ of pairwise disjoint sets of points, group assignment function g, and a vector $\overline{k} = (k_1, ..., k_m)$ of capacities of the m groups. It returns a feasible set S intersecting as many $N_p's$ as possible. This reduces to finding a maximum cardinality matching in an appropriately constructed bipartite graph.

Algorithm 2. GetReps(V, g, P, r)

Input: Set V, group assignment function g, subset $P \subseteq V$, and radius r.
Step 1: $N_p = \emptyset$
Step 2: **for each** $p \in P$ **do**:
Step 3: $N_p \leftarrow p$
Step 4: **for each** $q \in V$ **do**:
Step 5:   **for each** $p \in P$ **do**:
Step 6:   **if** $d(p,q) \leq r$ and N_p does not contain a point from q's group **then**:
Step 7: $N_p \leftarrow N_p \bigcup \{q\}$
Step 8: **Output** $\{N_p : p \in P\}$

The algorithm HittingSet() constructs the following bipartite graph. The left side vertex set contains K vertices, where K is the number of the input disjoint sets of points, and hence each of the vertices on the left side of the graph corresponds to a N_i. The right side vertex set is $A = \bigcup_{j=1}^{m} A_j$, where A_j contains k_j vertices for each group j. If N_i contains a point from group j, then its vertex is connected to all of those in A_j. Each matching H in this bipartite graph encodes a feasible subset $S = \bigcup_{i=1}^{K} N_i$ as follows. For each edge $e = (N_i, a) \in H$ where $a \in A_j$, add to S the point from N_i belonging to group j. Observe that since $|A_j| = k_j$ and H is a matching, S contains at most k_j points from group j. Moreover, $|S| = |H|$, and hence, a maximum cardinality matching in the bipartite graph encodes a set S intersecting as many of the N_i's as possible.

Algorithm 3. HittingSet($N, g, \overline{k}$)

Input: Collection $N = (N_1, ..., N_K)$ of pairwise disjoint sets of points, group assignment function g, and vector $\overline{k} = (k_1, ..., k_m)$ of capacities.
Step 1: Construct bipartite graph $G = (N, A, E)$ as follows:
Step 2: $A \leftarrow \bigcup_{j=1}^{m} A_j$ where A_j is a set of k_j vertices.
Step 3: **for each** N_i and **each** group j **do**:
Step 4:   **if** $\exists p \in N_i$ such that $g(p) = j$ **then**:
Step 5:   Connect N_i to all vertices in A_j.
Step 6: Find the maximum cardinality matching H of G.
Step 7: $S \leftarrow \emptyset$.
Step 8: **for each** edge (N_i, a) of H **do**:
Step 9:   Let s be a point in N_i from group j, where $a \in A_j$.
Step 10: $S \leftarrow S \bigcup \{s\}$.
Step 11: **Output** S.

Theorem 4.2 *[9]. The runtime of Algorithm 3 is $O(K^2 \cdot max_i |N_i|)$.*

With the above algorithms, we are now ready to introduce our main algorithm for the fair k-center problem with outliers. Algorithm 4 has three steps in total. In the first step, we apply the algorithm Outliers $(V, k, r, 3r)$ to get a set P of candidate points without outliers. In the second step, we use GetReps(V, g, P, r) to get a relatively large set, which finds representatives N_p of the groups in the neighbor of each $p \in P$. In the third step, we use HittingSet($\{N(p) : p \in P\}, g, \overline{k}$) to get a solution S that satisfies the fairness constraint.

In the first step we can delete at most z points, and in the next two steps we delete no more points. We guarantee that the outlier limit, and the third step satisfies the fairness constraint. So finally Algorithm 4 gets a feasible solution to the fair k-center problem with outliers. Next we will prove that the approximation ratio of Algorithm 4 is 4.

Algorithm 4. Fair k-center with outliers

Input: Set V, group assignment function g, vector $\overline{k} = (k_1, ..., k_m)$ of capacities, and radius r.

Step 1: $P \leftarrow$ Outliers $(V, k, r, 3r)$
Step 2: $\{N(p) : p \in P\} \leftarrow$ GetReps(V, g, P, r)
Step 3: $S \leftarrow$ HittingSet($\{N(p) : p \in P\}, g, \overline{k}$)

Theorem 4.3. *Algorithm 4 is a 4-approximation algorithm for the fair k-center problem with outliers.*

4.2   Distributed Fair k-Center Problem with Outliers

In this section, we consider the distributed fair k-center problem with outliers and give an algorithm for the problem. In the distributed fair k-center problem with outliers, the data points of V are stored on T machines and the goal is to choose a set S of k points and a set Z of z points such that $\max_{i \in V \setminus Z} d(i, S)$ is minimized.

We call the general distributed machines that store the initial data as the primary machines, and the machine that finally processes the aggregated data of all the primary machines is called the center machine.

In the primary machines, we use Algorithm 6, which contains a sub-algorithm Algorithm 5 to process the initial data and sends the results to the center machine. In the center machine, we use Algorithm 7, which contains a sub-algorithm Algorithm 8 to solve the distributed fair k-center problem with outliers.

Theorem 4.4 *([10]). Algorithm 5 is a greedy 2-approximation algorithm for the k-center problem.*

Our algorithms are based on the simple greedy algorithm of Dyer et al. [10]. Which, at each step, chooses a point with maximum distance to the current solution set and repeats k times.

The algorithm executed by each primary machine i is given by Algorithm 6, which consists of two main steps. In the first step, the machine uses Algorithm 5

Algorithm 5. Greedy(V, k)

Input: point set V, clustering number k, and distance function d.

Step 1: $S = \emptyset$

Step 2: Pick an arbitrary point $i \in V$.

Step 3: $S \leftarrow i$.

Step 4: while $\mid S \mid < k$ do.

Step 5:   choose j from V with the biggest $d(j, S)$.

Step 6: $S \leftarrow S \cup j$, $V - \{j\}$.

Output: S.

Algorithm 6. Distributed Fair k-center with ourliers in each primary machine i

---

Input: point set V_i, $1 \leq i \leq T$, clustering number k, and distance function d.

Step 1: Run Algorithm 5 Greedy$(V, k + z + 1)$ on each primary machine i and output a set of $k + z$ points $P_i \leftarrow \{p_1, ..., p_{k+z}\}$.

Step 2: $r_i \leftarrow \min_{j' : 1 \leq j' \leq k+z} d(p_j, p_{k+z+1})/2$

Step 3: $\{L(p) : p \in P_i\} \leftarrow$ GetReps$(V_i, g, P_i, 2r_i)$

Step 4: $L_i \leftarrow \cup_{p \in P_i} L(p)$

Step 5: For each point $p \in P_i$, machine i set $w_p = \mid \{v : v \in V_i, d(p, v) = d(P_i, v)\} \mid +1$

Output: (P_i, L_i, w_p).

---

to find $(k + z + 1)$ points. The first $(k + z)$ points constitute the set P_i. The point p_{k+z+1} is the farthest point from the set P_i, and it is at a distance $2r$ from P_i. Thus every point in V_i is within distance $2r$ from the set P_i.

In the second step, for each point $p \in P_i$, the machine computes a set $L(p)$ of local representatives in the vicinity of p. Finally, the set P_i and the set $L_i \leftarrow \cup_{p \in P_i} L(p)$ is sent to the center machine. Since L_i contains at most one point from any group, it has at most $m - 1$ points other than p. Since $\mid P_i \mid = k + z$, each machine sends at most $(k + z)m$ points to the center machine.

The algorithm executed by the center machine is given by Algorithm 7. The center machine receives messages (P_i, L_i, w_p) from the primary machines and constructs a candidate center set P by Algorithm 8. For each point $p \in P$, the center machine computes a set $N(p)$ of its global representatives, all of which are within distance $5r$ from p. Due to the separation between points in P, the sets $N(p)$ are pairwise disjoint. Finally, a feasible set S intersecting as many $N(p)$'s as possible is found and returned.

Algorithm 7. Distributed Fair k-center with ourliers in center machine i

---

Input: point set $P' = \cup_{i=1}^l P_i$, $L = \cup_{i=1}^l L_i$, clustering number k, and distance function d.

Step 1: $P \leftarrow$ Distribute Outliers $(P', k, 5r, 11r)$

Step 2: $\{N(p) : p \in P\} \leftarrow$ GetReps$(L, g, P, 5r)$

Step 3: $S \leftarrow$ HittingSet$(\{N(p) : p \in P\}, g, \bar{k})$

Output: S.

Algorithm 8. Distribute Outliers $(V, k, 5r, 11r)$

Input: Set V, integer k, and radius r.
Step 1: $V' = V$, $P = \emptyset$
Step 2: **While** $|P| \le k$ **do**:
Step 3:   For $\forall v \in V$ compute $B(v, 5r, V')$.
Step 4:   Let $v_{max} = argmax_{v \in V} \sum_{v' \in B(v,5r,V')} w_{v'}$.
Step 5: $P \leftarrow P \bigcup \{v_{max}\}$.
Step 6:   compute $B(v_{max}, 11r, V')$.
Step 7: $V' \leftarrow V' \backslash B(v_{max}, 11r, V')$.
Step 8: **Output** P.

Definition 4.1. *Let p be an arbitrary point in V. Suppose p is processed by machine i, that is, $p \in V_i$. Then $cov(p)$ is an arbitrary local pivot in P_i within distance $2r_i$ from p.*

Since the primary machines send only a small number of points to the center machine, it is possible that the optimal solution set S^* of the centers is lost in this process. In the next lemma, we claim that the set of points received by the center machine contains a good and feasible set of centers nevertheless.

Lemma 4.1. *The set $L = \cup_{i=1}^{l} L_i$ contains a feasible set, say B, whose clustering cost for $P' = \cup_{i=1}^{l} P_i$ is at most $5r$.*

The algorithm executed by the center machine is given by Algorithm 7. The center machine constructs a subset P of P' returned by the distributed machine such that points in P are pairwise separated by distance more than $11r$. P is called the set of global pivots. For each global pivot $p \in P$, the center machine computes a set $N(p) \subseteq L = \cup_{i=1}^{l} L_i$ of its global representatives, all of which are within distance $5r$ from p. Due to the separation points in P, the set $N(p)$ are pairwise disjoint. Finally a feasible set S intersecting as many $N(p)$'s as possible is found and returned (As before, it will be clear that S intersects all the $N(p)$'s)

Theorem 4.5. *The center machine returns a feasible set whose clustering cost is at most $18r$.*

In addition to the approximate ratio, we also need to prove the algorithm satisfies the outlier constraint. The number of points deleted by the algorithm will not exceed Z.

Let $O_1, O_2, ..., O_k$ denote the clusters in the optimal solution. A cluster in OPT is defined as a subset of the points in V, not including outliers identified by OPT. Our goal is to show that when our algorithm chooses each center, the set of points discarded from V' in Distribute Outliers() can be mapped to some cluster in the optimal solution. At the end of Distribute Outliers(), there should be at most z points in V', which are the outliers in the optimal solution. Knowing that we only discard points from V' close to centers we choose, this will imply the approximation bound.

For every point $v \in V$, which must fall into some V_i, we let $c(v)$ denote the closest point in P_i to v (i.e., $c(v)$ is the closest intermediate cluster center found by Greedy() to v). Consider the output of Distribute Outliers(), $P = \{p_1, p_2, ..., p_k\}$, ordered by how elements were added to P. We will say that an optimal cluster O_i is marked at Distribute Outliers() iteration j if there is a point $u \in O_i$ such that $c(u) \notin V'$ just before p_j is added to P. Essentially if a cluster is marked, we can make no guarantee about covering it within some radius of p_j (which will then be discarded). We begin by noting that when p_j is added to P that the weight of the points removed from V' is at least as large as the maximum number of points in an unmarked cluster in the optimal solution.

Lemma 4.2. *When p_j is added, then $\sum_{v' \in B(p_j, 5r, V')} w_{v'} \geq |O_i|$ for any marked cluster O_i.*

Given this result, the following lemma considers a point v that is in some cluster O_i. If $c(v)$ is within the ball $B(p_j, 5r, V')$ for p_j added to P, then intuitively, this means that we cover all of the points in O_i with $B(p_j, 11r, V')$. Another way to say this is that after we remove the ball $B(p_j, 11r, V')$, no points in O_i contribute weight to any point in V'.

Lemma 4.3. *Consider a p_j to be added to P. Say that $c(v) \in B(p_j, 5r, V')$ for some point $v \in O_i$ for some i. Then, for every point $u \in O_i$ either $c(u) \in B(p_j, 11r, V')$ or $c(u)$ has already been removed from V'.*

In the next lemma we are going to prove that the weight of the points in $\bigcup_{p_i : 1 \leq i \leq k} B(p_i, 11r, V')$ is at least as large as the number of points in $\bigcup_{1 \leq i \leq k} O_i$. Further, we know that $|\bigcup_{1 \leq i \leq k} O_i| = n - z$ since OPT has z outliers. Viewing the points in $B(p_i, 11r, V')$ as being assigned to p_i in the algorithm's solution then this shows that the number of points covered is as least as large as the number of points that the optimal solution covers. Hence, there cannot be more than z points uncovered by our algorithm.

Lemma 4.4. $\sum_{i=1}^{k} \sum_{u \in B(p_i, 11r, V')} w_u \geq n - z$

With the above lemma we proved the number of points deleted by the algorithm will not exceed Z.

5   Conclusions

In this paper, we consider the fair k-center problem with outliers and the distributed fair k-center problem with outliers. We have given the corresponding constant approximation ratio algorithms for the above two problems. For the fair k-center problem with outliers we give a 4-approximation algorithm and for the distributed fair k-center problem with outliers we give a 18-approximation algorithm.

Acknowledgements. The first author is supported by Beijing Natural Science Foundation Project No. Z200002 and National Natural Science Foundation of China (No. 12131003). The second author is supported by general research projects of Beijing Educations Committee in China (Grants KM201910005013). The third author is supported by the Natural Sciences and Engineering Research Council of Canada (NSERC) grant 06446 and Natural Science Foundation of China (Nos. 11771386, 11728104). The fourth author is supported by general program of science and technology development project of Beijing Municipal Education Commission (Grant KM201810005005).

References

1. Agarwal, P.K., Phillips, J.M.: An efficient algorithm for 2D Euclidean 2-center with outliers. In: Halperin, D., Mehlhorn, K. (eds.) ESA 2008. LNCS, vol. 5193, pp. 64–75. Springer, Heidelberg (2008). https://doi.org/10.1007/978-3-540-87744-8_6

2. Guha, S., Rastogi, R., Shim, K.: Techniques for clustering massive data sets. In: Clustering and Information Retrieval Network Theory and Applications, vol. 11, pp. 35–82. Springer, Boston (2004). https://doi.org/10.1007/978-1-4613-0227-8_2

3. Hassani, M., Mller, E., Seidl, T.: EDISKCO: energy efficient distributed in-sensor-network k-center clustering with outliers. In: KDD Workshop on Knowledge Discovery from Sensor Data, pp. 39–48 (2009)

4. Charikar, M., Khuller, S., Mount, D.M., Narasimhan, G.: Algorithms for facility location problems with outliers. In: SODA, pp. 642–651 (2001)

5. Bahmani, B., Moseley, B., Vattani, A., Kumar, R., Vassilvitskii, S.: Scalable k-Means++. Proc. VLDB Endow **5**(7), 622–633 (2012)

6. Balcan, M.-F., Ehrlich, S., Liang, Y.: Distributed k-means and k-median clustering on general communication topologies. In: NIPS, pp. 1995–2003 (2013)

7. Ene, A., Im, S., Moseley, B.: Fast clustering using MapReduce. KDD, pp. 681–689 (2011)

8. Mirzasoleiman, B., Karbasi, A., Sarkar, R., Krause, A.: Distributed submodular maximization: identifying representative elements in massive data. In: NIPS, pp. 2049–2057 (2013)

9. Chiplunkar, A., Kale, S., Ramamoorthy, S.N.: How to solve fair k-center in massive data models. In: ICML, pp. 1877–1886 (2020)

10. Dyer, M., Frieze, A.: A simple heuristic for the p-center problem. Oper. Res. Lett. **3**, 285–288 (1985)

11. Ahmadian, S., Epasto, A., Kumar, R., Mahdian, M.: Clustering without over-representation. In: KDD, pp. 267–275 (2019)

12. Bera, S.K., Chakrabarty, D., Flores, N., Negahbani, M.: Fair algorithms for clustering. In: NeurIPS, pp. 4955–4966 (2019)

13. Bandyapadhyay, S., Inamdar, T., Pai, S., Varadarajan, K.R.: A constant approximation for colorful k-center. ESA, 12:1–12:14 (2019)

14. Chierichetti, F., Kumar, R., Lattanzi, S., Vassilvitskii, S.: Fair clustering through fairlets. In: NIPS, pp. 5029–5037 (2017)

15. Chen, D.Z., Li, J., Liang, H., Wang, H.: Matroid and knapsack center problems. Algorithmica **75**(1), 27–52 (2015). https://doi.org/10.1007/s00453-015-0010-1

16. Teofilo, F.: Gonzalez: clustering to minimize the maximum intercluster distance. Theor. Comput. Sci. **38**, 293–306 (1985)

17. Hajiaghayi, M.T., Khandekar, R., Kortsarz, G.: Budgeted red-blue median and its generalizations. In: de Berg, M., Meyer, U. (eds.) ESA 2010. LNCS, vol. 6346, pp. 314–325. Springer, Heidelberg (2010). https://doi.org/10.1007/978-3-642-15775-2_27

18. Hsu, W.-L., Nemhauser, G.L.: Easy and hard bottleneck location problems. Discret. Appl. Math. **1**(3), 209–215 (1979)

19. Hochbaum, D.S., Shmoys, D.B.: A best possible heuristic for the k-center problem. Math. Oper. Res. **10**(2), 180–184 (1985)

20. Jia, X., Sheth, K., Svensson, O.: Fair colorful k-center clustering. Math. Program. 1–22 (2021). https://doi.org/10.1007/s10107-021-01674-7

21. Kale, S.: Small space stream summary for matroid center. APPROX-RANDOM, 20:1–20:22 (2019)

22. Kleindessner, M., Awasthi, P., Morgenstern, J.: Fair k-center clustering for data summarization. In: ICML, pp. 3448–3457 (2019)

23. Krishnaswamy, R., Kumar, A., Nagarajan, V., Sabharwal, Y., Saha, B.: The matroid median problem. In: SODA, pp. 1117–1130 (2011)

24. Kay, M., Matuszek, C., Munson, S.A.: Unequal representation and gender stereotypes in image search results for occupations. In: CHI, pp. 3819–3828 (2015)

25. Schmidt, M., Schwiegelshohn, C., Sohler, C.: Fair coresets and streaming algorithms for fair k-means. In: Bampis, E., Megow, N. (eds.) WAOA 2019. LNCS, vol. 11926, pp. 232–251. Springer, Cham (2020). https://doi.org/10.1007/978-3-030-39479-0_16

Multi-zone Residential HVAC Control with Satisfying Occupants' Thermal Comfort Requirements and Saving Energy via Reinforcement Learning

Zhengkai Ding[1,2], Qiming Fu[1,2](✉), Jianping Chen[2,3,4](✉), Hongjie Wu[1], You Lu[1,2], and Fuyuan Hu[1]

[1] School of Electronic and Information Engineering, SuZhou University of Science and Technology, Suzhou 215009, Jiangsu, China
`fqm_1@mail.usts.edu.cn`
[2] Jiangsu Province Key Laboratory of Intelligent Building Energy Efficiency, Suzhou University of Science and Technology, Suzhou 215009, Jiangsu, China
`alanjpchen@yahoo.com`
[3] School of Archirecture and Urban Planning, SuZhou University of Science and Technology, Suzhou 215009, Jiangsu, China
[4] Chongqing Industrial Big Data Innovation Center Co., Ltd., Chongqing 400707, China

Abstract. Residential HVAC system control has been focused on thermal comfort and energy consumption. Due to the complexity of the dynamic building thermal model, weather conditions and human activities, traditional methods such as rule-based control (RBC) and model predictive control (MPC) are difficult to learn a strategy that can save energy while satisfying occupants' thermal comfort requirements. To solve the above problem, we propose a method combining a thermal comfort prediction model and reinforcement learning to optimize residential multi-zone HVAC control. In this paper, we first design a hybrid model of Support Vector Regression and a Deep Neural Network (SVR-DNN) to predict thermal comfort value, which is taken as a part of the state and reward in reinforcement learning. Then we apply reinforcement learning algorithms (Q-learning, Deep Q-Network (DQN) and Deep Deterministic Policy Gradient (DDPG)) to respectively generate an optimal HVAC control strategy to maintain the stability of thermal comfort and minimize energy consumption. The experimental results show that our SVR-DNN model can improve thermal comfort prediction performance

This work was financially supported by Primary Research and Development Plan of China (No. 2020YFC2006602), National Natural Science Foundation of China (No. 62072324, No. 61876217, No. 61876121, No. 61772357), University Natural Science Foundation of Jiangsu Province (No. 21KJA520005), Primary Research and Development Plan of Jiangsu Province (No. BE2020026), Natural Science Foundation of Jiangsu Province (No. BK20190942).
The code and data are available at https://github.com/DZKK1234/Multi-zone-residential-HVAC-control.git.

© Springer Nature Switzerland AG 2022
H. Shen et al. (Eds.): PDCAT 2021, LNCS 13148, pp. 441–451, 2022.
https://doi.org/10.1007/978-3-030-96772-7_40

by 20.5% compared with the deep neural network (DNN); compared with rule-based control, DDPG, DQN and Q-learning based on SVR-DNN can reduce energy consumption by 11.89%, 8.41%, 6.51% and reduce thermal comfort violation by 91.8%, 43.2%, 25.4%.

Keywords: Multi-zone HVAC control · Reinforcement learning · Energy conservation · Thermal comfort

1   Introduction

Building energy consumption accounts for about 40%–50% of global energy consumption [1]. With the increasing urbanization, this inevitably leads to an increase in building density and building energy consumption. And a large part of building energy consumption comes from heating, ventilation and air-conditioning (HVAC) systems. Usually, occupants' thermal comfort in the indoor environment depends largely on HVAC systems. Considering that people spend 80%–90% of their day indoors, engineers need to consider not only energy savings but also improving the thermal comfort of the occupants' environment. Typically, people prefer heating in winter and cooling in summer to improve their thermal comfort. Therefore, it is really necessary to study energy-comfort-related control strategies to balance energy consumption and thermal comfort.

Human thermal comfort is an elusive quantity, affected by many factors which come from three main aspects: outdoor temperature and humidity, building environment and human-related factors. Firstly, outdoor temperature and humidity have a great impact on human comfort. For different outdoor temperature and humidity, the human body's response is different. Meanwhile, outdoor temperature and humidity also affect the HVAC system. If the outdoor temperature and humidity are appropriate, it is not necessary to turn on the HVAC system. Secondly, the building environment includes building materials, structures and internal heat sources. Different building materials and structures will affect temperature in the building and the occupants' thermal comfort. And the internal heat source will also affect the thermal conditions of the building and the thermal comfort of occupants. Thirdly, thermal comfort is subjective, so different occupants may have different thermal comfort under the same circumstance.

Currently, rule-based control (RBC) is usually used in HVAC systems. Because RBC is based on engineers' experience, it can not learn knowledge from historical data to save energy effectively or satisfy occupants' thermal comfort requirements. Model predictive control (MPC) [2], a model-based control method, usually solves HVAC control problems better than RBC. However, MPC requires a large amount of historical data and real-time monitoring data to establish an accurate model to save energy while meeting occupants' thermal comfort requirements. In the single-zone HVAC control problem, a low-order model can be established for MPC to solve the control problem. However, in the multi-zone HVAC control problem, it is necessary to consider not only the indoor and outdoor heat exchange but also the heat exchange between zones, which makes the building thermal model more complex. It is difficult to establish an accurate model for MPC to solve the multi-zone HVAC control problem. However, model-free control methods do not need to establish an accurate model to optimize HVAC control. Nowadays, model-free optimal control methods based on reinforcement learning (RL) show good adaptability and robustness in HVAC control problems.

In this paper, our objective is to minimize energy consumption under the condition of satisfying occupants' thermal comfort requirements in HVAC systems. We evaluate RBC and three RL algorithms: Q-learning for discrete control, Deep Q-Network for discrete action space control, Deep Deterministic Policy Gradient for continuous control in a multi-zone residential HVAC model. The main contributions of this paper are summarized as follows:

(1) We design a hybrid model based on Support Vector Regression (SVR) and a Deep Neural Network (DNN), called SVR-DNN, for predicting thermal comfort value which is taken as a part of the state and reward in reinforcement learning.
(2) The multi-zone residential HVAC problem, in which the heat exchange between zones and the change of occupants' number are considered, is formulated as a reinforcement learning problem. See Appendix for detailed formulation.
(3) We apply Q-learning, DQN and DDPG methods to optimize HVAC control in a multi-zone residential HVAC model and compare the performance of these three algorithms. We show that all three algorithms can reduce violation of thermal comfort and reduce energy consumption compared with rule-based control in multi-zone HVAC control.

2   Related Work

RL has been greatly developed in recent years, and as a result, many researchers have applied RL to deal with HVAC control problems. Qiu et al. [3] implemented Q-learning and the model-based controller to respectively optimize building HVAC systems to save energy. In [4], deep reinforcement learning (DRL) is applied to optimize the problem of the supply water temperature setpoint in a heating system and the well-trained agent can save energy between 5% and 12 %. Achieving energy savings from optimizing HVAC control equates to cost savings. Jiang et al. [5] proposed DQN with an action processor, saving close to 6% of total cost with demand charges, while close to 8% without demand charges.

Thermal comfort is the evaluation of people's subjective satisfaction with the environment. At present, many thermal comfort models have been proposed. Fanger et al. [6] proposed the classic steady-state model, which is based on a heat balance model. The model is designed by using Predicted Mean Vote-Predicted Percentage Dissatisfied (PMV-PPD) to express people's satisfaction with the environment. With the development of machine learning (ML), researchers have studied thermal comfort models based on ML algorithms. Zhou et al. [7] used the support vector machine (SVM) algorithm to develop a thermal comfort model with self-learning and self-correction ability. In [8], a model based on the Back Propagation (BP) neural network for individual thermal comfort was proposed.

At present, it is not only necessary to save energy for the HVAC system, but also to maintain the thermal comfort of occupants. In [9], the authors applied an MPC method to reduce energy consumption and keep the temperature in an acceptable range. Zenger et al. [10] implemented SARSA algorithm to maintain thermal comfort while saving energy. Du et al. [11] implemented DRL methods to address the issue of 2-zone residential HVAC control strategies that allow for the lower bound of the user comfort level (temperature) with energy savings but they did not consider the change of occupants' number and did not establish a thermal comfort prediction model. In summary, RL methods have been applied to HVAC control. Many papers discuss how to maintain thermal comfort while energy saving. We take this opportunity to study how to save energy with the emphasis on maintaining thermal comfort.

3   Theoretical Background

This section introduces the theoretical background of RL and DRL. We focus on Q-learning, DQN and DDPG. RL is a kind of trial and error learning through interaction with the environment. Its goal is to maximise a cumulative reward in the environmental interaction. The problem of RL can be modeled as a Markov Decision Process (MDP), which includes a quintuple $\langle \mathcal{S}, \mathcal{A}, r, p_1, p \rangle$. MDP is shown in Fig. 1.

Fig. 1. Model structure diagram of an MDP.

(1) $\mathcal{S}$ is the state space, $s_t \in \mathcal{S}$ indicates the state of the agent at time t.
(2) $\mathcal{A}$ is the action space, $a_t \in \mathcal{A}$ represents the action taken by the agent at time t.
(3) $r: \mathcal{S} \times \mathcal{A} \to \mathbb{R}$ is the reward function.
(4) p_1 is an initial state distribution with density $p_1(s_1)$.
(5) $p: \mathcal{S} \times \mathcal{S} \times \mathcal{A} \to [0, 1]$ is state transition probability distribution function satisfying the Markov property $p(s_{t+1}|s_1, a_1, \ldots, s_t, a_t) = p(s_{t+1}|s_t, a_t)$, for any trajectory $s_1, a_1, \ldots, s_T, a_T$ in state-action space.

A policy, denoted by $\pi : \mathcal{S} \times \mathcal{A} \to [0, 1]$, is used to select actions in MDPs. $\pi(a_t|s_t)$ represents the probability of selecting a_t in s_t. The agent uses one policy to interact with the environment to generate a trajectory of states, actions and rewards, $z_{1:T} = s_t, a_t, r_1, \ldots, s_T, a_T, r_T$ over $\mathcal{S} \times \mathcal{A} \times \mathbb{R}$. The return G_t is the total discounted reward from time-step t onwards, $G_t = \sum_{k=t}^{T} \gamma^{k-t} r(s_k, a_k)$, where $\gamma \in [0, 1]$, which is a discounted factor, is used to weighten the impact of the future reward on the return G_t. The value functions are defined as the expectation of return G_t: $V^\pi(s) = \mathbb{E}[G_t | S_t = s; \pi]$, $Q^\pi(s, a) = \mathbb{E}[G_t | S_t = s, A_t = a; \pi]$. The agent finds a policy to maximize the return G_t from the initial state, denoted by the performance objective $J(\pi) = \mathbb{E}[G_1 | \pi]$.

4   Methodology

In this section, we introduce our new ideas for energy conservation while maintaining thermal comfort well in residential buildings. Firstly, we design an SVR-DNN model to predict the thermal comfort value. A five-zone and three-occupant residential HVAC model [12] is used for simulation. The layout of the residential apartment is identified from multi-level residential buildings in Chongqing, China. We use real-world weather data from [13]. Then, the multi-zone HVAC control problem is formulated as an MDP, which can be processed by reinforcement learning algorithms. The control interval of the RL agent is set to 60 min. We implement RBC, Q-learning, DQN and DDPG(DQN and DDPG with two replay buffers) to evaluate their performances in the multi-zone HVAC control problem.

In the simulation environment of this paper, we transfer the indoor temperature and humidity data into the thermal comfort model to obtain the predicted thermal comfort value. The predicted thermal comfort value is taken as a part of the state and reward. And the reward is obtained through our designed reward function. Through learning, the agent gives an appropriate temperature setpoint to conserve energy while maintaining thermal comfort. The specific process is shown in Fig. 2 below.

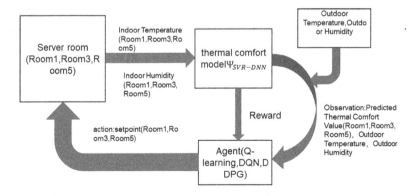

Fig. 2. Flowchart of multi-zone residential apartment simulation.

4.1   Thermal Comfort Prediction

We train a SVR-DNN model to predict thermal comfort. The structure diagram of SVR-DNN is shown in Fig. 3. The inputs of SVR-DNN are predicted value of SVR, indoor temperature and indoor humidity. The output of SVR-DNN is the predicted thermal comfort value. SVR-DNN has two hidden layers and one output neural unit.

4.2   Problem Formulation

State Space. The state space includes outdoor temperature $T_{out(t)}$, outdoor humidity $H_{out(t)}$, thermal comfort $M_{Roomk(t)}$ and ideal thermal comfort $M_{Roomk-ideal(t)}$ in three zones.

Action Space. The action space includes the temperature setpoints in three zones. HVAC systems will take actions according to different demands. In DQN and Q-learning, the action space is discrete, so we discretize the range of setpoints with a step size of $0.5\,^{\circ}\mathrm{C}$.

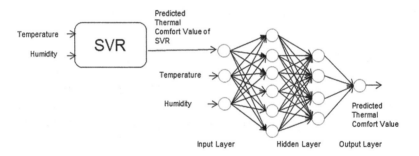

Fig. 3. The structure of SVR-DNN for predicting thermal comfort. The inputs of SVR-DNN are predicted value of SVR, indoor temperature and indoor humidity. The output of SVR-DNN is the predicted thermal comfort value.

Reword Function. Because it is necessary to consider energy saving under the condition of satisfying thermal comfort requirements, we define the reward function as:

$$r_t = -(\beta \sum_k |M_{Roomk(t)} - M_{Roomk-ideal(t)}| + \sum_k Q_t^k)/153, k = 1,3,5, \qquad (1)$$

where Q_t^k represents the energy consumption of $Roomk$ at time t. Since thermal comfort is the first consideration, multiply the first item by weight β to increase its impact on the reward function.

5   Experiments

5.1   SVR-DNN for Thermal Comfort Prediction

We select 899 samples under the same conditions in the ASHRAE [14], 80% for training and 20% for testing. These samples are selected in summer and under the condition of indoor air conditioning. We first train an SVR model. Then we take the predicted value of SVR, indoor temperature and indoor humidity as the input of the deep neural network. The occupants' thermal comfort value at time slot t as

$$M_t = \Psi_{SVR-DNN}(M_{SVR_t}, T_t, H_t). \tag{2}$$

The prediction error is shown in Table 1 below.

Table 1. Prediction error.

Model	DNN	SVR	XGBoost	LinearRegression	SVR-DNN
Prediction error(MSE)	0.329204	0.306900	0.336993	0.342541	0.261614

5.2   Performance of Q-Learning, DQN and DDPG

Convergence. In Fig. 4, the reward and thermal comfort violation of each episode of Q-learning, DQN and DDPG are presented during training. In this paper, we take May to September as an episode, a total of 50 training episodes. From Fig. 4(a), we note that the reward of DQN and DDPG is lower than that of Q-learning in the first few episodes. This is because both DQN and DDPG need to store transitions in the early stage, and they have not learned. On the contrary, Q-learning has begun to learn. At about 15 episodes, Q-learning tends to converge, which is due to the discretization of state space and action space, which greatly reduces the scope of exploration and converges quickly. However,

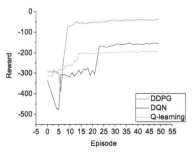

(a) Convergence of different RL methods.

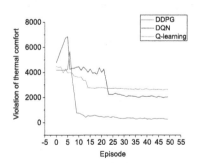

(b) Convergence of violation of thermal comfort via different RL methods.

Fig. 4. Convergence.

the reduction of exploration space will lead to insufficient exploration, resulting in low reward. The reward of Q-learning is the lowest of the three RL methods. The reward of DQN tends to converge after about 24 episodes. Due to the discretization of action space and the incomplete exploration of action space combination, the reward of DQN is lower than that of DDPG. Because DDPG can deal with continuous control problems, it can explore enough space so that it can find the optimal action to get higher reward. The reward of DDPG is the highest of the three RL methods. We present the violation of thermal comfort in each episode in Fig. 4(b). The violation of thermal comfort and reward have the opposite trend. The lower the violation of thermal comfort, the higher the reward, because we pay more attention to thermal comfort. The violation of thermal comfort has the same convergence trend as reward. The violation of Q-learning is the most, DQN is the second, and DDPG is the least. It can be seen from Fig. 4(a) and Fig. 4(b) that DDPG method has greater advantages in dealing with HVAC control problems. The learning effects of Q-learning and DQN are not as good as DDPG.

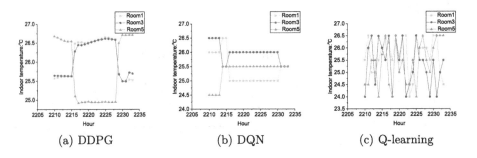

| (a) DDPG | (b) DQN | (c) Q-learning |

Fig. 5. Indoor temperature on August 1.

Analysis and Comparison of Indoor Temperature, Thermal Comfort and Energy Consumption. We take out the indoor temperature and thermal comfort on August 1 for detailed description and analysis. From Fig. 5(a) and Fig. 6, the indoor temperature and thermal comfort controlled by DDPG method are more regular, and the thermal comfort deviates little from the ideal thermal comfort we set. In Fig. 5(b), the temperature controlled by DQN is lower than that controlled by DDPG most of the day, which increases energy consumption. The performance of indoor temperature in Fig. 5(c) controlled by Q-learning is worse than DQN and DDPG. This is because Q-learning can only observe discrete space, and the knowledge learned is naturally less than DQN and DDPG. In Fig. 6, the comparison of thermal comfort of three rooms on August 1 is presented. DDPG based on SVR-DNN can maintain thermal comfort best in the three RL methods. DQN can only partially meet occupants' thermal comfort requirements. Q-learning can only satisfy a small part of thermal comfort requirements in a day, because it can only explore a limited space. We illustrate energy

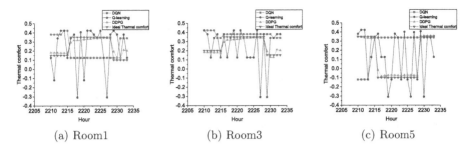

(a) Room1   (b) Room3   (c) Room5

Fig. 6. Thermal comfort on August 1

consumption and thermal comfort violation of different algorithms in Fig. 7(a). DDPG is the best among the four algorithms and RBC is the worst. Compared with RBC, DDPG, DQN and Q-learning based on SVR-DNN can reduce energy consumption by 11.89%, 8.41%, 6.51% and reduce thermal comfort by 91.8%, 43.2%, 25.4%. Compared with DQN and Q-learning based on SVR-DNN, DDPG based on SVR-DNN can reduce energy consumption by 3.80% and 5.76% respectively. For the violation of thermal comfort, DDPG based on SVR-DNN can reduce by 85.54% and 88.98% compared with DQN and Q-learning based on SVR-DNN. Compared with Q-learning based on SVR-DNN, DQN based on SVR-DNN can reduce energy consumption by 2.03% and thermal comfort by 23.84%. In Fig. 7(b) and Fig. 4(b), notice that too much or too little energy consumption will lead to great violation of thermal comfort. What we need is a method to learn the law of thermal comfort of occupants and reduce energy consumption. DDPG can better learn the law of occupants' thermal comfort and save energy while maintaining thermal comfort. DDPG, DQN and Q-learning can save energy and reduce violation of thermal comfort in the multi-zone HVAC control compared with RBC.

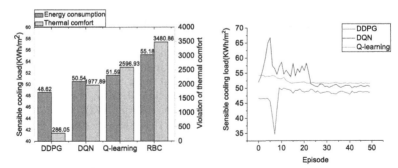

(a) The comparison of energy consumption and thermal comfort violation.   (b) The comparison of energy consumption.

Fig. 7. Energy consumption and thermal comfort violation.

6   Conclusion

In this paper, we proposed a method combining a thermal comfort prediction model and reinforcement learning to optimize residential multi-zone HVAC control. Firstly, we trained a hybrid model based on Support Vector Regression and a Deep Neural Network to predict thermal comfort value and used reinforcement learning algorithms to reduce energy consumption while maintaining occupants' thermal comfort. A multi-zone residential HVAC model was used to evaluate the performance of RL algorithms. The results show that our SVR-DNN model can improve thermal comfort prediction performance by 20.5% compared with the deep neural network(DNN); compared with rule-based control, DDPG, DQN and Q-learning based on SVR-DNN can reduce energy consumption by 11.89%, 8.41%, 6.51% and reduce thermal comfort violation by 91.8%, 43.2%, 25.4%.

In future work, we consider multi-agent RL algorithms to solve the multi-zone HVAC control problem. It is not limited to considering the strategic control of cooling months, but also considering that a strategy can maintain the thermal comfort of occupants and energy saving on a year-round basis. By the above researches, RL agents will adapt to different environments and can be implemented in the real world.

References

1. Pérez-Lombard, L., Ortiz, J., Pout, C.: A review on buildings energy consumption information. Energy Build. **40**(3), 394–398 (2008). https://doi.org/10.1016/j. enbuild.2007.03.007
2. Shepherd, A., Batty, W.: Fuzzy control strategies to provide cost and energy efficient high quality indoor environments in buildings with high occupant densities. Build. Serv. Eng. Res. Technol. **24**(1), 35–45 (2003)
3. Qiu, S., Li, Z., Li, Z., Li, J., Long, S., Li, X.: Model-free control method based on reinforcement learning for building cooling water systems: Validation by measured data-based simulation. Energy Build. **218**, 110055 (2020). https://doi.org/ 10.1016/j.enbuild.2020.110055
4. Brandi, S., Piscitelli, M.S., Martellacci, M., Capozzoli, A.: Deep reinforcement learning to optimise indoor temperature control and heating energy consumption in buildings. Energy Build. **224**, 110225 (2020)
5. Jiang, Z., et al.: Building HVAC control with reinforcement learning for reduction of energy cost and demand charge. Energy Build. **239**, 110833 (2021)
6. Shaw, E.W.: Thermal comfort: analysis and applications in environmental engineering, by p. o. fanger. 244 pp. danish technical press. copenhagen, denmark, 1970. danish kr. 76, 50. J. Roy. Soc. Promot. Health (1972)
7. Zhou, X., et al.: Data-driven thermal comfort model via support vector machine algorithms: insights from ashrae rp-884 database. Energy Build. **211**, 109795 (2020). https://doi.org/10.1016/j.enbuild.2020.109795
8. Liu, W., Lian, Z., Zhao, B.: A neural network evaluation model for individual thermal comfort. Energy Build. **39**(10), 1115–1122 (2007)
9. Wei, T., Zhu, Q., Maasoumy, M.: Co-scheduling of HVAC control, EV charging and battery usage for building energy efficiency. In: Chang, Y. (ed.) The IEEE/ACM International Conference on Computer-Aided Design, ICCAD 2014, San Jose, CA, USA, November 3–6, 2014, pp. 191–196. IEEE (2014)

10. Zenger, A., Schmidt, J., Krödel, M.: Towards the intelligent home: using reinforcement-learning for optimal heating control. In: Timm, I.J., Thimm, M. (eds.) KI 2013. LNCS (LNAI), vol. 8077, pp. 304–307. Springer, Heidelberg (2013). https://doi.org/10.1007/978-3-642-40942-4_30
11. Du, Y., et al.: Intelligent multi-zone residential HVAC control strategy based on deep reinforcement learning. Appl. Energy **281**, 116117 (2021)
12. Deng, J., Yao, R., Yu, W., Zhang, Q., Li, B.: Effectiveness of the thermal mass of external walls on residential buildings for part-time part-space heating and cooling using the state-space method. Energy Build. **190**, 155–171 (2019). https://doi.org/10.1016/j.enbuild.2019.02.029
13. Bureau, C.M., et al.: China Standard Weather Data for Analyzing Building Thermal Conditions, pp. 90–105. China Building Industry Publishing House, Beijing (2005)
14. Földváry Ličina, V., et al.: Development of the ashrae global thermal comfort database II. Build. Environ. **142**, 502–512 (2018). https://doi.org/10.1016/j.buildenv.2018.06.022

Approximating BP Maximization with Distorted-Based Strategy

Ruiqi Yang[1], Suixiang Gao[1], Lu Han[2], Gaidi Li[3(✉)], and Zhongrui Zhao[3]

[1] School of Mathematical Sciences, University of Chinese Academy Sciences, Beijing 100049, People's Republic of China
{yangruiqi,sxgao}@ucas.ac.cn
[2] School of Science, Beijing University of Posts and Telecommunications, Beijing 100876, People's Republic of China
hl@bupt.edu.cn
[3] Department of Operations Research and Information Engineering, Beijing University of Technology, Beijing 100124, People's Republic of China
ligd@bjut.edu.cn, zhaozhongrui@emails.biut.edu.cn

Abstract. We study a problem of maximizing the sum of a suBmodular and suPermodular (BP) function, denoted as $\max_{\mathcal{S} \subseteq \mathcal{V}, |\mathcal{S}| \leq k} \mathcal{G}(\mathcal{S}) + \mathcal{L}(\mathcal{S})$, where $\mathcal{G}(\cdot)$ is non-negative monotonic and submodular, $\mathcal{L}(\cdot)$ is monotonic and supermodular. In this paper, we consider the $\mathcal{K}$-cardinality constrained BP maximization under a streaming setting. Denote κ as the supermodular curvature of $\mathcal{L}$. Utilizing a distorted threshold-based technique, we present a first $(1 - \kappa)/(2 - \kappa)$-approximation semi-streaming algorithm and then implement it by lazily guessing the optimum threshold and yield a one pass, $\mathcal{O}(\varepsilon^{-1} \log((2 - \kappa)\mathcal{K}/(1 - \kappa)^2))$ memory complexity, $((1 - \kappa)/(2 - \kappa) - \mathcal{O}(\varepsilon))$-approximation. We further study the BP maximization with fairness constrains and develop a distorted greedy-based algorithm, which gets a $(1 - \kappa)/(2 - \kappa)$-approximation for the extended fair BP maximization.

Keywords: Submodular maximization · Stream model · Fairness · Approximation algorithms · Distorted threshold

1 Introduction

Submodularity plays an important role in developing algorithms for optimizing the utility functions with the diminishing returns. Maximizing submodular utility functions has been well-studied in the perspective of theoretical performance guarantees and also has been applied in social computing [11], data summarization [1], network monitoring [3,12], and just to name a few.

In this work, we study a problem of suBmodular+suPermodular (BP) maximization, which is formally stated as

$$\max_{\mathcal{S} \subseteq \mathcal{V}, |\mathcal{S}| \leq \mathcal{K}} \mathcal{G}(\mathcal{S}) + \mathcal{L}(\mathcal{S}) \tag{1}$$

© Springer Nature Switzerland AG 2022
H. Shen et al. (Eds.): PDCAT 2021, LNCS 13148, pp. 452–459, 2022.
https://doi.org/10.1007/978-3-030-96772-7_41

where $\mathcal{G}$ and $\mathcal{L}$ are non-negative non-decreasing submodular and supermodular functions, respectively. Indeed, we present a first distorted threshold-based semi-streaming algorithm and then implement it by lazily guessing the optimum threshold. We further study a more general fair BP maximization and develop a distorted fair greedy. The main results are listed as follows.

- We firstly present a distorted threshold-based algorithm, which achieves a $(1-\kappa)/(2-\kappa)$-approximation, where κ is the supermodular curvature of $\mathcal{L}$.
- We then implement our algorithm by lazily guessing the optimum threshold. With an increasing memory of $\mathcal{O}\left(\varepsilon^{-1}\log(2-\kappa)\mathcal{K}/(1-\kappa)^2\right)$, we develop a single pass full streaming algorithm, which obtains a $((1-\kappa)/(2-\kappa)-\mathcal{O}(\varepsilon))$-approximation.
- In last, we study a more general fair BP maximization. Utilizing a distorted greedy-based technique, we provide a $(1-\kappa)/(2-\kappa)$-approximation in time of $\mathcal{O}(n\mathcal{K})$.

1.1 Related Work

Streaming Submodular Maximization Algorithms. For the $\mathcal{K}$-cardinality constrained submodular maximization under streaming, there exists a natural local search procedure [7], which initially keeps the first $\mathcal{K}$ elements, and if the new visited element has a larger marginal value, then adds the new element to the solution, meanwhile deletes the former retained element with the maximum exchanged value. However, an example presented [1] implies that the performance of the local search degrades arbitrarily with $\mathcal{K}$. By setting a novelty threshold lower bound, [4] introduce an improved algorithm with 0.25-approximation with the memory complexity of $O(\mathcal{K})$. An efficient threshold-based streaming algorithm referred in [1], which attains a $(0.5-\varepsilon)$-approximation with the memory complexity of $O(\varepsilon^{-1}\mathcal{K}\log\mathcal{K})$ that independent on the input size of the stream. An improved threshold streaming algorithm is introduced by [14], which segmentally instantiates threshold values and gets $(0.5+10^{-14})$-approximation if the data are fed in a random order. If the data arrives in an arbitrary order, there exists no streaming algorithm with $(0.5+\varepsilon)$-approximation and memory complexity less than $O(|\mathcal{V}|/\mathcal{K})$ for any $\varepsilon>0$ [14]. Kazemi et al. [10] provide an improved streaming algorithm, which decreases the memory complexity from $O(\mathcal{K}\log\mathcal{K})$ to $O(\mathcal{K})$ and keeps the other performance guarantees at the same.

BP Maximization Algorithms. [2] introduce the constrained BP maximization and study two types of constraints, both $\mathcal{K}$-cardinality and p-matroid system, respectively. They accordingly present greedy-based algorithms with $(1-e^{-(1-\kappa^{\mathcal{L}})\kappa_{\mathcal{G}}})/\kappa_{\mathcal{G}}$-approximation and $(1-\kappa^{\mathcal{L}})/(\kappa_{\mathcal{G}}(1-\kappa^{\mathcal{L}})+p)$-approximation, where $\kappa_{\mathcal{G}}$ and $\kappa^{\mathcal{L}}$ individually represent the submodular curvature of $\mathcal{G}$ and the supermodular curvature of $\mathcal{L}$. [5] study the BP maximization under the online setting. They provide a $(1-\kappa_{\mathcal{G}})(1-\kappa^{\mathcal{L}})^3/(2-\kappa^{\mathcal{L}})^2$-competitive algorithm for the $\mathcal{K}$-cardinality constrained BP maximization and further develop a $(2-\kappa^{\mathcal{L}})/(3-\kappa^{\mathcal{L}})$-competitive algorithm for the p-matroid system constrained BP maximization. [15] extend the BP maximization to integer lattice and present a parameterized approximation algorithm with general submodular and supermodular curvatures. Recently, [13] introduce bifactor approximations for the constrained BP maximization based on distorted greedy strategy.

Organization. The rest of the paper is organized as follows. Section 2 gives some preliminary notations. Section 3 studies the $\mathcal{K}$-cardinality constrained BP maximization under streaming in detail. Indeed, Sect. 3.1 provides a distorted threshold-based algorithm. Section 3.2 presents a full distorted threshold-based algorithm for the $\mathcal{K}$-cardinality constrained BP maximization. Section 4 presents a distorted greedy-based algorithm for the fair BP maximization. Finally, Sect. 5 gives a conclusion for our work.

2   Preliminaries

Denote $\mathcal{V}$ as an element ground set, a set function $\mathcal{G} : 2^{\mathcal{V}} \to \mathbb{R}_+$ $\mathcal{V}$ is *submodular* if for any two subsets $\mathcal{A}, \mathcal{B} \subseteq \mathcal{V}$, one has $\mathcal{G}(\mathcal{A}) + \mathcal{G}(\mathcal{B}) \geq \mathcal{G}(\mathcal{A} \cup \mathcal{B}) + \mathcal{G}(\mathcal{A} \cap \mathcal{B})$. The function $\mathcal{G}$ is *non-negative* if $\mathcal{G}(\mathcal{A}) \geq 0$ for any $\mathcal{A} \subseteq \mathcal{V}$. Let $\mathcal{G}(u|\mathcal{A}) = \mathcal{G}(\mathcal{A} \cup \{u\}) - \mathcal{G}(\mathcal{A})$ be the marginal value of adding element u to set $\mathcal{A}$. The submodular function $\mathcal{G}$ is *non-decreasing* if $\mathcal{G}(u|\mathcal{A}) \geq 0$. Another description of submodular is presented as: $\mathcal{G}(u|\mathcal{S}) \geq \mathcal{G}(u|\mathcal{T}), \forall \mathcal{S} \subseteq \mathcal{T} \subseteq \mathcal{V}, u \notin \mathcal{V}$.

Conforti and Cornuéjols [6] introduce a parameter of (total) curvature of non-negative submodular functions and provide a more tighter performance guarantee for the $\mathcal{K}$-cardinality constrained submodular maximization problem. We now restate the total curvature of submodular functions.

Definition 1. *[6] The curvature of a non-negative submodular function $\mathcal{G}$ is defined as $\kappa_{\mathcal{G}} = 1 - \min_{u \in \mathcal{V}} \frac{\mathcal{G}(u|\mathcal{V} \setminus \{u\})}{\mathcal{G}(\{u\})}$.*

A set function $\mathcal{L} : 2^{\mathcal{V}} \to \mathbb{R}$ is supermodular if and only if $\mathcal{L}(u|\mathcal{S}) \leq \mathcal{L}(u|\mathcal{T})$ for any $\mathcal{S} \subseteq \mathcal{T} \subseteq \mathcal{V}$. A complementary parameter of supermodular curvature is introduced by [2] and we restate it below.

Definition 2. *[2] The supermodular curvature of a non-negative monotone non-decreasing supermodular function $\mathcal{L}$ is defined as $\kappa^{\mathcal{L}} = 1 - \min_{u \in \mathcal{V}} \frac{\mathcal{L}(u)}{\mathcal{L}(u|\mathcal{V} \setminus \{u\})}$.*

So, a remark for characterizing the relation of the defined two curvatures can be described as $\kappa_{\mathcal{G}}(\mathcal{A}) = \kappa^{\mathcal{G}(\mathcal{V}) - \mathcal{G}(\mathcal{V} \setminus \mathcal{A})}$ where $\mathcal{G}(\mathcal{V}) - \mathcal{G}(\mathcal{V} \setminus \mathcal{A})$ represents the dual of the non-negative monotone supermodular function $\mathcal{G}$ for any set $\mathcal{A}$. Denote $\kappa = \kappa^{\mathcal{L}}$ for clarity in our context.

Fair BP Maximization. In this model, assume there is a $\mathcal{P}$-partition for the elements and denote $\mathcal{P}_i$ as the ith part of the partition, i.e., $\mathcal{V} = \cup_i \mathcal{P}_i$. For any part $\mathcal{P}_i$, denote ℓ_i and u_i as the fairness lower and upper bounds constraints, respectively. The goal is to choose a subset $\mathcal{S}$ of size at most $\mathcal{K}$ satisfying $|\mathcal{S} \cap \mathcal{P}_i| \in [\ell_i, u_i]$ for any i, such that the sum of $\mathcal{G}(\mathcal{S}) + \mathcal{L}(\mathcal{S})$ is as large as possible. We formally describe this problem as

$$\max_{\mathcal{S} \in \mathcal{I}} \mathcal{G}(\mathcal{S}) + \mathcal{L}(\mathcal{S}) \tag{2}$$

Algorithm 1. Distorted Thresholding Algorithm

Input: Stream $\mathcal{V}$, integer $\mathcal{K}$, functions $\mathcal{G}$, $\mathcal{L}$ with supermodular curvature κ, $\alpha > 0$.

1: Set $\tau \leftarrow \frac{1}{\mathcal{K}} \cdot \{\mathcal{H}(\kappa) \cdot (\mathcal{G}(\mathcal{OPT}) + \alpha \cdot \mathcal{L}(\mathcal{OPT}))\}$, $\mathcal{H}(\kappa) \leftarrow \frac{1-\kappa}{2-\kappa}$, and $\mathcal{S} \leftarrow \emptyset$.
2: **while** there is a revealed element u from stream $\mathcal{V}$ **do**
3:     **if** $|\mathcal{S}| < \mathcal{K}$ and $\mathcal{G}(u|\mathcal{S}) + \alpha \cdot \mathcal{L}(\{u\}) \geq \tau$ **then**
4:         $\mathcal{S} \leftarrow \mathcal{S} \cup \{u\}$
5:     **end if**
6: **end while**
7: return $\mathcal{S}$

---

where $\mathcal{I} = \{\mathcal{S} \subseteq \mathcal{V} : |\mathcal{S}| \leq \mathcal{K}, |\mathcal{S} \cap \mathcal{P}_i| \in [\ell_i, u_i]$ for all $i\}$. Observe that our fairness BP maximization can be reduced to the BP maximization if $i = 1, u_i = \mathcal{K}$, and $\ell_i = 0$. If removing the lower bound constraints, the above problem (2) reduces to the BP maximization with a partition matroid.

In the paper, we emphasize the time complexity as the amount of oracle queries.

3   Streaming BP Maximization

Note that the greedy algorithm selects an element with the maximum marginal gain in every iteration for the centralized offline setting and guarantees that the value of chosen set has a significant amount comparing to the optimum. However, it is almost impossible to get the "best" elements, since all of them are revealed on the fly. To deal with the streaming submodular maximization, researchers develop an extended greedy strategy by introducing the threshold techniques. The key idea behind these ideas is to instantiate proper threshold values based on the optimum for the arriving elements.

We introduce a distorted threshold technique to the BP maximization and derive a distorted threshold-based streaming algorithm. In our algorithm, denote the distorted optimum threshold as $\tau = \frac{1}{\mathcal{K}} \cdot \{\mathcal{H}(\kappa) \cdot (\mathcal{G}(\mathcal{OPT}) + \alpha \cdot \mathcal{L}(\mathcal{OPT}))\}$. The chosen of the parameters $\alpha, \mathcal{H}(\kappa)$ are discussed in following section.

3.1   Distorted Threshold Algorithm

In this subsection, we present the distorted threshold algorithm, listed as Algorithm 1. Further, we discuss the main theoretical guarantees in detail.

The algorithm starts with an empty set, denoted by $\mathcal{S} = \emptyset$. If $|\mathcal{S}| < \mathcal{K}$ and u is the visited element at the current time, we add the revealed element u to $\mathcal{S}$ if the distorted marginal value no less than the distorted threshold, i.e., $\mathcal{G}(u|\mathcal{S}) + \alpha \cdot \mathcal{L}(\{u\}) \geq \tau$. The algorithm processes the next element until the stream is finished or the size of set $\mathcal{S}$ equals to the cardinality upper bound $\mathcal{K}$.

Our main result can be concluded as the following theorem and the proof is deferred to our full version.

Algorithm 2. Full-Distorted Thresholding Algorithm

Input: Stream $\mathcal{V}$, integer $\mathcal{K}$, functions $\mathcal{G}$, $\mathcal{L}$ with supermodular curvature κ, parameters $\alpha = 1$ and $\mathcal{H}(\kappa) = \frac{1-\kappa}{2-\kappa}$.

1: $\mathcal{M}_0 \leftarrow 0$
2: **while** there is a revealed element u from stream **do**
3:     $\mathcal{M}_t \leftarrow \max\{\mathcal{M}_{t-1}, \mathcal{H}(\kappa) \cdot (\mathcal{G}(u) + \alpha \cdot \mathcal{L}(u))\}$
4:     $\mathcal{O}_t \leftarrow \left\{ (1+\varepsilon)^i | (1+\varepsilon)^i \in \left[\frac{\mathcal{M}_t}{(1+\varepsilon)\mathcal{K}}, \frac{\mathcal{M}_t}{(1-\kappa)\mathcal{H}(\kappa)} \right] \right\}$
5:     delete threshold τ and sets $\mathcal{S}_\tau$ with $\tau < \frac{\mathcal{M}_t}{(1+\varepsilon)\mathcal{K}}$
6:     **for** $\tau \in \mathcal{O}_t$ **do**
7:         **if** τ is a new instantiated threshold **then**
8:             $\mathcal{S}_\tau \leftarrow \emptyset$
9:         **end if**
10:        **if** $|\mathcal{S}_\tau| < \mathcal{K}$ and $\mathcal{G}(u|\mathcal{S}_\tau) + \alpha \cdot \mathcal{L}(\{u\}) \geq \tau$ **then**
11:            $\mathcal{S}_\tau \leftarrow \mathcal{S}_\tau \cup \{u\}$
12:        **end if**
13:    **end for**
14: **end while**
15: **return** $S = \arg\max_\tau f(\mathcal{S}_\tau) + \mathcal{L}(\mathcal{S}_\tau)$

Theorem 1. *For the BP maximization under streaming, Algorithm 1 returns a solution $\mathcal{S}$, satisfying*

$$\frac{\mathcal{G}(\mathcal{S}) + \alpha \cdot \mathcal{L}(\mathcal{S})}{\mathcal{G}(\mathcal{OPT}) + \alpha \cdot \mathcal{L}(\mathcal{OPT})} \geq \frac{1-\kappa}{2-\kappa}.$$

3.2 Full Distorted Threshold Algorithm

In former section, we assume a prior for the threshold value τ based on the optimal value. Actually, we only can learn this value after the stream is finished. So, we embark on removing the above assumption and constructing a relaxed threshold interval following by the work of [1,9]. We claim that the approximation ratio does not lose too much and also the memory complexity does not increase sharply. The main pseudo codes are summarized by Algorithm 2.

It follows that

$$\max_{u \in \mathcal{V}} \mathcal{H}(\kappa) \cdot (\mathcal{G}(u) + \alpha \cdot \mathcal{L}(u)) \leq \mathcal{H}(\kappa) \cdot (\mathcal{G}(\mathcal{OPT}) + \alpha \cdot \mathcal{L}(\mathcal{OPT}))$$

$$\leq \frac{\mathcal{K}}{1-\kappa} \cdot \max_{u \in \mathcal{V}} \mathcal{H}(\kappa) \cdot (\mathcal{G}(u) + \alpha \cdot \mathcal{L}(u))$$

Consequently, if we have access to this maximum distorted singleton value $\mathcal{M} = \max_{u \in \mathcal{V}} \mathcal{H}(\kappa) \cdot (\mathcal{G}(u) + \alpha \cdot \mathcal{L}(u))$ in advance, then we would guess the threshold value τ with the form of $(1+\varepsilon)^i$ for some integer i among the range of $\left[\frac{\mathcal{M}}{(1+\varepsilon)\mathcal{K}}, \frac{\mathcal{M}}{1-\kappa} \right]$. Thus one can get a threshold $\tilde{\tau}$ subject to $\mathcal{K}\tilde{\tau} \leq$

Algorithm 3. Fair-Distorted-Greedy

Input: Element set $\mathcal{V}$, integer $\mathcal{K}$, functions $\mathcal{G}$, $\mathcal{L}$ with supermodular curvature κ,
     parameter $\alpha = \frac{2}{2-\kappa}$.
1: $\mathcal{S} \leftarrow \emptyset$
2: **while** $|\mathcal{S}| < \mathcal{K}$ **do**
3:     $\mathcal{U} \leftarrow \{u \in \mathcal{V} : \mathcal{S} \cup \{u\} \text{ is extendible}\}$
4:     $\mathcal{S} \leftarrow \mathcal{S} + \arg\max_{u \in \mathcal{U}} \mathcal{G}(u|\mathcal{S}) + \alpha \cdot \mathcal{L}(u)$
5: **end while**
6: return $\mathcal{S}$

$\mathcal{H}(\kappa) \cdot (\mathcal{G}(\mathcal{OPT}) + \alpha \cdot \mathcal{L}(\mathcal{OPT})) \leq (1 + \varepsilon)\mathcal{K}\tilde{\tau}$ and the amount of guesses is bounded by

$$\log_{1+\varepsilon} \frac{(1+\varepsilon)\mathcal{K} \cdot \max_{u \in \mathcal{V}} \mathcal{H}(\kappa) \cdot (\mathcal{G}(u) + \alpha \cdot \mathcal{L}(u))}{(1-\kappa) \cdot \max_{u \in \mathcal{V}} \mathcal{H}(\kappa) \cdot (\mathcal{G}(u) + \alpha \cdot \mathcal{L}(u))} \leq \mathcal{O}\left(\frac{1}{\varepsilon} \log \frac{\mathcal{K}}{1-\kappa}\right).$$

Actually, the value of $\max_{u \in \mathcal{V}} \mathcal{H}(\kappa) \cdot (\mathcal{G}(u) + \alpha \cdot \mathcal{L}(u))$ still can not be known in advance. Let $\mathcal{M}_t = \max_{u \in \mathcal{V}'} \mathcal{H}(\kappa) \cdot (\mathcal{G}(u) + \alpha \cdot \mathcal{L}(u))$ be the maximum singleton value at the time of t, where $\mathcal{V}'$ denotes the set of elements encountered at this time. We can utilize the value of $\frac{1}{(1+\varepsilon)\mathcal{K}} \cdot \max_{u \in \mathcal{V}'} \mathcal{H}(\kappa) \cdot (\mathcal{G}(u) + \alpha \cdot \mathcal{L}(u))$ as the lower bound of the threshold τ. Further, based on the value of single element seen so far, we get a relaxed upper bound for the guessing process by the following fact: If $\tau > \frac{1}{\mathcal{H}(\kappa)} \cdot \max_{u \in \mathcal{V}'} \mathcal{H}(\kappa) \cdot (\mathcal{G}(u) + \alpha \cdot \mathcal{L}(u))$, the elements of $\mathcal{V}'$ will not be added to $\mathcal{S}$. This implies that it suffices to explicitly maintain a copy of Algorithm 1 for values of τ that are equal to $(1 + \varepsilon)^i$ for some integer i and fall within the range $\left[\frac{\mathcal{M}_t}{(1+\varepsilon)\mathcal{K}}, \frac{\mathcal{M}_t}{(1-\kappa)\mathcal{H}(\kappa)}\right]$. The memory complexity can be bounded

$$\log_{1+\varepsilon} \frac{\frac{1}{(1-\kappa)\mathcal{H}(\kappa)} \cdot \max_{u \in V'} \mathcal{H}(\kappa) \cdot (\mathcal{G}(u) + \alpha \cdot \mathcal{L}(u))}{\frac{1}{(1+\varepsilon)\mathcal{K}} \cdot \max_{u \in V'} \mathcal{H}(\kappa) \cdot (\mathcal{G}(u) + \alpha \cdot \mathcal{L}(u))} \leq \mathcal{O}\left(\frac{1}{\varepsilon} \log \frac{\mathcal{K}}{(1-\kappa)\mathcal{H}(\kappa)}\right).$$

Now we conclude the results by the following theorem.

Theorem 2. *For any $\varepsilon > 0$, with $\mathcal{O}\left(\frac{1}{\varepsilon} \log \frac{(2-\kappa)\mathcal{K}}{(1-\kappa)^2}\right)$ memory complexity, Algorithm 2 makes one pass over the stream and gets a $\left(\frac{1-\kappa}{2-\kappa} - \mathcal{O}(\varepsilon)\right)$-approximation for the $\mathcal{K}$-cardinality constrained BP submodular maximization.*

4 Fairness in BP Maximization

In this section, we study the fair BP maximization and present a first fair distorted greedy for this problem. Consider the elegant greedy, which picks elements during the iterations with maximum marginal values by enumerating over the ground set. One easily conclude that the fairness constraints may be not satisfied when the global cardinality constraint is reached. To make sure the output of the chosen process is feasible, Halabi et al. [8] introduce a concept of extendable and we restate it here.

Definition 3. *[8] A set S is extendable if it is a subset $S \subseteq S'$ of some feasible solution set $S' \in \mathcal{I}$.*

Then it follows that a set S is extendable if and only if for any $\mathcal{P}_i$, $|S \cap \mathcal{P}_i| \leq u_i$ and $\sum_i \max\{|S \cap \mathcal{P}_i|, \ell_i\} \leq \mathcal{K}$. Actually, the extendability of sets encourages us to choose elements in a feasible manner.

Our fair distorted greedy starts with $S = \emptyset$ and selects at each iteration element with maximum distorted marginal value from an extendable set $\mathcal{U}$. We define $\mathcal{U} = \{u \in \mathcal{V} : S \cup \{u\}$ is extendable$\}$ and denote $\mathcal{G}(u|S) + \alpha \cdot \mathcal{L}(u)$ as the distorted marginal value of adding u to S. The algorithm returns the solution set S after processing $\mathcal{K}$ iterations.

We conclude that there exists a mapping between the solution set returned by the fair distorted greedy and the optimum.

Lemma 1. *There exists a mapping between $S = \{u_1, ..., u_\mathcal{K}\}$ and $\mathcal{OPT} = \{o_1, ..., o_\mathcal{K}\}$ satisfying*

- *for any i, either u_i and o_i are partitioned into the same group*
- *or, $\mathcal{P}[u_i] \neq \mathcal{P}[o_i]$ where $\mathcal{P}[u]$ denotes the part of u belong to, then $|S \cap \mathcal{P}[u_i]| > |\mathcal{OPT} \cap \mathcal{P}[u_i]|$ and $|S \cap \mathcal{P}[o_i]| < |\mathcal{OPT} \cap \mathcal{P}[u_i]|$.*

Following the above lemma, it concludes that $S \setminus \{u_i\} \cup \{o_i\}$ is feasible for any i. The main result is concluded as the following theorem and the proof is deferred to our full version.

Theorem 3. *Denote $\alpha = \frac{2}{2-\kappa}$. Algorithm 3 attains a $\frac{1-\kappa}{2-\kappa}$-approximation for the fair BP maximization.*

5   Conclusions

In this paper, we firstly consider the $\mathcal{K}$-cardinality constrained BP maximization under streaming fashion. Utilizing a distorted threshold-based technique, we develop a semi-streaming algorithm, which depends on a distorted optimum. We then implement the above algorithm by guessing the optimum distorted value and obtain a full streaming algorithm, which makes single pass over the stream, uses $\mathcal{O}\left(\frac{1}{\varepsilon} \log \frac{(2-\kappa)\mathcal{K}}{(1-\kappa)^2}\right)$ memory resource, and gets a $\left(\frac{1-\kappa}{2-\kappa} - \mathcal{O}(\varepsilon)\right)$-approximation for our BP maximization problem. Then we study a more general fair BP maximization. and present a distorted greedy-based algorithm, which performs a $\frac{1-\kappa}{2-\kappa}$-approximation. This arouses a natural research question: "If there exists a distorted threshold-based algorithm for the streaming fair BP maximization?" We believe this is an interesting open problem which needs further study.

Acknowledgements. The first two authors are supported by National Natural Foundation of China (No. 12101587), China Postdoctoral Science Foundation (No. 2021M703167), and Fundamental Research Funds for the Central Universities (No. EIE40108X2). The third author is supported by National Natural Science Foundation of China (No. 12001523). The fourth and fifth authors are supported by National Natural Science Foundation of China (No. 12131003) and Beijing Natural Science Foundation Project No. Z200002.

References

1. Badanidiyuru, A., Mirzasoleiman, B., Karbasi, A., Krause, A.: Streaming submodular maximization: massive data summarization on the fly. In: Proceedings of the 20th ACM SIGKDD International Conference on Knowledge Discovery and Data Mining, pp. 671–680 (2014)
2. Bai, W., Bilmes, J.: Greed is still good: maximizing monotone submodular+supermodular (BP) functions. In: Proceedings of the 35th International Conference on Machine Learning, vol. 80, pp. 304–313 (2018)
3. Bogunovic, I., Mitrović, S., Scarlett, J., Cevher, V.: Robust submodular maximization: a non-uniform partitioning approach. In: Proceedings of the 34th International Conference on Machine Learning, vol. 70, pp. 508–516 (2017)
4. Buchbinder, N., Feldman, M., Schwartz, R.: Online submodular maximization with preemption. In: Proceedings of the 26th Annual ACM-SIAM Symposium on Discrete Algorithms, pp. 1202–1216 (2015)
5. Liu, Z., Chen, L., Chang, H., Du, D., Zhang, X.: Online algorithms for BP functions maximization. Theoret. Comput. Sci. **858**, 114–121 (2021)
6. Conforti, M., Cornuéjols, G.: Submodular set functions, matroids and the greedy algorithm: tight worst-case bounds and some generalizations of the Rado-Edmonds theorem. Discret. Appl. Math. **7**(3), 251–274 (1984)
7. Gomes, R., Krause, A.: Budgeted nonparametric learning from data streams. In: Proceedings of the 27th International Conference on Machine Learning, pp. 391–398 (2010)
8. Halabi, M. E., Mitrovi, S., Norouzi-Fard, A., Tardos, J., Tarnawski, J.: Fairness in streaming submodular maximization: algorithms and hardness. In: Proceedings of Annual Conference on Neural Information Processing Systems (2020, to appear)
9. Kazemi, E., Minaee, S., Feldman, M., Karbasi, A.: Regularized submodular maximization at scale. In: Proceedings of the 38th International Conference on Machine Learning, pp. 5356–5366 (2021)
10. Kazemi, E., Mitrovic, M., Zadimoghaddam, M., Lattanzi, S., Karbasi, A.: Submodular streaming in all its glory: tight approximation, minimum memory and low adaptive complexity. In: Proceedings of the 36th International Conference on Machine Learning, pp. 3311–3320 (2019)
11. Kempe, D., Kleinberg, J., Tardos, É.: Maximizing the spread of influence through a social network. In: Proceedings of the 9th ACM SIGKDD International Conference on Knowledge Discovery and Data Mining, pp. 137–146 (2003)
12. Krause, A., McMahan, H.B., Guestrin, C., Gupta, A.: Robust submodular observation selection. J. Mach. Learn. Res. **9**(4), 2761–2801 (2008)
13. Liu, Z., Guo, L., Du, D., Xu, D., Zhang, X.: Maximization problems of balancing submodular relevance and supermodular diversity. J. Glob. Optim. **82**, 179–194 (2022). https://doi.org/10.1007/s10898-021-01063-6
14. Norouzi-Fard, A., Tarnawski, J., Mitrović, S., Zandieh, A., Mousavifar, A., Svensson, O.: Beyond 1/2-approximation for submodular maximization on massive data streams. In: Proceedings of the 35th International Conference on Machine Learning, pp. 3826–3835 (2018)
15. Zhang, Z., Du, D., Jiang, Y., Wu, C.: Maximizing DR-submodular+supermodular functions on the integer lattice subject to a cardinality constraint. J. Global Optim. **80**(3), 595–616 (2021). https://doi.org/10.1007/s10898-021-01014-1

Streaming Algorithms for Maximization of a Non-submodular Function with a Cardinality Constraint on the Integer Lattice

Jingjing Tan[1], Yue Sun[2], Yicheng Xu[3,4], and Juan Zou[5(✉)]

[1] School of Mathematics and Information Science, Weifang University,
Weifang 261061, People's Republic of China
[2] Beijing Institute for Scientific and Engineering Computing,
Beijing University of Technology, Beijing 100124, People's Republic of China
suny39@emails.bjut.edu.cn
[3] Shenzhen Institutes of Advanced Technology, Chinese Academy of Sciences,
Shenzhen 518055, People's Republic of China
yc.xu@siat.ac.cn
[4] Guangxi Key Laboratory of Cryptography and Information Security,
Guilin 541004, People's Republic of China
[5] School of Mathematical Sciences, Qufu Normal University, Qufu 273165,
People's Republic of China
zoujuanjn@163.com

Abstract. We consider the maximization of a monotone non-submodular function with a cardinality constraint on the integer lattice. As our main contribution, two streaming algorithms with provable good performance guarantee and reasonable query time complexity are proposed.

Keywords: Streaming algorithm · Non-submodular · Cardinality constraint · Integer lattice

1 Introduction

The submodular optimization problem is widely concerned in the combinatorial optimization area in recent decades [4,6–10,12,13,15,26–28,34]. There have been a lot of research about maximization of a monotone submodular function.

J. Tan—Supported by Natural Science Foundation of Shandong Province (Nos. ZR2017LA002, ZR2019MA022), and Doctoral research foundation of Weifang University (No. 2017BS02). Y. Sun—Supported by National Natural Science Foundation of China (No. 11871081). Y. Xu—Supported by Guangxi Key Laboratory of Cryptography and Information Security (No. GCIS202116) and Natural Science Foundation of China (No. 11901558). J. Zou—Supported by National Natural Science Foundation of China (11801310).

© Springer Nature Switzerland AG 2022
H. Shen et al. (Eds.): PDCAT 2021, LNCS 13148, pp. 460–465, 2022.
https://doi.org/10.1007/978-3-030-96772-7_42

Nemhauser et al. [25] first considers the cardinality constraint in the submodular maximization and propose a greedy algorithm achieving $(1-1/e)$-approximation. Feige [10] prove that the $(1-1/e)$-approximation is tight under the assumption $P = NP$. For the non-submodular set function, Bian et al. [2] prove that the standard greedy algorithm has a tight approximation ratio with cardinality constraint, based on the weak DR ratio introduced by Das et al. [8]. Many other excellent results of non-submodular optimization refer to [1,3,11,14,16–24,29–33,35,36].

In this paper, we are study streaming algorithms for maximization of a non-submodular function with a cardinality constraint on the integer lattice.

1.1 Problem Definition

We assume that the elements in the ground set $G = \{e_1, e_2, \cdots, e_n\}$ arrive one by one. Let s be a n-dimensional vector in $\mathbb{N}^G$, and denote the component of coordinate $e_i \in G$ of s as $s(e_i)$. We use $\mathbf{0}$ to denote the zero vector. χ_{e_i} is the standard unit vector. For any $S \subseteq G$, we denote $s(S) := \sum_{e_i \in S} s(e_i)$. $c \in \{N \cup \{\infty\}\}^G$ is a box. f is defined on $\mathscr{D}_c = \{s \in \mathbb{N}^G : s \leq c\}$, and $f(\mathbf{0}) = 0$. The problem is then described below

$$\max_{s \leq c, s(G) \leq k} f(s), \tag{1}$$

where $s(G) \leq k$ is the cardinality constraint and

$$s(G) = \sum_{e \in G} s(e).$$

1.2 Preliminaries

Let

$$(s \wedge t)(e) = \min\{s(e), t(e)\}$$

and

$$(s \vee t)(e) = \max\{s(e), t(e)\}$$

for each element $e \in G$.

$\mathscr{F}_c$ is denoted to be the set of all non-negative monotone DR-submodular functions.

Let s^* be the optimal solution vector, OPT be the optimal value.

Definition 1. *Suppose $f \in \mathscr{F}_c$, the DR ratio $\gamma_f(f)$ of f is the maximum scalar that satisfies*

$$\gamma_f(f)f(\chi_e|t) \leq f(\chi_e|s)$$

for any $e \in G$, $s, t \in \mathscr{D}_c$ with $s \leq t$ and $t + \chi_e \in \mathscr{D}_c$.

Definition 2. *Suppose $f \in \mathscr{F}_c$, the weak DR ratio $\gamma_f^w(f)$ of f is the maximum scalar that satisfies*

$$\gamma_f^w(f)(f(t) - f(s)) \leq \sum_{e \in \{t\} \backslash \{s\}} f(\chi_e | s)$$

for all $s, t \in \mathscr{D}_c$ with $s \leq t$.

In the following, we denote $\mathscr{F}_c^{\gamma_f, \gamma_f^w} = \{g \in \mathscr{F}_c : \gamma_f(f) = \gamma_f, \gamma_f^w(f) = \gamma_f^w\}$.

2   The Streaming Algorithm

In this section, we propose a streaming algorithm to approximate the NMCC which generalizes the DRSS algorithm in [33] on the integer lattice.

Algorithm 1. BinarySearch(f, s, c, e_i, k, τ)

Input: $f : \mathbb{N}^G \to \mathbb{R}^+$, stream of data G, $e \in G$, $s, c \in \mathbb{N}^G$, $k \in \mathbb{N}$, $\tau \in \mathbb{R}^+$.
Output: $\alpha \in \mathbb{R}^+$.

1: $\alpha_t \leftarrow \min\{c(e) - s(e), k - s(G)\}$;
2: $\alpha_s \leftarrow 1$;
3: **if** $\frac{f(\alpha_t \chi_e | s)}{\alpha_t} \geq \tau$, **then**
4:     return α_t.
5: **end if**
6: **if** $f(\chi_e | s) < \tau$, **then**
7:     return 0
8: **end if**
9: **while** $\alpha_t > \alpha_s + 1$, **do**
10:    $\rho = \lfloor \frac{\alpha_t + \alpha_s}{2} \rfloor$
11:    **if** $f(\rho \chi_e | s) \geq \tau$, **then**
12:        $\alpha_s = \rho$,
13:    **else**
14:        $\alpha_t = \rho$.
15:    **end if**
16: **end while**
17: **return** α_t

Let s_{i-1} be the output of the $(i - 1)$-th iteration and e_i be the element at the i-th iteration of Algorithm 2, and α_i is returned from Algorithm 1.

Lemma 1. *For the i-th iteration of Algorithm 2 with s_i, it holds that*

$$f(s_i) \geq \frac{\gamma_f v s_i(G)}{2\gamma_f k}. \tag{2}$$

Algorithm 2. Streaming Algorithm

Input: $f \in \mathscr{F}_c$, stream of data G, cardinality constraint k, $\varepsilon \in (0, 1)$.

Output: a vector $s \in \mathbb{N}^G$.

1: $m \leftarrow \max\limits_{e \in G} f(\chi_e)$;

2: $V_\varepsilon = \{(1+\varepsilon)^l | l \in N, \frac{\beta}{1+\varepsilon} \leq (1+\varepsilon)^l \leq \frac{km}{\gamma_f}\}$;

3: **for** $v \in V_\varepsilon$, **do**

4:     set $s^v \leftarrow \mathbf{0}$

5:     **for** $i = 1, \cdots, n$, **do**

6:         **if** $s^v(G) < k$, **then**

7:             $\alpha \leftarrow \mathbf{BinarySearch}\left(f, s^v, c, e_i, k, \frac{\gamma_f v / 2^{\gamma_f} - f(s^v)}{k - s^v(G)}\right)$;

8:             $s^v \leftarrow s^v + \alpha\chi_e$;

9:             **Return** s^v

10:         **end if**

11:     **end for**

12: **end for**

13: **return** s^v

Denote $\tilde{s}$ as the final output of Algorithm 2. For any $e \in \{s^*\} \setminus \{\tilde{s}\}$, consider the marginal gain of χ_e.

Lemma 2. *If $\tilde{s}(G) < k$, we have*

$$f(\chi_e | \tilde{s}) < \frac{v}{2^{\gamma_f} k},$$

where $e \in \{s^*\} \setminus \{\tilde{s}\}$.

Theorem 1. *For a given $\varepsilon \in (0, 1)$, Algorithm 2 is a two-pass $\min\{(1 - \varepsilon)\gamma_f / 2^{\gamma_f}, (1 - 1/\gamma_f^w 2^{\gamma_f})\}$-approximation algorithm for NMCC, with $O(\frac{k}{\varepsilon} \log \frac{k}{\varepsilon})$ memory complexity and $O(\frac{\log k}{\varepsilon} \log \frac{\log k}{\varepsilon})$ query times per element.*

References

1. Badanidiyuru, A., Mirzasoleiman, B., Karbasi, A., Krause, A.: Streaming submodular maximization: massive data summarization on the fly. In: Proceedings of KDD, pp. 671–680 (2014)
2. Bian, A.A., Buhmann, J.M., Krause, A., Tschiatschek, S.: Guarantees for greedy maximization of non-submodular functions with applications. In: Proceedings of ICML, pp. 498–507 (2017)
3. Bogunovic, I., Zhao, J., Y., Cevher, V.: Robust maximization of non-submodular objectives. In: Proceedings of AISTATS, pp. 890–899 (2018)
4. Balkanski, E., Rubinstein, A., Singer, Y.: An exponential speedup in parallel running time for submodular maximization without loss in approximation. In: Proceedings of SODA, pp. 283–302 (2019)

5. Calinescu, G., Chekuri, C., Pál, M., Vondrák, J.: Maximizing a submodular set function subject to a matroid constraint. SIAM J. Comput. **40**, 1740–1766 (2011)
6. Chekuri, C., Quanrud, K.: Submodular function maximization in parallel via the multilinear relaxation. In: Proceedings of SODA, pp. 303–322 (2019)
7. Das, A., Kempe, D.: Algorithms for subset selection in linear regression. In: Proceedings of STOC, pp. 45–54 (2008)
8. Das, A., Kempe, D.: Submodular meets spectral: greedy algorithms for subset selection, sparse approximation and dictionary selection. In: Proceedings of ICML, pp. 1057–1064 (2011)
9. Ene, A., Nguyen, H.L.: Submodular maximization with nearly-optimal approximation and adaptivity in nearly-linear time. In: Proceedings of SODA, pp. 274–282 (2019)
10. Feige, U.: A threshold of ln n for approximation set cover. J. ACM **32**, 65–82 (1998)
11. Feige, U., Izsak, R.: Welfare maximization and the supermodular degree. In: Proceedings of ITCS, pp. 247–256 (2013)
12. Golovin, D., Krause, A.: Adaptive submodularity: theory and applications in active learning and stochastic optimization. J. Artif. Intell. Res. **42**, 427–486 (2011)
13. Gong, S., Nong, Q., Liu, W., Fang, Q.: Parametric monotone function maximization with matroid constraints. J. Global Optim. **75**(3), 833–849 (2019). https://doi.org/10.1007/s10898-019-00800-2
14. Horel, T., Singer, Y.: Maximization of approximately submodular functions. In: Proceedings of NIPS, pp. 3045–3053 (2016)
15. Huang, C., Kakimura, N.: Improved streaming algorithms for maximising monotone submodular functions under a knapsack constraint. In: Proceedings of WADS, pp. 438–451 (2019)
16. Jiang, Y.J., Wang, Y.S., Xu, D.C., Yang, R.Q., Zhang, Y.: Streaming algorithm for maximizing a monotone non-submodular function under d-knapsack constraint. Optim. Lett. **14**, 1235–1248 (2020)
17. Krause, A., Leskovec, J., Guestrin, C., VanBriesen, J.M., Faloutsos, C.: Efficient sensor placement optimization for securing large water distribution networks. J. Water Resour. Plan. Manag. **134**, 516–526 (2008)
18. Krause, A., Singh, A., Guestrin, C.: Near-optimal sensor placements in gaussian processes: theory, efficient algorithms and empirical studies. J. Mach. Learn. Res. **9**, 235–284 (2008)
19. Kapralov, M., Post, I., Vondrák, J.: Online submodular welfare maximization: greedy is optimal. In: Proceedings of SODA, pp. 1216–1225 (2012)
20. Kempe, D., Kleinberg, J., Tardos, E.: Maximizing the spread of influence through a social network. In: Proceedings of KDD, pp. 137–146 (2003)
21. Khanna, R., Elenberg, E.R., Dimakis, A.G., Negahban S., Ghosh, J.: Scalable greedy feature selection via weak submodularity. In: Proceedings of ICAIS, pp. 1560–1568 (2017)
22. Kuhnle, A., Smith, J.D., Crawford, V.G., Thai, M.T.: Fast maximization of non-submodular, monotonic functions on the integer lattice. In: Proceedings of ICML, pp. 2791–2800 (2018)
23. Lawrence, N., Seeger, M., Herbrich, R.: Fast sparse Gaussian process methods: the informative vector machine. In: Proceedings of NIPS, pp. 625–632 (2003)
24. Lin, Y., Chen, W., Lui, J.C.S.: Bosting information spread: an algorithmic approach. In: Proceedings of ICDE, pp. 883–894 (2017)
25. Nemhauser, G.L., Wolsey, L.A., Fisher, M.L.: An analysis of approximations for maximizing submodular set functions. Math. Program. **14**, 265–294 (1978)

26. Norouzi-Fard, A., Tarnawski, J., Mitrovic, S., Zandieh, A., Mousavifar, A., Svensson, O.: Beyond 1/2-approximation for submodular maximization on massive data streams. In: Proceedings of ICML, pp. 3829–3838 (2018)

27. Sviridenko, M.: A note on maximizing a submodular set function subject to a knapsack constraint. Oper. Res. Lett. **32**, 41–43 (2004)

28. Shioura, A.: On the pipage rounding algorithm for submodular function maximization-a view from discrete convex analysis. Discrete Math. Algorithms Appl. **1**, 1–23 (2009)

29. Soma, T., Kakimura, N., Inaba, K., Kawarabayashi, K.: Optimal budget allocation: theoretical guarantee and efficient algorithm. In: Proceedings of ICML, pp. 351–359 (2014)

30. Soma, T., Yoshida, Y.: A generalization of submodular cover via the diminishing return property on the integer lattice. In: Proceedings of NIPS, pp. 847–855 (2014)

31. Soma, T., Yoshida, Y.: Maximization monotone submodular functions over the integer lattice. Math. Program. **172**, 539–563 (2018)

32. Wolsey, L.: Maximising real-valued submodular set function: primal and dual heuristics for location problems. Math. Oper. Res. **7**, 410–425 (1982)

33. Wang, Y., Xu, D., Wang, Y., Zhang, D.: Non-submodular maximization on massive data streams. J. Global Optim. **76**(4), 729–743 (2019). https://doi.org/10.1007/s10898-019-00840-8

34. Yang, R.Q., Xu, D.C., Jiang, Y.J., Wang, Y.S., Zhang, D.M.: Approximation robust parameterized submodular function maximization in large-scales. Asia Pac. J. Oper. Res. **36**, 195–220 (2019)

35. Zhang, Z.N., Du, D.L., Jiang, Y.J., Wu, C.C.: Maximizing DR-submodular+supermodular function on the integer lattice subject to a cardinality constraint. J. Glob. Optim. **80**, 595–616 (2021)

36. Zhu, X., Yu, J., Lee, W.D., Shan, S., Du, D.Z.: New domination sets in social networks. J. Glob. Optim. **48**, 633–642 (2010)

Adaptable Focal Loss for Imbalanced Text Classification

Lu Cao[1($\boxtimes$)], Xinyue Liu[1], and Hong Shen[2]

[1] Department of Intelligent Manufacturing, Wuyi University, Jiangmen, China
caolu20001742@163.com
[2] School of Data Science and Computer Science, Sun Yat-sen University, Guangzhou, China
shenh3@mail.sysu.edu.cn

Abstract. In this paper, we study the problem of imbalanced text classification based on the pre-trained language models. We propose the Adaptable Focal Loss (AFL) method to solve this problem. Firstly, we use the word embeddings from the pre-trained models to construct the sentence level prior by the sum of the word embeddings in the sentence. Then, we extend the Focal Loss, which is widely used in the field of object detection, by replacing the task-special parameters with the scaled-softmax of the distance between the fine-tuned embeddings and the prior embeddings from the pre-trained models. By removing the task-special parameters in Focal Loss, not only can the parameters of arbitrary imbalanced proportion distribution be adjusted automatically according to the task, but also the sentences that are difficult to classify can be given a higher weight. Experimental results show that our methods can easily combine with the common classifier models and significantly improve their performances.

Keywords: Imbalanced text classification · Pre-trained models · Adaptive training · Focal loss

1 Introduction

Text is the most common carrier of human beings to transmit information. With the rapid development of Internet technology, the demand for information technology and text processing has been increasing in recent years. Text classification [1–4], as one of the core issues in Natural Language Processing (NLP), has been widely studied by scholars and successfully applied to industry scenes. There are already many deep-learning based words on the text classification, which outperform the traditional methods, i.e., SVM [5], LDA [6].

At present, most text classification models generally believe that there is no significant difference in the number of different text labels classified, which may make the model's accuracy in predicting some weak labels far lower than all data sets. In actual scenes, the distribution of data labels will always be imbalanced to a certain extent. Even in some cases, such as spam classification, the distribution of data may be extremely imbalanced. In this case, if the positive-negative sample ratio is very high, the model

© Springer Nature Switzerland AG 2022
H. Shen et al. (Eds.): PDCAT 2021, LNCS 13148, pp. 466–475, 2022.
https://doi.org/10.1007/978-3-030-96772-7_43

only needs to predict all data as positive samples to achieve high classification accuracy. But it is obviously unreasonable. This requires the classification model not only to have a high classification accuracy for the whole data, but also to keep high classification accuracy for each kind of data sample. We propose an adaptive objective function based on a pre-trained language model to solve the problem of imbalanced text classification.

Recently, combining pre-trained language models and fine-tune models have become mainstream in many NLP task, i.e., text classification [7], text generation [8], etc. In this paper, we assume that the pre-trained embeddings are trained in the whole real word corpus for that all the pre-trained models are trained on enormous real world data. Li *et al.* [9] come up with this idea creatively, which uses the pre-trained embeddings to construct the topological order prior for each word. We extend this model and propose a scaled-softmax function to construct the sentence level prior for each sentence based on pre-trained word embeddings. We use the difference between the computed sentence prior and the fine-tuned sentence embedding to calculate an adaptable parameter and use the parameter to replace the task-specific parameter in Focal Loss. By removing the task-special parameters in Focal Loss, our model can not only reweight the higher weights to the disadvantage sentences, but higher weights to the sentences that are difficult to be classified for arbitrary texture data sets.

The content structure of this article is as follows: Firstly, we introduce the related knowledge of imbalanced learning and pre-training models. Secondly, we propose an adaptive loss function that combines pre-training language models. Then, the performance of our proposed new objective function is verified on multiple data sets. Finally, we make a summary.

2 Related Work

2.1 Imbalanced Learning

Many tasks in the real world suffer from the extreme imbalance in different groups. Imbalanced data distribution will have an adverse effect on the performance of the classification model [10]. At present, there are two traditional methods to solve the problem of imbalanced classification, one is data level [11–13], the other is algorithm level [14–16]. The data level methods use re-sampling to balance the size of different groups. Specifically, the over-sampling technique increases the number of samples by repeatedly sampling a small number of samples or generating minority class samples. While under-sampling technique divides the original data set into multiple small data sets with relatively balanced sample distributions. The algorithm level methods aim to solve this problem by using cost-sensitive objectives or adding cost-sensitive regularization. This method is mainly to improve the model itself, so that the model pays more attention to the minority samples. The mainstream method is to replace the original classification loss function with the cost sensitive loss. In 2016, Shrivastava *et al.* [17] proposed an online hard case mining (OHEM) algorithm. OHEM algorithm constructs training examples with the highest-loss examples by its loss function, and filters out the difficult samples that have a greater impact on classification and detection for retraining. Although the OHEM algorithm increases the weight of misclassified samples, it ignores samples which are easy to classify. In order to solve this problem, Lin *et al.* [18] proposed a new Focal Loss, which expands OHEM by reweighing misclassification, simple examples and difficult examples, and made the model pay more attention to the hard-to-distinguish samples by reducing the weight of easy-to-classify samples in training. The cost-sensitive function can be flexibly integrated into any classification algorithm, without adjusting the data set and directly optimizing cost-sensitive objectives through training. However, since the cost of misclassification is unknown and requires sufficient prior knowledge to make an accurate estimate, most of the cost-sensitive objectives need trade-off parameters related data set, which makes those methods rely too much on parameters tuning. This also brings difficulties to the setting of the cost matrix, and limits the application of cost-sensitive loss methods in any data sets. In this paper, we propose an adaptive focus loss function as an objective function to adapt to arbitrary text data sets without any re-sampling method.

2.2 Pre-trained Model

In the last few years, the pre-trained language models greatly promote the field of NLP, which makes breakthroughs in many NLP tasks. The goal of the pre-trained language model is to obtain general word vectors or initial model parameters based on large unsupervised corpus training, which provides an effective method for large-scale parameter learning of Deep Neural Network (DNN). The essence of pre-trained language model idea is that the model parameters are no longer randomly initialized, but pre-trained by some tasks, such as pre-training DNN on large data sets to obtain model parameters, and then applying the obtained model parameters to various specific downstream tasks to avoid training from scratch. The essence is to improve learning efficiency of different tasks by using transfer learning. Generally speaking, the pre-trained language model can be divided into two types: fine-tuning and feature-based methods. On the downstream tasks, we can easily fine-tune the specific parameters related to the task without training the model from scratch; or directly use the pre-trained representation as the initial representations or additional features. Given a sequence $s = [x_1, x_2, \ldots x_l]$ of l words, by using the pre-trained models, the embedding tensor of the sequence s can be represented as $e_s = [e_{x_1}, e_{x_2}, \ldots, e_{x_l}]$. Given a certain NLP task, suchlike text classification, the pre-trained model can be specialized by the module of the specific task (like Long Short-Term Multi-Layer Perceptron), or the pre-training representation can be used as the input of the model. Because all pre-training models are trained on the extremely large amounts of data, especially the models based on fine-tuning in recent years, the corpus used almost includes all common corpora, so we can approximately regard the obtained pre-trained embeddings as the prior distribution in the whole corpus.

3   Method

We first briefly declare the notations used in this paper. For a certain corpus $C = \{\{s_1 : y_1\}, \ldots, \{s_l : y_l\}\}$ of l sentences, where s_i is the i-th sentence and y_i is the label of it. Each sentence $s_i = \{w_1, \cdots, w_{|s_i|}\}$ consists of some words, and each word $w \in \mathcal{V}$ is in the vocabulary $\mathcal{V}$. For brevity, we consider the binary classification, and in this case, the class group $\mathcal{G} = \{y | y \in \{-1, 1\}\}$ consists of labels of sentences. In this paper, we assume that the label $y = -1$ to be advantage class (easy to classify) and $y = 1$ to be disadvantage class (hard to classify).

3.1 Focal Loss

The Focal Loss is first proposed in the field of object detection. In the field of object detection, an image can be segmented into hundreds or thousands of candidate objects consisting of foreground and background. However, there are only rare objects that are targeted objects compared with others (e.g., 1:1000), which is an extremely imbalanced classification task. In the terms of the Focal Loss, it can be seen as a cost-sensitive objective. The Focal Loss assigns different weights for each candidate of different types. The Focal Loss extends the cross entropy (CE) loss:

$$CE(p, y) = \begin{cases} -\log(p) & \text{if } y = 1, \\ -\log(1-p) & \text{otherwise.} \end{cases} \tag{1}$$

where $y \in \{-1, 1\}$ is the ground-truth label and $p \in [0, 1]$ is the output probability of the label $y = 1$, by using an additional notation p_t:

$$p_t = \begin{cases} p & \text{if } y = 1, \\ 1 - p & \text{otherwise.} \end{cases} \tag{2}$$

the Eq. 1 can be simplified as: $CE = -log(p_t)$.

The Focal Loss extends the balanced cross entropy:

$$CE = -\alpha \, log(p_t) \tag{3}$$

where the α is the trade-off parameter that balances cost of different types of misclassification, which is always set large for disadvantaged classes and small for advantaged classes. The Focal Loss extends the Eq. 3 by introducing an additional term: $(1 - p_t)^\gamma$ called modulating factor, the Focal Loss (FL) can be formulated as:

$$FL(p_t) = -\alpha(1 - log(p_t))^\gamma log(p_t) \tag{4}$$

where the $\gamma \in [0, 5]$ is the focusing parameter that controls the weight of misclassification.

By introducing modulation factors $(1 - p_t)^\gamma$ and trade-off parameters α, the focus loss function can not only focus on the difficult samples, but also assign higher weights to the weak samples. In other words, the focus loss solves the class imbalance problem from two aspects: (1) by introducing the trade-off parameters α to adjust the weight of majority class and minority class in the loss function to solve class imbalance problem; (2) by introducing the modulation factors $(1 - p_t)^\gamma$ to solve the problem of easy and difficult samples.

In the process of applying the Focal Loss, it is necessary to build parameter sets for different data sets, which constrains the applications of it. Inspired by the Focal Loss, we propose the Adaptable Focal Loss, which use the sum of the word level prior obtained to construct the sentence prior and replace the α by the scaled-softmax of learned sentence representations and the constructed sentence prior.

3.2 Adaptable Focal Loss

In order to minimize the tuning parameters of human intervention and adapt the sentence level imbalanced text classification, we design a function to construct the prior of sentence s:

$$e_s = \sum_{w \in s} e_w \tag{5}$$

where the e_w is the pre-trained embedding of word w. By using the Eq. 5, our model can easily capture the prior distribution, or in other words, the mean value of the sentence in the whole corpus.

For a task-specific fine-tune network Θ, the fine-tuned task-specific embedding of a sentence s is represented as $z_s = \Theta(z|e_s)$. In order to get the offsets of e_s and z_s, we use the scaled-softmax to calculate the distance of them and assign it to the focusing parameter in Focal Loss:

$$\gamma = \beta * \text{softmax}(D(e_s, z_s)) \tag{6}$$

where β is a scaling factor, which is set to equal to the length of γ in the Focal Loss (i.e., $\beta = 5$) in the paper, and D is a distance function. The Kullback-Leibler Divergence Distance can be expressed as:

$$D_{KL}(e_s, z_s) = KL(e_s, z_s) \tag{7}$$

Moreover, we set the trade-off parameter α as the inverse rating of the advantage and disadvantage examples. Finally, Adaptable Focal Loss (AF Loss) is formulated as:

$$\mathcal{L}_{AF} = \begin{cases} -(1-\alpha) * (1-p)^\gamma * \log(p) & \text{if } y = 1, \\ -\alpha * p^\gamma * \log(1-p) & \text{otherwise.} \end{cases} \tag{8}$$

where the $p = p_\phi(y|z_s)$ is the output probability of the classification network ϕ for the label y.

We find that Eq. 8 can adapt to the imbalance distribution and classification difficulty distribution for arbitrary data sets through parameters α and γ, respectively.

The steps for training the Adaptable Focal Loss are as follows:

(1) First, the pre-training word vector e_w of word w is obtained from the pre-training language model or pre-training word vector. Because all pre-training models are trained on a large amount of data, and the corpus used includes almost all public corpora, the pre-training word vectors obtained can be used as a prior distribution in the whole corpus approximately.

(2) According to Eq. 5, the prior sentence vector e_s is calculated from e_w.

(3) The hidden vector z_s is obtained by fine tuning network Θ training, $z_s = \Theta(z|e_s)$.

(4) Calculate the distance between e_s and z_s to obtain the adaptive modulation factor parameter γ.

(5) Pass the hidden vector through the classification network Φ to obtain the output probability of the label p, $p = p_\Phi(y|z_s)$. Up to now, the various parameters of the modulation factor $(1-p)^\gamma$ in the focus loss function have been set.

(6) Use the gradient descent method to calculate the adaptive focus loss function Eq. 8 and optimize it.
(7) Judge whether the termination condition is reached, and if the termination condition is reached, it ends. If the termination condition is not reached, the next batch of cycle will be entered.

4 Experiment and Analysis

4.1 Data Sets

Before describing the data sets, we first point out the way to construct the imbalanced data sets. For each data set/corpus C, we resample the sentences by their labels and make the distribution of different types of labels conform to the Bernoulli distribution with the parameter α, i.e., $y \sim B(|C|, \alpha)$, where the α is equal to the trade-off parameter in the Adaptable Focal Loss objective. We randomly choose 20% of the data set as the testing set and the remaining 80% of the data set as the training set. In our experiments, we use five real word data sets and the summary of the data sets are shown in Table 1.

Table 1. Statistics of the data set

Data sets	Number of classes	Average length	Size	Dictionary size
CR	2	20	1.8K	3K
TREC	6	10	5.4K	10K
SST	2	19	7.3K	16K
SUBJ	6	23	9.0K	21K
MR	2	20	9.5K	18K

4.2 Evaluation Criteria and Parameter Setting

Traditionally, the Mean Average Precision (MAP) is the main evaluation metric for the classification task. However, for the imbalanced classification, the MAP may cause some issues. For instance, the MAP for the disadvantage examples may be very low, but the MAP on the whole data sets is still at a high level. In this paper, we use the F1-measure as the evaluation metrics of our experiments, which is based on confusion matrix.

In order to evaluate our proposed Adaptable Focal Loss method, we use 4 pre-trained models for training, including AWD-LSTM, TextCNN, EIMo, and BERT. The embedding dimension of the word is set to 128, and the learning rate is equal to 0.001. The stretch of the sentence length is set to 64. The number of layers of the LSTM-based model (AWD-LSTM) is set to 2, TextCNN is set to 3. We use BERT-Base (12 layers, 768 hidden units, 16 heads) as the BERT baseline. ELMo is provided with 2-layer BiLSTM.

Table 2. F1 value of the model on all test sets.

Model	α	MR			SST			SUBJ			CR			TREC		
		0.2	1.0	5.0	0.2	1.0	5.0	0.2	1.0	5.0	0.2	1.0	5.0	0.2	1.0	5.0
AWD-LSTM	CEL	0.542	0.622	0.531	0.688	0.734	0.671	0.635	0.782	0.642	0.691	0.792	0.739	0.664	0.767	0.629
	FL	0.619	0.623	0.612	0.728	0.740	0.733	0.782	0.792	0.786	0.783	0.791	0.782	0.748	0.779	0.748
	RS	0.601	0.622	0.602	0.718	0.734	0.723	0.767	0.782	0.779	0.768	0.792	0.771	0.736	0.767	0.732
	AFL	**0.619**	**0.623**	**0.617**	**0.733**	**0.741**	**0.736**	**0.784**	**0.798**	**0.786**	**0.789**	**0.793**	**0.788**	**0.750**	**0.782**	**0.752**
TextCNN	CEL	0.534	0.619	0.527	0.663	0.732	0.665	0.636	0.778	0.639	0.691	0.793	0.764	0.659	0.752	0.631
	FL	**0.620**	0.622	0.618	0.731	0.736	0.712	0.779	0.789	0.783	0.779	0.794	0.783	0.750	0.778	0.747
	RS	0.617	0.619	0.612	0.723	0.732	0.699	0.774	0.778	0.771	0.771	0.793	0.768	0.744	0.759	0.726
	AFL	0.618	**0.624**	**0.620**	**0.733**	**0.736**	**0.723**	**0.785**	**0.793**	**0.783**	**0.786**	**0.794**	**0.788**	**0.754**	**0.780**	**0.761**
ELMo	CEL	0.578	0.623	0.583	0.713	0.739	0.728	0.727	0.804	0.734	0.735	0.811	0.759	0.738	0.796	0.722
	FL	**0.622**	0.626	0.619	0.732	0.743	0.735	0.786	0.803	0.791	0.792	0.814	0.783	0.765	0.801	0.755
	RS	0.619	0.623	0.620	0.729	0.739	0.727	0.787	0.804	0.779	0.793	0.811	0.780	0.770	0.794	0.753
	AFL	0.621	**0.627**	**0.620**	**0.735**	**0.744**	**0.741**	**0.792**	**0.804**	**0.799**	**0.798**	**0.816**	**0.794**	**0.793**	**0.801**	**0.784**
BERT	CEL	0.603	0.628	0.587	0.715	0.742	0.723	0.731	0.807	0.743	0.744	0.818	0.773	0.740	0.794	0.724
	FL	0.625	0.630	0.622	0.735	0.742	0.735	0.788	**0.812**	0.797	0.800	0.821	0.794	0.772	0.803	0.786
	RS	0.621	0.628	0.624	0.732	0.742	0.729	0.791	0.807	0.784	0.797	0.818	0.782	0.781	0.794	0.765
	AFL	**0.628**	**0.630**	**0.627**	**0.735**	**0.743**	**0.740**	**0.794**	0.809	**0.802**	**0.803**	**0.822**	**0.802**	**0.793**	**0.806**	**0.790**

In order to compare the effects of different objective functions, the following four objective functions are used for each baseline model: (1) Cross Entropy Loss (CEL); (2) Focal Loss (FL); (3) Re-Sampling (RS), resampling each data set of the sample with a probability inversely proportional to the number of samples in this class, so as to balance the proportion of positive and negative samples; (4) Adaptable Focal Loss (AFL).

4.3 Experimental Analysis

To verify the effectiveness of our proposed goal, we apply sentence-level text classification to five data sets mentioned in Sect. 4.1. Table 2 shows the results of text classification. We find that our Adaptable Focal Loss model has achieved significant advantages over all data sets in each classification network, especially for data sets with a shorter average sentence length, which illustrates the superiority of our method. The main reason why the performance of this model declines with the sentence length is that the prior error is positively correlated with the sentence length. At the same time, we notice that AFL using Kullback-Leibler Divergence Distance is less sensitive to sentence length, which indicates that Kullback-Leibler Divergence Distance is more robust to the modeling of prior distribution. Table 2 also shows the F1 value of various model under different distributions. Obviously, the F1 values of the Adaptable Focal Loss model are more stable and higher, which indicates that our AFL can better adapt to imbalanced data sets.

In order to study the impact of the degree of imbalance on model performance, we test two models (i.e., TextCNN, BERT) on SUBJ and SST datasets, and the imbalance coefficient α varies within the range of $[0.1, 25]$. The results are shown in Fig. 1. Figure 1 proves that Adaptable Focal Loss objective function can maintain high performance in both imbalance situations (i.e., positive sample advantage and negative sample advantage). Especially in the extreme case of $\alpha = 0.1$ or $\alpha = 25.6$, our method still has a high F1 value.

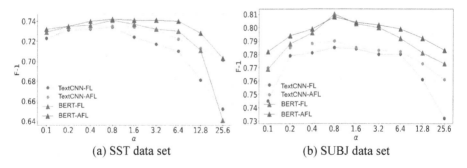

Fig. 1. The impact of data set imbalance on model performance.

5 Conclusion

In this paper, we propose an imbalanced text classification method with Adaptive Focus Loss from the cost function level. In the pre-training model, we use word embedding to build a sentence-level prior by embedding the sum of words in sentences, and calculate the offset of vectors and prior vectors after fine-tuning the current data set to replace the task-related parameters in the focus loss function, which can not only automatically adjust the parameters of arbitrary imbalanced distribution according to tasks, but also give higher weight to sentences that are difficult to classify. The proposed AFL algorithm shows excellent performance in many data sets and experimental environments. Nevertheless, when the sentence length is long, the adaptive objective function will still be plagued by performance degradation, which will be one of our future work directions.

Acknowledgments. This work is supported by the Key-Area Research and Development Program of Guangdong Province (No. 2020B010164003), National Key Research and Development Plan's Key Special Program on High Performance Computing of China (No. 2017YFB0203201), The National Natural Science Foundation of China (Grant No. 6177010044); Basic and Applied Basic Research Fund of Guangdong Province (Grant No. 2019A1515010716); Key Projects of Basic and Applied Basic Research in General Universities of Guangdong Province (Grant No. 2018KZDXM073); Special Project in key Areas of Artificial Intelligence in Guangdong Universities (No. 2019KZDZX1017).

References

1. Xu, W.D., Sun, H.Z., Deng, C., et al.: Variational autoencoder for semi-supervised text classification. In: 31st AAAI Conference on Artificial Intelligence, pp. 3358–3364. AAAI, CA (2017)
2. Zhang, T., Huang, M., Zhao, L.: Learning structured representation for text classification via reinforcement learning. In: 32nd AAAI Conference on Artificial Intelligence, pp. 6053–6060. AAAI, CA (2018)
3. You, R.H., Zhang, Z.H., Wang, Z.Y., et al.: AttentionXML: label tree-based attention-aware deep model for high-performance extreme multi-label text classification. Adv. Neural. Inf. Process. Syst. **32**, 5820–5830 (2019)
4. Liu, Y.X, Jin, X.M., Lan, Y., et al.: Adaptive region embedding for text classification. In: Proceedings of the AAAI Conference on Artificial Intelligence, pp. 7314–7321. AAAI, CA (2019)
5. Chen, X., Qiu, Z.Z.: Research on Chinese text classification based on WAE and SVM. In: 2021 3rd International Conference on Natural Language Processing (ICNLP), pp. 14–19. IEEE, NJ (2021)
6. Chen, Q.X., Yao, L.X., Yang, J.: Short text classification based on LDA topic model. In: 2016 International Conference on Audio, Language and Image Processing (ICALIP), pp. 749–753. IEEE, NJ (2016)
7. Radford, A., Wu, J., Child, R., et al.: Language models are unsupervised multitask learners. OpenAI blog **1**(8), 9 (2019)
8. Mikolov, T., Sutskever, I., Chen, K., et al.: Distributed representations of words and phrases and their compositionality. In: Advances in Neural Information Processing Systems, pp. 3111–3119. Curran Associates, NY (2013)
9. Li, Z.C., Wang, R., Chen, K.H., et al.: Data-dependent Gaussian prior objective for language generation. In: International Conference on Learning Representations (ICLR), pp. 1–18. ICLR (2020)
10. Fernández, A., del Río, S., Chawla, N.V., et al.: An insight into imbalanced big data classification: outcomes and challenges. Complex Intel. Syst. **3**(2), 105–120 (2017)

11. Li, Y.X., Chai, Y., Hu, Y.Q., et al.: Review of imbalanced data classification methods. Control Decis. **34**(4), 673–688 (2019)
12. Gu, X., Angelov, P.P., Soares, E.A.: A self-adaptive synthetic over-sampling technique for imbalanced classification. Int. J. Intell. Syst. **35**(6), 923–943 (2020)
13. Ng, W.W.Y., Hu, J.J., Yeung, D.S., et al.: Diversified sensitivity-based undersampling for imbalance classification problems. IEEE Trans. Cybern. **45**(11), 2402–2412 (2014)
14. Zhou, Z.H., Liu, X.Y.: Training cost-sensitive neural networks with methods addressing the class imbalance problem. IEEE Trans. Knowl. Data Eng. **18**(1), 63–77 (2005)
15. Khan, S.H., Hayat, M., Bennamoun, M., et al.: Cost-sensitive learning of deep feature representations from imbalanced data. IEEE Trans. Neural Netw. Learn. Syst. **29**(8), 3573–3587 (2017)
16. Castro, C.L., Braga, A.P.: Novel cost-sensitive approach to improve the multilayer perceptron performance on imbalanced data. IEEE Trans. Neural Netw. Learn. Syst. **24**(6), 888–899 (2013)
17. Shrivastava, A., Gupta, A., Girshick, R.: Training region-based object detectors with online hard example mining. In: IEEE Conference on Computer Vision and Pattern Recognition, pp. 761–769. IEEE, NJ (2016)
18. Lin, T.Y., Goyal, P., Girshick, R., et al.: Focal loss for dense object detection. In: IEEE Transactions on Pattern Analysis and Machine Intelligence, pp. 2980–2988. IEEE, NJ (2017)

Roman Amphitheater Classification Using Convolutional Neural Network and Data Augmentation

Haïfa Nakouri[1,2(✉)] (iD)

[1] LARODEC, Institut Supérieur de Gestion, Université de Tunis, Le Bardo, Tunisia
hayfa.nakouri@esen.tn
[2] ESEN, University of Manouba, Manouba, Tunisia

Abstract. In this paper, we propose a neural model to classify Roman amphitheater images into six groups corresponding to their locations: Rome, Eljem, Nîmes, Arles, Verona and Pula. The proposed neural structure makes essential use of convolutional neural networks for feature extraction and images classification. To avoid overfitting, data augmentation techniques have been deployed to expand the data set size by a magnitude of 16. This method is applied on the augmented training set and results show a substantial performance and high accuracy of 98.33% compared to state-of-the-art methods.

Keywords: Convolutional neural network · Data augmentation · Landmarks classification · Monument recognition

1 Introduction

Recognizing landmarks is a useful yet challenging task. Landmarks are easily recognizable and wellknown sites and buildings, such as monuments, tours, etc. They are the focal part of people's tours, due to their imposing physical, cultural and historical features. The explosion of personal digital photography, together with Internet, has led to the phenomenal growth of landmark photo sharing in many websites like Picasa, Google Images, Pinterest and many other social medias. With the extensive amount of landmark images in the Internet, landmark recognition becomes necessary, not only to visually recognize the presence of certain landmarks in an image, but also contributes to a worldwide landmarks indexing, in terms of geographical locations, popularity, historical pertinence, cultural values and social purposes. Besides, landmark recognition can be remarkably useful for many vision and multimedia applications. In fact, catching the visual features of landmarks provides clean landmark images for building virtual tourism [1]. Apart from content understanding, landmarks recognition also facilitates geolocation detection of images and videos. Moreover, organizing landmarks by category facilitates an intuitive themed exploration and navigation of landmarks in a local area. This would be relevant for a potential historical tour guide recommendation and visualization system.

© Springer Nature Switzerland AG 2022
H. Shen et al. (Eds.): PDCAT 2021, LNCS 13148, pp. 476–484, 2022.
https://doi.org/10.1007/978-3-030-96772-7_44

Unlike many existing landmark recognition and classification works, this study particularly sheds the light on ancient Roman amphitheaters classification. Roman amphitheaters are circular or oval in shape, and were used for events such as gladiator combats, chariot races, animal slayings and executions. Fragmentary remains of more than 230 Roman amphitheaters have been found in widely scattered areas throughout the provinces of the Roman Empire [2]. In this work, we focus on the classification of 6 among them whose shapes are still the best preserved and that did not fall into disrepair: the amphitheaters built at Rome, El Jem, Nîmes, Arles, Verona and Pula. As stated, we considered these six amphitheaters as they are the least ruined among the 230 Roman amphitheaters whose fragmentary remains were found. The second reason for choosing these amphitheaters is that touristically they are the six most visited Roman amphitheaters and thus the most photographed. Images of other amphitheaters are not as available as for these six. Besides, the most important architectural features of Roman amphitheaters are multi-storied, arcaded facades and were elaborately decorated with marble, stucco and statuary [2]. The main challenge in these amphitheaters classification is the high similarity between the six amphitheaters. On the other hand, having large data set is crucial for deep learning [3] and the performance of deep networks is heavily reliant on big data. It helps reduce or prevent overfitting when training a deep neural network [4]. The reality is that we usually are in a situation where no complete data set is available or where it is impractical to collect data from a single source. Since many application domain do not have access to big data, we can improve the performance of a model by augmenting the existing data.

In this paper, we propose a Convolutional Neural Network (CNN) framework for efficient ancient Roman amphitheater classification. The remainder of this paper is organised as follows: Sect. 2 presents the created data set, its preprocessing and the process of data augmentation. Section 3 describes the configuration of the used CNN. Section 4 provides experiments and results.

2 The Roman Amphitheater Data Set and Data Preprocessing

2.1 Data Set Collection and Preprocessing

The Roman amphitheater data set has been obtained after a three-months preparation period. Data was collected from free online stock images (e.g. images.google.com and images.baidu.com) and also from social media services namely Pinterest and Facebook. In this work, we only include images from the front view or side view. The reason is that side-viewed or front-viewed captures have a narrow field of view that captures better the architectural features of the landmark, which allows a more efficient learning performance and facilitates the identification of the theater [5]. Finally, we obtain a data set of 1910 images belonging to six classes. Each class name represents the city where the amphitheater is located. Each object type has an optimal viewing angle depending on the training data. For instance, many images of cups are taken from the side while many images of keyboards are taken from above [6]. In our case, a side view would be the optimal viewing angle since it depicts better the intrinsicality of each amphitheater. An above angle (e.g. taken by a drone) would give lookalike snapshots of circular or oval shapes to all six amphitheaters. Besides, previous research [6,7] showed that a network trained on normal camera images could be used on images taken by a drone with satisfactory results. On the other hand, a side view does not necessarily come from a fixed position and can naturally tilt offering thus various viewing angles. For these reasons, we retrained the model using images taken by hand-held camera, and this helped to improve the accuracy of classification.

For data preprocessing, a four-step technique was used. First, we manually clean the images by removing the background and replacing it with a plain black one. Moreover, since color has no importance in the classification of our images, we go for grayscale images to avoid false classification and complexities. Second, we move the amphitheater to the center of the image. Third, each image is manually cropped and resized to a 256×256 matrix. The image cropping is done manually so we can only keep the pixels covering the landmark. Nevertheless, numerous images contain occlusions that corrupt the structure of the amphitheater such as tourists, a camel, a bike, a tree, a statue, etc. This is intended as an additional challenge to the robustness of the network. Finally, each image is manually labeled to one of the 6 amphitheater classes: Rome, El Jem, Nîmes, Arles, Pula and Verona.

2.2 Data Augmentation

As stated and shown by Miki et al. [8], small number of training samples may lead to overfitting. One solution is to augment their size by creating fake data from the training set. Data augmentation implements a suite of techniques (e.g. geometric transformation, color space augmentation, kernel filters, random cropping, random erasing, etc.) that enhances the size and quality of training data sets such that better deep learning models can be built based on them [3]. For the Roman amphitheater data set, we equally and randomly divide the original data set that consists of 1910 images into a training set (957 images) and a validation set (953 images). Usually, the larger the validation set, the better. However, we considered a minimum size of training set so that, once augmented, we obtain at least a 16.000-sized training set to guarantee a more reliable training of data. After we split the data set into a training set and a test set, we only augment the training set. The validation set is used to estimate how our method works on real world data; thus, it should only contain real world data. Adding augmented data will not improve the accuracy of the validation. It will at best say something about how well our model responds to the data augmentation, and at worst ruin the validation results and interpretability. Considering the original training set, fake examples were generated by 7 different ways. The first data augmentation method is image rotation. We consider a rotation angle θ ranging from $-15°$ to $15°$ with a $5°$ step. Accordingly, this first augmentation method

Table 1. Effect of data augmentation on the data set size

Amphitheater	Size			
	Before augmentation		After augmentation	
	Training set	Test set	Training set	Test set
Rome	169	168	2873	168
El Jem	156	155	2652	155
Nîmes	155	154	2635	154
Arles	152	151	2584	151
Pula	165	165	2805	165
Verona	160	160	2720	160
Total	957	953	16269	953

allowed to create new samples of a size six times that of the original training set. Second, we apply the gamma correction method on the original training set [9] considering a 0.5 gamma value. The third augmentation method is noise injection. The fourth method for augmentation is contrast enhancement using histogram equalization [10]. The fifth data generation method is median filtering [11]. The sixth data augmentation method is performed by randomly cropping then rotating the image. Finally, five different optical distortions methods are applied to each image of the training set. Therefore, applying all the mentioned generation methods led to new samples of a size 16 times that of the original training set. Table 1 shows training set size after augmentation.

3   CNN Structure and Used Framework

Among deep structures, CNN have gained success in detection and classification. Compared to basic neural networks, CNNs have three major advantages: sparse interaction, parameter sharing and equivariance [12]. Moreover, CNNs have shown substantial gain over state-of-the-art classifiers such as linear regression, principal component analysis, SVM, linear discriminant approaches, etc. A typical CNN will include a convolutional layer, a nonlinear activation layer and a pooling layer. A characteristic that set apart the CNN from a regular neural network is taking into account the structure of the images while processing them. A regular neural network converts the input in a one dimensional array making the trained classifier less sensitive to positional changes [12]. The input of our CNN consists of standard grayscale images of size 256×256 each. Since the facade colors of the amphitheaters are pretty much the same, converting the image to grayscale will not bias the classification performance. All the hyperparameters selected in this study are the ones followed and used in open published literature [13,14]. The training algorithm was stochastic gradient descent with momentum (SGDM). Stochastic refers to the minibatch method whose size is set to 128. The initial learning rate is set to 0.001. The maximum of epochs is set to 8. The final structure of our 17-layer deep neural network is given in Table 2.

Table 2. CNN structure

Layer	Function	Filter	No. of filters	Stride	Padding	Weights	Bias	Activation
1	Image Input layer							$256 \times 256 \times 1$
2	Convolution + ReLU	3×3	16	[1 1]	[0 0]	$3 \times 3 \times 1 \times 16$	$1 \times 1 \times 16$	$254 \times 254 \times 16$
3	Pooling	2×2		[2 2]				$127 \times 127 \times 16$
4	Convolution + ReLU	3×3	32	[1 1]	[0 0]	$3 \times 3 \times 16 \times 32$	$1 \times 1 \times 32$	$125 \times 125 \times 32$
5	Pooling	2×2		[2 2]				$63 \times 63 \times 32$
6	Convolution + ReLU	3×3	64	[1 1]	[0 0]	$3 \times 3 \times 32 \times 64$	$1 \times 1 \times 64$	$61 \times 61 \times 64$
7	Pooling	2×2		[1 1]				$60 \times 60 \times 64$
8	Convolution + ReLU	3×3	128	[1 1]	[0 0]	$3 \times 3 \times 64 \times 128$	$1 \times 1 \times 128$	$58 \times 58 \times 128$
9	Pooling	2×2		[1 1]	·			$57 \times 57 \times 128$
10	Convolution + ReLU	3×3	64	[1 1]	[0 0]	$3 \times 3 \times 128 \times 64$	$1 \times 1 \times 64$	$55 \times 55 \times 64$
11	Pooling	2×2		[1 1]				$54 \times 54 \times 64$
12	Convolution + ReLU	3×3	32	[1 1]	[0 0]	$3 \times 3 \times 64 \times 32$	$1 \times 1 \times 32$	$52 \times 52 \times 32$
13	Pooling	2×2		[1 1]				$51 \times 51 \times 32$
14	Fully connected					32×83232	32×1	$1 \times 1 \times 32$
15	Fully connected					6×32	6×1	$1 \times 1 \times 6$
16	Softmax							$1 \times 1 \times 6$
17	Output							$1 \times 1 \times 6$

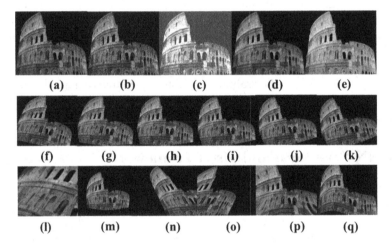

Fig. 1. Example of generated images for augmentation. (a): original cleaned image, (b): noised image, (c): histogram equalized image, (d): median filtered image, (e): 0.5 gamma corrected image, (f): $-15°$ rotated image, (g): $-10°$ rotated image, (h): $-5°$ rotated image, (i): $5°$ rotated image, (j): $10°$ rotated image, (k): $15°$ rotated image, (l): randomly cropped and rotated image, (m): image after barrel distortion, (n): image after left affine distortion, (o): image after right affine distortion, (p): image after pincushion distortion, (q): image after sinusoidal distortion

4 Experiments

4.1 Results of Data Augmentation

To give a preview of data augmentation, we consider an image of the Roman Colosseum and show the different images generated from it based on the different data generation techniques outlined in Sect. 2.2. Figure 1 captures the 16 images (from (b) to (q)) generated from original image (a). Images are generated by noise injection, histogram equalization, median filtering, gamma correction, image rotation with a rotation angle θ ranging from $-15°$ to $15°$ with a $5°$ step, random cropping and rotation then optical distortion using affine transformation, barrel, pincushion and sinusoidal distortions. As shown in Table 1, the overall training set expands 16 times its original size. In particular, the size of the training set increased from 957 to 16269 images. The goal of this boosted expansion is to help the network to deeply learn more interesting and stable features, and thus avoid overfitting.

4.2 Pooling Technique Comparison

To select the best pooling strategy, we compared the max-pooling and the average-pooling techniques on the same network structure. The overall accuracy of both pooling strategies is shown in Table 3. This result shows that max-pooling gives 0.33% better accuracy than average-pooling. Even though the max-pooling improvement is trivial, average-pooling is known for considering all elements in the region, and hence down-weighting the strong activations. Given the architectural similarity between the six amphitheaters, we would rather pool feature maps that highlight the most present features. Consequently, the max-pooling is considered in all combined layers.

4.3 Optimal Structure of CNN

Given the importance of convolutional layer and pooling layer, the proposed CNN contains six combined layers (convolutional layer + pooling layer) as shown in Table 2. To find the optimal number of combined layers, we trained and tested the same sets over 5 different numbers of combined layers. Results of the overall accuracy are finally presented in Table 4. CNNs with 3, 4, 5, 6 and 7 combined layers that led to overall accuracy of 96.18%, 97.57%, 98.15%, 98.33% and 97.32%, respectively. Therefore, 6 combined layers are selected for the proposed network structure.

Table 3. Pooling technique comparison

Pooling strategy	Overall accuracy
Max-pooling	98.33%
Average-pooling	98.00%

Table 4. CNN structure performance with different convolutional layers

Number of combined layers	Overall accuracy
3	96.18%
4	97.57%
5	98.15%
6 (proposed)	98.33%
7	97.32%

4.4 Classification Performance

In deep learning, an epoch means a training overall sample. An iteration means a training over 128 samples (minibatch size). For training, we set 8 epochs equal to $8 \times (16269/128) = 1016$ iterations. After training the network on the augmented data and tested it on the validation set, we achieved an overall accuracy of 98.33%. To assess the classification performance, we compare the proposed method with some popular state-of-the-art approaches: Principal Component Analysis (PCA), Discriminant Analysis (DA) approaches (LDA [15], 2D-LDA [16], SDA [17]), GLRAM [18], Robust GLRAM (RGLRAM) [19] and AlexNet [4]. We also trained the proposed neural structure on the original data set without augmentation. Compared to the cited methods, the proposed 17-layer neural structure performs the best with its 98.33% accuracy as depicted in Table 5. This experiment shows that CNNs outperform by far DA-based method despite the popularity of this latter for enhancing outer-class dissimilarity and inner-class similarity. Generally, Discriminant Analysis approaches always outperform PCA when modelling small data with well separated clusters [20]; however, their downperformance as shown in Table 5 can be explained by the high similarity between images from different classes given the matching architecture. From Table 5, we can also conclude that data augmentation has a positive effect on the classification performance. The reason for this is that variety of augmented images allow the CNN to train without resisting to data variation. Subsequently, the proposed data augmentation improved the recognition performance of our model by over 2%.

Table 5. CNN structure performance compared to Linear Discriminant approaches and non-augmented data

Approach	Overall accuracy
LDA	67.00%
RGLRAM	70.30%
SDA	72.00%
2D-LDA	83.90%
GLRAM	84.10%
PCA	93.00%
AlexNet	95.1%
CNN without augmentation	96.7%
CNN with augmentation (proposed)	98.33%

5   Conclusion

In this work, we developed a Roman amphitheater classification method based on a 17-layer CNN with data augmentation. Experiments show that the proposed CNN achieves a substantial classification performance of 98.33% outperforming that of the state-of-the-art methods namely Discriminant Analysis, Principal Component Analysis, GLRAM and the popular AlexNet. This study also highlights the positive impact that data augmentation has on the overall accuracy.

References

1. Snavely, N., Seitz, S.M., Szeliski, R.: Photo tourism: exploring photo collections in 3D. Trans. Graph. **25**(3), 835–846 (2006)
2. Smith, W., Anthon, C.: A Dictionary of Greek and Roman Antiquities (1871)
3. Shorten, C., Khoshgoftaar, T.M.: A survey on image data augmentation for deep learning. J. Big Data **6**, 60 (2019)
4. Krizhevsky, A., Sutskever, I., Hinton, G.E.: ImageNet classification with deep convolutional neural networks. In: Advances in Neural Information Processing Systems, vol. 25, pp. 1097–1105 (2012)
5. Zhu, J., et al.: Indoor topological localization using a visual landmark sequence. Remote Sens. **11**(1), 73 (2019)
6. Grip, L.: Vision Based Indoor Object Detection for a Drone, M.Sc. Thesis Dissertation, KTH, Stockholm, Sweden (2017)
7. Zheng, J., Yang, T., Liu, H., Su, T., Wan, L.: Accurate detection and localization of unmanned aerial vehicle swarms-enabled mobile edge computing system. IEEE Trans. Industr. Inf. **17**(7), 5059–5067 (2021)
8. Miki, Y., et al.: Classification of teeth in cone-beam CT using deep convolutional neural network. Comput. Biol. Med. **80**(C), 24–29 (2016)
9. Teh, V., Sim, K.S., Wong, E.K.: Brain early infarct detection using gamma correction extreme-level eliminating with weighting distribution. Scanning **38**(6), 842–856 (2016)

10. Pizer, S.M., et al.: Adaptive histogram equalization and its variations. Comput. Vis. Graph. Image Proces. **39**(3), 355–368 (1987)
11. Villar, S.A., Torcida, S., Acosta, G.G.: Median filtering: a new insight. J. Math. Imaging Vis. **58**(1), 130–146 (2017)
12. LeCun, Y., et al.: Backpropagation applied to handwritten zip code recognition. Neural Comput. **1**(4), 541–551 (1989)
13. Ghazi, M.M., Yanikoglu, B., Aptoula, E.: Plant identification using deep neural networks via optimization of transfer learning parameters. Neurocomputing **235**(C), 228–235 (2017)
14. Tabik, S., Peralta, D., Herrera-Poyatos, A., Herrera, F.: A snapshot of image preprocessing for convolutional neural networks: case study of MNIST. Int. J. Comput. Intell. Syst. **10**(1), 555–568 (2017)
15. Fukunaga, K.: Introduction to Statistical Pattern Recognition, 2nd edn. Academic Press Professional Inc., USA (1990)
16. Li, M., Yuan, B.: 2D-LDA: a statistical linear discriminant analysis for image matrix. Pattern Recogn. Lett. **26**(5), 527–532 (2005)
17. Zhu, M., Martínez, A.M.: Subclass discriminant analysis. IEEE Trans. Pattern Anal. Mach. Intell. **28**(8), 1274–1286 (2006)
18. Ye, J.: Generalized low rank approximations of matrices. Mach. Learn. **61**(1–3), 167–191 (2005)
19. Nakouri, H., Limam, M.: Robust generalized low rank approximation of matrices for image recognition. In: 2016 IEEE International Symposium on Signal Processing and Information Technology, ISSPIT 2016, Limassol, Cyprus, 12–14 December 2016, pp. 203–207 (2016)
20. Nakouri, H.: Two-dimensional subclass discriminant analysis for face recognition. Pattern Anal. Appl. **24**(1), 109–117 (2021)

Data-Hungry Issue in Personalized Product Search

Bin Wu[1], Yuehong Wu[2], and Shangsong Liang[1,3(✉)]

[1] School of Computer Science and Engineering, Sun Yat-sen University,
Guangzhou, China
wubin33@mail2.sysu.edu.cn, liangshangsong@gmail.com
[2] School of Politics and Law, Guangdong University of Technology,
Guangzhou, China
[3] Department of Machine Learning, Mohamed bin Zayed University
of Artificial Intelligence, Abu Dhabi, United Arab Emirates

Abstract. Product search has been receiving significant attention with the development of e-commerce. Existing works recognize the importance of personalization and focus on personalized product search. While these works have confirmed that personalization can improve the performance of product search, they all ignore the few-shot learning problems caused by personalization. Under the few-shot setting, personalized methods may suffer from the data-hungry issue. In this paper, we explore the data-hungry issue in personalized product search. We find that data-hungry issue exists under the few-shot setting caused by personalization, and degrades the performance under the few-shot setting when the input query consists of diverse intents. Furthermore, we illustrate that with such a data-hungry issue, the returned search results tend to be close to the products the user purchases most often, or the products the most users purchase in the market given the same query. The result in the further experiment confirms our conclusions.

Keywords: Data-hungry issue · Few-shot problem · Product search

1 Introduction

Due to the popularity of e-commerce, product search techniques [11] have received significant attention. The goal of product search is to retrieve a ranked list of products from a large number of products, in response to the user's input query. But only considering the content of the query is not sufficient. It has been shown that user preference has a direct impact on the product search [11,13,14]. The returned ranked list of products is supposed to be not only relevant to the input query, but also meet the user's preference underlying their own search records, which refer to personalized product search [2]. Based on this idea, the search results are different among users because of their various preferences, responding to the same input query.

© Springer Nature Switzerland AG 2022
H. Shen et al. (Eds.): PDCAT 2021, LNCS 13148, pp. 485–494, 2022.
https://doi.org/10.1007/978-3-030-96772-7_45

The existing methods [1,5] have confirmed that user preference extracted from user's search records can significantly improve the performance of product search. However, they all ignore the sparsity of individual search records when extracting user preference. In the real world, some users only have interacted with the search engine few times so that the search records are scarce, which refers to the few-shot learning problem [16]. Although the existing personalized methods for product search have confirmed the success of the overall performance, it is not clear whether personalization works well under the few-shot setting.

Data-hungry issue [12] is the common problem under the few-shot setting in machine learning. It refers to the fact that the model has an awful performance when there are little data, while it can achieve success with enough data. In this paper, we explore the data-hungry issue in personalized product search. Concretely, We aim to confirm whether the personalized methods suffer from the data-hungry issue in product search, and further explore when and how the data-hungry issue degrades the performance in product search.

Our contributions can be summarized as:

(1) Personalization causes the data-hungry issue under the few-shot setting. Personalization can improve the performance of product search when users' search records are redundant, but suffer from a degrading performance when the search records are scarce.
(2) Data-hungry issue degrades the performance in product search when meeting queries with diverse intents. When the intent of the query is less specific and relevant to many products, personalization can not play its effectiveness to help provide personalized services under the few-shot setting.
(3) Due to the data-hungry issue, the personalized methods tend to focus on the products that the user purchases most often or the products that the most users purchase in the market given the same query. It would lead to the result that the returned ranked list of products can not meet the user's personalized demand.

2   Related Work

Product search [11] has been studied for many years, whose goal is to retrieve a ranked list of products responding to the input query. In the early work [4,15], they focused only on the relationships between queries and products, ignoring the user personalized demand. Recently, an increasing number of works [1,2,8] recognized the important role of personalization, and studied the problem of personalized product search. Different from the product search, personalized product search aims to return a ranked list of products, which is not only relevant to the input query but also meets the user's preference behind her/his search records. Based on this idea, there were many works proposed to extract the user preference from the search records. Hierarchical Embedding Model (HEM) [2] was firstly proposed to explicitly model the users based on their search records to provide personalized services, and then some work considered using the specific mechanism to extract the user preference, such as RNN with attention mechanism [5] and the graph embedding [7,9]. Ai et al. [1] analyzed when and how personalization improves the performance in product search and proposed a zero-attention model to capture the user preference automatically. These existing methods have confirmed that personalization can improve performance; however, all of them have not taken into account the data-hungry issue under the few-shot setting caused by personalization. In this paper, we focus on the few-shot learning problem caused by personalization and explore the data-hungry issue in personalized product search.

3   Preliminaries

3.1   Problem Definition

The task of product search aims to retrieve a ranked list of products from all products $\mathcal{I}$, given the query q input by a user u, and the search records $\mathcal{S}$. The returned products are ranked by the conditional probability $p(i > i'|q, u, \mathcal{I}, \mathcal{S})$, indicating that user u may prefer product i to i' given the query q. The task can be defined mathematically as a mapping function f:

$$u, q, \mathcal{I}, \mathcal{S} \xrightarrow{f} p(i|q, u, \mathcal{I}, \mathcal{S}). \tag{1}$$

3.2   Non-personalized and Personalized Product Search

There are many existing methods [1,2,15] for the product search, which can be divided into two categories, non-personalized and personalized product search. The difference between them is whether the user model is considered. We introduce several state-of-the-state methods in the following.

For non-personalized product search $p(i|q)$, Latent Semantic Entities (LSE) [15] learns separate representations of queries and products, and the relationships between them, which returns the results by:

$$p(i|q) = \frac{\exp(g(\mathbf{q}) \cdot \mathbf{i})}{\sum_{i \in \mathcal{I}} \exp(g(\mathbf{q}) \cdot \mathbf{i})}, \tag{2}$$

where $\mathbf{q}$ and $\mathbf{i}$ are the representations of query and product, respectively, and g is the learnable mapping function between query and product.

Compared to the non-personalized methods, the core idea of the personalized product search $p(i|q, u)$ is to retrieve a ranked list of products, which are not only relevant to the input query, but also meet the user's interest behind her/his search records. Extended from LSE, Hierarchical Embedding Model (HEM) [2] jointly learns the representations of users, queries and products in the same latent space and returns the result by:

$$p(i|q) = \frac{\exp((\mathbf{q} + \mathbf{u}) \cdot \mathbf{i})}{\sum_{i \in \mathcal{I}} \exp((\mathbf{q} + \mathbf{u}) \cdot \mathbf{i})}, \tag{3}$$

where **u**, **q** and **i** are the learned representations of users, queries and products, respectively. Different from implicitly modeling users **u** in the HEM, the Attention-based Embedding Model (AEM) [1] explicitly models the users with an attention mechanism based on their current search records:

$$\mathbf{u} = \sum_{i \in \mathcal{I}_u} \frac{\exp(h(\mathbf{q}, \mathbf{i}))}{\sum_{i' \in \mathcal{I}_u} \exp(h(\mathbf{q}, \mathbf{i}'))} \cdot \mathbf{i}, \tag{4}$$

where $h(\mathbf{q}, \mathbf{i})$ is the attention function determining the attention weight of each product i in user's current search records to the input query q. To relax the constraints of the attention mechanism, the Zero Attention Model is proposed via introducing an zero vector in the attention mechanism when modeling users:

$$\mathbf{u} = \sum_{i \in \mathcal{I}_u} \frac{\exp(h(\mathbf{q}, \mathbf{i}))}{\exp(g(\mathbf{q}, \mathbf{0})) + \sum_{i' \in \mathcal{I}_u} \exp(h(\mathbf{q}, \mathbf{i}'))} \cdot \mathbf{i}. \tag{5}$$

These personalized methods have confirmed that the personalized search services can improve the overall performance of product search; however, the performance under the few-shot setting can not be explored, which may suffer from the data-hungry issue. In this paper, we explore the data-hungry issue under the few-shot setting caused by personalization in product search.

4   Data-Hungry Issue

Personalized product search aims to provide personalized services for users based on their queries and search records. Existing methods [1,2] aim to identify the user's preference from her/his search records. However, some users have interacted with the search engine only a few times so that their search records are scarce. Under such a few-shot scenario, it is difficult to capture the user's preference. Existing methods have confirmed that modeling users can improve the overall performance, but they do not take into account the performance with few search records. In this section, we illustrate (1) whether the personalized product search suffers from the data-hungry problem; (2) when the data-hungry issue degrades the performance under the few-shot setting; (3) how the data-hungry issue harms the performance of personalized product search.

4.1   Does Personalization Cause the Data-Hungry Issue?

Existing methods [1,2] have confirmed the benefit of personalization on the overall performance, but they can not take into account the performance under the few-shot setting, where users have few search records to be identified their preference. To evaluate the performance of the user with few search records, we divide the users into ten groups according to the number of their search records, with the balanced group sizes. Note that the ways of modeling users are different, and therefore, the measure of AEM and ZAM is different from that of HEM. AEM

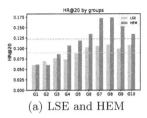 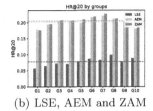

(a) LSE and HEM   (b) LSE, AEM and ZAM

Fig. 1. The performances (in terms of HR@20) by groups on *Video Games* dataset **according to the number of user's search records**. The dashed lines denote the overall performances of models.

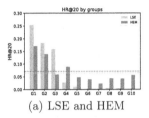 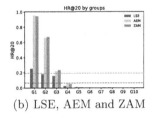

(a) LSE and HEM   (b) LSE, AEM and ZAM

Fig. 2. The performances (in terms of HR@20) by groups on **the 30% users with the least search records** of *Video Games* dataset **according to the diversity of query intents**. The dashed lines denote the overall performances.

and ZAM only count the current search records instead of all search records, because the user modeling is only on the current search records. We take all the users' search records to train the models and evaluate them on each group. The results can be seen in Fig. 1.

When comparing the methods of non-personalized and personalized product search, we can find that personalization can improve the overall performance of models. However, the performance in each group is different. For HEM, it outperforms the non-personalized methods (i.e., LSE) on the groups of users with more search records, but there is no significant improvement on the groups of users with few search records. For AEM and ZAM, while the performance on each group is improved, the performance on the groups of users with few search records is worse than the overall performance. In general, the personalized methods outperform the non-personalized one on the overall result, but the performance on the groups of users with few search records is not improved significantly, which refers to the data-hungry issue.

4.2   When Does Data-Hungry Issue Degrade the Performance?

The analysis in the above section has illustrated that personalization can not significantly improve the performances under the few-shot setting. However, it is still unclear when the personalization does not work under the few-shot settings.

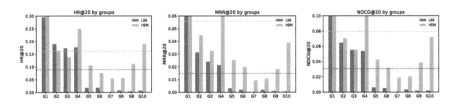

Fig. 3. The performances (in terms of HR@20, MRR@20 and NDCG@20) by groups on the **30% users with most search records** of *Video Games* dataset **according to the diversity of query intents.** The dashed lines denote the overall performances.

We take the users with few search records (occupying 30% of total) to find when the data-hungry issue degrades the performance under the few-shot setting.

Following the previous work [1], the difficulty of providing search services depends on the diversity of the query intent. We use the entropy of products relevant to the query, Entropy(q), to denote the diversity of query intent:

$$\text{Entropy}(q) = -\sum_{i \in \mathcal{I}_q} p(i|q) \log p(i|q) = -\sum_{i \in \mathcal{I}_q} \frac{|\mathcal{S}_{q,i}|}{|\mathcal{S}_q|} \log(\frac{|\mathcal{S}_{q,i}|}{|\mathcal{S}_q|}), \qquad (6)$$

where $\mathcal{I}_q$ and $\mathcal{S}_q$ are the sets of products and search records relevant to the query q, respectively, and the $\mathcal{S}_{q,i}$ is the set of search records related to the query q and the product i.

Figure 2 shows the performances of each group. We find that the methods for personalized product search can work and achieve the competitive performance on the groups with low entropy, where the query intents are specific so that it is easy to retrieve a ranked list of products to respond to the input query. However, the performance degrades significantly when the query carries diverse intents.

For HEM, we can see that it can outperform the non-personalized method (i.e., LSE) but not reach the overall performance, when the query carries diverse intents. To further confirm the impact of the few-shot setting, we take the users with enough search records for verification (also occupying 30% of total). The groups are divided according to the entropy of the product relevant to the query too and the results are shown in the same coordinate scale in Fig. 3. It illustrates that the HEM can perform better with enough search records on the groups even if the query carries diverse intents, compared to the performance under the few-shot setting. It confirms that the data-hungry issue still exists even if HEM can outperform the non-personalized methods under the few-shot setting.

The above analysis has demonstrated that the data-hungry issue degrades the performance under the few-shot setting, especially when the query carries diverse intents.

4.3 How Does Data-Hungry Issue Degrade the Performance?

In this section, we explore how the data-hungry issue degrades the performance. The previous section shows that the personalized methods have different performances on different purchase entropy of queries under the few-shot setting. But

Table 1. The MRR@20 between LSE and HEM, measuring the ranked list of products, whose targets are the two factors, respectively.

		G0	G1	G2	G3	G4	G5	G6	G7	G8	G9
The purchase frequency of **user**	LSE	.0010	.0022	.0034	.0031	.0064	.0063	.0076	.0073	.0052	.0050
	HEM	.3720	.3372	.3429	.3370	.3060	.2885	.2504	.2260	.1861	.1356
The purchase frequency of **query**	LSE	.0077	.0081	.0084	.0096	.0102	.0101	.0118	.0104	.0109	.0095
	HEM	.0162	.0188	.0246	.0373	.0408	.0502	.0608	.0569	.0535	.0339

Table 2. The MRR@20 between LSE, AEM and ZAM, measuring the ranked list of products, whose targets are the two factors, respectively.

		G0	G1	G2	G3	G4	G5	G6	G7	G8	G9
The purchase frequency of **user**	LSE	.0009	.0016	.0022	.0018	.0041	.0044	.0038	.0040	.0042	.0030
	AEM	.0031	.0026	.0064	.0087	.0083	.0110	.0107	.0052	.0087	.0039
	ZAM	.0028	.0025	.0047	.0046	.0049	.0076	.0089	.0047	.0068	.0037
The purchase frequency of **query**	LSE	.0077	.0080	.0084	.0096	.0101	.0100	.0117	.0104	.0109	.0095
	AEM	.0372	.0446	.0494	.0567	.0616	.0689	.0849	.0674	.0650	.0533
	ZAM	.0368	.0458	.0468	.0529	.0578	.0597	.0728	.0581	.0561	.0547

how the data-hungry issue leads to such results is not clear. We consider two factors affecting the biased result with the lack of user preference:

The Frequency of Purchases of Users. The user preference is extracted from the search records. If the records are scarce, the user preference tends to be close to the products the user purchases most often and the latest. To verify the influence of this factor, we count the frequency of purchases of each user in two ways because of the different ways to extract the user information in HEM and ZAM. **The Preference of Market.** Another potential factor is the market preference $p(i|q)$, which means that the search results tend to be close to the product the most users purchase given the same query. To verify the influence of this factor, we count the frequency of purchases given each query.

To recognize the influences of the above factors on the returned ranked list of products, a simple method is to evaluate the returned result with the target products deduced from the factors. We choose the highest frequency of products for each user and the highest frequency of products for each query as the target products for these two factors, respectively. Specifically, we use the mean reciprocal rank to show the relationship of the target products deduced from the factors and the returned ranked list of products.

The results of LSE and HEM can be seen in Table 1. We can find that the returned result has a close relationship with the product the user purchases most often and the relationship is more closely under the few-shot settings. It illustrates that the result returned by HEM is influenced by the frequency of purchases of the user, and this influence is intensified under the few-shot setting. It is the reason why the HEM can not perform well for the user when her/his search records are scarce, where the user preference can not be extracted properly.

The results of LSE, AEM and ZAM are shown in Table 2. Compared to the frequency of purchases of the user, the ranked list of products is influenced more by the market preferences. The results of the AEM and ZAM tend to be close to the products purchased by the most users in the market given the same query. When the query carries less diverse intents, the market preference can meet the user's demand because of the specificity of the query. When the query carries more diverse intents, the market preference only meets part of users' demands. It matches the results of AEM and ZAM shown in Fig. 2. In conclusion, the search results are influenced by the purchase frequency of users or the market preference under the few-shot setting, which leads to the data-hungry issue.

5   Experiment

In this section, we are interested in investing whether the data-hungry issue generalizes to other datasets.

We take Amazon product dataset provided by [10] as our experimental datasets, following the previous studies [1,2,12]. We extract four datasets (i.e., *Video Games*, *Pet Supplies*, *Toys and Games* and *Beauty*) for our experiments. Note that the *Video Games* is used to analyze the data-hungry issue in detail in the previous section. Following [1,2,12], we extract the query from the categories of products, as the query is not provided in the dataset because of the data privacy.

To measure the return ranked list of products, we take into account a number of widely used evaluation metrics, i.e., **HR@k**(Hit Ratio k) [3], **MRR@k** (Mean Reciprocal Rank at k) [3] and **NDCG@k** (Normalized Discounted Cumulative Gain at k) [6]. We set the depth of the evaluation metrics as 20, i.e., k = 20. In this paper, we show the average results of the test data.

Table 3 and Table 4 shows the performance of non-personalized methods (i.e., LSE) and the personalized method (i.e., HEM, AEM and ZAM) on groups of different number of search records on each experimental dataset. We find that the performances of personalized methods degrade under the few-shot learning in all datasets compared to the scenario with enough search records. It further confirms that the data-hungry issue exists in the personalized product search.

Table 3. The performances (i.e., HR@20, MRR@20 and NDCG@20) of LSE and HEM on each datasets when users with few records (i.e., the 30% users with the fewest records) and users with enough records (i.e., the 30% users with the most records).

		Pet supplies			Toys and games			Beauty		
		HR	MRR	NDCG	HR	MRR	NDCG	HR	MRR	NDCG
LSE	The least 30%	.2186	.0253	.0651	.1403	.0167	.0421	.1344	.0172	.0415
	The most 30%	.1910	.0215	.0565	.1182	.0153	.0364	.1211	.0154	.0374
HEM	The least 30%	.3026	.0607	.1123	.1634	.0263	.0553	.1240	.0182	.0403
	The most 30%	.2969	.0680	.1172	.1758	.0387	.0658	.1834	.0368	.0681

Table 4. The performances (i.e., HR@20, MRR@20 and NDCG@20) of LSE, AEM and ZAM on each datasets when users with few records (i.e., the 30% users with the fewest records) and users with enough records (i.e., the 30% users with the most records).

		Pet supplies			Toys and games			Beauty		
		HR	MRR	NDCG	HR	MRR	NDCG	HR	MRR	NDCG
LSE	The least 30%	.1986	.0203	.0551	.1312	.0156	.0372	.1230	.0163	.0389
	The most 30%	.1990	.0235	.0591	.1214	.0159	.0371	.1234	.0159	.0380
AEM	The least 30%	.3534	.0679	.1287	.1773	.0307	.0617	.1518	.0204	.0478
	The most 30%	.3761	.0739	.1386	.1997	.0344	.0694	.1738	.0235	.0549
ZAM	The least 30%	.3476	.0651	.1253	.2092	.0411	.0770	.1761	.0308	.0616
	The most 30%	.3863	.0762	.1426	.2337	.0425	.0833	.1872	.0358	.0681

6   Conclusion

In this paper, we focus on the data-hungry issue in personalized product search. While previous works have confirmed that the user preference extracted from the search records helps provide personalized services, they ignore the few-shot learning problem caused by personalization. Under the few-shot setting, it may suffer from the data-hungry issue. Therefore, We explore the data-hungry issue in personalized product search. We find that the data-hungry exists under the few-shot setting caused by personalization. The data-hungry issue degrades the performance under the few-shot setting when the input query carries diverse intents. With the data-hungry issue, the returned result tends to be close to the products the user purchase most often or the most users purchase in the market given the query. The further experimental results confirm the conclusions.

References

1. Ai, Q., Hill, D.N., Vishwanathan, S., Croft, W.B.: A zero attention model for personalized product search. In: Proceedings of the 28th ACM International Conference on Information and Knowledge Management, pp. 379–388 (2019)

2. Ai, Q., Zhang, Y., Bi, K., Chen, X., Croft, W.B.: Learning a hierarchical embedding model for personalized product search. In: Proceedings of the 40th International ACM SIGIR Conference on Research and Development in Information Retrieval, pp. 645–654 (2017)

3. Croft, W.B., Metzler, D., Strohman, T.: Search Engines: Information Retrieval in Practice, vol. 520. Addison-Wesley Reading (2010)

4. Duan, H., Zhai, C., Cheng, J., Gattani, A.: Supporting keyword search in product database: a probabilistic approach. Proc. VLDB Endow. 6(14), 1786–1797 (2013)

5. Guo, Y., Cheng, Z., Nie, L., Wang, Y., Ma, J., Kankanhalli, M.: Attentive long short-term preference modeling for personalized product search. ACM Trans. Inf. Syst. (TOIS) 37(2), 1–27 (2019)

6. Järvelin, K., Kekäläinen, J.: Cumulated gain-based evaluation of IR techniques. ACM Trans. Inf. Syst. (TOIS) 20(4), 422–446 (2002)

7. Liang, S., Tang, S., Meng, Z., Zhang, Q.: Cross-temporal snapshot alignment for dynamic networks. IEEE Trans. Knowl. Data Eng. (TKDE) (2022, to appear)

8. Liang, S., Yilmaz, E., Kanoulas, E.: Collaboratively tracking interests for user clustering in streams of short texts. IEEE Trans. Knowl. Data Eng. (TKDE) 31(2), 257–272 (2019)

9. Liu, S., Gu, W., Cong, G., Zhang, F.: Structural relationship representation learning with graph embedding for personalized product search. In: Proceedings of the 29th ACM International Conference on Information & Knowledge Management, pp. 915–924 (2020)

10. McAuley, J., Targett, C., Shi, Q., Van Den Hengel, A.: Image-based recommendations on styles and substitutes. In: Proceedings of the 38th International ACM SIGIR Conference on Research and Development in Information Retrieval, pp. 43–52 (2015)

11. Pan, Y., Meng, Z., Liang, S.: Personalized, sequential, attentive, metric-aware product search. ACM Tran. Inf. Syst. (TOIS) 10, 1–29 (2022)

12. van der Ploeg, T., Austin, P.C., Steyerberg, E.W.: Modern modelling techniques are data hungry: a simulation study for predicting dichotomous endpoints. BMC Med. Res. Methodol. 14(1), 1–13 (2014)

13. Sondhi, P., Sharma, M., Kolari, P., Zhai, C.: A taxonomy of queries for e-commerce search. In: The 41st International ACM SIGIR Conference on Research & Development in Information Retrieval, pp. 1245–1248 (2018)

14. Su, N., He, J., Liu, Y., Zhang, M., Ma, S.: User intent, behaviour, and perceived satisfaction in product search. In: Proceedings of the 11th ACM International Conference on Web Search and Data Mining, pp. 547–555 (2018)

15. Van Gysel, C., de Rijke, M., Kanoulas, E.: Learning latent vector spaces for product search. In: Proceedings of the 25th ACM International on Conference on Information and Knowledge Management, pp. 165–174 (2016)

16. Wang, Y., Yao, Q., Kwok, J.T., Ni, L.M.: Generalizing from a few examples: a survey on few-shot learning. ACM Comput. Surv. (CSUR) 53(3), 1–34 (2020)

Jointly Super Resolution and Degradation Learning on Unpaired Real-World Images

Xuankun Chen, Junhong Chen, and Dongyu Zhang$^{(\boxtimes)}$

Sun Yat-sen University, Guangzhou, China
zhangdy27@mail.sysu.edu.cn

Abstract. Recently super-resolution methods based on CNN have achieved amazing success. However, the effects of these methods on real-world images are not available. The main reason is that most of them use bicubic downsampling by default to obtain degraded low-resolution images, while the degradation process of real-world images is unknown. In our work, we argue that image degradation and super-resolution are tightly coupled. In order to complete this cycle, we propose a framework to jointly learn the degradation and super-resolution of real-world images. At the same time, in order to stabilize learning and optimize performance, we have combined a variety of image content losses. Our framework can not only achieve real-world super-resolution, but also generate paired unknown degraded datasets for other super-resolution methods. The experiments on the NTIRE2020 real-world SR dataset show the effectiveness of our model.

Keywords: Super-resolution · Real-world images · Deep learning

1 Introduction

Image super-resolution mainly aims to convert low-quality images into clear images, which is widely used in daily life. In recent years, due to the rise of convolutional neural network [1], the effect of image super-resolution has been significantly improved. Most methods focus on designing the network structure to improve the performance of specific datasets. Most of them are SISR (Single Image Super-Resolution) methods [2,3,9,11,13,18,21], which is using bicubic operation for downsampling to construct low/high-resolution training data pairs. While testing, the low-resolution images downsampled by bicubic kernel are fed into the network to get the generated results, then comparing with the groundtruth to calculate PSNR, SSIM and other metrics.

It is easy to obtain training datasets in this way, however, natural images are usually affected by sensor noise, compression artifacts or other corruptions encountered in applications. Only using the degradation representation of bicubic interpolation can not simulate real-world low resolution images. These methods can't work well on the natural data. Therefore, it is necessary to introduce an accurate degradation method to make the generated low-resolution images have the same domain attributes as the original images.

In our work, we propose a novel framework based on Generative Adversarial Networks(GAN) [4,16] to overcome the challenges of real-world super-resolution

© Springer Nature Switzerland AG 2022
H. Shen et al. (Eds.): PDCAT 2021, LNCS 13148, pp. 495–503, 2022.
https://doi.org/10.1007/978-3-030-96772-7_46

problems. By learning the degradation operation of real-world images, we avoid the problem of conversion between the training and test distribution caused by bicublc downsampling. Specifically, we train the degradation network from high-resolution images to real-world low-resolution images, and put the generated low-resolution images and real low-resolution images into the discriminator for discrimination. Thus, the low-resolution images matching the real-world distribution are obtained, witch enable us to learn the real-world super-resolution networks. At the same time, we also use the obtained real-world paired data to train a super-resolution network to construct the original high-resolution image.

In summary, our contributions are as follows:

- We proposed an unpaired super-resolution method to solve the super-resolution problem of unknown degraded real-world low-resolution images.
- By jointly learning super-resolution and degradation, it can also simulate the degradation of the real-world images, which can better provide the low/high-resolution data pairs of the real world for other methods.

2 Related Work

Since the rise of convolutional neural network (CNN), super-resolution methods based on deep learning have gradually entered people's field of vision. They have achieved strong performance in the task based on bicubic downsampled images. The pioneering work is completed by SRCNN [2], which used a three-layer network to learn the low/high-resolution mapping for SISR task. In the early stage, the most representative method is EDSR [13], which constructed a very deep and wide network by using residual structure and achieved outstanding performance. However, the methods above rely too much on L1 or L2 loss. Although these loss functions are closely related to metrics such as PSNR, they can not retain natural image features, which usually results in blurred textures. To improve the perceptual quality, SRGAN [11] introduced the adversarial loss and the perception loss based on VGG [17] feature layer. Although the PSNR is reduced, the image quality will be significantly improved. The enhanced version of SRGAN, ESRGAN [18], is also one of the state-of-the-art perception oriented models.

Despite the success of the above SISR methods, they can't get excellent test results in real-world images. Because the bicubic downsampling operation eliminates most high-frequency components, it significantly changes the natural features of the image, such as noise, artifacts and other corruptions encountered, which is inconsistent with the needs of the real world. Therefore, new solutions have been proposed to solve the problem of real-world data pair. CinCGAN [19] proposed a cycle-in-cycle network to learn both degradation network and super-resolution network. Lugmayr et al. [14] transferred and converted between the bicubic downsampled low-resolution image domain and the real-world low-resolution image domain. Maeda et al. [15] introduced a correction network to correct real-world images and then mapped them to the bicubic downsampled low-resolution image domain. Different from these methods, we omit the process of domain transfer and directly learn the degradation process from high-resolution images to real-world low-resolution images.

3   Proposed Method

In this work, we propose to jointly learn super-resolution and degradation within a unified disentangled image translation framework, as shown in Fig. 1. Inspired by Cycle-GAN [22], we construct a cycle network, which includes two branches. The one is to get low-resolution images Y_{LR} from the high-resolution images Y, through the degradation network G_{Down}, and then to get the high-resolution images Y_{HR} through the super-resolution network G_{Up}. The other one is the opposite. In order to get better training results, we also introduce discriminator D_{LR} and D_{HR}, making the generated results more like real-world images.

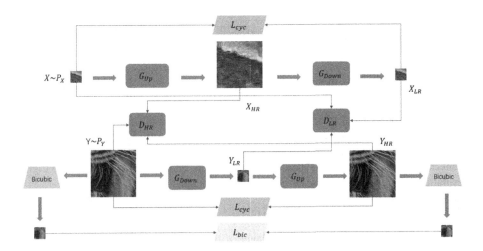

Fig. 1. The proposed training model architecture, where G_{Up} is the super-resolution network, G_{Down} is the degradation network, and the D_{HR} with the D_{LR} is the discriminator. The joint training helps to overcome the unpaired super-resolution problem and generate the real-world degradation low-resolution images.

3.1   Loss Function

Adversarial Loss. We impose an adversarial constraint [4] on both generators G_{Up} and G_{Down}. As an example, the adversarial loss for G_{Up} and D_{HR} can be expressed as:

$$L_{adv}(G_{Up}, D_{HR}, X, Y) = \mathbb{E}_{Y \sim P_Y}[log D_{HR}(Y)] \\ + \mathbb{E}_{X \sim P_X}[log(1 - D_{HR}(G_{Up}(X)))] \tag{1}$$

which is tasked to differentiate between the generated $G_{Up}(X)$ and images drawn from the input distribution P_Y. All the generated images will be put into the discriminator, the total adversarial loss is as follows:

$$L_{adv} = L_{adv}(G_{Up}, D_{HR}, X, Y) + L_{adv}(G_{Up}, D_{HR}, Y_{LR}, Y) \\ + L_{adv}(G_{Down}, D_{LR}, Y, X) + L_{adv}(G_{Down}, D_{LR}, X_{HR}, X) \tag{2}$$

Cycle Consistency Loss. Benefiting from the closed-loop in our framework, we employ two cycle-consistency losses [22] which self-supervise the super-resolution and degradation sub-networks to preserve the content information. Thus we define the cycle-consistency loss as:

$$
\begin{aligned}
L_{Cycle} = & \mathbb{E}_{X \sim P_X} [\|G_{Down}(G_{Up}(X)) - X\|_1] \\
& + \mathbb{E}_{Y \sim P_Y} [\|G_{Up}(G_{Down}(Y)) - Y\|_1]
\end{aligned}
\tag{3}
$$

Bicubic Loss. In addition to the adversarial losses and the cycle-consistency losses, for the low-resolution images generated by the degradation network, we also introduce the bicubic loss to preserve color composition and avoid color variation:

$$
\begin{aligned}
L_{bic} = & \mathbb{E}_{X \sim P_X} [\|G_{Down}(G_{Up}(X)) - Bic(G_{Up}(X))\|_1] \\
& + \mathbb{E}_{Y \sim P_Y} [\|G_{Down}(Y) - Bic(Y)\|_1]
\end{aligned}
\tag{4}
$$

where Bic is the bicubic downsampling operation.

Perceptual Loss. In our preliminary experiment, there are many artifacts in the generated high-resolution samples. In fact, the features extracted from the pre-trained deep network contain rich semantic information, and their distances can be used as the judgment of perceptual similarity. Therefore, we add perceptual loss [8] between the high-resolution images and the corresponding original images:

$$
L_{per} = \|\phi_l(G_{Up}(G_{Down}(Y))) - \phi_l(Y)\|_2^2
\tag{5}
$$

where $\phi_l(x)$ is the features of the l-th layer of the pre-trained CNN. Here we use the VGG-19 network pre-trained on ImageNet.

Full Objective. The full objective function is a weighted sum of all the loss functions:

$$
Loss = \lambda_{adv} L_{adv} + \lambda_{cycle} L_{cycle} + \lambda_{bic} L_{bic} + \lambda_{per} L_{per}
\tag{6}
$$

By imposing the full objective function, we alleviate the problem that paired low/high-resolution images are not accessible. In our framework, each super-resolution and degradation sub network is constrained by at least one unsupervised adversarial loss and one self-supervised cycle-consistency loss to ensure the domain of output images and preserve the content information.

3.2   Network Architecture

G_{Up} We use the structure of DBPN [6] as the generator. Through alternating iterative upsampling and downsampling units to back-propagate the projection error, it can correct the reconstruction results in the network many times. The upsampling unit generates more high-resolution space features, while the downsampling unit projects these features into low-resolution space. In this way, more high-resolution components can be retained and more depth features can be used effectively. We use the version of its 7-layer structure, whose structure of each layer includes two sub layer of upsampling and downsampling.

G_{Down}. Inspired by KernelGAN [5], we used a linear network without activation function to simulate the degradation process. The network is a 6-layer linear fully convolutional network with strides of 1: the first three Convolution kernels are 7×7, 5×5, 3×3, and the rest are 1×1, which make a receptive field of 13×13.

Discriminator. As for the discriminator of high-resolution images, we use five convolution layers with 3×3. The convolution layers, except for the first and the last layer, are followed by LeakyReLU with batch normalization. Besides, we use a patch discriminator [7, 12], which has a fixed receptive field. That is, each output value of the discriminator is only related to the patch of the locally fixed area. The patch loss will be fed back to the generator to optimize the gradient of local details. The discriminator of low-resolution images has the similar structure, but with a different stride in the initial layers.

4 Experiments

In this section, We first discuss the setup and datasets employed in our experiments. Next, we present comprehensive quantitative and qualitative evaluation of our approach. Finally, we perform an ablation study to validate training model structure.

4.1 Dataset and Evaluation Metrics

We use the DIV2K realistic-mild set as our training data. The realistic-mild set is generated by degrading DIV2K, consisting of 800 images with 2K resolution that are diverse in their content. It assumes that the degradation operators emulating the image acquisition process from a digital camera (such as blur kernel, decimation, downscaling strategy) can be estimated through training pairs of low and high-resolution images. The parameters of the degradation operators are fixed, while the randomly generated blur kernels and their resulting pixel shifts vary from image to image. Our experiments are performed with a scaling factor of $\times 4$. We randomly slice the high-resolution images into some 128×128 patches, and the low-resolution images into some 32×32 patches. Thus we expand our training data to 32590 images. We train our model using the above paired images but with "unpaired/unaligned" sampling.

For the case of the generated images, we use PSNR, SSIM and LPIPS as our evaluation metrics. PSNR and SSIM are commonly-used evaluation metrics for image restoration, which pay more attention to the fidelity of the image rather than visual quality. In contrast, LPIPS is a learned metric for perceptual similarity between two images, which uses a pre-trained network to extract image features, and then calculates the distance between the two features. It is worth noting that the smaller the LPIPS is, the closer the generated image is to the ground truth.

4.2   Training Details

Our framework is implemented using the PyTorch with four Titan Xp GPUs. We use the Adam optimizer [10] with $\beta 1 = 0.9$, $\beta 2 = 0.99$, and $\epsilon = 10^{-8}$ to train the generators and discriminators. We train our networks for more than $3 * 10^5$ iterations with the batch size of 32. In each iteration, low-resolution patches of 32×32 and high-resolution patches of corresponding size are extracted as inputs in an unaligned manner. We empirically set the balance weight λ_{adv}, λ_{cycle}, λ_{bic}, λ_{per} as 0.1, 10, 10, 0.5.

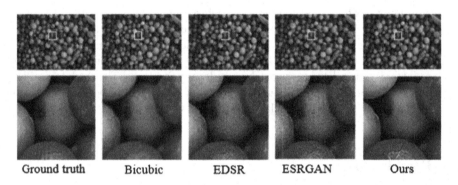

| Ground truth | Bicubic | EDSR | ESRGAN | Ours |

Fig. 2. Qualitative results on "0802" in the validation set of the NTIRE2020 Real World SR challenge Track 1 with scale factor×4 compared with EDSR and ESRGAN. The red area is cropped from different results and enlarged for visual convenient. (Color figure online)

(a)   (b)

Fig. 3. Our degradation network result(b) to "0815" groundtruth with scale factor×4 compared with bicubic downsampling(a). Our method can get more terrible low-resolution images similar to real-world.

4.3   Result

Compared with some state-of-the-art approaches for SISR, we demonstrate effectiveness of the proposed method. The results of perceptual image quality are shown in Fig. 2. Table 1 shows the average PSNR, SSIM and LPIPS [20] values of NTIRE2020 validation set with the different methods. From it we can inform that we get superior performance in all the metrics. We also show our degradation images in Fig. 3. Compared with the bicubic downsampling method, the images generated by our method have more complicated noise and artifacts, which is more like real-world images.

Table 1. The result compared with other methods.

Methods	PSNR	SSIM	LPIPS
Bicubic	25.49	0.670	0.49
ESRGAN	19.06	0.242	0.76
EDSR	25.31	0.638	0.58
ZSSR	25.13	0.626	0.61
Ours	**26.85**	**0.73**	**0.42**

4.4 Ablation Study

In this section, ablation study on our framework is conducted to evaluate the effectiveness of losses and network structure.

Effectiveness of Loss Functions. Denoting L_{per} as the perceptual loss, while L_{bic} as the bicubic loss, we investigate the effectiveness of the loss functions in Table 2. We remain our framework fixed and remove one of the losses while other losses keep the same. The performance drops demonstrate the benefits brought by the bicubic loss and the perceptual loss.

Effectiveness of Network Structure. We also test the single super-resolution sub-network. We remove the degradation sub-network, and remain the discriminator and the relative loss we used. The Table 2 also shows the metrics result, which proves that our total framework significantly improve the performance.

Table 2. The effectiveness of the loss functions and the network structure.

	Methods	PSNR	SSIM	LPIPS
Loss	Without L_{per}	26.02	0.68	0.47
	Without L_{bic}	25.59	0.66	0.46
	Full loss	**26.85**	**0.73**	**0.42**
Network	Single	24.74	0.533	0.54
	Full model	**26.85**	**0.73**	**0.42**

5 Conclusion

In this paper, we propose a disentangled framework which jointly learns super-resolution and degradation to deal with the real-world super-resolution problem. The degradation sub network is trained to generate realistic training data pairs for our super-resolution model, avoiding the artifacts caused by bicubic downsampling. We also introduce the bicubic loss to avoid color variation and the perceptual loss to remove unrealistic artifacts. Ablation study on each component shows the effectiveness of different modules. Experiments on real-world test images show that our framework has excellent performance, resulting in lower noise and better visual quality.

References

1. Imagenet classification with deep convolutional neural networks. Adv. Neural Inf. Process. Syst. **25**(2) (2012)
2. Chao, D., Chen, C.L., He, K., Tang, X.: Learning a deep convolutional network for image super-resolution. In: ECCV, pp. 184–199 (2014)
3. Dong, C., Loy, C.C., He, K., Tang, X.: Image super-resolution using deep convolutional networks. IEEE Trans. Pattern Anal. Mach. Intell. **38**(2), 295–307 (2016)
4. Goodfellow, I.J., et al.: Generative adversarial networks (2014)
5. Gu, J., Lu, H., Zuo, W., Dong, C.: Blind super-resolution with iterative kernel correction. In: IEEE, pp. 1604–1613 (2019)
6. Haris, M., Shakhnarovich, G., Ukita, N.: Deep back-projection networks for super-resolution. In: 2018 IEEE/CVF Conference on Computer Vision and Pattern Recognition, pp. 1664–1673 (2018). https://doi.org/10.1109/CVPR.2018.00179
7. Isola, P., Zhu, J.Y., Zhou, T., Efros, A.A.: Image-to-image translation with conditional adversarial networks. In: IEEE Conference on Computer Vision and Pattern Recognition (2016)
8. Johnson, J., Alahi, A., Fei-Fei, L.: Perceptual losses for real-time style transfer and super-resolution. In: Leibe, B., Matas, J., Sebe, N., Welling, M. (eds.) ECCV 2016. LNCS, vol. 9906, pp. 694–711. Springer, Cham (2016). https://doi.org/10.1007/978-3-319-46475-6_43
9. Kim, J., Lee, J.K., Lee, K.M.: Accurate image super-resolution using very deep convolutional networks. In: IEEE Conference on Computer Vision and Pattern Recognition, pp. 1646–1654 (2016)
10. Kingma, D., Ba, J.: Adam: a method for stochastic optimization. Comput. Sci. (2014)
11. Ledig, C., et al.: Photo-realistic single image super-resolution using a generative adversarial network. IEEE Computer Society (2016)
12. Li, C., Wand, M.: Precomputed real-time texture synthesis with Markovian generative adversarial networks. In: Leibe, B., Matas, J., Sebe, N., Welling, M. (eds.) ECCV 2016. LNCS, vol. 9907, pp. 702–716. Springer, Cham (2016). https://doi.org/10.1007/978-3-319-46487-9_43
13. Lim, B., Son, S., Kim, H., Nah, S., Lee, K.M.: Enhanced deep residual networks for single image super-resolution. In: 2017 IEEE Conference on Computer Vision and Pattern Recognition Workshops (CVPRW), pp. 136–144 (2017)
14. Lugmayr, A., Danelljan, M., Timofte, R.: Unsupervised learning for real-world super-resolution. In: 2019 IEEE/CVF International Conference on Computer Vision Workshop (ICCVW) (2020)
15. Maeda, S.: Unpaired image super-resolution using pseudo-supervision. In: 2020 IEEE/CVF Conference on Computer Vision and Pattern Recognition (CVPR), pp. 291–300 (2020)
16. Salimans, T., Goodfellow, I., Zaremba, W., Cheung, V., Radford, A., Chen, X.: Improved techniques for training gans. Adv. Neural Inf. Process. Syst. **29** (2016)
17. Simonyan, K., Zisserman, A.: Very deep convolutional networks for large-scale image recognition. Comput. Sci. (2014)
18. Wang, X., et al.: Esrgan: Enhanced super-resolution generative adversarial networks. In: European Conference on Computer Vision (2018)
19. Yuan, Y., Liu, S., Zhang, J., Zhang, Y., Dong, C., Lin, L.: Unsupervised image super-resolution using cycle-in-cycle generative adversarial networks. IEEE, pp. 701–710 (2018)

20. Zhang, R., Isola, P., Efros, A.A., Shechtman, E., Wang, O.: The unreasonable effectiveness of deep features as a perceptual metric. In: IEEE (2018)

21. Zhang, Y., Tian, Y., Kong, Y., Zhong, B., Fu, Y.: Residual dense network for image super-resolution. In: 2018 IEEE/CVF Conference on Computer Vision and Pattern Recognition, pp. 2472–2481 (2018)

22. Zhu, J.Y., Park, T., Isola, P., Efros, A.A.: Unpaired image-to-image translation using cycle-consistent adversarial networks. In: 2017 IEEE International Conference on Computer Vision (ICCV), pp. 2242–2251 (2017). https://doi.org/10.1109/ICCV.2017.244

Enhanced Discriminant Local Direction Pattern Learning for Robust Palmprint Identification

Siyuan Ma, Qintai Hu[✉], Shuping Zhao, Lin Jiang, and Wenyan Wu

Guangdong University of Technology, Guangzhou, China
huqt8@gdut.edu.cn

Abstract. Direction-based methods have been widely used in palmprint recognition methods. However, most existing palmprint direction patterns-based methods need rich prior knowledge, and usually ignores the relationships among different samples. Furthermore, how to make the extracted features more discriminative is also a dilemma to improving the recognition performance. To solve these problems, we propose to learn enhanced discriminative direction pattern in this study. We first extract the complete and stable local direction patterns, where a salient convolution average feature (EDL) is extracted from the palmprint image. Afterwards, a linear regression learning model is introduced to enhance the discriminant of EDL, such that the representation of the direction pattern can be improved. Experimental results on 4 real-world palmprint databases show that the proposed method can outperform the other state-of-the-art related methods.

Keywords: Robust palmprint identification · Complete and stable local direction feature · Discriminative projection learning

1 Introduction

In recent years, various biometrics technology, such as face, palmprint, voice and gait, has been successfully applied in real-word. Especially, palmprint recognition is a method of identification by palmprint features (visible or invisible to human eyes). Palmprint recognition is stable and reliable. which has attracted the interest of more and more researchers [1]. The existing palmprint recognition methods mainly include low-resolution palmprint, high-resolution palmprint, multispectral palmprint and 3-D palmprint recognition [2]. In recent years, the most commonly used method for palmprint recognition is low-resolution palmprint recognition.

In general, it is necessary to extract the features of the palmprint before the recognition of the palmprint, and it is important to preprocess the palmprint

This work is supported by the National Natural Science Foundation of China under Grant No. 62106052.

H. Shen et al. (Eds.): PDCAT 2021, LNCS 13148, pp. 504–511, 2022.
https://doi.org/10.1007/978-3-030-96772-7_47

before extraction. The preprocessing of the palmprint is to extract the region of interest (ROI). A variety of ROI methods have been proposed in the literature. After ROI pretreatment, the next step is to extract features from palmprint.

In the past decades, a variety of palmprint feature representation methods have been proposed in the literature for feature extraction. For example, Hui et al. [3] proposed a deep hashing network to extract discriminative features; Genovese et al. [4] based on Gabor responses and principal component analysis (PCA) to extract features. We can easily see that, most existing palmprint descriptors usually extracted features individually from each palmprint image, then fused them based on an addition scheme. In addition, most of these literatures extract hand-crafted features, which are heuristic and require strong prior knowledge. How to extract robust discriminant features from palmprint images, deeply excavate the similarity between different images of the same person, and simultaneously enlarge the difference between different images of the same person is always a key and challenging problem.

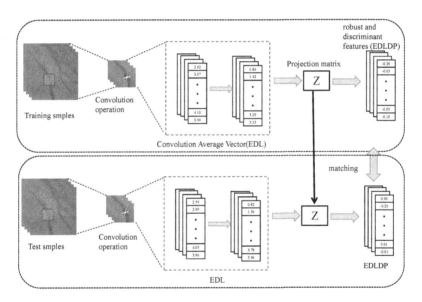

Fig. 1. The flow-chart of the proposed method. We first compute the convolution average vector for each palmprint image. Then, we learn mapping functions, which project EDL into EDLDP.

In this study, we propose an enhanced discriminant local directional pattern for robust palmprint identification (EDLDP). Specifically, we first extract features in 12 directions for each pixel of the palmprint image, and construct a new directional information container. Then, we propose a palmprint recognition method for joint enhancement to discriminate local directional patterns. This method is more stable and robust. Figure 1 outlines the pipeline of the proposed method. Experimental results on the widely used PolyU multispectral palmprint databases, IITD database and GPDS database clearly demonstrate the effectiveness of the proposed method.

The main contributions of this paper can be briefly summarized as follows:

(1) We propose a novel and informative convolution average vector for discriminant direction feature learning. EDL can more stably describe the characteristics of multiple dominant directions and the averaging of directions.
(2) We propose a joint learning model for enhanced discriminant palmprint direction feature encoding. In such manner, the representation of the original direction feature can be improved to achieve a better identification performance.
(3) We conduct extensive experiments on four real-world palmprint databases, including two contactless palmprint databases and two contact-based palmprint databases. Experimental results demonstrate that the proposed method is superior to state-of-the-art palmprint descriptors.

The remainder of this paper is organized as follows. Section 2 briefly presents a review for some related works. In Sect. 3, we introduce the proposed method. Experimental results and some related analysis are given in Sect. 4. Section 5 concludes this study.

2   Related Work

In this section, we briefly reviews two related topics of this paper, including the direction features of palmprint and discriminant regression feature Learning.

2.1   Direction Features of Palmprint

Plenty of lines in a palmprint carry rich direction features, which are insensitive to illumination changes. There have been extensive methods that exploited the direction features for palmprint recognition. Gabor filter can better characterize the direction feature of palmprint [5]. A 2D-Gabor filter is the product of a sinusoidal plane wave and a Gaussian nuclear function. The former is a tuning function and the latter is a window function. It can be divided into the real part and the imaginary part. In the study, the real part of Gabor filter is usually used to obtain the direction characteristics of the palmprintand

2.2   Discriminant Regression Feature Learning

Discriminant Regression feature learning refers to learning some mapping functions that can convert raw data into discriminative feature subspace. A variety of discriminative feature learning methods have been developed in recent years, such as dictionary-learning , transfer-learning , metric-learning and deep-learning, principal component analysis (PCA) and linear discriminant analysis (LDA).

Most existing learning-based methods learn palmprint regression features from raw-pixels of palmprint images. In this work, we learn novel and discriminative regression features from direction-based convolution for palmprint identification.

3 Proposed Methodology

In this section, we first introduce convolution average vector of palmprint. Then, we propose a enhanced discriminant local direction pattern learning for robust palmprint identification.

3.1 Convolution Average Vector

In general, we use a linear structure detector to extract the directional features of the palmprint, However, the black lines of the palmprint image usually have smaller gray values, the line-model of the Gabor template has larger values. Thus, in real application, we usually subtract the gray values of a palmprint image with 255 to obtain the "upside-down" palmprint image [7]. In practice, a bank of Gabor filters with directions of $\theta_i = (i-1)\pi/N_\theta$ is usually defined, where N_θ is used as the direction number of Gabor functions, and i is the corresponding direction index. To better characterize the direction of palmprint, in this paper N_θ is empirically set to 12 [8], the 12 Gabor templates with the directions is $(i-1)\pi/12 (i = 1, 2, \cdots, 12)$. The convolution between the Gabor functions and palmprint image I is as follow:

$$r_i(x, y) = G(\theta_i) * (255 - I(x, y)), \tag{1}$$

where $*$ denotes the convolution operator. A bank of Gabor functions with different directions can obtain a group of convolved results with the palmprint image. We obtain the EDL of a pixel by calculating the convolution average between a direction and the front neighboring direction as follow:

$$EDL = [(r_1 + r_2)/2, \cdots, (r_j + r_{j+1})/2, \cdots, (r_1 - r_{N_\theta})/2]. \tag{2}$$

EDL measures the convolution average between neighboring directions so that it can more stably describe how direction-based convolution response changes. Because the dimension of Gabor features increases sharply compared with the dimension of the original image after EDL, so a discriminative elite-net regularized Linear regression model (DENLR) is selected [9] to learn, the details of DENLR are in the next section.

3.2 Discriminant Elastic-Net Learning

Define the observed image features as $X = [x_1, \cdots, x_n] \in \Re^{d \times n}$, the target matrix as $Y = [y_1, \cdots, y_n]^T \in \Re^{n \times c}$.

By introducing the ε-dragging technique, DENLR model is used, its objective function is formulated as

$$\min_{Z} \zeta(Z) + \lambda_1 \|Z\|_* + \frac{\lambda_2}{2} \|Z\|_F^2, \tag{3}$$

where $\zeta(Z) = \|X^T Z - \bar{Y}\|_F^2$ and $\bar{Y}$ is the relaxed regression target matrix. To obtain an optimal $\bar{Y}$, an elaborate strategy is devised as follows. Let E be a constant matrix, and the i-th row and j-th column entry is defined as

$$E_{ij} = \begin{cases} +1, & \text{if } Y_{ij} = 1, \\ -1, & \text{if } Y_{ij} = 0. \end{cases} \tag{4}$$

Then we have $\bar{Y} = Y + E \odot M$, where $M \in \Re_1^{n \times c}$ is a learned nonnegative matrix. Thus, the DENLR model (5) is rewritten as follows

$$\min_{Z,M} \|X^T Z - (Y + E \odot M)\|_F^2 + \lambda_1 \|Z\|_* + \frac{\lambda_2}{2} \|Z\|_F^2, \tag{5}$$
$$\text{s.t. } M \geq 0.$$

Base on [9], we can equate (5) with (6)

$$\min_{Z,M,A,B} \|X^T Z - (Y + E \odot M)\|_F^2 + \frac{\lambda_1}{2} \left(\|A\|_F^2 + \|B\|_F^2 \right) + \frac{\lambda_2}{2} \|Z\|_F^2, \tag{6}$$
$$\text{s.t. } Z = AB, M \geq 0.$$

4   Experiments

In this section, we evaluate the performance of our proposed methods on publicly available databases, which conclude GPDS [10] databases, IITD database [11] and PolyU multispectral palmprint database [12]. It is worth pointing out that these databases are commonly used in Palmprint recognition and the existing methods have achieved decent results. Thus, challenging recognition results are convincing enough to verify the superiority of our methods.

4.1   Palmprint Databases

The GPDS database [10] contains 1000 samples collected by 100 volunteers. The ROIs with the size of 32×32 used in this study were provide by [10]. The IITD palmprint database [11] was captured using a contactless device, and there is no limit to the palm when collecting the database. In this study, we use the ROIs with the size of 32×32 from [11].

The PolyU multispectral palmprint database (M_Green and M_Blue) [12] collected 12000 palmprint images from 500 volunteers under two different illuminations, including green and blue spectra. In this study, the ROIs were extracted from the original database using the method in [13] with the size of 32×32.

Table 1. Accuracy (%) using different methods on contact-based databases (N = 4).

Method	GPDS	M_Blue	M_Green	IITD
Competitive	86.03	98.94	99.3	79.79
EBOCV	87.16	98.77	98.43	87.96
Ordinal	85.53	98.43	98.37	73.32
DOC	81.08	99.1	99.1	89.9
ResNet_50	93.91	62.2	67.61	95.57
AlexNet	90.5	92.21	74.27	88.18
EDLDP	**100**	**99.85**	**99.80**	**99.74**

4.2 Palmprint Identification

In this subsection, we evaluate the effectiveness of our method on palmprint identification. Palmprint identification is a one-against-many matching procedure to determine the identity. In our experiments, we randomly selected four samples as training samples. All methods were repeated ten times, several state-of-the-art palmprint recognition and image classification methods were implemented to be compared to the proposed method, including competitive code (Competitive) [4], EBOCV [14], Orinal [15], DOC [16], ResNet_50 [17] and AlexNet [18]. Besides, some popular deep learning-based methods including AlexNet and ResNet_50 were also implemented compared with the proposed method.

Table 1 illustrates the comparison results between our EDLDP and other state-of-the-art algorithms on palmprint identification. For E-BOCV, six directions are extracted to be encoded. Specifically, the results of Competitive, E-BOCV, Ordinal and DOC on the IITD, M_Green, M_Blue and GPDS databases are referred from [5,19]. AlexNet and ResNet_50 are two deep convolutional neural networks which have been pre-trained on the ImageNet database. In this work, we conducted identification using the 1-NN (Nearest Neighborhood, Euclidean distance) as the classifier to obtain the ARRs.

In order to further investigate the properties of the proposed method, the classification performances versus the different values of regularization parameters λ_1 and λ_2 are explicitly explored. To clearly show the results, we perform experiments on four databases, i.e., the extended GPDS, IITD, M_Green and M_Blue databases, to verify parameters sensitivity. Specifically, we tune the value of both parameters from $0.0001, 0.0005, 0.001, 0.005, 0.01, 0.05, 0.1, 0.5, 1$. Figure 2 shows the classification results of EDLDP over variations of parameters. In the parameter comparison experiment, after each parameter was set, the experiment was repeated for 5 times and the experimental results were averaged. From Fig. 2, we can observe that the performances of our models are not very sensitive to the settings of λ_1 and λ_2.

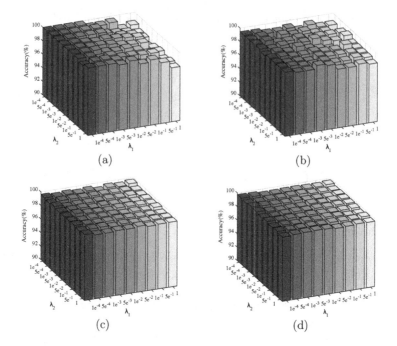

Fig. 2. Variations of EDLDP classification (%) versus the parameters λ_1 and λ_2 on the (a) GPDS, (b) IITD, (c) M_Green and (d) M_Blue databases. (Color figure online)

5   Conclusion

In this paper, we have proposed an enhanced discriminant local directional pattern for robust palmprint identification. Firstly, we have extracted the complete and stable local direction patterns, where a salient convolution average feature is extracted from the palmprint image. Afterwards, a linear regression learning model has been introduced to enhance the discriminant of EDL, such that the representation of the direction pattern has been improved. Experimental results on four real-world palmprint databases have shown that the proposed method outperforms the state-of-the-arts.

References

1. Zhao, S., Zhang, B.: Learning salient and discriminative descriptor for palmprint feature extraction and identification. IEEE Trans. Neural Netw. Learn. Syst. **31**(12), 5219–5230 (2020)
2. Fei, L., Zhang, B., Xu, Y., Guo, Z., Wen, J., Jia, W.: Learning discriminant direction binary palmprint descriptor. IEEE Trans. Image Process. **28**(8), 3808–3820 (2019)

3. Shao, H., Zhong, D.: One-shot cross-dataset palmprint recognition via adversarial domain adaptation. Neurocomputing **432**, 288–299 (2021). https://doi.org/10.1016/j.neucom.2020.12.072, https://www.sciencedirect.com/science/article/pii/S092523122031972X

4. Genovese, A., Piuri, V., Plataniotis, K.N., Scotti, F.: Palmnet: Gabor-PCA convolutional networks for touchless palmprint recognition. IEEE Trans. Inf. Forensics Secur. **14**(12), 3160–3174 (2019)

5. Zhao, S., Zhang, B.: Learning complete and discriminative direction pattern for robust palmprint recognition. IEEE Trans. Image Process. **30**, 1001–1014 (2021). https://doi.org/10.1109/TIP.2020.3039895

6. Cai, X., Ding, C., Nie, F., Huang, H.: On the equivalent of low-rank linear regressions and linear discriminant analysis based regressions. In: Proceedings of the 19th ACM SIGKDD International Conference on Knowledge Discovery and Data Mining, pp. 1124–1132. Association for Computing Machinery, New York, NY, USA (2013). https://doi.org/10.1145/2487575.2487701

7. Fei, L., Zhang, B., Xu, Y., Huang, D., Jia, W., Wen, J.: Local discriminant direction binary pattern for palmprint representation and recognition. IEEE Trans. Circ. Syst. Video Technol. **30**(2), 468–481 (2020). https://doi.org/10.1109/TCSVT.2019.2890835

8. Lu, J., Liong, V.E., Zhou, X., Zhou, J.: Learning compact binary face descriptor for face recognition. IEEE Trans. Pattern Anal. Mach. Intell. **37**(10), 2041–2056 (2015). https://doi.org/10.1109/TPAMI.2015.2408359

9. Zhang, Z., Lai, Z., Xu, Y., Shao, L., Wu, J., Xie, G.S.: Discriminative elastic-net regularized linear regression. Trans. Img. Proc. **26**(3), 1466–1481 (2017). https://doi.org/10.1109/TIP.2017.2651396

10. Gpds palmprint database. Accessed (2018). http://www.gpds.ulpgc.es

11. Kumar, A.: Incorporating cohort information for reliable palmprint authentication. In: 2008 Sixth Indian Conference on Computer Vision, Graphics & Image Processing, pp. 583–590. IEEE (2008)

12. Zhang, D., Guo, Z., Lu, G., Zhang, L., Zuo, W.: An online system of multispectral palmprint verification. IEEE Trans. Instrum. Measur. **59**(2), 480–490 (2010). https://doi.org/10.1109/TIM.2009.2028772

13. Jia, W., Huang, D.S., Zhang, D.: Palmprint verification based on robust line orientation code. Pattern Recogn. **41**(5), 1504–1513 (2008)

14. Zhang, L., Li, H., Niu, J.: Fragile bits in palmprint recognition. IEEE Sign. Process. Lett. **19**(10), 663–666 (2012). https://doi.org/10.1109/LSP.2012.2211589

15. Chu, R., Liao, S., Han, Y., Sun, Z., Li, S.Z., Tan, T.: Fusion of face and palmprint for personal identification based on ordinal features. In: 2007 IEEE Conference on Computer Vision and Pattern Recognition, pp. 1–2 (2007). https://doi.org/10.1109/CVPR.2007.383522

16. Fei, L., Xu, Y., Tang, W., Zhang, D.: Double-orientation code and nonlinear matching scheme for palmprint recognition. Pattern Recogn. **49**, 89–101 (2016)

17. He, K., Zhang, X., Ren, S., Sun, J.: Deep residual learning for image recognition. In: 2016 IEEE Conference on Computer Vision and Pattern Recognition (CVPR), pp. 770–778 (2016). https://doi.org/10.1109/CVPR.2016.90

18. Krizhevsky, A., Sutskever, I., Hinton, G.E.: Imagenet classification with deep convolutional neural networks. Commun. ACM **60**(6), 84–90 (2017). https://doi.org/10.1145/3065386

19. Zhao, S., Zhang, B.: Deep discriminative representation for generic palmprint recognition. Pattern Recogn. **98**, 107071 (2020)

Latent Multi-view Subspace Clustering Based on Schatten-P Norm

Yuqin Lu[1], Yilan Fu[1], Jiangzhong Cao[1(✉)], Shangsong Liang[2],
and Wing-kuen Ling[1]

[1] Guangdong University of Technology, Guangdong 510006, China
cjz510@gdut.edu.cn
[2] Sun Yat-sen University, Guangdong 510006, China

Abstract. In this paper, we aim at the research of rank minimization to find more accurate low-dimensional representations for multi-view subspace learning. The Schatten-p norm is utilized as the rank relaxation function for subspace learning to enhance its ability to recover the low rank matrices, and a multi-view subspace clustering algorithm via maximizing the original feature information is proposed under the assumption that each view is derived from a latent representation. With the Schatten-p norm, the proposed algorithm can improve the quality and robustness of the latent representations. The effectiveness of our method is validated through experiments on several benchmark datasets.

Keywords: Latent multi-view subspace clustering · Rank function · Schatten-p norm

1 Introduction

Clustering is a fundamental technique in many applications. When dealing with high-dimensional data, subspace clustering shows its advantage by clustering data points in a union of low-dimensional subspaces. In general, subspace clustering is applied on the learning of single view, which describes the data points from only one aspect. However, its performance depends greatly on the quality of the original features and is susceptible to noise and corruption. To improve clustering results for high-dimensional data, multiple views are utilized to gain a more comprehensive understanding of a data point. Multiple views of a data point include information derived from multiple sources of features, which describe a data point from different several aspects. Compared to single view, multi-view subspace clustering (MVSC) [3,21,22] is preferable for analyzing various types of data since different views can complement each other to form more robust and complete representations.

Supported by Natural Science Foundation of China (No. U1701266) and Guangdong Provincial Key Laboratory of Intellectual Property and Big Data (No. 2018B030322016).

H. Shen et al. (Eds.): PDCAT 2021, LNCS 13148, pp. 512–520, 2022.
https://doi.org/10.1007/978-3-030-96772-7_48

Early methods in this direction mainly focused on the learning of two views [1,4,6]. For example, the approach in [6] utilized a bipartite graph for connecting two types of features and further performed a standard spectral clustering on it to obtain the clustering result. However, the learning of two views is not sufficient as more and more high-dimensional data are collected from multiple sources. Hence, multi-view clustering has attracted a growing amount of attention among researchers. According to different expressions of the similarity within views and the consistency among views, we can divide multi-view clustering into three categories: multi-view canonical correlation clustering [18], multi-view matrix decomposition clustering [7,23] and multi-view subspace clustering [3,14,21]. Among them, multi-view subspace clustering (MVSC) is the most popular solution as it achieves the best results. MVSC methods usually generated a separate subspace representation for each view and reconstructed the data points on the original view directly. However, using each view alone is usually insufficient to fully describe the data points, thus making the reconstruction by using only one single view risky. In addition, various types of noises imposed to the data will further increase the difficulty for performing clustering. Therefore, finding a unified multiple view subspace representation matrix to simultaneously incorporate the difference and complementarity among all views became a challenging problem. More recently, the research on multi-view subspace clustering was focused on performing subspace clustering based on latent representations. For single-view setting, there were several methods, such as Latent Space Sparse Subspace Clustering (LS3C) [16] and Latent Low-Rank Representation (LatLRR) [13] that were based on latent representation. For multi-view setting, some methods [8,19] explicitly learned a shared representation from multiple views under the assumption that all views originate from the same latent representation and jointly optimized it with a common subspace representation matrix. This could essentially give a full picture of the data and reveal the latent structure shared by different views. On this basis, unlike LS3C that directly performed dimensionality reduction on the original single view data, [22] proposed to integrate the latent representation learning and multi-view subspace clustering into a unified framework and utilize the complementarity among views to improve the performance of subspace clustering. Nevertheless, when the singular value is too large, the nuclear norm function as the relaxation of the rank function will lead to suboptimal solution [9]. Moreover, the Schatten-p norm with a decomposable formula is another option that's commonly used as the rank relaxation function. It is a more accurate approximation of the rank function.

In this paper, the Schatten-p norm is introduced to approximate the rank function in latent multi-view subspace clustering. Our experimental results demonstrate that our proposed method can effectively improve the performance of subspace clustering.

2 The Schatten P-Norm Based Multi-view Low Rank Representation Framework

Latent multi-view subspace clustering [22] uses the data points of latent representation for performing clustering, which is mainly aimed at mining the

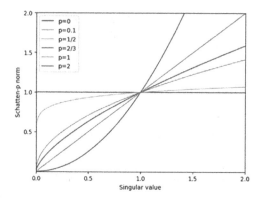

Fig. 1. The input-output relationship of the Schatten-p norm.

complementarity among different views. This paper uses the Schatten-p norm to replace the conventional nuclear norm in latent multi-view subspace clustering. It is worth noting that the Schatten-p norm approaches to the rank function as p approaches to 0, hence the better clustering results. Moreover, due to the complementarity of the multi-view information, the latent multi-view representation is able to describe the data more comprehensively than a single view, thereby producing more promising clustering results.

2.1 Introduction to Schatten-P Norm

Consider applying the singular value decomposition on $X \in R^{m \times n}$. Then, we have $X = U diag(\sigma_i(X))V^T$, where $\sigma_i(X)$ denotes the ith singular value. The Schatten-p norm of X is defined as

$$\|X\|_{S_p} = (\sum_{i=1}^{\min(m,n)} \sigma_i^p(X))^{\frac{1}{p}}. \tag{1}$$

Therefore, the Schatten-p norm of a matrix X to the power p can be written as:

$$\|X\|_{S_p}^p = \sum_{i=1}^{\min(m,n)} \sigma_i^p. \tag{2}$$

Note that the Schatten-p norm includes the nuclear norm ($p=1$) and the Frobenius norm ($p=2$). Figure 1 shows the input-output relationship of the Schatten-p norm. When $p \to 0$, the Schatten-p norm approximates the rank function.

2.2 Objective Function

The subspace clustering is guaranteed by imposing the constraints on the reasonable latent representation and the subspace reconstruction, while the latent representation is guaranteed by the complementation of the multiple views and improved by the subspace reconstruction. Considering the robustness to outliers and the low rank property, we have:

$$\min_{(P,H,Z,E_h,E_r)} \quad \|E_h\|_{2,1} + \lambda_1 \|E_r\|_{2,1} + \lambda_2 \|Z\|_{S_p}^p$$

$$\text{s.t. } X = PH + E_h, \ H = HZ + E_r \text{ and } PP^T = I. \tag{3}$$

where $\|\cdot\|_{S_p}$ represents the Schatten-p norm, $\|\cdot\|_{1,2}$ represents the $l_{1,2}$ norm, X represents the observations of different views, H represents the shared latent representation, P represents the reconstruction models, Z is the reconstruction coefficient matrix and E represents the error term. The columns of E_h and E_r, can further be concatenated together and optimized jointly. Then, the final objective function becomes the following:

$$\min_{(P,H,Z,E_h,E_r)} \quad \|E\|_{2,1} + \lambda \|Z\|_{S_p}^p$$

$$\text{s.t. } X = PH + E_h, \ H = HZ + E_r,$$

$$E = [E_h; E_r] \text{ and } PP^T = I. \tag{4}$$

2.3 Model Optimization

Although the objective function is not convex for all variables P, H, Z, E_h, and E_r, the Augmented Lagrangian Multiplier (ALM) approach is an effective method for solving the problem. It fixes other variables and leaves a single variable for optimization at each sub-problem. Since it is difficult to solve Z directly, the variable J is introduced and we let $J = Z$. The objective function can then be transformed from (4) into the ALM form:

$$\min_{(P,H,Z,E_h,E_r)} \quad \mathfrak{I}(P,H,Z,E_h,E_r,J) = \|E\|_{2,1} + \lambda \|J\|_{S_p}^p$$

$$+ tr(Y_1^T(X - PH - E_h)) + tr(Y_2^T(H - HZ - E_r)) + tr(Y_3^T(J - Z))$$

$$+ \frac{\mu}{2}(\|Y_1 - X + PH + E_h\|_F^2 + \|Y_2 - H + HZ + E_r\|_F^2 + \|Y_3 - J + Z\|_F^2)$$

$$\text{s.t. } PP^T = I. \tag{5}$$

The update is shown in Algorithm 1.

3 Experiments

3.1 Datasets

To demonstrate the effectiveness of our proposed method, we used the following five image datasets for our experiments. They are design patent dataset[1], ORL dataset [2], Coil-20 dataset [17], Extend Yale B dataset [10], and Yaleface

---

[1] https://iplab.gpnu.edu.cn/info/1044/1608.htm.

Algorithm 1. Improved latent MVSC algorithm.

Input: X: Multi-view matrices:$\{X^{(1)}, \cdots, X^{(V)}\}$; λ: the hyper-parameter; H: the latent representation; K: the dimension.

Initialization: $P_0 = I, E_{r,0} = 0, E_{h,0} = 0, J_0 = 0, Z_0 = 0, Y_{1,0} = 0, Y_{2,0} = 0, Y_{3,0} = 0, H_0$ as a random matrix, $k = 0, \mu_0 = 10^{-6}, \rho = 1.1, \varepsilon = 10^{-4}$, and $\overline{\mu} = 10^6$

while not converged **do**

    Update P through $P = U_Z V_Z^T$ and $(Y_1^T - \mu(Y_1 - X + E_h)^T)H = U_Z D_Z V_Z^T$;

    Update H through $\frac{P^T Y_1 + Y_2^T (Z-I)}{\mu} - P^T(Y_1 - X + E_h) - (Y_2 + E_r)^T(Z - I) = (H(Z - I)(Z - T)^T + P^T PH)$;

    Update Z through $Z = (H^T H + I)^{-1}(\frac{H^T Y_2 + Y_3}{\mu} + (J - Y_3 - H^T(Y_2 - H + E_r)))$;

    Update J through $\mu J_{m,n} + \lambda p \left| J_{m,n}^{p-1} \right| \text{sgn}(J_{m,n}) + C_{m,n} = 0.$;

    Update E through $\mathfrak{I}_E(E) = \|E\|_{2,1} tr(Y_1^T(X - PH - E_h)) + tr(Y_2^T(H - HZ - E_r)) + \frac{\mu}{2}(\|Y_1 - X + PH + E_h\|_F^2 + \|Y_2 - H + HZ + E_r\|_F^2)$;

    Update Y_1 ; Y_2 and Y_3 through $Y_{1,k+1} = Y_{1,k} + \mu_k(X_k - P_k H_k - E_{h,k})$, $Y_{2,k+1} = Y_{2,k} + \mu_k(H_k - H_k Z_k - E_{r,k})$ and $Y_{3,k+1} = Y_{3,k} + \mu_k(J_k - Z_k)$ respectively

    Update μ via $\mu_{k+1} = \min(\rho\mu, \overline{\mu})$.

    Check the convergence conditions:

    $\|X - P_k H_k - E_{h,k}\|_\infty < \varepsilon, \|H_k - H_k Z_k - E_{r,k}\|_\infty < \varepsilon$ or $\|J_k - Z_k\|_\infty < \varepsilon$;

end while

Construct the similarity matrix $S = \frac{\left|(Z^v)^T + Z^v\right|}{s}$;

Calculate the Laplacian matrix L and obtain the eigen matrix F. Here, the columns of F are the eigenvectors of L corresponding to the largest k eigenvalues of L. Finally, the K means algorithm is used for performing the clustering.

Output: The multi-view representation Z

---

dataset [20]. The details of these five datasets can be found in the corresponding references. Figure 2 shows some sample images of the these five datasets. First, the color images are converted into grayscale images. Then, three features are extracted, including the local binary (LBP) map [15], the local directional gradient histogram (HoG) [5] and the Gabor filtered texture [5]. These three features are employed because different features reflect different information of the images. The multi-view training set used in our experiments is constructed with these three features.

3.2   Experimental Results

In this section, we first analyzed the effect of different values of p on the clustering results. In our experiments, we utilized the design patent dataset for validation and repeated 30 times to obtain the average values of ACC (accuracy) and NMI (normalized mutual information). Note that higher values indicate better performance for both metrics. As can be seen in Fig. 3, the highest values for NMI and ACC are achieved when the value of p is equal to 0.1. Therefore, in the following experiments, we set p = 0.1.

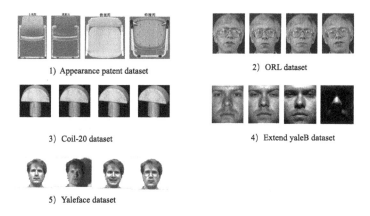

1) Appearance patent dataset

2) ORL dataset

3) Coil-20 dataset

4) Extend yaleB dataset

5) Yaleface dataset

Fig. 2. Sample images of the datasets used in our experiments.

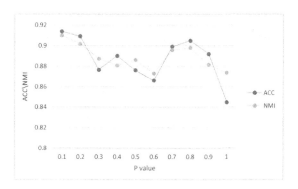

Fig. 3. Performance of clustering with different values of p.

To evaluate the clustering performance, we compared our method with some typical algorithms based on single view and multiple views, including LRR_{BestSV} [12], DiMSC [3], FMR [11], LMSC [22], and LT_MSC [21].

For evaluation metrics, we use NMI (normalized mutual information) and ACC (accuracy), we run 30 times for each method and report the mean values and standard deviations. Tables 1, 2, 3, 4 and 5 show the NIM and ACC measured by various methods on the above five datasets, respectively. It can be seen that our proposed method outperforms other methods on all five datasets, especially on the design patent dataset and the Coil-20 dataset. The results show that combining multiple views and using the Schatten-p norm as an approximation of rank function minimization yields better and more stable results.

Table 1. Performances comparison of clustering for design patent dataset.

Methods	ACC	NMI
LRR$_{BestSV}$	0.8371 ± 0.0640	0.8104 ± 0.0249
DiMSC	0.7462 ± 0.0008	0.6597 ± 0.0008
FMR	0.7783 ± 0.0599	0.8407 ± 0.0261
LT_MSC	0.7558 ± 0.0026	0.8712 ± 0.0009
LMSC	0.7568 ± 0.0073	0.8601 ± 0.0173
Sp_LMSC	**0.9094 ± 0.0500**	**0.8984 ± 0.0292**

Table 2. Performances comparison of clustering for ORL dataset.

Methods	ACC	NMI
LRR$_{BestSV}$	0.7362 ± 0.0226	0.8774 ± 0.0096
DiMSC	0.6684 ± 0.0216	0.8173 ± 0.0096
FMR	0.2580 ± 0.0145	0.5121 ± 0.012
LT_MSC	0.7631 ± 0.0180	0.8948 ± 0.0069
LMSC	0.6408 ± 0.0266	0.8250 ± 0.0117
Sp_LMSC	**0.7894 ± 0.0240**	**0.9021 ± 0.0127**

Table 3. Performances comparison of clustering for Coil-20 dataset.

Methods	ACC	NMI
LRR$_{BestSV}$	0.8551 ± 0.0571	0.8758 ± 0.0424
DiMSC	0.6478 ± 0.0185	0.5860 ± 0.0117
FMR	0.7856 ± 0.0102	0.8354 ± 0.0150
LT_MSC	0.8217 ± 0.0530	0.8844 ± 0.0302
LMSC	0.8829 ± 0.0415	0.9066 ± 0.0178
Sp_LMSC	**0.9692 ± 0.0025**	**0.9544 ± 0.0029**

Table 4. Performances comparison of clustering for Extend Yale B dataset

Methods	ACC	NMI
LRR$_{BestSV}$	0.5847 ± 0.0100	0.5959 ± 0.0053
DiMSC	0.4903± 0.0259	0.4723 ± 0.0197
FMR	0.5128 ± 0.0176	0.5311 ± 0.0145
LT_MSC	0.5649 ± 0.0337	0.6018 ± 0.0159
LMSC	0.4258 ± 0.0363	0.4573 ± 0.1023
Sp_LMSC	**0.6257 ± 0.0119**	**0.6696 ± 0.0135**

Table 5. Performances comparison of clustering for Yaleface dataset.

Methods	ACC	NMI
LRR$_{BestSV}$	0.6395 ± 0.0262	0.7005 ± 0.0095
DiMSC	0.6224 ± 0.0364	0.6875 ± 0.0226
FMR	0.6309 ± 0.0269	0.6889 ± 0.0208
LT_MSC	0.5591 ± 0.0290	0.6529 ± 0.0146
LMSC	0.6432 ± 0.0196	0.7109 ± 0.0189
Sp_LMSC	**0.6644 ± 0.0263**	**0.7120 ± 0.0178**

4   Conclusion

This paper proposed a MVSC algorithm via maximizing the original feature information under the assumption that each view is derived from a latent representation. By using the Schatten-p norm approach, it achieves the better rank minimization compared with the conventional nuclear norm approach and improves the quality of low-dimensional representations for subspace learning. The effectiveness of our proposed method is demonstrated via comparing with five classical algorithms on five datasets.

References

1. Bickel, S., Scheffer, T.: Multi-view clustering. In: ICDM, vol. 4, pp. 19–26 (2004)
2. Cai, D., He, X., Hu, Y., Han, J., Huang, T.: Learning a spatially smooth subspace for face recognition. In: CVPR, pp. 1–7. IEEE (2007)
3. Cao, X., Zhang, C., Fu, H., Liu, S., Zhang, H.: Diversity-induced multi-view subspace clustering. In: CVPR, pp. 586–594 (2015)
4. Chaudhuri, K., Kakade, S.M., Livescu, K., Sridharan, K.: Multi-view clustering via canonical correlation analysis. In: AICML, pp. 129–136 (2009)
5. Dalal, N., Triggs, B.: Histograms of oriented gradients for human detection. In: CVPR, vol. 1, pp. 886–893. IEEE (2005)
6. De Sa, V.R.: Spectral clustering with two views. In: ICML Workshop on Learning with Multiple Views, pp. 20–27 (2005)
7. Deng, C., Lv, Z., Liu, W., Huang, J., Tao, D., Gao, X.: Multi-view matrix decomposition: a new scheme for exploring discriminative information. In: IJCAI (2015)
8. Guo, Y.: Convex subspace representation learning from multi-view data. In: AAAI, vol. 27, no. 1, pp. 387–393 (2013)
9. Hu, Y., Zhang, D., Ye, J., Li, X., He, X.: Fast and accurate matrix completion via truncated nuclear norm regularization. PAMI **35**(9), 2117–2130 (2012)
10. Lee, K.C., Ho, J., Kriegman, D.J.: Acquiring linear subspaces for face recognition under variable lighting. PAMI **27**(5), 684–698 (2005)
11. Li, R., Zhang, C., Hu, Q., Zhu, P., Wang, Z.: Flexible multi-view representation learning for subspace clustering. In: IJCAI, pp. 2916–2922 (2019)
12. Liu, G., Lin, Z., Yan, S., Sun, J., Yu, Y., Ma, Y.: Robust recovery of subspace structures by low-rank representation. PAMI **35**(1), 171–184 (2012)

13. Liu, G., Yan, S.: Latent low-rank representation for subspace segmentation and feature extraction. In: ICCV, pp. 1615–1622. IEEE (2011)
14. Lu, C., Yan, S., Lin, Z.: Convex sparse spectral clustering: single-view to multi-view. IEEE Trans. Image Process. **25**(6), 2833–2843 (2016)
15. Ojala, T., Pietikainen, M., Maenpaa, T.: Multiresolution gray-scale and rotation invariant texture classification with local binary patterns. PAMI **24**(7), 971–987 (2002)
16. Patel, V.M., Van Nguyen, H., Vidal, R.: Latent space sparse subspace clustering. In: CVPR, pp. 225–232 (2013)
17. Rate, C., Retrieval, C.: Columbia object image library (coil-20). Computer (2011)
18. Vinokourov, A., Cristianini, N., Shawe-Taylor, J.: Inferring a semantic representation of text via cross-language correlation analysis. NIPS **15**, 1497–1504 (2002)
19. White, M., Yu, Y., Zhang, X., Schuurmans, D.: Convex multi-view subspace learning. In: NIPS, pp. 1682–1690. Lake Tahoe, Nevada (2012)
20. Xu, Y., Fang, X., Li, X., Yang, J., You, J., Liu, H., Teng, S.: Data uncertainty in face recognition. IEEE Trans. Cybern. **44**(10), 1950–1961 (2014)
21. Zhang, C., Fu, H., Liu, S., Liu, G., Cao, X.: Low-rank tensor constrained multiview subspace clustering. In: ICCV, pp. 1582–1590 (2015)
22. Zhang, C., Hu, Q., Fu, H., Zhu, P., Cao, X.: Latent multi-view subspace clustering. In: CVPR, pp. 4279–4287 (2017)
23. Zhao, H., Ding, Z., Fu, Y.: Multi-view clustering via deep matrix factorization. In: AAAI (2017)

Security and Privacy

MOFIT: An Efficient Access Control Scheme with Attribute Merging and Outsourcing Capability for Fog-Enhanced IoT

Richa Sarma[✉] and Ferdous Ahmed Barbhuiya

Indian Institute of Information Technology Guwahati, Guwahati, India
{richa,ferdous}@iiitg.ac.in

Abstract. The advancement of technology in the modern era has accelerated the growth of Internet of things (IoT) resulting in an exponential increase in the number of connected devices and the generated data. This encouraged the development of paradigm fog computing, which facilitates data analysis and processing at the edge. Along with fog, cloud co-exists to provide various services such as massive storage, processing resources, etc. However, data storage and computation at multiple levels raise the risk of data security. Ciphertext-policy attribute-based encryption (CP-ABE) is a well-known cryptographic technique for providing fine-grained access control. Unfortunately, the existing CP-ABE schemes do not support the functionality of *attribute merging*. Therefore, we propose a CP-ABE scheme named MOFIT that solves this long-standing problem. Additionally, expensive encryption and decryption operations are outsourced to fog nodes, which reduces the computation overhead of resource-constrained IoT devices. Further, the task of attribute merging is also outsourced to the third party. The size of the secret key held by the data user is constant and remains unaltered during any updates. According to security and performance analysis, MOFIT is secure and suitable for IoT applications.

Keywords: Access control · IoT · Fog · Cloud · Attribute merging

1 Introduction

Cloud computing has emerged as a potential paradigm in the IT sector as it facilitates flexible on demand resources. However, the widespread use and popularity of IoT have imposed several challenges to the centralised cloud. As the number of IoT devices is increasing exponentially, sending all the large and frequent data generated by them to the distant cloud severely affects network bandwidth. In cases of latency-sensitive services like health monitoring, firefighting, etc., the cloud-IoT architecture suffers from transmission delay between the user's request and the cloud's response. Further, the IoT devices may not have a stable internet connection to connect to the geographically dispersed cloud. Therefore, to

© Springer Nature Switzerland AG 2022
H. Shen et al. (Eds.): PDCAT 2021, LNCS 13148, pp. 523–535, 2022.
https://doi.org/10.1007/978-3-030-96772-7_49

address the aforesaid issues, the paradigm Fog Computing [3] has been introduced, which involves using the computing and storage capabilities of networking devices such as switches, routers, etc. (known as fog nodes). These nodes are positioned between the cloud and end-devices, and some cloud-based services can be moved to the fog nodes, located near the end-users. Therefore, fog computing can be viewed as an extension of cloud computing at the edge that bridges IoT devices and the cloud, and enhances service quality. However, outsourcing the storage and computation of sensitive data to third parties (fog nodes and cloud) increases the risk of data security as such entities may access, disclose users' privacy, and even may share the data illegally. As a result, data security has become a primary concern of data owners. A solution is to allow data owners to encrypt their data before outsourcing. Traditional cryptosystems are not deemed adequate for this purpose since they do not provide efficient access control over encrypted data [7]. Ciphertext-policy attribute-based encryption (CP-ABE) [2] is a recently developed cryptosystem which provides fine-grained access control over encrypted data. In this cryptosystem, the encrypted data and the decryption keys are linked with the attributes (age, gender, department, etc.). The data owner encrypts his data using an attribute-based access policy, and any user having the decryption key of attributes that satisfies the access policy can decrypt the ciphertext.

The problem with the CP-ABE scheme is that it involves computationally expensive pairing and exponentiation operations, which restricts its usage for resource-constrained IoT devices. Green et al. [4] presented a CP-ABE scheme that outsources the decryption operations. In their scheme, a transformation key is generated through which the proxy partly decrypts the ciphertext and forwards it to the user, which greatly reduces the computation overhead of the data user. Similarly, the works [8,11,12] were proposed, which supports decryption outsourcing. Additionally, Zuo et al. [12] supports fog computing environment. But, for resource-constrained IoT devices, encryption also involves complex operations, which is challenging. Sarma et al. [9] presented a scheme that supports both encryption and decryption outsourcing to the fog nodes, which lowers the computation cost of the resource-constrained data owners and users. However, it does not support *attribute merging* functionality. As a matter of fact, none of the existing works support *attribute merging*.

The functionality of *attribute merging* is required when any existing attribute of the system is merged with another attribute. For example, consider an engineering college, which has IT and CSE departments. Suppose the college authorities want to merge the IT department with the CSE department. So, in this case, the authority needs to update the attribute IT with the attribute CSE in the system. This involves issuing keys related to attribute CSE to those users, who previously held attribute keys related to IT. Further, all the ciphertexts previously encrypted with the attribute IT needs to be updated with the attribute CSE. In CP-ABE systems, attribute merging is challenging as the same attributes are held by numerous users and used in several ciphertexts but it is a desirable feature for modern systems.

Contributions: In the following, we summarize the key contributions of MOFIT,

- It supports merging of different attributes of the system i.e. attribute merging, without disrupting the system. Additionally, the attribute merging task is handled by the third party that remarkably lowers the overhead on the user side.
- Considering the resource-limited nature of IoT devices, the complex operations involved during encryption and decryption are offloaded to the fog nodes. All the attribute-related expensive operations are performed by the fog nodes, leaving only a small and constant amount of computation for the data owner and user. Further, the data user needs to store only a constant size secret key, which remains unchanged even during any update.
- The conducted security and performance analysis shows that MOFIT is efficient and secure for IoT devices.

To the best of our knowledge, the proposed scheme MOFIT is the only scheme that supports the functionality of attribute merging.

Table 1. Notations

Notation	Description
G, G_T	Multiplicative cyclic groups
Γ	Access tree
$\mathbb{U}, |\mathbb{U}|$	Attribute universe and number of attributes in $\mathbb{U}$, respectively
$\mathbb{S}$	User's attribute set
k	Number of attributes held by the user
t	Number of attributes in Γ of ciphertext
a_k, a_l	Merging and merged attribute, respectively
m	Number of merging attributes
T_G, T_{G_T}	Time for an exponentiation operation in G and G_T, respectively
C_e	Time for a bilinear pairing operation

2   Background

In this section, we discuss some fundamental definitions.

Access Tree [10]: An access tree Γ is a way to express an access structure or access policy. In Γ, the non-leaf node x is a threshold gate that may be an AND or OR. For AND gate, $d_x = num_x$, and for OR gate, $d_x = 1$, where d_x and num_x denote the threshold value and the number of children of node x, respectively. In Γ, each leaf node x denotes an attribute and for such node $d_x = 1$. The attribute associated to the leaf node x is denoted by $att(x)$. Similarly, the parent and index of node x are represented by $parent(x)$ and $index(x)$, respectively.

Bilinear Pairing [5]: Let G and G_T be two bilinear pairing groups, where G is the source group with generator g, and G_T is the target group. Let p be their common order. The bilinear map $e : G \times G \to G_T$ has the following properties.

Bilinearity: $e(g_1^a, g_2^b) = e(g_1, g_2)^{ab}$, $\forall g_1, g_2 \in G$ and $a, b \in Z_p$.
Non-degeneracy: $e(g, g) \neq 1$.
Computable: $\forall\, g_1, g_2 \in G$, $e(g_1, g_2)$ must be computable.

Decisional Bilinear Diffie-Hellman Assumption (DBDH) [6]: For a computationally efficient bilinear map e, where $e : G \times G \to G_T$ and g is the generator of G, the challenger randomly selects the components $a, b, s \in Z_p$ and $R \in G_T$. The DBDH assumption thus says that the tuples (g, g^a, g^b, g^s, R) and $(g, g^a, g^b, g^s, e(g, g)^{abs})$ can not be differentiated with non-negligible advantage by any probabilistic polynomial-time algorithm.

3   System Model

The entities of the proposed Cloud-Fog-IoT system MOFIT are shown in Fig. 1.

Key Authority (KA). In MOFIT, the Key Authority KA manages the system, generates public parameters, and issues decryption keys to the legitimate users. Further, during attribute merging, it updates the public parameters and generates the update keys required to update the ciphertexts and attribute keys.

Cloud Service Provider (CSP). It provides numerous services to the end-users that primarily involve data storage to reduce the storage overhead of resource-limited data owners. Additionally, in MOFIT, when attributes are merged, it updates the corresponding ciphertexts and user's attribute keys.

Fog Node. It is an entity deployed close to the users. It partly encrypts and decrypts the ciphertext, which reduces the computation overhead of the user. Further, during attribute merging, the fog node generates the update keys required to update the ciphertexts.

Data Owner. It is an entity who owns the file. Before outsourcing, the data owner encrypts the file under an access policy of attributes to curtail the unauthorized access of the outsourced data.

Data User. It is an entity who wishes to access the file stored in the cloud. In MOFIT, to decrypt a ciphertext, a user must possess adequate attributes required to satisfy the access policy of the ciphertext.

Assumptions on Each Entity: The entity KA is fully trusted, as such it will not collude with other entities. CSP and fog nodes are considered as honest but curious entities i.e. they will carry out the responsibilities entrusted to them honestly but may be curious to learn about the received data. Further, users may not be honest and may attempt to collude with other users to get unauthorized access to the outsourced data.

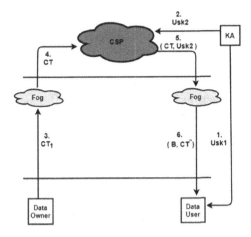

Fig. 1. Proposed system: MOFIT

4   Proposed Scheme: MOFIT

MOFIT is comprised of four phases, which are discussed as follows,

1. **Setup** $(\sigma) \rightarrow (PP, MSK)$**:** In this phase, system setup is done by the key
   authority KA. The KA takes security parameter σ as input, and chooses a
   pairing group G with large prime order p. It selects generator g, bilinear map
   $e : G \times G \rightarrow G_T$, and computes $e(g,g) \in G_T$. It also selects the elements
   $\beta, \alpha \in Z_p$ randomly, and computes $h = g^\beta$. Then, for each attribute $a_j \in$
   $\mathbb{U}$ ($1 \leq j \leq |\mathbb{U}|$), it randomly chooses $t_j \in Z_p$. Finally, it sets the master
   secret key MSK and public parameter PP as follows,

$$MSK = \{\beta, \alpha, \{t_j | a_j \in \mathbb{U}\}\}$$
$$PP = \{G, g, h, e(g,g)^\alpha, \{PK_j = g^{t_j} | a_j \in \mathbb{U}\}\}$$

2. **Key Generation** $(PP, MSK, \mathbb{S}) \rightarrow (U_{sk})$**:** In this phase, decryption key of
   a user u_{id} is generated by the KA. At first, the KA authenticates the user
   and allocates a set of attributes $\mathbb{S}$ to the legitimate user u_{id}. Then, it chooses
   a user-specific random number $r \in Z_p$ and also selects $\lambda \in Z_p$ randomly. It
   generates the decryption key U_{sk}, where $U_{sk} = \{U_{sk1}, U_{sk2}\}$ as follows,

$$U_{sk1} = \{D = g^{\alpha+\beta r}\},$$
$$U_{sk2} = \{D' = g^{\beta r}h^\lambda, D'' = g^\lambda, \forall a_j \in \mathbb{S} : D_j = g^{\beta r t_j^{-1}}\}$$

   Finally, the KA sends U_{sk1} securely to the user u_{id}, whereas attribute key U_{sk2}
   is sent to the cloud for storage. It may be noted that the secret key U_{sk1} stored
   by the user u_{id} is of constant size.

3. **Encryption.** In this phase, the plaintext of the data owner is encrypted. At
   first, the owner partially encrypts the message M using *Encrypt.Owner* algorithm and sends the partially encrypted ciphertext to the nearest fog node.

Next, the fog node using *Encrypt.Fog* algorithm re-encrypts it to facilitate data sharing and finally sends it to the cloud for storage. The detailed working of these algorithms are as follows,

- *Encrypt.Owner* $(M, PP, \Gamma) \rightarrow (CT_1)$: In this phase, the data owner partially encrypts the message M. At first, it randomly chooses $s \in Z_p$. It also chooses an access structure Γ, partially encrypts the message M, and generates the partial ciphertext CT_1 as follows,

$$CT_1 = \left\{ \Gamma, \widetilde{C} = M.e(g, g,)^{\alpha s}, C' = g^s, C'' = h^s \right\}$$

The data owner sends CT_1 for further encryption to the nearest fog node.

- *Encrypt.Fog* $(PP, CT_1) \rightarrow (CT)$: On receiving CT_1, the fog node selects a polynomial q_x of degree $d_x = k_x - 1$ for each node $x \in \Gamma$, where k_x is the threshold value for x. Further, it chooses $\overline{s} \in Z_p$ randomly for root node R of Γ, and sets $q_R(0) = \overline{s}$. In case of any other node x, it chooses a polynomial of degree d_x such that $q_x(0) = q_{parent(x)}(index(x))$. Additionally, it re-computes the components C' and C'' of CT_1 as $\widetilde{C'} = g^s g^{\overline{s}}$ and $\widetilde{C''} = h^s h^{\overline{s}}\}$, respectively. It also computes the component $\{C_j = g^{t_j q_x(0)}, \forall a_j = att(x) \in X\}$, where X is an attribute set related to the leaf nodes in Γ. Finally, it sets the final ciphertext as CT and sends it to the cloud for storage.

$$CT = \left\{ \begin{matrix} \Gamma, \widetilde{C} = M.e(g, g,)^{\alpha s}, C' = g^s, \widetilde{C'} = g^s g^{\overline{s}}, \widetilde{C''} = h^s h^{\overline{s}}, \\ \{\forall a_j = att(x) \in X : C_j = g^{t_j q_x(0)}\} \end{matrix} \right\}$$

4. **Decryption.** In this phase, ciphertext is decrypted and the plaintext is retrieved. It comprises of algorithms *Decrypt.Fog* and *Decrypt.User*. At first, the fog node using Decrypt.Fog algorithm partially decrypts the ciphertext and then, the data user using Decrypt.User algorithm further decrypts the partially decrypted ciphertext and accesses the message. The detailed working of these algorithms are as follows,

- *Decrypt.Fog* $(PP, CT, U_{sk2}) \rightarrow B$: On user's request, the cloud provides the user's attribute key U_{sk2} along with the ciphertext CT to the fog node. At first, the fog node divides CT into CT' and CT'', such that $CT' = \{\widetilde{C'}, \widetilde{C''}, \{\forall a_j \in X : C_j\}\}$ and $CT'' = \{\widetilde{C}, C'\}$. Then, it executes a recursive decryption algorithm $Node.Decrypt(CT', U_{sk2}, x)$, for all $x \in \Gamma$ as follows,

(a) Consider $a_j = att(x)$, if x is a leaf node. For $a_j \notin S$, the function $Node.Decrypt\ (CT', U_{sk2}, x)$ returns $\perp$. Further, for $att(x) \in S$, it does the following,

$$Node.Decrypt(CT', U_{sk2}, x) = e(D_j, C_j) = e(g^{\beta r t_j^{-1}}, g^{t_j q_x(0)})$$
$$= e(g, g)^{\beta r q_x(0)}$$

(b) For every node x, if x is a non-leaf node, the algorithm $Node.Decrypt$ (CT', U_{sk2}, x) is executed. Additionally, $Node.Decrypt(CT', U_{sk2}, z)$ is also called for all the child nodes of x, referred as z, and the output is stored in F_z. Let S_x represent a set of child nodes z, which is of size k_x and $F_z \neq \perp$. If no such set exists then $F_z = \perp$, else F_x is computed as,

$$F_x = \prod_{z \in S_x} F_z^{\Delta_{j,S'_x}(0)} = \prod_{z \in S_x} e(g,g)^{r\beta q_z(0)})^{\Delta_{j,S'_x}(0)} = e(g,g)^{r\beta q_x(0)}$$

where $j = \text{index}(z)$, $S'_x = \{\text{index}(z) : z \in S_x\}$.

(c) Finally, if the attribute set satisfies the access policy Γ, $Node.Decrypt$ (CT', U_{sk2}, z) calls root R of Γ and stores the output as F_R,

$$F_R = Node.Decrypt(CT', U_{sk2}, z) = e(g,g)^{r\beta q_R(0)} = e(g,g)^{\beta r \overline{s}}$$

(d) The fog node computes the component $\widetilde{A}$. Further, using $\widetilde{A}$ and F_R, it generates the partially decrypted ciphertext B as follows,

$$\widetilde{A} = \frac{e(D', \widetilde{C'})}{e(D'', \widetilde{C''})} = \frac{e(g^{r\beta}h^\lambda, g^s g^{\overline{s}})}{e(g^\lambda, h^s h^{\overline{s}})} = e(g,g)^{r\beta(s+\overline{s})}$$

$$B = \frac{\widetilde{A}}{F_R} = \frac{e(g,g)^{r\beta(s+\overline{s})}}{e(g,g)^{r\beta\overline{s}}} = e(g,g)^{r\beta s}$$

Finally, the fog node sends the partly decrypted ciphertext B to the corresponding user u_{id}, along with CT''.

• $Decrypt.User(CT'', B, U_{sk1}) \to M$: The data user u_{id} using it's secret key U_{sk1} decrypts the ciphertext and retrieves the message M as follows,

$$\frac{\widetilde{C} \cdot B}{e(C', D)} = \frac{M \cdot e(g,g)^{\alpha s} e(g,g)^{\beta rs}}{e(g^s, g^{\alpha + \beta r})} = M$$

5. **Attribute Merging.** Suppose in an engineering college, the authorities want to merge the IT department with the CSE department. Let the attributes IT and CSE be denoted as a_k and a_l, respectively. Therefore, in that case, all the components related to attribute a_k are required to be updated to attribute a_l. The attributes a_k and a_l may be called merging attribute and merged attribute, respectively. It includes the following,

• $PP.Update$ $(PP, a_k) \to (PP')$: In this phase, the KA updates the public attribute key component of PP as follows,

$$PP' = \left\{ \begin{array}{ll} G, g, h, e(g,g)^\alpha, \forall a_j \in \mathbb{U} : & \text{if } a_j \neq a_k, PK_j = g^{t_j} \\ & \text{else} \quad \text{remove } PK_k \end{array} \right\}$$

• $Ukey.Gen$ $(MSK, a_k, a_l) \to (U'_v, U''_v)$: The KA takes the master secret key MSK components t_k and t_l of attribute a_k and a_l, respectively, which are generated during system setup and outputs update keys U'_v and U''_v. It generates the update key U'_v for updating the attribute key of the user who posses attribute a_k in its attribute set $\mathbb{S}$. Similarly, it generates U''_v to update the ciphertexts possessing attribute a_k in their access policy Γ.

$$U'_v = t_k/t_l \qquad\qquad U''_v = t_l/t_k$$

Then, it sends the update keys U'_v and U''_v to the CSP.

• $KeyGen.Update\ (U_{sk2}, U'_v) \rightarrow (U'_{sk2})$: In this phase, the attribute key U_{sk2} of the user who possess attribute a_k in its attribute set $\mathbb{S}$ is updated using update key U'_v. The updated attribute key U'_{sk2} comprises of components related to attribute a_l. The CSP updates the attribute key U_{sk2} as,

$$U'_{sk2} = \left\{ \begin{array}{l} D' = g^{\beta r} h^\lambda, D'' = g^\lambda, \forall a_j \in \mathbb{S}: \quad \text{if } a_j \neq a_k, \ D_j = g^{\beta r t_j^{-1}} \\ \qquad\qquad\qquad\qquad\qquad\qquad\quad \text{else } D_{k \rightarrow l} = g^{\beta r t_k^{-1}}.U'_v \end{array} \right\}$$

• $CT.Update\ (CT, U''_v) \rightarrow (\overline{CT})$: Using this algorithm, the CSP updates those stored ciphertexts which possess attribute a_k in their access policy Γ. The ciphertext update mechanism varies in accordance with the structure of the access policy Γ of the ciphertext. Hence, the following three cases arise,

- Case 1: $\Gamma = (a_k \vee a_l)$.

When Γ contains an OR gate between a merging attribute a_k and merged attribute a_l, the CSP updates the ciphertext as follows.

$$\overline{CT} = \left\{ \begin{array}{c} \Gamma, \widetilde{C} = M.e(g,g,)^{\alpha s}, C' = g^s, \widetilde{C'} = g^s g^{\overline{s}}, \widetilde{C''} = h^s h^{\overline{s}}, \\ \forall a_j = att(x) \in X : \text{if } a_j \neq a_k, C_j = g^{t_j q_x(0)} \\ \text{else remove } C_k \end{array} \right\}$$

- Case 2: $\Gamma = (a_k \vee a_j) \vee a_j \neq a_l$.

When Γ contains an OR gate between a merging attribute a_k and any attribute $a_j \in \mathbb{U}$ except the merged attribute a_l, the fog node computes $Q_{x'} = \frac{q_{a_l}(0)}{q_{a_k}(0)}$ using $q_x(0)$ for $x = \{a_l, a_k\}$ used during $Encrypt.Fog$ phase, and sends it to the CSP. Next, the CSP taking $Q_{x'}$ and the update key U''_v as input, updates the ciphertext as,

$$\overline{CT} = \left\{ \begin{array}{c} \Gamma, \widetilde{C} = M.e(g,g,)^{\alpha s}, C' = g^s, \widetilde{C'} = g^s g^{\overline{s}}, \widetilde{C''} = h^s h^{\overline{s}}, \\ \forall a_j = att(x) \in X : \text{if } a_j \neq a_k, C_j = g^{t_j q_x(0)} \\ \text{else } C_{k \rightarrow l} = g^{t_k q_{a_k}(0)} Q_{x'} U''_v \end{array} \right\}$$

- Case 3: $\Gamma = (a_k \wedge a_j) \vee a_j \neq a_l$.

When Γ contains an AND gate between a merging attribute a_k and any attribute $a_j \in \mathbb{U}$ except the merged attribute a_l, the ciphertext update mechanism is same as Case 2.

5   Security Proof

Through theorem 1, the Chosen-Plaintext Attack (CPA) security proof of MOFIT is shown.

Theorem 1. *If there is a probabilistic polynomial-time PPT adversary $\mathcal{A}$ who can win MOFIT with a non-negligible advantage $\varepsilon > 0$, then the construction of a PPT simulator $\mathcal{B}$ can be done, which can solve DBDH problem with $\frac{\varepsilon}{2}$ advantage.*

Proof. Let G and G_T be bilinear groups, where g is the generator of G and p is their common order. Also, let e be a mapping function such that $e : G \times G \to G_T$. In the security game, the challenger $\mathcal{C}$ selects $s, a, b \in Z_p$ randomly, chooses $\vartheta \in \{0, 1\}$ and also chooses a random element $R \in G_T$. Further, if $\vartheta = 0$, it sets $Z = e(g, g)^{abs}$, else for $\vartheta = 1$, it sets $Z = R$. Then, it sends the components $< g, A, B, S, Z > = < g, g^a, g^b, g^s, Z >$ to the simulator $\mathcal{B}$ and requests to output ϑ. Next, $\mathcal{B}$ acts as a challenger to respond to this challenge in the following game.

- *Initialization.* In this phase, the adversary $\mathcal{A}$ chooses an access structure A^* in which it wishes to challenge and gives it to simulator $\mathcal{B}$.
- *Setup.* In the setup phase, the following is done by the simulator $\mathcal{B}$.
  At first, $\mathcal{B}$ randomly selects $\alpha' \in Z_p$ and sets $\alpha = \alpha' + ab$. Next, it calculates $u = e(g, g)^\alpha = e(g, g)^{\alpha'} \cdot e(g, g)^{ab}$, $h = g^\beta = g^b = B$. Then, for all $a_j \in \mathbb{U}$, $\mathcal{B}$ selects $v_j \in Z_p$ randomly and calculates $PK_j = g^{bv_j^{-1}} = g^{t_j}$ for $t_j = bv_j^{-1}$
  Finally, $\mathcal{B}$ gives the public parameter $PP = \{h, u, \{PK_j | \forall a_j \in \mathbb{U}\}$ to $\mathcal{A}$.
- *Phase 1.* Adversary $\mathcal{A}$ issues an attribute set $\mathbb{S}$ to simulator $\mathcal{B}$ and queries the secret keys. In fact, $\mathcal{A}$ can submit any random attribute set $\mathbb{S}$, for $\mathbb{S} \subseteq \mathbb{U}$ and $\mathbb{S} \nvDash A^*$ as many times as it wishes to $\mathcal{B}$. Simulator $\mathcal{B}$ randomly selects $r' \in Z_p$ and sets $r = r' - a$. Further, it generates $U_{sk1} = \{D = g^\alpha g^{\beta r} = g^{(\alpha'+ab)} g^{b(r'-a)} = g^{\alpha'+br'} = g^{\alpha'}.B^{r'}\}$ and $U_{sk2} = \{D' = g^{\beta r} h^\lambda = g^{\beta(r'-a)} h^\lambda = B^{(r'-a)} h^\lambda, D'' = g^\lambda, \forall a_j \in \mathbb{S} : D_j = g^{b^{-1} v_j r b} = g^{t_j^{-1}(r'-a)b} = B^{t_j^{-1}(r'-a)}\}$. Then, $\mathcal{B}$ issues the keys U_{sk1} and U_{sk2} to $\mathcal{A}$.
  Additionally, whenever any attribute merging occurs, the newly added attribute should be provided to $\mathcal{A}$ in such that a way that the new attribute set should not satisfy A^*.
- *Challenge.* The adversary $\mathcal{A}$ selects two challenge messages m_0 and m_1, which are of equal lengths and gives those to simulator $\mathcal{B}$. Then, $\mathcal{B}$ randomly selects $s \in Z_p$. It also randomly selects $\vartheta \in \{0, 1\}$ and outputs CT_1^*, where $CT_1^* = \{A^*, \widetilde{C} = m_\vartheta.e(g, g)^{\alpha s} = m_\vartheta.e(g, g)^{(\alpha'+ab)s} = m_\vartheta Z e(g, g)^{\alpha' s}, C' = g^s = S, C'' = h^s = g^{\beta s} = B^s\}$. Again, it randomly chooses $\overline{s} \in Z_p$ and outputs $CT^* = \{A^*, \widetilde{C} = m_\vartheta Z e(g, g)^{\alpha' s}, C' = S, \widetilde{C'} = g^s \cdot g^{\overline{s}} = S \cdot g^{\overline{s}}, \widetilde{C''} = h^s h^{\overline{s}} = g^{\beta(s+\overline{s})} = B^{(s+\overline{s})}\}$. At last, the ciphertext $CT^* = \{A^*, \widetilde{C}, C', \widetilde{C'}, \widetilde{C''}, C_j | \forall a_j \in A^*\}$ is sent to $\mathcal{A}$.
- *Phase 2.* The *Phase 1* is repeated.
- *Guess.* The adversary $\mathcal{A}$ generates his guess ϑ' of ϑ and gives it to simulator $\mathcal{B}$. Therefore, in the aforesaid game, if $\vartheta' = \vartheta$, then $\mathcal{B}$ outputs 0 to show that $Z = e(g, g)^{abs}$ else, to guess $Z = R$, the simulator $\mathcal{B}$ outputs 1 .
  Case 1: If $Z = e(g, g)^{abs}$, it implies CT^* is an available ciphertext. Therefore, $\mathcal{A}'s$ advantage is ε and thus, $Pr[\mathcal{B}(g, g^a, g^b, g^s, Z = e(g, g)^{abs}) = 0] = \frac{1}{2} + \varepsilon$.
  Case 2: If $Z = R$, it implies CT^* is random from $\mathcal{A}'s$ view and has no knowledge about ϑ. Thus, $Pr[\mathcal{B}(g, g^a, g^b, g^s, Z = R) = 0] = \frac{1}{2}$., in the DBDH security game, the overall advantage of simulator $\mathcal{B}$ is $\frac{1}{2}(Pr[\mathcal{B}(g, g^a, g^b, g^s, Z = e(g, g)^{abs}) = 0] + Pr[\mathcal{B}(g, g^a, g^b, g^s, Z = R) = 0]) - \frac{1}{2} = \frac{1}{2}(\frac{1}{2} + \varepsilon + \frac{1}{2}) - \frac{1}{2} = \frac{\varepsilon}{2}$

6   Performance Analysis

In this section, the performance of MOFIT is compared with the closely related schemes [8,9,11,12].

Comparison of Functionalities: The functionalities of MOFIT are compared to those of the works [8,9,11,12], as shown in Table 2. It can be seen that only MOFIT provides the features: attribute merging, encryption and decryption outsourcing, supports the fog computing environment, and is highly efficient[1] at the same time.

Table 2. Functional analysis

Schemes	Attribute merging	Encryption outsourcing	Decryption outsourcing	High efficiency	Fog computing
[12]	✗	✗	✔	✗	✔
[8]	✗	✗	✔	✗	✗
[9]	✗	✔	✔	✗	✔
[11]	✗	✗	✔	✗	✗
MOFIT	✔	✔	✔	✔	✔

Comparison of Computational Cost: The time required to execute different algorithms of MOFIT and the existing works [8,9,11,12] is shown through Table 3 and the notations can be found in Table 1. Starting from the key generation, we can see that in all the schemes, the time required for key generation grows in proportion to the number of attributes held by the user i.e. k. But, the time required by MOFIT is significantly less than the scheme [9] and similar to the schemes [8,11,12]. It can be noticed from the table that in schemes [8,11,12], the encryption time on data owner rises in proportion to the number of attributes linked to the access policy i.e. t. But, in MOFIT and the scheme [9], all such complex operations are offloaded to fog nodes, which leaves only a small and constant amount of computation for resource-limited data owners. Further, in comparison to scheme [9], MOFIT puts less encryption overhead on the data owner and the fog node, which makes the overall encryption time of MOFIT efficient. During decryption, in MOFIT and the schemes [8,9,11,12] complex attribute related operations are offloaded to a third party and the resource-limited data users need to do only a small and constant amount of computation. It can be observed that the decryption overhead on the data user in the schemes [11,12] and [8] is $2T_{G_T}$ and T_{G_T}, respectively, whereas in MOFIT and the scheme [9] it requires C_e time, which is higher than the schemes [8,11,12] but computationally tolerant by resource-limited data users. It can be noticed that the outsourced decryption time of the schemes [9,11,12] is significantly higher than MOFIT, which makes

---

[1] Key storage cost on data user is constant and expensive operations of encryption, decryption, and attribute merging are offloaded to the third party.

the overall decryption time of MOFIT efficient. Only MOFIT supports the functionality of attribute merging. The attribute merging time varies in accordance with the structure of access policy embedded in the ciphertext and as such three cases are considered, represented by Case 1–3, which have been discussed in Sect. 4. It can be observed from the table that the time required for attribute merging in Case 1 is less than in Cases 2 and 3 as in the former case only key update operation is required which takes mT_G time, whereas in the other two cases key update as well as ciphertext update operations are performed, which takes $2mT_G$ time.

Table 3. Computational cost comparison **DO:** Data owner, **EE:** External entity, **DU:** Data user

Algorithms	[11]	[9]	[8]	[12]	MOFIT
Key Generation	$(1 + k)T_G$	$(4 + 4k)T_G$	$(1 + k)T_G$	$(1 + k)T_G$	$(3 + k)T_G$
Encryption	**DO**	**DO**	**DO**	**DO**	**DO**
	$(2 + t)T_G + T_{G_T}$	$3T_G + T_{G_T}$	$(1 + t)T_G + T_{G_T}$	$(2 + t)T_G + T_{G_T}$	$2T_G + T_{G_T}$
	EE	**EE**	**EE**	**EE**	**EE**
	–	$2(1 + 2t)T_G$	–	–	$(2 + t)T_G$
Decryption	**DU**	**DU**	**DU**	**DU**	**DU**
	$2T_{G_T}$	C_e	T_{G_T}	$2T_{G_T}$	C_e
	EE	**EE**	**EE**	**EE**	**EE**
	$(3 + 3t)C_e$	$(2 + 3t)C_e$	$(1 + t)C_e$	$(3 + 3t)C_e$	$(2 + t)C_e$
Attribute Merging					**Case 1**
	–	–	–	–	mT_G
					Case 2
	–	–	–	–	$2mT_G$
					Case 3
	–	–	–	–	$2mT_G$

Experimental Analysis: The performance of MOFIT is compared with two recently published works (Zuo et al. [12], Sarma et al. [9]), which support IoT-fog-cloud framework like MOFIT, in this section. All the three schemes have been implemented using Pairing-Based Cryptography library (PBC) [1] in a commodity Laptop having Ubuntu 16.04 (64-bit) with an Intel Core i5 CPU running at 2.40 GHz and 3 GB RAM. A super-singular curve $y^2 = x^3 + x$ of degree 2 with group order 160 bit and base field of 512 bits has been chosen. Figure 2 shows the time required to execute the algorithms *Key generation*, *Encryption*, *Decryption*, and *Attribute merging* by varying the number of attributes. The results are the average of 10 trials. Starting from the key generation phase, it can be observed from Fig. 2(a) that the time required by MOFIT is significantly less than Sarma et al. and almost similar to Zuo et al. Next, Fig. 2(b) shows the encryption time on data owner. It can be noticed that in MOFIT and Sarma et al., the encryption time on data owner is small and constant, whereas in Zuo et al. it rises in proportion to the number of attributes in the access policy. This is because, in MOFIT and Sarma et al., all the complex operations related to the attributes are outsourced to the fog node, whereas in the case of Zuo et al., all

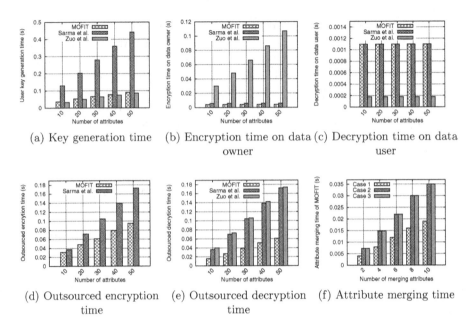

(a) Key generation time   (b) Encryption time on data (c) Decryption time on data
owner   user

(d) Outsourced encryption   (e) Outsourced decryption   (f) Attribute merging time
time   time

Fig. 2. Experimental results

such computations are done by the data owner. Further, it can be noticed that
MOFIT incurs less encryption overhead on the data owner than Sarma et al. The
time required for decryption on the data user has been shown through Fig. 2(c).
In all the three schemes, as the complex decryption operations are outsourced to
the fog node, the time required to execute the decryption operation by the data
user is small and constant. The data user in MOFIT and Sarma et al. needs
to execute only a pairing operation requiring 0.00114s and in Zuo et al., two
exponentiation operations on G_T is required which takes 0.00019 s, where it may
be noticed that both the values are computationally tolerant. Figures 2 (d) and
(e) show the outsourced encryption and decryption time, respectively on the fog
node. Only MOFIT and Sarma et al. support outsourced encryption and it can
be seen from Fig. 2 (d) that MOFIT requires significantly less time than Sarma
et al. Further, all the three schemes outsource decryption operation to the fog
node but it can be observed from Fig. 2 (e) that MOFIT requires considerably less
time than the other two schemes. Furthermore, only MOFIT supports attribute
merging. The time required by MOFIT during attribute merging has been shown
in Fig. 2 (f), where we have considered all the three cases, which have been
discussed in Sect. 4. It can be noticed that the attribute merging time rises in
proportion to the number of merging attributes. The time required for attribute
merging in Case 1 is less than in Cases 2 and 3, as in the former case only key
update operation is required whereas in the other two cases key update along
with ciphertext update operations are performed.

7   Conclusion

To realize fine-grained data access control, an attribute-based data sharing scheme named MOFIT has been proposed which addresses the issue of *attribute merging*. It also supports outsourcing of expensive encryption and decryption operations to fog nodes, leaving only a small and constant amount of computation to be performed locally on the user's device. Additionally, the task of attribute merging is also outsourced to the third party. The scheme is designed in such a way that the resource-constrained data user needs to store only a constant size key which remains unchanged throughout. Further, MOFIT is found to be secure against Chosen-plaintext attack under DBDH assumption. From the performance analysis, we can conclude that MOFIT can be efficiently employed for data sharing in IoT applications.

References

1. Pairing-Based Cryptography (PBC) library. http://crypto.stanford.edu/pbc/. Accessed 20 Oct 2021
2. Bethencourt, J., Sahai, A., Waters, B.: Ciphertext-policy attribute-based encryption. In: IEEE Symposium on Security and Privacy, pp. 321–334 (2007)
3. Bonomi, F., Milito, R., Zhu, J., Addepalli, S.: Fog computing and its role in the Internet of Things. In: MCC Workshop on Mobile Cloud Computing, pp. 13–16. ACM (2012)
4. Green, M., Hohenberger, S., Waters, B.: Outsourcing the decryption of ABE ciphertexts. In: USENIX Conference on Security, pp. 34–34. SEC 2011 (2011)
5. Guo, R., Yang, G., Shi, H., Zhang, Y., Zheng, D.: O3-R-CP-ABE: an efficient and revocable attribute-based encryption scheme in the cloud-assisted IoMT system. IEEE Internet Things J. **8**(11), 8949–8963 (2021)
6. He, Y., Wang, H., Li, Y., Huang, K., Leung, V.C.M., Yu, F.R., Ming, Z.: An efficient ciphertext-policy attribute-based encryption scheme supporting collaborative decryption with blockchain. IEEE Internet Things J. 1 (2021)
7. Horváth, M.: Attribute-based encryption optimized for cloud computing. In: Italiano, G.F., Margaria-Steffen, T., Pokorný, J., Quisquater, J.-J., Wattenhofer, R. (eds.) SOFSEM 2015. LNCS, vol. 8939, pp. 566–577. Springer, Heidelberg (2015). https://doi.org/10.1007/978-3-662-46078-8_47
8. Liu, H., Zhu, P., Chen, Z., Zhang, P., Jiang, Z.L.: Attribute-based encryption scheme supporting decryption outsourcing and attribute revocation in cloud storage. In: IEEE International Conference on Embedded and Ubiquitous Computing, vol. 1, pp. 556–561 (2017)
9. Sarma, R., Kumar, C., Barbhuiya, F.A.: Pac-fit: An efficient privacy preserving access control scheme for fog-enabled IoT. Sustain. Comput. Inform. Syst. **30**, 100527 (2021)
10. Yu, S., Wang, C., Ren, K., Lou, W.: Attribute based data sharing with attribute revocation. In: International Symposium on Information, Computer and Communications Security, pp. 261–270 (2010)
11. Zuo, C., Shao, J., Wei, G., Xie, M., Ji, M.: Chosen ciphertext secure attribute-based encryption with outsourced decryption. In: Liu, J.K., Steinfeld, R. (eds.) ACISP 2016. LNCS, vol. 9722, pp. 495–508. Springer, Cham (2016). https://doi.org/10.1007/978-3-319-40253-6_30
12. Zuo, C., Shao, J., Wei, G., Xie, M., Ji, M.: CCA-secure ABE with outsourced decryption for fog computing. Future Gen. Comp. Sys. **78**, 730–738 (2018)

RepBFL: Reputation Based Blockchain-Enabled Federated Learning Framework for Data Sharing in Internet of Vehicles

Haoyu Chen[1], Naiyue Chen[1(✉)], He Liu[1], Honglei Zhang[1], Jiabo Xu[1], Huaping Chen[2], and Yidong Li[1]

[1] School of Computer and Information Technology, Beijing Jiaotong University, Beijing 100044, China
{hychen95,nychen,liuhe1996,honglei.zhang,18281280,ydli}@bjtu.edu.cn
[2] QI-ANXIN Technology Group Inc., Beijing 100044, China
chenhuaping@qianxin.com

Abstract. Internet of Vehicles (IoV) enables the integration of smart vehicles with Internet and collaborative analysis from shared data among vehicles. Machine learning technologies show significant advantages and efficiency for data analysis in IoV. However, the user data could be sensitive in nature, and the reliability and efficiency of sharing these data is hard to guarantee. Moreover, due to the intermittent and unreliable communications of various distributed vehicles, the traditional machine learning algorithms are not suitable for heterogeneous IoV network. In this paper, we propose a novel reputation mechanism framework that integrates the IoV with blockchain and federated learning named RepBFL. In this framework, blockchain is used to protect the shared data between the vehicles. The Road Side Units (RSU) select the high reputation vehicular nodes to share their data for federated learning. To enhance the security and reliability of the data sharing process, we develop the reputation calculated mechanism to evaluate the reliability of all vehicles in IoV. The proposed framework is feasible for the large heterogeneous vehicular networks and perform the collaborative data analysis in distributed vehicles. The experimental results show that the proposed approach can improve the data sharing efficiency. Furthermore, the reputation mechanism is able to deal with malicious behaviors effectively.

Keywords: Data sharing · Internet of Vehicles · Reputation mechanism · Federated learning · Blockchain

Supported in part by the Fundamental Research Funds for the Central Universities(2021YJS304) and 2020 Industrial Internet Innovation and Development Project.

H. Shen et al. (Eds.): PDCAT 2021, LNCS 13148, pp. 536–547, 2022.
https://doi.org/10.1007/978-3-030-96772-7_50

1   Introduction

Internet of Vehicles (IoV) is an open heterogeneous network composed of vehicular Ad-Hoc Network (VANET) and Mobile Internet. The IoV network provides a platform for vehicles to communicate and share data with their neighbors, e.g., time stamped location, traffic conditions and weather data, etc. It not only facilitates to establish secure and reliable intelligent transportation system (ITS), but also provides vehicles extensive high-quality service. However, due to the high mobility and variability of vehicular networks, it brings serious challenges to the computing efficiency and privacy preserving of vehicles in IoV. There may be some malicious nodes in the network, deliberately broadcasting false messages to affect the decision-making and normal driving of other vehicles. Therefore, the security of IoV network is directly related to the personal information security and life safety.

Federated learning based data sharing process is a promising distributed machine learning method for training a global model on decentralized data. Federated learning addresses the privacy concerns to a large content that local model training by all participants only use own data and share the model training parameter to servers during the transmission process. This mechanism can not only achieve efficient communication and improve the quality of IoV application, but also reduce the risk of privacy leakage. Thus, federated learning achieves vehicular intelligence by learning from distributed data in a privacy preserved manner [1].

To combat the security issue, blockchain has become a promising technology that can provide solutions towards the distributed security issues [2,3]. The blockchain adopts decentralized storage and consensus mechanism to guarantee data security. It also uses cryptographic methods to ensure that data cannot be tampered or forged. With these advanced features, blockchain based federated learning has attracted significant attention in secure data sharing process [4–7].

However, there remain several issues in applying federated learning to the real world. Most existing federated learning paradigms allow all nodes participate in training process. Due to difference of computing skills, biases or malicious tampering, federated learning is vulnerable to adversarial manipulations by malicious participants, which can negatively impact the learned model. For instance, malicious participants can corrupt the global model via poisoning their local training data (known as data poisoning attacks) or their local model updates sent to the server (called local model poisoning attacks) [8]. To address the aforementioned issues, we propose a novel *Reputation based Blockchain-enabled Federated Learning* (RepBFL) framework. We summarize our contributions below:

- We propose RepBFL framework to provides security and effective mechanism for each vehicles in IoV while preventing unreliable nodes participating in model training.
- RepBFL utilizes a reputation mechanism to iteratively evaluate the credibility of all participant in IoV. Moreover, the reputation of each participant is not only based on its own shared data, but also based on the evaluation computed from other participating vehicles.

- Experiments demonstrate that our proposed framework can effectively evaluate the credibility of nodes and is robust against the malicious attacks while maintaining competitive accuracy.

The remainder of this paper is organized as follows. We first give the overview of related literature in Sect. 2 and problem setting in Sect. 3. Then, we develop our proposed RepBFL framework to achieve secure data sharing in IoV in Sect. 4. Next, we analyze the security of the proposed solution in Sect. 5. Finally, the numerical results are provided in Sect. 6, and conclusions are made in Sect. 7.

2   Related Work

The concept of trusted data sharing has drawn much attention recently, as a promising approach to address the issue of security and reliability in vehicular data sharing process. Recently, federated learning has emerged for edge nodes collaboratively training a shared model while keeping all the data on their own devices [9]. However, multiple studies showed that the global model's accuracy can be significantly decreased by malicious clients [10,11]. Malicious clients can substantially degrade the testing accuracy of a global model via carefully tampering their model updates sent to the server. The adversary will launch malicious attacks to disturb the federated learning process, which causes the central server and edge nodes are vulnerable to be comprised. To address these security challenges, previous work has explored the federated learning framework design or attack defenses methods [12].

In order to deal with the security issues during the data sharing process, blockchain technology has been widely studied in IoV to establish distributed trust. One popular domain is using blockchain for trust management and data sharing. Wang et al. [13] proposed a blockchain-enabled vehicular edge computing (VEC) system for secure and efficient resource sharing, in which a permissioned blockchain architecture was introduced to incentivize parked vehicles (PV) in an effective and safe way has great potential to join the vehicle network to share its idle computing and network resources. Yang et al. [14] proposed a decentralized trust management system for vehicle networks based on blockchain technology. Vehicles can use Bayesian inference models to verify messages received from neighboring vehicles. All RSUs jointly maintain an updated, reliable and consistent trust zone. Jiang et al. [15] researched how to extend the blockchain technology to the application of the vehicle network, and proposed a model for the outward transmission of blockchain data and Kang et al. [16] proposed a reputation-based data sharing scheme to ensure high-quality data sharing between vehicles.

Besides, it is crucial to guarantee privacy-preserving during the data sharing process. Luo et al. [17] proposed a trust-based location privacy protection scheme based on blockchain in VANET, in which a trust-based anonymous cloaking region construction procedure was by introducing the proposed trust management method into distributed k-anonymity. Lu et al. [18] proposed an asynchronous joint learning scheme for learning models from edge data, and Gai et al.

[19] proposed a privacy-preserving approach solving the task allocation problem in edge computing that utilizes blockchain's characteristics. They also explored the implementation of differential privacy technique in blockchain system, in order to prevent information on blocks from data mining-based attacks.

However, most existing works still cannot guarantee the reliability of shared data from each vehicle. As a result, the secure mechanism may be broken by strong attacks, which is carefully craft the model updates sent from the malicious clients to the server. It is necessary to improve existing blockchain and federated learning algorithms towards secure data sharing in IoV, which can improve the learning efficiency and guarantee the reliability of the shared data. In this case, we propose a reputation based blockchain-enabled federated learning framework for trusted data sharing process in IoV.

3   System Model

The RepBFL framework utilizes reputation mechanism to guarantee the quality and reliability of data sharing process in IoV and implement the blockchain-based federated learning method to learn the shared data. The RepBFL framework is presented in Fig. 1, in which consists of reputation layer and learning layer. For the learning layer, vehicles follow diverse driving route and continuously collect environmental data in different regions to implement federated learning process. In order to incentive more participating vehicles to share their data and improve the security of the sharing and learning process, blockchain is adopted for recording the shared data collected by the vehicles. In the reputation layer, reputation mechanism is utilized to avoid the malicious vehicular nodes and guarantee the reliability of the shared data. Furthermore, the reputation value can be the fundamental basis of the node selection, which can select the representative vehicular nodes to improve the learning efficiency.

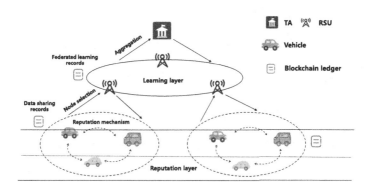

Fig. 1. The architecture of RepBFL framework

There are three crucial components in IoV includes Trusted Authority (TA), Road Side Units (RSU) and Vehicle. We provide a short summary for each role as follows.

TA. TA is the trusted security and the highest authority center in IoV, which is responsible for registration, identity verification and global aggregation in federated learning. After local training by RSUs, the TA collects current local data model from the RSUs and perform the global aggregation.

RSU. RSUs are widely deployed on the roadside based on the variety of locations and communication ranges. It can not only ensure that the devices constantly collect the real-time data shared by vehicles, but also make it possible to train the federated learning model using the new shared data in time. Moreover, RSUs are responsible for calculating the reputation value of vehicles in their area and selecting the high reputation vehicles as shared data within their communication ranges, which can improve the efficiency of federated learning and guarantee the reliability of shared data.

Vehicle. Vehicles are responsible for periodically collecting and broadcasting the current position, direction, acceleration, road conditions, traffic incidents, surrounding environmental data and other safety information, which make the traffic management system and other vehicles have a better perception of the traffic environment. There are multiple vehicular chains in each RSU area, in which different chains can record vehicular shared data to guarantee the security of data sharing process.

4   Reputation Model

Vehicles can share data and perform transactions through direct communication in IoV. However, the openness of IoV network cannot avoid the nodes with malicious behavior, which makes vehicles often do not know each other and lack mutual trust. Therefore, it is necessary to design a secure and efficient method, which can establish trusted mechanism for vehicles to share their data and avoid unqualified data to affect the training efficiency and accuracy. In this paper, we propose a reputation calculation mechanism for each vehicles in IoV to evaluate the reliability of vehicles.

The reputation mechanism proposed in this paper is divided into two layers: the first layer is the reward layer; the other layer is the penalty layer. In the reward layer, it gives the vehicles reward based on the quality of shared data and the evaluation of the other vehicles. Penalty layer is the punishment of negative sharing process which will decrease the reputation.

Local Reputation. Local reputation is calculated based on the contribution of shared data. In order to reflect the objectivity and accuracy, we consider the following factors to calculate local reputation.

Accuracy Contribution: Accuracy contribution (Ac) is the degree to which the model accuracy is improved [5]. Assume that the loss of global model before and after t-th slot of V_i are denoted as l_i^{t-1} and l_i^t respectively. When the loss of global model reduces after the t-th round, $l_i^t < l_i^{t-1}$, it means the shared data is useful. Then the Ac of V_i in t-th round is calculated as Eq. 1.

$$Ac_t = \log_2 \left[1 + \frac{-\left(l_i^t - l_i^{t-1}\right)}{l_i^{t-1}} \right] \tag{1}$$

Sharing Frequency: Sharing frequency (L_f) is the number of times that a vehicular node communicates to share its own data in time window T. The higher sharing frequency means the node has a positive attitude. In a period of time T, the more communications are made, the more scores will be earned correspondingly.

Sharing Quantity: Sharing quantity (L_q) is the amount of data shared by a vehicle in one time. It reflects the willingness of vehicular nodes to share data. The more data shared, the more contribution the node made, so the reputation will be correspondingly higher.

In addition, we use L_f^s and L_q^s to indicate the number of successful sharing frequency and successful sharing quantity according to the Ac. When the uploaded parameters is useful for the global model, $Ac > 0$, it means the shared data is successful. We consider that all of vehicles have the same evaluation criteria to calculate their local reputation. According the factors, we have the local reputation L_i as Eq. 2.

$$L_i = \frac{L_f^s \cdot L_q^s}{L_f \cdot L_q} \tag{2}$$

Global Reputation. Global reputation is calculated based on the evaluation of other vehicles in the same communication area. It reflects the feedback given by other nodes according to the quality of the data shared by the V_i. After V_i performs data sharing process, other nodes will evaluate the quality of the shared data and give their own evaluations in each round. The related factors for different evaluation are as follows.

Feedback: Feedback (f) is the appreciation of other vehicle for V_i. The positive interaction means that the vehicles believe that the shared data by V_i is useful and true. f_p is the number of positive feedback and f_n is the number of negative feedback. If V_i receives more positive feedback, it will increase the overall global reputation. On the contrary, if V_i receives more negative feedback, it will decrease the overall global reputation. One problem here is that we cannot know the reliability of other vehicles. If there are colluding malicious nodes in system, they will deliberately give more positive feedback to themselves. Therefore, we introduce credibility factor (C) for evaluating the credibility of vehicles.

$$f_i = \frac{f_p}{f_p + f_n} \tag{3}$$

Credibility: C is the credibility of participating vehicular nodes. If the credibility of a node is higher, the evaluation it gives is more trustworthy. In contrast, the evaluation given by a node with low credibility is not credible. Thus, the credibility of V_i is defined as:

$$C_i^e = \begin{cases} 0.5, & e = 0 \\ \sum_{i=1}^{e} (1 - |G_i^e - L_i^e|), & e > 0 \end{cases} \tag{4}$$

where C is related to the current reputation and credibility of other evaluated nodes in round e. Then the global reputation can be calculated as Eq. 5.

$$G_i = \frac{\sum_{k=1}^{e} f_i * C_i}{e} \tag{5}$$

Time Decay. In actual situation, the weight of reputation should be different in each iteration. The recent data sharing process has a higher impact on the reputation calculated. The weight of historical data sharing process will decrease with time growth. When a new sharing process occurs, because the total number has changed, we not only need to calculate the time decay factor of the new process, but also need to update the time decay factor of the historical process.

$$t = T_i - t_0 \tag{6}$$

$$T_i = \frac{t}{(t + \sum_{i=1}^{e} t_i)} \tag{7}$$

where T_i is the current time, t_0 is the initial time, with the t-th data sharing process of V_i. According to the above factors, the reward layer R_i can be calculated by Eq. 8.

$$R_i = (\alpha * L_i + \beta * G_i) \cdot T_i \tag{8}$$

Here, the parameter α represents the weight of local reputation and β represents the weight of global reputation, where $\alpha + \beta = 1$.

Penalty Reputation. It should notice that the penalty for the malicious data sharing process should be larger than that for reward because the malicious attack is more destructive. The punishment for giving a wrong sharing process as positive should be larger than that for denying a correct one. The penalty reputation has no attenuation factor, which will not decrease its value with the increase of time. Therefore, the penalty value of V_i is calculated as Eq. 9.

$$P_i = \frac{f_n}{f_p + f_n} \tag{9}$$

The reputation mechanism will determine whether a node is trusted node. If the score is lower than threshold λ, it will be determined as an untrusted node and the node will be isolated from the system. Then the final reputation value of V_i in t-th round is calculated as Eq. 10.

$$F_i = \gamma R_i - \delta P_i \tag{10}$$

Here, the parameter γ represents the weight of reward layer and δ represents the weight of penalty layer, where $\gamma + \delta = 1$.

Based on the reputation mechanism, the reliability of all vehicles in IoV can be evaluated. Then RSU can select the vehicles with high reputation to share their data and join the FL process.

5 Security Analysis

In this section, we analyze the security guarantee of our RepBFL framework. There are mainly two challenges for trusted data sharing in IoV: the reliability of shared data and the training efficiency of global model. In the reliability of shared data, the malicious vehicles may share wrong or redundant data to reduce the availability of entire shared data. However, our RepBFL method has the penalty mechanism which can decrease the reputation value of the malicious vehicles. If the reputation value of vehicle is below the threshold, it will be isolated from the system. In addition, we select the vehicles with high reputation for federated learning. If a vehicle wants to participate the model training, it should have high reputation by sharing more positive data, which can guarantee the quality of shared data.

Moreover, malicious attackers may register a large number of new users to join the network and cause collusion among nodes to affect the reputation of framed nodes. However, the new participating nodes have low reputation in our RepBFL. If a node wants to improve its reputation, it needs to share high-quality data for a long time to improve its local reputation. At the same time, the credibility factor can evaluate the assessed weights of different vehicular nodes. Honest nodes with high reputation will have greater assessed credibility and higher confidence for the evaluation of global reputation. In addition, the credibility of a new node is also very low, and the collusion of malicious new nodes cannot greatly improve or reduce the global reputation. Therefore, it will not have great impact on the reputation mechanism.

6 Performance Evaluation

In this section, we evaluate the performance of our proposed RepBFL model for data sharing in IoV. We first investigate the performance of shared data for federated learning. Then we test the proposed reputation mechanism in vehicular evaluation. Finally, we discuss the security performance of the reputation method by using different number of malicious vehicular nodes.

6.1   Experimental Setting

For the learning evaluation part, we conduct the evaluation on the MNIST dataset. In order to simulate the actual situation, the dataset is first split into 20 shards with a randomly sharded equally-sized portion of the entire dataset without overlap, and then the shards are assigned to 20 providers.

The data sharing task is to share the local data of each vehicular node to RSU for federated learning. The Convolutional Neural Network (CNN) model is adopted as local training model. We consider $N_{RSU} = 20$ and each RSU has 10 vehicles in their own communication area. The honest vehicular node shares the right data following a uniform distribution over 10 classes for the RSU trains the local model, while each malicious vehicular node shares the dataset with falsified data samples or add the noise on the raw data. As a result, these malicious vehicular nodes will share low-quality data to decrease the model learning accuracy.

When calculating reputation, we consider different number of compromised vehicular node. Here, the compromised vehicle may intentionally generate falsified reputation opinions to misguide other vehicular reputation calculated. We set the initial reputation value F of all vehicles to 0.5, and then establish our RepBFL framework.

6.2   Numerical Results

Performance of Our Approach. We first evaluate the accuracy and loss of the proposed scheme on the MNIST dataset with a various number of malicious vehicles. In addition, to test the destructive of the malicious vehicles, we set different number of malicious vehicles in the experiments. The malicious vehicles will provide low-quality data for model training. The low-quality data derived by disturbing the original parameters with random noise. The accuracy and loss results are shown in Fig. 2.

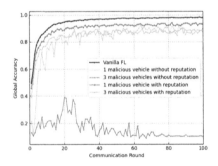

Fig. 2. The accuracy of global model with various numbers of vehicles under reputation and non-reputation

We choose different numbers of malicious vehicles as the comparative group with our proposed framework. The results show that FL is not capable of filtering out malfunction or malicious attacks during the global model construction. The global accuracy of the most basic FL, termed Vanilla FL, cannot achieve good accuracy under the malicious attacks. We can see that the increase of malicious nodes has a dramatically impact on performance. On the contrary, we can observe that our approach will have good accuracy, which can prove the superiority of our RepBFL framework. Furthermore, the learning accuracy of our model is not sacrificed in different number of malicious vehicles. This effectively proves that the RepBFL framework can improve the learning accuracy in IoV. The results indicate that it is vital importance to optimize the selection of participating nodes, which can guarantee the performance significantly. Therefore, we verify our proposed reputation mechanism in the next part.

In summary, we can observe that the reputation mechanism can guarantee the global accuracy with the increase of malicious vehicular nodes. The stable accuracy is due to our reputation mechanism can evaluate the reliability of vehicular nodes for selecting the vehicles with high reputation to share their data, which can guarantee the quality of the shared data. Meanwhile, the vehicular nodes with low reputation can be isolated by our reputation mechanism.

Security of Reputation Mechanism. Then, the security performance of our proposed RepBFL scheme is discussed.

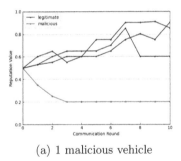
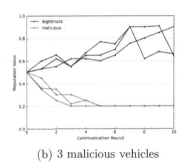

(a) 1 malicious vehicle   (b) 3 malicious vehicles

Fig. 3. Reputation value with various numbers of malicious vehicles

To analyze the effect of our proposed reputation mechanism, we compare and analyze various numbers of malicious vehicles on the reputation value under a fixed threshold $\lambda = 0.2$. From Fig. 3(a) and Fig. 3(b) we can see that, the increase of malicious vehicles cannot degrade the reputation mechanism dramatically.The reputation of normal vehicles can increase according to their shared data. The reputation value of malicious vehicles will decrease and isolate until their value below the reputation threshold. This mechanism can avoid the misleading by compromised vehicles and attacks by malicious vehicles.

Furthermore, a vehicle is not always trusted and reliable. The reputation value is not always constant, it can change with different performance of their data sharing process. Although a vehicle has high reputation, it will decrease if the vehicle cannot share its data or share disturbing data. The honest vehicles can increase their reputation value by continuously sharing high-quality data. The malicious vehicles have low reputation value, and the reputation declines dramatically.

In summary, these results confirm our expectations about the advantages derived from the adoption of reputation mechanism for data sharing process in IoV. The reason can be elucidated as that the RepBFL utilizes the reputation mechanism to evaluate the reputation of all vehicles in IoV, which can reflect the reliability of their shared data. The process can find the vehicles with high reputation to share their data, consequently increasing the final learning accuracy. These characteristics of reputation mechanism are suitable in traffic scenarios, especially in IoV, where multiple vehicles and RSU can cooperate with each other to provide more high-quality services.

7   Conclusion

In this paper, we proposed a novel reputation based blockchain-enabled federated learning framework in IoV for secure data sharing process. In order to ensure the reliability of data sharing process, we proposed a reputation mechanism, which can evaluate the reliability of all vehicles in IoV. The vehicles with high reputation value can share their collected data to RSU for federated learning and each node can maintain its own data. Furthermore, we conducted the security analysis and numerical performance evaluation. The results show that our proposed reputation mechanism has great advantages in avoiding the malicious attacks, which can guarantee the security and reliability of the data sharing process in IoV.

References

1. McMahan, B., Moore, E., Ramage, D., Hampson, S., Arcas, B.A.: Communication-efficient learning of deep networks from decentralized data. In: Proceedings of the 20th International Conference on Artificial Intelligence and Statistics, AISTATS 2017, Fort Lauderdale, FL, USA, vol. 54, pp. 1273–1282. PMLR (2017)
2. Mollah, M.B., et al.: Blockchain for the internet of vehicles towards intelligent transportation systems: a survey. IEEE Internet Things J. 8(6), 4157–4185 (2021)
3. Xiao, L., et al.: A reinforcement learning and blockchain-based trust mechanism for edge networks. IEEE Trans. Commun. 68(9), 5460–5470 (2020)
4. Chai, H., Leng, S., Chen, Y., Zhang, K.: A hierarchical blockchain-enabled federated learning algorithm for knowledge sharing in internet of vehicles. IEEE Trans. Intell. Transp. Syst. 22(7), 3975–3986 (2021)
5. Zou, Y., Shen, F., Yan, F., Lin, J., Qiu, Y.: Reputation-based regional federated learning for knowledge trading in blockchain-enhanced IOV. In: 2021 IEEE Wireless Communications and Networking Conference (WCNC), pp. 1–6. IEEE (2021)

6. Liu, L., et al.: Blockchain-enabled secure data sharing scheme in mobile-edge computing: an asynchronous advantage actor-critic learning approach. IEEE Internet Things J. **8**(4), 2342–2353 (2021)
7. Erdemir, E.N., Dragotti, P.L., Gündüz, D.: Privacy-aware time-series data sharing with deep reinforcement learning. IEEE Trans. Inf. Forensics Secur. **16**, 389–401 (2021)
8. Cao, X., Fang, M., Liu, J., Gong, N.Z.: Fltrust: Byzantine-robust federated learning via trust bootstrapping. In: 28th Annual Network and Distributed System Security Symposium, NDSS 2021, virtually, 21–25 February 2021. The Internet Society (2021)
9. Zhang, J., Wu, Y., Pan, R.: Incentive mechanism for horizontal federated learning based on reputation and reverse auction. In: Proceedings of the Web Conference 2021, pp. 947–956 (2021)
10. Warnat-Herresthal, S., et al.: Swarm learning for decentralized and confidential clinical machine learning. Nature **594**(7862), 265–270 (2021)
11. Wei, K., et al.: Federated learning with differential privacy: algorithms and performance analysis. IEEE Trans. Inf. Forensics Secur. **15**, 3454–3469 (2020)
12. Hu, R., Guo, Y., Li, H., Pei, Q., Gong, Y.: Personalized federated learning with differential privacy. IEEE Internet Things J. **7**(10), 9530–9539 (2020)
13. Wang, S., Huang, X., Yu, R., Zhang, Y., Hossain, E.: Permissioned blockchain for efficient and secure resource sharing in vehicular edge computing. arXiv preprint arXiv:1906.06319 (2019)
14. Yang, Z., Yang, K., Lei, L., Zheng, K., Leung, V.C.: Blockchain-based decentralized trust management in vehicular networks. IEEE Internet Things J. **6**(2), 1495–1505 (2018)
15. Jiang, T., Fang, H., Wang, H.: Blockchain-based internet of vehicles: distributed network architecture and performance analysis. IEEE Internet Things J. **6**(3), 4640–4649 (2018)
16. Kang, J., Yu, R., Huang, X., Wu, M., Maharjan, S., Xie, S., Zhang, Y.: Blockchain for secure and efficient data sharing in vehicular edge computing and networks. IEEE Internet Things J. **6**(3), 4660–4670 (2018)
17. Luo, B., Li, X., Weng, J., Guo, J., Ma, J.: Blockchain enabled trust-based location privacy protection scheme in vanet. IEEE Trans. Veh. Technol. **69**(2), 2034–2048 (2019)
18. Lu, Y., Huang, X., Zhang, K., Maharjan, S., Zhang, Y.: Blockchain empowered asynchronous federated learning for secure data sharing in internet of vehicles. IEEE Trans. Veh. Technol. **69**(4), 4298–4311 (2020)
19. Gai, K., Wu, Y., Zhu, L., Zhang, Z., Qiu, M.: Differential privacy-based blockchain for industrial Internet-of-Things. IEEE Trans. Ind. Inform. **16**(6), 4156–4165 (2019)

Multimodal Fusion Representation Learning Based on Differential Privacy

Chaoxin Cai, Yingpeng Sang$^{(\boxtimes)}$ ⓘ, Jinghao Huang, Maliang Zhang, and Weizheng Li

School of Computer Science and Engineering,
Sun Yat-sen University, Guangzhou, China
{caichx6,huangjh279,zhangmliang3,liwzh56}@mail2.sysu.edu.cn,
sangyp@mail.sysu.edu.cn

Abstract. Multimodal data for a certain target can often play a complementary role in information integration, but the diversification of the modal brings difficulties to the training of the model. Further, previous differential privacy works are only performed on a single modality. To tackle the problem, we choose deep representation learning to map different modalities data into the same subspace. This method of fusing multiple modalities uses low-rank decomposition based on Canonical Polyadic (CP) decomposition to implicitly obtain a high-dimensional tensor rich in mutual fusion information between multiple modalities, but explicitly obtain a low-dimensional representation. The perturbation that satisfies differential privacy is then carried out in the dimensional subspace. Experimental results show that it satisfies the data utility requirement while remaining suited privacy guarantee.

Keywords: Differential privacy · Multimodal fusion · Representation learning

1 Introduction

Humans perceive the world in diversified forms and types. Various modalities data can give humans comprehensive information to make more correct judgments. In recent years, the amount of multimodal data collected by expanding devices has been extremely increasing, including sensory data such as voice, text, images, and non-sensory data such as demographic data and other structured data. Specifically, information about an individual is usually multimodal, such as demographic data, CT image data and text description data for patients, text comments, image information and demographic information for netizens in social networks. It is natural and common to describe one target objects in different modalities.

Single modality sometimes cannot make better judgments. For example, when detecting human crying [1], vocal information is far more helpful than video information. Study [14] have shown that multimodal data classifiers are

ⓒ Springer Nature Switzerland AG 2022
H. Shen et al. (Eds.): PDCAT 2021, LNCS 13148, pp. 548–559, 2022.
https://doi.org/10.1007/978-3-030-96772-7_51

often better than monomodal data classifiers. Therefore, the integration of multiple modal data can often make better decisions, which is more in line with the way of human understanding the world.

Among various methods, multimodal fusion has attracted much attention for its flexibility in fusing at different levels(feature level or decision level) and capturing mutual information between modalities [1].

Recently, differential privacy has become the gold standard in the field of privacy protection. Based on random response and information theory, differential privacy solves the problem of protecting personal privacy while allowing third-party data collectors to analyze the common characteristics of data. Besides, it provides measurable privacy protection rules. However, the diversity of modality results in various Differential Privacy mechanisms, which are difficult to be unified under the same multimodal differential privacy framework. Although the method based on gradient descent is suitable for various data types, its clipping of gradient will lead to the unfairness of few sample learning [10]. What we are exploring here is non-gradient method.

To tackle the problem, we propose a framework for multimodal deep learning guaranteed by local differential privacy. Unlike federated learning which requires a lot of communication cost, local differential privacy, especially the perturbed fusion representation that meets given privacy budget, has extremely less communication cost when the dimension is much smaller than the original multimodal data. Specifically, our contributions are as follows:

- To the best of our knowledge, we are the first to propose differential privacy mechanism for the multimodal learning. We firstly train the various modalities in the local setting to a common subspace, and get representations with rich information using low rank fusion method based on Canonical Polyadic (CP) decomposition, then perturb them with guarantee of differential privacy to form protected representations, which can be aggregated by any third party.
- We propose a general framework to suit the fusion of various types of modalities. The framework consists of Encoding module, Perturbation module and Aggregation module. The machine learning models utilized in the Encoding and Aggregation modules are replaceable to suit the requirement of specific modality and learning tasks.
- Experimental results on various multimodal datasets show that data processed by our privacy protection method remain high utility even in low privacy budget.

The reminder of this paper is organized as follows: Sect. 2 introduces preliminary concepts about multimodal representation fusion, different privacy and binary encoding methods. Section 3 presents our work in detail of three module: encoding, perturbation and aggregation module. Section 4 describes used datasets and experimental setup. In Sect. 5, experimental results are shown as well as further discussion. Section 6 summarizes related works and Sect. 7 concludes the paper.

2   Preliminaries

2.1   Multimodal Representation Fusion

With the development of deep representation learning, we can map the data with uneven spatial distribution into a dense subspace through constraints. Multimodal fusion can use the characteristics of representation learning to fuse different modalities into the same subspace, and make good use of the complementary information between different modalities in the process of fusion.

In the previous multimodal representation fusion methods, the representations of different modalities are trained respectively at first, then mathematical operations such as max and min are carried out, and finally the representations are simply concatenated or fully connected to the next layer. In this way, the internal information of the same modality can be learned, but the common information among different modalities are ignored.

Recently, in Tensor Fusion Network (TFN) [19], different modalities representation are regarded as n-fold Cartesian space, e.g., 3D cube for three modalities, then fused these modalities by outer product. Obviously, this method will bring curse of dimensionality: the amount of calculation will increase exponentially with the number of modalities. To solve that, a low rank fusion method based on CP decomposition was proposed in [11] to calculate the fusion representation without explicit calculation on outer product.

2.2   Differential Privacy

For two adjacent dataset D and D' where only one record differs, and all their subset S, we says an algorithm M satisfies ϵ-differential privacy if:

$$Pr[M(D) \in S] \leq e^{\epsilon} Pr[M(D') \in S] \tag{1}$$

we call ϵ the privacy budget which means the protection level of data. The lower the budget, the better the protection, but usually the lower the data utility. Based on this definition, Centralized Differential Privacy (CDP) and Local Differential Privacy (LDP) frameworks are proposed according to whether the aggregation server is trusted or not.

2.3   Binary Encoding Methods

Although LDP methods vary for different types of modalities, the data of various modalities can be encoded into binary vectors. Then perturbations can be applied to these encoded vectors to avoid the problem of disunity.

Unary Encoding (UE). The unary encoding perturbs a binary vector B and outputs B' as follows:

$$Pr[B'[i] = 1] = \begin{cases} p, & if\ B[i] = 1 \\ q, & if\ B[i] = 0 \end{cases} \tag{2}$$

The unary encoding satisfies ϵ-LDP for

$$\epsilon = \ln \frac{p(1-q)}{(1-p)q} \tag{3}$$

B is the vector after encoding. B' is the adjacent vector of B. Among different choices for p and q, there are Symmetric Unary Encoding and Optimized Unary Encoding algorithms [17].

Symmetric Unary Encoding (SUE). RAPPOR's implementation [4] chooses $p = 0.75$ and $q = 0.25$ such that $p + q = 1$, making the treatment of 1 and 0 symmetric.

$$p = \frac{e^{\epsilon/2}}{e^{\epsilon/2}+1}, \quad q = \frac{1}{e^{\epsilon/2}+1} \tag{4}$$

Changing one bit of the vector has the greatest impact on 2 bits difference between the two vector, so the sensitivity is 2 here. In Eq. (4), $\epsilon/2$ can be replaced by $\epsilon/\Delta f$.

Optimized Unary Encoding (OUE). When the relative number of either 0 or 1 in the binary vector is obviously large, we can use the ratio of unchanged bits to flipped bits to allocate different privacy budgets respectively. For example, when there are more 1s than 0s, we can allocate more privacy budgets to 1 to maintain utility:

$$\frac{p}{1-p} = e^{\epsilon_1}, \quad \frac{1-q}{q} = e^{\epsilon_2}, \quad where \ \epsilon = \epsilon_1 + \epsilon_2 \tag{5}$$

Optimized Multiple Encoding (OME). Suppose the length of fusion representation is r, then for OUE and SUE, the sensitivity Δf are both $2r$ because they are binary vectors. When the representation value is real, we can extract the vector into a binary matrix [12], that is, for $\vec{x} = \{x_1, x_2, ..., x_r\}$, each x_i can be transformed into a length-l binary vector $\vec{x_{b_i}}$ to obtain a binary matrix $X = \{\vec{x_{b_1}}, \vec{x_{b_2}}, .., \vec{x_{b_r}}\}$. In this case, the sensitivity Δf is rl. The choices of p and q are in Eq. (6) and Eq. (7).

$$p = Pr\{1 \rightarrow 1\} = \begin{cases} \dfrac{\lambda}{1+\lambda}, & for \quad i \in 2n \\ \dfrac{1}{1+\lambda^3}, & for \quad i \in 2n+1 \end{cases} \tag{6}$$

$$q = Pr\{0 \rightarrow 1\} = \frac{1}{1+\lambda e^{\frac{\epsilon}{rl}}} \tag{7}$$

3   Our Framework

Our framework consists of three modules. Firstly, the encoding module takes different modalities of data as input and outputs the fusion representation. The fusion representation is obtained by low rank multimodal representation fusion, as Fig. 1 shows. Secondly, the perturbation module transforms values of the fusion representation into a binary matrix. For each vector extracted by one value, since OME scales well even if the domain size d is large, we apply OME mechanism given fixed privacy budget. Finally, the aggregation module trains the perturbed binary matrix.

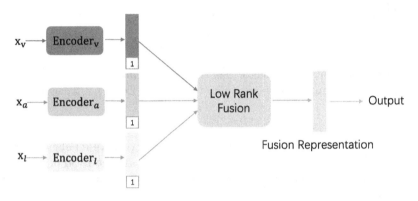

Fig. 1. The low rank multimodal fusion module, which uses different encoders for corresponding modalities (here are three modalities) to gain pioneer representations, then fuses them implicitly to a cube tensor by decomposing the fusion tensor weights into CP decomposition forms but directly calculate with the pioneer representations. This avoids exponentially increasing the amount of computation [11].

3.1   Encoding Module

Encoding module encodes original modalities data into one fusion representation. In the first step, original modalities data are encoded into corresponding representations by sub-encoders. In the second step, the fusion representation is obtained by these representations. An approach to gain the fusion representation is by outer product. As Eq. (8) shows, $\mathbf{Z}_m$ means representation of the m-th modality, d_m is the representation size of each modality, and $\otimes$ is outer product. However, this fusion by outer product is time-consuming. We utilize a network architecture with weight $\mathbb{W}$ to transform $\mathbb{Z}$ into a vector z_{fusion}, i.e., $z_{fusion} = \mathbb{W} \cdot \mathbb{Z}$.

The CP decomposition [8] decomposes an Nth-order tensor into a linear combination of rank-1 tensors, as illustrated in Eq. (9). $\mathbf{B}$ is the N-th order tensor of size $I_1 \times I_2 \times ... \times I_N$. $\mathbf{b}_1^{(1)} \circ \mathbf{b}_2^{(2)} \circ ... \mathbf{b}_r^{(N)}$ is outer product among vectors $\mathbf{b}_r^{(i)}$ from dimension i until rank R. We apply CP decomposition to the network weight $\mathbb{W}$, and adopt the method in [11] to decompose $\mathbb{W}$ into matrix $\mathbf{W}_m^{(i)}$ made up of rank-1 vectors, i.e., $\mathbb{W} = \sum_{i=1}^{r} \bigotimes_{m=1}^{M} \mathbf{W}_m^{(i)}$.

$$\mathbb{Z} = \bigotimes_{m=1}^{M} \mathbf{Z}_m, \quad \mathbf{Z}_m \in \mathbb{R}^{d_m} \tag{8}$$

$$\mathbf{B} \cong \sum_{r=1}^{R} \lambda_r \mathbf{b}_\mathbf{r}^{(1)} \circ \mathbf{b}_\mathbf{r}^{(2)} \circ ... \mathbf{b}_\mathbf{r}^{(N)}, \quad \mathbf{B} \in \mathbb{R}^{I_1 \times I_2 \times ... \times I_N} \tag{9}$$

$$z_{fusion} = (\sum_{i=1}^{R} \bigotimes_{m=1}^{M} \mathbf{W}_m^{(i)}) \cdot \mathbb{Z} = \bigwedge_{m=1}^{M} [\sum_{i=1}^{R} \mathbf{W}_m^{(i)} \cdot \mathbf{Z}_m] \tag{10}$$

According to [19], the fusion tensor $\mathbb{Z}$ created by outer product can be decomposed together with the weight in the network. As Eq. (10) shows, $\bigotimes$ is outer product between matrices, $\bigwedge$ means the element-wise product, $\cdot$ is the dot product with the effect of tensor contractions, and finally a vector z_{fusion} is obtained. Thus we can gain the fusion representation z_{fusion} without explicit calculation of the tensors. This low rank trick remains efficiency and performance. Concretely, this derivation reduces the computation complexity from $O(d_y \prod_{m=1}^{M} d_m)$ to $O(d_y \cdot R \cdot \sum_{m=1}^{M} d_m)$, where d_y is the size of vector z_{fusion}.

3.2 Perturbation Module

After gaining the fusion representation z_{fusion}, we adopt Optimized Multiple Encoding (OME) to convert each z_{fusion_i} to a binary vector with fixed length l, then perturb each bit in the light of Eq. (6) and Eq. (7). We follow the intuition that 0s and 1s happen at different ratios and each ratio owns its privacy budget, as Eq. (5) shows. Further, the odds of 0 and 1 bits flipping should satisfy Eq. (6) and Eq. (7). When the representation size and vector extracting size are fixed, if randomization factor λ is constant, lower ϵ values and higher rl will result in higher q value. The schematic diagram of perturbation is shown in Fig. 2.

Fusion Representation

Fig. 2. The perturbation module

3.3 Aggregation Module

In the aggregation module, the untrusted third party can use its well-designed network to analyze the data and train the model. Since the input is a low dimensional embedding, it will lighten the burden of input. Each sample corresponds to a label, so we can input more samples in a batch for faster training to achieve memory utilization. Besides, the network structure can be flexible to adapt to different privacy budget for specific problem requirement.

4 Experiments

4.1 Datasets

We perform our framework on three representative multimodal datasets including the Multimodal Corpus of Sentiment Intensity (CMU-MOSI) [20], the Persuasive Opinion Multimedia (POM) [16] and Interactive Emotional Dyadic Motion Capture Database (IEMOCAP) [3].

1. *CMU-MOSI*: The dataset is a collection of 2199 viewpoint video clips, including audio, transcript and video information. Each opinion video is annotated with sentiment in the range of [–3,3] from highly negative to highly positive.
2. *POM*: The datasets were obtained from a social multimedia website called ExpoTV.com, including 1000 movie review videos with a half getting 5-star rating and other half getting 1 or 2-star rating. These videos are annotated for 16 speaker sentimental traits which ranges from –3 to +3. Besides, verbatim transcriptions are also included to make up this multimodal dataset.
3. *IEMOCAP*: The audio-visual dataset collects 12 h recording of 10 actors' facial expressions, head and hand movements information together with word-level text information and audio information. The actors performed selected emotional scripts and improvised hypothetical scenes designed to trigger specific types of emotions (happiness, anger, sadness, frustration and neutral state). The label our experiment carries on includes angry, sad, neutral and happy.

In order to better test the generalization performance of the model, we divide the dataset into training set, validation set and test set, use the training set to train the data, find the model with the smallest error through the validation set, and finally use the test set to test the performance. Since our goal is not to train the model, but to obtain the representation output, we merge the training set and validation set in the perturbation module and aggregation training module.

4.2 Experiment Details

For the regression task, we use $L1$ loss as the loss function. Finally we evaluate its MAE, $F1$ score and the correlation coefficient between the output and the label. For the classification task, we use log cross entropy as its loss function.

For different modalities, we use subnetwork as encoders, as illustrated in Fig. 1. For video and audio information, we simply apply fully connected network. For text information, we also apply a simple Long Short-Term Memory (LSTM) network because here we focus on our framework instead of searching for network structure. Before training the subnetwork, we preprocess the multimodal data by aligning them at the word-level.

In the perturbation, we compare OME, OUE and SUE perturbation methods. The most fundamental difference among them is the choice of p and q. As shown in Table 1, we compare the changes of $F1$ score and accuracy with the increasing privacy budget in different orders (include non-privacy results).

The aggregation module is made up of a three-layer fully connected network, which can be replaced by other well-designed network. It is worth noting that even such a simple network can restore the multimodal data with differential privacy to the same accuracy as the cases where there is no perturbation module.

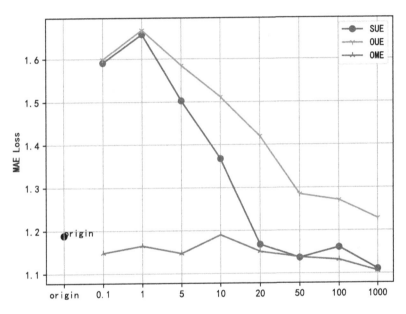

Fig. 3. The test results on MAE loss for models trained on dataset CMU-MOSI, where the horizontal axis means privacy budget ϵ. The "origin" means non-perturbation by differential privacy.

Table 1. Performance under SUE, OUE and OME mechanisms in IEMOCAP dataset.

		F1 score					Accuracy				
		Origin	$\epsilon = 1$	$\epsilon = 10$	$\epsilon = 100$	$\epsilon = 1000$	Origin	$\epsilon = 1$	$\epsilon = 10$	$\epsilon = 100$	$\epsilon = 1000$
SUE	Sad	0.8367	0.6916	0.7252	0.7979	0.8289	83.05%	69.19%	72.81%	79.21%	82.73%
	Happy	0.8321	0.7662	0.7901	0.8201	0.8494	84.65%	78.57%	80.81%	84.97%	84.90%
	Neutral	0.6779	0.5093	0.5504	0.6217	0.6354	68.02%	52.67%	56.50%	65.14%	64.71%
	Angry	0.8650	0.6810	0.6958	0.8350	0.8309	86.25%	71.22%	71.00%	82.62%	82.09%
OUE	Sad	0.8335	0.6708	0.6818	0.8012	0.8226	82.73%	66.95%	68.34%	80.06%	81.98%
	Happy	0.8290	0.7715	0.7727	0.8266	0.8249	84.33%	79.64%	78.68%	83.80%	83.48%
	Neutral	0.6795	0.5019	0.5037	0.6349	0.6194	68.23%	51.81%	52.35%	65.46%	63.65%
	Angry	0.8719	0.6487	0.6714	0.8125	0.8255	86.89%	66.95%	69.08%	80.17%	81.56%
OME	Sad	0.8382	0.8039	0.8088	0.8027	0.8238	83.37%	81.13%	80.60%	80.06%	82.09%
	Happy	0.8369	0.8219	0.8385	0.8281	0.8281	85.29%	83.26%	84.75%	84.01%	84.01%
	Neutral	0.6805	0.6353	0.6203	0.6271	0.6431	68.23%	65.88%	65.99%	64.50%	65.46%
	Angry	0.8674	0.8049	0.8192	0.8192	0.8347	86.46%	82.52%	83.05%	80.81%	82.52%

5   Results and Discussion

We train multimodal fusion representations with differential privacy in EMO-CAP dataset shown in Table 1. It is obviously to see both $f1$ score and accuracy increase when more privacy budgets ϵ are given. Besides, the OME mechanism remains stable under different ϵ and performs well even in tight budget. We assume that part of the reason is rl acts as an actor of normalization for ϵ, which allows ϵ to have a larger shift range while the accuracy is still high. The other reason is it may play the role of regularization and avoid over fitting.

As shown in Fig. 3, our framework demonstrates the similar phenomenon in CMU-MOSI dataset. Under all three mechanisms, the MAE loss have the same trend of decreasing when ϵ increases.

In experiments on POM dataset employing OME, we can find accuracy gets higher when larger ϵ is given, as Fig. 4 (a) shows. Compared with the other two mechanisms, OME remains the highest accuracy as well as stability. In the meantime, we can find few samples may influence the result like label 3 in both Fig. 4 (a) and (b). We assume that the phenomenon is due to overfitting during training process.

It is worth mentioning that the multimodal fusion representation based on differential privacy itself ensures certain security on the neural network model. When there is no data perturbation, the attacker may attack the neural network alone, by inferring members by parameters, as well as inferring specific modalities. The fusion of modalities greatly increases the difficulty of this type of attacks. Once the attack is slightly biased, The diversity of modalities also amplifies the noise.

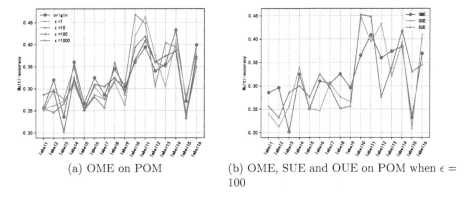

(a) OME on POM   (b) OME, SUE and OUE on POM when $\epsilon = 100$

Fig. 4. Experimental results on POM dataset. Figure (a) is OME on POM dataset ranging from different privacy budgets ϵ. Figure (b) shows results of OME, OUE and SUE on POM dataset when $\epsilon = 100$. In the horizontal axis labels represent all sentimental labels in POM. In the vertical axis values represent multitask classification accuracy.

6 Related Work

There have been many works on privacy protection for data of single modality, but few works for multimodal data fusion. An extension of differential privacy E_{d_x}- privacy was proposed in [6], at the text level of the bag of words, in which the clues about the author's style are deleted while keeping the text content as unchanged as possible. Moreover, another new differential privacy mechanism was proposed in [5] which defines the "m-neighborhood" notion to adapt to the image data. Concretely, it allows to protect sensitive information under at most m pixels.

Most previous works on multimodal fusion can be divided into three categories according to the level where the information is fused [1], i.e., early fusion (fusion at the feature level) [7,18], late fusion (fusion at the decision level) [9,13] and hybrid fusion (fusion at both level) [2,15]. The most universal technique of late fusion is to use different models for different modalities, such as Hidden Markov Model for audio and Support Vector Machine for image [1]. Among these works, linear weighted method is the most common one used to combine different modalities. However, this method must be carefully designed and still fails to capture nonlinear relationships.

Neural network was first used in [20] to connect the sub network layers of different modalities to the same network layer, aiming to achieve simple multimodal fusion. However, this fusion lacks the interaction information between modalities. [19] used the outer product method to fuse the information of different modalities, but the computational complexity is too high, and the amount of computation increases exponentially with the number of modalities. On the basis of this work, [11] used the low rank decomposition based on CP decomposition to decompose the gradient weight, and implicitly calculated the low dimensional representation vector, and avoided the explicit calculation of high-dimensional tensor, so as to reduce the computational complexity.

7   Conclusions

We propose a learning framework for multimodal fusion representation based on differential privacy. The framework is designed for general purposes of multimodal fusion, and consists of encoding, perturbation, aggregation modules. The machine learning models in the modules are replaceable to suit requirements of various modalities and specific problem settings. Experiments on three most popular multimodal datasets demonstrate the high performance on data utility and privacy protection of the framework.

Acknowledgement. This work was supported by the Science and Technology Program of Guangzhou, China (No. 201904010209), and the Science and Technology Program of Guangdong Province, China (No. 2017A010101039).

References

1. Atrey, P.K., Hossain, M.A., El Saddik, A., Kankanhalli, M.S.: Multimodal fusion for multimedia analysis: a survey. Multimedia Syst. **16**(6), 345–379 (2010). https://doi.org/10.1007/s00530-010-0182-0, http://link.springer.com/10.1007/s00530-010-0182-0

2. Bendjebbour, A., Delignon, Y., Fouque, L., Samson, V., Pieczynski, W.: Multisensor image segmentation using dempster-shafer fusion in markov fields context. IEEE Trans. Geosci. Remote Sens. **39**(8), 1789–1798 (2001)

3. Busso, C., et al.: Iemocap: interactive emotional dyadic motion capture database. Lang. Resour. Eval. **42**(4), 335–359 (2008)

4. Erlingsson, Ú., Pihur, V., Korolova, A.: Rappor: Randomized aggregatable privacy-preserving ordinal response. In: Proceedings of the 2014 ACM SIGSAC Conference on Computer and Communications Security, pp. 1054–1067 (2014)

5. Fan, L.: Image pixelization with differential privacy. In: Kerschbaum, F., Paraboschi, S. (eds.) DBSec 2018. LNCS, vol. 10980, pp. 148–162. Springer, Cham (2018). https://doi.org/10.1007/978-3-319-95729-6_10

6. Fernandes, N., Dras, M., McIver, A.: Generalised differential privacy for text document processing. In: Nielson, F., Sands, D. (eds.) POST 2019. LNCS, vol. 11426, pp. 123–148. Springer, Cham (2019). https://doi.org/10.1007/978-3-030-17138-4_6

7. Foresti, G.L., Snidaro, L.: A distributed sensor network for video surveillance of outdoor environments. In: Proceedings. International Conference on Image Processing, vol. 1, pp. I-I. IEEE (2002)

8. Hitchcock, F.L.: Multiple invariants and generalized rank of a p-way matrix or tensor. J. Math. Phys. **7**(1–4), 39–79 (1928)

9. Iyengar, G., Nock, H.J., Neti, C.: Audio-visual synchrony for detection of monologues in video archives. In: 2003 IEEE International Conference on Acoustics, Speech, and Signal Processing, 2003. Proceedings. (ICASSP 2003), vol. 5, p. V-772. IEEE (2003)

10. Liu, W., et al.: Fair differential privacy can mitigate the disparate impact on model accuracy (2020)

11. Liu, Z., Shen, Y., Lakshminarasimhan, V.B., Liang, P.P., Zadeh, A., Morency, L.P.: Efficient low-rank multimodal fusion with modality-specific factors. arXiv:1806.00064 (2018). http://arxiv.org/abs/1806.00064

12. Lyu, L., Li, Y., He, X., Xiao, T.: Towards differentially private text representations. arXiv:2006.14170 (2020). http://arxiv.org/abs/2006.14170

13. Neti, C., et al.: Joint processing of audio and visual information for multimedia indexing and human-computer interaction. In: RIAO, pp. 294–301. Citeseer (2000)

14. Ngiam, J., Khosla, A., Kim, M., Nam, J., Lee, H., Ng, A.Y.: Multimodal deep learning, p. 8 (2011)

15. Ni, J., Ma, X., Xu, L., Wang, J.: An image recognition method based on multiple BP neural networks fusion. In: International Conference on Information Acquisition, 2004. Proceedings, pp. 323–326. IEEE (2004)

16. Park, S., Shim, H.S., Chatterjee, M., Sagae, K., Morency, L.P.: Computational analysis of persuasiveness in social multimedia: A novel dataset and multimodal prediction approach. In: Proceedings of the 16th International Conference on Multimodal Interaction, pp. 50–57 (2014)

17. Wang, T., Blocki, J., Li, N., Jha, S.: Locally differentially private protocols for frequency estimation. In: 26th {USENIX} Security Symposium ({USENIX} Security 17), pp. 729–745 (2017)

18. Yang, M.T., Wang, S.C., Lin, Y.Y.: A multimodal fusion system for people detection and tracking. Int. J. Imaging Syst. Technol. 15(2), 131–142 (2005)

19. Zadeh, A., Chen, M., Poria, S., Cambria, E., Morency, L.P.: Tensor fusion network for multimodal sentiment analysis. arXiv preprint arXiv:1707.07250 (2017)

20. Zadeh, A., Zellers, R., Pincus, E., Morency, L.P.: Multimodal sentiment intensity analysis in videos: facial gestures and verbal messages. IEEE Intell. Syst. 31(6), 82–88 (2016)

Efficient List Decoding Applied to ECC^2

Peidong Guan^{1,2}, Yunqi Wan^3, Zhuoran Zhang^{1,2}, and Fangguo Zhang$^{1,2(\boxtimes)}$

^{1} School of Computer Science and Engineering, Sun Yat-sen University,
Guangzhou 510006, China
isszhfg@mail.sysu.edu.cn
^{2} Guangdong Key Laboratory of Information Security Technology,
Guangzhou 510006, China
^{3} School of Electronics and Information Technology, Sun Yat-sen University,
Guangzhou, China

Abstract. ECC^2 is an public key encryption system based on elliptic code. It can resist known attacks based on the special structures of algebraic geometric code. However, the computational overhead of decryption of ECC^2 is unsatisfactory, because the list decoding algorithm occupies a major part of the computational overhead of decryption of ECC^2. Therefore, we propose our module basis reduction interpolation of list decoding for elliptic code to speed up the decryption of ECC^2. The algorithm we proposed is based on the theory of Gröbner basis of modules. By implementing our proposed algorithm combined with ECC^2, it shows that the proposed algorithm performs better than the list decoding algorithms used in ECC^2.

Keywords: Code-based cryptography · Elliptic codes · List decoding · Gröbner Basis · ECC^2

1 Introduction

List decoding is an efficient decoding algorithm with a long history. It was first proposed by Eilas [6] in the 1950s. Sudan [12], in 1997, proposed a polynomial time algorithm for some low rate Reed-Solomon (RS) codes. Later, Shokrollahi and Wasserman [11] extended this algorithm from RS codes to algebraic geometric (AG) codes. We denote this algorithm as SW list decoding. In 1999, Guruswami and Sudan [7] optimized the previous list decoding algorithm and improved the error-correcting capacity for RS codes and AG codes to $n - \sqrt{nk}$. We denote this algorithm as GS list decoding. Based on the Gröbner basis theory and the Berlekamp-Massey-Sakata algorithm, Sahata [10] proposed fast interpolation methods for the original and improved versions of list decoding of one-point AG codes. Lee and O'Sullivan [9] proposed an interpolation algorithm of

---

Supported by Guangdong Major Project of Basic and Applied Basic Research (2019B030302008) and the National Natural Science Foundation of China (No. 61972429).

H. Shen et al. (Eds.): PDCAT 2021, LNCS 13148, pp. 560–567, 2022.
https://doi.org/10.1007/978-3-030-96772-7_52

GS list decoding of RS code based on the theory of Gröbner bases of modules. Later, they proposed an interpolation algorithm of Hermitian codes using Gröbner bases [8]. Beelen and Brander further reduced the complexity in finding the interpolation polynomial for a class of AG codes [4]. Wan [13] proposed an efficient list decoding algorithm of elliptic code.

In addition to extensive research in the academic field, list decoding for AG codes is widely used in communication engineering. Besides, it plays an important role in cryptography. For example, it can be used to solve ECDLP [15] and to reduce the key sizes for McEliece cryptosystems [3]. Zhang, Zhang and Guan proposed an encryption system ECC^2 [16] based on elliptic code and proved its security. ECC^2 encryption system uses list decoding for AG codes which is the key to resisting known attacks against AG codes. The authors selected GS list decoding and SW list decoding in the decryption algorithm. However, both algorithms are not efficient enough to put ECC^2 in to practice, so we consider using list decoding based on Gröbner basis theory in ECC^2.

Unfortunately, the Gröbner basis algorithms mentioned above only focus on codes generated by all points on a curve, since such codes perform best in the communication field. This design will result in a special structure of the code, which can lead to efficient attacks if they are used in ECC^2. In more detail, ECC^2 uses elliptic code with carefully chosen points on the curve in order to hide the structure of the curve and the codes. As a consequence, all the above algorithms based on Gröbner basis can not be applied in the decryption of ECC^2.

Our Contributions: We extend the results of Wan [13] so that for the elliptic code choosing n arbitrary points, list decoding based on the theory of Gröbner bases of modules can work for the decryption of ECC^2. Then, we analyse the performance of our implementation which shows it performs better than the GS and SW list decoding.

Organization: The rest of paper is organized as follows. In Section 2, we introduce the preliminaries of elliptic code, list decoding algorithm and ECC^2. In Section 3, we present our improved module basis reduction algorithm. In Section 4, we implement ECC^2 with different algorithms and show the performance of them.

2   Preliminaries

2.1   Elliptic Code and List Decoding

Let $\mathbb{F}_q$ be a finite field of size q. Elliptic curves $\mathcal{E}$ over $\mathbb{F}_q$ are defined by a nonsingular Weierstrass equation

$$\mathcal{E} : y^2 + a_1 xy + a_3 y = x^3 + a_2 x^2 + a_4 x + a_6, \tag{1}$$

where coefficients of curves are $a_1, a_2, a_3, a_4, a_6 \in \mathbb{F}_q$. Let $\mathbb{F}_q(\mathcal{E})$ denotes the function field defined over elliptic curve $\mathcal{E}$. For any $f \in \mathbb{F}_q(\mathcal{E})$, the order of f at a rational point $P \in \mathcal{E}$ is denoted by $v_P(f)$. Let $f \in \mathbb{F}_q(\mathcal{E})$ and $f \neq 0$, then the function f can be associated with a principle divisor which is defined as $div(f) = \sum_P v_P(f)P$. Let $G = \sum_P n_P P$ be any divisor of degree k on $\mathcal{E}$, where $n_P \in \mathbb{Z}/\{0\}$. Let $\mathcal{L}(G)$ be a set of rational functions $f \in \mathbb{F}_q(\mathcal{E})$ such that $\mathcal{L}(G)$ can be denoted by $\mathcal{L}(G) = \{f \mid div(f) + G \succ 0, f \in \mathbb{F}_q(\mathcal{E}), f \neq 0\} \cup \{0\}$, where $\succ$ denotes that all the coefficients of a divisor are non-negative.

Let $P_1, P_2, \cdots, P_n \in \mathbb{F}_q$ are n distinct affine points on $\mathcal{E}$. Define $D = P_1 + P_2 + \cdots + P_n$ be a divisor on $\mathcal{E}$ and define $G = k\mathcal{O}$ with $k < n$. For vector space $\mathcal{L}(G)$, we can obtain that $\{\phi_0, \phi_1, \cdots, \phi_{k-1}\} = \{1, x, y, x^2, xy, x^3, x^2y, \cdots, x^i y^j \mid j = \{0,1\}, 2i + 3j = k\}$ is a pole basis of $\mathcal{L}(G)$. Let $f \in \mathcal{L}(G)$ denote the message polynomial which can be taken in the form

$$f(x, y) = f_0\phi_0 + f_1\phi_1 + \cdots + f_{k-1}\phi_{k-1}, \tag{2}$$

where $f_0, f_1, \cdots, f_{k-1}$ denote the message. Then an $[n, k]$ elliptic code is defined as

$$\mathcal{C}(D, G) = \{(f(P_1), \cdots, f(P_n)) \mid f \in \mathcal{L}(G)\} \subseteq \mathbb{F}_q^n. \tag{3}$$

For $[n, k, d]$ linear code, list decoding algorithm is a way to obtain all the codewords within distance $n - \sqrt{nk}$ from a received word. Let $r = (r_1, r_2, \cdots, r_n) \in \mathbb{F}_q^n$ be a received word after channel corruption, then construct a set of n interpolation points which can be taken in the form $\mathbf{P} = \{(P_1, r_1), \cdots, (P_n, r_n)\}$. List decoding of elliptic code consists of two main steps: interpolation and root finding. Interpolation step is to construct a minimal polynomial $Q(x, y, z)$ which interpolates the n interpolation points in $\mathbf{P}$ with a multiplicity m. Root finding step is to find the z-roots of the interpolation polynomial $Q(x, y, z)$ with $z = f \in \mathcal{L}(G)$ and $Q(x, y, f) = 0$. One of the roots of $Q(x, y, z)$ that satisfies $z \in \mathcal{L}(G)$ is the message before coding.

2.2   ECC²

Take 1^λ as security level, then the public key encryption system ECC^2 based on elliptic codes can be specified as follows:

– **KeyGen**(1^λ)
   1. Generate parameters param $= (q, n, k, t)$.
   2. Choose random elements $a, b \in \mathbb{F}_q$, such that the elliptic curve $\mathcal{E} : y^2 = x^3 + ax + b$ has p rational points, where p is prime.
   3. Run ECGen [16] to generate the set $R = \{r_i\}_{i=1}^n$ and a point P. Then generates the elliptic code $\mathcal{C}$ in form (3) with $D = \sum_{i=1}^n r_i P$, $G = k\mathcal{O}$. The generator matrix of $\mathcal{C}$ is denoted as G. Transform the matrix G to the systematic form $[I \mid G^{pub}]$ where I is identity matrix.
   4. Output pk $= G^{pub}$ and sk $= (a, P, R)$.
– **Encrypt**(pk, $m \in \mathbb{F}_q^t$)
   1. Choose $r_1 \in \mathbb{F}_q^k$ randomly. Choose random vector $e \in \mathbb{F}_q^n$ of weight t.
   2. Set $r_2 = (e_{i_1}, e_{i_2}, \cdots, e_{i_t}) \in \mathbb{F}_q^t$ as the non-zero coordinates of e with the original order, where $e_{i_j} \neq 0$ and $i_j < i_k$ for $j < k$.

3. Calculate $c_1 = r_1 \cdot [I \mid G^{pub}] + e$, and $c_2 = m + r_2$.
4. The cipher-text is $c = c_1 \parallel c_2$.

- **Decrypt**(sk, c)
  1. Recover the elliptic curve parameter b by solving $y_P^2 = x_P^3 + ax_P + b$ and get $\mathcal{E} : y^2 = x^3 + ax + b$. Recover the divisors $D = \sum_{i=1}^{n} r_i P$ and $G = k\mathcal{O}$.
  2. Calculate $e = c_1 - \text{ListD}(\mathcal{E}, D, G, c_1, t)$, where $\text{ListD}(\mathcal{E}, D, G, c_1, t)$ is the list decoding algorithm for elliptic code.
  3. Set $r_2 = (e_{i_1}, \cdots, e_{i_t})$, and finally get the message $m = c_2 - r_2$.

3 The Module Basis Reduction Interpolation of List Decoding for Elliptic Code

Our module based reduction(MBR) interpolation consists of two procedures: basis construction and module basis reduction. The basis construction step is to construct a basis of $\mathbb{F}_q[x]$-module which consists of all the polynomials that satisfy the interpolation constraints. The module basis reduction step is to reduce the basis above to a Gröbner basis of the module. Before presenting the basis construction step, there are some preliminaries that should be known.

Let the elliptic curves $\mathcal{E}$ over $\mathbb{F}_q$ are defined by Weierstrass equation in the form $y^2 = x^3 + ax + b$, where $a, b \in \mathbb{F}_q, 4a^3 + 27b^2 \neq 0 \in \mathbb{F}_q$ and q is prime. Let $\mathbb{F}_q(\mathcal{E})[z]$ be a polynomial ring over algebraic function field $\mathbb{F}_q(\mathcal{E})$. Let the monomial set of polynomial ring $\mathbb{F}_q(\mathcal{E})[z]$ be $\{x^\alpha y^\beta z^\gamma \mid 0 \leq \alpha, 0 \leq \beta \leq 1, 0 \leq \gamma\}$.

Define the $(1, k)$-weighted degree of monomial $\phi_a z^\gamma \in \mathbb{F}_q(\mathcal{E})[z]$ is $deg_{1,k}(\phi_a z^\gamma) = -v_\infty(\phi_a) + k\gamma$. Then we define the monomial order $>_k$ on $\mathbb{F}_q(\mathcal{E})[z]$. For two monomials $x^{\alpha_1} y^{\beta_1} z^{\gamma_1}, x^{\alpha_2} y^{\beta_2} z^{\gamma_2} \in \mathbb{F}_q(\mathcal{E})[z]$, we have $x^{\alpha_1} y^{\beta_1} z^{\gamma_1} >_k x^{\alpha_2} y^{\beta_2} z^{\gamma_2}$ if $deg_{1,k}(x^{\alpha_1} y^{\beta_1} z^{\gamma_1}) > deg_{1,k}(x^{\alpha_2} y^{\beta_2} z^{\gamma_2})$ or if $deg_{1,k}(x^{\alpha_1} y^{\beta_1} z^{\gamma_1}) = deg_{1,k}(x^{\alpha_2} y^{\beta_2} z^{\gamma_2})$ and $\gamma_1 > \gamma_2$. Define the z-degree of polynomial $f \in \mathbb{F}_q(\mathcal{E})[z]$ is the degree of f in z over $\mathbb{F}_q(\mathcal{E})$, denoted as $z\text{-}deg(f)$.

Given a polynomial $Q \in \mathbb{F}_q(\mathcal{E})[z]$, the $(1, k)$-weighted degree of Q is the maximum $(1, k)$-weighted degree of monomial in Q with respect to the monomial order $>_k$. Given a polynomial $Q \in \mathbb{F}_q(\mathcal{E})[z]$, the leading term of Q is the monomial appearing in Q which is the maxmium monomial with respect to the order $>_k$. The leading term of Q is denoted as $lt(Q)$. The leading coefficient of Q is the coefficient of $lt(Q)$ and is denoted as $lc(Q)$.

3.1 Basis Construction

Our basis construction firstly designs functions which interpolate n points of elliptic curve $\mathcal{E}$. For elliptic code $\mathcal{C}(D, G)$, it fixs n distinct points from elliptic curve $\mathcal{E}$. Define divisor $D_\eta = P_1 + \cdots + P_n + (-(P_1 + \cdots + P_n)) - (n+1)\mathcal{O}$. It holds that divisor D_η is a principle divisor. Define divisors $D_{h_i} = P_1 + \cdots + P_{i-1} + P_{i+1} + \cdots + P_n + (-(P_1 + \cdots + P_{i-1} + P_{i+1} + \cdots + P_n)) - n\mathcal{O}$, where $i = 1, \cdots, n$. Then construct n functions $h_i' \in \mathbb{F}_q(\mathcal{E})$ that satisfy $div(h_i') = D_{h_i}$ and let $h_i = \frac{h_i'}{h_i'(P_i)}$. Fix a positive integer m which is used to represent the multiplicity parameter of list decoding. Define $h_r = \sum_{i=1}^{n} r_i h_i \in \mathbb{F}_q(\mathcal{E})$. According to the definition of h_i, we have $h_r(P_i) = r_i$ where $i = 1, \cdots, n$. Define $I_{r,m}$ an ideal of the polynomial ring $\mathbb{F}_q(\mathcal{E})[z]$ and $I_{r,m} = \langle z - h_v, \eta \rangle^m$. Ideal $I_{r,m}$ consists of all the polynomials that interpolate all points in $\mathbf{P}$ with a multiplicity m.

Let l be a positive integer, which is the list size parameter of list decoding. Define $\mathbb{F}_q(\mathcal{E})[z]_l = \{f \in \mathbb{F}_q(\mathcal{E})[z] \mid z\text{-}deg(f) \le l\}$, then $\mathbb{F}_q(\mathcal{E})[z]_l$ is a free module over $\mathbb{F}_q(\mathcal{E})$ with a basis $\{1, z, \cdots, z^l\}$. Define $I_{r,m,l} = I_{r,m} \cap \mathbb{F}_q(\mathcal{E})[z]_l$, it holds that $I_{r,m,l}$ is a submodule of $\mathbb{F}_q(\mathcal{E})[z]$ over $\mathbb{F}_q(\mathcal{E})$. By computing the Gröbner basis of $I_{r,m,l}$, it can be efficient to find the minimal element of $I_{r,m}$ with respect to $>_k$.

Proposition 1. $I_{r,m,l}$ *is a module over* $\mathbb{F}_q(\mathcal{E})$, *it has a set of generators consisting of* $G_i, 0 \le i \le l$, *where*

$$G_i = \begin{cases} (z - h_r)^i \eta^{m-i} & 0 \le i \le m, \\ z^{i-m}(z - h_r)^m & m < i \le l. \end{cases} \tag{4}$$

According to Proposition 1, a generator for $I_{r,m,l}$ as a module over $\mathbb{F}_q[x]$ is $H = \{y^j G_i \mid 0 \le i \le l, 0 \le j \le 1\}$.

Define a set $S = \{(\gamma, \beta) \mid 0 \le \gamma \le l, 0 \le \beta \le 1\}$, and define a function $ind : \mathbb{F}_q(\mathcal{E})[z]_l \to S$. Function ind takes a element f of $\mathbb{F}_q(\mathcal{E})[z]_l$ as input. We can obtain $lt(f)$ from the input f. Assume $lt(f) = a_{\alpha,\beta,\gamma} x^\alpha y^\beta z^\gamma$, then $ind(f) = (\gamma, \beta)$. Let $H_{i,j} = y^j G_i$, for $0 \le i \le l, 0 \le j \le 1$, and let

$$H_{i,j} = \sum_{(\gamma, \beta) \in S} h_{i,j,\gamma,\beta} y^\beta z^\gamma,$$

where $h_{i,j,\gamma,\beta} \in \mathbb{F}_q[x]$. Define the degree of $f' \in \mathbb{F}_q[x]$ to be the largest power of monomial with the largest power of x in f', denoted by $deg(f')$. Now we finish the basis construction and get the basis H of $I_{r,m,l}$.

3.2 Module Basis Reduction

After basis construction of $I_{r,m,l}$, it's time to reduce the basis H of the submodule $I_{r,m,l}$ over $\mathbb{F}_q(\mathcal{E})$ to a Gröbner basis which contains the interpolation polynomial of list decoding.

The module basis reduction step is stated as Algorithm 1. The idea of Algorithm 1 is to update the basis H until $ind(H_{i,j}) = (i, j), \forall (i, j) \in S$, so that $H_{i,j}, 0 \le i \le l, 0 \le j \le 1$ is a Gröbner basis of $I_{r,m,l}$ by Buchberger's criterion [5]. Algorithm 1 is also an optimized version of Buchberger's algorithm and the correctness proof of Algorithm 1 is similar to the proof of Algorithm G in [8].

After running Algorithm 1, the basis H satisfies $ind(H_{i,j}) = (i, j), \forall (i, j) \in S$. It means that we obtain the Gröbner basis of $I_{r,m,l}$, and we can get the interpolation polynomial Q which satisfies the constraints of list decoding by choosing the minimal polynomial of H with respect to $>_k$. Finally, we use the polynomial factorization algorithm proposed by Wu [14] to efficiently find the z-roots of Q. One of the z-roots of Q is the message encoded by the elliptic code.

Algorithm 1: The Module Based Interpolation Algorithm

Input: The finite field $\mathbb{F}_q$, an elliptic curve $\mathcal{E}$, the code parameters n, k, received codeword r, interpolation parameters m, l and the basis H of $I_{r,m,l}$;

Output: The interpolation polynomial Q of list decoding

1   **if** $ind(H_{0,0}) \neq (0,0)$ **and** $ind(H_{0,1}) \neq (0,1)$ **then**

2   Swap $H_{0,0}$ and $H_{0,1}$;

3   **end**

4   **for** $i = 1$ *to* l **do**

5   **while** $ind(H_{i,0}) \neq (i,*)$ **or** $ind(H_{i,1}) \neq (i,*)$ **or** $ind(H_{i,0}) = ind(H_{i,1})$ **do**

6   **for** $j = 0$ *to* 1 **do**

7   **while** $ind(H_{i,j}) \neq (i,*)$ **do**

8   Set $s \leftarrow ind(H_{i,j})$, assume $s = (\gamma, \beta)$;

9   Set $d \leftarrow deg(h_{i,j,\gamma,\beta}) - deg(h_{\gamma,\beta,\gamma,\beta})$;

10   Set $c \leftarrow lc(h_{i,j,\gamma,\beta})lc(h_{\gamma,\beta,\gamma,\beta})^{-1}$;

11   **if** $d \geq 0$ **then**

12   Set $H_{i,j} \leftarrow H_{i,j} - cx^d H_{\gamma,\beta}$;

13   **else**

14   Set $T \leftarrow H_{\gamma,\beta}$;

15   Set $H_{\gamma,\beta} \leftarrow H_{i,j}$;

16   Set $H_{i,j} \leftarrow x^{-d} H_{i,j} - cT$;

17   **end**

18   **end**

19   **end**

20   **while** $ind(H_{i,0}) = ind(H_{i,1})$ **do**

21   Set $s \leftarrow ind(H_{i,0})$, assume $s = (i, \beta)$;

22   **if** $deg(h_{i,0,i,\beta}) > deg(h_{i,1,i,\beta})$ **then**

23   Set $sign_h \leftarrow 0$ and $sign_l \leftarrow 1$;

24   **else**

25   Set $sign_h \leftarrow 1$ and $sign_l \leftarrow 0$;

26   **end**

27   Set $d \leftarrow deg(h_{i,sign_h,i,\beta}) - deg(h_{i,sign_l,i,\beta})$;

28   Set $c \leftarrow lc(h_{i,sign_h,i,\beta})lc(h_{i,sign_l,i,\beta})^{-1}$;

29   Set $H_{i,sign_h} \leftarrow H_{i,sign_h} - cx^d H_{i,sign_l}$;

30   **end**

31   **end**

32   **if** $ind(H_{i,0}) \neq (i,0)$ **and** $ind(H_{i,1}) \neq (i,1)$ **then**

33   Swap $H_{i,0}$ and $H_{i,1}$;

34   **end**

35   **end**

36   **return** *the smallest element in H with respect to $>_k$.*

---

4   Performance

In this section, we use the MBR interpolation of list decoding on the decryption of ECC^2 and analyse the performance. Moreover, we compare the performance of ECC^2 with that of Classic McEliece [1] which is a round-3 submission to NIST's Post-Quantum Cryptography Standardization Project [2]. We find that our MBR interpolation performs better in running time than SW list decoding and our MBR interpolation performs better in key sizes than Classic McEliece.

According to [16], in order to keep security of the encryption system and reduce the complexity of the MBR interpolation algorithm, we choose the appropriate parameters for ECC^2 as in Table 1. Our MBR interpolation algorithm with the parameters for ECC^2 has the parameters which are multiplicity parameter $m = 3$ and list size parameter $l = 4$ for $1^\lambda = 2^{128}$ and $1^\lambda = 2^{256}$.

After programming our MBR interpolation algorithm and reprogramming the SW list decoding with OpenSSL, we get the computational cost and the key sizes of them. Meanwhile, we show the performance of Classic McEliece as a comparison.

Table 1. Computational time and key sizes of ECC^2 and Classic McEliece. All computational time is expressed in CPU cycles and all key sizes are expressed in bytes. The time as well as key sizes of mceliece348864 and mceliece6688128 are from [1].

1^λ	Algorithm	q	n	k	t	Average time	PK size	SK size
2^{128}	ECC^2.SW.Enc	134807	521	150	196	4411314	125212	1179
2^{128}	ECC^2.SW.Dec	134807	521	150	196	1333533835		
2^{128}	Our MBR.Enc	127079	410	205	106	3093021	89304	878
2^{128}	Our MBR.Dec	127079	410	205	106	551506970		
2^{128}	Mceliece348864.Enc	–	3488	2720	–	44350	261120	6492
2^{128}	Mceliece348864.Dec	–	3488	2720	–	134745		
2^{256}	ECC^2.SW.Enc	561307	1031	322	364	9994042	570745	2585
2^{256}	ECC^2.SW.Dec	561307	1031	322	364	9669511992		
2^{256}	Our MBR.Enc	481001	770	385	204	7026536	352035	1836
2^{256}	Our MBR.Dec	481001	770	385	204	1726689977		
2^{256}	Mceliece6688128.Enc	–	6688	5024	–	151721	1044992	13932
2^{256}	Mceliece6688128.Dec	–	6688	5024	–	323957		

Time. The program of our implementation is compiled with GCC 9.3.0. It is run on a computer running on Windows10 with Intel Core i7-9700K @3.60 GHz CPU and 32.00 GB RAM. Without loss of generality, we run our program 10000 times and give statistics on running time in Table 1.

According to Table 1, it is obvious that the MBR interpolation algorithm performs better in decryption speed than ECC^2.GS and ECC^2.SW. Compared with Classic McEliece, the computational cost of ECC^2 with MBR interpolation is about 4000 times of that of Classic McEliece. Although there is still a big gap compared with Classic McEliece, the running time of the encryption system ECC^2 shows that ECC^2 could be applied in real life.

Space. Now we analyse the key sizes of ECC^2. For Classic McEliece, the public key sizes of mceliece348864 and mceliece6688128 are bigger than that of ECC^2. Table 1 reports the key sizes of ECC^2 and Classic McEliece. Hence, our MBR interpolation ECC^2 system performs better in key sizes than ECC^2.SW. Although the running time of our MBR interpolation ECC^2 is longer than that of Classic McEliece, the key sizes of it are shorter than Classic McEliece.

References

1. Classic McEliece: conservative code-based cryptography. https://classic.mceliece.org/index.html Accessed 10 Oct 2020
2. Post-Quantum Cryptography PQC. https://csrc.nist.gov/Projects/post-quantum-cryptography/round-3-submissions Accessed 26 Sep 2021
3. Barbier, M., Barreto, P.: Key reduction of McEliece's cryptosystem using list decoding. In: IEEE International Symposium on Information Theory Proceedings, pp. 2681–2685 (2011)
4. Beelen, P., Brander, K.: Efficient list decoding of a class of algebraic geometry codes. Adv. Math. Commun. **4**(4), 485–518 (2010)
5. Cox, D.A., Little, J., O'Shea, D.: Using Algebraic Geometry, 2nd edn. Springer, New York (2005). https://doi.org/10.1007/b138611
6. Elias, P.: List decoding for noisy channels. Research Laboratory of Electronics, Massachusetts Institute of Technology (1957)
7. Guruswami, V., Sudan, M.: Improved decoding of reed-Solomon and algebraic-geometry codes. IEEE Trans. Inf. Theor. **45**(6), 1757–1767 (1999)
8. Lee, K., O'Sullivan, M.: List decoding of Hermitian codes using gröbner bases. J. Symbolic Comput. **44**(12), 1662–1675 (2005)
9. Lee, K., O'Sullivan, M.: List decoding of reed-Solomon codes from a gröbner basis perspective. J. Symbolic Comput. **43**(9), 645–658 (2008)
10. Sakata, S.: On fast interpolation method for Guruswami-Sudan list decoding of one-point algebraic-geometry codes. In: Boztaş, S., Shparlinski, I.E. (eds.) AAECC 2001. LNCS, vol. 2227, pp. 172–181. Springer, Heidelberg (2001). https://doi.org/10.1007/3-540-45624-4_18
11. Shokrollahi, M., Wasserman, H.: List decoding of algebraic-geometric codes. IEEE Trans. Inf. Theor. **45**(2), 432–437 (1999)
12. Sudan, M.: Decoding of reed-solomon codes beyond the error-correction bound. J. Complex. **13**(1), 180–193 (1997)
13. Wan, Y., Chen, L., Zhang, F.: Guruswami-Sudan decoding of elliptic codes through module basis reduction. IEEE Trans. Inf. Theor. **67**(11), 7197–7209 (2021)
14. Wu, X., Siegel, P.: Efficient root-finding algorithm with applications to list decoding of algebraic-geometric codes. IEEE Trans. Inf. Theor. **47**(6), 2579–2587 (2001)
15. Zhang F., Liu, S.: Solving ECDLP via list decoding. In: Steinfeld, R., Yuen, T. (eds.) Provable Security. ProvSec 2019. Lecture Notes in Computer Science, vol. 11821, pp. 222–244. Springer, Cham (2019). https://doi.org/10.1007/978-3-030-31919-9_13
16. Zhang, F., Zhang, Z., Guan, P.: ECC2: Error correcting code and elliptic curve based cryptosystem. Inf. Sci. **526**, 301–320 (2020)

Federated Data Integration for Heterogeneous Partitions Based on Differential Privacy

Jinghao Huang, Yingpeng Sang$^{(\boxtimes)}$ ⓘ, Chaoxin Cai, Weizheng Li,
and Maliang Zhang

School of Computer Science and Engineering, Sun Yat-sen University,
Guangzhou, China
sangyp@mail.sysu.edu.cn

Abstract. Federated learning has recently become a research hotspot in distributed learning, and its purpose is to jointly train machine learning models on the premise of protecting privacy. However, there are some problems with federated learning. Each machine learning algorithm must be modified in order to complete the training. The data partitioning is either horizontal or vertical, which is not flexible enough. In addition, there are many rounds of communication during the training process, so the training efficiency is low. In order to address these problems, we propose a generic federated integration method for multiple data sources. The method can integrate data in arbitrary partitions, protect the privacy based on differential privacy, and reduce communication cost based on singular value decomposition. After the data are modelled in this method, they can be transferred to the center for purpose of federated learning. Our method includes four algorithms. We give a theoretical proof on the method's satisfying of differential privacy. Finally, experiments are conducted to demonstrate the performance of the method in prediction accuracy and data compression.

Keywords: Differential privacy · Singular value decomposition · Federated data integration · Data partition

1 Introduction

With the advent of the data age, while we can mine value from big data, privacy leaks also arise. People's sensitive data such as identity information, social relations, health data, address, if not effectively protected, privacy will be abused, which may have a serious impact on personal work and life.

The general mode in traditional federated learning [1] is that the data is stored locally and the parameters are passed to the central server through local training for aggregation, but this mode has two disadvantages. One is poor versatility, and each algorithm has to undergo complicated transformations to meet

© Springer Nature Switzerland AG 2022
H. Shen et al. (Eds.): PDCAT 2021, LNCS 13148, pp. 568–575, 2022.
https://doi.org/10.1007/978-3-030-96772-7_53

local training requirements. The second is the time-consuming training of algorithms, because the training iterations require network communication between the central server and the data nodes. In addition, the model training is performed on the data nodes with uneven computing power. It needs to wait for each node to complete the training before the central server can aggregate. These disadvantages can be avoided by applying differential privacy on the local data, then one round of transferring of the local data to the central node.

In addition, the main paradigms of traditional federated learning include vertical federated learning (each data owner provides all samples of a certain attribute) and horizontal federated learning (each data owner provides all attributes of some samples) [1]. However, in practice, the data segmentation is not perfect. One data owner may only have some attributes for some samples, and thus the data partitioning among owners will be heterogeneous. For example, the rapid proliferation of Internet of Things (IoT) calls for data mining and learning securely and reliably in distributed systems [2]. However, IoT devices can only collect part of the features data of some users, so cannot meet the needs of federated learning for data partition.

Few existing methods can solve the problem that data owners hold data in a heterogeneous way. This paper aims to propose a generic algorithm that allows the samples and attributes of each data owner in the heterogeneous partitions to be integrated to the central server under the premise of protecting privacy, and to maximize the use of the owner's data for machine learning tasks. We also provide client-level differential privacy protection on the owner's data, before they are transmitted to the central server, to minimize the risk of information leakage. The main contributions of this paper are as follows. We propose a generic federated integration method on heterogeneous partitions, assuming that the central server is untrustworthy. This method can integrate arbitrary data segments across clients to construct the training set, without modifying the algorithms, and the applicable type of learning tasks is not limited, including supervised learning, semi-supervised learning, etc. We design four sub-algorithms for the federated integration. The communication complexity of data transmission is minimized and we also prove that the method obeys ε-differential privacy.

2   Related Work

Differential privacy is a common technique for privacy protection. [3,4] put forward the concept of differential privacy. Differential privacy has flexible combination characteristics, the differential privacy mechanism can be used in combination [5]. In terms of differential privacy implementation mechanism, [3] proposed an exponential mechanism, which was applied to continuous variable. [6] proposed an exponential mechanism, which solved the problem that the Laplace mechanism was only applicable to numerical variables, and the exponential mechanism was applicable to categorical variable queries. Differential privacy mechanisms have been applied to many machine learning algorithms and statistical problems, including random forest classification algorithms [7], stochastic gradient descent algorithm [8], etc. [9] pointed out that local differential privacy (LDP) broke the shackles of the trusted third party, and allowed users to perturb their data locally, thus providing much stronger privacy protection.

Singular value decomposition is an important matrix decomposition, which has important applications in signal processing [10], image compression [11], and other fields. [12] introduced differential privacy into singular value decomposition of the collaborative filtering task, but this method was only applicable to the user-item evaluation matrix, but not to all types of matrices.

3   Our Method

The goal of our *generic federated integration* is to negotiate a matrix among the heterogeneous data owned by the data holders. Before the data is sent to the central server, we use differential privacy to protect the data and then transmit it to the server to ensure the security of private information. Figure 1 introduces related concepts. Assuming that there are k data holders, $\{H_1, \ldots, H_k\}$, they hold part of the features of different samples, and then upload the data to the central server after adding differential privacy to form a feature-label matrix $\mathbf{D}$ for federated integration. The meaning of label is general, if it is a classification problem, label is the classification value, if it is a regression problem, label is the target value. Each blue box in Fig. 1 represents a data holder matrix $\mathbf{D}_i$ owned by a data holder. Each $\mathbf{D}_i$ requires a user-ID vector $\mathbf{u}_i$ and a feature-schema vector $\mathbf{f}_i$ to define the meaning of each element. $\mathbf{f}_i$ is a list of feature names. The $\mathbf{D}_i$s are *heterogeneous* means the user-ID and feature-schema vectors are different among users. Even in a single data holder's matrix $\mathbf{D}_i$, some elements may be missing, so there are many block matrices $\mathbf{B}_{ij}$ in the matrix $\mathbf{D}_i$.

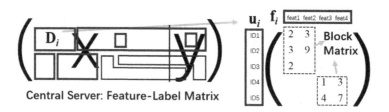

Central Server: Feature-Label Matrix

Fig. 1. Related concepts

3.1   Multi-Party Feature-Label Matrix Negotiation Algorithm

Each data holder has different features and different samples, and this algorithm aims to find a uniform feature-schema vector and user-ID vector on the central server, and form the data source matrix $\mathbf{D_S}$, the elements of which are H_i ($i = 1, \ldots, k$), specifying the source of each pair of feature and user-ID. A data holder H_i's ID-feature list L_i is $\{[\text{hash}(\text{ID}_1) : \text{feat}_1, \text{feat}_2, \ldots], [\text{hash}(\text{ID}_2) : \text{feat}_3, \ldots], \ldots\}$.

By hashing the ID, Algorithm 1 ensures that other data holders and the central server cannot know true IDs of the local samples, nor can the samples be identified to specific entities through ID.

Algorithm 1. Multi-Party Feature-Label Matrix Negotiation

Input: ID-feature list L_i, missing rate threshold T
Output: data source matrix $\mathbf{D_S}$, feature set $\mathbb{F}$, sample set $\mathbb{U}$

1: Each data holder sends his ID-feature list to the central server.
2: (Feature Negotiation) Central server performs statistics on the features sent by the data holder. For each feature, if the missing rate is less than T, the feature is included, and the feature set used for federated integration is denoted as $\mathbb{F}$.
3: (Sample Negotiation) Central server performs statistics on each sample and calculates the missing rate of the sample in $\mathbb{F}$. If the missing rate is less than the threshold T, the sample is included in the federated integration, and the sample set used for federated integration is denoted as $\mathbb{U}$.
4: Determine $\mathbf{D_S}$. If a value for a certain feature $feat_i$ of some user ID_j is missing on all data holders, the central server will fill the missing value with the average of $feat_i$ values on all the other user-IDs. If more than two data holders have a value at $(ID_j, feat_i)$, the central server must coordinate and specify which data holder's value will be preserved. The server can randomly designate a data holder, or select the holder with a higher credibility.

Algorithm 2. Matrix Block Recognition

Input: data holder matrix $\mathbf{D}_i$ with dimensions $m \times n$
Output: block information list BIL_i

1: Convert $\mathbf{D}_i$ to a 0-1 matrix, if the element at this position must be transmitted, it is recorded as 1, otherwise it is recorded as 0.
2: Initialize an empty list $visited$, and an empty queue Q.
3: **for** i = 1 to m **do**
4:     **for** j = 1 to n **do**
5:         **if** $(i, j) \notin visited$ **then**
6:             Put (i, j) into $visited$, put (i, j) and its 4-neighbor index C_{ij} into Q, if the element is not in $visited$ and the value is 1.
7:         **else**
8:             **continue**
9:         **while** Q is no empty **do**
10:             Get an element (i', j') from Q head, let $(i, j) = (i', j')$.
11:             Update the connected domain range $max_i, min_i, max_j, min_j$.
12:             Put (i, j) into $visited$, put (i, j) and its 4-neighbor index C_{ij} into Q, if the element is not in $visited$ and the value is 1.
13:             Get a connected domain Dom_p, where its scale is m_p, n_p, its upper left corner element index is x_p, y_p.
14:             Put m_p, n_p, x_p, y_p into block information list BIL_i.

3.2   Matrix Block Recognition Algorithm

After executing Algorithm 1, the preserved features and user-IDs will be fed back to the corresponding data holders. The data holder i can determine the required user-ID vector $\mathbf{u}_i$ and feature-schema vector $\mathbf{f}_i$, then decide his data holder matrix $\mathbf{D}_i$, which should be transmitted to the central server. In $\mathbf{D}_i$, part of the elements is missing, because a certain feature of a sample should be uploaded by other data holders. We propose the Matrix Block Recognition algorithm in order to find all block matrices in $\mathbf{D}_i$. Based on the idea of connected domain recognition which checks the connectivity between matrix elements, our algorithm finds matrix elements that are connected to each other. Suppose an element index is (i, j), its 4-neighbor index list C_{ij} is $[(i - 1, j), (i + 1, j), (i, j - 1), (i, j + 1)]$. A list *visited* will record the coordinates of the element after it is accessed. A queue Q is used to find each connected domain. The algorithm can be shown in Algorithm 2.

3.3   DP-based Singular Value Decomposition Algorithm

For each block matrix $\mathbf{B}_{ij}$ obtained through Algorithm 2, we propose a differential privacy-based singular value decomposition algorithm (DP-SVD) so that the data meets differential privacy before being transmitted to the central server. At the same time, a low-rank approximation of SVD is performed for each block, where some singular values are removed to achieve matrix compression, reducing the amount of data transmission in each block. The precision is lost after the matrix is recovered by the central server, but the introduced error also provides privacy protection.

In Algorithm 3, according to the theorem in [3, 6], if the feature is a categorical variable, the exponential mechanism is used, and if the variable is a continuous variable, the Laplace mechanism is used.

Algorithm 3. DP-SVD

Input: data holder matrix $\mathbf{D}_i$, the number of features n_i, block information list BIL_i, block matrix $\mathbf{B}_{ij}$, compression dimension r_{ij}, block scale threshold T_b, threshold of block missing rate T_m, privacy budget ε_i
  Output: approximate matrices list $[(\mathbf{U}_{m \times r}, \mathbf{\Sigma}_{r \times r}, \mathbf{V}_{n \times r}), ...]$
1: **for** each feature of $\mathbf{D}_i$ **do**
2:    Add ε_i / n_i - differential privacy to this feature, get matrix with noise $\mathbf{D}_i'$ and $\mathbf{B}_{ij}'$.
3: **for** each block matrix $\mathbf{B}_{ij}'$, it scale is m_{ij}, n_{ij} **do**
4:    **if** $\min(m_{ij}, n_{ij}) < T_b$ or the missing rate of $\mathbf{B}_{ij}' > T_m$ **then**
5:        Transfer $\mathbf{B}_{ij}'$ to central server directly.
6:    **else**
7:        If the value is categorical variable, use label encoder to become a numerical value. Use 0 to fill the missing value in $\mathbf{B}_{ij}'$.
8:        $(\mathbf{U}_{m \times r_{ij}}, \mathbf{\Sigma}_{r_{ij} \times r_{ij}}, \mathbf{V}_{n \times r_{ij}}) \approx \mathrm{SVD}(\mathbf{B}_{ij}', r_{ij})$, r_{ij} is compression dimension. Transfer $(\mathbf{U}_{m \times r_{ij}}, \mathbf{\Sigma}_{r_{ij} \times r_{ij}}, \mathbf{V}_{n \times r_{ij}})$ to central server.

3.4   Optimal Compression Dimension Model of SVD

Since the approximate SVD brings errors into the data, we should optimize the compression dimension r in SVD. We consider two goals: the least error of recovery and the least amount of transmission. Suppose the original matrix $(m \times n)$ is $\mathbf{M}$, the matrix after differential privacy is $\mathbf{M}'$, and $\mathbf{M}'$ is decomposed by SVD. $\mathbf{M}'$ after approximate recovery is R. We use $error = \|\mathbf{M}' - \mathbf{R}\|_F/(mn)$ to represent error of recovery, where $\|\cdot\|_F$ means matrix $Frobenius$-norm. We use $scale = r(m+n+1)$ of $\mathbf{U}_{m \times r}, \mathbf{\Sigma}_{r \times r}, \mathbf{V}_{n \times r}$ to represent amount of transmission. For each r, we can calculate $scale_r$ and $error_r$. Then we standardize $scale_r$ and $error_r$ respectively using Z-score, and get $sScale_r, sError_r$. The model is $\min_r w_1 * sScale_r + w_2 * sError_r$, $s.t.$ $r \in [1, \min(m, n)], r(m + n + 1) < mn$. w_1, w_2 are the weight of two parts. The optimal value $r_{optimal}$ of the objective function can be obtained by traversing r under the restricted conditions.

3.5   Privacy Budget Allocation Strategy

Given a global privacy budget ε, in order to ensure data utility, the privacy budget ε_i used by each data holder should be the largest. Our method satisfies $\max_{1 \leq i \leq n} \varepsilon_i$ - DP. Therefore, we set $\varepsilon_i = \varepsilon, (i = 1, \ldots k)$. For each feature in $\mathbf{D}_i$, set $\varepsilon_{ij} = \varepsilon_i/n$, where n is the number of features. The sensitivity of feature j is $\max_i d_{ij} - \min_i d_{ij}$, where d_{ij} is an element of data holder matrix.

Algorithm 4. Generic Federated Integration Method

Input: privacy budget ε

Output: Feature-Label matrix $\mathbf{D}$

1: Execute Multi-Party Feature-Label Matrix Negotiation Algorithm.
2: **for** each data holder **do**
3:     Execute Matrix Block Recognition Algorithm in $\mathbf{D}_i$.
4:     Execute DP-SVD Algorithm in $\mathbf{D}_i$, let $\varepsilon_i = \varepsilon$, $r_{ij} = r_{ij,optimal}$.
5:     Transmit the data (added noise) to the central server.
6: The central server reconstructs feature-label matrix $\mathbf{D}$, executes modeling in $\mathbf{D}$.

Theorem 1. *Our generic federated integration method satisfies ε-DP.*

Proof. For each feature in $\mathbf{D}_i$. According to the sequential composition theorem in [5], the privacy budget of $\mathbf{D}_i$ is $\sum_{j=1}^n \varepsilon_{ij} = n * (\varepsilon_i/n) = \varepsilon_i$.

For all data holders, $\mathbf{D}_i(i = 1, \ldots, k)$ are disjoint subsets. According to the parallel composition theorem in [5], the privacy budget of our method is $\max_{1 \leq i \leq k} \varepsilon_i = \max_{1 \leq i \leq k} \varepsilon = \varepsilon$. Therefore, our method satisfies ε - DP.

4 Experiments

We use the Breast Cancer Wisconsin Data Set [13] for integration. This data set is a binary classification problem for judging whether breast lumps are benign or not. This data set belongs to private data in the field of personal health and is very suitable for demonstration of federated integration. The data set includes 32 features, including radius, area, texture, etc. ID is used to indicate the identity of the patient. SVM, kNN, naive Bayes, back propagation neural network, random forest, softmax regression are used as classifiers. The experimental parameters are the privacy budget ε and the number of partitions. We segment the samples and features to simulate multiple data holders.

The result of the experiments is shown in Fig. 2, the baseline means the performance of the model when differential privacy is not added. Accuracy in the test set is used as a performance metric. Accuracy is defined as $num_{correct}/num_{all}$.

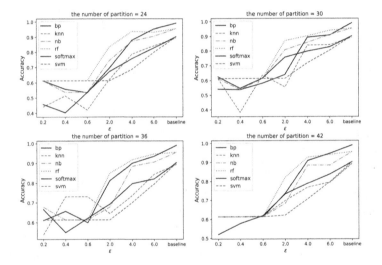

Fig. 2. The result of Breast Cancer Wisconsin (Diagnostic) Data Set.

The results show that with the increase of ε, the accuracy of the model is closer to the baseline models. While the algorithm in this paper protects privacy, the performance of subsequent model learning is also guaranteed. The average compression rate of DP-SVD is **44.94%**. The results show that our method compresses the amount of data that needs to be transmitted. Compression rate means dividing the number of transmission matrix elements using compression by the number of transmission matrix elements without SVD.

5   Conclusion

In this paper, we propose a generic federated integration method, which avoids the problems of federated learning that need to modify machine learning algorithms, inflexible data partitioning, and low training efficiency. The method has strong versatility, can process category features and continuous features simultaneously, and can be applied to different data mining tasks. Theoretical analysis and experiments show that our algorithm performs well in privacy protection, prediction accuracy, and data compression.

Acknowledgement. This work was supported by the Science and Technology Program of Guangzhou, China (No. 201904010209), and the Science and Technology Program of Guangdong Province, China (No. 2017A010101039).

References

1. Yang, Q., Liu, Y., Chen, T., Tong, Y.: Federated machine learning: concept and applications. ACM Trans. Intell. Syst. Technol. (TIST) **10**(2), 1–19 (2019)
2. Ma, Z., Xiao, M., Xiao, Y., Pang, Z., Poor, H.V., Vucetic, B.: High-reliability and low-latency wireless communication for internet of things: challenges, fundamentals, and enabling technologies. IEEE Internet Things J. **6**(5), 7946–7970 (2019)
3. Alvim, M.S., Chatzikokolakis, K., McIver, A., Morgan, C., Palamidessi, C., Smith, G.: Differential privacy. Presented at the (2020). https://doi.org/10.1007/978-3-319-96131-6_23
4. Dwork, C., McSherry, F., Nissim, K., Smith, A.: Calibrating noise to sensitivity in private data analysis. In: Halevi, S., Rabin, T. (eds.) TCC 2006. LNCS, vol. 3876, pp. 265–284. Springer, Heidelberg (2006). https://doi.org/10.1007/11681878_14
5. McSherry, F.D.: Privacy integrated queries: an extensible platform for privacy-preserving data analysis. In: Proceedings of the 2009 ACM SIGMOD International Conference on Management of Data, pp. 19–30 (2009)
6. McSherry, F., Talwar, K.: Mechanism design via differential privacy. In: 48th Annual IEEE Symposium on Foundations of Computer Science (FOCS 2007), pp. 94–103. IEEE (2007)
7. Hou, J., Li, Q., Meng, S., Ni, Z., Chen, Y., Liu, Y.: Dprf: a differential privacy protection random forest. IEEE Access **7**, 130707–130720 (2019)
8. Abadi, M., et al.: Deep learning with differential privacy. In: Proceedings of the 2016 ACM SIGSAC Conference on Computer and Communications Security, pp. 308–318 (2016)
9. Xiong, X., Liu, S., Li, D., Cai, Z., Niu, X.: A comprehensive survey on local differential privacy. Secur. Commun. Netw. **2020**, 1–29 (2020)
10. Van Der Veen, A.J., Deprettere, E.F., Swindlehurst, A.L.: Subspace-based signal analysis using singular value decomposition. Proc. IEEE **81**(9), 1277–1308 (1993)
11. Abdi, H.: Singular value decomposition (SVD) and generalized singular value decomposition. In: Encyclopedia of measurement and statistics, pp. 907–912 (2007)
12. Xian, Z., Li, Q., Huang, X., Li, L.: New SVD-based collaborative filtering algorithms with differential privacy. J. Intell. Fuzzy Sys. **33**(4), 2133–2144 (2017)
13. William W., Nick S., O.L.: Breast cancer wisconsin (diagnostic) data set (1995). https://archive.ics.uci.edu/ml/datasets/Breast+Cancer+Wisconsin+(Diagnostic)

Patient-Chain: Patient-centered Healthcare System a Blockchain-based Technology in Dealing with Emergencies

Hai Trieu Le[1], Lam Nguyen Tran Thanh[2], Hong Khanh Vo[3],
Hoang Huong Luong[3], Khoi Nguyen Huynh Tuan[3], Tuan Dao Anh[3],
The Anh Nguyen[3], Khang Hy Nguyen Vuong[3], and Ha Xuan Son[4(✉)]

[1] Can Tho University of Technology, Can Tho City, Vietnam
[2] Ho Chi Minh University of Technology, Ho Chi Minh city, Vietnam
[3] FPT University, Can Tho City, Vietnam
{khanhvh,khoinhtce140133,tuandace140502,anhntce160237,
hynvkce140237}@fpt.edu.vn
[4] Insubria University, Varese, Italy
sha@uninsubria.it

Abstract. Medical healthcare currently plays a vital role for humans in society. For each patient, personal health records are critical and sensitive assets, so how to manage them effectively is becoming exciting research to solve. Many types of research in managing and operating personal health records have been introduced; however, dealing with patients' data in emergency cases remains an uncertain issue. When emergencies happen in reality, using a traditional access system is challenging for patients to consent medical staff, i.e., nurses or doctors, to access their data. Besides, there is no secured record management of patient' data, which reveals highly confidential personal information, such as what happened, when, and who has access to such information. Thus, this paper proposes a control and management system regarding emergency access to protect the patients' data called the Patient-Chain platform: a patient-centred healthcare system, a Blockchain-based technology in dealing with emergencies. The Patient-Chain system is built based on permitted Blockchain Hyperledger Fabric, defines several rules and regulations by using smart contracts and time duration to deal with emergencies. The patients also restrict the time to access the data in such urgent cases-several algorithms representing how the system works are also provided to make readers understand the proposed management system.

Keywords: Emergency access · Blockchain · Hyperledger fabric · Privacy & security · Personal health record

1 Introduction

Human health is currently considered the most valuable asset, so all the latest and most influential scientific and technical achievements are applied to the

© Springer Nature Switzerland AG 2022
H. Shen et al. (Eds.): PDCAT 2021, LNCS 13148, pp. 576–583, 2022.
https://doi.org/10.1007/978-3-030-96772-7_54

health care fields. In the industrial revolution 4.0, Blockchain and the Internet of Things are emerging technologies being applied to the medical field to enhance the ability to examine, treat, manage and monitor patients. The purpose of applying these technologies is to allow continuous monitoring of the patient's health status anywhere in the world, especially for patients with underlying diseases.

Patients are considered the center of medical examination and treatment services, especially fee-based services, so their health data is becoming more and more critical, and it is necessary to have a system to ensure data confidentiality. There are many studies towards the confidentiality of patient's health parameters [1], but these studies have not focused on emergency emergencies. For emergencies, patients will not actively decide who can access their medical records, so that emergency treatment will be challenging. This shortage creates a significant weakness when applying new technologies to the medical field.

Due to their sensitivity and privacy, systems typically allow patients to designate some of the doctors and nurses they treat and limit everyone else. However, such pre-determining of access [2–6] would be the main limitation because, in emergencies, it is not possible to ensure that designated doctors and nurses are available when the patient needs emergency care.

To alleviate these problems, ensure secure access handling in emergencies, and maintain a secure transaction log, we recommend a Patient-Chain framework to leverage a distributed and immutable shared ledger called Blockchain technology. **Blockchain** is a decentralized architecture that has an immutable distributed ledger in which all transactions are recorded. In the Patient-Chain system, there are five main types of user groups: patient, doctor, medical, nurse and insurance agent.

2   Related Work

2.1   Emergency Access Control for Personal Healthcare Records

Zhang et al. [7] proposed an online system for polling to provide available access for urgent control to a personal health record. For every emergency access request, the system controls the right access based on the collected views of the patient's predefined emergency contact information and additional online enrolled physicians. In another research published by Thummavet and Vasupongayya [8], they proposed a framework to deal with personal health record data in emergency cases. The main challenge in such emergency conditions is how emergency staff and doctors obtain their patients' data when they are incapable of providing information. Another system that uses fingerprints of patients is proposed in Guan et al. [9]. This system allows doctors to obtain quick access permission of personal health records by using patients' fingerprints. In this system, patients' fingerprints served as a permission key for the doctor to access and obtain the necessary information. The server administers compared the presented data and the original data saved on the database.

In the research of Rabieh et al. [10], a secure medical records access plan was designed to provide emergency access for the patients using a cloud server. In this case, an emergency center could decrypt a patient's medical records without exposing the secret key used to encrypt them with the guidance of the patients' smartphone and the cloud server.

2.2   Blockchain-Based Technology Application in Health Care System

Ichikawa et al. [11] developed a mHealth scheme for cognitive-behavioral treatment for sleeplessness practicing a smartphone application. The volunteer's data information obtained by the application was saved in JSON format and forwarded to the blockchain HF system. They confirmed the data update process under circumstances where all the validating peers were working routinely.

An implementation that utilized smart contracts as mediators were proposed by [12] to access electronic health records in a largescale information system. In this paper, the problem of accessibility and data privacy issues in healthcare is emphasized. The current version of the Ethereum platform is the base idea of the suggested architecture, in which smart contracts play the core role in the system.

MeDShare [13] was another efficient blockchain-based management system to handle medical records. This system was implemented to use cloud repositories that manage shared medical records and data among medical big data entities. It guaranteed data provenance, security, auditing, and user verification via cryptographic keys. The mechanism of MedShare is divided into four main layers, including user, data query, data structuring and provenance, and an existing database infrastructure layer.

In the research of Duong-Trung et al. [6,14], a patient-centric care system was built based on a smart contract mechanism. It is also introduced in [15], where the system consisted of five main parties: doctor, medical man, nurse, insurance man, and patients; in which, patients were the heart of the system.

3   Patient-Chain System Architecture

In an emergency case, accessing personal health records can provide the necessary medical treatment for patients. Nevertheless, when the patient is unconscious, it is complicated for them to control access to their health record and provide their information to doctor or nurse. Therefore, it requires an automatic system control to manage the medical record and to be able to access or share the health record data during the medication or post-treatment monitoring. Due to the sensitivity of the data, it is compulsory to keep the data complete, securely saved, and can be accessed only based on the patient's approval quickly and expediently. Hence, in this paper, we apply private Blockchain. Hyperledger Fabric technology network to create a framework of a personal health record. By operating Permissioned blockchain technology, this paper provides emergency access to expedite the consent management and speed up PHR data fetch from the PHR system. A smart contract is developed to enable patients to impose permission access control policy [16,17] for their data efficiently and allow personal health record data for sharing with emergency doctors during emergencies.

The patient-Chain system defines some permission access rules through Hyperledger Fabric. In this paper framework, the medical staff, i.e., doctors or nurses, can initiate an emergency request at the medical center, then send it directly to the data management service center. This request is sent under the restrictions of the patient's rules through the framework. Personal health data is saved via the blockchain network or, in other words, is kept in their health record. There may be multiple accesses from different participants. Nevertheless, the authority is only given to staff who have granular access rights from the database according to the permissions. The data requests are also updated frequently by the blockchain network. Hence, the patients, after recovering, can see who already accessed and took their data.

In our system, a smart contract plays an important role. All the transactions are concerned with authorization, and data fetching from the ledger are executed through smart contracts (a business, logic). The proposed framework operates based on the smart contracts of the ledger, which makes the system protected, effective, and auditable. Figure 1 shows the proposed Blockchain-based design of the Patient-Chain system for emergency control in healthcare. This system consists of five actors: patients, doctors, nurses, medical men, and insurance men. The detailed explanation of the entities is as follows.

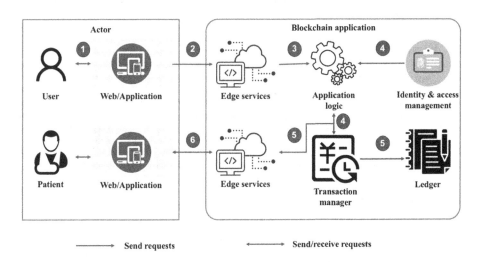

Fig. 1. Patient-Chain workflow

Figure 1 includes six main steps from the beginning, the **User** (i.e., medical staff) send the requirement to collect the patient information in the emergencies; eventually, the patient information is synced on the web/application. In the first step, the User, nurses or doctors, initiates an emergency request at the medical center equipment, send it to the edge service for processing data. Then, the second step checks the validity of the data sent from the requests to avoid missing data when the User makes the request at the edge services. After checking, the data will be sent to the compute module at the **Application logic**. Next step, these modules conduct data format before storing into the system, **ID_user** is also collected to store to identify the person making the transaction; in addition to the immutability of data, transparency is also a strong point of the blockchain system when it allows identifying which User made a transaction and when it was made. Then, in the fourth step, when an emergency request is initiated, the system will send request information to the **Transaction manager** for storage with the waiting state. At that time, **Application logic** also sends an emergency case message to the patient with a preset timeout. If the patient finds some problems (i.e., from the malicious user requests), they will reject the request. **Application Logic** updates the request again with the reject status. Conversely, if the system does not receive the message within the waiting time, **Application logic** will update the request with approval status and grant access to the patient's database to the doctor and nurse. Finally, **Transaction manager** includes the API tasked with storing or querying data. When an emergency request is sent, the **Transaction manager** will store emergency information with a waiting status, which can be updated to change to reject or approve depending on whether the patient has a response to the system or not. In many cases, individuals may attempt to gain unauthorized access to patient data, so the confirmation or denial of a patient's emergency request is essential in this model.

4   Evaluation

4.1   Environment Setting

This section measures the response time and results of requests sent to and processed by smart contracts. The measurements are performed on a computer with Intel® Core™ i5-3340M CPU configuration @ 2.70 GHz × 4, 8 GB RAM. Moreover, the authors provide the sources codes for the proof of concept, instruction of installation. Interesting readers might refer to our GitHub repository[1].

4.2   The Four Scenarios

This paper test our proposed model with four scenarios in two characteristics, i.e., the number of request result and the latency of request as following:

1. In the first scenario, we compare the requests' results and the corresponding latency with the emergency data initialization function. With the first 5 cases corresponding to the number of requests from 1000 to 5000. With the subsequent 5 cases corresponding to the number of requests from 6000 to 10,000, the number of successful requests.

---

[1] https://github.com/Masquerade0127/emergency-blockchain

2. In this scenario, the article measures the patient's data initialization function and parallels the latency of this function; the number of workers is changed with two workers. The first 5 request cases correspond to the number of requests from 1000 to 5000, 2 workers for 5 cases then correspond to the number of requests increasing from 6000 to 10,000.

3. In the third scenario, the study presents the results of the emergency data query feature; the number of workers is now adjusted to 10 for all 10 data query cases.

4. In this scenario, the study measures the results of the patient data query feature; the number of workers used is 10 for 10 cases. In general, requests are handled quite stably, with the number of successful requests being more than 20,000 requests while the number of failed requests is only from 0 to 2 requests.

The result of these scenario is shown in Fig. 2.

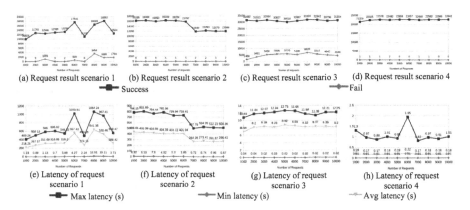

Fig. 2. The results of #request success and # request failure and The latency (max/min/average) of the requests to initiate emergency data of four scenarios

4.3   Future Work

For the deployment aspect, further works will be deployed in the practical environment. We plan to set up Patient-Chain model in the IoHT (Internet of Healthcare Things) platform. Specifically, the sensors, wearable devices collect the health and fitness information and store in the medical data center. These information can be exploited by the medical staff if necessary for the emergency situations [18–20]. For the privacy aspect, we will exploit attribute-based access control (ABAC) [3,4] to manage the authorization process of the SIP-MBA Platform via the dynamic policy approach [16,17,21].

5 Conclusion

The proposed system in this paper provides privacy protection and security policy to manage patients' data in urgent situations. Technically, the system is built based on Hyperledger Fabric and Smart Contract, a permissioned based blockchain technology. The proposed framework deals with the problems of getting access to a patient's data when emergencies arise and considers the problems of setting suitable rules for accessing the emergency control management of personal health records. The system is implemented through Hyperledger Fabric to evaluate the efficiency of our framework. Our experimental results also confirm that this system can ensure the privacy and security of sensitive patient data.

References

1. Thanh, L.N.T., et al.: IoHT-MBA: an internet of healthcare Things (IoHT) platform based on microservice and Brokerless architecture. Int. J. Adv. Comput. Sci. Appl. **12**(7) (2021). http://dx.doi.org/10.14569/IJACSA.2021.0120768, https://doi.org/10.14569/IJACSA.2021.0120768

2. Son, H.X., Chen, E.: Towards a fine-grained access control mechanism for privacy protection and policy conflict resolution. Int. J. Adv. Comput. Sci. Appl. **10**(2), 507–516 (2019)

3. Son, H.X., Hoang, N.M.: A novel attribute-based access control system for fine-grained privacy protection. In: Proceedings of the 3rd International Conference on Cryptography, Security and Privacy, pp. 76–80 (2019)

4. Hoang, N.M., Son, H.X.: A dynamic solution for finegrained policy conflict resolution. In: Proceedings of the 3rd International Conference on Cryptography, Security and Privacy, pp. 116–120 (2019)

5. Duong-Trung, N., et al.: On Components of a patient-centered healthcare system using smart contract. In: Proceedings of the 2020 4th International Conference on Cryptography, Security and Privacy, New York, pp. 31–35. Association for Computing Machinery (2020). https://doi.org/10.1145/3377644.3377668

6. Duong-Trung, N., et al.: Smart care: integrating blockchain technology into the design of patient-centered healthcare systems. In: Proceedings of the 2020 4th International Conference on Cryptography, Security and Privacy, ICCSP 2020, New York, pp. 105–109. Association for Computing Machinery (2020). https://doi.org/10.1145/3377644.3377667

7. Zhang, Y., et al.: Emergency access for online personally controlled health records system. Inf. Health Soc. Care **37**(3), 190–202 (2012)

8. Thummavet, P., Vasupongayya, S.: A novel personal health record system for handling emergency situations. In: 2013 International Computer Science and Engineering Conference (ICSEC), pp. 266–271. IEEE (2013)

9. Guan, S., Wang, Y., Shen, J.: Fingerprint-based access to personally controlled health records in emergency situations. Sci. Chin. Inf. Sci. **61**(5), 059103 (2018)

10. Rabieh, K., et al.: A secure and cloud-based medical records access scheme for on-road emergencies. In: 2018 15th IEEE Annual Consumer Communications & Networking Conference (CCNC), pp. 1–8. IEEE (2018)

11. Ichikawa, D., Kashiyama, M., Ueno, T.: Tamper-resistant mobile health using blockchain technology. JMIR mHealth and uHealth **5**(7), e111 (2017)

12. da Conceição, A.F., et al.: Eletronic health records using blockchain technology. arXiv preprint arXiv:1804.10078 (2018)
13. Xia, Q.I., et al.: MeDShare: trust-less medical data sharing among cloud service providers via blockchain. IEEE Access **5**, 14757–14767 (2017)
14. Duong-Trung, N., et al.: On components of a patient-centered healthcare system using smart contract. In: Proceedings of the 2020 4th International Conference on Cryptography, Security and Privacy, pp. 31–35 (2020)
15. Son, H.X., Nguyen, M.H., Vo, H.K., Nguyen, T.P.: Toward an privacy protection based on access control model in hybrid cloud for healthcare systems. In: Martínez Álvarez, F., Troncoso Lora, A., Sáez Muñoz, J.A., Quintián, H., Corchado, E. (eds.) CISIS/ICEUTE -2019. AISC, vol. 951, pp. 77–86. Springer, Cham (2020). https://doi.org/10.1007/978-3-030-20005-3_8
16. Xuan, S.H., et al.: Rew-xac: an approach to rewriting request for elastic abac enforcement with dynamic policies. In: 2016 International Conference on Advanced Computing and Applications (ACOMP), pp. 25–31. IEEE (2016)
17. Son, H.X., Dang, T.K., Massacci, F.: REW-SMT: a new approach for rewriting XACML request with dynamic big data security policies. In: Wang, G., Atiquzzaman, M., Yan, Z., Choo, K.-K.R. (eds.) SpaCCS 2017. LNCS, vol. 10656, pp. 501–515. Springer, Cham (2017). https://doi.org/10.1007/978-3-319-72389-1_40
18. Thanh, L.N.T., et al.: UIP2SOP: a unique IoT network applying single sign-on and message queue protocol. IJACSA **12**(6), 19–30 (2021)
19. Thanh, L.N.T., et al.: Toward a security IoT platform with high rate transmission and low energy consumption. In: Gervasi, O., et al. (eds.) ICCSA 2021. LNCS, vol. 12949, pp. 647–662. Springer, Cham (2021). https://doi.org/10.1007/978-3-030-86653-2_47
20. Nguyen, T.T.L., et al.: Toward a unique IoT network via single sign-on protocol and message queue. In: Saeed, K., Dvorský, J. (eds.) CISIM 2021. LNCS, vol. 12883, pp. 270–284. Springer, Cham (2021). https://doi.org/10.1007/978-3-030-84340-3_22
21. Thi, Q.N.T., Dang, T.K., Van, H.L., Son, H.X.: Using JSON to specify privacy preserving-enabled attribute-based access control policies. In: Wang, G., Atiquzzaman, M., Yan, Z., Choo, K.-K.R. (eds.) SpaCCS 2017. LNCS, vol. 10656, pp. 561–570. Springer, Cham (2017). https://doi.org/10.1007/978-3-319-72389-1_44

A Differential Privacy Image Publishing Method Based on Wavelet Transform

Guifen Zhang[1,2], Hangui Wei[1], Lina Ge[1,2(✉)], and Xia Qin[1]

[1] School of Artificial Intelligence, Guangxi University for Nationalities, Nanning, China
66436539@qq.com
[2] Key Laboratory of Network Communication Engineering, Guangxi University
for Nationalities, Nanning, China

Abstract. Image is an important information-bearing medium with many important attributes. If the image data is released directly, personal privacy will be compromised. This paper aims at how to use the method of differential privacy to protect the privacy of image data and make the image data have high usability. In this paper, a WIP method based on wavelet change is proposed. Firstly, wavelet transform is used to compress the image. Then, noise is added to the main features after transformation to obtain the published image satisfying the differential privacy. It solves the problem of low usability of large images and the problem that Fourier transform cannot deal with abrupt signal. Experimental results show that compared with similar methods in the frequency domain, the denoised image obtained by the proposed WIP method is more distinguishable and the information entropy is closer to the original image. The accuracy is 10% higher than other methods. Compared with other frequency-domain methods for image differential privacy protection, the proposed WIP method has higher usability and robustness.

Keywords: Image processing · Differential privacy · Privacy protection · The wavelet transform

1 Introduction

To solve the problem of the privacy protection of image data, Hill, Kamijo et al. proposed to use pixelation [1], bluring [2] and P3 system [3] to process images. By using standard image blurring techniques, such as pixelation and blurring, to obscure areas of interest, including faces and text. However, these methods are ineffective in protecting privacy. [4] uses homomorphic encryption algorithms to encrypt medical images and then send them to the cloud without damaging confidentiality. [5] provides an effective and practical privacy protection scale-invariant feature transform scheme for encrypted images. It can achieve higher computational efficiency and perform correct feature key point detection, accurate feature point description and image matching. There are still some shortcomings in these schemes. One is that the efficiency and security aspects of sharing data can be challenging. And untrusted servers often calculate characteristics that reveal private information. In addition, homomorphic encryption, garbled characters [6], or multiple

H. Shen et al. (Eds.): PDCAT 2021, LNCS 13148, pp. 584–595, 2022.
https://doi.org/10.1007/978-3-030-96772-7_55

independent servers [7] all potentially limit the feasibility of extracting complex features and enabling time-critical applications.

Differential privacy [8] is a new privacy protection technology with rigorous mathematical logic and scientific theoretical proof. In order to solve the above problems, this technology can provide a more stringent method for protecting the privacy of image data. Image data privacy protection methods have been relatively mature. However, there are few studies using differential privacy methods.

2   Differential Privacy Protection for Image Publishing

Differential privacy involves perturbations of input or output values. It maps a definite input to an uncertain output, to achieve the real data fuzzy, to ensure privacy protection. [9] proposes a differential privacy publishing method that uses Fourier transform compression to obtain the main information of image data and then adds Laplace noise. [10] proposes a method that uses singular value decomposition (SVD) to extract the singular values representing the main features of the image, and then adds disturbance to the singular value matrix to achieve differential privacy protection. [11] proposes a sliding window method to make image data one-dimensional. By including image features as comprehensively as possible, dynamically allocating privacy budget and adding Laplace noise, image usability and privacy are improved. There are few researches on differential privacy protection that disturb the image itself. Generally, the image publishing methods of differential privacy mainly focus on the image publishing of social network. [12–15] design social network graph data publishing methods that satisfy differential privacy based on image data attributes, privacy risk assessment based on ranking, uncertainty perception and fairness mechanism, respectively.

Matrix A is a face graphics matrix. It is compressed and transformed based on frequency domain technology to obtain the matrix B representing the feature information of face image. Add noise disturbance to B, and then use inverse transformation to recover A, and then get A'. Two kinds of errors are going to occur in the process of obtaining A'. The first is the noise error $LE(A')$ caused by the addition of noise using the Laplace mechanism. The second is the face image matrix A' in the process of inverse transformation caused by the reconstruction error $RE(A')$. Then, the overall error of the published face image A' can be expressed as formula (1):

$$Error(A') = RE(A') + LE(A') \tag{1}$$

The usability of face image is improved by reducing the overall error of A' of published face image as much as possible.

2.1   Laplace's Method

The differential privacy protection of LAP method is to directly use Laplace noise to disturb the face image matrix and release the disturbed data. For A given face data image $A'_{m \times n}$ with the size $m \times n$, according to the Laplace mechanism, to satisfy ε-differential privacy, the LAP method adds Laplace noise to each value in the face image matrix of A, which can be expressed as: $a'_i = a_i + Lap(\Delta A / \varepsilon)$.

According to the error calculation method in [9], the total error of LAP $Error_{LAP}(A')$ can be expressed as formula (2):

$$Error_{LAP}(A') = LE(A') = E\left(\sum_{i=1}^{n} Error(a'_i)\right) = E\left(\sum_{i=1}^{n}(a'_i - a_i)^2\right)$$

$$= E\left(\sum_{i=1}^{n}\left(a_i - a_i + \sum_{j=1}^{m} lap\left(\frac{\Delta_1 A}{\varepsilon}\right)\right)^2\right) = \sum_{i=1}^{n} \frac{2\,m(\Delta_1 A)^2}{\varepsilon^2} = 2\,mn\left(\frac{\Delta_1 A}{\varepsilon}\right)^2$$

$$= 2\,mn\left(\frac{\max\limits_{j}\sum_{i=1}^{m}|a_{ij}|}{\varepsilon}\right)^2$$

(2)

Where, E is expectation, $\max\limits_{j}\sum_{i=1}^{m}|a_{ij}|$ represents the maximum column norm of the matrix, a'_i represents the vector form of the matrix, and a_{ij} represents the matrix element or image pixel.

The error generated by the LAP algorithm mainly comes from the noise error $LE(A')$ of the Laplace mechanism. This noise error is proportional to the parameters m and n and inversely proportional to the privacy parameter ε. At the same degree of privacy protection, when the size of the image data $m \times n$ is larger, then the value of $LE(A')$ will become too larger, making the face image usability of the whole algorithm reduced.

2.2 Fourier Transform Method

For the problem of the above LAP image differential privacy algorithm, the following scheme is proposed in [9].

By adding noise to the Fourier coefficient of the face image after the Fourier transform, the Laplace mechanism disturbance of the main information of the image can be realized, so that the compression of the image can meet ε-difference privacy, and reduce the noise error of $LE(A')$.

Meanwhile, the former $k \times k$ coefficients of Fourier transform are extracted in a heuristic way to ensure that the image features are not damaged and the reconstruction error $RE(A')$ is reduced as much as possible.

In order to improve the usability of Laplace mechanism, [9] proposed the FIP method of differential privacy based on Fourier transform technology.

The steps of FIP algorithm are: Make a compression transformation by using Fourier transform technology to face image matrix A which A is a face image matrix. Extract the first $k \times k$ Fourier coefficients containing the feature information of the image and add the noise disturbance.

The Fourier transform coefficient is denoted by vector: $F^k = (F_1, F_2, \ldots, F_k)$. The noise Fourier coefficient vector $\tilde{F}^k$ can be expressed as: $\tilde{F}^k = (\tilde{F}_1, \tilde{F}_2, \ldots, \tilde{F}_k)$, where $\tilde{F}_i = F_i + lap(\Delta_1 F^k/\varepsilon)(1 \leq i \leq k)$.

The total error value $Error_{FIP}(A')$ of the FIP algorithm is mainly related to the extracted Fourier coefficient and the privacy parameter ε. The smaller the value of k, the smaller the error $LE(A')$ caused by the Laplace noise. However, the value of the resulting reconstruction error $RE(A')$ is larger. On the contrary, the larger the value of k, the smaller the value of the resulting reconstruction error $RE(A')$. However, the error $LE(A')$ caused by the Laplace noise is larger.

Fourier coefficient vector matrix F^k to a certain extent represents the features of human face images. When the value of k is smaller, the feature information of the image is less, and the usability of the face image will be reduced.

Fourier transform is complicated and difficult to deal with abrupt signal, while wavelet transform has two special properties, oscillation and attenuation, which can solve this problem well.

So, this paper proposes a differential privacy image data publishing algorithm based on wavelet transform WIP (Wavelet Analysis Facial Image Publication).

3   The Method of WIP

The total error value of the FIP algorithm is related to the number of Fourier coefficients extracted and the privacy parameter ε. When the value of k is smaller, the error noise $LE(A')$ caused by the Laplace noise is smaller, but the value of the reconstruction error $RE(A')$ is larger. On the contrary, the greater the value of k, the smaller the value of the reconstruction error $RE(A')$, but the greater the error $LE(A')$ caused by the Laplace noise.

Fourier coefficient vector matrix F^k to a certain extent represents the features of the face image, when the k value of F^k is smaller, then, the image of the feature information is less, the usability of the face image will be reduced.

WIP method will use the wavelet transform technology to compress the image, and add noise disturbance to the low-frequency coefficient matrix containing the main information to ensure that ε-differential privacy can be met and $LE(A')$ can be reduced. Then use the primary wavelet transform to guaranteed the image features not to be damaged as much as possible and the reconstruction error $RE(A')$ is reduced.

3.1   Algorithm Design

The FIP algorithm obtains the relatively evenly distributed in the Fourier coefficient characteristic information through the way of Fourier transform. The neighborhood matrix is obtained by extracting the former $k \times k$ Fourier transform coefficients. Although the noise error $LE(A')$ caused by the Laplace mechanism is reduced, most of the feature information of the image is destroyed, thus reducing the usability of the image data. The Fourier transform has the disadvantage that the characteristic information is evenly divided into the coefficient matrix. Therefore, this paper adopts the wavelet transform technology to compress the image.

In image processing, the main characteristics of the image data can be concentrated on the low-frequency matrix after the wavelet transform of the image data. The detail information, contour information and edge information of the image are concentrated on the high frequency coefficient. Figure 1 describes the process of the wavelet transform diagram. The face image matrix is extracted from wavelet coefficient matrix CA, CH, CV,

CD by wavelet transform. The low-frequency coefficient matrix *CA* is an approximate image, which contains the main characteristic information of the original image. High-frequency coefficient matrix *CH*, *CV* and *CD* are the details of the image. After multiple wavelet transform, more low frequency coefficient approximation image can be obtained.

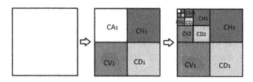

Fig. 1. The wavelet transform process

The WIP method proposed in this paper mainly uses the compression technology of wavelet transform to compress the face image data. In order to obtain better usability, it only uses the wavelet decomposition once. So, it retains some image detail. It then disturbed the low-frequency coefficient matrix of wavelet transform by adding noise conforming to Laplace mechanism, and then released after disturbance. The pseudocode for the algorithm is shown in Algorithm 1 as following.

Algorithm 1:WIP

Input: Image matrix A, privacy parameter ε
Output: Image matrix A' met ε-differential privacy protection
1) c←DWT(A)   // Apply the wavelet transform A
2) CA←(CA,CH,CV,CD)←c // Take the low frequency coefficient matrix of the wavelet
transform
3) For r from 1 to m
4)   For c from 1 to n
5)   CA' (r,c) ←CA(r,c) + lap($\Delta A/\varepsilon$)
6)   End for
7) End for
8) (CH,CV,CD) = 0 // Set the high frequency coefficients to zero
9) C' ← (CA',CA,CH,CV,CD)
10) A' ← IDWT(C')

The size of a face image matrix *A* is $m \times n$. First, the face image matrix *A* is transformed by two-dimensional discrete wavelet transform technology. Then, the low frequency matrix *CA* containing the main information is extracted from the obtained wavelet coefficient matrix *C*. Finally, the Laplace mechanism is used to add Laplace noise to the coefficients in the low frequency coefficient matrix *CA*. Thus, the low frequency coefficient matrix *CA'* after noise is obtained, That is $CA'(r,c) \leftarrow CA(r,c) + lap(\Delta A/\varepsilon)$. For reconstruction, the high frequency coefficient matrix is filled with 0 and merged with the low frequency coefficient matrix. The noisy wavelet coefficient matrix *C'* is obtained. Finally, the image data *A'* is reconstructed by IDWT technology for publication.

3.2 Algorithm Error Analysis

The method of measuring error in this paper is to calculate the expectation of mean square error. According to step 2 of Algorithm 1, the WIP algorithm obtains the low-frequency coefficient CA of the coefficient matrix, that is, the matrix of the first $r \times c$ of the wavelet coefficient. Then, in step 7 to Step 9, set the high-frequency coefficient matrix CH, CV and CD to zero. A new wavelet coefficient matrix is formed together with the low frequency coefficient matrix CA. Then the IDWT function is used to reconstruct the face image data A' for publishing.

Since the wavelet coefficients of magnitude $(m\text{-}r) \times (n\text{-}c)$ are ignored, the reconstruction error $RE(A')$ is generated, which can be expressed in formula (3):

$$RE(A') = CH + CV + CD = \sqrt{\sum_{i=k+1}^{m} \sum_{j=k+1}^{n} C_{ij}^2} \tag{3}$$

where $r = m/2$, $c = n/2$.

According to steps 3 to 5 of the Algorithm 1, the noise error of the WIP method mainly comes from the noise added to the wavelet low-frequency coefficient matrix CA. Therefore, according to the Laplace mechanism, the noise error $LE(A')$ can be calculated by the method of the square root of expectation, then formula (4) is given:

$$LE(A') = E\left(\sqrt{\sum_{i=1}^{r} \sum_{j=1}^{c} (\Delta_1 CA_{ij}/\varepsilon)^2}\right) \leq \sum_{i=1}^{c} \frac{2r(\Delta_1 CA)^2}{\varepsilon^2}$$
$$= \sqrt{2\,mn\left(\frac{\Delta_1 CA}{\varepsilon}\right)^2} = \sqrt{2rc} \frac{\sum_{i=1}^{r} \sum_{j=1}^{c} |CA_{ij}|}{\varepsilon} \tag{4}$$

According to formula (4) of total error calculation, the total error $Error_{WIP}(A')$ of algorithm 1 is composed of reconstruction error $RE(A')$ and noise error $LE(A')$, which is expressed as formula (5):

$$Error_{WIP}(A') = E\left(RE(A') + LE(A')\right) \leq \sum_{i=r}^{m} \sum_{j=c}^{n} |C_{ij}| + \sqrt{2rc} \frac{\sum_{i=1}^{r} \sum_{j=1}^{c} |CA_{ij}|}{\varepsilon} \tag{5}$$

In particular, when the image is $n \times n$ or the wavelet transform coefficients are reduced to a square matrix of $n \times n$, the noise error $LE(A')$ of Algorithm 1 is expressed in the form of vector matrix as formula (6):

$$LE(A') = E\left(\sqrt{\sum_{i=k+1}^{n} |F_{i-1}|^2}\right) \tag{6}$$

The reconstruction error $RE(A')$ of Algorithm 1 can be expressed in formula (7):

$$RE(A') = \left(\sqrt{\sum_{i=1}^{k} 4\left(\frac{\Delta_1 F^k}{\varepsilon}\right)^2}\right) \tag{7}$$

Then the total error of Algorithm 1 can be expressed as formula (8):

$$\text{Error}_{WIP}\left(A'\right) = RE\left(A'\right) + LE\left(A'\right) = \left(\sqrt{\sum_{i=1}^{k} 4(\frac{\Delta_1 F^k}{\varepsilon})^2}\right) + \left(\sqrt{\sum_{i=k+1}^{n} |F_{i-1}|^2}\right)$$

$$= \sqrt{\sum_{i=k+1}^{n} |F_{i-1}|^2} + \frac{\sqrt{2}k\Delta_1 F^k}{\varepsilon} \tag{8}$$

Where $k = n/2$.

It can be seen from formula (5) that the error value of Algorithm 1 depends on the number of layers of wavelet transform. If you take multiple wavelet transforms, then r and n will become smaller. That is, the value of k in formula (8) will be smaller, and the error $LE(A')$ caused by Laplace noise will also be smaller. The value of the resulting reconstruction error $RE(A')$ is larger. However, compared with the FIP method, the neighbor coefficient matrix obtained contains more feature information of face image. Setting the high-frequency coefficient matrix to zero can reduce the interference of filtering to a certain extent, Then the proposed method in this paper obtain a certain noise reduction effect.

4 Experiments and Analysis

4.1 Experimental Environment

This experiment is carried out under windows10 system. The programming language is MATLAB. The main databases used are YALE Face Database (YALE University) and its expanded YALEB face database (YALEB), JAFFE face database (ATR) for expression recognition (Japan), and ORL face database (Cambridge University). Some information about the four face datasets can be seen in Table 1. (https://blog.51cto.com/shanyou/309 8359).

Table 1. Data sets information table

Data set name	Data set size	Number of people included	Sample number per person	Image size
YALE	150	15	10	195 × 231
JAFFE	200	10	20	256 × 256
ORL	400	40	10	92 × 112
YALEB	2280	38	60	168 × 192

The algorithm is verified by the usability of single image data and the accuracy of face data classification and verification.

4.2 Usability Analysis

In order to study the usability of the algorithm based on the frequency domain, the image identifiability and the image information entropy generated by the three algorithms in different data sets are compared to measure the usability of the three algorithms.

According to the method in [9], the image identifications are tested experimentally on the gray scale face image of the classic image Lena, as shown in Fig. 2. In Fig. 3, the noise distribution results of the three algorithms (LAP method [9], FIP method [9] and WIP method) under Lean gray image are shown.

Fig. 2. Lena original image

In Fig. 3, the noise distribution results of the three algorithms (LAP method [9], FIP method [9] and WIP method) under Lean gray image are shown.

(a) Adding noisy images under the LAP method   (b) Adding noisy images under the FIP method   (c) Adding noisy images under the WIP method

Fig. 3. Noise enhancement in three frequency-domain methods of lean image

As shown in Fig. 3, the images obtained by the WIP method are significantly improved over those obtained by the LAP and FIP methods. The LAP algorithm can hardly see Lena's image. The FIP algorithm can see the outline of Lena more vaguely. The WIP algorithm can be clearly reserved for the image that sees Lena. So, it shows that the WIP algorithm makes more information retention of Lena image feature information, and the WIP algorithm is better in terms of recognition rate.

In order to further study the usability comparison of the three algorithms, we examine the information entropy comparison results of the three algorithms under the Laplace mechanism by means of image information entropy. In Fig. 4 (a) to (d), non-DP, LAP, FIP and WIP algorithms without differential privacy are shown respectively in the classic Lena image and three real face databases, as well as the comparison graph of image information entropy when privacy parameter ε is 0.1, 0.5, 0.9 and 1.3.

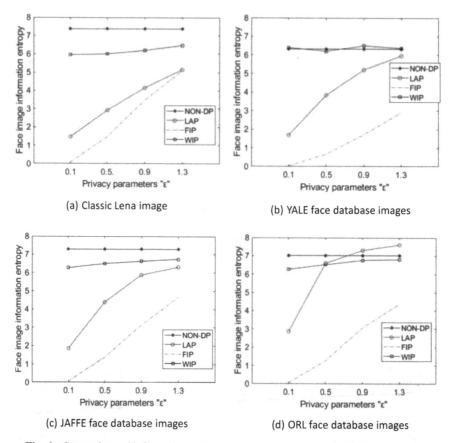

Fig. 4. Comparison of information entropy in different cases of ε under five image data

From the comparison of information entropy from (a) to (e) in Fig. 4, it can be seen that under the LAP method, the information entropy of images in all databases increases with the increase of privacy parameter ε, and gradually approaches the non-DP information entropy curve. The information entropy of FIP method in Lena image and YALE database is relatively stable and close to non-DP. However, in JAFFE database, ORL database and YALEB database, there is a rising trend from very low, and a big gap with the non-DP information entropy curve. That's because the JAFFE database, ORL database and YALEB database have a lot of contrast, a lot of local changes in lighting and posture, and the Fourier transform is less capable of dealing with that kind of abrupt information. The WIP method presents a relatively stable trend in all data sets, which is close to the non-DP image information entropy curve. This is because the wavelet transform makes up for the weakness of Fourier transform. When processing the external environment image signal in the image, the face image features can be extracted better, and the image information can be retained at a larger scale, and the robustness is stronger.

Therefore, it can be seen from Fig. 4 that the WIP method proposed in this paper has higher usability and robustness than the LAP method and the FIP method.

4.3   Validity Analysis

In addition to analyzing the usability of the algorithm by comparing the recognition and information entropy of the single noised image data, the validity of the algorithm needs to be analyzed by the accuracy in face image classification and verification.

In order to verify the accuracy of the three algorithms in face image classification and verification, the combined method of Support Vector Machine (SVM) and Principal Components Analysis (PCA) was used for face image classification and verification.

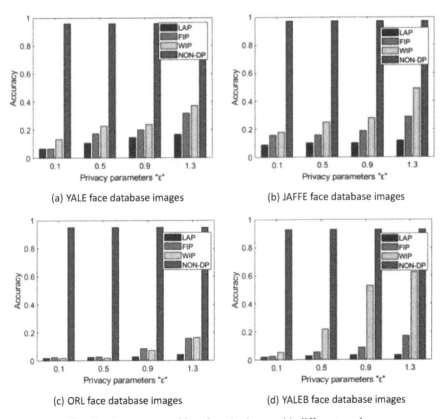

(a) YALE face database images   (b) JAFFE face database images

(c) ORL face database images   (d) YALEB face database images

Fig. 5. The accuracy of four face databases with different ε values

The verification method adopts MATLAB platform, and takes 50% of each person's image sample in the face image database as training data and 50% as verification data. Then, PCA method is used to reduce dimension and extract features of face image matrix. Combined with the covariance matrix, the centralization matrix was used to replace the original matrix to remove the correlation of face image matrix. Finally, the classification function of SVM was used to classify and verify the images with the removal of correlation. The experimental results were evaluated by the accuracy of face image classification and verification.

The experiment was based on four real face databases, and the value of privacy parameters ε is set to 0.1, 0.3, 0.5 and 1.3, respectively. PCA + SVM method was used to conduct the experiment and compare the three privacy protection methods with Laplace mechanism. The experimental results are shown in Fig. 5.

As shown in Fig. 5, the accuracy of the three image differential privacy protection methods in the four databases increases with the increase of privacy parameter ε. When $\varepsilon = 0.1$, the accuracy of LAP method and FIP method is almost equal, and the accuracy of WIP method is higher, which is almost twice that of LAP method and FIP method. With the increase of ε, the gap between the three kinds of accuracy gradually becomes obvious. The LAP method is growing slowly. When $\varepsilon = 0.9$, the difference between FIP method and WIP method is the smallest. However, it is still not higher than WIP method. When ε values are 0.5, 0.9 and 1.3, the accuracy of WIP method is about 5% higher than FIP method, and 10% to 20% higher than LAP method. Therefore, the WIP method is more efficient and usable than LAP algorithm and FIP algorithm.

5   Conclusion

Data distortion technology is easy to cause large area image distortion problem and the security of the published image is weak. The encryption technology is highly complicated and its actual use is easily limited. However, if anonymous publishing method is adopted, once the attacker has acquired certain background knowledge, he can obtain access rights and image data through background knowledge attack, resulting in privacy disclosure. Therefore, based on the privacy protection technology of differential privacy, this paper proposes the image data privacy protection method based on differential privacy from the perspective of frequency domain.

In this paper, the WIP method based on wavelet transform is proposed to solve the disadvantages of LAP method, such as poor usability and Fourier transform can not deal with abrupt signal. It is proved by theory that the WIP method satisfies ε-differential privacy. The experimental results of single image processing and face image verification show that the WIP method has stronger robustness and usability than LAP method and FIP method.

However, when the frequency domain method is used to compress and transform the image data, the feature extraction of the main information is not accurate enough when the Laplace noise is added to the image data based on the operation in the frequency domain, which makes the overall usability less than the image differential privacy protection method under the algebraic method. Next, it may concern that try to use the tree structure combined with wavelet transform to compress the face image, and then according to the compression process and results of the reasonable use of Laplace mechanism.

Acknowledgment. This work is partially supported by the National Natural Science Foundation of China (No. 61862007).

References

1. Kamijo, S., Matsushita, Y., Ikeuchi, K., et al.: Traffic monitoring and accident detection at intersections. IEEE Trans. Intell. Transp. Syst. **1**(2), 108–118 (2000)
2. Hill, S., Zhou, Z., Saul, L., et al.: On the (in) effectiveness of mosaicing and blurring as tools for document redaction. Proc. Priv. Enhancing Technol. **2016**(4), 403–417 (2016)
3. Ra, M.R., Govindan, R., Ortega, A.: P3: toward privacy-preserving photo sharing. Comput. Sci. **1**(2), 515–528 (2013)
4. Vengadapurvaja, A.M., Nisha, G., Aarthy, R., et al.: An efficient homomorphic medical image encryption algorithm for cloud storage security. Procedia Comput. Sci. **115**(1), 643–650 (2017)
5. Jiang, L., Xu, C., Wang, X., et al.: Secure outsourcing SIFT: efficient and privacy-preserving image feature extraction in the encrypted domain. IEEE Trans. Dependable Secure Comput. **17**(1), 179–193 (2017)
6. Wang, S., Nassar, M., Atallah, M., Malluhi, Q.: Secure and private outsourcing of shape-based feature extraction. In: Qing, S., Zhou, J., Liu, D. (eds.) Information and Communications Security. ICICS 2013. Lecture Notes in Computer Science, vol. 8233, pp. 90–99 Springer, Cham (2013). https://doi.org/10.1007/978-3-319-02726-5_7
7. Wang, Q., Hu, S., Ren, K., et al.: Catch me in the dark: effective privacy-preserving outsourcing of feature extractions over image data. In: IEEE INFOCOM 2016-The 35th Annual IEEE International Conference on Computer Communications, vol. 2, no. 2, pp. 1–9. IEEE (2016)
8. Guo, J.M., Prasetyo, H.: False-positive-free SVD-based image watermarking. J. Vis. Commun. Image Represent. **25**(5), 1149–1163 (2014)
9. Zhang, X.J., Fu, C.C., Meng, X.F.: Facial image publication with differential privacy. J. Image Graph. **23**(9), 1305–1315 (2018)
10. Zhang, X.J., Fu, C.C., Meng, X.F.: Private facial image publication through matrix decomposition. J. Image Graph. **25**(04), 0655–0668 (2020)
11. Liu, C., Yang, J., Zhao, W., et al.: Face image publication based on differential privacy. Wirel. Commun. Mob. Comput. **2021**, 1–20 (2021)
12. Jorgensen, Z., Yu, T., Cormode, G.: Publishing attributed social graphs with formal privacy guarantee. In: Proceedings of the 2016 international conference on management of data, vol. 4, no. 1, pp. 107–122 (2016)
13. Biega, J.A., Gummadi, K.P., Mele, I., et al.: R-susceptibility: An ir-centric approach to assessing privacy risks for users in online communities. In: Proceedings of the 39th International ACM SIGIR Conference on Research and Development in Information Retrieval vol. 2, no. 1, pp. 365–374 (2016)
14. Xiao, D., Eltabakh, M.Y., Kong, X.: Sharing uncertain graphs using syntactic private graph models. In: 2018 IEEE 34th International Conference on Data Engineering (ICDE), vol. 1, no. 2, pp. 1336–1339. IEEE (2018)
15. Zheng, X., Luo, G., Cai, Z.: A fair mechanism for private data publication in online social networks. IEEE Trans. Netw. Sci. Eng. **7**(2), 880–891 (2018)

Traffic Matrix Prediction Based on Differential Privacy and LSTM

Weizheng Li, Yingpeng Sang$^{(\boxtimes)}$ ⓘ, Maliang Zhang, Jinghao Huang, and Chaoxin Cai

School of Computer Science and Engineering, Sun Yat-sen University, Guangzhou, China
sangyp@mail.sysu.edu.cn,
{liwzh56,zhangmliang3,huangjh279,caichx6}@mail2.sysu.edu.cn

Abstract. The traffic matrix (TM) is an important type of information in network management, which is needed in network load balancing and routing configuration. Due to technical and cost reasons, it is difficult to directly measure the matrix, but we can use prediction instead of direct measurement. The Long Short-Term Memory(LSTM) model in deep learning is very suitable for time series forecasting problems. However, due to the characteristics of deep learning, the data samples used to train the network will leave their own traces on the final model, which allows attackers to restore training samples through member inference attacks, causing privacy leakage. This paper focuses on combining the differential privacy mechanism with the LSTM model. In the gradient descent stage of training, a well-controlled noise is added to protect the final model. In the experiments, we verify the feasibility of the method proposed in this paper on the data set Abilene.

Keywords: Traffic matrix prediction · Long short-term memory · Differential privacy

1 Introduction

Traffic matrix (TM) is used to represent the traffic of all nodes in a network in a certain period of time and it has temporal attributes. Traffic matrix plays a very important role in network load management and routing configuration [6]. An OD pair consist of the original and destination nodes, which can be a link among routers [11]. Generally, routing configuration information and link traffic are used to estimate the traffic matrix [8].

With the development of deep learning in recent years, many scholars began to utilize depth neural network to predict traffic matrix. Because in a network, the network traffic has self-similarity and long-range dependence, so the time series model can be applied to predict the traffic matrix [10]. In [7], the deep belief networks (DBN) model was trained to predict and estimate the traffic matrix.

However, due to the characteristics of deep learning, the training data may leave their own traces on the final model, which makes the model be attacked

H. Shen et al. (Eds.): PDCAT 2021, LNCS 13148, pp. 596–603, 2022.
https://doi.org/10.1007/978-3-030-96772-7_56

by membership inference attack. Differential privacy [4] is one of state-of-the-art privacy protection mechanism, which ensures that even if the adversary possesses all the ancestors of sensitive data, they cannot infer any information about any particular record with a high degree of confidence from the published learning model. Motivated by this, we propose to apply differential privacy mechanism in the training process of Long Short-Term Memory (LSTM) to ensure that the published model will not cause privacy disclosure of training data.

In summary, the main contributions of this paper are as follows. We propose an LSTM model combined with differential privacy mechanism, which is used to predict the traffic matrix. The prediction accuracy and privacy protection of the model are evaluated by adjusting the privacy budget. Through this work, the released model will not be subject to member reasoning attacks and leakage of training samples. For the OD pair whose prediction rate changes greatly after adding noise, we also analyze the statistical characteristics of its original data and give a conclusion.

2   Related Work

In [9], independently and identically distributed Poisson distribution was used to model the time-varying characteristics of OD pairs. The traffic matrix problem can be transformed into using a neural network to train a predictor. Its input is a series of previous traffic matrices, and its output is the traffic matrix to be predicted at a certain time [3]. In recent years, many scholars have proposed different time series models to solve this problem. [7] used the deep belief network(DBN) model to predict and estimate the traffic matrix, and used the principal components analysis (PCA) method as the control group. Experiments showed that the DBN model has achieved good accuracy. In [5], the flow of OD pair in a certain period was proved to be not only related to the earlier flow, but also affected by other ODs on the flow. This phenomenon is called Inter-flow correlations.

In [12], how to apply differential privacy in deep learning model was discussed, which mainly has three directions. The first is to add noise to the original data set, which can be regarded as data preprocessing. However, it is a great challenge to operate on large dataset. The second direction is to add privacy protection mechanism in training stage. [1] proposed an algorithm called DP-SGD. In the process of gradient descent, the algorithm clips the gradient and then adds noise, and can track the privacy consumption in the whole training process. The third direction is to add privacy protection in the output layer.

3   Traffic Matrix Prediction Methods

In this section, we mainly introduce the traffic matrix prediction problem and the application of differential privacy mechanism in deep learning.

3.1   Traffic Matrix Prediction

We assume that there are N nodes in a network, then there are $N \times N$ OD pairs (all possible pairs of original and destination nodes). In a certain period of time, the traffic from node i to node j is denoted as $x_{i,j}$. A matrix with the size of $N \times N$ is used to characterize the traffic size of all OD pairs in a certain time period t. This matrix is called the traffic matrix and denoted as X_t.

The problem we are facing now is to train a predictor whose input is sequence $(X_{t-k}, X_{t-k+1}, \dots, X_{t-1})$ and output is X_t. In order to predict the traffic size of a specific OD pair in a certain period of time in the future, we use a set of previous data as input and output as the result we need.

3.2   Long Short-Term Memory

Figure 1 shows the internal structure of the LSTM. Usually, the output c_t is based on the c_{t-1} transmitted from the previous state plus some values, while h_t is often very different under different nodes. The main internal structure of LSTM consists of three gates:

– Input gate: this gate selectively remembers the input of this stage. It mainly selects and memorizes the input x_t.

$$i_t = \sigma(W_i \cdot [h_{t-1}, x_t] + b_i) \tag{1}$$

$$\hat{c}_t = tanh(W_c \cdot [h_{t-1}, x_t] + b_c) \tag{2}$$

– Forget gate: this gate determines how much of the upper state is retained.

$$f_t = \sigma(W_f \cdot [h_{t-1}, x_t] + b_f) \tag{3}$$

– Output gate: this gate determines how much of the current state is output to the subsequent network.

$$o_t = \sigma(W_o \cdot [h_{t-1}, x_t] + b_o) \tag{4}$$

$$c_t = f_t \cdot c_{t-1} + i_t \cdot \hat{c}_t \tag{5}$$

$$h_t = o_t \cdot tanh(c_t) \tag{6}$$

3.3   Differential Privacy With Deep Learning

In this section, we focus on the differential privacy mechanism and how to deploy differential privacy on the deep learning model.

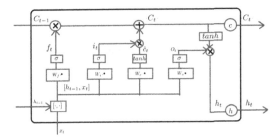

Fig. 1. The structure of LSTM.

Definition Of Differential Privacy. Differential privacy provides a powerful privacy guarantee for algorithms dealing with aggregated databases. It is defined in the context of adjacent databases, which are different only in a single data record.

The following is the mathematical definition of differential privacy: A randomize mechanism $M : D \xrightarrow{R}$ with domain D and range R satisfies (ε, δ)-differential privacy, if for any two adjacent inputs d, $d' \in D$ and for any subset of outputs $S \subseteq R$ it holds that

$$Pr[M(d) \in S] \le e^{\varepsilon} Pr[M(d') \in S] + \delta \tag{7}$$

By adjusting the privacy budget parameter ε, the accuracy of the model and the degree of privacy disclosure can be controlled.

Differentially Private SGD Algorithm. Following [12], our algorithm mainly includes two steps. Firstly, the sensitivity of each sample is reduced by clipping the gradient of the sample, and then noise is added to the gradient in batches before uploading the parameters. Secondly, the privacy consumption of the whole training is tracked by the composition theorem of differential privacy. Algorithm 1 describes how to add noise to the gradient descent process.

$L(\theta)$ is the loss function of the whole model. In each step of SGD, we calculate the gradient $\nabla_{\theta} L(\theta, x_i)$ of a batch of samples, then clip the l_2 norm of each gradient, compute the average, add noise, and finally update the parameters by back propagation.

4   Experiments Results and Analysis

In this section, we will validate the accuracy of traffic matrix prediction on the proposed model. Moreover, we will compare the changes in the practicability of the prediction model after adding differential privacy. In this experiment, the data set used is Abilene. The Abilene network [2] is mainly used for education and research, which consists of 12 nodes and 54 undirected links. There are 144 OD pairs in this data set. Finally, we analyze the OD pairs whose prediction rate changes greatly before and after adding noise, and discuss the reasons.

Algorithm 1. Differentially private SGD

Input: Examples $x_1, \ldots, x_N$, loss function $L(\theta) = \frac{1}{N}\sum_i L(\theta, x_i)$. Parameters : learning rate η_t, noise scale σ, group size L, gradient norm bound C.

Initialize θ_0 randomly

for $t \in [T]$ **do**

    Take a random sample L_t with sampling probability L/N

    Compute gradient

    For each $i \in L_t$,comupte $g_t(x_i) \leftarrow \nabla_{\theta_t} L(\theta_t, x_i)$

    Clip gradient

    $\bar{g}_t(x_i) \leftarrow g_t(x_i)/max(1, \frac{\|g_t(x_i)\|_2}{C})$

    Add noise

    $\tilde{g}_t \leftarrow \frac{1}{L}\left(\sum_i \bar{g}_t(x_i) + N(0, \sigma^2 C^2 I)\right)$

    Descent

    $\theta_{t+1} \leftarrow \theta_t - \eta_t \tilde{g}_t$

end for

Output: θ_T and compute the overall privacy cost (ε, δ) using a privacy accounting method.

4.1 Performance Metrics

In order to effectively evaluate our proposed method, we use Mean Absolute Percentage Error (MAPE) as the evaluation index. The metric can be expressed by the following formula:

$$MAPE = \frac{100\%}{n} \sum_{i=1}^{n} |\frac{\hat{y}_i - y_i}{y_i}| \tag{8}$$

where $\hat{y}_i$ represents the predicted value, and y_i represents the true value.

4.2 Results and Analysis

The cumulative distribution function (CDF) curve of MAPE results is plotted for different input steps. In Fig. 2, k is used to represent the input step size, which means that the previous k number values are used to predict the flow value at the next moment. We can see that the LSTM network captures the long-distance dependence of the OD pair well. In the LSTM without differential privacy, more than 50% of the data has a MAPE lower than 50%, and in the DP-LSTM network, more than 40% of the data has a MAPE lower than 50%. In the 4 sets of experiments with different k, when $k = 20$, the model performs best. In Table 1, it shows the drop rate of the model's prediction rate after adding noise at different input step lengths.

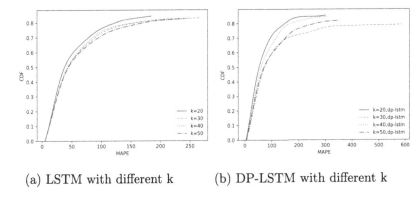

(a) LSTM with different k   (b) DP-LSTM with different k

Fig. 2. The MAPE result of different k

The degree of reduction in the usability of the model is related to the magnitude of the added noise. Through Fig. 3, we observe that the amount of noise added is negatively correlated with the prediction accuracy of the model. This shows that we need to make a trade-off between protection level and prediction accuracy.

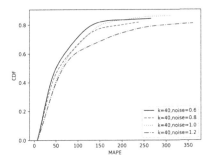

Fig. 3. The MAPE result of different noise level on LSTM

In addition, we find that the prediction rate of some OD pairs did not drop much after adding noise, while on some OD pairs it changed greatly after adding noise. In Fig. 4(a), we plot the relationship between the MAPE metric of the OD pair and the absolute difference of the model prediction rate after adding differential privacy. Through the scatter plot, it can be found that the data points are concentrated in the lower left corner of the graph, which shows that when the LSTM model without DP performs better on some OD pairs, the performance of the model will not drop too much after adding noise to these pairs. However, when the model without DP performs poorly, the performance of it will get even worse when noise is added. In addition, Fig. 4(b) demonstrates the relationship between the decline in performance and the variance of OD-pair

Table 1. Model prediction rate after add noise.

K	MAPE decrease percentage
20	12.96%
30	22.52%
40	16.73%
50	19.96%

intra-flow values. The scatter plot shows that the smaller the variance of the OD pair, the less likely the addition of noise will affect the model, but the statistical feature of variance cannot fully explain the degree of influence of differential privacy on the model.

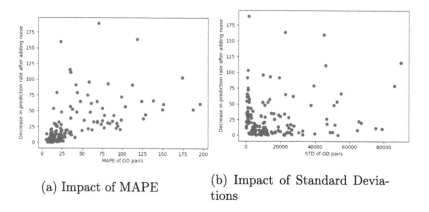

(a) Impact of MAPE

(b) Impact of Standard Deviations

Fig. 4. Impact of MAPE and standard deviations

5   Conclusions

The traffic matrix is an indispensable type of information in network management, and the time series model can be used to predict the traffic matrix to be used in the future. LSTM is a model that is very suitable for this type of problem in deep learning. However, due to the inherent characteristics of deep learning, it is vulnerable to attacks. This paper focuses on combining the differential privacy mechanism with the LSTM model, so that the usability of the model is maintained while protecting the privacy of traffic data. In the experiments, it can be concluded that after adding noise, the prediction accuracy of the model can be compromised to a very low degree, and it can still be released as an excellent predictor. Moreover, by analyzing the characteristics of the original data, we discuss some reasons why some OD pairs behave abnormally after adding noise.

Acknowledgement. This work was supported by the Science and Technology Program of Guangzhou, China (No. 201904010209), and the Science and Technology Program of Guangdong Province, China (No. 2017A010101039). The corresponding author is Yingpeng Sang.

References

1. Abadi, M., et al.: Deep learning with differential privacy. In: Proceedings of the 2016 ACM SIGSAC Conference on Computer and Communications Security, pp. 308–318 (2016)
2. Abilene. http://www.cs.utexas.edu/yzhang/research/abilenetm/ (2004)
3. Brockwell, P.J., Davis, R.A.: Introduction to Time Series and Forecasting. STS, Springer, Cham (2016). https://doi.org/10.1007/978-3-319-29854-2
4. Dwork, C.: Differential privacy. In: Bugliesi, M., Preneel, B., Sassone, V., Wegener, I. (eds.) ICALP 2006. LNCS, vol. 4052, pp. 1–12. Springer, Heidelberg (2006). https://doi.org/10.1007/11787006_1
5. Gao, K., et al.: Incorporating intra-flow dependencies and inter-flow correlations for traffic matrix prediction. In: 2020 IEEE/ACM 28th International Symposium on Quality of Service (IWQoS), pp. 1–10. IEEE (2020)
6. Mardani, M. and Giannakis, G.B.: Robust network traffic estimation via sparsity and low rank. In: 2013 IEEE International Conference on Acoustics, Speech and Signal Processing, pp. 4529–4533. IEEE (2013)
7. Nie, L., Jiang, D., Guo, L., Shui, Yu.: Traffic matrix prediction and estimation based on deep learning in large-scale IP backbone networks. J. Netw. Comput. Appl. **76**, 16–22 (2016)
8. Soule, A., et al. Traffic matrices: balancing measurements, inference and modeling. In: Proceedings of the 2005 ACM SIGMETRICS International Conference on Measurement and Modeling of Computer Systems, pp. 362–373 (2005)
9. Tune, P., Roughan, M.: Spatiotemporal traffic matrix synthesis. In: Proceedings of the 2015 ACM Conference on Special Interest Group on Data Communication, pp. 579–592 (2015)
10. Ke, X., Shen, M., Cui, Y., Ye, M., Zhong, Y.: A model approach to the estimation of peer-to-peer traffic matrices. IEEE Trans. Parallel Distrib. Syst. **25**(5), 1101–1111 (2013)
11. Zhang, Y., Roughan, M., Duffield, N., Greenberg, A.: Fast accurate computation of large-scale IP traffic matrices from link loads. ACM SIGMETRICS Perform. Eval. Rev. **31**(1), 206–217 (2003)
12. Zhao, J., Chen, Y., Zhang, W.: Differential privacy preservation in deep learning: challenges, opportunities and solutions. IEEE Access **7**, 48901–48911 (2019)

A Blockchain-Based Continuous Query Differential Privacy Algorithm

Heng Ouyang[1], Hongqin Lyu[1], Shigong Long[1,2(✉)], Hai Liu[1,2],
and Hongfa Ding[2,3]

[1] College of Computer Science and Technology, Guizhou University,
Guiyang 550025, Guizhou, China
526796467@qq.cpm
[2] State Key Laboratory of Public Big Data, Guizhou University,
Guiyang 550025, Guizhou, China
[3] School of Information, Guizhou University of Finance and Economics,
Guiyang 550025, China

Abstract. In the differential privacy interactive framework, data sets need to be used to answer multiple queries. With the gradual consumption of the privacy budget, the risk of privacy disclosure increases. Therefore, it is essential to save and track the consumption of the privacy budget, which should not exceed the limit given by the privacy budget. Therefore, firstly, this paper optimizes the Gaussian mechanism to reduce the query response time; Then a Continuous Query Differential Privacy Mechanism (CQDPM) is designed to save the overhead of privacy budget and improve the availability of data; Use the blockchain to record the privacy budget to facilitate the query of the usage of the privacy budget; Finally, a data integrity verification algorithm is proposed by using blockchain. Experiments show that the proposed mechanism reduces the query response time, effectively saves the privacy budget overhead under the same privacy budget limit, and has higher data availability.

Keywords: Differential privacy · Gaussian mechanism · Blockchain

1 Introduction

More and more information is collected for publishing and analysis, which can bring significant social benefits, such as providing better services, publishing official statistics, providing data mining or machine learning tasks, but at the same time, it will lead to the disclosure of personal privacy data. To solve the problem of privacy disclosure in data publishing, Dwork et al. proposed differential privacy protection in 2006 [3]: differential privacy protection is a privacy protection technology based on data distortion, and then add noise to distort sensitive data, and the processed data can still maintain some statistical characteristics.

Differential privacy protection can be divided into the interactive framework and the non-interactive framework [18]. In the non-interactive framework, the

© Springer Nature Switzerland AG 2022
H. Shen et al. (Eds.): PDCAT 2021, LNCS 13148, pp. 604–615, 2022.
https://doi.org/10.1007/978-3-030-96772-7_57

data owner publishes the disturbance results of all queries at one time or publishes a data set disturbed by noise, that is, the synthetic data set, for all possible queries proposed by the user. The user can query the synthetic data set directly. In the interactive framework, the user puts forward a query request to the data owner, adds noise satisfying differential privacy to the real query results, obtains the disturbing results, and returns the results to the user. In this process, the data set is isolated from the user; the user cannot touch the whole data set to achieve privacy protection.

In the traditional interactive framework, users will consume a certain amount of privacy budget for every query, resulting in fewer queries supported by a dataset and being vulnerable to repeated attacks [8]. To Solving these problems, this paper proposes CQDPM , which stores the usage of privacy budget in the blockchain network and records the disturbing results locally. When encountering the same type of query, the previous noise answer can be reused partially or completely. Especially when encountering the same query as before, the framework will directly return the previous results to the user to effectively resist repeated attacks.

The main contributions of this paper are as follows:

1) This paper uses the Newton downhill method to iteratively calculate the value and improve the Gaussian analysis mechanism (AGM) proposed by Balle et al. [1]. Under the same precision, the query response time is reduced.
2) A differential privacy protection mechanism (CQDPM) for continuous query is designed, which improves the availability of data compared with the algorithm of Zhao et al. [17]. A data integrity verification algorithm is proposed to ensure the security of records.
3) We conducted experiments using real data sets. Numerical results show that our proposed algorithm reduces the query response time and effectively saves the privacy overhead, and the data availability after disturbance is higher.

2   Related Work

2.1   Differential Privacy Interactive Framework

In the interactive publishing framework, Dwork et al. [5] first applied the Laplace mechanism to the interactive framework, adding Laplace noise directly before publishing the query results, but it can provide few queries. After that, Roth et al. Proposed the median mechanism [12], which divides queries into "hard query" and "easy query". Among them, the query results of "easy query" can be approximated by the "hard query" results, which can effectively improve the query times under a sure accuracy. Hardt et al. Proposed the multiplicative weight mechanism (PMW) [9], which is an iterative mechanism. Laplace noise interference is applied to the query results, and the interference results are compared with the previous query results. If the difference is less than the preset threshold, the "approximate" result of the previous query is used to replace this query, but the framework is only limited to counting queries. The accuracy and query times are improved to a certain extent. However, none of the above frameworks can effectively prevent repeated attacks. Yang et al. [15] proposed reusing noise response but did not quantify the proportion of noise reuse. Zhao et al. Proposed blockchain-based reuse noise (BBRN) [17], which records the disturbing results and the privacy budget in the distributed blockchain network. Due to the tamper-proof characteristics of the blockchain, its data security is high, but the query response time of the mechanism is exponentially correlated with the number of queries.

Compared with the mechanism of Zhao et al., the CQDPM proposed in this paper stores the disturbing results in the local server, which reduces the query response time, but brings the risk of record tampering. Therefore, an integrity verification algorithm is proposed to ensure the security of records. For the noise disturbance mechanism, the Gaussian mechanism is optimized to reduce the number of iterations. In the interactive framework, the privacy budget and other parameters of each query customized by the user rather than added adaptively by the algorithm, so it is essential to track the consumption of the privacy budget. The mechanism records the privacy budget by using the blockchain to facilitate the query of the usage of the privacy budget.

2.2 Gaussian Mechanism

Dwork et al. [3] proposed a Gaussian mechanism in 2006. Gaussian mechanism achieves the purpose of differential privacy protection by adding noise obeying Gaussian distribution to query results. Moreover, the privacy loss random variables constitute an independent Gaussian distribution, so the Gaussian mechanism has a more straightforward analysis method. At present, some researches on the Gaussian mechanism are worth learning from. When the Gaussian mechanism meets $(\varepsilon, \delta) - \mathrm{ADP}$, the value σ_{2006} is at least: $\sigma_{2006} \geq \sqrt{2\log 2/\delta}/\varepsilon$, and the global sensitivity is 1. Subsequently, Dwork et al. [6] optimized the satisfaction conditions when meeting $(\varepsilon, \delta) - \mathrm{ADP}$ in 2014: $\sigma_{2014} \geq \sqrt{2\log 1.25/\delta}/\varepsilon$. When Balle et al. [1] reanalyzed the Gaussian mechanism in 2018, they found the limitations and suboptimal of Dwork et al. Therefore, they proposed the analytical Gaussian mechanism (AGM). However, since σ_{AGM} has no closed expression, In 2019, when Zhao et al. [16] sacrificed a small accuracy, σ_{2019} can be calculated directly by expression to simplify the calculation process. Under the same conditions, the size relationship of their calculated values is: $\sigma_{2006} > \sigma_{2014} > \sigma_{2019} > \sigma_{AGM}$.

3   Basic Knowledge

Table 1 defines the symbols used in this article.

3.1   Differential Privacy

Definition 1 (Differential Privacy [4]). A randomized function $A(\mathcal{D})$ is (ε, δ) - differentially private if for all pairs of databases $(\mathcal{D}, \mathcal{D}')$ with $d_H(\mathcal{D}, \mathcal{D}') = 1$ and all measurable subsets of outputs $\mathcal{O}$:

Table 1. Symbol summary

Symbol	Describe
(ε, δ)	Privacy parameters
$\mathbb{F}(\cdot)$	Probability density function
$\Delta_2 Q$	Global sensitivity of query Q
σ^2	Variance of Gaussian distribution
$\widehat{Q}_m(\mathcal{D})$	The result after the m-th query disturbance
r	Reuse ratio
$L_{M,\mathcal{D},\mathcal{D}'}(Y)$	Privacy loss function
$\Phi(\cdot)$	Standard Gaussian distribution function
$\mathbb{N}\left(0, \sigma^2\right)$	Gaussian distribution with mean value of 0 and variance of σ^2
$H(\cdot)$	Hash function
$Q_m(\mathcal{D})$	The m-th query results without noise
$\Phi(\cdot)'$	Derivative of standard Gaussian distribution function

$$\mathbb{P}(A(\mathcal{D}) \in \mathcal{O}) \leq e^{\varepsilon} \mathbb{P}\left(A\left(\mathcal{D}'\right) \in \mathcal{O}\right) + \delta$$

Intuitively, $(\varepsilon, 0)$- differentially privacy ensures that for every run of algorithm A the outputis almost equally likely to be observed on every neighboring database. This condition isrelaxed by (ε, δ)- differentially privacy since it allows that given a random output O from $A(\mathcal{D})$, it may be possible to find a database $\mathcal{D}'$ such that O is more likely to beproduced on $\mathcal{D}'$ that it is when the database is $\mathcal{D}$. In both cases the similarity is defined by the factor e^{ε} while the probability ofdeviating from this similarity is δ.

Definition 2 (Global Sensitivity [14]). upposing f is a random query function of a sequence, and $f : D \rightarrow R^d$, D_1 and D_2 are two data sets with at most one difference, the global sensitivity of f is shown as the following:

$$\Delta_f = \max_{D_1, D_2} \|f(D_1) - f(D_2)\|_1$$

In addition to global sensitivity, there are local sensitivity and smoothing sensitivity. Refer to specific literature [11], which is not described here.

Definition 3 (Privacy loss function [7]). Consider running an algorithm $\mathcal{M}$ on a pair of databases $\mathcal{D}, \mathcal{D}'$. The privacy loss function $L_{M,\mathcal{D},\mathcal{D}'}(Y)$ can be expressed as the distance between two probabilities that M acts on adjacent data sets $\mathcal{D}$ and $\mathcal{D}'$ and outputs the same random variable Y. It is defined as follows:

$$L_{M,\mathcal{D},\mathcal{D}'}(Y) = \ln\left(\frac{\mathbb{F}_{M(\mathcal{D})}(Y)}{\mathbb{F}_{M(\mathcal{D}')}(Y)}\right)$$

Where $\mathbb{F}_{M(\mathcal{D})}(Y)$ is the probability density function of the output random variable $Y = (\mathcal{D})$. if the Gaussian mechanism is selected to add noise, then

$L_{M,D,D'}(Y) \sim \mathbb{N}\left(\Delta_2 f^2/2\sigma^2, \Delta_2 f^2/\sigma^2\right)$[13]. We can extend it to multiple random mechanisms and set a set of random mechanisms $M_1, M_2, \cdots, M_n$. When this set of mechanisms acts on adjacent data sets $\mathcal{D}$ and $\mathcal{D}'$, the output result is random variable Y_i, represented by $Y_i = M(\mathcal{D})$. Then:

$$L_{(M_1, M_2, \cdots, M_n), \mathcal{D}, \mathcal{D}'}(Y_1, Y_2, \cdots, Y_n) = \ln \frac{\mathbb{F}\left(\bigcap_{i=1}^n Y_i = M_i(\mathcal{D})\right)}{\mathbb{F}\left(\bigcap_{i=1}^n Y_i = M_i(\mathcal{D}')\right)}$$

4   Optimize AMG Variance Calculation Method

Lemma 1. Let the global sensitivity of $M : \mathbb{R}^{|\mathcal{D}|} \to \mathbb{Y}$ be $\Delta_2 f$, and for any $\varepsilon \geq 0, \quad 0 < \delta < 1$, the necessary and sufficient condition for $M(\mathcal{D}) = f(\mathcal{D}) + \mathbb{N}\left(0, \sigma^2\right)$ to satisfy (ε, δ) - differential privacy is:

$$\Phi\left(\frac{\Delta_2 f}{2\sigma} - \frac{\varepsilon\sigma}{\Delta_2 f}\right) - e^\varepsilon \Phi\left(-\frac{\Delta_2 f}{2\sigma} - \frac{\varepsilon\sigma}{\Delta_2 f}\right) \leq \delta \tag{1}$$

Lemma 1 is Theorem 8 in reference [1], where $\Phi(\cdot)$ is the standard normal distribution. To satisfy the privacy guarantee of (ε, δ)-differential privacy, the noise variance σ^2 of formula (1) needs to be calculated.

Corollary 1. σ **Solving Algorithm** Set $\sigma = \alpha \Delta_2 f/\sqrt{2\varepsilon}$, where $\alpha > 0$ takes the formula in Lemma 1 (1):

$$\mathcal{B}_\varepsilon(\alpha) = \Phi\left(\varepsilon\left(1 - \alpha^2\right)/\alpha\sqrt{2\varepsilon}\right) - e^\varepsilon \Phi\left(-\varepsilon\left(1 + \alpha^2\right)/\alpha\sqrt{2\varepsilon}\right) - \delta \tag{2}$$

Formula (1) The second item on the right $-\varepsilon\left(1 + \alpha^2\right)/\alpha\sqrt{2\varepsilon} \leq 0$, and the first item on the right are divided into the following three cases:

1) $\varepsilon\left(1 - \alpha^2\right)/\alpha\sqrt{2\varepsilon} < 0, \quad \alpha > 1$
   Make $u = \alpha^2/2 + 1/2\alpha^2 - 1$, then: $\mathcal{B}_\varepsilon^-(u) = \Phi(-\sqrt{\varepsilon u}) - e^\varepsilon \Phi(-\sqrt{\varepsilon(u+2)}) - \delta$
2) $\varepsilon\left(1 - \alpha^2\right)/\alpha\sqrt{2\varepsilon} > 0, \quad \alpha < 1$
   Make $v = \alpha^2/2 + 1/2\alpha^2 - 1$, then: $\mathcal{B}_\varepsilon^+(v) = \Phi(\sqrt{\varepsilon v}) - e^\varepsilon \Phi(-\sqrt{\varepsilon(v+2)}) - \delta$
3) $\varepsilon\left(1 - \alpha^2\right)/\alpha\sqrt{2\varepsilon} = 0, \quad \alpha = 1$:
   $\mathcal{B}_u^-(0) = \mathcal{B}_v^+(0) = \Phi(0) - e^\varepsilon \Phi(-\sqrt{2\varepsilon}) - \delta = \delta(\varepsilon) - \delta$

From Corollary 1, we can see that $\lim_{v \to \infty} \mathcal{B}_\varepsilon^+(v) = 1 - \delta$ and $\lim_{v \to 0} \mathcal{B}_\varepsilon^+(v) = -\delta$, and $\mathcal{B}_\varepsilon^+(v)$ monotonically increasing functions, so they have and only have one root. According to the characteristics of $\mathcal{B}_\varepsilon^+(v)$ function, we find that it satisfies the convergence condition of Newton's downhill method for finding roots ($\mathcal{B}_\varepsilon^-(u)$ homology). Therefore, Corollary 1 output satisfies the noise variance of (ε, δ) - differential privacy, where $\varepsilon > 0, \quad 0 < \delta < 1$. Implemented by Algorithm 1.

Algorithm 1 uses the error function $\mathrm{erf}(x) = 2/\sqrt{\pi} \int_0^x e^{-t^2} dt$ to calculate the Gaussian distribution, and $\Phi(x) = \frac{1}{2} + \mathrm{erf}(x/\sqrt{2})/2$ can be obtained.

5   Continuous Query Differential Privacy Mechanism

5.1   Blockchain

Since the advent of Bitcoin in 2008 [10], Blockchain technology has attracted wide attention. Blockchain is a decentralized, shared account that uses cryptographic techniques to guarantee that data on the chain cannot be tampered with or forged [2]. This paper proposes a CQDPM for continuous queries. Because the allocation of the privacy budget is not adaptive, it consumes the privacy budget according to query requirements. Therefore, it is essential to control and track the consumption of the privacy budget. Considering the characteristics of Blockchain, this paper records the privacy budget and consumption in the Blockchain network. This ensures that the privacy budget will not be tampered with, and at the same time, it is easy to query the usage of the privacy budget. Finally, due to the security of local records, relying on the Blockchain network, a data integrity verification algorithm is proposed. The hash values of each record from the local server are recorded in the Blockchain network separately. Whether the integrity of the data is damaged or not, only the hash values of the data are compared. The security of records in the local server is improved.

Algorithm 1: Newton iterative variance calculation algorithm

Input: Dataset $\mathcal{D}$, Query Q, Sensitivity $\Delta_2 Q$, Privacy parameters (ε, δ)
Output: Noise variance σ^2

1 Computer $\delta_0 = \Phi(0) - e^\varepsilon \Phi(-\sqrt{2\varepsilon})$
2 **if** $\delta > \delta_0$ **then**
3   funciton $B_\varepsilon^+(v) = \Phi(\sqrt{\varepsilon v}) - e^\varepsilon \Phi(-\sqrt{\varepsilon(v+2)}) - \delta$
4   Computer $B_\varepsilon^+(v)' = \Phi(\sqrt{\varepsilon v})' - e^\varepsilon \Phi(-\sqrt{\varepsilon(v+2)})$
5   **while** $\left(B_\varepsilon^+(v^*) < tol\,\right)$ **do**
6 | Computer $u^* = u - B_\varepsilon^-(u)/B_\varepsilon^-(u)'$
7   **end**
8 **end**
9 Computer $\alpha = \sqrt{1 - v^*/2} - \sqrt{v^*/2}$
10 **else if** $\delta < \delta_0$ **then**
11   function $B_\varepsilon^-(u) = \Phi(-\sqrt{\varepsilon u}) - e^\varepsilon \Phi(-\sqrt{\varepsilon(u+2)}) - \delta$
12   Computer $B_\varepsilon^-(u)' = \Phi(-\sqrt{\varepsilon u})' - e^\varepsilon \Phi(-\sqrt{\varepsilon(u+2)})'$
13   **while** $\left(B_\varepsilon^-(u^*) < tol\right)$ **do**
14 | $u^* = u - B_\varepsilon^-(u)/B_\varepsilon^-(u)'$
15   **end**
16 **end**
17 Computer $\alpha = \sqrt{1 - u^*/2} - \sqrt{u^*/2}$
18 **else**
19 | $\alpha = 1$
20 **end**
21 **return** $\sigma^2 = \left(\alpha \Delta_2 Q / \sqrt{2\varepsilon}\right)^2$

5.2   Noise Reuse in Differential Privacy

To answer how to reuse noise in continuous queries with different privacy guarantees, Zhao et al. Proposed a new method of reusing noise in Theorem 1 of document [3] to minimize the ratio of privacy cost. In this paper, we give Lemma 2.

Lemma 2. Query $Q_1, Q_2, \cdots, Q_{m-1}$ has been answered before answering query Q_m. if Q_m is a T-type query, Q_j has the same query type as Q_m, $j \in (1, 2, \cdots, m-1)$, at this time, you can reuse the noise that has answered $\widehat{Q}_j(\mathcal{D})$ to answer $\widehat{Q}_m(\mathcal{D})$. Set the noise reuse rate r; $0 \le r \le 1$, $\sigma_m^2 - r^2\sigma_j^2 > 0$ is satisfied, and $\widehat{Q}_j(\mathcal{D}) - Q_j(\mathcal{D}) \sim \mathbb{N}\left(0, \sigma_j^2\right)$, then $\widehat{Q}_m(\mathcal{D})$:

$$Q_m(\mathcal{D}) + r\left(\widehat{Q}_j(\mathcal{D}) - Q_j(\mathcal{D})\right) + \mathbb{N}\left(0, \sigma_m^2 - r^2\sigma_j^2\right) = \widehat{Q}_m(\mathcal{D}) \tag{3}$$

where $Q(\mathcal{D})$ represents the exact result of the query, $\widehat{Q}(\mathcal{D})$ represents the result after disturbance, and σ^2 is the output of Algorithm 1. Now it is necessary to determine the specific value of noise reuse rate r. According to the definition of privacy loss function in the three sections of this paper, this paper gives Corollary 2.

Corollary 2. Calculation of r. Because Q_m and Q_j are of the same type, $Q_m(\mathcal{D}) = Q_j(\mathcal{D})$ and the global sensitivity is $\Delta Q_m = \Delta Q_j$, the following results are obtained:

1. If you have answered $Q_1, Q_2, \cdots, Q_{m-1}$ before answering the same type of query Q_m, the privacy loss function $L_{(\widehat{Q}, \widehat{Q}_2, \cdots, \widehat{Q}_m), \mathcal{D}, \mathcal{D}'}(Y_i) \sim \mathbb{N}(V(\mathcal{D}, \mathcal{D}')/2, V(\mathcal{D}, \mathcal{D}'))$, and the privacy loss function $L_{(\widehat{Q}_1, \widehat{Q}_2, \cdots, \widehat{Q}_m), \mathcal{D}, \mathcal{D}'}(Y_i) \sim \mathbb{N}(U(\mathcal{D}, \mathcal{D}')/2, U(\mathcal{D}, \mathcal{D}'))$ after answering Q_m. Of which:

$$U(\mathcal{D}, \mathcal{D}') = V(\mathcal{D}, \mathcal{D}') + \{\|Q_m(\mathcal{D}) - Q_m(\mathcal{D}')\|_2\}^2 (1 - r)/\sigma_m^2 - r^2\sigma_j^2 \tag{4}$$

   In particular, when $m = 1, U(\mathcal{D}, \mathcal{D}') = 0 + \Delta Q^2/\sigma^2$.
2. In order to minimize the total privacy cost, we regard the second term on the right in formula (4) as a function of r, which can give the optimal ratio:

$$r = \begin{cases} 1 & \sigma_m \ge \sigma_j \text{ and } Q_m \in T \\ (\sigma_m/\sigma_j)^2 & \sigma_m < \sigma_j \text{ and } Q_m \in T \\ 0 & Q_m \notin T \end{cases} \tag{5}$$

Where $T\{\}$ represents a collection of query types, according to the value of noise reuse ratio given by inference 2, Algorithm 2 realizes the reuse noise response. When reusing noise, the algorithm needs to compare the corresponding data of the same query type, so it is necessary to record the privacy parameters, query type, disturbance result and σ after each response to the query result.

5.3   Local Data Integrity Verification

In order to prevent malicious modification of data, Algorithm 3 is proposed based on the characteristics of the Hash function to verify whether the record is modified.

Algorithm 2: Continuous Query Differential Privacy Mechanism

Input: Dataset $\mathcal{D}$, Type of Q_m: $Q \in t$, Variance σ_m^2, parameters $(\varepsilon_m, \delta_m)$
Output: Results after disturbance $\widehat{Q}_m(\mathcal{D})$

1   **if** *Query type t of Q_m met for the first time* **then**
2   Computer $\varepsilon_r = \varepsilon_r - \varepsilon_m$
3   **if** $\varepsilon_r \geq 0$ **then**
4   Computer $\widehat{Q}_m(\mathcal{D}) = Q_m(\mathcal{D}) + \mathbb{N}\left(0, \sigma_m^2\right)$
5       $h_m = H\left(\widehat{Q}_m(\mathcal{D}), t, \varepsilon_m, \delta_m, \sigma_m^2\right)$
6   Blockchain record h_m, ε_r
7   **return** $\widehat{Q}_m(\mathcal{D})$
8   **end**
9   **end**
10 **else**
11   **if** $\sigma_m^2 = \left\{\sigma_j^2 \mid \sigma_j^2 \in t\right\}$ **then**
12   **return** $\widehat{Q}_j(\mathcal{D})$
13   **end**
14 **end**
15 **else** $\sigma_m^2 < \min\left\{\sigma_j^2 \mid \sigma_j^2 \in t\right\}$
16   Computer $\left(\alpha\Delta_2 Q/\sqrt{2\varepsilon}\right)^{-2} = \sigma_m^{-2} - \sigma_j^{-2}$
17   Computer $\varepsilon_r = \varepsilon_r - \varepsilon_l$
18   **if** $\varepsilon_r \geq 0$ **then**
19   Let $r = \left(\sigma_m^2/\sigma_j^2\right)$
20   Computer $\widehat{Q}_m(\mathcal{D}) = Q_m(\mathcal{D}) + r\left(\widehat{Q}_j(\mathcal{D}) - Q_m(\mathcal{D})\right) + \mathbb{N}\left(0, \sigma_m^2 - r\sigma_j^2\right)$
21       $h_m = H\left(\widehat{Q}_m(\mathcal{D}), t, \varepsilon_m, \delta_m, \sigma_m^2\right)$
22   Blockchain record h_m, ε_r
23   **return** $\widehat{Q}_m(\mathcal{D})$
24   **end**
25 **end**
26 **else** $\sigma_m^2 > \max\left\{\sigma_j^2 \in t \mid \sigma_j^2 < \sigma_m^2\right\}$
27   Computer $\widehat{Q}_m(\mathcal{D}) = \widehat{Q}_j(\mathcal{D}) + \mathbb{N}\left(0, \sigma_m^2 - \sigma_j^2\right)$
28     $h_m = H\left(\widehat{Q}_m(\mathcal{D}), t, \varepsilon_m, \delta_m, \sigma_m^2\right)$
29   Blockchain record h_m, ε_r
30   **return** $\widehat{Q}_m(\mathcal{D})$
31 **end**

Algorithm 3: Data integrity verification

Input: $R[i]$
Output: True or False

1   Computer: $h_i = H(R[i])$
2   Compare: $h_i == h_j \, of \, Blockchain$

---

6   Experimental Analysis

6.1   Experimental Environment

In this experiment, using the American community survey sample provided by IPUMS (integrated public use microdata Series), we selected 10000 data from 17293 data in 2019. Each data includes four attributes: Total personal income, Total family income, Age and Sex. Five types of query types are considered: average individual income, average family income, the proportion of men, the proportion of women, $\geq$ per capita income of 60 years old. The sensitivity of each query is 10, 9.7, 0.0001, 0.0001, 10. For the privacy parameters of each query, ε_i samples randomly from $[0.1, 1]$, and δ_i samples randomly from $(10^{-5}, 10^{-4})$.

6.2   Comparison of Time Efficiency of Algorithm 1

Algorithm 1 optimizes the calculation method of Gaussian mechanism variance, uses the Newton downhill method to search for the optimal v^*, u^* iteratively, and theoretically shows that Algorithm 1 satisfies (ε, δ) - differential privacy. In order to improve the response efficiency under the interactive framework, the number of iterations and response time is compared with the AGM algorithm.

It can be seen from Fig. 1. a) and 1. b). Under the same accuracy, the number of iterations after optimization is nearly 60% lower than the dichotomy used by AGM, and the iteration time is about 50% lower. Among them, the red algorithm is 1, and the black is the AGM algorithm.

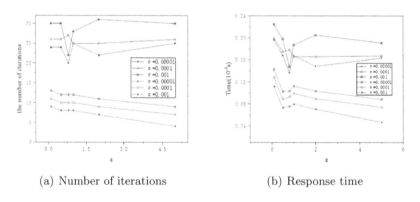

| (a) Number of iterations | (b) Response time |

Fig. 1. Comparison between Algorithm 1 and AGM algorithm (Color figure online)

6.3   Time Efficiency Comparison of CQDPM

An experiment is designed to verify the effectiveness of Algorithm 2 in saving privacy budget. Under the same conditions, 40 above five types of query requests are randomized. Compared with the traditional algorithm that does not reuse noise disturbance, the two algorithms have less consumption of privacy budget.

As shown from Fig. 2. a), Algorithm 2 significantly saves the privacy budget and reduces the privacy budget consumption by about 62% compared with the traditional algorithm. As the number of queries increase, the consumption of the privacy budget tends to a specific value. Randomize 50 queries, compare the absolute error of Algorithm 2 and BBNR algorithm, and the calculation formula is: $\left|\widehat{Q}_m(\mathcal{D}) - Q_m(\mathcal{D})\right|$. Verify the availability of Algorithm 2 on real data sets.

As can be seen from Fig. 2. b), Algorithm 2 improves the effectiveness of data compared with the BBNR algorithm of Zhao et al. The comparison of absolute error can also be considered the comparison of added noise.

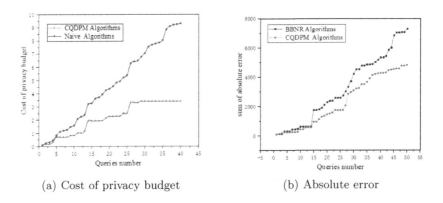

(a) Cost of privacy budget   (b) Absolute error

Fig. 2. Comparison between CQDPM and existing algorithms

Finally, we compare the response efficiency with the BBNR algorithm. Since the time complexity of blockchain increases greatly with the increase of the number of records, this paper records the query results in the local rather than the distributed storage blockchain system. When responding to a new query, you only need to compare it in the local record without requesting the blockchain system, which reduces the query response time.

The experiment uses the truffle framework to compile and deploy the smart contract, and deploys the smart contract to the Ropsten test network through the services provided by infra. We randomly collected 100 bytes32 type data and gradually recorded it into the smart contract.

In Fig. 3, the response time fluctuates obviously due to the blockchain network. Nevertheless, the response time of the CQDPM has been improved greatly. CQDPM is efficient for the response efficiency of interactive queries.

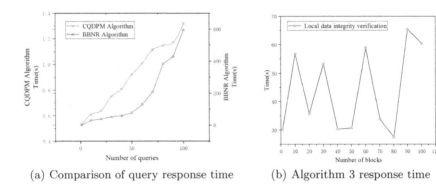

(a) Comparison of query response time   (b) Algorithm 3 response time

Fig. 3. Comparison of efficiency

7   Summary

This paper study the problem of "fast consumption of privacy budget in differential privacy interactive query, resulting in a small number of queries". The noise reuse proposed by Zhao et al. Effectively solves this problem but brings slow response speed. In an interactive query framework, the response speed of the query is as essential as the number of queries that the data set can provide. Therefore, this paper designs a CQDPM, which can reuse noise to improve the number of queries and reduce the query response time significantly, and improve data availability to a certain extent. At the same time, this paper analyzes the shortcomings and limitations of the Gaussian mechanism and uses the Newton downhill method to calculate the noise variance iteratively. From the experiment, it can be seen that the iterative efficiency is improved by about 50%. Finally, Algorithm 3 is proposed to verify the integrity of data in the local server. In terms of security, there are also corresponding guarantees. Because the query type is preset, the type is relatively fixed. In the future, the internal relationship between query statements will be used to expand the types of query types and further improve the practicability of the mechanism proposed in this paper.

Acknowledge. Thanks to the National Natural Science Foundation of China (NO. 62062020)(NO. 62002081)(NO. 62002080)

References

1. Balle, B., Wang, Y.X.: Improving the gaussian mechanism for differential privacy: analytical calibration and optimal denoising. In: International Conference on Machine Learning, pp. 394–403. PMLR (2018)
2. Christidis, K., Devetsikiotis, M.: Blockchains and smart contracts for the internet of things. IEEE Access **4**, 2292–2303 (2016)
3. Dwork, C., Kenthapadi, K., McSherry, F., Mironov, I., Naor, M.: Our data, ourselves: privacy via distributed noise generation. In: Vaudenay, S. (ed.) EUROCRYPT 2006. LNCS, vol. 4004, pp. 486–503. Springer, Heidelberg (2006). https://doi.org/10.1007/11761679_29

4. Dwork, C., Lei, J.: Differential privacy and robust statistics. In: Proceedings of the Forty-First Annual ACM Symposium on Theory of Computing, pp. 371–380 (2009)
5. Dwork, C., McSherry, F., Nissim, K., Smith, A.: Calibrating noise to sensitivity in private data analysis. In: Halevi, S., Rabin, T. (eds.) TCC 2006. LNCS, vol. 3876, pp. 265–284. Springer, Heidelberg (2006). https://doi.org/10.1007/11681878_14
6. Dwork, C., Roth, A., et al.: The algorithmic foundations of differential privacy. Found. Trends Theor. Comput. Sci. **9**(3–4), 211–407 (2014)
7. Dwork, C., Rothblum, G.N.: Concentrated differential privacy. arXiv preprint arXiv:1603.01887 (2016)
8. Hao, C., Peng, C., Zhang, P.: Selection method of differential privacy protection parameter under repeated attack. Comput. Eng. **44**(7), 145–149 (2018)
9. Hardt, M., Rothblum, G.N.: A multiplicative weights mechanism for privacy-preserving data analysis. In: 2010 IEEE 51st Annual Symposium on Foundations of Computer Science, pp. 61–70. IEEE (2010)
10. Nakamoto, S.: Bitcoin: a peer-to-peer electronic cash system. Decentralized Bus. Rev. 21260 (2008)
11. Nissim, K., Raskhodnikova, S., Smith, A.: Smooth sensitivity and sampling in private data analysis. In: Proceedings of the Thirty-Ninth Annual ACM Symposium on Theory of Computing, pp. 75–84 (2007)
12. Roth, A., Roughgarden, T.: Interactive privacy via the median mechanism. In: Proceedings of the Forty-Second ACM Symposium on Theory of Computing, pp. 765–774 (2010)
13. Sommer, D.M., Meiser, S., Mohammadi, E.: Privacy loss classes: the central limit theorem in differential privacy. Proc. Priv. Enhancing Technol. **2019**(2), 245–269 (2019)
14. Wang, D., Long, S.: Boosting the accuracy of differentially private in weighted social networks. Multimedia Tools Appl. **78**(24), 34801–34817 (2019). https://doi.org/10.1007/s11042-019-08092-0
15. Yang, M., Margheri, A., Hu, R., Sassone, V.: Differentially private data sharing in a cloud federation with blockchain. IEEE Cloud Comput. **5**(6), 69–79 (2018)
16. Zhao, J., et al.: Reviewing and improving the gaussian mechanism for differential privacy. arXiv preprint arXiv:1911.12060 (2019)
17. Zhao, Y., et al.: A blockchain-based approach for saving and tracking differential-privacy cost. IEEE Internet Things J. **8**(11), 8865–8882 (2021)
18. Zhu, T., Li, G., Zhou, W., Yu, P.S.: Differential Privacy and Applications. AIS, vol. 69. Springer, Cham (2017). https://doi.org/10.1007/978-3-319-62004-6

Formalization and Verification of Group Communication CoAP Using CSP

Sini Chen, Ran Li, and Huibiao Zhu[✉]

Shanghai Key Laboratory of Trustworthy Computing, East China Normal University,
Shanghai, China
hbzhu@sei.ecnu.edu.cn

Abstract. With the rapid expansion of Internet of Things (IoT), Constrained Application Protocol (CoAP) is developed to enable those devices with small memory, constrained computing power and limited ability to communicate with other nodes in the network. Meanwhile, group communication is very useful for managing and controlling a set of homogeneous devices in many IoT scenarios. Thus, many scholars are devoted to expanding CoAP to enable group communication. Furthermore, because CoAP is widely applicated in transportation, health care, industrial and many other areas, the security and consistency of data is of great importance. In this paper, we adopt Communicating Sequential Processes (CSP) to model group communication CoAP, and we use model checker Process Analysis Toolkit (PAT) to verify six properties of our model, including deadlock freedom, divergence freedom, data reachability, data leakage, client faking and entity manager faking. The verification results show that the original architecture has the security risk of data leakage. So we enhance it by adding message authentication code in the process. In the light of the new verification results, it can be found that we succeed in eliminating the possibility of data leakage.

Keywords: Group communication · CoAP · CSP · Modeling · Verification

1 Introduction

The expansion of Internet of Things (IoT) market is changing the way people live and work tremendously in many aspects, including transportation, healthcare, industrial automation, etc. [1]. The Constrained Application Protocol (CoAP), an application level protocol created by IETF group, aims to enable tiny devices to utilize RESTful interactions. The basic communication model for CoAP is based on the client-server model [2]. However, group communication can be quite useful in practical scenarios of IoT, thus it has been recently supported by CoAP. This can be implemented with IP multi-cast [3] or an observe-based group communication scheme [4].

In the meantime, IoT devices generate, exchange and consume potentially sensitive and safety-critical data [5]. Moreover, in the IoT ecosystem, users can

© Springer Nature Switzerland AG 2022
H. Shen et al. (Eds.): PDCAT 2021, LNCS 13148, pp. 616–628, 2022.
https://doi.org/10.1007/978-3-030-96772-7_58

remotely access IoT devices by using application message brokers or middle-ware technologies. These characters make IoT prone to cyber criminals [6]. Therefore, security and integrity are rather important requirements. However, from those existing works concerning security of group communication CoAP, we find that they mainly take the approach of implementing the protocol, and analyzing the security performance with data collected in experiments [7,8]. Experiment data is prone to a variety of external factors. There may still exist potential security issues in group communication CoAP.

In this paper, we adopt a formal method to verify the security of group communication CoAP. We choose Communicating Sequential Processes (CSP) [9] to model the architecture, which has the accuracy of mathematical proof. And we use Process Analysis Toolkit (PAT) to verify six properties: deadlock freedom, divergence freedom, data reachability, data leakage, client faking and entity manager faking. The verification results show that data leakage is possible with the presence of an intruder. On this basis, we introduce message authentication code (MAC) [10] as an improvement and formalize a new model to address the problem. The new verification results indicate the improved model achieves higher security. The works we have done in this paper is shown in Fig. 1.

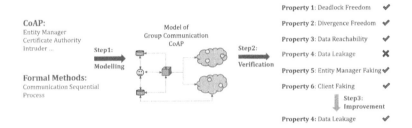

Fig. 1. Works done in this paper.

This paper is organized as follows. Section 1 gives a brief introduction of group communication CoAP and process algebra CSP. Section 3 illustrates detailed modeling of group communication CoAP. In Section 4, we use PAT to verify six properties of the original model and make improvements accordingly. Finally, we draw a conclusion and give the future work in Section 5.

2 Background

In this section, we give a brief explanation of the architecture and message flow of group communication CoAP. We also introduce the process algebra CSP.

2.1 Overall Architecture of Group Communication CoAP

In this paper, we adopt the observe-based group communication scheme. Under this scheme, entities participating in communication include:

- **Entity**: A set of resources is called an entity. One CoAP request is capable of manipulating all resources in one entity.
- **Entity Manager**: It manages multiple entities. Theoretically, users can select the Entity Manager based on the size and topology of the network.
- **Resource Directory**: It records detailed information of resources.

Furthermore, the security of CoAP depends on Datagram Transport Layer Security (DTLS) binding [11] in the absence of built-in security mechanisms. There are four security patterns: **No-Sec, Pre-shared-Key (PSK), Raw-Public-Key (RPK)** and **Certificate**. In our architecture, we should ensure the security of the content as well as reduce the cost of communication.

Thus, we make the following assumptions: the communication between client and entity manager adopts **Certificate** pattern. **RPK** pattern is selected for the communication between other nodes.

The RPK pattern we adopted is implemented with ECDHE [12] algorithm. Based on those assumptions, we introduce a new entity, **Certificate Authority**, to issue and manage digital certificates. The overall architecture of group communication CoAP is shown in Fig. 2.

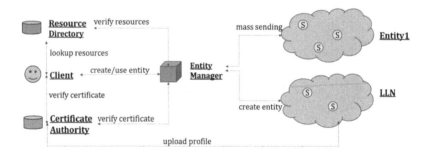

Fig. 2. Architecture of group communication CoAP.

2.2   Working Mechanism of Group Communication CoAP

Entity manager provides the client with three main functions: Entity Creation, Entity Usage and Entity Manipulation.

- **Entity Creation:** The client interacts with the entity manager to create an entity with designated resources. Figure 3 demonstrates the detailed process.
  1. Resources in the network send their own profiles to the resource directory and the resource directory returns an acknowledgement (ACK).
  2. The client sends a resource query to the resource directory.
  3. The resource directory sends back the information of existing qualified resources to the client.
  4. The client initiates a request to create an entity to the entity manager. Payload includes specific resources, its own certificate, and expected operation on the return value.

5. The entity manager forwards the certificate to the certificate authority for verification and gets the verification result. If the result is valid, it proceeds to the next step. Otherwise, it fails.
6. The entity manager verifies whether the resource is valid through the resource directory. If the result is valid, it proceeds to the next step. Otherwise, it fails. The verification here includes two aspects: all members actually exist and provide expected functionality.
7. The entity manager integrates and stores the information of the group of resources and assigns an URL to the freshly created entity. Then it returns an ACK including the assigned URL together with the certificate of itself back to the client.
8. The client forwards the certificate to the certification authority for verification as is described in step 5.
9. The client returns an ACK. The entity is created successfully and can continue subsequent communications.

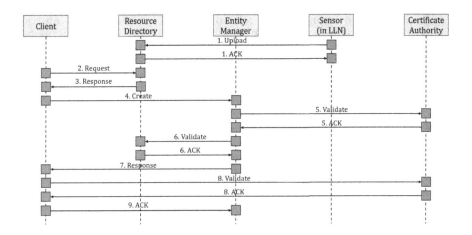

Fig. 3. Interactions among entities in entity creation phase.

– **Entity Usage:** User can manage all members in an entity by only one CoAP request to the entity manager. Figure 4 illustrates this process.
  1. The client sends a request to the entity manager to request the data of Entity1.
  2. The entity manager sends requests to all resources in Entity1 respectively.
  3. The entity manager waits for the data returned, until the amount of data meets the requirement.
  4. The entity manager processes the collected data and returns it to the user.

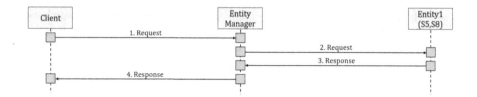

Fig. 4. Interactions among entities in entity usage phase.

– **Entity Modification:** After creation of an entity, it is possible that client wants to make some modifications, like adding new members. The process is similar to entity creation. Therefore, we combine the two.

2.3 CSP

CSP is a process algebra proposed by C.A.R.Hoare. Since CSP's introduction in 1978, it has been improved and refined, and has evolved into an abstract language that is highly mature and capable of describing message exchanges among processes. Part of CSP syntax used in our model are described as follows.

$$P, Q \ ::= SKIP \mid STOP \mid a \rightarrow P \mid c?x \rightarrow P \mid c!v \rightarrow P$$
$$\mid P \square Q \mid P \parallel Q \mid P \lhd b \rhd Q \mid P; Q$$

– $SKIP$: The process terminates properly.
– $STOP$: The process reaches deadlock.
– $a \rightarrow P$: After the execution of event a, process P is executed.
– $c?x \rightarrow P$: The process accepts value from the channel c, assigns it to variable x, and then starts executing process P.
– $c!v \rightarrow P$: The process sends value v through the channel c, and then starts executing process P.
– $P \square Q$: It stands for general choice between the process P and process Q.
– $P \parallel Q$: Process P and process Q run in parallel.
– $P \lhd b \rhd Q$: If boolean expression b equals true, then process P is executed, otherwise process Q is executed.
– $P; Q$: After successful termination of process P, process Q is executed.

3 Modeling Group Communication CoAP

3.1 Sets, Messages and Channels

To facilitate the procedure of modeling, we first define the following sets. For those entities participating in the communication, we have: **Clients** for clients. **EMs** for entity managers. **Sensors** for constrained resources, including sensors in the network, etc. **RDs** for resource directories. **Entities** for client-created entities, which consist several constrained resources. **CA** for certificate authority.

And we define **UnconEntities** denotes the set of clients and entity managers. **ConEntities** denotes the set of resource directories and sensors.

Furthermore, all entities defined above have their own keys, clients and entity managers have certificates, entities have their unique identifiers. So we define: **Cert** for certificates, **Content** for data, **Id** for entities' identifiers, **State** for the two states true and false and **Key** for the set of public keys (kPUB), private keys (kPRI) used in Certificate pattern and public key generated by the ECDHE algorithm (kECDHE) used in RPK pattern. Based on the sets defined above, we generalize the messages:

$$MSG_{cert} = {}_{def}\{msg_{req}a.b.cert, msg_{rsp}a.b.state \mid a, b \in UnconEntities \cup CA,$$
$$cert \in Cert, \ state \in State\}$$
$$MSG_{ack} = {}_{def}\{msg_{ack}a.b.ack, msg_{ack}c.d.ack.cert \mid a \in ConEntities \cup CA,$$
$$b \in ConEntities \cup UnconEntities, c, d \in UnconEntities,$$
$$cert \in Cert, ack \in State\}$$
$$MSG_{data} = {}_{def}\{msg_{dreq}a.b.cert.id, msg_{drsp}a.b.cert.id.E(k, c), msg_{dreq1}c.d,$$
$$msg_{drsp1}c.d.E(k, c) \mid a, b \in UnconEntities, c, d \in ConEntities,$$
$$k \in Key, c \in Content\}$$

$$MSG_{cre} = {}_{def}\{msg_{cre}a.b.cert.E(k, c) \mid a, b \in UnconEntities, cert \in Cert,$$
$$k \in Key, c \in Content\}$$
$$MSG_{rsc} = {}_{def}\{msg_{rsc}a.b.E(k, c) \mid a, b \in ConEntities \cup UnconEntities\}$$

MSG_{cert} includes messages used in the process of certificate verification. For example, $msg_{req}a.b.cert$ denotes that node a (possibly a client or an entity manager), sends a certificate cert to node b (certificate authority), requesting validation of $cert$. Likewise, we have MSG_{ack} consisting acknowledgements, MSG_{rsc} representing any messages transferred to or from resource directory, MSG_{cre} including messages involved in the process of creating an entity and MSG_{data} for messages involved in the process of using an entity.

Here, $E(k, msg)$ indicates that the key k is used to encrypt msg. $D(k^{-1}, E(k, msg))$ states that the key k^{-1} is used to decrypt message msg which is encrypted by the key k. It should be noted that $msg_{dreq1}c.d$ denotes that node c (entity manager) sends requests to all members in node d (entity) respectively.

To model the communications between parties, we introduces two sets of channels. **COM_PATH** consists channels between legals nodes.

$$ComCCA, \ ComCRD, \ ComCEM, \ ComEMRD, \ ComEEM, \ ComSRD$$

While **INTRUDER_PATH** consists channels being intruded.

$$FakeCEM, \ FakeEMC, \ InterceptCEM, \ InterceptEMC$$
$$FakeEEM, \ FakeEME, \ InterceptEEM, \ InterceptEME$$

Com∗ stands for the channels for legal nodes to communicate. *Fake*∗ and *Intercept*∗ denote the channels with existence of an intruder. The former implies that the intruder can pretend to be a legal node to communicate with others, while the latter implies that the intruder can intercept messages transferred between legal nodes. Intuitively, *ComCCA* denotes the channel between Client and Certificate Authority. The rest can be interpreted in the same manner.

3.2   Overall Modeling

We construct two models *SystemC* and *SystemU*, denoting the entity-creating phase and the entity-using phase respectively. Combining *SystemC* and *SystemU* we get the whole system without the existence of intruder, and we name it *System0*. *SYSTEM* represents the whole system considering the presence of intruders.

$$SystemC =_{def} S[\|COM\_PATH\|] RD[\|COM\_PATH\|] C[\|COM\_PATH\|]$$
$$EM[\|COM\_PATH\|] CA$$
$$SystemU =_{def} C[\|COM\_PATH\|] EM[\|COM\_PATH\|] E$$
$$Syetem0 =_{def} SystemC\|SystemU$$
$$SYSTEM = System0[\|INTRUDER\_PATH\|] Intruder$$

Here, we abbreviate clients as C, sensors as S, resource directories as RD, entity managers as EM, certificate authorities as CA and entities as E. Then we introduce the process above in detail.

3.3   Client Modeling

The client participates in communicating with the resource directory to look up resources and the entity manager to manipulate the resources. We use general choice □ to split different scenarios of communication and formalize the model of the client as below.

$$\mathbf{C} =_{def} ECDHE\_key\_exchange \rightarrow ComCRD!msg_{rsc}C.RD.E(k_{ECDHE}, msg)$$
$$\rightarrow ComCRD?msg_{rsc}RD.C.E(k_{ECDHE}, msg) \rightarrow C$$
$$\square\ ComCEM!msg_{cre}C.EM.cert_C.E(k_{PUB}, msg)$$
$$\rightarrow ComCEM?msg_{ack}EM.C.cert_{EM}.E(k_{PUB}, msg)$$
$$\rightarrow ComCCA!msg_{req}C.CA.cert_{EM}$$
$$\rightarrow ComCCA?msg_{rsp}CA.C.cert_{EM}.verified$$
$$\rightarrow (success \rightarrow C) \triangleleft verified == true \triangleright (fail \rightarrow C)$$
$$\square\ ComCEM!msg_{dreq}C.EM.cert_C.id_E$$
$$\rightarrow ComCEM?msg_{drsp}EM.C.cert_{EM}.id_E.E(k_{PUB}, msg) \rightarrow C$$

In the first part, we describe the behavior of looking up resource directory. The client and the resource directory conduct an ECDHE key exchange. The details of key generation and exchange belong to DTLS protocol, which is not the focus of this paper, and it is simplified as an event **ECDHE_key_exchange**.

After the exchange, the client gains a key K_{ECDHE} which is used in subsequent communications. As we have described previously, the client sends a request to the resource directory with payload message, which carries the information about the target resource encrypted with K_{ECDHE}. Afterwards the resource directory sends back responses with contents also encrypted with K_{ECDHE}.

In the second part, we describe the behavior of requesting to create a new entity. The client and the entity manager use certificates to establish connections through the Transport Layer Security (TLS) protocol. The exact procedure of establishing connection is also not in the domain of this paper, so we assume that the connection has been established beforehand in our model and a pair of public key and private key have already been assigned to each party. The messages transferred through the channel $ComCEM$ is encrypted by the sender's public key, and it can only be decrypted by the receiver's private key.

As to the third part, it's quite similar to the first part, so we don't go into much detail here.

Above is the model established when there is no intruder. Moreover, we need to take the presence of intruders into our considerations. According to our assumptions, the intruder is capable of eavesdropping channels and faking messages. The relationship among client, entity manager and intruder is described in Fig. 5. We simulate those behaviors by renaming as below.

$$C' =_{def} C[[ComCEM!\{|ComCEM|\} \leftarrow ComCEM!\{|ComCEM|\},$$
$$ComCEM!\{|ComCEM|\} \leftarrow InterceptCEM!\{|ComCEM|\},$$
$$ComCEM?\{|ComCEM|\} \leftarrow ComCEM?\{|ComCEM|\},$$
$$ComCEM?\{|ComCEM|\} \leftarrow FakeEMC?\{|ComCEM|\}]]$$

Symbol $\{|x|\}$ denotes the set of messages which can be transmitted through channel x. The first and second parts indicate that either the client sends a true message to the entity manager through channel $ComCEM$ or the message is eavesdropped. The third and fourth parts indicate that either the client receives a true message from the entity manager through channel $ComCEM$ or the client receives a false message produced by the intruder through channel $FakeEMC$.

Due to limitation of space, we leave out detailed modeling of other entities except for the intruder.

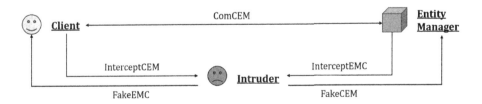

Fig. 5. Channels with existence of intruder.

3.4   Intruder Modeling

We assume the intruder can intercept legal channels, make a series of reasoning through the existing message (such as encryption and decryption, but we do not allow the intruder to guess the key) and fake new messages based on the information above and sent to legal nodes. We first define a set **Fact**, which includes all facts that can be obtained by intruder. Theoretically, the intruder can obtain all nodes in the network, and get all certificates, public keys and encrypted messages through channels.

$$Fact =\ _{def} ConstrainedEntities \cup UnconstrainedEntities \cup CA \cup Cert \cup Key$$
$$\cup \{k, c \mid k \in Key, c \in Content\} \cup \{E(k, c) \mid k \in Key, c \in Content\}$$

Based on the facts, the intruder can make inferences as below. The first inference signifies that if the intruder have the key k and the content c, then he can get the texture of c encrypted by k. Likewise, the second one shows if the intruder gets k^{-1}, he can decrypt $E(k, c)$ and get the plain-text of c. The last one demonstrates that if the intruder can get fact f from set F, then he can undoubtedly get f from a bigger set F'.

$$\{k, c\} \mapsto E(k, c) \qquad \{k^{-1}, E(k, c)\} \mapsto c \qquad F \mapsto f \wedge F \subseteq F' \Rightarrow F' \mapsto f$$

Next, we introduce a method **info(msg)**, which represents that the intruder can get fact f directly from intercepted message. For example, the intruder intercepts a piece of message $msg_{req} a.b.cert$ from channel, then he can know that this is a message from node a to node b, and get the content c encrypted by the key k. Then we define channel **Deduce** to describe the behaviors above. We give the model of the intruder as below.

$$Intruder(F) =\ _{def} {}_{msg \in MSG} Intercept.msg \to Intruder(F \cup Info(msg))$$
$$\Box\ _{msg \in MSG \cap Info(msg) \in I} Fake.msg \to Intruder(F)$$
$$\Box\ _{f \in Fact, f \notin F, F \mapsto f} Init\{data\_leakage\_success = false\} \to Deduce.f.F$$
$$\to ((data\_leakage\_success = true \to$$
$$Intruder(F \cup f)) \lhd (f == Data) \rhd (Intruder(F)))$$

The first line indicates that the intruder can intercept messages from channel **Intercept**, obtain the content and store in set **F**. The second line shows intruder's ability to forge a message and send it through channel **Fake**. The rest represents deductions through channel **Deduce**. In the process of constantly collecting and reasoning, if the intruder can crack the encryption and obtain the original data, it means the data is compromised. In addition, we define set IK to denote facts originally obtained by the intruder.

$$IK =\ _{def} \{ConsEntities, UnconsEntities, CA, kPUB\}$$

Finally, we finish the modeling of intruder:

$$Intruder =\ _{def} Intruder(IK)$$

4   Verification and Improvement

We conduct verification of the model through model checker **PAT** to verify six properties, including deadlock freedom, divergence freedom, data reachability, data leakage, client faking and entity manager faking. From the verification results, we improve the origin model by introducing message authentication code into it.

4.1   Verification

Property 1: Deadlock Freedom
Deadlock means the system is blocked and no further operation can be done. PAT provides us with a primitive:

$$\#assert\ System()\ deadlockfree;$$

Property 2: Divergence Freedom
Divergence refers to the state in which the system enters an infinite loop. We also have a primitive:

$$\#assert\ System()\ divergencefree;$$

Property 3: Data Reachability
CoAP should ensure that clients can successfully obtain the requested information. Then we have:

$$\#define\ Data\_Reachability\ data\_reachability\_success\ ==\ true;$$
$$\#assert\ CoAP\ reaches\ Data\_Reachability\_Success;$$

We define a state $Data\_Reachability\_Success$ in which variable $data\_reach$ $ability\_success$ is set to true. The assert statement is used to judge whether the system can reach the state after execution.

Property 4: Data Leakage
If an intruder can decrypt the information obtained on the channel and get the content of the information, then we face the problem of data leakage. We have:

$$\#define\ Data\_Leakage\_Success\ data\_leakage\_success\ ==\ true;$$
$$\#assert\ CoAP\ reaches\ Data\_Leakage\_Success;$$

Property 5: Client Faking
Supposing the intruder successfully disguises itself as a user and communicates with other entities, we run into the problem of client faking. We have:

$$\#define\ Client\_Faking\_Success\ client\_faking\_success\ ==\ true;$$
$$\#assert\ CoAP\ reaches\ Client\_Faking\_Success;$$

Property 6: Entity Manager Faking
If the intruder has the ability to pretend to be an entity manager and communicates with other entities, we encounter with the problem of entity manager faking. We have:

$$\#define\ EM\_Faking\_Success\ em\_faking\_success\ ==\ true;$$

$$\#assert\ CoAP\ reaches\ EM\_Faking\_Success;$$

4.2 Verification Results

According to verification results shown in Fig. 6, **Deadlock Freedom, Divergence Freedom** and **Data Reachability** all passed validation. This means our system will terminate normally and the client can get the requested data. **Client Faking** and **Entity Faking** both failed validation. It signifies that the intruder cannot disguise himself as a normal node in the network. However, **Data Leakage** also passed validation, showing potential risk of leaking data.

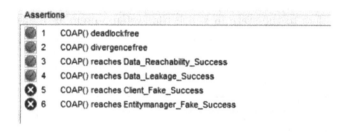

Fig. 6. Verification results of the original model.

4.3 Attack and Improvements

```
Output
********Verification Result********
The Assertion (COAP() reaches Data_Leakage_Success) is VALID.
The following trace leads to a state where the condition is satisfied.
<Init -> ECDHE_key_generation2 -> FakeCEM.CertC.E_id -> InterceptEME.E_id -> FakeEEM.E_id.K_ECDHE.Msg -> [if((enkey == true))] ->
InterceptEMC.CertEM.E_id.Msg>
```

Fig. 7. Possible trace of data leakage.

The counter example returned by PAT is presented in Fig. 7. In this case, the intruder lies between entity and entity manager, conducting ECDHE algorithm with both sides respectively, and gets two pairs of keys. Then, in the subsequent communications, the intruder disguises himself as an entity manager, receives the request sent by the user. Afterwards it sends the request to the target entity, waits for the entity to return data, then disguises himself as an entity, and sends

Fig. 8. Man-in-the-middle attack.

the data just received to the entity manager to deceive the entity manager. This is actually a classic **man-in-the-middle-attack** [13], shown in Fig. 8.

We can take preventive measures against man-in-the-middle attack, that is, enforcing an authentication mechanism. There are many means of authentication mechanism. For example, certificate authentication is one of them, but certificate authentication brings heavy resource consumption. According to our hypothesis, the resources in the entity are limited and can not bear the additional cost brought by the certificate. Therefore, we consider adding a more lightweight authentication mechanism - **message authentication code** (MAC).

We introduce MAC into our model by adding an event **MAC_authentication** to indicate that the two parties have conducted MAC signature exchange. This prohibits the intruder from initiating ECDHE key exchange with both the entity manager and the entity. For example,

$$E =_{def} MAC\_authentication \rightarrow ComEEM?msg_{dreq1}EM.E_{id} \rightarrow$$
$$ComEEM!msg_{drsp1}E_{id}.EM.A(mac, E(k_{ECDHE}, msg)) \rightarrow E$$

In our new model, although the intruder can obtain the encrypted and hashed information, he cannot decrypt it. Because of the introduction of message authentication code, in the process of ECDHE key exchange, intruders can no longer fake entities and entity managers to establish links with the two parties, implement man-in-the-middle attack, obtain two sets of keys, and then decrypt the plain-text of the message. The verification results of our new model are shown in Fig. 9.

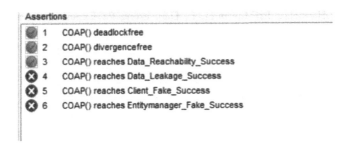

Fig. 9. Verification results of the improved model.

5   Conclusion and Future Work

In this paper, we have applied process algebra CSP to describe and model the group communication CoAP protocol, and used the verification tool PAT to verify the constructed model. The results show that the protocol has potential security risk of data leakage. To solve the problem, we proposed an improved method of using message authentication code, and verify the improved model again. It can be found that the problem of data leakage will not occur again. Considering that CoAP mainly works in LLN and the message may face packet loss in transmission, probabilistic CSP [14] will be introduced in the future.

Acknowledgement. This work was partly supported by the National Key Research and Development Program of China under Grant No. $2018_{YFB}2101300$, the National Natural Science Foundation of China under Grant Nos. 61872145 and 62032024, and Shanghai Trusted Industry Internet Software Collaborative Innovation Center.

References

1. Gubbi, J., Buyya, R., Marusic, S., Palaniswami, M.: Internet of things (IoT): a vision, architectural elements, and future directions. Future Gener. Comput. Syst. **29**(7), 1645–1660 (2013)
2. Bormann, C.: Angelo paolo castellani, zach shelby: CoAP: an application protocol for billions of tiny internet nodes. IEEE Internet Comput. **16**(2), 62–67 (2012)
3. Rahman, A., Dijk, E.: Group communication for the constrained application protocol (CoAP). RFC **7390**, 1–46 (2014)
4. Ishaq, I., Hoebeke, J., Moerman, I., Demeester, P.: Observing CoAP groups efficiently. Ad Hoc Netw. **37**, 368–388 (2016)
5. Sadeghi, A.-R., Wachsmann, C., Waidner, M.: Security and privacy challenges in industrial internet of things. DAC **54**(1–54), 6 (2015)
6. Tushir, B., Sehgal, H., Nair, R., Dezfouli, B., Liu, Y.: The impact of DoS attacks on resource-constrained IoT devices: a study on the mirai attack. CoRR abs/2104.09041 (2021)
7. Capossele, A., Cervo, V., De Cicco, G., Petrioli, C.: Security as a CoAP resource: an optimized DTLS implementation for the IoT. In: ICC 2015, pp. 549–554 (2015)
8. Ishaq, I., Hoebeke, J., Moerman, I., Demeester, P.: Experimental evaluation of unicast and multicast CoAP group communication. Sensors **16**(7), 1137 (2016)
9. Hoare, C.A.R.: Communicating Sequential Processes. Prentice-Hall, Hoboken (1985). ISBN 0-13-153271-5
10. Lambert, S.M.: Exploiting the power of message authentication codes. Inf. Syst. Secur. **3**(3), 53–63 (1994)
11. Tschofenig, H., Fossati, T.: Transport layer security (TLS)/Datagram transport layer security (DTLS) profiles for the internet of things. RFC **7925**, 1–61 (2016)
12. McGrew, D.A., Bailey, D.V., Campagna, M.J., Dugal, R.: AES-CCM elliptic curve cryptography (ECC) cipher suites for TLS. RFC **7251**, 1–10 (2014)
13. Desmedt, Y.: Man-in-the-middle attack. In: van Tilborg, H.C.A. (eds.) Encyclopedia of Cryptography and Security. Springer, Boston (2005). https://doi.org/10.1007/0-387-23483-7_241
14. Lowe, G.: Probabilistic and prioritized models of timed CSP. Theor. Comput. Sci. **138**(2), 315–352 (1995)

Author Index

Printed in the United States
by Baker & Taylor Publisher Services